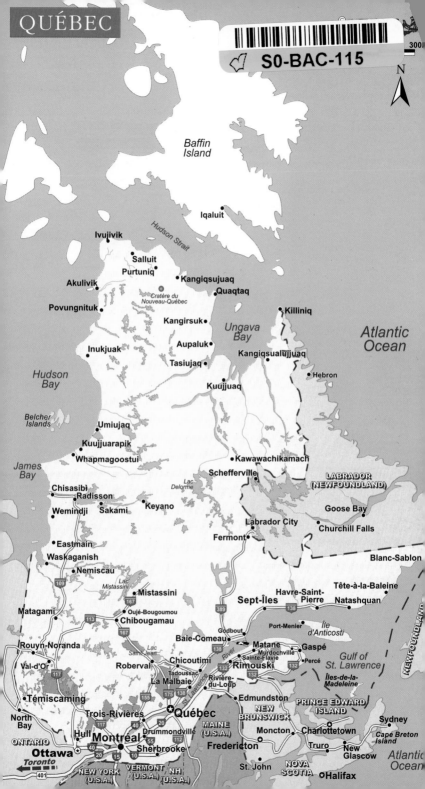

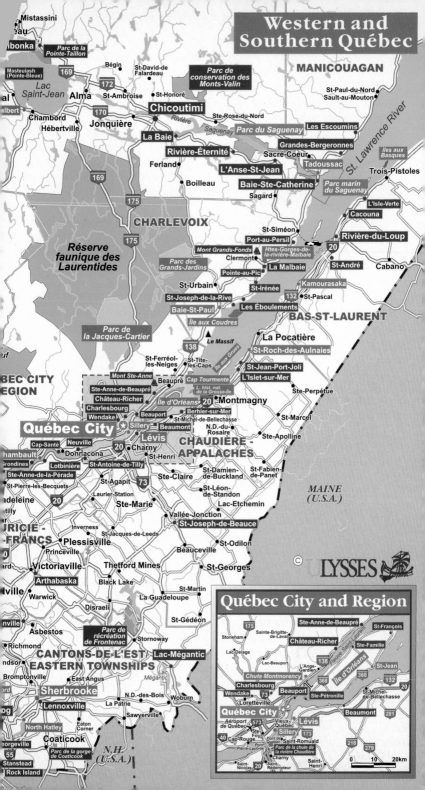

QUÉBEC

2nd edition

ULYSSES
TRAVEL PUBLICATIONS
Travel better... enjoy more

Editorial *Series Director:* Claude Morneau; *Project Supervisor:* Pascale Couture; *Editors:* Claude Morneau, Jennifer McMorran.

Research and Composition *Authors:* François Rémillard (Exploring); Benoit Prieur (Portrait) *Contributors:* Gabriel Audet, Caroline Béliveau, Virginie Bonneau, Daniel Desjardins, Simon Dubé, Claude Feuiltault, Sophie Gaches, François Hénault, Isabelle Gosselin, Judith Lefebvre, Alain Legault, Guiseppe Marcario, Stéphane G. Marceau, Claude Morneau, Yves Ouellet, Francis Plourde, Joël Pomerleau, Marc Rigole, Steve Rioux, Sylvie Rivard, Christian Roy, Yves Séguin, Marcel Verrault.

Production *Design:* Patrick Farei (Atoll Direction); *English Editing;* Jennifer McMorran, Sarah Kresh; *Translation:* T. Kendrick, D. Berglas, N. Meredith, E. Tilson, C. Wood, S. Kresh, D. Gauthier, E. Pahmer, *Cartography:* André Duchesne, Patrick Thivierge (Assistant); *Layout:* Tara Salman, Christian Roy, Stéphane Marceau.

Illustrations *Cover Photo:* Grant V. Faint (Image Bank); *Interior Photos:* Guy Dagenais, Michel Gagné, Serge Gosselin, H. Hughes, Diane de Koninck, John Mameamskum, Perry Mastrovito, Georges Mestokosho, Roger Michel, Audrey Mitchell, Roch Nadeau, Sean O'Neill, Monique Papatie, Clotilde Pelletier, Carlos Pineda, François Rémillard, Philippe Renault, Régent Sioui, B. Terry; *Chapter Headings:* Jennifer McMorran; *Drawings:* Lorette Pierson, Steve Rioux.

Thanks to SODEC and the Department of Canadian Heritage for their financial support.

Distributors

AUSTRALIA:
Little Hills Press
11/37-43 Alexander St.
Crows Nest NSW 2065
☎ (612) 437-6995
Fax: (612) 438-5762

BELGIUM AND LUXEMBOURG:
Vander
Vrijwilligerlaan 321
B-1150 Brussel
☎ (02) 762 98 04
Fax: (02) 762 06 62

CANADA:
Ulysses Books & Maps
4176 Saint-Denis
Montréal, Québec
H2W 2M5
☎ (514) 843-9882, ext.2232
or 1-800-748-9171
Fax: 514-843-9448
www.ulysse.ca

GERMANY AND AUSTRIA:
Brettschneider
Fernreisebedarf
Feldfirchner Strasse 2
D-85551 Heimstetten
München
☎ 89-99 02 03 30
Fax: 89-99 02 03 31

GREAT BRITAIN AND IRELAND:
World Leisure Marketing
9 Downing Road
West Meadows, Derby
UK DE21 6HA
☎ 1 332 34 33 32
Fax: 1 332 34 04 64

ITALY:
Centro Cartografico del Riccio
Via di Soffiano 164/A
50143 Firenze
☎ (055) 71 33 33
Fax: (055) 71 63 50

NETHERLANDS:
Nilsson & Lamm
Pampuslaan 212-214
1380 AD Weesp (NL)
☎ 0294-465044
Fax: 0294-415054
E-mail: nilam@euronet.nl

PORTUGAL:
Dinapress
Lg. Dr. Antonio de Sousa de Macedo, 2
Lisboa 1200
☎ (1) 395 52 70
Fax: (1) 395 03 90

SCANDINAVIA:
Scanvik
Esplanaden 8B
1263 Copenhagen K
DK
☎ (45) 33.12.77.66
Fax: (45) 33.91.28.82

SPAIN:
Altaïr
Balmes 69
E-08007 Barcelona
☎ 454 29 66
Fax: 451 25 59
E-mail: altair@globalcom.es

SWITZERLAND:
OLF
P.O. Box 1061
CH-1701 Fribourg
☎ (026) 467.51.11
Fax: (026) 467.54.66

U.S.A.:
The Globe Pequot Press
6 Business Park Road
P.O. Box 833
Old Saybrook, CT 06475
☎ 1-800-243-0495
Fax: 1-800-820-2329
E-mail: sales@globe-pequot.com

Other countries, contact Ulysses Books & Maps (Montréal), Fax: (514) 843-9448

Canadian Cataloguing in Publication Data

Canadian Cataloguing in Publication
Rémillard, François
        Québec   2nd edition
        (Ulysses travel guides)
        Translation of: Le Québec
        Includes index.
        ISBN 2-921444-78-X
        1. Quebec (Province) - Guidebooks. 2. Québec (Province) - Tours. I. Title. II. Series
FC2907.Q322513 1998   917.1404'4   C97-940021-X
F1952.Q322513 1998

"Eastward, the view down the St. Lawrence towards the Gulf is the finest of all, scarcely surpassed by anything in the world. Your eye follows the range of lofty mountains until their blue summits are blended and lost in the blue of the sky."

Susanna Moodie, at Grosse Isle

TABLE OF CONTENTS

Help make Ulysses Travel Guides even better!

The information contained in this guide was correct at press time. However, mistakes can slip in, omissions are always possible, places can disappear, etc. The authors and publisher hereby disclaim any liability for loss or damage resulting from omissions or errors.

We value your comments, corrections and suggestions, as they allow us to keep each guide up to date. The best contributions will be rewarded with a free book from Ulysses Travel Publications. All you have to do is write us at the following address and indicate which title you would be interested in receiving (see the list at the end of guide).

Ulysses Travel Publications
4176 Rue Saint-Denis
Montréal, Québec
Canada H2W 2M5
www.ulysse.ca
E-mail: guiduly@ulysse.ca

LIST OF MAPS

TABLE OF SYMBOLS

🌴	Ulysses' favourite
☎	Telephone number
≠	Fax number
≡	Air conditioning
⊗	Ceiling fan
≈	Pool
ℜ	Restaurant
◉	Whirlpool
ℝ	Refrigerator
K	Kitchenette
△	Sauna
#	Screen
☺	Exercise room
♿	Handicapped-accessible rooms
♥	Restos du Coeur member
tv	Colour television
fb	Full-board (lodging + 3 meals)
½b	Half-board (lodging + 2 meals)
pb	Private bathroom
sb	Shared bathroom
ps	Private shower
hw	Hot water
½b	half-board (lodging + 2 meals)
bkfst	Breakfast

ATTRACTION CLASSIFICATION

★	Interesting
★★	Worth a visit
★★★	Not to be missed

HOTEL CLASSIFICATION

The prices in the guide are for one room in the high season, double occupancy, not including taxes.

RESTAURANT CLASSIFICATION

$	$10 or less
$$	$10 to $20
$$$	$20 to $30
$$$$	$30 or more

The prices in the guide are for a meal for one person, not including taxes, drinks or tip.

All prices in this guide are in Canadian dollars.

Map Symbols

?	Tourist Information (Permanent)	⚓	Church
?	Tourist Information (Seasonal)	⊠	Border Crossing
	Golf Course		Look Out
A	Camp Ground		Métro Station
	Downhill Ski Centre		Steam Train
	Museum		Whale-watching Centre
	Car Ferry	⚓	Port or Marina
	Ferry		Aquaculture Centre
	Bus Station		Train Station
H	Hospital		Bike Path
P	Parking Lot		Ulysses Travel Bookshop
	Sanctuary or monastery		Casino

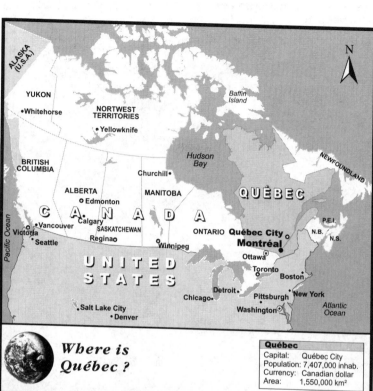

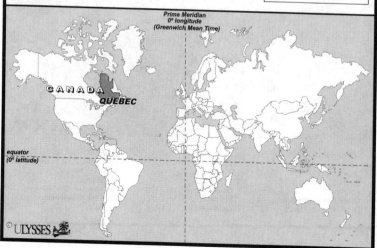

Where is
Québec ?

Québec
Capital: Québec City
Population: 7,407,000 inhab.
Currency: Canadian dollar
Area: 1,550,000 km²

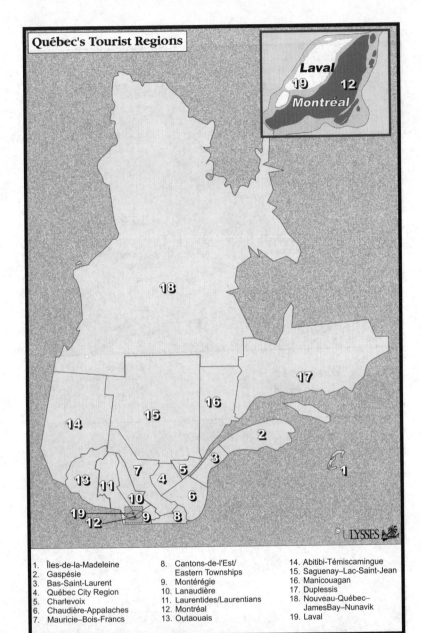

Québec's Tourist Regions

	Laval	
19		12
Montréal		

18

17

16

15

14

2

3

7 5

13 11 4

10 6

19 9

12 8

© ULYSSES

1. Îles-de-la-Madeleine
2. Gaspésie
3. Bas-Saint-Laurent
4. Québec City Region
5. Charlevoix
6. Chaudière-Appalaches
7. Mauricie–Bois-Francs

8. Cantons-de-l'Est/
   Eastern Townships
9. Montérégie
10. Lanaudière
11. Laurentides/Laurentians
12. Montréal
13. Outaouais

14. Abitibi-Témiscamingue
15. Saguenay–Lac-Saint-Jean
16. Manicouagan
17. Duplessis
18. Nouveau-Québec–
    JamesBay–Nunavik
19. Laval

PORTRAIT

Situated in the extreme northeast of the American continent, Québec is Canada's largest province. It covers a surface area of 1,550,000 square kilometres, roughly equivalent to the size of France, Germany and the Iberian peninsula put together, or slightly larger than the state of Alaska. With the exception of certain southern regions, Québec is sparsely populated and is characterized by an expansive wilderness of lakes, rivers and forests. The province forms a huge northern peninsula, with James Bay and Hudson Bay to the west, Hudson Strait and Ungava Bay to the north, and the Gulf of St. Lawrence to the south. Québec also has very long land borders which it shares with Ontario to the west and southwest, with New Brunswick and the state of Maine to the southeast, with the states of New York, Vermont and New Hampshire to the south and with Labrador, part of the province of Newfoundland, to the northeast.

Québec's borders changed several times prior to 1927, when the province was defined as we know it today. With Canadian Confederation in 1867, Québec occupied the territory previously known as Lower Canada, which corresponds to what is now southern Québec. Soon, Québec expanded northward. By 1898, it included the region between Abitibi and the Rivière Eastmain, and in 1912, the province grew once again when Nouveau Québec, was added in the north. In 1927, London's Privy Council decided in favour of Newfoundland in its dispute with Québec over the immense territory of Labrador.

GEOGRAPHY

Québec's geography is dominated by the St. Lawrence River, the Appalachian Mountain range and the Canadian Shield, three of the most significant geographical formations in North America. More than a thousand kilometres long, the St. Lawrence is the largest river leading to the Atlantic Ocean on the continent. The river has its source at the Great Lakes and is also fed by a number of major waterways, such as the Ottawa, the Richelieu, the Saguenay and the Manicouagan. Traditionally the primary route into the continent, the St. Lawrence played a central part in Québec's development. Even today, most of the province's population lives along the river, particularly in the Montréal region where nearly half the province's population resides. To the south, near the American border, the Appalachian mountains cross the St. Lawrence lowlands from southwestern Québec to the Gaspé peninsula. The hilly scenery of these regions is very similar to that of New England, although the mountains rarely exceed one thousand metres in height. The remaining 80% of Québec's land mass is part of the Canadian Shield, a very old, heavily eroded mountain range extending over all of northern Québec. This region of the province has a tiny population and abundant natural resources, including vast forests and mighty rivers, some of which are used in the production of hydroelectric power.

Settling the Land

Traces of the seigneurial system used by the first colonists to settle the land, can still be seen today in the St. Lawrence lowlands. Land was divided into long tracts running inland from the water. In order to give the maximum number of colonists access to the river, which was the only thoroughfare navigable by canoe in the summer and by sled in the winter. When all the land next to the river had been settled, another set of tracts was cleared along a road, called a *rang*, literally row, at the far end of the previously established tracts. Much of the land remains divided like this, and farmers still live as they would have years ago, working long and narrow fields. In certain other regions, close to the American border, the first European settlers were British and they cleared the land according to a system of townships, which involved dividing the territory into squares. This system survives in some parts of the Cantons de l'Est (which means literally Eastern Townships) region, though it disappeared in many others with the massive influx of French settlers who imposed the seigneurial system.

FLORA

As a result of climatic differences, the vegetation in northern Québec is sparse, while that found in the south is quite lush (at least in the summer). Québec's flora can be divided into four zones from north to south: the tundra, the taiga, the Boreal forest, and the deciduous forest.

The tundra occupies the northernmost reaches of Québec, principally along Hudson Bay and Ungava Bay. With a month-long growing season and severe winters during which the ground is frozen several metres deep, vegetation in the tundra is limited to mosses, lichens and very small trees.

The taiga, an area of transition between the tundra and the Boreal forest, covers more than

a third of Québec and is characterized by sparse, very slow-growing trees such as spruce and larch.

The Boreal forest covers a huge section of the province, from the edge of the taiga to the banks of the St. Lawrence in some regions. This is a very homogeneous zone made up of coniferous trees, primarily white pine, black pine, grey pine, balsam fir and larch. This forest is an important source of lumber and wood pulp.

The deciduous forest is in fact made up of coniferous and deciduous trees and covers the regions south of the St. Lawrence River to the American border. Along with a variety of coniferous trees, this zone is rich in maple, birch, spruce and aspen.

FAUNA

Québec's vast and varied wilderness boasts a richly diverse fauna. A multitude of animal species populates its immense forests, plains and arctic regions, and its seas, lakes and rivers are teeming with fish and aquatic animals. The following are some of Québec's most common animal species. Please see colour section on Québec's wildlife.

A BRIEF HISTORY

By the time European settlers arrived in the New World, a mosaic of indigenous peoples had already been living on the continent for thousands of years. The ancestors of these people were nomads who had crossed the Bering Strait from northern Asia toward the end of the ice age, more than 12,000 years ago, and slowly populated the continent. Over the following millennia, as the glaciers receded, some of these groups began to settle in the northernmost parts of the continent, including the peninsula now known as Québec. A variety of native peoples, belonging to three language groups (Algonquian, Iroquoian and Inuit), were thus sharing the territory when the Europeans first began to explore North America. Established societies with very diverse ways of life occupied this vast region. For example, native peoples occupying in the river valley of the St. Lawrence lived primarily on fish, game, and food they grew themselves, while communities farther north depended mostly on meat gathered during hunting expeditions. All, however, made ample use of the canoe as a means of travelling along the "paths that walk", and maintained very close trade relations with the neighbouring nations. These societies, well-adapted to the rigours and distinctive features of the territory, were quickly marginalised with the onset of European colonization at the beginning of the 16th century.

New France

During his first exploration of the mouth of the St. Lawrence and the shores of what is now Newfoundland, the French explorer Jacques Cartier came in contact with fishermen from various parts of Europe. In fact, these waters were first explored by the Vikings sometime around the year 900, and were being visited regularly by European cod fishermen and whalers. However, Jacques Cartier's three voyages, which began in 1534, did represent an important step forward, as they established the first official contact between whites and the peoples and territory of this part of North America. On these expeditions, the Breton navigator sailed far up the St. Lawrence to the villages of Stadacona (now Québec City) and Hochelaga (on the island of Montréal). However, as Cartier's mandate from the king of France had been to find gold or a passage to Asia, his discoveries were considered unimportant and uninteresting. For several decades after this "failure", the French crown forgot about this distant, inhospitable place.

French interest in North America was rekindled when fur coats and hats became increasingly fashionable and therefore profitable in Europe. As the fur trade required a direct and constant link with local suppliers, a permanent presence in the New World was indispensable. Throughout the end of the 16th century, various unsuccessful attempts at setting up trading posts on the Atlantic coast and in the interior of the continent were made. Finally, in 1608, under the leadership of Samuel de Champlain, the first permanent outpost was set up. Champlain and his men chose a location at the foot of a large cliff overlooking a considerable narrowing of the St. Lawrence. The collection of fortified buildings they constructed was named the Abitation de Québec (kebec is an Algonquian word meaning "where the river narrows"). During that first harsh winter in Québec, 20 of the 28 men

posted there died of scurvy or malnutrition before ships carrying fresh supplies arrived in the spring of 1609. When Samuel de Champlain died on Christmas Day, in 1635, there were about three hundred pioneers living in New France.

Between 1627 and 1663, the Compagnies des Cents Associés held a monopoly on the fur trade and ensured the slow growth of the colony. Meanwhile, French religious orders became more and more interested in New France. The Récollets arrived first, in 1615; they were replaced by the Jesuits, who began arriving in 1632. Determined to convert the natives, the Jesuits settled deep in the interior of the continent, near the shores of Georgian Bay, where they founded the Sainte-Marie-des-Huron mission. The Huron people, it can be assumed, put up with the presence of the Jesuits to maintain the trading arrangements they had established with the French. The mission was nevertheless abandoned after five Jesuits were killed during the Huron-Iroquois war of 1648-1649. This war was part of an extensive offensive campaign launched by the powerful Iroquois Five Nations between 1645 and 1655 and intended to wipe out all rival nations. The Huron, Pétun, Neutrals and Erie nations, each at least 10,000 strong, were almost completely annihilated within the space of ten years. The offensive also threatened the existence of the French colony. In 1660 and 1661, Iroquois warriors mounted strikes all over New France, destroying crops and bringing about a decline in the fur trade. Louis the XIV, the king of France, decided to take the situation in hand. In 1663, he dissolved the Compagnies des Cents Associés and took on the responsibility of administering the colony himself officially declaring New France, with its three thousand settlers (or *habitants*), a French province.

Emigration to New France continued under the royal regime. Most people sent over were agricultural workers, though some also belonged to the military. In 1665, for example, the Carignan-Salières regiment was dispatched to the New World to fight the Iroquois. The Crown also took steps to encourage the natural growth of the population, which had theretofore been hindered by the lack of unmarried female immigrants. Between 1663 and 1673, 800 young women, known as the *filles du roi*, and each provided with a dowry, were sent to find husbands in the New World. This period of the history of New France was also the glorious era of the *coureurs des bois*.

Abandoning their land for the fur trade, these intrepid young men travelled into the heart of the continent to deal directly with native trappers. The primary occupation of most colonists, however, remained farming.

Society revolved around the seigneurial system. Land in New France was divided into seigneuries which in turn were divided into *rotures*. The long narrow lots running perpendicular to the rivers (most notably the St. Lawrence) gave everyone access to the water. Serfs were expected to pay an annual sum to their seigneur and to do certain tasks for them. Since the territory was so vast and so sparsely populated, however, colonists in New France enjoyed much higher profits once all their debts were paid than their counterparts in France.

The territorial claims made by the French in North America increased rapidly during this era as a result of expeditions made by religious orders, *coureurs des bois* and explorers, to whom we owe the discovery of most of the North American continent. New France reached its peak at the beginning of the 18th century. At this time, it had a monopoly on the North American fur trade, it had control of the St. Lawrence and was beginning to develop Louisiana. New France was thus able to contain the expansion of the more populous British colonies located between the Atlantic and the Appalachians. This changed following military dedeat in Europe and the Treaty of Utrecht (1713) where France relinquished control of Hudson Bay, Newfoundland and Acadia to the British. France thereby lost a large stake in the fur trade, as well as certain strategic military locations, all of which severely weakened its position in North America and marked the beginning of the end of New France. Over the following years, the stakes continued to mount. In 1755, British colonel Charles Lawrence took what he viewed as a preventive measure and ordered the deportation of the Acadians, French-speaking settlers living in what is now Nova Scotia. At least 7,000 Acadians, who had been considered British citizens since 1713, were displaced as a result of this directive. The fight for control of the colony came to an end several years later. Though Montréal was last to fall in 1760, it was the infamous battle of the Plains of Abraham a year before, where Montcalm's and Wolfe's troops met, that sealed the fate of New France with the loss of Québec City. At the time of the British Conquest, the population of the colony had risen to 60,000. Of this number, 8,967 lived in Québec City, and 5,733 lived in Montréal.

British Rule

With the Treaty of Paris of 1763, French Canada, holdings east of the Mississippi and what remained of Acadia were officially ceded to England. For former subjects of the French crown, the first years under British rule were difficult ones. Territorial divisions dictated by the Royal Proclamation of 1763 denied the colony control of the fur trade, the most dynamic sector of its economy. In addition, the introduction of British civil law and the refusal to recognize the authority of the Pope put an end to both the seigneurial system and the Catholic hierarchy, the pillars on which French colonial society had been based. Finally the Test Oath, required of anyone in a high-ranking administrative position, discriminated against French Canadians, since it denied the transubstantiation of the Eucharist and the authority of the Pope. A large segment of the French elite returned to France while English merchants gradually took control of most businesses.

England, however, soon agreed to do away with the Royal Proclamation. To better resist the trend towards independence in its 13 colonies to the south, it sought to secure its place in Canada by gaining the favour of the population. In 1774, the Québec Act replaced the Royal Proclamation, introducing policies much more appropriate to a French Catholic colony.

The Canadian population remained French, until the end of the American Revolution when Canada experienced the arrival of a first big wave of Anglo-Saxon colonists. The new arrivals were Loyalists, Americans wishing to remain faithful to the British crown. Most moved to the Maritimes (formerly Acadia) and around Lake Ontario, but some also settled in regions inhabited strictly by francophones. With the arrival of these new colonists, British authorities passed the Constitution Act of 1791, which divided Canada into two provinces. Upper Canada, situated west of the Rivière Outaouais and mainly populated by anglophones, would be governed by British civil law. Lower Canada, which was mostly francophone, would be governed according to the French tradition of common law. In addition, the Act planted the seeds of a parliamentary system in Canada by creating a Legislative Assembly in each province.

Meanwhile, Napoleon's Continental System forced Britain to get its lumber from Canada. From an economic standpoint, this was good for the colony. The development of a new industry was especially timely, as the fur trade, the original reason for the existence of the colony, was in steady decline. In 1821, the take-over of the Montréal-based Northwest Company by the Hudson's Bay Company marked the end of Montréal as the centre of the North American fur trade. Meanwhile, rural Québec suffered through an agricultural crisis caused by the exhaustion of farmlands and rapid population growth resulting from high birth rates among French-Canadian families, whose diet consisted almost entirely of pea soup and buckwheat pancakes (*galettes*).

These economic difficulties and the struggle for power between francophones and anglophones in Lower Canada combined to spark the Patriotes Rebellion of 1837 and 1838. The period of political conflict which fuelled the rebellion was initiated by the 1834 publication of the *92 Résolutions*, a scathing indictment of British colonial policy. The authors of the resolutions, a group of parliamentarians led by Louis-Joseph Papineau, decided to hold back from voting on the budget until Britain addressed their demands. Britain's response came in 1837 in the form of the *10 Resolutions*, written by Lord Russell, which categorically refused any compromise with their opponents in Lower Canada. In the fall of 1837, Montréal was the scene of violent clashes between the Fils de la Liberté (Sons of Liberty), made up of young French Canadians, and the Doric Club, comprised of Loyalists. Further confrontations occurred in the Richelieu valley region and in the county of Deux-Montagnes, where small insurgent groups stood up to the British army before being crushed. The following year, in an attempt to rekindle the rebellion, a group of Patriotes met with the same fate in Napierville where they confronted 7,000 British troops. This time, however, colonial authorities sent a strong message to prospective rebels. In 1839, they hanged 12 Patriotes and deported many others.

When hostilities first broke out, London had sent an emissary, Lord Durham, to study the problems in the colonies. Expecting to find a population rebelling against colonial authority, Durham found instead two peoples, one French and one British in battle. The solution he later proposed in his report, known as the Durham Report, was radical. He suggested to authorities in Britain that gradual efforts should be made to assimilate French Canadians.

The Union Act, laid down by the British government in 1840, was largely based on the conclusions of the Durham Report. A new parliamentary system was introduced giving the two former colonies the same number of delegates, despite the fact that Lower Canada had a much larger population than Upper Canada. Financial responsibilities were also divided equally between the provinces, and English was made the sole official language. As armed insurrection had proven futile in the past, French Canada's political class sought to align itself with progressive anglophones in an attempt to resist these changes. Later the struggle for responsible government became the central goal of this coalition.

The agricultural crisis, furthermore, remained as severe as ever in Lower Canada. Intensified by the constant arrival of immigrants and by the high birth rate, the situation resulted in a massive emigration of French Canadians to the United States. Between 1840 and 1850, 40,000 French Canadians left the country to seek employment in the factories of New England. To counteract this exodus, the Catholic Church and the government launched an extensive campaign to colonize outlying regions, such as Lac Saint-Jean. The harsh life in these newly settled regions, where colonists worked as farmers in the summer and lumberjacks in the winter, is poignantly depicted in Louis Hémon's novel *Maria Chapdelaine*. Nevertheless, the mass exodus from Québec did not stop until the beginning of the next century. It is estimated that about 750,000 French Canadians left the province between 1840 and 1930. From this point of view, the colonization campaign, which doubled the amount of farmland in Lower Canada, ended in failure. The swelling population of rural Québec was not effectively absorbed until several decades later with the start of industrialization.

The Canadian economy received a serious blow during this era when Britain abandoned its policy of mercantilism and preferential tariffs for its colonies. To cushion the effects of this change in British policy, United Canada signed a treaty in 1854, making it possible for certain goods to enter the United States without import duties. Canada's economy began to recover slightly but the treaty was revoked in

1866, under pressure from American industrialists. Resolving these economic difficulties was the impetus behind canadian confederation in 1867.

Confederation

Under Canadian Confederation, Lower Canada became the Province of Québec. Three other provinces, Nova Scotia, New Brunswick, and Ontario (formerly Upper Canada) joined the Confederation, which would eventually unite a vast territory stretching from the Atlantic to the Pacific Ocean. For French Canadians, this new political system reinforced their minority status, which began with the Union Act of 1840. The creation of two levels of government did, however, grant Québec jurisdiction over education, culture and civil law.

Confederation was slow to bring about positive economic change. The economy fluctuated for three decades before experiencing a real boom. The first years after Confederation did, however, see the development of local industry (thanks to the implementation of protective tariffs), the creation of a large, unified market and the development of the railway system across the territory. The industrial revolution that had begun in the mid 19th century picked up again in the 1880s. While Montréal remained the undisputed centre of this movement, it was felt in many smaller towns. The lumber industry, which had been one of the mainsprings of the economy during the 19th century, began exporting more cut wood than raw lumber, giving rise to a processing industry. Montréal was also the hub of the expanding railroad, leading the city to specialize in the production of rolling stock. The leather goods, clothing and food industries also enjoyed significant growth in Québec. This period of growth was also marked by the emergence of the brand-new textile industry, which would remain for many years Québec's flagship industry. Benefitting from a huge pool of unskilled labour, the textile industries initially employed mostly women and children.

This wave of industrialization accelerated the pace of urbanization and created a large and poor working class clustered near the factories. Montréal's working-class neighbourhoods were terribly unhealthy. Infant mortality in these areas was twice that of wealthy neighbourhoods.

Québec's cities were going through tremendous changes, and the situation in rural areas finally began to improve. Dairy production was gradually replacing subsistence farming, contributing to an improved standard of living among farmers.

In 1885, the tragic hanging of Louis Riel once again highlighted the opposition between Canada's two language groups francophones and anglophones. Having led Métis and aboriginal rebels in the western part of the country, Riel, a French-speaking, Catholic Métis (a semi-nomadic group descended from French traders and aboriginals) was found guilty of high treason and sentenced to death. French-Canadian public opinion was strongly in favour of a commuted sentence, while anglophones took the opposite view. The federal government under John A. Macdonald ultimately went ahead with the execution, and the reaction was quick and angry among the people of Québec.

The Golden Age of Economic Liberalism

With the beginning of the 20th century, a period of prodigious economic growth in Québec started and last until the Great Depression of the 1930s. Sharing the optimism and euphoria of Canadians, Prime Minister Wilfrid Laurier predicted that the 20th century would be Canada's.

Québec manufacturers profited during this period of growth. Thanks to new technology and new markets, the province's, abundance of natural resources was the principal catalyst of this second wave of industrialization. Central to the new era was the production of electrical power. With its numerous powerful rivers, Québec became a major producer of hydroelectric power in a matter of years. The resulting availability of affordable energy attracted industries with large electricity needs. Aluminum smelters and chemical plants were constructed in the vicinity of hydroelectric power stations. The mining industry also began to enjoy modest growth during this period with the development of asbestos mines in the Eastern Townships and copper, gold, zinc and silver mines in Abitibi. Above all, Québec's pulp and paper industry found huge markets in the United States, due to the depletion of American forests and the rise of the popular press. To promote the development of processing industries in Québec the exportation of logs was forbidden by the provincial government in 1910.

This new period of industrialization differed from the first one in several ways. Taking place largely outside the major cities, it led to an increase in urban growth in outlying regions. In some cases, cities sprang up in a matter of a few years. Unlike the manufacturing industries, the exploitation of natural resources required more qualified workers and a level of financing far beyond local means. Britain's stake in the economy, which up until now had been the largest, gave way to the triumphant rise of American capitalism.

Despite rapid changes in Québec society (by 1921, half the population was living in urban centres), the church was still highly influential. With 85% of the overall population, including virtually all French Canadians, as members the Catholic Church was a major political force in the province. Because of the control it wielded over education, health care and social services, its authority was inescapable. The Catholic Church, moreover, did not hesitate to intervene in the political arena, often confronting politicians it considered to be too liberal.

When World War I began, the Canadian government gave its full support to Britain without hesitation. A significant number of French Canadians voluntarily enrolled in the army, although the percentage of volunteers per capita was far lower than that in other provinces. This lack of enthusiasm can doubtless be attributed both to Québec's long severed ties with France and, what is more important, to francophones' somewhat ambivalent feelings toward Britain. Canada soon set a goal of inducting 500,000 men. Since there were not enough volunteers, the government voted, in 1917, to introduce conscription. Reaction to this in Québec was violent and marked by fights, bombings and riots. In the end, conscription failed to appreciably increase the number of French-Canadian recruits. Instead, it simply underlined out once again the ongoing friction between English and French Canada.

The Great Depression

Between 1929 and 1945, two international-scale events, the Depression and World War II, greatly disrupted the country's political, economic and social progress. The Great Depression of the 1930s, originally viewed as a cyclical, temporary crisis, lengthened into a decade-long nightmare and put an end to Québec's rapid economic expansion. With Canada strongly dependent on foreign markets, the country as a whole was hard hit by the international stock market crash. Québec was unevenly affected. With its economy based to a large extent on exports, Montréal, along with towns dependent on the development of natural resources, took the hardest blows. The textile and food industries, which sold to the Canadian market, held up better during the first years of the Depression, before foundering as well. The trend towards urbanization slowed as people began to view the countryside as a refuge where they could grow their own food. Poverty became more and more widespread, and unemployment levels reached 27% in 1933. Governments were at a loss in the face of this crisis, which they had expected to be short-lived. The Québec government started by introducing massive public works projects to provide jobs for the unemployed. As this proved insufficient, more direct help was gradually given. Very timidly put forward at first, since unemployment had always been considered a personal problem, these measures later helped many Quebecers. The federal government was also compelled to question the merits of economic liberalism and to redefine the role of the state. Part of this trend included establishing the Bank of Canada in 1935, which permitted greater control over the monetary and financial system. However, it was not until the ensuing war years that a full-scale welfare state was created. In the meantime, the crisis led to the proliferation of political ideologies in Québec. The most popular of these, traditional nationalism, put great emphasis on values such as rural life, family, religion and language.

World War II

World War II began in 1939, and Canada became officially involved September 10th of that year. The Canadian economy received a much-needed boost as industry set out to modernize the country's military equipment and to meet the requirements of the Allies. Canada's close ties to Great Britain and the United States gave it an important diplomatic role, as indicated by the conferences held in Québec in 1943 and 1944. Early in the war, however, the problem of conscription surfaced again. While the federal government wanted to avoid the issue, mounting pressure from the country's anglophones forced a plebiscite on the issue. The results once again showed the division between francophones and anglophones: 80% of English Canadians voted in favour of conscription, while the same percentage of French Canadians were opposed to the idea. Mixed feelings toward Britain and France left French Canadians very reluctant to become involved in the fighting. However, they were forced to follow the will of the majority. In the end, 600,000 Canadians were recruited, 42,000 of whom died in action.

Québec was profoundly changed by the war. Its economy became much stronger and more diversified than before. As far as relations between Ottawa and Québec City were concerned, the federal government's massive intervention during the war marked the beginning of its increased role in the economy and of the relative marginalization of provincial governments. In addition, the contact thousands of Quebecers had with European life and the jobs women held in the factories modified people's expectations. The winds of change were blowing, but were to come up against a serious obstacle: Premier Maurice Duplessis and his political allies.

1945-1960: The Duplessis Era

The end of World War II signalled a period of considerable economic growth, during which consumer demands repressed by the economic crisis and wartime rationing could finally be satisfied. Despite a few fluctuations, the economy performed spectacularly until 1957. However, this prosperity affected Québec's various social and ethnic groups unequally. Many workers, particularly non-unionized ones, continued to receive relatively low wages. - Furthermore, the anglophone minority in Québec still enjoyed a far superior standard of living than the francophone majority. A francophone employee with the same skills and experience as an anglophone employee would routinely be paid less. With an economy largely controlled by English Canadians and Americans, French Canadians were held back. To some degree, francophones lived as second class citizens in their own province.

Be that as it may, the economic growth encouraged a stable political environment, such that the leader of the Union Nationale Party, Maurice Duplessis, remained in power as Pre-

mier of Québec from 1944 until he died in 1959. Duplessis's influence characterized this era, often referred to as *la grande noirceur*, or the great darkness. The Duplessis ideology was based on a sometimes paradoxical amalgam of traditional nationalism, conservatism and unbridled capitalism. He professed a respect for rural life, religion and authority, while at the same time providing major foreign business interests with highly favourable opportunities to exploit Québec's natural resources. In his mind, a cheap work force was one of those resources and it had to be preserved. To this end, he fought fiercely against unionization, not hesitating to use intimidation tactics when he felt it was necessary. These years were marked by many strikes but it was the asbestos strike of 1949 that most influenced the collective conscience. While Maurice Duplessis was the dominant personality of this period, his rule could only have been sustained through the tacit collaboration of much of the traditional and business elite, both francophone and anglophone. The church, seemingly at the height of its glory during these years, felt its authority weakening, which prompted it to support the Duplessis government in full measure.

Despite Duplessis's iron hand, opposing voices nonetheless emerged. The Liberal Party of Québec had difficulty getting organized, and so opposition came mainly from outside the parliamentary structure. Artists and writers made their anger known by publishing the *Refus Global*, a bitter attack on the repressive atmosphere in Québec. The most organized opposition came from union leaders, journalists and the intellectual community. All these groups wanted modernization for Québec and endorsed the same neo-liberalist economic credo favouring a strong welfare system. However, from quite early on, two different camps developed among these reformists. Certain individuals, such as Gérard Pelletier and Pierre Trudeau, believed modernization would result from a strong federal government, while neo-nationalists like André Laurendeau wanted change through a more powerful provincial government. These two groups, which quickly overshadowed traditionalism during the Quiet Revolution, would remain at odds with each other throughout modern Québec history.

The Quiet Revolution

In 1960, the Liberal Party under Jean Lesage was elected on a platform of change and stayed in power until 1966. This period, referred to as the Révolution Tranquille, or Quiet Revolution, was indeed marked by a veritable race for modernism. Over the course of just a few years, Québec caught up to the modern world. Control of education, health care and social services meant the provincial government played a bigger role in society.. The church, thus stripped of its main spheres of influence, lost its authority and eventually its following, as dissatisfied Québec catholics moved away from the church. State control of the production of hydro-electricity increased the provincial government's interests in the economy. Powerful economic reources thus permitted the government to establish itself, and French Canadians in general, in the business world. The great vitality brought to Québec society through the Quiet Revolution was symbolized by two events of international scope that took place in Montréal: Expo '67 and the 1976 Olympics.

The lively nature of Québec society in the 1960s engendered a number of new ideological movements, particularly on the left. The extreme was the Front de Libération du Québec (FLQ), a small group of radicals who wanted to "decolonize" Québec, which launched a series of terrorist strikes in Montréal. In October 1970, the FLQ abducted James Cross, a British diplomat, and Jean Laporte, a Québec cabinet minister. The Canadian Prime Minister at the time, Pierre Elliot Trudeau, fearing a political uprising, called for the War Measures Act to be enforced. The Canadian army took to the streets of Montréal, thousands of searches were carried out and hundreds of innocent people temporarily imprisoned. Shortly afterward, Pierre Laporte was found dead. The crisis finally ended when the James Cross'kidnappers agreed to let him go in exchange for their safe conduct to Cuba. During this entire crisis, and long afterwards, Trudeau was severely criticized for invoking the War Measures Act. Some accused him of having done so mainly to quash the growing Québec independence movement.

The most significant political phenomenon in Québec between 1960 and 1980 was the rapid rise of moderate nationalism. Breaking with the traditionalism of the past, this new vision of

nationalism championed a strong, open and modern Québec with increased powers for the provincial government, and, ultimately, political independence for the province. The nationalist forces rallied around René Lévesque, founder of the Mouvement Souveraineté-Association and then, in 1968, the Parti Québécois. After two elections, which saw only a handful of its representatives elected to Parliament, a stunning 1976 victory brought the Parti Québécois to power. With a mandate to negotiate sovereignty for Québec, the party called a referendum in 1980. From the beginning, the referendum campaign revived the division between Québec sovereigntists and federalists. The struggle was intense and mobilized the entire population right up until the vote. Finally after a campaign based on promises of a new style of federalism, the "No" (no to sovereignty association) side won out with 60% of the vote. Despite this loss, sovereigntists were consoled by how far their cause had come in only a few years. From a marginal trend in the 1960 s, nationalism quickly proved itself to be a major political movement. The night of the defeat, Parti Québécois leader René Lévesque,charisma intact, vowed to his supporters that victory would be their's "next time."

Since 1980: Breaks and Continuity

The independence movement and desire for self-determination amongst Quebecers engendered by the Quiet Revolution suffered a great setback with the loss of the referendum on sovereignty. For many, the 1980s began with a post-referendum depression, accentuated by a period of economic crisis in Canada unmatched since the 1930s. As the economy improved slightly over time, the unemployment rate remained very high and government spending resulted in a massive deficit. Like many other western governments, Québec had to reassess the policies of the past, though some feared that the new direction chosen would sacrifice the achievements of the Quiet Revolution.

The 1980s and early 1990s were a time of streamlining and one that saw the creation of global markets and the consolidation of large economic blocks. Canada and the United States signed the Free-Trade Agreement in 1989. The 1994 North American Free Trade Agreement (NAFTA) brought Mexico into this

A Brief Summary of Québec's History

More than 12,000 years ago: Nomads from Northern Asia cross the Bering Strait and gradually populate the Americas. With the melting of the glaciers, some of them settle on the peninsula now known as Québec: these are the ancestors of the aboriginal nations.

1534: Jacques Cartier, a navigator from Saint-Malo in Brittany, France, makes the first of three explorations of the Gulf and St. Lawrence River. These were the first official French contacts with this territory.

1608: Samuel de Champlain and his men found Québec City, marking the beginning of a permanent French presence in North America.

1663: New France officially becomes a French province. Colonization continues.

1759: Québec City falls to British forces. Four years later, the King of France officially relinquishes all of New France, which now has a population of about 60,000 colonists of French origin.

1837-1838: The British army suppresses the Patriotes rebellion.

1840: Following the Durham Report, the Union Act seeks to create an English majority and eventually assimilate French Canadians.

1867: This year marks the birth of Canadian Confederation. Four provinces, including Québec, sign the agreement. Six others eventually follow suit.

1914-1918: Canada participates in World War I. Anglophones and francophones disagree about the level of participation of the country. Canada comes out of the conflict very divided.

1929-1939: The economic crash hits Québec hard. In 1933, unemployment reaches 27%.

1939-1945: Canada participates in World War II. Once again, anglophones and francophones are divided on the issue of conscription.

1944-1959: Premier Maurice Duplessis leads Québec with a strong hand. This period is known as the *"grande noirceur"*, or "great darkness".

1960: The Liberal Party is elected, marking the beginning of the *Révolution Tranquille*, or Quiet Revolution.

October 1970: A small terrorist group, the Front de Libération du Québec (FLQ), kidnaps a British diplomat and a Québec cabinet minister, igniting a serious political crisis.

November 1976: A party favouring independence for Québec, the Parti Québécois, wins the provincial election.

May 1980: A majority of the Québec population votes against holding negotiations aimed at Québec independence.

1982: The Canadian Constitution is repatriated without Québec's consent.

June 1990: The failure of the Meech Lake Accord on the Canadian Constitution is poorly accepted in Québec. Following this, opinion polls show that a majority of Quebecers are in favour of Québec sovereignty.

October 22, 1992: The federal government and the provinces organize a referendum on new constitutional offers. Considered unacceptable, these are rejected by a majority of Quebecers and Canadians.

October 30, 1995: The Parti Québecois government holds a referendum on the sovereignty of Québec: 49.4% of Quebecers vote "yes" to a sovereignty project and 50.6% vote "no".

market, creating the largest tariff-free market in the world.

From a political standpoint, the question of Québec's political status surfaced again. In the early 1990s, the sovereigntist movement regained surprising momentum, spurred along by Quebecers' resentment at the failure in June 1990 of the Meech Lake Accord, an agreement aimed at reintegrating Québec into the "constitutional family" by giving it special status (see p 25). The governing bodies involved, in an attempt to resolve this impasse, called for a Canada-wide referendum on a new constitutional offer, held on October 26, 1992. The offer was flatly rejected everywhere in Canada, but for differing reasons. The federal election of October 25, 1993, saw the sovereigntist Bloc Québécois win two-thirds of the ridings in Québec and form the official opposition in the Canadian Parliament. The next year, the Parti Québecois was elected in Québec; high on its agenda was the holding of a referendum on the sovereignty of Québec.

Less than one year after its election, the Parti Québecois, launched a referendum campaign, as promised, for the sovereignty of Québec. As with the first referendum, 15 years earlier in 1980, the Québec population was very divided on the issue. This time, however, the results were unbelievably close. The suspense lasted right until the last ballot was counted on referendum day, October 30, 1995. The results would tell of a population divided: 49.4% of Quebecers voted "yes" to the sovereignty project of Québec and 50.6% voted "no". Some 28,000 votes separated the two options! Unbelievable! The profound question of Québec's political status thus remained unresolved following this referendum, which in effect only served to underline the division that exists within the population. One thing remains certain, however, the "national question" will remain at the forefront of Québec politics in the coming years.

POLITICS

The British North America Act is the constitutional document on which Canadian Confederation is based. It creates a division of powers between the levels of government. In addition to a central government based in Ottawa, therefore, the ten Canadian provinces each has a government with the power to legislate in certain domains. The constitutional conflict between Québec and the Canadian government is largely a product of disagreements over precisely how these powers should be divided.

Based on the British model, Canada and Québec's political systems give legislative power to a parliament elected by universal suffrage. In Québec, the Parliament is called the Assemblée Nationale. It has 125 seats, each representing a riding in the province. In Ottawa, power belongs to the House of Commons, with members from regions across the country. The federal government also has an Upper Chamber, the Senate. This institution has gradually had all its real power reduced and its future is now unclear. In an election, the party with the most elected representatives forms the government. These elections are held about every four years, and function according to the single ballot majority system. This kind of system generally leaves room for only two major political parties. It also, however, has the advantage of ensuring great stability between each election, while making it possible to identify each member of Parliament with a particular riding.

Federal Politics

At the federal level, two parties, the Liberal Party and the Conservative Party, have each governed the country at various times since Confederation in 1867. Quebecers and French-speaking Canadians in general have, until recently, strongly supported the Liberal Party.

The first three French-speaking Prime Ministers of Canada, moreover, represented this party. The Conservative Party, long associated with British imperialism and with the implementation of conscription in 1917, has traditionally made little room for francophones. Recently, the Conservative Party has shown signs of greater openness. In 1984, the party was thus voted into power in a federal election, and retained that power in the next election in 1988, with tremendous support from Québec. They were, however, defeated by the Liberal Party in the election of October 25, 1993, which placed Jean Chrétien at the head of Canadian government. This election lead to a spectacular rearrangement of Canada's political map and signalled the rise of two new federal political parties: the Reform Party and the Bloc Québécois. The Reform Party, a populist right-wing party, elected 52 members of parliament, almost exclusively from Western Canada. The Bloc Québécois won 54 seats, in effect more than two thirds of the seats in Québec. Born out of the Meech Lake fiasco, the Bloc Québécois's goal is to promote Québec sovereignty at the federal level. Meanwhile, the Progressive Conservative Party, up until then in power, and the New Democratic Party, the eternal third-place finishers on the federal scene, were virtually wiped off that map.

The results of the 1993 federal election were confirmed during the most recent election in the spring of 1997. The Liberal Party was re-elected, though with a smaller majority despite massive support from Ontario, the most populous Canadian province. The Reform Party was once again the big winner in the West, claiming even more seats than in the previous election. The Bloc Québécois's performance was not as strong as in 1993. They nevertheless won 45 of the 75 seats in Québec. As for the Progressive Conservatives and the New Democrats, they regained some of their former strengths thanks to voters in Atlantic Canada. The Canadian political map has never been so complex. The Liberal Party's inability to gain much support outside of Ontario, Reform's performance in the West and the large contingent of Bloc Québécois members of parliament certainly puts in question the idea of a Canadian consensus.

Provincial Politics

Two political parties dominate Québec politics. Lucien Bouchard, head of the Parti Québécois

(PQ) and Premier since January 1996, succeeded Jacques Parizeau, who was elected under the same banner in 1994. This relatively young party previously lead the provincial government from 1976 to 1985; it was then led by the charismatic René Lévesque. The PQ's opposition is essentially composed of the Liberal Party of Québec, which was at the head of the Québec government from 1985 to 1994, when Robert Bourassa was leader of the party. The party's new leader, Jean Charest, the former head of the federal Conservatives, has yet to prove his leadership abilities but is nevertheless very popular with the people. His move to Québec politics promises to change the playing field when it comes to the major source of disagreement between these two parties: the political status of Québec. Since it was founded, the Parti Québécois has pursued the objective of gaining political sovereignty for Québec. The Liberal Party, on the other hand, has sought more power for the provincial government, though it remains loyal to the Canadian federalist system.

Federal-Provincial Relations

Over the course of the last 35 years, federal-provincial relations and the conflicts between federalists and Québec sovereigntists, have dominated politics in Canada. This ongoing dispute continues to fuel public debate. Since the Quiet Revolution, successive Québec governments have all considered themselves representatives of a distinct society, demanding special status for Québec and greater independence from the federal government. Faced with the prospect of Québec autonomy, the federal government has resisted vigorously, arguing that there is only one Canada and that Québec is one province like the others. During this same thirty year period, the federal government had been attempting to repatriate the Canadian constitution in London, a task that requires the support of the provinces. While Québec did not oppose the repatriation of the constitution, it decided that such a development could be an opportunity to bring about a major revision of its place in the country and an increase of its powers. However, the province's demands were never met by the federal government, and Québec, long supported by other provinces, responded by blocking the repatriation of the Constitution at the federal-provincial conferences of 1964 and 1971.

The Referendum of 1980

The stakes were much higher once the Parti Québécois took power in 1976. This party, whose reason for being was the creation of a sovereign Québec, worried the federal government and Québec's federalist forces. In 1980, the PQ decided to hold a referendum on sovereignty, asking Quebecers to give the party a mandate to negotiate a sovereignty-association with the rest of the country. The referendum campaign that followed was a showdown between federalist forces, represented by the Liberal Party of Québec and the Canadian government, and sovereigntist forces, represented by the Parti Québécois. This clash of the two main views that had defined the contemporary political scene in Québec also took on the appearance of a fight to the finish between two men, Pierre Elliot Trudeau and René Lévesque. After a long battle, marked by a good deal of demagoguery, the campaign concluded on May, 20, 1980, with 60% of Quebecers voting against the negotiation of sovereignty association. Taking into account the anglophone vote, the results showed that the francophone population was about evenly split on the issue. The vote came as a serious jolt to those who had dreamed of an independent state with a francophone majority in North America. On referendum day 1980, a majority of Quebecers decided to give federalism another chance and placed their future in Pierre Elliot Trudeau's hands. Trudeau, without being very specific about what he meant, promised that voting No in the referendum meant voting Yes to a new Canada.

Quebecers were quick to discover, however, that Trudeau's new federalism did not address their province's traditional demands. In November of 1981, Trudeau called a federal-provincial conference with the goal of repatriating the Constitution. Québec, with the support of certain other provinces, intended to block the federal project, but a spectacular turnaround occurred in a late-night meeting to which Québec was not invited. Following this event, which became known as the "night of the long knives", the federal government imposed a new constitutional pact on Québec in 1982, knowing full well that the Québec National Assembly was fiercely opposed to signing it. Not only were Québec's language laws placed in jeopardy and provincial powers not increased, but the new constitutional pact

also removed the Québec government's veto right on all constitutional amendments. Having won the referendum victory, the federalists thus attempted to silence Québec's separatist impulses once and for all. The Federal Liberal Party has since then never succeeded in electing a majority of members of parliament in Québec.

From Meech Lake to Charlottetown

After a break of several years, the constitutional saga entered a new and tumultuous era with the elections of Brian Mulroney in Ottawa (1984) and the Liberal Party led by Robert Bourassa in Québec (1985). Bringing Québec back into the constitutional fold with "honour and enthusiasm" became a priority for the new Canadian Prime Minister. In 1987, the federal government and the ten provinces drew up an agreement, known as the Meech Lake Accord, which called for constitutional changes in response to a minimum of Québec's traditional demands. To become official, the Accord had to be ratified by the Legislative Assemblies of the ten provinces before June 24, 1990. This seemed simple enough. However, the situation turned into a monumental fiasco when certain provincial premiers were elected out of office and replaced by opponents of the deal, when the Premier of Newfoundland changed his mind on the matter, and when public opinion in English Canada turned against the agreement, considered too advantageous to Québec. After a number of hopeless attempts to save it, what was to have been a "great national reconciliation" ended in resounding failure. By coincidence, June 24, the day the Meech Lake Accord failed to win approval, is Québec's national holiday, Saint-Jean-Baptiste Day. Hundreds of thousands of frustrated Quebecers took to the streets that day. In an attempt to avert a major swing towards sovereignty, Premier Bourassa resolved to present the federal government with an ultimatum. He announced that a referendum would be held before October 26, 1992, either on an acceptable federalist offer or on the proposition of sovereignty for Québec. Until the last moment, Robert Bourassa trully believed the other provinces and the federal government would produce, for the first time in the recent history of the country, an agreement responding to the demands of a majority of Quebecers. However, as the referendum date came near and it became clear that this was not going to happen, he put aside his threats and once again entered into negotiations with the other provinces and the federal government. A general agreement, the Charlottetown Accord, was thrown together in a few days. This was presented not only as a response to Québec's aspirations, but also to those of the other Canadian provinces and Canada's aboriginal peoples. To be ratified, however, this agreement would have to be accepted by a majority of the population of each province. October 26, 1992, the date originally planned for a provincial referendum on Québec's future, was kept as the date for this Canada-wide referendum. Bourassa promised to succeed in "selling" the package to the people of Québec. However, from the beginning, a majority of Quebecers were fiercely opposed to the deal and Bourassa even lost the support of certain militants within his own party. The rejection of the agreement by Quebecers was therefore no surprise. It was refected by a number of other provinces as well, though for completely opposite reasons. The matter of Québec's political status thus remained unresolved.

again found themselves engaged in the campaign of their lives, one whose outcome would determine the nature of Québec's political status. From the start of the campaign, both sides realized that the population was divided. No one could have predicted such a close race, however. The night of the referendum, every single ballot had to be counted before the results were known: 50.6% of Quebecers voted no to the sovereignty project while 49.4% voted yes! Incredible. A mere 28,000 votes separated the two options; Québec was literally split right down the middle. It was no surprise therefore when the leaders of the sovereignty movement, who had lost by so little, announced the night of the vote that another referendum would be called very soon. There is no doubt that for the next few years, the Québec political scene will be dominated by the question of Québec's political status. The day after the vote, Jacques Parizeau resigned as head of the Parti Québecois and Premier of Québec. He was replaced by Lucien Bouchard, until then head of the Bloc Québécois.

No: 50.6% - Yes: 49.4%

THE ECONOMY

Tired of the endless discussions throughout Canada on the Québec issue, Quebecers were anxious for the situation to be resolved. The opportunity presented itself with the 1993 federal election. With the election of the Bloc Québécois as official opposition in the Canadian Parliament, sovereigntist Quebecers could now show their support for Québec sovereignty at the federal level. In the beginning, the Bloc only expected a small showing, enough to make the sovereigntist case in Ottawa, the federal capital, but what occurred was a veritable landslide in Québec. The party won two thirds of the province's ridings and became the official opposition in Ottawa. The following year, the Québec population was called upon to elect a new provincial government, and it chose the Parti Québecois, the principal proponent of Québec sovereignty for the last quarter century. And so with a strong sovereigntist force in the Canadian Parliament and the Parti Québecois at the head of the Québec government, Quebecers would once again be given a choice between sovereignty and Canadian federalism.

After a few months a referendum was set for October 30, 1995. Fifteen years after the 1980 referendum, federalists and sovereigntists once

Long avoided by a majority of francophones, the world of business now occupies a particularly important place within Québec society. Since the 1960s, it has become a vehicle through which francophones have sought to take control of their own destiny, something that represents a significant social change. Until the Quiet Revolution, French students usually studied law or medicine or joined the clergy. The business world was seen as shallow, and controlled by anglophones, was also largely inaccessible. Francophones attitudes have changed drastically in the last 30 years: indifference has given away to a clear desire for direct involvement in Québec's economy. Today, a large proportion of students in the province study business administration. In fact, Québec is now turning out more graduates in this field than any other province. Media attention on the success of Québec entrepreneurs has helped to fuel this trend. The increased business activity among francophones has overshadowed Anglo-Canadian and American interests in the province. Over the last few years, there has been a reduction of a foreign presence, particularly from the United States, in the Québec economy. This is explained by many factors, including a climate of political uncertainty, the energy of local entrepreneurs, federal laws controlling investments by outsiders and the decline in certain sectors controlled by American investors. However, the impact of the 1989 Free Trade Agreement between Canada and the United States and of the 1994 agreement which includes Mexico in that market may reverse this trend.

The Government's Role

As in many western countries, government influence over business has been reduced over the past ten years. Despite this trend, the government remains, in many ways, an important player in the development of the economy. In fact, it is now the largest employer in Québec, boasting a large number of highly qualified management-level employees, as well as being active in stimulating the economy. The expansion of Hydro-Québec is a good example of the Québec government's successful intervention in business. From the time of Premier Jean Lesage, Hydro-Québec has had an almost exclusive monopoly on the production and distribution of hydro-electricity in Québec. This vital public enterprise, through the great sweep of its activities, has propelled the success of many private businesses in Québec. As well, certain engineering firms owe their growth, in Québec and beyond, to experience gained through participation in the construction of Hydro-Québec's immense hydro-electric projects. The Québec government has also had at its disposal over the last few decades a number of powerful investment tools for economic development, the most famous being the Caisse de Dépot et de Placement. This institution, which manages capital from the retirement funds of a huge number of Québec workers, has become a financial giant. While making only modest investments in its first few years, the Caisse de Dépot et de Placement began to provide massive support for Québec businesses after the Parti Québécois came to power in 1976. Today, it has one of the biggest stock portfolios in Canada. Presently, the concern exists that too much public intervention can be bad for an economy, but in a small economy like Québec's, the need for strong state involvement is generally agreed on.

Québec's Economic Future

Québec's economy is going through a period of great change, largely resulting from a move away from industrialization, as is seen in many western countries. The effects have been a diversification of the economy, a reduction in mining and the decline of certain traditional industries. At the same time there has been growth in several new and promising sectors. In addition, because of its abundance of affordable electrical power, Québec has become the world's third largest producer of molten aluminium and is an important centre for the processing of various other metals. As well, industries creating finished products in the fields of transportation, machinery and electrical appliances are important to Québec's economy. The Bombarbier company, for example, which began as a family snowmobile business, has expanded to become a major producer of rail and air transport products. Despite recent trends, natural resources remain a key asset for Québec. By harnessing certain powerful rivers in northern Québec, Hydro-Québec stands to produce a colossal amount of electrical power, 25,600 MW. With domestic demand for electricity now satisfied, plans are in the works to turn water into money by developing new hydro-electric power stations to meet the needs of several northeastern American states. This development strategy however, has not been unanimously approved by economists and it is coming up against vigorous opposition from environmental and aboriginal groups. Forest industries continue to have a significant place in Québec's economy, providing 100,000 jobs, and representing for 10% of the GDP. Lastly, the decline in the metal market around the world has resulted in a decrease in the once profitable mining of iron, asbestos, copper and zinc. Only gold production, with an annual total of 52,000 tonnes, has increased.

The recent restructuring of Québec's economy did not occur without some adverse consequences. Over the last ten years, the unemployment rate in the province has consistently hovered at about 10%. A shortage of jobs has hit certain parts of Montréal and a number of outlying regions particularly hard. In addition, the middle class has experienced an increasingly lower standard of living, while the rich have become richer. The progress made since the Quiet Revolution, particularly regarding the domination of the Québec economy

PORTRAIT

by Quebecers, is significant, but Québec faces many other important challenges before its economy can guarantee the development of a more harmonious society.

POPULATION

As is the case in the rest of America, the people of Québec have a diverse ancestry. The aboriginal peoples were joined by French colonists in the 16th century, the descendants of whom represent a majority of the current population. Over the last two centuries, Québec has experienced waves of immigration from all over the world, particularly from Britain and the United States. A 1991 census put Québec's population at nearly 7 million.

Aboriginal Peoples

The original inhabitants of Québec, the Inuits and other native groups, now represent less than 1% of Québec's total population. The ancestors of these peoples crossed the Bering straight from Northern Asia more than 12,000 years ago and moved into the region which would come to be known as Québec in successive waves several thousand years later. When Jacques Cartier "discovered" the region around the Gulf of St. Lawrence in the name of François I, the King of France, the area had already been home to a number of civilizations for thousands of years. During that period, the territory was populated by a complex mosaic of indigenous cultures, each with its own language, way of life and religious practices. With lifestyles adapted to climate and to the particularities of the landscape, northern populations survived by hunting and fishing, while the peoples of the St. Lawrence valley grew much of their food. The aboriginal population of Québec did not have a written language. Their history comes to us through oral tradition and from explorers' journals and anthropological research.

With the arrival of the first European colonists in the 16th century, these ancient civilizations went into decline. Unlike the European conquest of certain other regions in the Americas, clashes between colonists and aboriginals are not common to Québec history. The low population density of the vast territory allowed the first settlers to establish their small colonies without directly challenging the indigenous population, which for a long time had a far greater population. However, Québec aboriginals did suffer enormously during the first years of European colonization with the introduction of certain illnesses, such as influenza, measles and tuberculosis. In some areas, nearly half the aboriginal population was wiped out as a result of these diseases. Further devastation resulted as aboriginal groups engaged in bloody warfare against each other (using firearms provided by colonists) for control of the fur trade, a business introduced by the Europeans. Between 1645 and 1655, the confederation of five Iroquois nations nearly wiped out some of Canada's native groups. The destruction of aboriginal civilizations continued with losses of territory to the unrelenting spread of colonization. While the aboriginals of Québec were rarely the target of European military aggression, they were nevertheless soon overpowered by the colonists.

There are roughly 60,000 aboriginals presently living in Québec, three quarters of whom live in small communities scattered across the province. Though some of these groups live in areas where they can hunt and fish, in most cases traditional lifestyles have not survived. With the loss of their culture and the resulting sense of alienation, aboriginals endure major social problems. In recent years, however, Québec aboriginals have managed to attract increased attention from the media, leading to a sensitization on the part of government and the rest of the population to their issues. The international success of Kashtin, a Montagnais musical duo, has created awareness. Aboriginal land claims and issues of self-government have attracted much more attention, however. Particularly during the summer of 1990, when, for two months, armed Mohawks barricaded one of the main bridges connecting Montréal to the south shore of the St. Lawrence. The incident forced native concerns to the forefront. Two years later, an important step was taken with a project to reform the Canadian constitution to include a provision for native self-government. While a majority of Quebecers and Canadians voted against this constitutional reform package, called the Charlottetown Accord, on October 26, 1992, they did so in response to other, unrelated provisions. In fact, native claims enjoy strong support throughout the country.

The eleven aboriginal nations of Québec are regrouped into three distinct cultural families. The Abenaki, Algonquin, Attikamek, Cree,

Malecite, Micmac, Montagnais, and Naskapi are all part of the Algonquian culture, while the Wendat-Huron and the Mohawk are Iroquoian. The Inuit, for their part form a culture entirely their own. Here follows a brief description of each of the eleven native nations, in alphabetical order.

Originally occupying the region that is now New England, where many still live, the **Waban Aki (Abenaki)** settled first in Sillery (near Québec City) around 1675, then in 1684 next to falls of the Rivière Chaudière. The Waban Aki (Abenaki) had close ties with the French colonists, and shared many of their ancestral skills with them, including it seems the art of making of maple syrup. During the colcnial wars the Waban Aki (Abenaki) sided with the French, they also participated in the defence of the colony against British invaders, who were established to the south. In 1700 a group of them settled permanently in Odanak, a village that was later sacked during the British conquest in 1759. Today there are two Waban Aki (Abenaki) villages in Québec, Odanak and Wôlinak, located on the south shore of the St. Lawrence between the cities of Sorel and Bécancour. Of the 1,600 Waban Aki (Abenaki) living in Québec, about 350 live in one of the two villages. The baskets woven of hay and ash, for which the Waban Aki (Abenaki) are famous, are still made in these villages, however most Waban Aki (Abenaki) work in the neighbouring cities or elsewhere in Québec. The Waban Aki (Abenaki) language has practically disappeared.

Having lived in more or less remote areas away from the city centres, the **Anishnabe (Algonquin)** were able to preserve their nomadic way of life, living off the land, hunting, fishing and gathering.The traditional activities of the Algonquin were upset with the arrival of lumberjacks and prospectors to the Abitibi region in the middle of the last century. Their way of life thus became less nomadic. In Québec there are approximately 6,500 Anishnabe (Algonquin), 4,000 of which live in the communities of Grand-Lac-Victoria, Lac-Rapide and Maniwaki, in the Outaouais region, and Hunter's Point, Kebaowek, Lac-Simon, Pikogan, Témiscaming and Winneway, in Abitibi-Témiscamingue. The Anishnabe (Algonquin) language is still used in most of these communities.

Almost completely decimated during the 17th century as a result of epidemics and Iroquois wars, the **Attikamekw** took refuge with the

Cree, or Montagnais, peoples before integrating with a group from Lake Superior known as the O'pimittish Ininivac, who later settled in the Haute-Mauricie. The 4,000 Attikamekw in Québec still live in this region, mainly in the villages of Manouane, Weymontachie and Obedjiwan. The Attikamekw have remained close to nature working in forestry and advocating the development of resources while preserving the balance of nature. The Attikamekw language which is similar to Montagnais, is still spoken by the populations of all three communities.

Remarkably well adapted to the land and the rigours of the climate, the **Ndooheenoo (Cree)** have lived in Northern Québec for about the last 5,000 years. Despite their remote isolation, the Ndooheenoo (Cree) came into regular contact with Europeans very early. From the 17th century on, fur-trading with non-native merchants constituted one of the principal economic activities of the Ndooheenoo (Cree) nation. The decline in the fur-trade and the Canadian and Québec governments increased interest in the development of Québec 's far north, starting in the 1950's, have had a profound effect on the interaction between the Ndooheenoo (Cree) and their environment. However it was the signing in 1975 of the Convention de la Baie-James et du Nord Québécois, by the governments of Québec and Canada that really changed the Ndooheenoo (Cree) way of life. This signing allowed Hydro-Québec to construct hydro-electric dams on some of the strongest rivers of the region, in exchange the Ndooheenoo (Cree) were given 225 million dollars, ownership of 13,696 square kilometres and exclusive hunting and fishing rights in a territory measuring 151,580 square kilometres. The convention provided the Ndooheenoo (Cree) with the resources to take an active part in the economic development of their region, as shown by the number of dynamic enterprises undertaken by this nation in the last ten years. The 10,500 Ndooheenoo (Cree) of Québec today live in 9 villages: Waskaganish, Eastmain, Wemindji and Chisasibi, on the shores of James Bay; Whapmagoostui, near Hudson Bay; Nemiscau, Waswanipi and Mistissini, in the interior; and Oujé-Bougoumou, near the city of Chibougamau. The Ndooheenoo (Cree) language is still used by most of the population.

The **Inuit**, sometimes still erroneously called Eskimo, have lived for about 4,500 years in extreme northern Québec, in a region known in Inuktitut as Nunavik, which means "land to live off". Right up to the beginning of the 20th century, the Inuit still lived as their ancestors had, hunting with traditional weapons and living in igloos. The adaptation to a more modern lifestyle only occurred in the last few decades, and is still very new. Like the Cree, the Inuit also signed the Convention de la Baie-James et du Nord Québécois. Among other things, this convention granted the Inuit a greater degree of independence and self-government. They administer most of the services in Nunavik, and will eventually receive a regional government. The monetary compensation received by the Inuit is managed by the Société Makivik, and provides the Inuit with the tools necessary to play a larger role in the economic development of their region. In fact, thanks to Société Makivik, the Inuit of Québec are the owners of Air Inuit and First Air airline companies, which play a dominant role in air transport in Northern Canada. The 6,850 Inuit in Québec live in 14 villages located on the shores of Hudson Bay (Kuujjuarapik, Umiujaq, Inukjuak, Payungnituk, Akulivik), of Hudson Strait (Ivujivik, Salluit, Kangiqsujjuaq, Quaqtag) and of Ungava Bay (Kangirsuk, Aupaluk, Tasiujaq, Kuujjuaq and Kangiqsualujjuaq). A few dozen Inuit live in Chisasibi. The language of the Inuit, Inuktitut, is used in these communities. In Inuit schools it is the only language of instruction from kindergarten to third grade. Even though the Inuit have adopted a more modern lifestyle their ancestral culture and values remain significant.

Scattered across the territory the **Welustuk (Malecite)**, who were for a long time known as Etchemins, number only about 270 in Québec. They are also the only aboriginal nation not organized in at least one village. However, in 1827 the government created the first native reserve for them, on the shores of the Rivière Verte, in the Bas-St-Laurent region. The reserve was eventually bought back by the government because the Welustuk (Malecite) hardly ever used it and preferred to remain nomadic. In the end the Welustuk (Malecite) never settled down in one community, and were eventually integrated into neighbouring white communities. Even though the language is no longer spoken and no village exists, the Welustuk (Malécite) have had a chief and band-council since 1987.

The **Mïgmaq (Micmac)**, who number just under 4,000 in Québec, settled in the Gaspésie region and formed the villages of Restigouche and Gesgapegiag or lived with non-natives in Gaspé and the surroundings. Definitely one of the first Aboriginals nations, if not the first, to come into contact with Europeans, the Mïgmaqs

(Micmacs) were living on the shores of the St. Lawrence and the coast of the Atlantic Ocean when colonists arrived. Known as accomplished seamen, the MïgMaq (Micmac) also established temporary and permanent camps on various of the islands in the Gulf of St. Lawrence. With the economic development of the region, many Micmac have become lumberjacks and workers. A considerable number of **Mïgmaq (Micmac)** still speak the language, which is now taught in the two community schools.

When the Europeans arrived, the **Kanien'Kahaka (Mohawks)** formed one of the five Iroquois nations of the powerful Five-Nation Confederation, which was at the heart of the fur-trade war in the 17th century. Despite their association with this sophisticated political system, the Kanien'Kahaka (Mohawk) were still very independent and ambitious. Later, after they had become more sedentary, many became very skilled craftsmen, particularly as specialized steel workers. The Kanien'Kahaka (Mohawks) have an international reputation, even today, as expert craftsmen with steel on skyscrapers and bridges. Numbering around 12,000, the **Kanien'Kahaka** (Mohawks) are the largest group of aboriginal in Québec. They live mainly in three villages: Kahnawake, located close to Montréal, on the south shore of the St. Lawrence; Akwesasne, in the southwest corner of the province and overlapping the borders of Québec, Ontario and the state of New York; Kanesatake, about 50 kilometres west of Montréal on the shores of the Lac des Deux-Montagnes. Recall that land-claims by the Kanesatake Kanien'Kahaka (Mohawks) were at the centre of a crisis during the summer of 1990. Though many Kanien'Kahaka (Mohawks) have adapted to modern North American culture, others still live according to their ancestral teachings, based on the Great Law of Peace. **Kanien'Kahaka** (Mohawk) society is traditionally matrilinear, as such the clan mothers choose the chief. The Kanien'Kahaka (Mohawk) language is still spoken by several members of the communities.

Isolated across the vast regions of the Côte-Nord and the Basse-Côte-Nord, the **Innuat (Montagnais)** lived essentially by hunting, fishing, gathering and by the fur-trade up until the beginning of this century. The arrival of the mining and forestry industries as well as the construction of hydro-electric dams completely disrupted their way of life. Their culture remains nevertheless very vibrant, and the

Innuat (Montagnais) language is still spoken in most communities, especially the more isolated ones. The musical group Kashtin, from Uashat-Maliotenam, whose success in Europe and America is proof positive of the vital culture of this nation, as is the recent publication of the first Montagnais-French dictionary. In number the 12,000 Innuat (Montagnais) form the second largest aboriginal nation in Québec. They live in seven communities: Les Escoumins, Betsiamites, Uashat-Maliotenam in the Côte-Nord; Mingan, Natashquan, La Romaine and Pakuashipi in the Basse-Côte-Nord; Mashteulatsh in Lac-Saint-Jean, and Matimekosh near Schefferville.

The **Naskapi** nation has only one village in Canada, Kawawachikamach, founded in 1984 and located in northern Québec, a few kilometres from Schefferville. In accordance with the Convention du Nord-Est Québécois, the 475 Naskapis of Kawawachikamach own 285 square kilometres of territory and have exclusive hunting, fishing and trapping rights in a 4 144 square-kilometre territory. The Naskapis, who have only recently embraced modern culture, still hunt caribou, whose flesh and fur allow them to survive the harsh conditions of the arctic tundra. The Naskapi language is still spoken by the whole population.

When the first French colonists arrived the **Wendat-Huron** inhabited about twenty large villages in southeastern Ontario on the shores of Georgian Bay. Besides being excellent farmers they controlled an extensive commercial empire, which stretched from the Great Lakes to the Rivière Saguenay and Hudson Bay, and quite became naturally the main trading partners of the French merchants in the early years of colonization. However, this economically profitable relationship did not last, for within a few years the Wendat-Huron population was decimated, first by epidemics in 1634 and 1639, and then by repeated Iroquois attacks starting in 1640. In 1649 the remaining 300 Wendat-Hurons took refuge on the outskirts of Québec City, then settled on Île d'Orléans in 1657, then finally near the Rivière Saint-Charles in 1697, where the village of Wendake now sits. Located near Loretteville, this economically flourishing community is the only Wendat-Huron village in Québec. Of the approximate 2,500 Wendat-Hurons that live in Québec, about 950 live in Wendake. Some of the goods produced in Wendake, such as the moccasins, canoes and snowshoes, are known

worldwide. The Huron language is no longer used in Québec.

Francophones

A large percentage of Québec's francophones are descendants of the original French colonists who arrived in the country between 1608 and 1759. These immigrants arrived gradually. By 1663 there were only 3,000 settlers in New France. With an increased number of immigrants starting to arrive and with settlers starting families, the population of Québec stood at about 60,000 at the time of the British conquest of 1759. The settlers were mostly farmers from western France.

Today, after just over two centuries, the descendants of these 60,000 French-Canadians number in the millions, seven million of whom still live in Canada. Some interesting comparisons have been made between Québec's sharp rate of population growth and the growth rates seen elsewhere between 1760 and 1960. For example, while the population of the world during this same two hundred year period grew three times, and the population of Europe grew five times, the population of francophone Canada grew eighty times. This statistic is particularly surprising given that immigration from France had dwindled to almost nothing and that there were very few marriages between British and French families (with the exception of a number of Irish-French unions). In addition, between 1840 and 1930, about 900,000 Quebecers, most of them francophone, left Canada for the United States. This phenomenal growth of Canada's French population resulted largely from a remarkably high birth rate. Indeed, for a long time, French-Canadian women had an average of eight children. Families of 15 or 20 children were not unusual. This trend can be attributed to the influence of the Catholic church which sought to counterbalance the growth of the Protestant church in Canada. Interestingly, francophone Quebecers now have one of the lowest birth rates in the world, similar to that found in Germany and other western European countries.

The French majority in Québec had long been deprived of control over the economy of the province. In 1960, on average, francophones earned 66% of what anglophones did. With the Quiet Revolution, francophones began to take control of their economy. At the same time, they stopped thinking of themselves as French-Canadians and began to define themselves as Quebecers. Québec's total population, 82% of which is francophone, is characterized by an increasing number of immigrants.

Anglophones

Anglophones were for a long time stereotyped as Protestant and rich. In reality, Anglo-Quebecers have always been a diversified group. While anglophones may have been paid more on average, there have always been anglophones in every socio-economic group. The integration of anglophone immigrants from many backgrounds into Québec society has created a particularly heterogenous minority.

The first anglophone settlers arrived in Québec after the conquest of 1759. Most were merchants and they represented a small fraction of the total population. A second wave of English-speaking immigrants arrived from the United States between 1783 and the beginning of the 19th century. Of this group, many were British loyalists and others were simply farmers looking for land. Throughout the 19th century, immigrants from the British Isles arrived in Québec in great numbers. These British, Scottish and Irish arrivals, who were often dispossessed in their own country or the victims of famine, generally settled in the Eastern Townships, the Outaouais region or in Montréal. The declining number of immigrants from Great Britain at the end of the 19th century has been made up for by the integration of newcomers from a variety of other places.Immigrants from countries other than France or Great Britain have generally preferred to adopt the English language, feeling that this was necessary for economic success. For the same reason, a number of francophones have become assimilated into Québec's anglophone culture. A breakdown of the anglophone population according to origin shows that 60% of the population have British origins, 15% have French origins, 8% have Jewish origins and 3% have Italian origins.

English-speaking Quebecers currently represent just over 10% of the total population of the province. Three quarters of this group lives in Montréal, most in the west end of the city. They have their own institutions (schools, universities, hospitals, media) which function just as francophone institutions do. Anglophones represent a fairly large economic force, though unlike several decades ago, anglophones no longer dominate Québec's economy. The rise of the independence movement, Québec francophones's increasing role in the economy and the creation of linguistic laws aimed at protecting the French language have shaken up the anglophone community.Though many have simply left the province, the majority has stayed and has adapted. For example, 60% of anglophones surveyed say that they can speak French. This demonstrates a marked increase. Francophones and anglophones may differ on certain issues, but anglophones generally feel a profound attachment to Québec and particularly to Montréal, a city they played a major role in building.

Quebecers of Other Ethnic Origins

Immigrants from elsewhere besides France, Great Britain and the United States really only started to arrive at the beginning of the 20th century. In the first part of the century, before the economic crisis of the 1930s and World War II put a stop to immigration to Québec, most new arrivals were of Jewish and Italian descent. During the era of post-war prosperity, immigrants began to come in even greater numbers than before. Most originated in Southern and Eastern Europe. Starting in the 1960s, Québec began to see the arrival of immigrants from every continent. The greatest number came from Indochina and Haiti. At present, Quebecers of Italian, Jewish and Greek origin represent the largest ethnic minorities.

Even though these new arrivals tended to preserve their own culture as much as possible, they eventually adopted either the English or the French language, and were then integrated into that particular community. This integration was until recently the source of significant social tensions. Not so long ago immigrants for the most part were assimilated into the anglophone community, which threatened to completely reverse the linguistic balance, and therefore create a split within Québec's population between francophones and the rest of the population, known as allophones. Promoted in 1977, Bill 101, was intended to remedy this situation, by encouraging immigrants to integrate into the language of the majority by forcing new arrivals into French schools. However following pressures by the anglophone community in Québec and the rest of Canada, the law gradually lost its authority.

ARCHITECTURE

The 17th and 18th Centuries

A Vast Territory to Defend and Develop

During the Age of Enlightenment the immense French territory in America was something to behold. In 1750, New France stretched from Acadia to the estuary of the Mississippi and from the foothills of the Appalachians to those of the Rockies. Explorers and soldiers who forged these unknown territories were usually content just to bury plaques of tin or terracotta in significant places (promontories, river mouths) claiming them for the King of France. Sometimes a small fort was erected to defend a critical pass. These buildings occasionally gave rise to villages, which years later grew into the large cities of the American Midwest like Detroit or Pittsburgh. The hinterland remained for the most part untouched. This was native territory, visited sporadically by white fur trappers, and Jesuit missionaries. The population of French origin which reached about 65,000 souls in 1759, was concentrated in the valley of the St. Lawrence between Tadoussac and Montréal. Close to a quarter of this total lived in the three towns that lined the river (Québec city: pop. 8,400, Trois-Rivières: pop. 650 and Montréal: pop. 5,200), this represented a higher proportion of urban population than in France at the same time (22% in Canada compared to only 17% in France)!

The feeling of insecurity on the part of inhabitants as well as the King's desire to protect his colony, led the citizens of the towns and villages of New France to surround their settlements with fortified enclosures made of stone or wood, designed according to the principles of Vauban, military engineer of Louis XIV. These strongholds, financially supported by the Crown, were completed by a network of forts intended to slow the advancement of the enemy. Their walls had to be designed to withstand both the surprise attacks by hostile native tribes and the British Army, who were arriving by sea in warships equipped with heavy artillery weapons. By the end of the French Regime, Montréal and Québec City were both typical French provincial towns well-protected within their walls. Inside, the streets were lined with churches whose steeples reached above the walls, convents, colleges, hospitals and a few aristocratic and bourgeois homes surrounded by French gardens. Added to that would be a *place d'armes* (parade ground) and a market square.

For a long time the rivers, in particular the St. Lawrence, were the roads of New France. These water-ways became punctuated by portage routes, which often developed into tiny hamlets with little else besides an inn and a chapel. It was not until 1734 that a land route suitable for vehicles between Montréal and Québec City was opened. The Chemin du Roy (more or less the present Route 138), as it was called, was only passable in summer, during the winter the frozen river once again became the main thoroughfare. In 1750, the trip from Québec City to Montréal along the Chemin du Roy took five days.

The banks of the St. Lawrence River and Rivière Richelieu were slowly cleared and farmed. The King of France, who had chosen the seigneurial system to develop Canada, conceded long rectangles of land, perpendicular to the water, to individuals and religious communities who in exchange kept hearth and home and recruited new colonists. These new colonists in turn promised to pay the *cens* (tax) and swear *foi et hommage* (faith and homage) to their seigneur. Under the French Regime, few seigneurs actually fulfilled their obligations, finding their land too isolated and exposed to Iroquois and British attacks, while others used their land as hunting grounds or for speculation. It was not until the end of the 18th century that most of the seigneuries granted between 1626 and 1758 were actually cleared and planted.

The seigneuries were developed according to a strict model, that shaped the countryside of the valley of the St. Lawrence River and that of the Richelieu. Close to the river that supplied the seigneury would sit the seigneur's *domaine*, which included the manor house and wind or water mill, intended to grind the grains harvested by the workers into flour. The *commune*, a common pasture land, was also located on the river bank. A small village would be located to the side, generally including a simple church and five or six stone or wooden houses. The rest of the seigneury consisted of long narrow strips of land, laid out in successive rows, called *rangs*, and conceded to the colonists parcel by parcel as the number of families grew. Each strip was linked one to the other by *côtes*, roads bordering the narrow edge of the land concessions, and by *montées* which traversed the seigneury perpendicularly to the *rangs* and the *côtes*. The seigneurial system was abolished in 1854, however the division of land in *rangs* is still visible today.

French Architecture Adapted for the Québec Context

Of the enemies to do battle with, the cold was without a doubt the most dreaded. After rather difficult and often tragic beginnings, during which some colonists froze to death because their only shelter was a rickety wood cabin with paper windows, French architecture slowly adapted to the long winters. It had to overcome the shortage of skilled workers, in particular stone-cutters, as well as the lack of the necessary materials on the local market, like glass for the windows and slate for the roofs which otherwise had to be shipped in at great expense. As such the architecture of the French Regime is an architecture of colonization, pure and economic, where each element has a specific function, essential to the wellbeing of the inhabitants.

The French Regime house consisted of a modest rubble-stone rectangle squared off by two chimneys, and topped with a double-sloped roof covered with cedar shingles. Openings in the walls were few and far between and filled with small casement windows, since larger pieces of glass did not usually survive the ocean passage. The door was made of moulded panels. The interior remained rustic, since the priority was heating. The number of rooms was limited to the number of chimneys, since each room had to be heated. Starting in 1740, several buildings were equipped with cast iron stoves, forged at the Saint-Maurice ironworks. Occasionally stone sinks and built-in cupboards were found, and even more rarely, Louis XV style panelling. Seigneurial manors were architecturally similar to the houses of prosperous farms. There were exceptions, particularly with busy seigneurs or with religious communities where the manor also served as a convent. These manors took on the allure of veritable castles, the most famous being the Château de Longueuil, which no longer exists.

The architecture of the towns varied little from that of the country. The first priority remained of course the eternal battle with the cold, added to this however was the prevention of fires, which could easily result in tragedy in the absence of an effective fire-fighting system. Two edicts written by New France Intendants in 1721 and in 1727 pertained to construction inside the town walls. Wooden houses with mansard roofs, and their dangerous wooden shingles were forbidden; all buildings had to be made of stone and had to equipped with firebreak walls; attic floors had to be covered with terracotta tiles. Those who could not afford to obey such strict standards built up small communities outside the walls. Few examples remain of these wood houses, whose architecture was sober and functional.

Certain buildings were always more sophisticated. As expected in this colony settled by a devout society, the churches and chapels were the most elaborate. Some were even adorned with beautiful baroque façades of cut stone. Even more important though were the bright interiors, decorated with numerous Louis-XIV and Louis-XV style wood embellishments, painted white and gold leafed, which appeared in the first half of the 18th century. Most of the churches and chapels in the cities therefore were built with respect to the classic French urban perspectives. Unfortunately these perspectives were eliminated during the 19th century to ease traffic circulation... In the cities you might come upon *hôtels particuliers* with yards and gardens, more prominent however were three and four story buildings, occupied by businesses and built close to the street. These occasionally included a workshop and stone-vaulted basements for the storing of merchandise. A few beautiful examples of these basements can be found surrounding the Place Royale de Québec (see p 338).

After the Conquest

New France was devastated by the Seven Years' War, leaving many of its most beautiful buildings in ruins. What the British Conquest of 1760 did not succeed in destroying, the American invasion of 1775 and the War of 1812 did. Despite the political turmoil, however, the architectural vocabulary remained the same up until the end of the 18th century because the British population was too small to have an impact, and all the businessmen and labourers remained essentially French Canadian. The English Palladian style of architecture, influenced by the work of Andreo Palladio in Italy, was only visible after 1780 following the construction of a few homes for the British dignitaries and the high-ranking military officers posted in Québec City.

The 19th Century

The Evolution of a Tradition

The combination of the French Regime and Palladian architectural styles as well as the Regency trend formed the basis of Traditional Québec architecture, which reached its peak in the 19th century. It differed from the style of the previous century mainly by a lengthening of the drip moulding, which extended out to cover the long balcony across the front of the house. The elaborate and gabled drip mouldings of Regency cottages, inspired by Oriental architecture found a new function here. The balconies served as a halfway point between inside and outside, and as a place to relax in the summer. They also prevented snow from blocking windows and doors in the winter. Other particularly useful innovations of note were the decreased slope of the roofs, which avoided the inevitable wall of snow that would come falling down each time the unlucky inhabitant stepped outside, the raising of the masonry brick foundation to separate the house from the ground, and the installation of chimneys against the walls instead of in the middle thereby creating a better distribution of heat.

The windows remained French, but became more numerous and the number of panes decreased from 12 to 6; a storm window was added in the winter and a sNdooheenoo (Cree)n in the summer for the maximum comfort of those inside. Around 1820, the summer kitchen was introduced, a sort of lean-to positioned on the north side of the house, therefore exposed to cold winds. This room was cooler in summer and closed in winter. It was used to store perishables, while at the same time protecting the main house from chilling winter winds. Eventually the shingle roof was replaced by sheet metal, a material that is both resistant and non-flammable and which was used also on steeples and churches.

Churches also benefited from the contribution of Palladianism, thanks mostly to the Baillargé family from Québec City who revolutionized the art of building churches in Québec. This dynasty of architects added Palladian windows and pediments to the façades. They also added Louis XVI elements to the liturgical furniture.

At the other end of the scale Louis-Amable Quévillon (1749-1823) assembled every sumptuous element of the French Regime, to create his highly decorated diamond and star patterned ceilings.

The population of the villages of Québec was growing rapidly, leading to the enlargement or replacement of several churches of the French Regime. The Catholic nuns built convents and colleges for the education of boys and girls. In every region a new class of professionals including notaries, lawyers and doctors were building large homes. Traditional Québec villages established in this era differed from Ontarian and American villages; they consisted of country-style homes located very close together, so close they were almost duplexes; commercial buildings were rare, so boutiques and stores were located in buildings that resembled the residential dwellings. This style is explained by the townspeople's fear of fire (most of these village homes were made of wood), and by the Catholic Church's negative attitude towards the expansion of commerce.

American and British Immigration

Following the signing of the Treaty of Versailles in 1783, recognizing the independence of the United States, a number of Americans loyal to the crown of England took refuge in what remained of British North America, namely Canada. They brought with them a decidedly Georgian style of architecture from New England, characterized by the use of red brick, and white wooden accents. These new arrivals settled in areas left vacant by the French Regime, which the British colonial government divided into townships in the first half of the 19th century. Most of these townships are located in the Eastern Townships (see p 199) and the Outaouais (Ottawa Valley) regions (see p 272).

Québec City and Montréal also received a large number of Scottish and Irish immigrants between 1800 and 1850. They brought with them the severe but elegant neoclassical style of architecture, such as is seen in Dublin and in Glasgow. As a result cut stone definitively replaced rubble stone around 1810. Sash windows and columned porticoes became more common in urban settings, as did all manner of Greek and ancient Roman inspired architectural styles (pediments, Tuscan pilasters, parapets with palmettes). The first democratically elected municipal governments undertook the lighting and paving of the streets. This was also the era of large-scale engineering projects such as the dredging of the Canal de Lachine (1821-1825) and the appearance of shipyards larger than any ever seen before. This bustle of economic activity also attracted the rural French-Canadian population to the cities, such that the population of Montréal surpassed that of Québec City around 1830, and reached the 100,000 mark in 1860.

The Reign of Historicism

The building of the Protestant orphanage in Québec City in 1823, and in particular that of the Église Notre-Dame in Montréal between 1824 and 1829, both of which are Gothic Revival, announced the arrival of historicism in Québec architecture. Originally quite marginal, historicism would come to dominate the skyline of Québec's cities and towns in the second half of the 19th century. It is defined by the use of decorative elements taken from different architectural epochs in history, which were popularized thanks to archeological discoveries, the invention of photography, and the popularity of historic novels across the world.

An array of architectural styles influenced by ancient trends appeared almost simultaneously just before, and during, the reign of Queen Victoria (1837-1901), which explains why all these styles, so different one from the other, are all united under the simplified architectural term "Victorian". America being sufficiently removed from the Middle-Ages and the Renaissance models was not affected by the pastiche elements that for so long influenced Europe. As such North-American Victorian architecture was altogether new. It employed a backward looking style, that was meaningful only to North Americans.

The Gothic Revival style with its pointed arches, pinnacles and battlements, was for a long time reserved for churches, since the Middle Ages, from which it originated, was a period of great religious fervour. Similarly the Renaissance Revival style was favoured by the Bourgeois class for the building of sumptuous residences, since the Italian Renaissance corresponded to birth of a powerful middle class. The Second Empire style is associated with Napoleon III's refinement of Paris. The mansard roofs, covered in slate, were used repeatedly in Québec residential architecture and in a whole series of public buildings. Their popularity is a result of the French heritage of

Québec's society, but also the vogue of the style throughout North America between 1865 and 1900. Also not to be forgotten are the Romanesque Revival style characterized by compound arches, and short squat columns, the Queen Anne style, used in the suburbs of the new middle class, and in particular the Château Style, a mixture of the architecture of Scottish manors and Loire châteaux, which became, over the years, a sort of Canadian "National Style".

Victor Bourgeau (in the region of Montréal) and Joseph Ferdinand Peachy (in the region of Québec City), showed their talents well in the building of innumerable historicistic parochial churches, for all tastes and budgets. Bourgeau worked with a neoclassical vocabulary originally, as much a product of Brit John Ostell as the church architecture of the French Regime, before gradually turning towards Gothic Revival, and then Romanesque Revival. Peachy left his mark through a series of Renaissance Revival and Second Empire works.

Industrialization and Comfort

The Victorian era might seem contradictory, since while it looked backward in terms of its architectural style, it looked decidedly forward when it came to comfort. As such the technological innovations that made life much more agreeable are often overlooked: running water, automatic hot water heaters, more washrooms, central heating, telephones and electricity. Among the permanent changes to the buildings that are of note were the popularity of bay-windows, bow-windows and box-windows, as well as the use of flat roofs covered with tar and pebbles which retained the snow until it melted creating a natural insulator. Some of the more complex roofs belonging to religious and public buildings were covered with richly ornamented copper, which over the years acquired a rich green hue as a result of oxidation (verdigris).

In the second half of the 19th century, the railroad finally linked the major centres effectively. The railway also lead to the development of land north of the St. Lawrence (Saguenay—Lac-Saint-Jean, Laurentians and Témiscamingue) thereby helping French-Canadian farmers extend the boundary of settled land in Québec. The Industrial Revolution transformed the cities into manufacturing centres for primary goods. Workers' neighbourhoods sprouted like weeds around the factories, well-serviced by a net-work of tramways, originally horse-drawn (1861), then electrified (1892). The cities of Montréal and Québec City became bustling and business-oriented. Large stores, theatres, bank and insurance company headquarters opened their doors, attracting even more workers. Meanwhile the rest of Québec, essentially agriculturally-oriented was still anchored in tradition. It remained relatively isolated up until the middle of the 20th century.

The 20th Century

The Standard Urban Dwelling

The record birth rate in rural Québec around 1900, where families with 12 children were common, began to overburden the land. New regions such as Abitibi were opened up for settlement by the clergy, yet the attraction of the city proved insurmountable, despite the meagre wages. These uprooted workers longed for aspects of their country homes in the city: galleries and balconies, numerous well-lighted-rooms, a lot of storage space, which might also serve as henhouse or stables if necessary. It all had to be inexpensive to heat and relatively easy to maintain. Thus the Montréal-style dwelling was born!

Its exterior staircases, which wound their way tightly to the second floor in the limited space between the sidewalk and balcony, avoided the need to heat an interior stairwell. The balconies were reminiscent of rural galleries, leading directly into the homes (one or two per floor), which each had their own exterior entrance. Between 1900 and 1930 thousands of these duplexes, triplexes, quadruplexes, and quintuplexes were built along Montréal's straight streets. These two- and three-story buildings, with wooden frames and built on to each other, were covered either with local limestone, or brick. Even though the dwelling was supposed to be economical each one was adorned with a decorative cornice or parapet, balconies with Tuscan columns and beautiful *art nouveau* inspired stained-glass windows.

During the same era, a whole series of one-industry towns (paper or mining) were being born across Québec. These urban areas were created by the industries, and therefore equipped with a precise urban plan from the beginning. This included a well-designed public and residential architecture, renowned architectural works, modelled after English city-gardens.

Back to Basics

The École des Beaux-Arts de Paris, whose teachings engendered rigorous principles of architectural composition (symmetry, monumentalism), as well as a blend of French classicism, received a positive response among enlightened French-Canadians at the beginning of the 20th century. They sought to make a torch of the Beaux-Arts style, signalling the French presence in America. The twin columns, wrought-iron balconies supported by stone brackets and decorated railings were also found in the wealthy Anglo-Saxon neighbourhoods, for whom the Beaux-Arts style represented the tradition of Parisian refinement.

This timid back-to-basics movement on the part of French Canadians, took on much larger proportions with the descendants of English and Scottish merchants, making pilgrimages back across the Atlantic to rediscover the ruins of such and such Welsh Manor, or such and such Scottish farm-house that Grandfather grew up in. The British Arts and Crafts Movement found among these people enthusiasts of Herefordshire tiles, Elizabethan wainscotting, and Tudor chimneys. These people, who were sensitized to Great Britain's rural architecture and planned to reproduce it in Québec, were ironically the first to attempt to save some of the rural architecture of the French Regime, which was in sad decline in 1920. At the beginning of the thirties, some new buildings inspired by New France styling were being constructed. The Quiet Revolution during the sixties fortunately awakened a larger portion of the population to the importance of the traditions of their French heritage. It was the beginning of an era of painstaking restoration. However, while a part of the heritage was put on a pedestal, another part, that of the 19th century was shoved off by the wrecking ball! The destruction went on until the eighties. Efforts continue today to stave off the deterioration caused by the massive wave of demolition whose results have been compared to those of a military bombardment, and which left vacant lots scattered across the cities.

North American Influence

The favourable contacts that Québec architects and artists maintained with their colleagues in Paris, Brussels and London, did not deter them from opting out for America at the beginning of the 20th century. And so the first skyscrapers pierced the Montréal sky in 1928, following the definitive repeal of a ruling limiting the height of buildings to ten stories. Celebrated architects from the United States, designed many of Montréal's towers, giving the downtown core it present, decidedly North-American skyline. The geometric and aerodynamic French Art-Deco style, of which there are several examples in all regions of Québec, was replaced by Modern American architecture following the Second World War. Expo '67 presented the perfect opportunity to provide Montréal and the whole province with bold and representative examples of international architecture.

The Quiet Revolution of the sixties corresponds to a massive expansion of the suburbs and the construction of major public infrastructures. Since then, new highways crisscross Québec; huge schools, hospitals, cultural centres, and museums opened in towns where before there was only a church and a convent. Northern Québec received considerably more attention with the construction of major hydro-electric complexes. Cities underwent radical transformations in these respects : construction of the Métro (subway system) in Montréal, vast modern government complexes in Québec City, etc.

At the beginning of the eighties, the weariness resulting from the *ad nauseam* repetition of the same formulas put forward by the modernists, provoked a return to the styles of the past by way of post-modernism which freely combines reflective glass and polished granite in compositions which echo Art Deco and neoclassicism. The nineties for their own part present two opposing ideas : the culmination of post-modernism, in the form of a Romantic architecture, and the search for a new ultra-modern style of architecture, making use of new materials, computers and electronics.

THE ARTS

The aspirations and the concerns of a society are reflected in the work of its artists. For a long time, artistic expression in Québec

presented an image of a people constantly on the defensive, tormented by an unsatisfactory present situation and filled with doubt over the future. However, after World War II, and particularly after the Quiet Revolution, Québec culture evolved and became more affirming. Open to outside influences, and often very innovative, Québec culture is now remarkably vital.

Québec Literature

Literary output in Québec began with the writings of early explorers, like Jacques Cartier, and members of religious communities. These manuscripts were usually intended to describe the New World to authorities back in France. The lifestyles of the aboriginals, the geography of the region and the beginnings of colonization were the topics most often covered by authors of the period, such as Père Sagard (*Le Grand Voyage au Pays Hurons*, 1632) and Baron de La Hontan *(Nouveaux Voyages en Amérique Septentrionale,* 1703).

The oral tradition dominated literature during 18th century and the beginning of the 19th century. Later, the legends that had been passed down over generations, involving such things as ghosts, werewolves and pacts with the devil, were put down in writing. It was not until the end of the 19th century that Québec produced a more advanced literary movement. Most of the literary output of this period dealt with the theme of survival and reflected nationalist, religious and conservative values. The romanticization of life in the country, far from the temptations of the city, was a common element. Glorifying the past, particularly the period of French rule, was another common theme in the literature of the time. With the exception of certain works, most of the novels from this period are only of socio-historic interest.

Traditionalism continued to profoundly influence literary creation until 1930, when certain new literary movements began to emerge. The École Littéraire de Montréal (Montréal Literary School), and particularly the works of the poet Émile Nelligan, who was inspired by Baudelaire, Rimbaud, Verlaine and Rodenbach, stood in contrast to the prevailing style of the time. Nelligan, who remains a mythical figure, wrote poetry at a very young age, before lapsing into mental illness. Rural life remained an important ingredient of Québec fiction during this period, though certain authors began to put country life in a different light. Louis Hémon, in *Maria Chapdelaine* (1916), presented rural life more realistically, while Albert Laberge (*La Scouine*, 1918) presented the mediocrity of a country existence.

During the Great Depression and World War II, Québec literature began to reflect modernism. Literature with a rural setting, which continued to dominate, gradually began to incorporate themes of alienation. Another major step was taken when cities, where most of Québec's population actually lived, began to be used as settings in francophone fiction, in books such as *Bonheur d'Occasion* (*The Tin Flute* 1945), by Franco-Manitoban Gabrielle Roy.

Modernism became a particularly strong literary force with the end of the war, despite Maurice Duplessis's repressive administration. Two genres of fiction dominated during this period. The urban novel, and the psychological novel. Québec poetry entered a golden era distinguished by the work of a multitude of writers such as Gaston Miron, Alain Grandbois, Anne Hébert, Rina Lasnier and Claude Gauvreau. This era essentially saw the birth of Québec theatre as well. With regard to essay writing, the *Refus Global* (1948), signed by a group of painters, was the most incisive of many diatribes critical of the Duplessis administration.

Québec writers gained greater prominence with the political and social vitality brought about by the Quiet Revolution in the 1960s. A great number of political essays, such as *Nègre Blanc d'Amérique* (1968), by Pierre Vallière reflected an era of reappraisal, conflict and cultural upheaval. Through the plays of Marcel Dubé and those of rising talents such as Michel Tremblay, Québec theatre truly came into its own during this period. The use by novelists, poets and dramatists of idiomatic French-Canadian speech, called *joual*, was an important literary breakthrough of the time.

Contemporary literature is rich and diversified. New writers, such as Victor-Lévy Beaulieu, Alice Parizeau, Roch Carrier, Jacques Poulin, Louis Caron, Yves Beauchemin and Christian Mistral, have joined the ranks of previously established authors.

Music and Song

Music entered a modern era in Québec after World War II. In 1961, Québec hosted an international festival of *musique actuelle* (experimental music). Also in the 1960's, large orchestras, most notably the Orchestre Symphonique de Montréal (OSM), began to attract bigger crowds. Several important music festivals are held throughout Québec, including the festival of *musique actuelle* in Victoriaville and the summer festival in the Lanaudière region.

Popular culture is an important part of Québec culture and when it comes to pop-culture Quebecers are leaders. Be it Celine Dion at the Grammies, comedians or the Cirque du Soleil. Humour plays an important part in the culture and this is reflected in the ongoing popularity of comedians with a particularly theatrical bent. The Cirque du Soleil, which now includes a number of troupes performing around the world, has literally reinvented the circus.

The popular song, which has always been important to Québec folk culture, gained further popularity after World War I with the rise of radio and the improved quality of music recordings. The greatest success was known by La Bolduc (Marie Travers), who sang popular songs in idiomatic French. In the 1950s, the prevailing popular music trend involved adapting American songs or reinterpreting songs from France. As a result, certain talented Québec song writers working at the time, like Raymond Levesque and Felix Leclerc, were virtually ignored until the 1960s.

With the Quiet Revolution, song writing in Québec entered a new and vital era. Singers like Claude Leveille, Jean-Pierre Ferland, Gilles Vigneault et Claude Gauthier won over crowds with nationalist and culturally significant lyrics. In 1968, Robert Charlebois made an important contribution to the Québec music scene by producing the first French-language rock album. Currently, established performers like Plume Latraverse, Michel Rivard, Diane Dufresne, Pauline Julien, Claude Dubois, Richard Seguin, Paul Piche are being joined by newcomers like Jean Leloup, Joe Bocan, Sylvie Bernard, Vilains Pingouins and Richard Desjardins. The most well known name these days is Celine Dion, who

Softimage

Founded in 1986 by Montrealer Daniel Langlois, Softimage, particularly renowned for its expertise in 3D animation, has quickly become the world leader in the development of advanced digital media creation. Since 1990, a great number of major special effects movies, including *Jurassic Park, The Mask, Casper, Twister* and *Dragon Heart*, among others, were created with the help of Softimage software.

Two years after having put its shares on the American stock market, Softimage amalgamated with Microsoft. Following this agreement, Daniel Langlois was named Microsoft's Senior Director of Advanced Authoring Technology. Since computer-generated images were first developed, Langlois has consistently drawn simultaneous recognition and international honours, as much for his entrepreneurship as for his artistic work (named Canada's Entrepreneur of the Year in 1994, honorary doctor in administration at the Université de Sherbrooke in 1996, Personality of the Year by the daily paper *La Presse*; received the Industrial Research Association's Entrepreneur award and was invited to speak at the prestigious Americas Society in New York). On the artistic front, Langlois designed and produced the first stereoscopic 3D computer animation film in IMAX format, presented at the Vancouver Expo in 1986. In 1985, he also co-directed the short *Tony de Petrie*, which won several international awards and was applauded as a milestone in the history of computer animation.

With the comfortable success of his enterprise, in 1997, Langlois gave his name to a foundation that aims to foster the broadcasting and creation of artistic works. He thus took over the defunct Montreal Festival of New Cinema and restructured the event as the Montreal International Festival of Cinema & New Media. In 1998, a cinema complex meant for *cinema d'auteur* and artistic creation with the aid of technology will see the light of day on St. Laurent Boulevard, just around the corner from Softimage's head office.

sings in both French and English. Her amazing voice has made her *the* pop diva around the world. There is also the particular achievement of songwriter Luc Plamondon and his participation in the production of *Starmania*. In addition, certain non-francophone artists, like Leonard Cohen and the group Kashtin, enjoy a strong international reputation.

Visual Arts

Visual art in Québec through most of the 19th century displayed a rather antiquated aesthetic. With the support of major art collectors in Montréal, Québec artists began to experiment somewhat towards the end of the 19th century and the beginning of the 20th century. Landscape artists, including Lucius R. O'Brien, achieved a certain success during this period. The Barbizon school, characterized by representations of rural life, was also influential. Inspired by the La Haye school, painters like Edmund Morris began to introduce a suggestion of subjectivism into their work.

The works of Ozias Leduc, which are attributed to the Symbolism trend, began to show a tendency towards the subjective interpretation of reality, as did the sculptures of Alfred Laliberté at the beginning of the 20th century. Some works completed around this time exhibit a certain receptiveness of European styles, among them the paintings of Suzor-Côté. It is however, in the work of James Wilson Morrice, who was inspired by Matisse, that the influence of the European School is most explicitly detectable. Morrice, who died in 1924, is considered by most as the forerunner of modern art in Québec . It would, however, take several years, marked notably by the work of Marc-Aurèle Fortin, landscape and urban artist, before the visual arts in Québec were in line with contemporary trends.

Québec modern art began to affirm itself during World War II thanks to the leaders of the group, Alfred Pellan and Paul-Émile Borduas. In the 1950s, two major trends developed in Québec's art community. The most significant of these involved non-figurative works, of which there were two general categories: abstract expressionism, as seen in the works of

Marcelle Ferron, Marcel Barbeau, Pierre Gauvreau and Jean-Paul Riopelle, and geometric abstraction, represented by artists such as Jean-Paul Jérôme, Fernand Toupin, Louis Belzile and Redolphe de Repentigny. The other major trend in art was a new wave of figurative painting by artists including Jean Dallaire and Jean-Paul Lemieux.

Post-war trends continued into the 1960s. The emergence of new painters, such as Guido Molinari, Claude Tousignant and Yves Gaucher brought increased attention to the geometric abstraction style. Engraving and print-making became more common mediums of expression, art "happenings" were frequent and artists began to be asked to provide work for public places. Styles and influences diversified greatly in the early 1970s, resulting in the eclectic art scene found in Québec today.

Cinema

While some full-length films were made earlier, the birth of Québec cinema really did not occur until after World War II. Between 1947 and 1953, independent producers brought a number of literary adaptations to the screen, including *Un Homme et Son Péché* (1948), *Seraphin* (1949), *La Petite Aurore l'Enfant Martyre* (1951) and *Tit-Coq* (1952). However, the arrival of television in the early 1950s resulted in a ten-year period of stagnation for the Québec film industry.

A cinematic renaissance during the 1960s occurred largely thanks to the support of the National Film Board (NFB-ONF). With documentaries and realistic films, directors focused primarily on a critique of Québec society. Later, the full-length feature film dominated with the success of certain directors like Claude Jutras (*Mon Oncle Antoine,* 1971), Jean-Claude Lord (*Les Colombes,* 1972), Gilles Carle (*La Vraie Nature de Bernadette,* 1972), Michel Brault (*Les Ordres,* 1974), Jean Beaudin (*J.A. Martin Photographe,* 1977) and Frank Mankiewicz (*Les Bons Débarras,* 1979). The NFB-ONF and other government agencies provided most of the funding for these largely uncommercial works.

Import feature films of recent years include those of Denys Arcand (*Le Déclin de l'Empire Américain,* 1986, and *Jésus de Montréal,* 1989, both available in English), Jean-Claude Lauzon (*Un Zoo la Nuit,* 1987, and *Léolo,* 1992), Léa Pool (*À Corps Perdu,* 1988) and Jean Beaudin (*Being at Home With Claude,* 1992). Director Frédérick Back won an Academy Award in 1988 for his superb animated film, *The Man who Planted Trees.*

PRACTICAL INFORMATION

I nformation in this chapter will help you to better plan your trip, not only well in advance, but once you've arrived in Québec. Important details on entrance formalities and other procedures, as well as general information, have been compiled for English-speaking visitors from other countries. Finally, we explain how to use this guide. All this said, we wish you happy travels in Québec!

ENTRANCE FORMALITIES

Passports

A valid passport is usually sufficient for most visitors planning to stay less than three months; visas are not required. A three-month extension is possible, but a return ticket and proof of sufficient funds to cover this extension may be required.

Caution: some countries do not have an agreement with Canada concerning health and accident insurance, so it is advisable to have the appropriate coverage. For more information, see the section entitled **"Health"** on page 60.

Extended Visits

Visitors must submit a request to extend their visit **in writing** and **before** the expiration of their visa (the date is usually written in your passport) to an Immigration Canada office. To make a request you must have a valid passport, a return ticket, proof of sufficient funds to cover the stay, as well as the $65 non-refundable filing-fee. In some cases (work, study), however, the request must be made **before** arriving in Canada.

EMBASSIES AND CONSULATES

Abroad

Australia
Canadian Consulate General: Level 5, Quay West, 111 Harrington Road, Sydney, N.S.W., Australia 2000, ☎(61) 2364-3000, ≠(61) 2364-3098.

Belgium
Canadian Embassy: 2 Avenue de Tervueren, 1040 Brussels, ☎(2) 735.60.40, ≠(2) 732.67.90, Métro Mérode

Denmark
Canadian Embassy: Kr. Bernikowsgade 1, DK=1105 Copenhagen K, Denmark, ☎(45)12.22.99, ⊷(45)14.05.85

Finland
Canadian Embassy: Pohjos Esplanadi 25 B, 00100 Helsinki, Finland, ☎(9) 171-141, ⊷(9) 601-060.

Germany
Canadian Consulate General: Internationales Handelzentrum, Friedrichstrasse 95, 23rd Floor, 10117 Berlin, Germany, ☎(30) 261.11.61, ⊷(30) 262.92.06.

Great Britain
Canada High Commission: Macdonald House, One Grosvenor Square, London W1X 0AB, England, ☎(171) 258-6600, ⊷(171) 258-6384.

Italy
Canadian Embassy: Via G.B. de Rossi 27, 00161 Rome, ☎(6) 44.59.81, ⊷(6) 44.59.87.

Netherlands
Canadian Embassy: Parkstraat 25, 2514JD The Hague, Netherlands, ☎(70) 361-4111, ⊷(70) 365-6283.

Norway
Canadian Embassy: Oscars Gate 20, Oslo 3, Norway, ☎(47) 46.69.55, ⊷(47) 69.34.67.

Spain
Canadian Embassy: Edificio Goya, Calle Nuñez de Balboa 35, 28001 Madrid, ☎(1) 431.43.00, ⊷(1) 431.23.67.

Sweden
Canadian Embassy: Tegelbacken 4, 7th floor, Stockholm, Sweden, ☎(8) 613-9900, ⊷(8) 24.24.91.

Switzerland
Canadian Embassy: Kirchenfeldstrasse 88, 3000 Berne 6, ☎(31) 532.63.81, (31) ⊷352.73.15.

United States
Canadian Embassy: 501 Pennsylvania Avenue, N.W., Washington, DC, 20001, ☎(202) 682-1740, ⊷(202) 682-7726.

Canadian Consulate General: Suite 400 South Tower, One CNN Center, Atlanta, Georgia, 30303-2705, ☎(404) 577-6810 or 577-1512, ⊷(404) 524-5046.

Canadian Consulate General: Three Copley Place, Suite 400, Boston, Massachusetts, 02116, ☎(617) 262-3760, ⊷(617) 262-3415.

Canadian Consulate General: Two Prudential Plaza, 180 N. Stetson Avenue, Suite 2400, Chicago, Illinois, 60601, ☎(312) 616-1860, ⊷(312) 616-1877.

Canadian Consulate General: St. Paul Place, Suite 1700, 750 N. St. Paul Street, Dallas, Texas, 75201, ☎(214) 922-9806, ⊷(214) 922-9815.

Canadian Consulate General: 600 Renaissance Center, Suite 1100, Detroit, Michigan, 48234-1798, ☎(313) 567-2085, ⊷(313) 567-2164.

Canadian Consulate General: 300 South Grande Avenue, 10th Floor, California Plaza, Los Angeles, California, 90071, ☎(213) 687-7432, ⊷(213) 620-8827.

Canadian Consulate General: Suite 900, 701 Fourth Avenue South, Minneapolis, Minnesota, 55415-1899, ☎(612) 333-4641, ⊷(612) 332-4061.

Canadian Consulate General: 1251 Avenue of the Americas, New York, New York, 10020-1175, ☎(212) 596-1600, ⊷(212) 596-1793.

Canadian Consulate General: One Marine Midland Center, Suite 3000, Buffalo, New York, 14203-2884, ☎(716) 852-1247, ⊷(716) 852-4340.

Canadian Consulate General: 412 Plaza 600, Sixth and Stewart Streets, Seattle, Washington, 98101-1286, ☎(206) 442-1777, ⊷(206) 443-1782.

In Montreal

Australia
Australian High Commission: (no office in Montréal), 50 O'Connor Street, Ottawa, Ontario, K1N 5R2, ☎(613) 236-0841, ⊷(613) 236-4376.

Belgium
Consulate General of Belgium: 999 Boulevard de Maisonneuve Ouest, suite 1250, Montréal, H3A 3C8, ☎(514) 849-7394, ⊷(514) 844-3170.

Denmark
Consulate General of Denmark: 1 Place-Ville-Marie, 35th Floor, Montréal, H3B 4M4, ☎(514) 871-8977.

Finland
Consulate General of Finland: 800 Carré Victoria, Suite 3400, Montréal, H4Z 1E9, ☎(514) 397-7600.

Germany
Consulate General of Germany: 1250 Boulevard René-Lévesque Ouest, Suite 4315, Montréal, H3B 4X1, ☎(514) 931-2277.

Great Britain
British Consulate General: 1155 Rue University, Suite 901, Montréal, H3B 3A7, ☎(514) 866-5863.

Italy
Consulate General of Italy: 3489 Rue Drummond, Montréal, H3G 1Z6, ☎(514) 849-8351, ≈(514) 499-9471.

Netherlands
Consulate General of the Netherlands: 1002 Rue Sherbrooke Ouest, Suite 2201, Montréal, H3A 3L6, ☎(514) 849-4247, ≈(514) 849-8260.

Norway
Consulate General of Norway: 1155 Boul. René-Lévesque Ouest, Suite 3900, Montréal H3B 3V2, ☎(514) 874-9087.

Spain
Consulate General of Spain: 1 Westmount Square, Montréal, H3Z 2P9, ☎(514) 935-5235, ≈(514) 935-4655.

Sweden
Consulate General of Sweden: Tour de la Bourse, 800 Carré Victoria, 34th Floor, Montréal, H4Z 1E9, ☎(514) 866-4019, ≈(514) 397-7600.

Switzerland
Consulate General of Switzerland: 1572 Avenue Dr Penfield, Montréal, H3G 1C4, ☎(514) 932-7181, ≈(514) 932-9028.

United States
American Consulate General: Place Félix-Martin, 1155 Rue Saint-Alexandre, Montréal, H2Z 1Z2, ☎(514) 398-9695, ≈(514) 398-9748.

Mailing address: C.P. 65 Stations Desjardins, Montréal, H5B 1G1.

TOURIST INFORMATION

Québec is divided into 19 tourist regions. Each region has its own regional tourist associations, called the Associations Touristiques Régionales or ATR, responsible for the distribution of information on the region. Basic information guides are published for each tourist region, and are available free of charge from these associations and offices, or from the Délégations Générales du Québec outside of Québec. In Montréal, Québec City, and Laval, tourist information is available from official tourist offices.

Various guides and maps exist that might prove very useful for visitors seeking more information on certain aspects of Québec. Note that most of these are in French. Guides for specific regions include *Gaspésie-Bas-Saint-Laurent-Îles-de-la-Madeleine* (Éditions Ulysse; available in French only), *Charlevoix-Saguenay-Lac-Saint-Jean* (Éditions Ulysse; available in French only) and *Montréal* (Ulysses Travel Publications). And for outdoor enthusiasts: *25 Randonnées à Vélo au Québec* (Éditions Tricycle; a French-language guide to bicycle tours in Québec), *Répertoire des Sentiers de Vélo de Montagne* (Éditions Tricycle; a French-language guide to mountain-bike trails), *Hiking in Québec* (Ulysses Travel Publications), the map *Les Parcours Canotables du Québec* (Fédération Québécoise du Canot-Camping; a French-language map of canoeable rivers and lakes in Québec), *Ski-de-Fond au Québec* (a French-language guidebook to cross-country skiing in Québec, Éditions Ulysse) and *Motoneige au Québec* (a French-language guidebook to snowmobiling in Québec). For information on accommodations: *Affordable Bed and Breakfasts in Québec* (Ulysses Travel Publications), or, try a guide in French to country inns in Québec called *Le Guide des Auberges et Relais de Campagne du Québec* (Édition de l'Homme), finally mapmakers Carthothèque Géo-Montage publishes a series of Québec regional maps, as well as a map on cycling in Québec.

Abroad

Belgium
Délégation Générale du Québec: 46 Avenue des Arts, 7e étage, 1040 Bruxelles, ☎(2) 512.00.36, Métro Art-Loi.

Comission Canadienne du Tourisme: Rue Amèricaine, 27, 1060 Bruxelles, ☎(2) 538-5792, ⋈(2) 539-2433.

Canada
Bureau du Québec: 20 Queen St., West, Suite 1504, Box 13, Toronto, Ontario, M5H 3S3, ☎(416) 977-6060, ⋈(416) 596-1407.

Germany
Destination Québec: c/o MEKS, GmbH, Vautierstrasse 92, D-40235 Düsseldorf, Germany, ☎(211) 914-26-0, ⋈(211) 914-26-14.

Great Britain
Destination Québec: c/o Aurora Marketing, Suite 154, 4th Floor, 35-37 Grosvenor Gardens House, Grosvenor Gardens, Victoria, London, SW1W 0BS, England, ☎(171) 233-8011, ⋈(171) 233-7203.

Switzerland
Welcome to Canada!: 22, Freihofstrasse, 8700 Küsnacht, ☎(1) 910 90 01, ⋈910 38 24.

United States
Tour & Travel: 84-03 Chapin Pkwy, Floor 3, Jamaica Queens, New York 11432, ☎(718) 657-1727, ⋈(718) 206-9114.

MC & IT: 420 East 55th Street, New York, NY 10022, ☎(212) 317-1711, ⋈(212) 317-1881.

In Québec

For information on the different Tourist Regions, call **toll-free**:

from the region of Montréal, ☎873-2015;
from Québec, United States or Canada, ☎1-800-363-7777.

You can also write to: **Tourisme Québec**, Case Postale 979, Montréal H3C 2W3.

In Montréal

For detailed information, maps, flyers, accommodation information for Montréal and all the tourist regions of Québec:

Infotouriste 1001 Rue du Square-Dorchester, Métro Peel.

Ulysses Travel Bookshop 4176 Rue Saint-Denis, ☎(514) 843-9447, Métro Mont-Royal or
560 Président-Kennedy, ☎(514) 843-7222, Métro McGill.

In Québec City

Maison du Tourisme de Québec 12 Rue Sainte-Anne, Québec G1R 3X2.

Ulysses Travel Bookshop 4 Boul. René-Lévesque Est, Québec, ☎(418) 529-5349.

Centre d'Information de l'Office du Tourisme et des Congrès de la Communauté Urbaine de Québec 835 Avenue Wildfrid Laurier, QC, G1R 2L3, ☎(418) 649-2608.

Grand Nord Québécois–Ministère du Tourisme Direction des projets du Grand Nord Québécois, 960 Boulevard René-Lévesque Est, bureau 400, Québec, G1R 2B5, ☎(418) 643-9131, ⋈(418) 643-0549.

AIRPORTS

There are two major airports in the province of Québec: **Dorval** and **Mirabel**. A third one, in **Québec City** is much smaller and serves only a limited number of destinations, although it does receive some international flights. The Dorval and Québec City airports are intended for international and domestic flights whereas Mirabel Airport handles only chartered flights.

Dorval Airport

Location

Dorval airport is located approximately 20 kilometres from downtown Montréal, and is 20 minutes by car. To get downtown from here, take Highway 20 E. to the junction of

Highway 720 (the Ville-Marie), follow signs for "Centre-ville, Vieux-Montréal".

Information

For information regarding airport services (arrivals, departures, other information), an information counter is open from 6am to 10pm seven days a week; ☎(514) 633-3105.

Buses

From Dorval to downtown: with the Connaisseur Bus Company (☎514-934-1222). Schedules vary, so it's best to contact the company after arriving at Dorval airport. The bus stops at the Hôtel Reine-Elizabeth *(900 Boul. René-Lévesque Ouest, Métro Bonaventure)*, the Château Champlain, the Centre Sheraton and the Voyageur Bus Terminal *(505 Boul. de Maisonneuve Est, Métro Berri-UQAM)*. Free for children under five. Cost: $9 one way and $16.50 return.

Car Rentals

The major car rental companies, such as Tilden, Hertz, Avis, Budget and Thrifty, have offices at the airport.

Limousines

Limousine Montréal provides limo service (☎514-333-5466). Cost: four passengers, $40 one way; 6 passengers, $80 one way; 10 passengers, $125 one way.

Foreign Exchange

A Thomas Cook counter is open from 6am to 11pm, but a commission is charged. Better exchange rates are available in downtown Montréal (see p 88).

Lost and Found

☎(514) 633-3094

Mirabel Airport

Location

This airport is located approximately 50 kilometres north of Montréal, in Mirabel. To reach downtown Montréal from Mirabel, follow the Autoroute des Laurentides (Hwy 15) S. until it intersects with Autoroute Métropolitaine (Hwy 40) E., which you follow for a few kilometres, then continue once again on the 15 S. (which is now called Autoroute Décarie) until Autoroute Ville-Marie (Hwy 720). Follow the signs for "Centre-ville, Vieux-Montréal". The trip takes 40 to 60 minutes *(☎514-476-3010 or 1-800-465-1213)*.

Information

For information on airport services (arrivals, departures, and other information), visit the information counter, it is open daily from 8am to 11:30pm. There is also a 24-hour telephone service *(☎514-476-3010 or 1-800-465-1213)*.

Buses

From Mirabel to downtown Montréal: the Connaisseur Bus Company offers a shuttle service (☎514-934-1222). Because the schedule changes often, it is best to get information upon arriving at Mirabel. The bus stops at the Hôtel Reine-Elizabeth (Queen Elizabeth Hotel), (Rue Mansfield, Métro Bonaventure) and at the Voyageur Bus Terminal *(505 Boul. de Maisonneuve Est, Métro Berri-UQAM). Cost: $7.25 one-way, $10.25 return (free for children under five)*.

From Dorval to Mirabel: with the Connaisseur Bus Company *(☎514-934-1222)*. Daily departures from 9:20am to 10:30pm. Cost: $12 one-way and $16 return.

Limousine

Limousine service is provided by Limousine Montréal Inc. *(☎514-333-5466)*. Cost: 4 passengers, $70 + tax one way and $140 return; 6 passengers, $115 + tax one way and $230 + tax return; 10 passengers, $150 + tax one way.

PRACTICAL INFORMATION

Car Rentals

All the large car rental companies: Avis, Hertz, Tilden, Budget, and Thrifty, have offices at the airport (see p 86).

Foreign Exchange

The Royal Bank of Canada is open during flight arrivals and departures, but they charge a commission. Better exchange rates are available in downtown Montréal (see p 88). This bank, however, has various automatic teller machines for currency exchange of the more common currencies.

Lost and Found

☎(514) 476-3010

Jean-Lesage Airport (Québec City)

Location

Though small, the Québec City airport handles international flights. It is located on the periphery of Sainte-Foy and Ancienne-Lorette. To get there from Vieux-Québec, take Boulevard Laurier heading west to Autoroute Henri-IV (Hwy 40 N.). From there take Boulevard Hamel going west and follow it until the Route de l'Aéroport: 510 Rue Principale, Sainte-Foy, G2E 5W1, ☎418-640-2600, ≈418-640-2656.

Public Transportation

There is a bus from the airport to the downtown area, with only two daily departures, at 8am and at 5pm.

Airport Shuttle

A company called La Québécoise (☎418-872-5525, ≈872-0294), travels between the airport and several hotels in the downtown area of Québec City. A one-way trip costs $8 to Sainte-Foy and $9 to Québec for adults and half price for children.

Car Rentals

Various car rental agencies, such as Budget, Thrifty, Hertz and Tilden, are located at the airport.

Foreign Exchange

The Thomas Cook foreign exchange office is open every day from 8am to 9pm.

Lost and Found

☎(418) 640-2765.

CUSTOMS

If you are bringing gifts into Québec, remember that certain restrictions apply: **Smokers** (minimum age is 16) can bring in a maximum of 200 cigarettes, 50 cigars, 400 g of tobacco, and 400 tobacco sticks. **Wine and alcohol**: the limit is 1.1 litres; in practice, however, two bottles per person are usually allowed. The limit for beer is 24 cans or bottles, the 355 ml size.

There are very strict rules regarding the importation of **plants, flowers, food** and other **vegetation**; it is therefore not advisable to bring any of these types of products into the country. If it is absolutely necessary, contact the Customs-Agriculture service of the Canadian embassy **before** leaving.

If you are travelling with your **pets**, you will need a health certificate (available from your veterinarian) as well as a rabies vaccination certificate. It is important to remember that the vaccination must be carried out **at least** 30 days **before** your departure and should not have been administered more than one year ago.

Tax reimbursements for visitors: it is possible to get reimbursed for the taxes paid on purchases made while in Québec (see p 57).

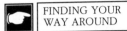

FINDING YOUR
WAY AROUND

By Car

Good road conditions and cheaper oil prices than in other parts of the world make driving an ideal way to travel all over Québec. Excellent road maps published in Québec and regional maps can be found in bookstores and in tourist information centres.

Things to Consider

Driver's License: As a general rule, foreign driver's licenses are valid for six months from the arrival date in Canada.

Winter Driving: Although roads are generally in good condition, the dangers brought on by drastic climatic conditions must be taken into consideration. Roads are often transformed into virtual skating rinks by black ice. Wind is also a factor, causing blowing snow, and reducing visibility to almost nil. All these factors, which Quebecers are used to, require prudent driving. If you plan on driving through remote areas, be sure to bring along a blanket and some supplies should your car break down.

Driving and the Highway Code: Turning right on a red light and turning from a one-way to another one-way on a red light are both **forbidden** in Québec. Priority to the right is the law here, however is not always observed so pay attention. Signs marked "Arrêt" or "Stop" against a red background must always be respected. Come to a complete stop even if there is no apparent danger.

Traffic lights are often located on the opposite side of the intersection, so be careful to stop on the stop line, a white line on the pavement before the intersection. When a school bus (usually yellow in colour) has stopped and has its signals flashing, you must come to a complete stop, no matter what direction you are travelling in. Failing to stop at the flashing signals is considered a serious offense, and carries a heavy penalty. Wearing of seatbelts in the front and back seats is compulsory at all times.

There are no tolls on Québec highways, and the speed limit on highways *(autoroutes)* is 100 km/h. The speed limit on secondary highways is 90 km/h, and 50 km/h in urban areas.

Gas Stations: Because Canada produces its own crude oil, gasoline prices are less expensive than in Europe. However, due to hidden taxes, gas prices in Québec are considerably higher than those in the United States and in Western Canada. Some gas stations (especially in the downtown areas) might ask for payment in advance as a security measure, especially after 11pm.

Car Rentals

Many travel agencies have agreements with the major car rental companies (Avis, Budget, Hertz, etc.) and offer good values; contracts often include added bonuses (reduced ticket prices for shows, etc.). Package deals usually prove to be a good deal. However if you cannot get a package it is cheaper to rent your car here than it is from abroad.

One good way to save on rental costs and meet local Quebecers is through a group of organized hitchhikers known as ALLO-STOP (see p 56), where rides are organized and costs are shared.

When renting a car, find out if:

The contract includes unlimited kilometres and if the insurance offered provides full coverage (accident, property damage, hospital costs for you and passengers, theft).

Caution:

To rent a car in Québec, you must be at least 21 years of age and have had a driver's license for **at least** one year. If you are between 21 and 25, certain companies (for example Avis, Thrifty, Budget) will ask for a $500 deposit, and in some cases they will also charge an extra sum for each day you rent the car. These conditions do not apply for those over 25 years of age.

A credit card is extremely useful for the deposit to avoid tying up large sums of money, and can in some cases (gold cards) cover the insurance.

Most rental cars have an automatic transmission, however you can request a car with a manual shift. Child safety seats cost extra.

PRACTICAL
INFORMATION

Renting an R.V.
(Motorhomes or Camper-Trailers)

This is a fairly expensive way to get around, but beyond the price it is an excellent way to discover the great outdoors. As with the car rental, however, a package deal organized through a travel agency is the most inexpensive. Your travel agent can provide you with more information.

Because of high demand and the short camping season, it is necessary to reserve early to have a good choice of trailers. When planning a summer holiday it is best to reserve by January or February at the latest.

Remember to examine the insurance coverage carefully as these vehicles are very expensive. Make sure the kitchen utensils and the bedding are included in the rental price.

Here is a helpful address should you decide to rent on the spot. There are many other companies listed in the Yellow Pages phone book under the heading *Véhicules Récréatifs* (recreation vehicles):

Cruise Canada, ☎(514) 628-7093, ⁼628-7103

Accidents and Emergencies

In case of serious accident, fire or other emergency, dial 911 in the Montréal area and 0 elsewhere.

If you run into trouble on the highway, pull onto the shoulder of the road and turn the hazard lights on. If it is a rental car, contact the rental company as soon as possible. Always file an accident report. If a disagreement arises over who was at fault in an accident, ask for police help.

If you are planning a long trip, and decide to buy a car, it is a good idea to become a member of the Canadian Automobile Association, or C.A.A., which can offer help throughout Québec and Canada. If you are a member in your home country of an equivalent association (U.S.A.: American Automobile Association; Switzerland: Automobile Club de Suisse; Belgium: Royal Automobile Touring Club de Belgique; Great-Britain: Automobile Association; Australia: Australian Automobile Association), you have the right to some free services. For further information, contact your association or the C.A.A. in Montréal:

C.A.A. 1180 Drummond, H3G 2R7, ☎(514) 861-7111.

By Bus

While a car may be the easiest way to get around, buses are relatively cheap and provide access to most of Québec. With the exception of city buses, which are government run, long-distance bus companies are privately run; several companies cover the region.

Smoking is prohibited on most bus lines and pets are not allowed. In general, children under five travel free of charge and people aged 60 and over are granted significant discounts.

Travel Times from Montréal by Bus

Québec City:	2 h 45 min
Saint-Jovite:	2 h
Saint-Sauveur:	1 h 30 min
Val-David, Sainte-Agathe:	1 h 50 min
Sherbrooke:	2 h
Trois-Rivières:	1 h 30 min
Rimouski:	6 h 40 min
Toronto:	6 h 10 min
Ottawa:	2 h 10 min
Gaspé:	15 h

The *TourPass*

The various bus companies offer what is called a *TourPass*. It is a ticket that allows you to travel throughout Québec and most of Ontario. It costs $230 and is valid for 14 consecutive days between May 1 and October 29. It is possible to extend the ticket for a maximum of six days at a cost of $22.79 per additional day. This extension must however be purchased at the same time as the *TourPass*. When purchased in advance the *TourPass* costs $150 (from March 1 to April 22). A 50 % reduction is offered to children under 12, children under five travel free-of-charge. For information:

In Montréal: Terminus Voyageur, 505 Boulevard de Maisonneuve Est, ☎(514) 842-2281
In Québec City: Gare du Palais, 320 Rue Abraham-Martin, ☎(514) 525-3000.

© ULYSSES

Table of distances (km/mi)

Via the shortest route

Example: The distance between Québec City and Chicoutimi in 211 km/131mi.

1 mile = 1.62 kilometres
1 kilometre = 0.62 mile

	Baie-Comeau	Boston (Mass.)	Charlottetown (P.E.I.)	Chibougamau	Chicoutimi	Gaspé	Halifax (N.S.)	Hull / Ottawa	Montréal	New York (N.Y.)	Niagara Falls (Ont.)	Québec City	Rouyn-Noranda	Sherbrooke	Toronto (Ont.)
Boston (Mass.)	1040/645														
Charlottetown (P.E.I.)	724/449	1081/670													
Chibougamau	679/421	1152/714	1347/835												
Chicoutimi	316/196	849/526	992/615	363/225											
Gaspé	337/209	1247/773	867/538	1039/644	649/402										
Halifax (N.S.)	807/500	1165/722	265/164	1430/887	1076/667	952/590									
Hull / Ottawa	869/539	701/435	1404/870	725/450	662/410	1124/697	1488/923								
Montréal	676/419	512/317	1194/740	700/434	464/288	930/577	1290/800	207/128							
New York (N.Y.)	1239/768	352/218	1308/811	1421/881	1550/961	1919/1190	1508/935	543/337	608/377						
Niagara Falls (Ont.)	1334/827	767/476	1836/1138	1298/805	1590/986	1916/1188	1919/1190	670/415	638/396	685/425					
Québec City	422/262	648/402	984/610	515/319	211/131	700/434	1056/655	451/280	253/157	834/517	858/532				
Rouyn-Noranda	1304/808	1136/704	1833/1136	493/306	831/515	1559/967	1916/1188	536/332	638/396	1246/773	827/513	877/544			
Sherbrooke	662/410	426/264	1187/736	724/449	451/280	915/567	1271/788	347/215	147/91	657/407	925/574	240/149	782/485		
Toronto (Ont.)	1224/759	906/562	1746/1083	1124/697	1000/620	1476/915	1828/1133	399/247	546/339	823/510	141/87	802/497	606/376	693/430	
Trois-Rivières	545/338	566/351	1089/675	574/356	338/210	808/501	1173/726	331/205	142/88	750/465	814/505	130/81	747/463	158/98	688/427

PRACTICAL INFORMATION

Bus Tours

Some companies also offer package deals on excursions of a day or more, which (depending on the length of the tour) include accommodation and guided tours. There is quite a variety of tours available, too many to list here. For further information on these tours, contact the Tourist Information Centres in Montréal or Québec City.

By Train

Travelling by train can prove very interesting, particularly when covering great distances, as these provide an excellent level of comfort. **VIA Rail Canada** (see inset) is the main railway company, transporting passengers all across Canada.

The **Québec North Shore & Labrador Railway Company** *(100 Retty Street, P.O. 1000, Sept-Iles, G4R 4L5, Tel. 418-968-7803)*, for its part, only serves two lines in the northeast: Sept-Iles to Schefferville (once a week) and Sept-Iles to Wabush-Labrador City (twice a week).

By Boat

There is an almost endless list of possible cruises and boating excursions available throughout Québec. River boat trips on what are known as *bateau-mouche* (sightseeing boats) are also available. In some cases naturalists are present to give interesting presentations on the ecosystem of the area, providing insights into the flora and fauna. Although many options are offered, some of them deserve mention:

From Montréal

For thrill-seekers who don't mind a bumpy and wet ride, try going down the Rapides de Lachine.
Cruise around the Îles de Boucherville .
Take a night cruise and enjoy a stunning view of the lights of Montréal.

From Québec

Tour of Île d'Orléans.

Saguenay

Sightseeing trip to the Saguenay fjord. This is the only navigable fjord in North America, its depth reaches 275 metres in some places.

On the St. Lawrence

Several sightseeing trips around the islands (île aux Coudres, île aux Lièvres) and whale watching cruises. Croisières AML *(124 Rue Saint-Pierre, Québec, ☎418-692-1159, ≈692-0845)* organize cruises between Montréal and Québec City.

The North Shore

Trips along the Côte-Nord from Sept-Îles to Blanc-Sablon, passing by Île d'Anticosti as well as through 12 towns accessible only by boat.

The Îles-de-la-Madeleine

Sightseeing trips around the islands.

A boat takes passengers weekly from Montréal to Cap-aux-Meules, although it is really more of a cargo boat. Information and reservations: ☎(418) 986-6600, ≈986-6198.

For pleasure-boating enthusiasts, the Fédération de Voile du Québec publishes the *Guide Nautique du Saint-Laurent* in French, which describes the various marinas and the different services offered on site. Always bring along warm clothing, even in summer, as it can get cool on the open water.

By Ferry

Ferries cross the St. Lawrence and other waterways at several points. Given their large number and the frequent timetable changes, we cannot list them all. For further information, check the section of the guide on the region you want to visit. Ask beforehand if you plan on bringing your car on the ferry, as not all ferries can accommodate automobiles.

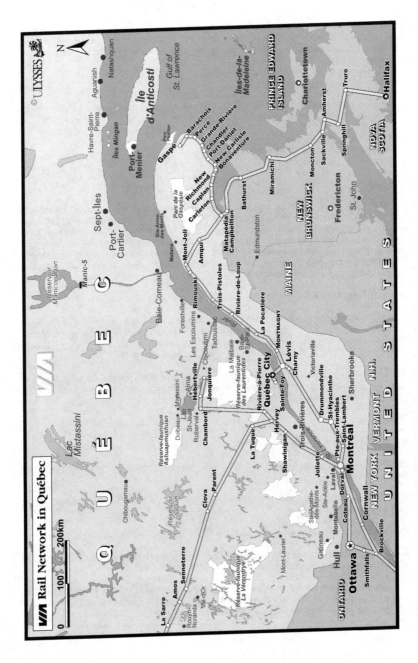

Rail Network in Québec

VIA Rail: the pleasure of discovering Québec by train

In this land where the highway is king, the train offers memorable and enjoyable experiences when it comes to exploring Québec and eastern Canada. Comfortably ensconced in plush seats, passengers can thus leisurely contemplate the passing landscape that, in many respects, can appear altogether new.

Journeys

Modern and rapid (reaching up to 150 km/h), **VIA Rail** trains connect eastern Canadian cities in good time. Here are a few examples of distances from Montreal:

Ottawa:	2 hours
Québec City:	2 hours 50 minutes
Toronto:	4 hours
Gaspé:	17 hours
Halifax:	20 hours

VIA Rail also provides regular service to New Brunswick and Nova Scotia. Particularly interesting is the transcontinental *Chaleur*, which leaves from Montreal and follows the river all the way to Gaspé via Carleton, New Carlisle and Percé, among other cities. The *Abitibi* train, for its part, acquaints passengers with the Lanaudière, Mauricie and Abitibi-Témiscamingue regions. There is also the *Saguenay*, which travels to Saguenay—Lac-Saint-Jean, the land of Marie Chapdelaine. And of course, the train also links Montreal and Québec City, travelling though Montérégie and Bois-Francs.

Economy Class or First Class?

Economy class cars are equipped with comfortable seats and wide aisles and, for a slight surcharge, passengers can have something to eat as well. If you enjoy being waited on hand and foot, opt for first class, where the price of your ticket includes access to a sitting room, priority boarding and meals served with wine and spirits at your seat.

Some trains are equipped with a Skyline car. This car's café and saloon are great places to enjoy the company of other passengers. These cars have large panoramic windows whence you can admire the passing landscape.

Discounts

VIA Rail offers several kinds of discounts:

Outside peak hours, during low season (up to 40%, depending on destinations), upon reserving five days in advance.

Student discounts (10% all year round or 40% if reservation is made five days ahead, except during the holiday season).

Discounts for people 60 years of age and over (10% also applicable on off-peak days).

Special rates for children (2 to 11 years old, half price; free for those under 2 years of age accompanied by an adult).

Another option is the Canrailpass, which entitles you to unlimited travel throughout Canada. This pass offers good value for the money as it also includes a special car rental rate. If you are planning to visit Western Canada consider this ticket.

For any additional information, check out the VIA website at www. viarail.ca, or call your travel agent or the VIA office in your area:

In Canada: ☎1-800-561-8630 or contact your travel agent.

In Australia: Walshes World, ☎(02) 9318 1044, ⚏(02) 9318 2753.

In Italy: Gastaldi Tours, ☎(10) 24 511, ⚏(10) 28 0354.

In the Netherlands: Incento B.V., ☎(035) 69 55111, ⚏(035) 69 55155.

In New Zealand: Walshes World, ☎(09) 379-3708, ⚏(09) 309-0725.

In Switzerland: Touring Club Suisse, ☎(22) 737 1313, ⚏(22) 737 1590. Western Tours, Zurich, ☎(01) 268 2323, ⚏(01) 268 2373

In the United Kingdom: Leisurail, ☎01733-335-599, ⚏01733-505-451, or Airsavers at ☎0141-303-0308, ⚏041-303-0306.

In the United States: ☎1-800-561-3949 or contact Amtrak or your travel agent.

By Plane

Flying is by far the most expensive mode of transportation; however, some airline companies, especially the regional ones, regularly offer special rates (off season, short stays). Once again, it is wise to shop around and compare prices.

Two large companies provide regular flights:

Inter-Canadian: travels to various Québec destinations such as Québec City, Gaspé, Baie-Comeau, Sept-Îles, and many others. Information in Montréal ☎(514) 631-9802, ⚏847-2055; in Québec City ☎(418) 692-0912.

Air Alliance: subsidiary of Air Canada that services many destinations, such as Saguenay, Québec, Gaspé, the Îles-de-la-Madeleine. Information in Montréal Air Canada, ☎(514) 393-3333, ⚏393-6710; in Québec City ☎1-800-361-8620.

Québec's Far North

Two other companies, which are owned and operated by native communities, provide regular flights to Québec's far north.

Air Creebec: services include Chibougamau, Chisasibi, Matagami, Wemindji among others. Flights depart from Val d'Or. For more information: Air Creebec (☎1-800-567-6567), reservations ☎(819) 825-3355, ⚏825-0208.

Air Inuit: services include Inukjuak, Kuujjuarapik, Ivujivik, among others. Information: Air Inuit (☎1-800-361-2965); ☎(514) 636-9445, ⚏839-3180.

By Seaplane

Not the most conventional means of transportation, a seaplane is perhaps the most exciting to get an overview of a region or city. For visitors on a tight schedule it is an ideal way to see the massive James Bay hydroelectric complexes, or to reach the Native reserves and outfitters for short fishing or hunting trips. Flights over Montréal and the surrounding area, and Saguenay, Lac-Saint-Jean, Charlevoix, Québec and the Laurentians are also available. In fact this service is offered in most tourist regions. As schedules change often, it is best to get information on departure times directly from the company.

By Bicycle

Bicycling is very popular in Québec, especially in the cities like Montréal. Bicycle paths have been set up so that cyclists can get around easily and safely, but caution is always recommended, even on these paths. Bicycle touring is possible throughout Québec (see p 77).

Hitchhiking

There are two types: "free" hitchhiking, which is prohibited on highways, and "organized" hitchhiking with a group called Allo-Stop. "Free" hitchhiking is more common, especially during the summer, and easier to do outside the large city centres.

"Organized" hitchhiking, or ridesharing, with Allo-Stop works very well in all seasons. This efficient company pairs drivers who want to share their car for a small payment with passengers needing a ride. A membership card is required and costs $6 for a passenger and $7 for a driver per year. The driver receives part (a-pproximately 60 %) of the fees paid by the passengers. Destinations include virtually everywhere in the province of Québec, as well as the rest of Canada and the United States.

Examples of ALLO-STOP prices :

Montréal-Québec : $15
Montréal-Saguenay : $30
Montréal-Tadoussac : $30
Montréal-Toronto : $26

Children under five cannot travel with Allo-Stop because of a regulation requiring the use of child safety-seats. Not all drivers accept smokers, and not all passengers want to be exposed to smoke, so check on this ahead of time.

For registration and information:

Allo-Stop Montréal, 4317 Rue Saint-Denis, Montréal, H2J 2K9, ☎(514) 985-3032 or 985-3044.

Allo-Stop Québec, 467 Rue Saint-Jean, Québec, G1R 1P3, ☎(418) 522-3430.

CURRENCY

The monetary unit is the dollar ($), which is divided into cents (¢). One dollar = 100 cents.

Bills come in 5-, 10-, 20-, 50-, 100-, 500- and 1000- dollar denominations, and coins come in 1-, 5-, 10-, 25- cent pieces and in 1- and 2-dollar coins.

Francophones sometimes speak of *"piastres"* and *"sous"* which are dollars and cents respectively. On occasion, especially in popular language, you might be asked for a *"trente sous"* (thirty-cent piece), what they really want is a 25 cent piece. As well, *"cenne noir"* (black cent) is a one-cent piece! In English, Europeans may be surprised to hear "pennies" (1¢), "nickels" (5¢), "dimes" (10¢), "quarters" (25¢) and "loonies" ($1).

MONEY AND BANKING

Exchange

Most banks readily exchange American and European currency but almost all will charge **commission**. There are exchange offices that have longer hours, and some don't take commission. Just remember to **ask about fees** and **to compare rates**.

Traveller's Cheques

Remember that Canadian dollars are different from American dollars. If you do not plan on travelling to the United States on the same trip, it is best to get your travellers cheques in Canadian dollars. Traveller's cheques are ac-cepted in most large stores and hotels, however it is easier and to your advantage to change your cheques at an exchange office.

Credit Cards

Most major credit cards are accepted at stores, restaurants and hotels. While the main advantage of credit cards is that they allow visitors to avoid carrying a large sums of money, using a credit card makes leaving a deposit for car rental much easier, also some cards, gold cards for example, automatically insure you when you rent a car. In addition, the exchange rate with a credit card is generally better. The most commonly accepted credit cards are Visa, Master Card, and American Express.

Credit cards offer a chance to avoid service charges when exchanging money. By

Exchange Rates

$1 US	=	$1.39 CAN	$1 CAN	=	$0.70 US
1 £	=	$2.40 CAN	$1 CAN	=	£0.42
$1 Aust	=	$1.14 CAN	$1 CAN	=	$0.95 Aust
$1 NZ	=	$1.06 CAN	$1 CAN	=	$1.05 NZ
1 fl	=	$0.95 CAN	$1 CAN	=	1.33 fl
1 SF	=	$0.98 CAN	$1 CAN	=	1.02 SF
10 BF	=	$0.41 CAN	$1 CAN	=	24.39 BF
1 DM	=	$0.85 CAN	$1 CAN	=	1.18 DM
10 pesetas	=	$0.10 CAN	$1 CAN	=	99 pesetas
1000 lire	=	$0.87 CAN	$1 CAN	=	1148 lire

overpaying your credit card (to avoid interest charges) you can then withdraw against it. You can thus avoid carrying large amounts of money or travellers' cheques. Withdrawals can be made directly from an automatic teller if you have a personal identification number for your card.

Banks

Banks can be found almost everywhere and most offer the standard services to tourists. Visitors who choose to stay in Québec for a long period of time should note that **non-residents** cannot open bank accounts. If this is the case, the best way to have ready money is to use traveller's cheques. Withdrawing money from foreign accounts is expensive. However, several automatic tellers machines accept foreign bank cards, so that you can withdraw directly from your account. Money orders are another means of having money sent from abroad. No commission is charged but it takes time. People who have residence status, permanent or not (such as landed-immigrants, students), can open a bank account. A passport and proof of residence status are required.

TAXES AND TIPPING

Taxes

The ticket price on items usually **does not include tax**. There are two taxes, the GST (federal Goods and Services Tax, TPS in French) of 7 % and the PST (provincial sales

tax, TVQ in French) at 7.5 % on goods and on services. They are cumulative, therefore you must add 14.5 % in taxes to the price of most items and to restaurant and hotel prices.

There are some exceptions to this taxation system, such as books, which are only taxed 7% and food (except for ready made meals), which is not taxed at all.

Tax Refunds for Non-Residents

Non-residents can be refunded for taxes paid on their purchases made while in Québec. To obtain a refund, it is important to keep your receipts. A separate form for each tax (federal and provincial) must be filled out to obtain a refund. Conditions under which refunds are awarded are different for the GST and the PST. For further information, call ☎1-800-668-4748 (for GST) and ☎(514) 873-4692 (for PST).

Tipping

Tipping applies to all table services, that is in restaurants or other places in which customers are served at their tables (fast food service is therefore not included in this category). Tipping is also compulsory in bars, nightclubs and taxis.

Depending on the quality of the service, patrons must give approximately 15% of the bill before tax. Unlike in Europe, the tip is not included in the bill, and clients must calculate the amount themselves and give it to the waitress or waiter; service and tip are one and the same in North America.

PRACTICAL INFORMATION

BUSINESS HOURS AND HOLIDAYS

Business Hours

Stores

The law respecting business hours allows stores to be open the following hours:

Monday to Wednesday from 8am to 9pm; though most stores open at 10am and close at 6pm
Thursday and Friday from 8am to 9pm; though most open at 10am
Saturday from 8am to 5pm; though most open at 10am
Sunday from 8am to 5pm; most open at noon, but not all stores are open Sundays.

Dépanneurs (convenience stores that sell food) are found throughout Québec and are open later, sometimes 24 hours a day.

Banks

Banks are open Monday to Friday from 10am to 3pm. Most are open on Thursdays and Fridays, until 6pm or even 8pm.

Post Offices

Large post offices are open from 8am to 5:45pm. There are several smaller post offices throughout Québec, located in shopping malls, *dépanneurs*, and even pharmacies; these post offices are open much later than the larger ones.

Holidays

Here is a list of public holidays in Québec. Most administrative offices and banks are closed on these days.

January 1st and 2nd
Easter Monday
3rd Monday in May: Fête de Dollard, also called Victoria Day
June 24:   Saint-Jean-Baptiste Day
(Québec's national holiday)
July 1st: Canada Day

1st Monday in September: Labour Day
2nd Monday in October: Thanksgiving
November 11:   Remembrance Day
(only banks and federal government services are closed)
December 25 and 26

TIME DIFFERENCE

Québec is six hours behind continental Europe and three hours ahead of the North American west coast. The entire province of Québec (save for the Îles-de-la-Madeleine, which are an hour ahead) operates on "Eastern Standard Time". Keep in mind that there are several time zones across Canada. Daylight Savings Time (+1 hour) starts the first Sunday in April.

CLIMATE AND CLOTHING

Climate

Québec's seasonal extremes are something which set the province apart from much of the world. Temperatures can climb to above 30°C in summer and drop to -25°C in winter. Visiting Québec during the two "main" seasons (summer and winter) is like having visited two totally different countries, with the seasons influencing not only the scenery, but the lifestyles and behaviour of the province's residents.

Winter

Mon pays ce n'est pas un pays,
c'est l'hiver...

- Gilles Vigneault

Mid-November to the end of March is the best season for skiing, snowmobiling, skating, snowshoeing and other winter sports. In general, there are five or six large snow storms per winter. Howling wind often makes the temperatures bitterly cold, causing "drifting snow" (very fine snow that is blown by the wind). One bright spot is that though it may be freezing, the number of hours of sunshine are greater than in Europe.

Spring

Spring is short, lasting roughly from the end of March to the end of May, and heralded by the arrival of "slush", a mixture of melted snow and mud. As the snow disappears, long-buried plants and grass, yellowed by frost and mud, come to life again. Nature's welcomed reawakening is spectacular.

Summer

Summer in Québec blossoms from the end of May to the end of August and may surprise some who think of Québec as a land of snow and igloos. The heat can be quite extreme and often seems much hotter because of the accompanying humidity. The vegetation becomes lush, and don't be surprised to see some rather exotic looking red and green peppers growing in window boxes, the temperature is almost high enough to fool you into thinking you are in Mexico! City streets are decorated with flowers, and restaurant terraces are always full. It is also the season when festivals of all kinds are held all across Québec (see the **"Festivals"** section p 66).

Fall

The fall colours can last from September to November. Maple trees form one of the most beautiful living pictures on the North American continent. Leaves are transformed into a kaleidoscope of colours from bright green to scarlet red, to golden yellow. The days will stay warm for a while, but eventually the days and especially the nights will be quite cold.

Indian Summer

This relatively short period (only a few days) during the late fall are like summer's triumphant return! Referred to as Indian Summer, it is in fact the result of warm air currents from the Gulf of Mexico. This time of the year is called Indian Summer because it represented the last hunt before winter. Natives took advantage of the warm weather to stock up on provisions before the cold weather arrived.

Clothing

Because of the extremes of the Québec climate, it is important to pack according to the season.

Winter

Sweaters, gloves, hat (called a "tuque" here), scarf... and you are now ready to tackle winter... well, almost! Here are a few pieces of advice:

Bring a long coat that has a hood. If there is no hood, buy a hat or a pair of earmuffs to protect your auditory extremities!

If you value your shoes, buy a pair of rubber-overshoes, or galoshes which slip over regular footwear, and protect shoes from the corrosive effects of the salt used to melt the ice on streets and sidewalks. These are easy to find and are inexpensive.

Many visitors may find stores, Métro stations and other public places too hot in winter. It is a good idea to take off your scarf and undo your jacket once you enter one of these places.

When out window shopping, do not hesitate to warm up inside some stores, and while you are at it do a little browsing.

If you plan on doing any skiing, bring sunglasses.

Summer

Come equipped with short-sleeved shirts, lightweight shirts and pants, shorts, and sunglasses; a sweater is sometimes needed for the evenings.

Spring and Fall

A sweater, a jacket, a scarf, and an umbrella will all come in handy for these in-between seasons.

PRACTICAL INFORMATION

INSURANCE

Cancellation Insurance

Your travel agent will usually offer you
cancellation insurance when you buy your
airline ticket or vacation package. This
insurance allows you to be reimbursed for the
ticket or package deal if your trip must be
cancelled due to serious illness or death.
Healthy people are unlikely to need this protection, which is therefore only of relative use.

Theft Insurance

Most residential insurance policies protect
some of your goods from theft, even if the
theft occurs in a foreign country. To make a
claim, you must fill out a police report. It may
not be necessary to take out further insurance,
depending on the amount covered by your
current home policy. As policies vary
considerably, you are advised to check with
your insurance company. European visitors
should take out baggage insurance.

Life Insurance

Several airline companies offer a life insurance
plan included in the price of the airplane ticket.
However, many travellers already have this
type of insurance and do not require additional
coverage.

Health Insurance

This is the most useful kind of insurance for
travellers, and should be purchased before your
departure. Your insurance plan should be as
complete as possible because health care costs
add up quickly. When buying insurance, make
sure it covers all types of medical costs, such
as hospitalization, nursing services and doctor's
fees. Make sure your limit is high enough, as
these expenses can be costly. A repatriation
clause is also vital in case the required care is
not available on site. Furthermore, since you
may have to pay immediately, check your
policy to see what provisions it includes for

such situations. To avoid any problems during
your vacation, always keep proof of your insurance policy on your person.

HEALTH

Vaccinations are not necessary for people
coming from Europe, the United States and
Australia. On the other hand, it is strongly
suggested, particularly for medium or long-term
stays, that visitors take out health and accident
insurance. There are different types so it is best
to shop around. Bring along all medication,
especially prescription medicine. Unless
otherwise stated, the water is drinkable
throughout Québec.

In the winter, moisturizing lotion and lip balm
are useful for people with sensitive skin, since
the air in many buildings is very dry.

During the summer, always protect yourself
against sunburn. It is often hard to feel your
skin getting burned by the sun on windy days.
Do not forget to bring sun screen!

Safety

There is far less violence in Québec, compared
to the United States. A genuine non-violence
policy is advocated throughout the province.
The city of Montréal even boasts a monument
to peace built out of 12,700 war toys given up
voluntarily by Montréal-area children. The
monument, designed by Linda Covit, is on
display at Jarry Park (Métro Jarry) in Montréal.

By taking the normal precautions, there is no
need to worry about your personal security.
Most municipalities in Québec have the **911**
service, allowing you to dial only three digits to
reach the police, firefighters or ambulance
service, in case of emergency. You can also
dial **0** to contact an operator who will supply
you with the appropriate numbers.

DISABLED PEOPLE

The Keroul Association publishes a free
bilingual guide called ***Tourism Access***, which
lists places that are accessible to the disabled
throughout the province. They have lists of
similar organizations throughout Canada and

around the world. Kéroul also publishes a magazine for disabled travellers called, *Le baladeur*.

For information:

KEROUL (tourism for the disabled), 4545 Avenue Pierre-de-Coubertin, C.P.1000, Succursale M., Montréal, H1V 3R2, ☎(514) 252-3104, ⏚(514) 254-0766.

Association Québécoise de Loisir pour Personnes Handicapées, 4545 Avenue Pierre-de-Coubertin, C.P.1000, Succursale M, Montréal, H1V 3R2, ☎(514) 252-3144.

SENIOR CITIZENS

Older people who would like to meet people their age can do so through the organization listed below which provides information about the activities and local clubs throughout Québec.

For further information:

Fédération de l'Âge d'Or du Québec, 4545, Avenue Pierre-de-Coubertin, C.P. 1000, Succursale M, Montréal, H1V 3R2, ☎(514) 252-3017.

Reduced transportation fares and entertainment tickets are often made available to seniors. Do not hesitate to ask.

CHILDREN

Children in Québec are treated like royalty. Facilities are available almost everywhere you go, whether it be transportation or leisure activities. Generally children under five travel for free, and those under 12 are eligible for fare reductions. The same rules apply for various leisure activities and shows. Find out before you purchase tickets. High chairs and children's menus are available in most restaurants, while a few of the larger stores provide a babysitting service while parents shop.

TELECOMMUNICATIONS

Local area codes are clearly indicated in the "Practical Information" section of every

chapter. Dialling these codes is unnecessary if the call is local. For long distance calls, dial 1 for the United States and Canada, followed by the appropriate area code and the subscriber's number. Phone numbers preceded by 1-800 or 1-888 allow you to reach the subscriber without charge if calling from Canada, and often from the US as well. If you wish to contact an operator, dial 0.

When calling abroad you can use a local operator and pay local phone rates. First dial 011 then the international country code and then the phone number.

Country codes

United Kingdom: 44
Ireland: 353
Australia: 61
New Zealand: 64
Belgium: 32
Switzerland: 41
Italy: 39
Spain: 34
Netherlands: 31
Germany: 49

For example, to call Belgium, dial 011-32, followed by the area code (Antwerp 3, Brussels 2, Ghent 91, Liège 41) and the subscriber's number. To call Switzerland, dial 001-41, followed by the area code (Bern 31, Geneva 22, Lausanne 21, Zurich 1) and the subscriber's phone number.

Another way to call abroad is by using the direct access numbers below to contact an operator in your home country.

United States:
AT&T, ☎1-800-CALL ATT,
MCI, ☎1-800-888-8000
British Telecom Direct:
☎1-800-408-6420 or 1-800-363-4144
Australia Telstra Direct:
☎1-800-663-0683
New Zealand Telecom Direct:
☎1-800-663-0684

Considerably less expensive to use than in Europe, public phones are scattered throughout the city, easy to use and some even accept credit cards. Local calls cost $0.25 for unlimited time. For long distance calls, equip yourselves with quarters ($0.25 coins), or purchase a $10, $15 or $20 smart card ("La Puce"), on sale at newsstands. As an example,

PRACTICAL INFORMATION

a call from Montreal to Québec City will cost $2.50 for the first three minutes and $0.38 for every additional minute. Calling a private residence will cost even less. Paying by credit card or with the prepaid "HELLO!" card is also possible, but be advised that calling by such means is considerably more expensive.

 EXPLORING

Every chapter in this guide leads you through one of Québec's 19 tourist regions, including major tourist attractions, followed by an historical and cultural description. Attractions are classified according to a star system, allowing you to quickly see what are the must-sees.

★   Interesting
★★   Worth a visit
★★★   Not to be missed

The name of each attraction is followed by its address and phone number. Prices included therein are admission fees for one adult. It is best to make inquiries, for several places offer discounts for children, students, senior citizens and families. Several are only open during the summer. Even in the off-season, however, some of these places welcome groups upon request.

 ACCOMMODATIONS

A wide choice of accommodation to fit every budget is available in most regions of Québec. Most places are very comfortable and can offer a number of extra services. Prices vary according to the type of accommodation, but remember to add the 7% G.S.T. (federal Goods and Services Tax) and the 7% provincial tax. These taxes are refundable to non-residents (see p 57). Please note that as of April 1997, a new tax takes effect on accommodation rates in Quebec. It was introduced to support the tourist infrastructures of all regions. Visitors will thus incur this $2/night tax (regardless of the total of your bill) in establishments in the Montreal, Québec City, Laval and Outaouais regions, for the time being, with the rest of Québec following suite before long.

When reserving in advance, which is strongly recommended during the summer months, a credit card is indispensable for the deposit, as payment for the first night is often required in advance.

There is a reservation service in the Montréal and Québec City (summer only) tourist information centres. It is called Hospitalité Canada, and takes care of visitors' hotel reservations for free:

1001 Rue du Square-Dorchester, Montréal, Québec, H3B 4V4, ☎(514) 393-9049, ≈393-8942.

12 Rue Sainte-Anne, Québec, Québec, G1R 3X2, ☎(418) 694-1602 or 1-800-665-1528.

Hotels

Hotels rooms abound, and range from modest to luxurious. Most hotel rooms come equipped with a private bathroom.

Bed and Breakfasts

Unlike hotels, rooms in private homes are not always equipped with a bathroom. Bed and breakfasts are well distributed throughout most of Québec, and besides the obvious price advantage is the unique family atmosphere. They also provide the opportunity to experience a regional architecture, many of the small houses are quite picturesque. Credit cards are not always accepted in bed and breakfasts. Prices for a room also include breakfast.

In Québec bed and breakfasts are known as **Gîtes du Passant**. In order to be a Gîte du Passant, a bed and breakfast must be a member of the Fédération des Agricotours du Québec and must conform to regulations and norms meant to ensure an impeccable stay. Each year, the Fédération, in collaboration with Ulysses Travel Publications, produces the guide *Affordable Bed and Breakfasts in Québec*, which lists, for each region, a variety of accommodations, and the services offered by each one. In addition to bed and breakfasts, the guide also lists the addresses for farm-stays as well as country houses for rent.

Motels

There are many motels throughout the province, that tend to be cheaper and lacking in atmosphere. They are particularly useful when pressed for time.

Youth Hostels

Youth hostel addresses are listed in the "Accommodation" section for the cities in which they are located.

University Residences

Due to certain restrictions, this can be a complicated alternative. Residences are only available during the summer (mid-May to mid-August); reservations must be made several months in advance, usually by paying the first night with a credit card.

This type of accommodation, however, is less costly than the "traditional" alternatives, and making the effort to reserve early can be worthwhile. Visitors with valid student cards can expect to pay approximately $20 plus tax, while non students can expect to pay around $33. Bedding is included in the price, and there is usually a cafeteria in the building (meals are not included in the price).

Staying in Native Communities

The opportunities for staying in Native communities are limited but are becoming more popular. As the reserves are managed by Native groups, in some cases it is necessary to obtain authorization from the Band Council to visit.

Camping

Next to being put up by friends, camping is the most inexpensive form of accommodation. Unfortunately, unless you have winter-camping gear, camping is limited to a short period of the year, from June to August. Services provided by campgrounds can vary considerably.

Campsites can be either private or publicly owned. The prices listed in this guide apply to campsites without connections for tents, and vary depending on additional services. Take note that campgrounds are not subject to the accommodation tax.

The Conseil du Développement du Camping au Québec, in collaboration with the Fédération Québécoise de Camping et Caravaning publishes an annual guide entitled *Camping-Caravaning*, which lists 300 campgrounds and their services. It is available for free from the regional tourist associations or from the Fédération Québécoise de Camping et Caravaning.

Fédération Québécoise de Camping et Caravaning: 4545, Pierre-de-Coubertin, C.P. 1000, Succursale M, Montréal, H1V 3R2, ☎(514) 252-3003.

 RESTAURANTS

Though you may have learned differently in your French classes, Quebecers refer to breakfast as *déjeuner*, lunch as *dîner*, and dinner as *souper*. Many restaurants offer a "daily special" (called *spécial du jour*), a complete meal for one price, which is usually less expensive than ordering individual items from the menu à la carte. Served only at lunch, the price usually includes a choice of appetizers and main dishes, plus coffee and sometimes dessert. In the evenings, a table d'hôte (same formula, but slightly more expensive) is also an attractive possibility.

Prices in this guide are for a meal for one person, before taxes and tip (See "Taxes and Tipping", p 57).

$	$10 or less
$$	$10 to $20
$$$	$20 to $30
$$$$	$30 or more

These prices are often based on the cost of evening table d'hôtes, but remember that lunchtime meals are often considerably less expensive.

"Bring Your Own Wine" Restaurants

Restaurants exist where you can bring your own wine. This interesting phenomenon is a result of the fact that in order to sell alcohol a restaurant must have an alcohol permit, which is very expensive. Restaurants who want to offer their clientele a less expensive menu opt for a special type of permit that allows their patrons to bring their own bottle of wine. In most cases, a sign in the restaurant window indicates whether alcohol can be purchased on the premises (*permis d'alcool*) or if you should bring your own (*apportez votre vin*). Besides the alcohol permit, there is also a bar permit. Restaurants with only the alcohol permit can sell alcohol, beer and wine, but only if they are accompanied by a meal. Restaurants with both permits can sell you just a drink, even if you do not order a meal.

Cafés

Many people in Québec are *espresso* connoisseurs. Numerous little restaurants with a relaxed, convivial atmosphere also serve as cafés. Every city has some, especially Montreal and Québec, and several are institutions in certain parts of the city. Coffee reigns supreme in these places, but good, small meals are also served such as soups, salads or *croques-monsieur*, and, of course, croissants and desserts!

Sugar Shack or *Cabane à sucre*

Called "sugaring-off" at the "sugar-shack" in English, this is a true Québécois tradition. Sap begins to rise in the trees at the beginning of the spring thaw. Taps are inserted in the maple trees in order to retrieve the sap. After a rather involved boiling process, the sap is transformed into a sugary syrup known as maple syrup. In the early spring Quebecers from across the province venture off into the countryside (to the maple groves) to spend the day at the sugar shack, dining on such specialties as eggs with maple syrup and deep fried lard (called *oreilles de Christ* - Christ's ears). After this, it is time for *la tire*, hot maple syrup which is poured on snow, hardening into a delicious toffee which you roll onto a stick and enjoy!

 BARS AND NIGHTCLUBS

Most pub-style bars do not have a cover charge (although in winter there is usually a mandatory coat-check). Expect to pay a few dollars to get into discos on weekends. Québec nightlife is particularly lively, and it doesn't hurt that the sale of alcohol continues until 3am. Some bars remain open past this hour but serve only soft drinks. Drinking establishments that only have a tavern or brasserie permit must close at midnight. In small towns, restaurants also frequently serve as bars. Those seeking entertainment come nightfall should therefore consult the "Restaurant" sections in every chapter as well as those in the "Entertainment" sections.

Happy Hours or *Heures Joyeuses* (5pm to 7pm and two for one)

Bars in the downtown areas offer two for one specials during *Heures Joyeuses* (usually from 5pm to 7pm). During these hours you can buy two beers for the price of one, or drinks are offered at a reduced price. Some snack bars and dessert places also offer the same discounts. A recent Québec law prohibits the advertising of these specials, so if you are interested, ask your waiter or waitress.

WINE, BEER AND ALCOHOL

In Québec, the provincial government is responsible for regulating alcohol, sold in liquor stores known as Société des Alcool du Québec (S.A.Q.). If you wish to purchase wine, imported beer or hard liquor, you must go to a branch of the S.A.Q. Some, known as "Sélection", offer a more varied and specialized selection of wines and spirits. S.A.Q. outlets can be found throughout the city, but their opening hours are fairly limited, with the exception of so-called "Express" branches, open later but offering a more limited choice. As a general rule, their opening hours are the same as those of stores. Convenience and grocery stores have authorization to sell Canadian beer and a few wines, but the choice is slim and the quality of wines mediocre.

You must be at least 18 years old to purchase alcohol, the sale of which is not permitted after 11pm.

Beer

Two huge breweries share the largest part of the beer market in Québec: Labatt and Molson-O'Keefe. They each produce different types of

THE SEASONS
IN QUÉBEC

Québec folk-singer Gilles Vigneault said it best, *"Mon pays ce n'est pays un pays, c'est l'hiver"*, my country is not a country it is winter. Though this long cold season is so closely associated with Québec, all four seasons leave their mark on the province: the cold freezes waterfalls into walls of ice in winter, waters rise and the plants come to life with the spring thaw, bright sun and sometimes unbearable heat waves last through the summer, Indian summer is this last season's final hurrah before the brilliant spectacle of the fall colours. Quebecers have learned to make the most of the many incarnations of their home, heading to the mountains, forests, lakes and mighty rivers no matter what the season...

The calls of frogs and robins herald the arrival of spring: tiny buds on trees and bushes slowly grow into leaves and flowers, dandelions blanket the fields and the fresh smell of the earth returns to the air...

The St. Lawrence lowlands still bear the stamp of the old French seigneurial system, which divided the land into long, narrow rectangular plots in order to give the greatest number of colonists possible access to the waterways. Beyond the farm houses lined up along the *rangs,* the fields run on as far as the eye can see.

A fisherman's life is a hard one requiring backbreaking work, endurance, patience – but which would you prefer: the recycled air of a lawyer's or accountant's office, or the fresh sea air, the wind, your nets and your office extending across half the globe?

Whale-watching: the thrill of observing these giant, magnificent creatures make their way through the St. Lawrence at the mouth of the Saguenay.

The far-off
and mysterious
Îles-de-la-Madeleine
have been sculpted
by the wind
and the sea.

Land of lakes and
rivers, Québec is a
choice spot for a
slew of water sports:
canoeing, kayaking,
sailing, windsurfing,
fishing, rafting...
and the list goes on.

Country house, summer cottage or lakefront chalet... call it what you will, it is the dream of many an urban dweller in this province. What better way to pass the summer than out in the country, far from the heat and humidity of the city.

When fall arrives, the forests of Québec ignite with colour. This blaze of red, orange and gold transforms the countryside and is best experienced during those last warm days of Indian Summer.

As soon as the waterways and lakes freeze over, the shacks go up, the hole in the ice is drilled and ice-fishing, called *pêche blanche* here, season begins.

There can be more to conquering Québec's winter wilderness than a warm tuque; two modes of winter transportation have become two of the hottest outdoor activities when temperatures fall below zero: snowmobiling and dogsledding.

beer, mostly pale beers, with varying levels of alcohol. In bars, restaurants, and discos, draft beer is cheaper than bottled beer.

Besides these large breweries, some interesting independant micro-breweries have developed in the past few years. The variety and taste of these beers make them quite popular in Québec. However, because they are micro brews, they are not available everywhere. Here are a few of the micro-brewery beers: Unibroue (Maudite, Blanche de Chambly and Fin du Monde), McAuslan (Griffon, St-Ambroise), Le Cheval Blanc (Cap Tourmente, Berlue), Les Brasseurs du Nord (Boréale) and GMT (Belle Gueule).

Wine

Surprising as it may seem, Québec produces a small variety of wines, mostly white. Grapes are grown in the Eastern Townships region. Tours (see p 199) of the area can help you discover this beautiful region. Apple cider is also produced in Québec, mostly in the Montérégie Region.

GAY AND LESBIAN LIFE

In 1977, Québec became the second state in the world, after Holland, to include in its charter the principle of not discriminating on the basis of sexual orientation. Quebecers' attitudes towards homosexuality are, in general, open and tolerant. Montréal and Québec City offer many services to the gay and lesbian community. In Montréal, most of these services are concentrated in the part of town known as **The Village**, located on Rue Sainte-Catherine, between Amherst and Papineau streets, as well as on the adjoining streets. The gay village in Québec City is found on Rue Saint-Jean-Baptiste, outside the walls. Below is a list of a few of the available services.

Two telephone lines provide details on the activities in the city : **Gai-Info** (☎768-0199), which is bilingual, and **The Gay Line** (☎990-1414), in English only. There is also the gay and lesbian bookstore **L'Androgyne**, located at 3636 Boulevard Saint-Laurent and the **Centre Communautaire des Gais et Lesbiennes**, 1311 Sherbrooke Est, ☎528-8424. The latter organizes various activities, such as dances, language courses, music, etc. The Pa-

rade de la Fierté Gaie et Lesbienne (Gay and Lesbian Pride March), which is part of **Divers/Cité**, takes place at the end of June on Rue Sainte-Catherine, and ends with various performances at the Parc Campbell (information ☎285-4011).

Two free magazines called, *RG* and *Fugues* are available in bars. They are monthly publications and contain information concerning the gay and lesbian communities. *Fugues* contains a section called *Gazelle*, which deals with lesbian issues.

 ADVICE FOR SMOKERS

Smoking is prohibited in most shopping centres, on buses and on the Métro and in government offices.

Most public places (restaurants, cafés) have smoking and non-smoking sections. Cigarettes are sold in bars, grocery stores, newspaper and magazine shops.

 SHOPPING

In most cases prices are fixed and as indicated. Do not be surprised, however, if you hear someone asking a store clerk if something is *"en vente"*, meaning on sale.

What to Buy?

Electronics: One of the biggest manufacturers of telecommunications products is located in Montreal. It therefore might be a good idea to buy some gadgets such as answering machines, fax machines or cordless telephones and cellular phones. However, be aware that these devices may require a special adaptor for use in your home country. Importing these items may be illegal in certain European countries.

Compact Discs: Compact discs are much less expensive than in Europe, however, they may be more expensive than in the United States.

Books: Books by Québec francophone authors are ideal purchases for those interested in the francophone culture. English-language Quebecers and Canadian literature is easier to find here than elsewhere in the world. In addition, American books are sold in the English bookstores throughout the province at better prices than in Europe. A wide selection of French-language books is available.

Furs and Leather: Clothes made from animal skins are of very good quality and their prices are relatively low. Approximately 80% of fur items in Canada are made in the "fur area" of Montréal.

Maple syrup: There are many varieties of maple syrup. Some are thicker and more syrupy than others, some are dark and some are light in colour, and some have more sugar than others; in any case, it would be sinful to pass up a chance to at least try a few!

Blueberry wine: This wine is made from blueberries and is available in most stores of the Sociéte des Alcools du Québec (S.A.Q.) (liquor stores).

Local Wine: Local wines are available in the Eastern Townships.

Dandelion *(Pissentlit)* Wine: This is a dry white wine made from a wild flower. It is available in the Beauce region.

Mead *(Hydromel)*: A honey wine.

Apple Cider: Made in the Montérégie region, along with many other apple-based products (vinegar, butter, alcohol, etc.).

Liqueurs: Many different liqueurs are produced locally. Try the famous peach schnapps and *"Caribou"*, a very strong grain liqueur.

Local Arts & Crafts: These consist of paintings, sculptures, woodwork, ceramics, coppered enamel, weaving, etc.

Native Arts & Crafts: There are beautiful native sculptures made from different types of stone that are generally quite expensive. Make sure the sculpture is authentic by asking for a certificate of authenticity issued by the Canadian government. Good quality imitations are widely available and are much less expensive.

FESTIVALS AND EVENTS

Québec's coloured history and distinct culturally diverse population are well represented by a variety of cultural activities

each year. Given the impressive number (approximately 240) of festivals, annual expositions, exhibitions, fairs, gatherings and otherwise, it is impossible to list them all. We have, however selected a few of the highlights, which are described in the "Entertainment" sections of each chapter, and a list of them can be found in the box below. The *Bottin des Fêtes et Festivals du Québec*, published by the Société des Fêtes et Festivals du Québec (☎514-252-3037), provides a complete list and is available in magazine stores.

Calendar of Events

February

Montreal
La Fête des Neiges (winter festival)

Hull - Ottawa (Outaouais)
Winterlude

Québec City
Québec Winter Carnival
International Pee-Wee Hockey Tournament

Chicoutimi (Saguenay—Lac-Saint-Jean)
Le Carnaval-Souvenir de Chicoutimi

May

Plessisville (Mauricie—Bois-Francs)
Le Festival de l'érable de Plessisville (maple festival)

Victoriaville (Mauricie—Bois-Francs)
Le Festival de musique actuelle de Victoriaville (Victoriaville New Music Festival)

June

Montreal
The Benson & Hedges International Fireworks Competition
Les Francofolies (French music festival)
Molson Canadian Grand Prix
Le Tour de l'île de Montréal (cycling marathon)

Saint-Gabriel-de-Brandon (Lanaudière)
Le Maski-Courons

Saint-Jean-Port-Joli (Chaudière-Appalaches)
La Fête internationale de la Sculpture (International Sculpture Festival)

Matane (Gaspésie)
Le Festival de la Crevette (shrimp festival)

Tadoussac (Manicouagan)
Le Festival de la Chanson de Tadoussac (song festival)

July

Montreal
The Benson & Hedges International Fireworks Competition
The Montreal International Jazz Festival
The Just for Laughs Comedy Festival
Les Francofolies

Kahnawake (Montérégie)
The Pow Wow

Saint-Hyacinthe (Montérégie)
L'Exposition régionale agricole de Saint-Hyacinthe (Regional Agricultural Fair)

Sorel (Montérégie)
Le Festival de la Gibelotte de Sorel ("gibelotte" (fish stew) festival)

Valleyfield (Montérégie)
Valleyfield International Regatta

Granby (Eastern Townships)
Le Symposium international de sculpture de l'Estriade (international symposium of sculpture)

Magog (Eastern Townships)
La Traversée internationale du lac Memphrémagog (Lake Memphrémagog International Swimming Marathon)

Orford (Eastern Townships)
The Orford Festival

Joliette (Lanaudière)
Lanaudière International Festival

Hull - Ottawa (Outaouais)
The Ottawa and Hull International Jazz Festival

Drummondville (Mauricie—Bois-Francs)
World Folklore Festival

Québec City
The Québec City Summer Festival

Beauport (Greater Québec Area)

Les Grands feux Loto-Québec (musical fireworks show)

Saint-Jean-Chrysostome (Chaudière-Appalaches)
Le Festivent

Mont-Saint-Pierre (Gaspésie)
La Fête du Vol Libre (hand-gliding event)

Saint-Irénée (Charlevoix)
Le Festival international du Domaine Forget

Roberval (Saguenay—Lac-Saint-Jean)
La Traversée internationale du lac Saint-Jean (swimming marathon)

Baie-Comeau (Manicouagan)
Le Festival international de Jazz et Blues (international jazz and blues festival)

August

Montreal
The World Film Festival (WFF)

Chambly
La Fête de Saint-Louis

Saint-Jean-sur-Richelieu (Montérégie)
Le Festival des montgolfières (hot air balloon festival)

Saint-Paul-de-l'île-aux-Noix (Montérégie)
Festival Nautique de Saint-Paul-de-l'île-aux-Noix

Orford (Eastern Townships)
The Orford Festival

Repentigny (Lanaudière)
The Canadian International Junior Tennis Tournament

Mont Tremblant (Laurentians)
Le Festival de Blues de Mont Tremblant (blues festival)
Le Festival de la Musique (music festival)

Aylmer (Outaouais)
La fête de l'été d'Aylmer (summer festival)

Trois-Rivières (Mauricie—Bois-Francs)
Player's Grand Prix

Québec City
Expo-Québec
Plein art ("fresh art")

PRACTICAL INFORMATION

Beauport (Greater Québec Area)
Les Grands feux Loto-Québec (musical fireworks show)

Montmagny (Chaudière-Appalaches)
World Accordion Jamboree

Ile du Havre Aubert (Iles-de-la-Madeleine)
Sand Castle Competition

Saint-Irénée (Charlevoix)
Le Festival international du Domaine Forget

Baie-Saint-Paul (Charlevoix)
Symposium of Young Canadian Painters

September

Chambly (Montérégie)
Le Festi-Bière (beer fest)

Granby (Eastern Townships)
Le Festival de la chanson de Granby (song festival)

Saint-Donat (Lanaudière)
Autumn Colours Weekend

Laurentians
Le Festival des Couleurs (autumn colours festival)

Val-Morin (Laurentians)
Les couleurs en vélo (cycling event)

Gatineau (Outaouais)
Hot Air Balloon Festival

Saint-Tite (Mauricie—Bois Francs)
Western Festival

Rimouski (Bas-Saint-Laurent)
Le Festi-Jazz (jazz fest)
Le Carrousel international du film de Rimouski (film festival)

Baie-Saint-Paul (Charlevoix)
Rêves d'automne (Autumn Dreams)

October

Montreal
The Montreal International Festival of Cinema and New Media

Laurentians
Le Festival des couleurs (autumn colours festival)

Rouyn-Noranda (Abitibi-Témiscamingue)
Le Festival du cinéma international en Abitibi-Témiscamingue (international film festival)

Trois-Rivières (Mauricie—Bois-Francs)
International Poetry Festival

Montmagny (Chaudière-Appalaches)
Le Festival de l'Oie Blanche (Snow Goose Festival)

November

Saint-Denis (Montérégie)
La Fête des Patriotes

WORK AND STUDY

Studying in Québec

To study in Québec, individuals from outside Canada must first obtain a C.A.Q. (Certificat d'Acceptation du Québec) issued by the Ministère des Communautés Culturelles et de l'Immigration du Québec, as well as a federal permit allowing an extended visit.

To obtain these documents, you must **first** be registered at a college or university for at least six months, with a minimum of 24 hours of classes per week. You must also provide proof of financial resources necessary to pay your living expenses and tuition. Moreover, you must have medical and hospitalization insurance and a medical exam may be required.

Student Employment

If you have obtained a residence permit to study in Québec, you have the right to work under certain conditions. Working on campus as a research assistant, or work providing experience in your field of study, are just some of the possibilities offered to students.

Spouses of students admitted as visitors can also work for the duration of the student's stay. The laws, however, change regularly, so it is best to obtain information from the Délégation Générale du Québec or Canadian consulate of your home country (see p 46).

Working in Québec

Working Under Temporary Contract

All the paperwork must be done from your home country. Your Canadian employer must make a request at a Canada Employment Centre. If the job offer is deemed admissible, you will have to appear before the Québec Delegation who will evaluate your abilities, and inform you as to the next steps to take.

Remember that if you have not received a working visa, it is against the law to work in the country. As well, the work permit is valid only for the job and the employer with which you applied, and were accepted, and only for the duration of this job.

Caution: authorization to work in Québec does **not** mean that you can stay on as an immigrant (see below).

Au Pair Work

As with other temporary work, a request for a permit must be made by the employer, and is only valid for this job. The employee must reside with the employer.

Seasonal Work

This type of work is concentrated in the agricultural field and varies from picking apples to agricultural training courses. Obtaining a work visa beforehand is required. Contact the Canadian embassy or consulate in your home country for additional information.

IMMIGRATING TO QUÉBEC

Canada remains one of the few countries that still accepts large numbers of immigrants per year. Although a special qualification or a job offer are considered an advantage, Canada accepts immigrants from all social conditions, and not having a specialized diploma or training should not discourage you. A few years ago, Québec began selecting its own immigrants, so you can send your request to the Délégation du Québec (see p 46), otherwise contact the nearest Canadian consulate. The ability to speak French is an asset when applying to immigrate, and once here immigrants are encouraged to learn and speak French.

There are two fundamental rules to remember: Always (if possible) take the necessary steps from your country of residence before arriving. Be patient and persevere. Reviewing a file takes on average one year, sometimes more.

PETS

Dogs on a leash are permitted in most public parks in cities. Consequently most parks in the backcountry do not allow domestic animals. Bringing your pet onto hiking trails with you is not recommended. Small pets are allowed on the public transportation systems in cities, as long as they are in a cage or well controlled by the owner. Pets are generally not allowed in stores, however, many Quebecers tie their pets up near the entrance while they run in. Pets are not allowed in restaurants, although some establishments with terraces permit pets.

WEIGHTS AND MEASURES

Although the metric system has been in use in Canada for more than 10 years, some people continue to use the Imperial system in casual conversation. Here a some equivalents:

Weights
1 pound (lb) = 454 grams (g)
1 kilogram (kg) = 2.2 pounds (lbs)

Linear Measure
1 inch = 2.54 centimetres (cm)
1 foot (ft) = 30 centimetres (cm)
1 mile = 1.6 kilometres (km)
1 kilometre (km) = 0.63 miles
1 metre (m) = 39.37 inches

Land Measure
1 acre = 0.4 hectare
1 hectare = 2.471 acres

Volume Measure
1 U.S. gallon (gal) = 3.79 litres
1 U.S. gallon (gal) = 0.83 imperial gallon

Temperature
To convert °F into °C: subtract 32, divide by 9, multiply by 5
To convert °C into °F: multiply by 9, divide by 5, add 32.

PRACTICAL INFORMATION

Québec Cuisine

Although many restaurant dishes are similar to those served in France or the United States, some of them are prepared in a typically Québécois way. These unique dishes should definitely be tasted:

La soupe aux pois (pea soup)
La tourtière (meat pie)
Le pâté chinois (also known as shepherd's pie, layered pie consisting of ground beef, potatoes, and corn)
Les cretons (a type of pâté of ground pork cooked with onions in fat)
Le jambon au sirop d'érable (ham with maple syrup)
Les fèves au lard (baked beans)
Le ragoût de pattes de cochon (pigs' feet stew)
Le cipaille (layered pie with different types of meat)
La tarte aux pacanes (pecan pie)
La tarte au sucre (sugar pie)
La tarte aux bleuets (blueberry pie)
Le sucre à la crème (creamy maple-syrup fudge)

In the country, you may also have the opportunity to enjoy some exceptional regional specialties like venison, hare, beaver, Atlantic salmon, Arctic char and Abitibi caviar.

The Corporation de la Cuisine Régionale au Québec has been promoting regional Québec cuisine ever since the organization's establishment in 1993. In the fall of 1997, they published in collaboration with Les Éditions Ulysse, *Le Québec Gourmande*, a French-language guide to restaurants and producers who have helped the development of this cuisine throughout Québec.

DRUGS

Recreational drugs are against the law and not tolerated (even "soft" drugs). Drug users and dealers caught with drugs in their possession risk severe consequences.

ELECTRICITY

Voltage is 110 volts throughout Canada, the same as in the United States. Electricity plugs have two parallel, flat pins. Adaptors are available here.

FOLKLORE

Québec's rich folklore offers an interesting insight into the history and culture of the province. The organization below regroups various regional committees aimed at the preservation and development of folklore. Several activities are organized depending on the seasons and locations. For more information:

Association Québécoise des Loisirs Folkloriques, 4545, Pierre-de-Coubertin, C.P. 1000, Succursale M, Montréal, H1V 3R2, ☎(514) 252-3022.

HAIRDRESSERS

As in restaurants, a tip of 15% before taxes is standard.

LAUNDROMATS

Laundromats and dry cleaners are found almost everywhere in urban areas. In most cases, detergent is sold on site. Although change machines are sometimes provided, it is best to bring plenty of quarters (25¢) with you.

MARKETS

There are many markets in Québec, some of which are covered in winter. These are interesting places not only for their great prices, but also for their atmosphere.

MOVIE THEATRES

There are no ushers and therefore no tips.

MUSEUMS

Most museums charge admission. Reduced prices are available for people over 60, for children, and for students. Call the museum for further details.

ÉCONOMUSÉES

This new form of living and educational museums is now to be found throughout Quebec. The aim of these museums is to showcase Québec's traditional culture and economy. They are thereby housed in forges, flour mills, sculpture studios and other places in which visitors can sometimes observe artisans at work.

NEWSPAPERS

International newspapers can easily be found in the cities. The major Québec newspapers are: in French *Le Devoir*, *La Presse*, *Le Journal de Montréal* from Montréal and *Le Soleil*, from Québec City; and in English *The Gazette* from Montréal. Three free weekly newspapers called, *Voir* (in French—Québec City and Montréal editions), *The Mirror* and *Hour* are also published in Montréal with information on activities and entertainment.

PHARMACIES

In addition to the smaller drug stores, there are large pharmacy chains which sell everything from chocolate to laundry detergent, as well as the more traditional items such as cough drops and headache medications.

RELIGION

Almost all religions are represented. Unlike English Canada, the majority of the Québec population is Catholic, although most Quebecers are not practising Catholics.

RESTROOMS

Public restrooms can be found in most shopping centres. If you cannot find one, it usually is not a problem to use one in a bar or restaurant.

WEATHER

For road conditions, call ☎(514) 873-4121; for weather forecasts, call ☎(514) 636-3302.

THE LANGUAGE OF QUÉBEC

Language in Québec is a hot issue. Quebecers are very proud of their unique version of French, and have struggled long and hard to preserve it while surrounded on all sides by English. The accent and vocabulary are different from European French, and can be surprising at first, but have a charm all their own.

French of English?

When writing a guide to a place where the use and preservation of language are a part of daily life, certain decisions have to be made. We have tried to keep our combined use of English and French consistent throughout the guide. The official language in Québec is French, so when listing attractions and addresses, we have kept the titles in French, except with federal sites, which have official names in both languages, and with certain sites, in Montréal and the Eastern Townships, for example, that have two names as well. This will allow readers to make the connection between the guide and the signs they will be seeing. The terms used in these titles are in the glossary at the end of the guide, but we are confident that after a couple of days, you will not even need to check!

English style has been used in the text itself, to preserve readability. In areas such as Montréal, Ottawa-Hull, and the Eastern Townships, visitors will hear English almost as much as French. English-speaking visitors to these areas will often be able to take a break from practising their French, if they want. Just remember, a valiant effort and a sincere smile go a long way! A complete list of all the local expressions would be too long to include in the guide. Travellers interested in knowing a bit more on the subject can refer to the *Dictionnaire de la Langue Québécoise* by Léandre Bergeron, published by Éditions VLB, or the excellent *Dictionnaire Pratique des Expressions Québécoises*, published by Éditions Logiques.

PRACTICAL INFORMATION

Glossary of Unique Québec Expressions

achaler: to bother someone

blonde: a girlfriend

breuvage: in general, all non-alcoholic beverages

carosse: an airport or store cart

cenne: a penny

c'est pas pire: an expression warning of the banality of a situation or thing;
                      also means: that's not too bad (according to the tone of
                      voice)

char: automobile

chum: friend, buddy, boyfriend; ex: *mon chum* for a male friend
                      and *ma chumme* for a female friend

dépanneur: a convenience store, (to be *en panne* means out of order,
                      not working)

dispendieux: something that is expensive; ex: a car that is *dispendieuse*

donner un bec: to give a friendly kiss, the word bec means "mouth" or
                      "beak" in a figurative sense; ex: se sucrer le bec = to eat
                      sweets

être tanné: to have enough of a situation, at the end of one's rope

jaser: to chat

la valise du char: the trunk of a car

le fun: a good time, to be good or great

liqueur: a flavoured, non-alcoholic drink, a soft drink

niaiseux: a stupid person or situation; ex : a person who seems "niai-
                      seuse", *une situation niaiseuse*

plate: used to describe an unpleasant situation; ex: missing the
                      bus, *c'est plate!*

Learning French

Travellers hoping to learn the language of Molière while in Québec can hope to absorb it as they go, or might prefer to opt for French lessons. In-depth courses are offered at CÉGEPS and universities, while the private schools usually offer more courses of varying lengths and difficulties. Here are a few schools to check out:

Centre Linguista ☎(514) 397-1736
Language Studies Canada ☎(514) 499-9911
Berlitz Language Centre ☎(514) 288-3111.

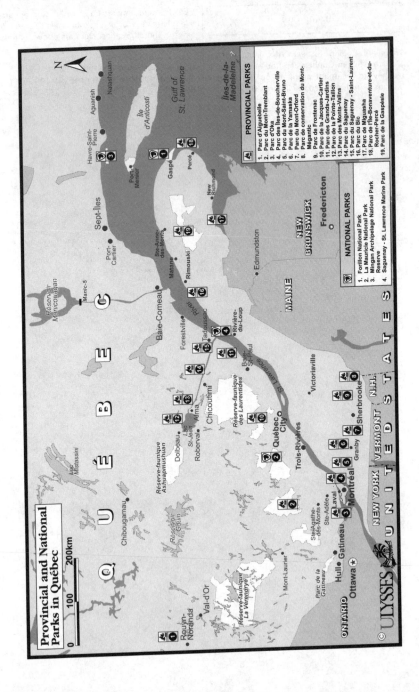

Provincial and National Parks in Québec

0 100 200km

PROVINCIAL PARKS

1. Parc d'Aiguebelle
2. Parc du Mont-Tremblant
3. Parc d'Oka
4. Parc des Îles-de-Boucherville
5. Parc du Mont-Saint-Bruno
6. Parc de la Yamaska
7. Parc du Mont-Orford
8. Parc de conservation du Mont-Mégantic
9. Parc de Frontenac
10. Parc de la Jacques-Cartier
11. Parc de la Pointe-Taillon
12. Parc des Monts-Valins
13. Parc du Saguenay
14. Parc du Saguenay - Saint-Laurent
15. Parc du Bic
16. Parc de Miguasha
17. Parc de l'Île-Bonaventure-et-du-Rocher-Percé
18. Parc de la Gaspésie

NATIONAL PARKS

1. Forillon National Park
2. La Mauricie National Park
3. Mingan Archipelago National Park Reserve
4. Saguenay - St. Lawrence Marine Park

© ULYSSES

OUTDOORS

Québec's huge open spaces and spectacular countryside make it an ideal spot for all types of outdoor sports and activities. This chapter outlines the various kind of outdoor recreation practised in Québec. However, what follows is in no way a complete list of the multitude of choices available to visitors in each region. For each activity or sport the basic information needed to organize an outing is given, along with the address of the specific federation or organization in charge of the activity. Refer to the specific regional chapter to find out which activities can be done where. In the interest of clarity we have categorized the activities as either winter or summer recreation.

Le Regroupement Loisir Québec

This private non-profit organization groups together more than 100 national organizations (federations, movements, associations) - responsible for the promotion of various sports or activities. Its goal is to provide these organizations with the financial and technical support they need. Most of the organization's offices are located in Montréal's Olympic Stadium.

Regroupement Loisir Québec
4545 Av Pierre-de-Coubertin
C.P. 1000, Succursale M
Montréal H1V 3R2
☎(514) 252-3000

 PARKS AND RESERVES

Throughout Québec there are national parks administered by the federal government, and provincial parks administered by the Québec government. Most of the parks offer a variety of services and facilities: information centres, maps of the parks, nature interpretation programs, guides, lodging information (B&B, inns, camping) and restaurant information.

Since these services often depend on the season and are not available in all parks, it is best to check with the park offices ahead of time. It is possible to reserve campsites (except backwoods sites), shelters and chalets (in provincial parks). Reservations are not accepted for campsites in the national parks.

In most parks, networks of marked trails, many kilometres in length, traverse the area permitting amateurs and experts alike to take advantage of the activities offered: hiking, canoeing, cross-country skiing and even snowmobiling. Backwoods campsites and shelters are set up along the trails in some parks. Some of the backwoods sites are quite basic, without even running water, so be sure to be well-prepared. Some trails lead deep into forests far from civilization so it is advisable to stick to the marked trails. Maps with the various trails, campsites and shelters are very helpful and available for most parks.

National Parks

There are four national parks within the province of Québec: Forillon National Park in Gaspé, La Mauricie National Park in the Cœur-du-Québec region, Mingan Archipelago National Park Reserve in the Duplessis region and the Saguenay Marine Park. Aside from these parks, the Canadian Parks Service also runs various National Historic Sites.

More information is available on these parks by contacting the following offices:

Canadian Parks Service
Minister of the Environment
3 Passage du Chien d'Or
C.P. 6060,
Québec G1R 4V7
☎(418) 648-4177 or 800-463-6769
≐(418) 648-4234

Heritage Canada - Parks Canada
200 Boulevard René-Lévesque
Tour Ouest, 6e Étage
Montréal, H2Z 1X4
☎(514) 283-2332
≐(514) 496-4841

Provincial Parks

There are two categories of provincial parks: conservation parks or recreational parks. The first category was created as a means of conserving natural spaces and most of the organized activities revolve around the observation of nature. Absolutely no exploitation of the parks' resources is permitted. The second category offers more activities. A certain amount of exploitation of the natural resources (forestry for example) is allowed, but closely regulated. Fishing is permitted in the recreational parks, but you must have a permit and follow addition regulations. Hunting is not permitted in the parks. There are 16 recreational and conservation parks in Québec, including Parc du Bic, Parc du Mont-Orford, Parc de Frontenac, Parc du Saguenay, Parc de la Gas-

pésie, Parc du Mont-Tremblant, Parc des Îles-de-Boucherville and Parc du Mont-Saint-Bruno.

Ministère de l'Environnement et de la Faune
675 Boulevard René-Lévesque E.
Québec, G1R 5V7
☎(418) 521-3830 or 800-561-1616
≐(418) 646-5974
www.mef.gouv.qc.ca

5199 Rue Sherbrooke E., Bureau 3860
Montréal, H1T 3X9
☎(514) 374-2417
≐(514) 873-5662

Réserves Fauniques

Réserves Fauniques (Provincial Wildlife Reserves) which extend over larger areas than the other parks. Organized fishing and hunting are permitted here. Many provincial wildlife reserves have been established in Québec: La Vérendrye, Saint-Maurice, Laurentide, Portneuf, Mastigouche, Rouge-Matawin, Papineau-Labelle and Chic-Chocs. They are administered by the Société des Établissements de Plein Air du Québec (SÉPAQ) *(☎1-800-665-6527)*. The SÉPAQ distributes a yearly French-language publication called *Activités Services*, which outlines the different activities and services offered in the parks and wildlife reserves of the province of Québec.

Zones D'Exploitation Controlés and Outfitters

The Zones d'Exploitation Contrôlée (ZEC), or controlled development zones, are also Québec government property. They're not generally set up for visitors like parks and wildlife reserves but hunting and fishing are practised here. Outfitters, called *pourvoiries* in Québec, are private establishments specially set up for hunting and fishing. Some just have rustic huts and others welcome you in luxurious inns with elaborate menus.

Jardins du Québec

The province of Québec has wonderful gardens where it's a pleasure to discover landscapes of unparalleled beauty. Along with historical buildings, artwork and ancestral traditions, gardens are considered an integral part of Québec heritage.

In 1989 the Association Des Jardins du Québec brought together the great gardens of Québec to promote ornamental horticulture and to let nature lovers know about them. Allow yourself be led down the 'garden path'!

SUMMER ACTIVITIES

As soon as the temperature inches above 0^0C and the ice starts to melt, Quebecers and visitors alike start to look forward to days in the country. While your choice of clothing will vary with the season, do not forget that evenings and nights are often quite chilly (except in July and August). In certain regions of the province regardless of the temperature, a long-sleeved shirt is indispensable unless you want to serve yourself as dinner to the mosquitoes and black flies. If you plan on venturing into the woods in the month of June, bring insect repellent and use it!

 Hiking

Hiking is accessible to all and is practised all over Québec. Many of the parks have hiking trails of varying length and difficulty. A few have longer trails that head deep into the wilderness for 20 to 40 km. Respect the trail markings and always leave well prepared when you follow these trails. Maps which show the trails, campsites and shelters are available. Reservations for shelters in wildlife reserves as well as those in Parc de la Gaspésie and Parc de la Jacques-Cartier can be made as of the month of May by calling ☎1-800-665-6527 or ☎(418) 890-6527 or by faxing ⌐418-528-6025.

An excellent guide called *Hiking in Québec* (Ulysses Travel Publications) is available in bookstores and camping stores. A hiking guide with something for everyone, it suggests various trails and trips, and classifies them according to their length and level of difficulty. The Fédération Québécoise de la Marche (Québec Hiking Federation) (☎514-252-3157), promotes hiking, snowshoeing and city walking, and can also provide information.

 Biking

Exploring by bike is one of the most rewarding ways to discover the diverse regions of Québec. There is quite a variety of publications to help organize your two-wheeled excursions. The Association Vélo-Québec publishes cycling maps in conjunction with Éditions Tricycle. The following maps and guides are available in most travel bookstores:

Carte du Québec Cyclable: map in french with general information.

Cinq Week-ends en Estrie: a bilingual map of the Eastern Townships by bike.

The Great Montréal Bike Path Guide is available in English.

25 Randonnées à Vélo au Québec is a cycling guide available in French.

Vélo Mag: general information French-language magazine.

Mountain-bike trails have been cleared in most of the parks. Check with the information desk of the particular park or buy the French language guide *Répertoire des Sentiers de Vélo de Montagne*, which lists mountain-bike trails in Québec.

For information :

Maison des Cyclistes
1251 Rachel E.
Montréal H2J 2J9
☎(514) 521-3711 or 521-VELO (521-8356),
www.velo.qc.ca

There is another association called Le Monde à Bicyclette (911 Rue Jean-Talon E., Bureau 126, Montréal, ☎514-270-4884), whose horizons stretch a bit farther. It publishes a small free newsletter called *Le Monde à Bicyclette* available in French only.

The Centre Infotouriste distributes free-of-charge a complete map of the bike-paths of Montreal. Cycling these paths is an exciting way to get to know Montréal in the summer. If you have time, use the map to tour the whole island!

Every June the Groupe Vélo association organizes the Tour de l'Ile, tour of the island of

OUTDOORS

Montréal by bike. Information is available directly from Vélo-Québec. Reservations are required and can be made from outside Montréal. The registration period begins in April, and places go fast.

Many bike shops have bikes for rent. Check with Vélo-Québec or the local tourist office to locate a place; otherwise look in the *Yellow Pages* under *"Bicyclettes-Location"* or "Bicycle-Rental". Insurance is a good idea. Some places also include theft insurance in the rental fee, but be sure to check this when you rent.

  ## Canoeing and Rafting

Québec's vast territory is spotted with a multitude of lakes and rivers, making it a canoe enthusiast's dream. Many of the parks and Réserves Fauniques are departure points for canoe trips of one or more days. For the longer trips backwoods campsites are available for canoeists. Maps of the canoe trips and trails, as well as canoe-rental services are available at the information centre of a park. River rafting is most popular in the springtime when water levels are high after the spring thaw.

An excellent map, *Les Parcours Canotables du Québec*, (Canoe Trips of Québec) as well as the book *Rivières et Lacs Canotables du Québec* (Éditions de L'Homme), a French language guide to the canoeable rivers and lakes of Québec, are both available in travel bookstores. A series of map-guides for rivers (up to 125 different maps) is available as well as a guide for beginners called *Canot-Camping,* available only in French. Contact the Fédération Québécoise du Canot-camping which is a part of the Regroupement Loisir Québec for information (☎514-252-3001, ⊸514-254-1363).

 ## Beaches

The shores of Québec's rivers and countless lakes are lined with everything from fine white sand to pebbles to boulders. You should not have any trouble finding one that suits your sport or style of sunbathing. Unfortunately, swimming in the waters around the island of Montréal is no longer possible because of the pollution in the St. Lawrence and the Rivière des Prairies. The city does, however, run a public beach on Île-Notre-Dame where you can splash about in filtered river water. Beware

though this place is very popular and access is limited; get there early!

 ## Nudism

Nudism is an accepted activity in certain areas of Québec. The Nudist Federation, Fédération Québécoise de Naturisme promotes these activities. As well as publishing a magazine called *Au Naturel*, the federation puts out a guide each summer and organizes activities in the winter (under wraps of course!). Members of the International Federation of Nudists have certain privileges when they present their I.F.N. passport. For information contact the Federation itself or the Regroupement Loisir Québec (☎514-252-3014, ⊸514-254-1363).

 ## Pleasure Boating

La Fédération de Voile du Québec (Québec Sailing Federation) organizes clubs, schools and associations involved in sailing and pleasure boating. The federation coordinates teaching programmes and a data base of important information. Aside from l'*Annuaire de la Voile* a French language listing of clubs and schools, they publish a seasonal bilingual periodical, *Le Bulletin Voile Québec*. For information, check with the federation itself which is part of the Regroupement Loisir Québec (☎514-252-3097, ⊸514-252-3158). The *Guide des Marinas du Québec*, in French, which lists the facilities in every marina in the province is available in bookstores and boating supply stores and could also prove useful.

 ## Waterskiing

La Fédération Québécoise de Ski Nautique (Québec Federation of Waterskiiing) provides information, guide-books and lessons. It also publishes a French-language newsletter called *Ski Nautique Québec*. For information contact the federation through the Regroupement Loisir Québec (☎514-252-3092)

  ## Hunting and Fishing

Hunting and fishing are both strictly regulated. Given the complexity of the regulations it is a good idea to check with the Ministère de l'Environnement et de la Faune *(150 Boulevard René-Lévesque Est, Québec G1R 4Y3, ☎418-643-3127 or 1-800-561-1616)*. Free bilingual brochures containing the essentials with respect to the hunting and fishing regulations and restrictions are available.

As a general rule the following applies:

A Québec permit is required to hunt or fish. Permits are available in most sporting stores and from outfitters. Hunting of migratory birds is only permitted with a federal permit which can be purchased in any post office. A certificate to bear fire-arms or a permit by the province or country of origin is required when requesting this type of permit.

At the time of this guide's publication, a fishing permit is $13.82 ($45.19 for non-residents) or $30.93 for salmon fishing ($94.77 for non-residents).

A hunting permit costs $42 for caribou ($227 for non-residents), $34 for black bear and deer, and $45 for moose, ($245 for non-residents). The permit for small game is $12 ($106 for non-residents), for hare and rabbit is $13. These prices are subject to change. A permit to hunt moose is limited to a specific zone defined by the government. Permits are issued depending on the hunting zone, time of year, the species and the existing quotas. It is a good idea to obtain your permit well in advance since there are numerous restrictions.

Fishing and hunting seasons are established by the province and must be respected at all times. The season depends on the type of game: deer is usually at the beginning of November; moose from mid-September to mid-October; caribou in summer or winter, depending on the zone; bear from mid-September to mid-November; partridge from mid-September to the end of December; hare from mid-September to March. While hunting, always wear an orange fluorescent singlet. Hunting at night is not permitted. In the interests of conservation, the number of game is limited, and protected species cannot be hunted. All hunters must declare their kill at one of the registration centres (most of which are located on access roads to the hunting zones) within 48 hours of leaving the zone.

Hunting and fishing are permitted in the wildlife reserves and parks according to certain rules.

Reservations are required for access to waterways. For more information check directly with the park or reserve office where you plan to hunt or fish.

 Birdwatching

In addition to the national parks there are many other interesting bird-watching spots throughout Quebec. We recommend two interesting guides:

Les Meilleurs Sites d'Observation des Oiseaux du Québec, published by Éditions Québec-Science.

Peterson's Field Guide: All the Birds of Eastern and Central North America, published by Houghton Mifflin.

 Whale-watching

The St. Lawrence is teeming with diverse marine life. A large part of it is made up of countless marine mammals, including many species of whales (belugas, finback-whales and blue whales). Whale-watching expeditions are popular in the tourist regions of Charlevoix, Saguenay - Lac-Saint-Jean, Bas-Saint-Laurent, Manicouagan, Duplessis and the Gaspésie. For more information refer to the section in the guide which describes each region.

 Golf

Groomed golf courses exist in all corners of Québec. A map called *Le Golf au Québec* as well as the guide *Maxi-Golf* should provide all the teeing-off information necessary. Both are available in travel bookstores and the Centre Infotouriste in Montréal.

 Horseback Riding

Many horse stables offer lessons or trail rides. Some even organize longer trips of more than one day. Both types of riding, English and Western are available depending on the stable. As the two styles are very different check which one is offered when making reservations. Some provincial parks have horseback riding trails.

Québec à Cheval (Québec on horseback) is an organization that promotes horseback riding. They distribute an annual French publication free-of-charge called *Découvrir le Québec à Cheval* (Discovering Québec on Horseback). Instructional courses are also offered. For more information check with Québec à Cheval which is part of the Regroupement Loisir Québec (☎514-252-3002, ⚏514-251-8038).

 ## Scuba Diving

Most of the regions of Québec offer dive sites, and there are at least 200 diving centres, schools or clubs. There is also a treatment centre for diving accident victims : Urgence Hyperbarre à l'Hôpital Sacré-Coeur de Montréal (☎514-338-2222). For more complete information on diving in Québec contact the Fédération Québécoise des Activités Subaquatiques (Québec Federation of Underwater Activities) (☎514-252-3009).

 ## Climbing

Climbing enthusiasts can practise their sport in summer and in winter, when there are ice walls for climbers of all levels. Adequate and reliable equipment (often rented on site) and a firm grasp of the basic techniques are particularly important in this sport. Some climbing centres offer beginners' courses.

For information concerning ice and rock climbing activities, beginner courses and more advanced courses, contact the Fédération Québécoise de la Montagne also part of the Regroupement Loisir Québec (☎514-252-3004, ⚏514-254-1363). A French language magazine called *Le Mousqueton*, (which means the karabiner), is available free of charge from the Regroupement.

  ## Hang-gliding and Paragliding

The sport of hang-gliding has existed in Québec since the seventies. The mountains and cliffs most conducive to this sport are located in the regions of Gaspésie, Charlevoix and in the Appalachians and Laurentides. Paragliding is a relatively new sport in Québec. These sports are dangerous and can only be attempted after following a course led by an accredited instructor. For more information contact the Association Québécoise de Vol Libre (The Québec Association of Hang-gliding and Paragliding) (☎252-3055).

WINTER ACTIVITIES

A road map called *Sports d'Hiver Québec* (Québec Winter Sports) outlines the various winter sports practiced in Québec. It contains a list of facilities organized by location and sport and directions on how to get there. This map is available in most travel bookstores and the Centre Infotouriste in Montréal. The Minister of Tourism also publishes a brochure describing various winter sports and activities.

 ## Downhill Skiing

There are many downhill skiing centres in Québec. Some of these have lighting systems and offer night skiing. The hotels located near the ski hills often offer package-deals including accommodation, meals and lift tickets. Check when reserving your room.

Lift tickets are very expensive; in an effort to accommodate all types of skiers most centres offer half-day passes, whole-day and night-passes. Some centres have even started offering skiing by the hour. There is a ticket called a *billet à prix réduit* (reduced-price ticket) which allows access to one of the 40 alpine ski centres associated with Ski Québec. The ticket good for a day, is 25 to 30 percent cheaper than a regular ticket and sold by Ski Québec. It must be purchased in advance. As well as saving you money, the ticket price goes toward promoting the sport of downhill skiing in Québec for pro skiers and disabled athletes. For information, contact Ski Québec, part of the Regroupement Loisir Québec (☎514-252-3089, ⚏514-254-1499).

 ## Cross-country Skiing

There are many parks and ski centres with well kept cross-country trails. In most ski centres you can rent equipment by the day. Many places offer longer trails, with shelters alongside them offering accommodation for skiers. To ensure a spot in a shelter, reservations are required. Call ☎1-800-665-6527 or ☎418-890-6527 from mid-october on. A map called *Répertoire du Ski au Québec* is also available in French from bookstores. For skiers on longer trails, some ski centres offer a service that delivers food to the shelter by snowmobile.

 ## Snowshoeing

Reinvented today as a leisure pastime, the snowshoe was first invented by Amerindians as a means of transportation through deep snow. There is no association in Québec for enthusiasts of this sport, which mainly takes place in cross-country ski-centres.

 ## Snowmobiling

Now this is a popular Québec sport! It was after all a Quebecer named Joseph-Armand Bombardier who invented the snowmobile, thereby giving life to one of the most important industries of Québec, now involved in the building of airplanes and railway materials.

A network of more than 26,000 km of cleared snowmobile trails crisscross Québec. Trails cross diverse regions and lead adventurers into the heart of the wilderness. Along the trails are all the necessities for snowmobiling: repair services, heated sheds, fuel, and food services. It is possible to rent a snowmobile and the necessary equipment in certain snowmobiling centres. The Minister of Tourism offers a free brochure called *Vacances d'Hiver* (Winter Vacation) which describes seven networks of snowmobile trails. A map called *Sentiers de Motoneige à Travers le Québec* (Snowmobile Trails Across Quebec) is also available. It indicates the location of trails, service centres, and towns where equipment can be rented.

To use the trail, you must have the vehicles registration paper and a membership card. The membership card is available from the Fédération des Clubs de Motoneigistes. No-fault insurance is strongly recommended.

Certain safety rules apply. A helmet is mandatory and driving on public roads is forbidden unless the trail follows it. Headlights and brake lights must be lit at all times. The speed-limit is

60 km/h. It is preferable to ride in groups. Lastly always stick to cleared trails.

For information, contact the Fédération des Clubs de Motoneigistes du Québec, part of the Regroupement Loisir Québec (☎514-252-3076, ⊷514-254-2066)

 ## Dogsledding

Used by the Inuit for transportation in the old days, today dogsledding has become a respected sporting activity. Competitive events abound in northern countries all over the world. In recent years, tourist centres have started offering dogsled trips running anywhere from a few hours to a few days in length. In the latter case the tour organizer provides the necessary equipment and shelter. In general you can expect to cover 30 km to 60 km per day and this sport is more demanding than it looks, so good physical fitness is essential for long trips. For those of you with your own team and sled, the Réserve Faunique Saint-Maurice (☎819-646-5687) has cleared trails for dogsleds. Throughout the guide are addresses of tourist centres which offer dogsled trips.

 ## Skating

Most municipalities have public skating rinks set up in parks, on rivers or lakes. Some places have rental services, and even a little hut where you and your skates can warm up.

 ## Ice-fishing

This sport has become more and more popular in recent years. The basic idea, as the name suggests, is to fish through the ice. A small wooden shack built on the ice keeps you warm during the long hours of waiting for the big one! The main regions for this sport are the Eastern Townships, Mauricie - Bois-Francs, and Saguenay - Lac-Saint-Jean regions. This guide mentions various spots for ice-fishing.

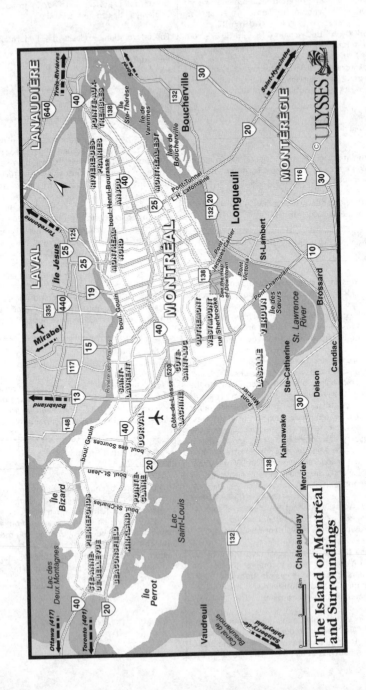

The Island of Montréal and Surroundings

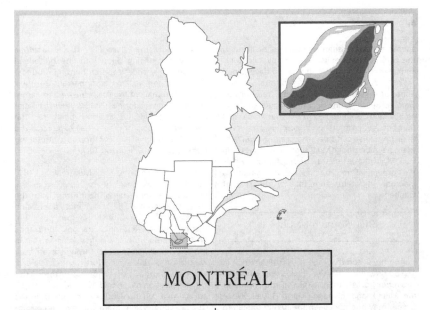

MONTRÉAL

A city of paradoxes at the crossroads of America and Europe, seen as both Latin and northern, cosmopolitan and unmistakably the metropolis of Québec, Montreal holds nothing back. It succeeds in delighting American tourists with its so-called European charm, but also manages to surprise overseas travellers with its haphazard character and nonchalance. Montréal is an enchanting city to visit, an exhilarating place to discover; it is generous, friendly and not at all mundane. And, when it comes time to celebrate jazz, film, humour, singing or Saint-Jean-Baptiste Day, hundreds of thousands of people flood into the streets, turning events into warm public gatherings. This festive spirit lasts all year in the city's countless cafés, nightclubs and bars of all different kinds, which are constantly packed by a joyful, urban crowd. While Montrealers know how to party, they also enjoy celebrating the arts. With French and North American influences, as well as the vitality of new arrivals, Montréal is an international city and the primary centre of culture in Québec. The abundance of high quality work produced here, most notably in the fields of theatre, fashion, literature and music, attests to the dynamism and creativity of the local population. The city has also earned an enviable reputation among food-lovers; many believe that one can eat better in Montréal than anywhere else in North America.

Montréal's richly varied urban landscape illustrates the different stages of the city's evolution. The oldest buildings in Vieux-Montréal or old-Montréal predate the glass skyscrapers downtown by a period of over three centuries during which the city was in constant expansion. The splendour of Montréal's countless churches, the neoclassical bank façades of the banks along Rue Saint-Jacques, the flat-roofed little houses in the working-class neighbourhoods and the sumptuous residences of the "Golden Square Mile" all bear witness, like so much else here, to the city's recent and not so recent history. Montréal's important role, both past and present, as the province's main centre of artistic and intellectual activity, and as a large industrial, financial, commercial and port city, is eloquently reflected in its rich architectural heritage.

Though its towering glass and concrete skyline gives it the appearance of a big North American city, Montréal is above all a city of narrow streets, of neighbourhoods, each with its own church, handful of businesses, corner delicatessen, brasserie or tavern. Over the years, the city has also been shaped by an increasingly cosmopolitan population. The division between the east and west (between French-speakers and English-speakers) still exists to a certain degree, although it no longer stirs up the same feelings. The "two solitudes" have developed a greater respect for one another, and in spite of all their differences, appreciate the distinct advantages of living in this Québec metropolis. Over the past century, immigrants from all over the world have joined these two main elements of Montreal society. Some of these minorities, notably the Italians, Greeks, Jews, Chinese and Portuguese, have established communities in specific areas, and thus succeeded in preserving certain aspects of their particular cultures. The great diversity of these neighbourhoods and their inhabitants help give Montréal a unique charm. Although it is the provincial metropolis, its population is markedly different from that of the rest of Québec.

Brief History of Montreal

During his second voyage to North America in 1535, Jacques Cartier sailed up the St. Lawrence to Montréal, explored the shores of the island and climbed Mont Royal. While Cartier may not have been the first European to visit the island, which is located at the confluence of two rivers now known as the St. Lawrence River and the Ottawa River, he was nevertheless the first to report its existence. In those days, the aboriginals referred to it as Hochelaga. At the time of Cartier's arrival, a large fortified town populated by about 1,000 Iroquoian stretched across the sides of Mont Royal. This town was evidently destroyed or abandoned a few years later, since when the great explorer Samuel de Champlain, founder of Québec City, came here in 1611, he found no trace of it. He did note, however, that the island would make a very good spot for a trading post.

It was not the fur trade, however, that gave rise to the founding of Montréal. Originally named Ville-Marie, the city was established by a group of devout French citizens who came here in hopes of converting the natives to Christianity. Under the direction of Paul de Chomedey, Sieur de Maisonneuve, 50 men and four women, including Jeanne Mance, founded Ville-Marie on May 18, 1642. Their plans soon came up against Iroquois opposition, however—so much so that until the signing of a peace treaty in 1701, the French and the Iroquois engaged in such constant conflict that the very existence of the settlement was threatened on a number of occasions.

Although Montréal was originally founded for the glory of Christianity, merchants quickly replaced members of religious orders and other bearers of the "word". The numerous waterways leading deep into the hinterland provided easy access to rich hunting grounds. Montréal soon became an important business hub, and remained the main fur-trading centre in North America for nearly 150 years. The city also served as the starting point for the coureurs des bois (trappers) and explorers who set out to discover the vast territory stretching from Louisiana to Hudson Bay.

After the British army took Montréal in 1760, the Scots took over the fur trade from the French. The city became the metropolis of the country during the 1820s, when its population surpassed Québec City. From that point on, Montréal underwent rapid changes; thousands of immigrants from the British Isles settled in the city, or simply passed through it on their way to other regions in North America. For a certain period of time, before the industrialization of the mid-19th century began attracting a continual influx of people from the Québec countryside, there was even an Anglo-Saxon majority here.

By the turn of the 20th century, Montréal had become a major industrial city, whose upper class residents controlled 70% of the wealth in Canada. The industrial revolution had also generated a large working class, composed mainly of French Canadians and Irish, who lived in wretched conditions. Meanwhile, immigrants from outside Great Britain—particularly Jews from Eastern Europe, Germans and Italians—began to pour into the city, which was quickly beginning to take on a cosmopolitan character.

During the 20th century, Montréal grew continually, swallowing up neighbouring towns and villages, due to the steady influx of both rural Quebecers and immigrants. Starting in the 1950s, the city even began spreading beyond the island itself, turning the adjacent countryside into a suburban zone. Its economic centre gradually shifted from Old Montréal to the area around Boulevard Dorchester (now Boulevard René-Lévesque), where glass and concrete skyscrapers have since sprouted up.

In the 1960s and 1970s, Mayor Jean Drapeau, who has often been accused of megalomania, strengthened "his" city's international reputation by bringing about the construction of a subway system in 1966, and by organizing large-scale events. Montréal hosted the 1967 World Fair (Expo '67), the 1976 Summer Olympics and the 1980 Floralies

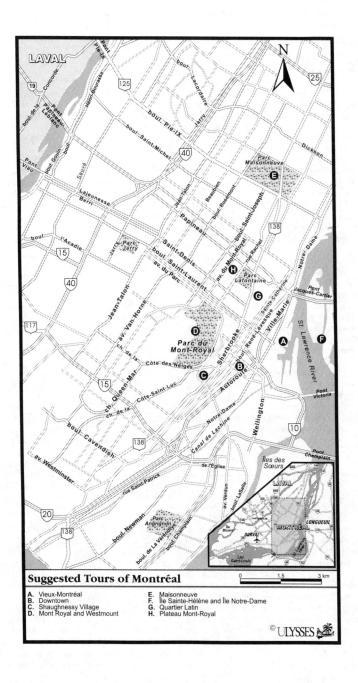

Suggested Tours of Montréal

A.	Vieux-Montréal	**E.**	Maisonneuve
B.	Downtown	**F.**	Île Sainte-Hélène and Île Notre-Dame
C.	Shaughnessy Village	**G.**	Quartier Latin
D.	Mont Royal and Westmount	**H.**	Plateau Mont-Royal

© ULYSSES

MONTRÉAL

Internationales. Montrealers celebrated the 350th anniversary of their city in 1992.

FINDING YOUR WAY AROUND

There are 28 municipalities on the island of Montréal, which measures 32 kilometres at its longest point by 16 kilometres at its widest. Montréal proper, with a population of about one million, is the main urban area in the Communauté Urbaine de Montréal (Montréal Urban Community), which encompasses all of the boroughs on the island. Greater Montréal also includes the Rive-Sud (South Shore), Laval and the Rive-Nord (North Shore), for a grand total of 3,200,000 inhabitants (1991). The downtown area runs along the St. Lawrence, south of Mont Royal (234 m), which is one of the 10 hills of the Montérégie region.

To help visitors explore a few of the city's most beautiful neighbourhoods, we have outlined the following nine walking tours, which crisscross Montréal and the municipalities adjacent to it: **Tour A: Vieux-Montréal ★★★** (see p 88), **Tour B: Downtown ★★★** (see p 100), **Tour C: Village Shaughnessy ★★** (see p 110), **Tour D: Mont Royal and Westmount ★★** (see p 113), **Tour E: Maisonneuve ★★** (see p 118), **Tour F: Île Sainte-Hélène and Île Notre-Dame ★★** (see p 123), **Tour G: Quartier Latin ★★** (see p 127), **Tour H: Plateau Mont-Royal ★** (see p 130), and **Tour I: Laval** (see p 134). For more Montréal tours, please see the Ulysses Travel Guide *Montréal*.

By Car

There are two possible routes from Québec City. The first is via Highway 20 W. to the Pont Champlain, then follow Autoroute Bonaventure (10) straight into the centre of town, the other route is via Highway 40 W. to Autoroute Décarie (15), and follow the signs for downtown, *centre-ville*.

Visitors arriving from Ottawa should take Highway 40 E. to Autoroute Décarie (15), then follow the signs for downtown, while those arriving from Toronto should take Highway 20 E. onto the island, then follow the signs for downtown via Autoroute Ville-Marie (720).

Visitors arriving from the United States on Highway 10 (Autoroute des Cantons de l'Est) or Highway 15 will enter Montréal by way the Pont Champlain and Autoroute Bonaventure (10).

To reach Laval: From Montréal, cross the Pont Pie-IX, and take the Boulevard Lévesque Est Exit (on the right). Turn left onto Boulevard Lévesque Est to the tip of Île Jésus.

Car Rentals

Avis: 1225 Rue Metcalfe, ☎(514) 866-7906
Budget: 1240 Rue Guy, ☎(514) 937-9121; Complexe Desjardins, ☎(514) 842-9931
Hertz: 1475 Rue Aylmer, ☎(514) 842-8537
Tilden: 1200 Rue Stanley, ☎(514) 878-2771
Via Route: 1255 Rue Mackay, ☎(514) 871-1166

Airports

Mirabel Airport: see p 47
Dorval Airport: see p 46

Bus Stations

---

505 Boulevard de Maisonneuve Est, ☎514-842-2281, Métro Berri-UQAM.

Train Station

Gare Centrale: 935 Rue de la Gauchetière Ouest, ☎514-871-7765, 800-361-5390 (from Québec) or 800-561-8630 (from Canada), ☎871-7766, Métro Bonaventure.

Public Transportation

Montréal's Métro (subway) and bus network covers the entire metropolitan region. A $45 pass entitles the holder to unlimited use of these services on the island for one month. For shorter stays, visitors can purchase six tickets for the price of $7.75, or single tickets at $1.85 apiece. If a trip involves a transfer (from the bus to the Métro or vice versa), the passenger must ask the bus driver for a transfer ticket when boarding or take one from

MONTRÉAL

a transfer machine in the Métro station. Free subway maps and timetables for each line are available inside all stations.

For more information on the public transportation system, call: **STCUM**, ☎288-6287 (A-U-T-O-B-U-S).

Laval: 10765 Rue Lajeunesse (at the corner of Henri-Bourassa Boulevard and Lajeunesse Street); for information : ☎ (514) 688-6520.

Taxis

Co-op Taxi: ☎(514) 725-9885.
Diamond: ☎(514) 273-6331.
Taxi LaSalle: ☎(514) 277-25.52

PRACTICAL INFORMATION

Area code: ☎514

Tourist Information

Centre Infotouriste (Peel Métro station): 1001 Rue du Square-Dorchester (at the corner of Metcalfe and Square-Dorchester), ☎(514) 873-2015, www.tourisme-montreal.org

The centre is open from 8am to 7pm, every day during summer, and from 9am to 6pm every day from November to April.

There is a small tourist booth, which provides information only on Montréal, at 174 Rue Notre-Dame Est (Champ-de-Mars Métro station)

Laval: 2900 Boulevard Saint-Martin Ouest, Chomedey, ☎(514) 682-5522.

Foreign Exchange

A number of downtown banks offer currency exchange services. In most cases, there is a service charge. Foreign exchange offices don't always charge a fee, so it is best to inquire beforehand. Most banks are able to exchange U.S. currency.

Bank of America Canada: 1230 Rue Peel, ☎392-9100

National Bank of Canada: 1001 Rue Sainte-Catherine Ouest, ☎281-9640.
Forexco: 1250 Rue Peel, ☎879-1300.
Thomas Cook: 625 Boulevard René-Lévesque Ouest, ☎397-4029.

Automatic teller machines capable of exchanging foreign currency have been installed in Complexe Desjardins (on Sainte-Catherine Ouest, between Jeanne-Mance and Saint-Urbain). They are open from 6am to 2am. These machines can provide Canadian funds in exchange for various foreign currencies, or American or French funds for Canadian currency. There are similar machines at Mirabel Airport.

Post Office

1250 Rue University: ☎283-4506.
1250 Rue Sainte-Catherine Est: ☎522-5191.

EXPLORING

Tour A: Vieux-Montréal ★★★
(two days)

In the 18th century, Montréal, like Québec City, was surrounded by stone fortifications. Between 1801 and 1817, these ramparts were demolished due to the efforts of local merchants, who saw them as an obstacle to the city's development. The network of old streets, compressed after nearly a century of confinement, nevertheless remained in place. Today's Vieux-Montréal, or Old Montréal, thus corresponds quite closely to the area covered by the fortified city. During the 19th century, this area became the hub of commercial and financial activity in Canada. Banks and insurance companies built sumptuous head offices here, leading to the demolition of almost all buildings erected under the French Regime. The area was later abandoned for nearly 40 years in favour of the modern downtown area of today. Finally, the long process of putting new life into Old Montréal got underway during the preparations for Expo '67, and continues today with numerous conversion and restoration projects.

The tour begins at the west end of Old Montréal, on Rue McGill, which marks the site

of the surrounding wall that once separated the city from the Faubourg des Récollets (Métro Square-Victoria). Visitors will notice a considerable difference between the urban fabric of the modern downtown area behind them, with its wide boulevards lined with glass and steel skyscrapers, and the old part of the city, whose narrow, compact streets are crowded with stone buildings.

The numbers following the names of attractions refer to the map of Vieux-Montréal.

The **Tour de la Bourse ★ (1)** *(Place de la Bourse)*, or the stock exchange tower, dominates the surroundings. It was erected in 1964 according to a design by the famous Italian engineers Luigi Moretti and Pier Luigi Nervi, to whom we owe the Palazzo dello Sport (sports stadium) in Rome and the Exhibition Centre in Turin. The elegant 47-floor black tower houses the offices and trading floor of the exchange. It is one of many buildings in this city designed by foreign talents. Its construction was intended to breathe new life into the business section of the old city, which was deserted after the stock market crash of1929 in favour of the area around Square Dorchester. According to the initial plan, there were supposed to be two, or even three, identical towers.

In the 19th century, **Square Victoria (2)** was a Victorian garden surrounded by Second-Empire and Renaissance-Revival-style stores and office buildings. Only the narrow building at 751 Rue McGill survives from that era. North of Rue Saint-Antoine, visitors will find a **statue of Queen Victoria**, executed in 1872 by English sculptor Marshall Wood, as well as an authentic Art-Nouveau-style **Parisian Métro railing**. The latter, designed by Hector Guimard in 1900 and given to the city of Montréal by the city of Paris for Expo '67, was installed at one of the entrances to the Square-Victoria Métro station.

The headquarters of the two organizations that control civil aviation in the world, IATA (the International Air Transport Association) and ICOA (the International Civil Aviation Organization) are located in Montréal. The latter is a United Nations organization that was founded in 1947. It recently gained the new **Maison de l'OACI (3)** *(at the corner of University and Saint-Antoine Ouest)* to house the delegations of its 183 member countries. The back of the building, which has been connected to the Cité Internationale de Montréal, is visible from Square Victoria. Completed in 1996, it was designed by architect Ken London, who was inspired somewhat by Scandinavian architecture of the 1930s.

Enter the covered passageway of the Centre de Commerce Mondial.

World Trade Centres are exchange organizations intended to promote international trade. Montréal's **Centre de Commerce Mondial ★ (4)** *(Rue McGill)*, completed in 1991, is a new structure hidden behind an entire block of old façades. An impressive glassed-in passageway stretches 180 metres through the centre of the building, along a portion of the Ruelle des Fortifications, a lane marking the former location of the northern wall of the fortified city. Alongside the passageway, visitors will find a fountain and an elegant stone stairway, which provide the setting for a statue of Amphitirite, Poseidon's wife, taken from the municipal fountain in Saint-Mihiel-de-la-Meuse, France. This work dates back to the mid-18th century; it was executed by Barthélémy Guibal, a sculptor from Nîmes, France, who also designed the fountains gracing Place Stanislas in Nancy, France.

Climb the stairway, then walk along the passageway to the modest entrance of the lobby of the Hôtel Inter-Continental. Turn right onto the footbridge leading to the Nordheimer building.

This edifice was restored in order to accommodate the hotel's reception halls, which are linked to the trade centre. Erected in 1888, the building originally housed a piano store and a small concert hall, where many great artists performed, including Maurice Ravel and Sarah Bernhardt. The interior, with its combination of dark woodwork, moulded plaster and mosaics, is typical of the late 19th century, characterized by exuberant eclecticism and lively polychromy. The façade, facing Rue Saint-Jacques, combines Romanesque Revival elements, as adapted by American architect Henry Hobson Richardson, with elements from the Chicago School, notably the many-windowed metallic roof.

Exit via 363 Rue Saint-Jacques.

Rue Saint-Jacques was the main artery of Canadian high finance for over a century. This role is reflected in its rich and varied architecture, which serves as a veritable encyclopedia of styles from 1830 to 1930. In those years, the banks, insurance companies and department stores, as well as the nation's railway and shipping companies, were largely controlled by Montrealers of Scottish extraction, who had come to the colonies to make their fortune.

Begun in 1928 according to plans by New York skyscraper specialists York and Sawyer, the former head office of the **Banque Royale** ★★ (5) *(360 Rue Saint-Jacques)*, or Royal Bank, was one of the last buildings erected during this era of prosperity. The 22-floor tower has a base inspired by Florentine palazzos, which corresponds to the scale of the neighbouring buildings. Inside the edifice, visitors can admire the high ceilings of this "temple of finance," built at a time when banks needed impressive buildings to win customers' confidence. The walls of the great hall are emblazoned with the heraldic insignia of eight of the 10 Canadian provinces, as well as those of Montréal (St. George's cross) and Halifax (a yellow bird), where the bank was founded in 1861.

The **Banque Molson** ★ (6) *(288 Rue Saint-Jacques)*, or Molson bank, was founded in 1854 by the Molson family, famous for the brewery established by their ancestor, John Molson (1763-1836), in 1786. The Molson Bank, like other banks at the time, even printed its own paper money — an indication of the power wielded by its owners, who contributed greatly to the city's development. The head office of

the family business looks more like a patrician residence than an anonymous bank. Completed in 1866, it is one of the earliest examples of the Second Empire, or Napoleon III, style to have been erected in Canada. This French style, modelled on the Louvre and the Paris Opera, was extremely popular in North America between 1865 and 1890. Above the entrance, visitors will see the sandstone carvings of the heads of William Molson and two of his children. The Molson Bank merged with the Bank of Montréal in 1925.

Walk along Rue Saint-Jacques; you'll soon come to Place d'Armes.

The square, which is in fact shaped more like a trapezoid, is surrounded by several noteworthy buildings. The **Banque de Montréal** ★★ (7) *(119 Rue Saint-Jacques, Métro Place-d'Armes)*, or Bank of Montreal, founded in 1817 by a group of merchants, is the country's oldest banking institution. Its present head office takes up an entire block on the north side of Place d'Armes. A magnificent building by John Wells, built in 1847 and modelled after the Roman Pantheon, it occupies the place of honour in the centre of the block, and offers customer banking. Its Corinthian portico is a monument to the commercial power of the Scottish merchants who founded the institution. The capitals of the columns, severely damaged by pollution, were replaced in 1970 with aluminum replicas. The pediment includes a bas-relief depicting the bank's coat of arms carved out of Binney stone in Scotland by Her Majesty's sculptor, Sir John Steele.

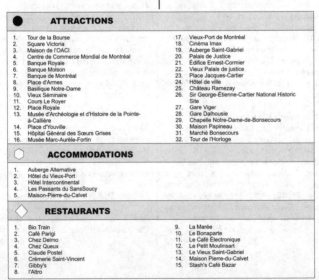

ATTRACTIONS

1. Tour de la Bourse	17. Vieux-Port de Montréal
2. Square Victoria	18. Cinéma Imax
3. Maison de l'OACI	19. Auberge Saint-Gabriel
4. Centre de Commerce Mondial de Montréal	20. Palais de Justice
5. Banque Royale	21. Édifice Ernest-Cormier
6. Banque Molson	22. Vieux Palais de justice
7. Banque de Montréal	23. Place Jacques-Cartier
8. Place d'Armes	24. Hôtel de ville
9. Basilique Notre-Dame	25. Château Ramezay
10. Vieux Séminaire	26. Sir George-Étienne-Cartier National Historic
11. Cours Le Royer	Site
12. Place Royale	27. Gare Viger
13. Musée d'Archéologie et d'Histoire de la Pointe-	28. Gare Dalhousie
à-Callière	29. Chapelle Notre-Dame-de-Bonsecours
14. Place d'Youville	30. Maison Papineau
15. Hôpital Général des Sœurs Grises	31. Marché Bonsecours
16. Musée Marc-Aurèle-Fortin	32. Tour de l'Horloge

ACCOMMODATIONS

1. Auberge Alternative
2. Hôtel du Vieux-Port
3. Hôtel Intercontinental
4. Les Passants du SansSoucy
5. Maison-Pierre-du-Calvet

RESTAURANTS

1. Bio Train	9. La Marée
2. Café Parigi	10. Le Bonaparte
3. Chez Delmo	11. Le Café Électronique
4. Chez Queux	12. Le Petit Moulinsart
5. Claude Postel	13. Le Vieux Saint-Gabriel
6. Crémerie Saint-Vincent	14. Maison Pierre-du-Calvet
7. Gibby's	15. Stash's Café Bazar
8. l'Altro	

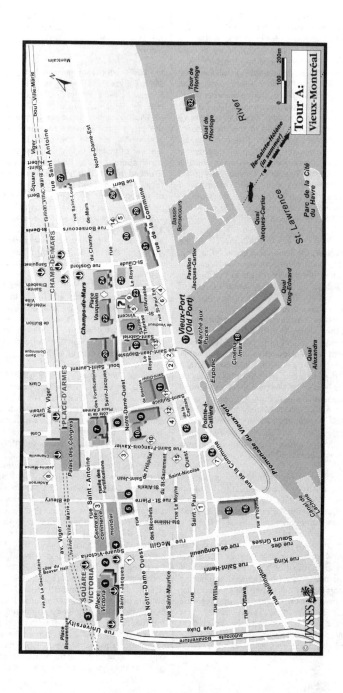

Tour A: Vieux-Montréal

MONTRÉAL

The interior was almost entirely redone in 1904-05, according to plans by celebrated New York architects McKim, Mead and White (Boston Library, Columbia University in New York City). On this occasion, the bank was endowed with a splendid banking hall, designed in the style of a Roman basilica, with green syenite columns, gilded bronze ornamentation and beige marble counters. A small **Numismatic museum** *(free admission; Mon to Fri, 9am to 5pm)* located in the lobby of the more recent building displays bills from different eras, as well as an amusing collection of mechanical piggy banks. Across from the museum, visitors will find four bas-reliefs carved out of an artificial stone called *coade*, which once graced the façade of the bank's original head office. These were executed in 1819, after drawings by English sculptor John Bacon.

Under the French Regime, **Place d'Armes ★★ (8)** was the heart of the city. Used for military manoeuvres and religious processions, the square was also the location of the Gadoys well, the city's main source of potable water. In 1847, the square was transformed into a lovely, fenced-in Victorian garden, which was destroyed at the beginning of the 20th century in order to make room for a tramway terminal. In the meantime, a **monument to Maisonneuve** was erected in 1895. Executed by sculptor Philippe Hébert, it shows the founder of Montréal, Paul de Chomedey, Sieur de Maisonneuve, surrounded by prominent figures from the city's early history, namely Jeanne Mance, founder of the Hôtel-Dieu (hospital), Lambert Closse, along with his dog Pilote, and Charles Lemoyne, head of a family of famous explorers. An Iroquois warrior completes the tableau.

The surprising red sandstone tower at number 511 Place d'Armes was erected in 1888 for the New York Life insurance company according to a design by architects Babb, Cook and Willard. Although it only has eight floors, it is regarded as Montréal's first skyscraper. The stone used for the facing was imported from Scotland. At the time, this type of stone was transported in the holds of ships, where it served as ballast until it was sold to building contractors at the pier. The edifice next door *(507 Place-d'Armes)* is adorned with beautiful Art Deco details. It was one of the first buildings over 10 stories to be erected in Montréal after a regulation restricting the height of structures was repealed in 1927.

On the south side of the Place d'Armes, visitors will find the Basilique Notre-Dame and the Vieux Séminaire, which are described below.

In 1663, the seigneury of the island of Montréal was acquired by the Sulpicians from Paris, who remained its undisputed masters up until the British conquest of 1760. In addition to distributing land to colonists and laying out the city's first streets, the Sulpicians were responsible for the construction of a large number of buildings, including Montréal's first parish church (1673). Dedicated to *Notre Dame* (Our Lady), this church had a beautiful Baroque façade, which faced straight down the centre of the street of the same name, creating a pleasant perspective characteristic of classical French town-planning. At the beginning of the 19th century, however, this rustic little church cut a sorry figure when compared to the Anglican cathedral on Rue Notre-Dame and the new Catholic cathedral on Rue Saint-Denis, neither of which remains today. The Sulpicians therefore decided to make a decisive move to surpass their rivals once and for all. In 1823, to the great displeasure of local architects, they commissioned New York architect James O'Donnell, who came from an Irish Protestant background, to design the largest and most original church north of Mexico.

Basilique Notre-Dame ★★★ (9) *(110 Rue Notre-Dame Ouest, ☎842-2925)*, built between 1824 and 1829, is a true North American masterpiece of Gothic Revival architecture. It should be seen not as a replica of a European cathedral, but rather as a fundamentally neoclassical structure characteristic of the Industrial Revolution, complemented by a medieval-style decor which foreshadowed the historicism of the Victorian era. These elements make the building remarkable. O'Donnell was so pleased with his work that he converted to Catholicism before dying, so that he could be buried under the church. Between 1874 and 1880, the original interior, considered too austere, was replaced by the fabulous polychromatic decorations found today. Executed by Victor Bourgeau, then the leading architect of religious buildings in the Montréal region, along with about 50 artists, it is made entirely of wood, painted and gilded with gold leaf. Particularly noteworthy features include the baptistery, decorated with frescoes by Ozias Leduc, and the powerful electro-pneumatic Casavant organ with its 5,772 pipes, often used during the numerous concerts given at the basilica. Lastly, there are the

Basilique Notre-Dame

stained-glass windows by Francis Chigot, a master glass artist from France, which depict various episodes in the history of Montréal. They were installed in honour of the church's 100th anniversary.

To the right of the chancel, a passage leads to the Chapelle du Sacré-Cœur (Sacred Heart Chapel), added to the back of the church in 1888. Nicknamed the Chapelle des Mariages (Wedding Chapel) because of the countless nuptials held there every year, it was seriously damaged by fire in 1978. The spiral staircases and the side galleries are all that remain of the exuberant, Spanish-style Gothic-Revival decor of the original. The architects Jodoin, Lamarre and Pratte decided to tie these vestiges in with a modern design, completed in 1981, and included a lovely sectioned vault with skylights, a large bronze reredos by Charles Daudelin and a Guilbault-Thérien mechanical organ. To the right, on the way out of the chapel, visitors will find the small **Musée de la Basilique** *(closed to the public)*, a museum displaying various treasures, including embroidered liturgical clothing as well as the episcopal throne and personal effects of Monseigneur de Pontbriand, the last bishop of New France.

The **Vieux Séminaire ★ (10)** *(116 Rue Notre-Dame Ouest)*, or old seminary, was built in 1683 in the style of a Parisian *hôtel particulier*, with a courtyard in front and a garden in back. It is the oldest building in the city. For more than three centuries, it has been occupied by Sulpician priests, who, under the French Regime, used it as a manor from which they managed their vast seigneury. At the time of the building's construction, Montréal had barely 500 inhabitants, and was constantly being terrorized by Iroquois attacks. Under those circumstances, the seminary, albeit modest in appearance, represented a precious haven of European civilization in the middle of a wild, isolated land. The public clock at the top of the façade was installed in 1701, and may be the oldest one of its kind in the Americas.

Take Rue Saint-Sulpice, which runs alongside the basilica.

Old Montréal contains a large number of 19th-century warehouses with stone frames used to store the goods unloaded from ships at the nearby port. Certain elements of their design — their large glass surfaces, intended to reduce the need for artificial gas lighting and consequently the risk of fire; their wide open interior spaces; the austere style of their

facing, given the Victorian context in which they were built and their cast-iron framed American counterparts — make these buildings the natural precursors of modern architecture.

The immense warehouses of the **Cours Le Royer ★ (11)** *(Rue Saint-Sulpice)* belonged to the *religieuses hospitalières* of Saint-Joseph. These nursing sisters of Saint-Joseph rented them out to importers. Designed between 1860 and 1871 by Michel Laurent and Victor Bourgeau, who seldom worked on commercial structures, they are located on the site of Montréal's first Hôtel-Dieu (hospital), founded by Jeanne Mance in 1643. The warehouses, covering a total of 43,000 square metres, were converted into apartments and offices between 1977 and 1986. The small Rue Le Royer was excavated to make room for an underground parking lot, now covered by a pleasant pedestrian mall.

Turn right on Rue Saint-Paul, towards Place Royale, which lies on the left-hand side of the street.

Montréal's oldest public square, **Place Royale (12)** dates back to 1657. Originally a market square, it later became a pretty Victorian garden surrounded by a cast-iron fence. In 1991, it was raised in order to make room for an archaeological observation site. It now links the Musée d'Archéologie de la Pointe-à-Callière to the **Vieille Douane**, the old customs house, on the north side. The latter is a lovely example of British neoclassical architecture transplanted into a Canadian setting. The building's austere lines, accentuated by the facing, made of local grey stone, are offset by the appropriate proportions and simplified references to antiquity. The old customs house was built in 1836 according to drawings by John Ostell, who had just arrived in Montréal.

The **Musée d'Archéologie et d'Histoire de la Pointe-à-Callière ★★** (13) *(8$; Sep to Jun, Tue to Fri 10am to 5pm, Sat and Sun 11am to 5pm; Jul to Sep, Tue to Fri 10am to 6pm, Sat and Sun 11am to 6pm; 350 Place Royale, Pointe-à-Callière, ☎872-9150)*. This archaeology and history museum lies on the exact site where Montréal was founded on May 18, 1642. The Rivière Saint-Pierre used to flow alongside the area now occupied by Place d'Youville, while the muddy banks of the St. Lawrence reached almost as far as the present-day Rue de la Commune. The first colonists built Fort Ville-Marie out of earth and wooden posts on the isolated point of land created by these two bodies of water. Threatened by Iroquois flotillas and flooding, the leaders of the colony soon decided to establish the town on Coteau Saint-Louis, the hill now bisected by Rue Notre-Dame. The site of the fort was then occupied by a cemetery and the château of Governor de Callière, hence the name.

The museum uses the most advanced techniques available to provide visitors with a survey of the city's history. Attractions include a multimedia presentation, a visit to the vestiges discovered on the site, excellent models showing the different stages of Place Royale's development, holographic conversations and thematic exhibitions. Designed by architect Dan Hanganu, the museum was erected for the celebrations of the city's 350th anniversary in 1992.

Head towards Place d'Youville, to the right of the museum.

Stretching from Place Royale to Rue McGill, **Place d'Youville (14)** owes its elongated shape to its location on top of the bed of the Rivière Saint-Pierre, which was canalized in 1832. In the middle of the square stands the **Centre d'Histoire de Montréal** *($4.50; May to Sep, every day 9am to 5pm; Sep to May, closed Mon 10am to 5pm, closed Dec 8 to Jan 5; 335 Place d'Youville, ☎872-3207)*, a small, unpretentious historical museum presenting temporary exhibitions on various themes related to life in Montréal. The building itself is the former fire station number 3, one of only a few examples of Flemish-style architecture in Québec. The Marché Sainte-Anne once lay to the west of Rue Saint-Pierre and was, from 1840 to 1849, the seat of the Parliament of United Canada. In 1849, the Orangemen burned the building after a law intended to compensate both French and English victims of the rebellion of 1837-38 was adopted. The event marked the end of Montréal's political vocation.

Turn left on Rue Saint-Pierre.

The Sœurs de la Charité (Sisters of Charity) are better known as the Sœurs Grises (Grey Nuns), a nickname given these nuns falsely accused of selling alcohol to the natives and thus getting them tipsy (in French, *gris* means both grey and tipsy). In 1747, the founder of the community, Saint Marguerite d'Youville, took charge of the former Hôpital des Frères Charon, established in 1693, and transformed it into the **Hôpital**

Général des Sœurs Grises ★ (15) *(138 Rue Saint-Pierre)*, a shelter for the city's homeless children. The west wing and the ruins of this complex built during the 17th and 18th centuries in the shape of an "H". The other part, which made up another of the old city's classical perspectives, was torn open when Rue Saint-Pierre was extended through the middle of the chapel. The right transept and a part of the apse, visible on the right, have been reinforced in order to accommodate a work of art representing the text of the congregation's letters patent.

The small **Musée Marc-Aurèle-Fortin (16)** *($4, students and seniors $2, children free; Tue to Sun 11am to 5pm; 118 Rue Saint-Pierre, ☎845-6108)*, which has only a few rooms, is entirely dedicated to the work of Marc-Aurèle Fortin. Using his own unique style, Fortin painted picturesque Québec scenes. Paintings executed on a black background and majestic trees are just a couple of his trademarks. The museum has some lovely pieces.

Head across Rue de la Commune to the Promenade du Vieux-Port, which runs alongside the St. Lawrence.

The Port of Montréal is the largest inland port on the continent. It stretches 25 km along the St. Lawrence, from Cité du Havre to the refineries in the east end. The **Vieux-Port de Montréal ★★ (17)**, or old port, corresponds to the historic portion of the port, located in front of the old city. Abandoned because of its obsolescence, it was revamped between 1983 and 1992, following the example of various other centrally-located North American ports. The old port encompasses a pleasant park, laid out on the embankments and coupled with a promenade, which runs alongside the piers or *quai*, offering a "window" on the river and the few shipping activities that have fortunately been maintained. The layout accents the view of the water, the downtown area and Rue de la Commune, whose wall of neoclassical, grey stone warehouses stands before the city, one of the only examples of so-called "waterfront planning" in North America.

From the port, visitors can set off on an excursion on the river and the Lachine canal aboard **Le Bateau Mouche** *($18, children $9; May to Oct, departures every day at 10am, noon, 2pm, 4pm, 7pm; Quai Jacques-Cartier; ☎849-9952)*, whose glass roof enables passengers to fully appreciate the beauty of the

MONTRÉAL

surroundings. The *navettes fluviales* or river shuttles *($3.25; late May to mid-Oct, every day 11am to 7pm; Quai Jacques-Cartier, ☎281-8000)* ferry passengers to Île Sainte-Hélène and Longueuil, offering a spectacular view of the old port and Old Montréal along the way.

On the right, directly in line with Rue McGill, visitors will find the mouth of the **Canal de Lachine**, inaugurated in 1825. This waterway made it possible to bypass the formidable rapids known as the Rapides de Lachine upriver from Montréal, thus providing access to the Great Lakes and the American Midwest. The canal also became the cradle of the industrial revolution in Canada, since the spinning and flour-mills were able to use it as a source of power, as well as a direct means of taking in supplies and sending out shipments (from the boat to the factory and vice versa). Closed in 1959 when the seaway was opened, the canal was then turned over to the Canadian Parks Services. A bicycle path now runs alongside it, continuing on to the vieux-port or old port. The locks, restored in 1991, lie adjacent to a park and a boldly-designed lock-keeper's house. Behind the locks stands the last of the old port's towering **grain silos**. Erected in 1905, this reinforced concrete structure excited the admiration of Walter Gropius and Le Corbusier when they came here on a study trip. It is now illuminated as if it were a monument. In front, visitors will see the strange pile of cubes that form Habitat '67 (see p 123) on the right, and the **Gare Maritime Iberville** *(☎496-7678)*, the harbour station for liners cruising the St. Lawrence, on the left.

The former warehouses at **Quai King-Edward**, to the east, now house various seasonal expositions, a flea market, a café, and most importantly, the **Cinéma Imax ★ (18)** *(Quai King-Edward, Champ-de-Mars or Place-d'Armes Métro, ☎496-4629)*, a marvel of Canadian technology. The cinema projects truer than life films, shot with a special camera, onto a giant screen (see p 156). At the far end of the pier, there is a lookout, commanding a stunning view of Old Montréal, framed by the downtown skyline.

Walk along the promenade to **Boulevard Saint-Laurent**, one of the city's main arteries, which serves as the dividing line between east and west not only as far as place names and addresses are concerned, but also from an ethnic point of view. Traditionally, there has always been a higher concentration of English-speakers in the western part of the city, and French-speakers in the eastern part, while ethnic minorities of all different origins are concentrated along Boulevard Saint-Laurent.

Head up Boulevard Saint-Laurent to Rue Saint-Paul. Turn right, then left on to a narrow street named Rue Saint-Gabriel.

It was on this street that Richard Dulong opened an inn in 1754. Today, the **Auberge Saint-Gabriel (19)** *(426 Rue Saint-Gabriel)*, the oldest Canadian inn still open, operates only as a restaurant (see "Restaurants" chapter, p 144). It occupies a group of 18th-century buildings with sturdy fieldstone walls.

Turn right on Rue Notre-Dame.

Having passed through the financial and warehouse districts, visitors now enter an area dominated by civic and legal institutions; no less than three courthouses lie clustered along Rue Notre-Dame. Inaugurated in 1971, the massive new **Palais de Justice (20)** *(1 Rue Notre-Dame Est)*, or courthouse, dwarfs the surroundings. A sculpture by Charles Daudelin entitled *Allegrocube* lies on its steps. A mechanism makes it possible to open and close this stylized "hand of Justice."

From the time it was inaugurated in 1926 until it closed in 1970, the **Édifice Ernest-Cormier ★ (21)** *(100 Rue Notre-Dame Est)* was used for criminal proceedings. The former courthouse was converted into a conservatory, and was named after its architect, the illustrious Ernest Cormier, who also designed the main pavilion of the Université de Montréal and the doors of the United Nations Headquarters in New York City. The Courthouse is graced with outstanding bronze sconces, cast in Paris at the workshops of Edgar Brandt. Their installation in 1925 ushered in the Art Deco style in Canada. The main hall, faced with travertine and topped by three dome-shaped skylights, is worth a quick visit.

The **Vieux Palais de Justice ★ (22)** *(155 Rue Notre-Dame Est)*, the oldest courthouse in Montréal, was built between 1849 and 1856, according to a design by John Ostell and Henri-Maurice Perrault, on the site of the first courthouse, which was erected in 1800. It is another fine example of Canadian neoclassical architecture. After the courts were divided in 1926, the old Palais was used for civil cases, judged according to the Napoleonic Code. Since the opening of the new Palais to its left,

Hôtel de Ville

the old Palais has been converted into an annex of City Hall, located to the right.

Place Jacques-Cartier ★ (23) was laid out on the site once occupied by the Château de Vaudreuil, which burned down in 1803. The former Montréal residence of the governor of New France was without question the most elegant private home in the city. Designed by engineer Gaspard Chaussegros de Léry in 1723, it had a horseshoe-shaped staircase, leading up to a handsome cut-stone portal, two projecting pavilions (one on each side of the main part of the building), and a formal garden that extended as far as Rue Notre-Dame. After the fire, the property was purchased by local merchants, who decided to give the government a small strip of land, on the condition that a public market be established there, thus increasing the value of the adjacent property, which remained in private hands. This explains Place Jacques-Cartier's oblong shape.

Merchants of British descent sought various means of ensuring their visibility and publicly expressing their patriotism in Montréal. They quickly formed a much larger community in Montréal than in Québec City, where the government and military headquarters were located. In 1809, they were the first in the world to erect a monument to Admiral Horatio Nelson, who defeated the combined French and Spanish fleets in the Battle of Trafalgar. Supposedly, they even got the French-Canadian merchants drunk in order to extort a financial

contribution from them for the project. The base of the **Colonne Nelson**, or the Nelson Column, was designed and executed in London, according to plans by architect Robert Mitchell. It is decorated with bas-reliefs depicting the exploits of the famous Admiral at Abukir, Copenhagen, and of course Trafalgar. The statue of Nelson at the top was originally made of *coade* artificial stone, but after being damaged time and time again by protestors, it was finally replaced by a fibre-glass replica in 1981. The column is the oldest extant monument in Montréal. At the other end of Place Jacques-Cartier, visitors will see the **Quai Jacques-Cartier** and the river, while **Rue Saint-Amable** lies tucked away on the right, at the halfway mark. During summer, artists and artisans gather on this little street, selling jewellery, drawings, etchings and caricatures.

Under the French Regime, Montréal, following the example of Québec City and Trois-Rivières, had its own governor, not to be confused with the governor of New France as a whole. The situation was the same under the English Regime. It wasn't until 1833 that the first elected mayor, Jacques Viger, took control of the city. This man, who was passionately interested in history, gave Montréal its motto (*Concordia Salus*) and coat of arms, composed of the four symbols of the "founding" peoples, namely the fleur-de-lys, the Irish clover, the Scottish thistle and the English rose, all linked together by the Canadian beaver.

MONTRÉAL

After occupying a number of inadequate buildings for decades (a notable example was the Hayes aqueduct, an edifice containing an immense reservoir of water, which cracked one day while a meeting was being held in the council chamber immediately below; it's easy to imagine what happened next), the municipal administration finally moved into its present home in 1878. The **Hôtel de Ville ★ (24)** *(275 Rue Notre-Dame Est)*, or City Hall, a fine example of the Second-Empire, or Napoleon III, style, is the work of Henri-Maurice Perrault, who also designed the neighbouring courthouse. In 1922, a fire (yet another!) destroyed the interior and roof of the building, later restored in 1926, after the model of the city hall in Tours, France. Exhibitions are occasionally presented in the main hall, which is accessible via the main entrance. Visitors may also be interested to know that it was from the balcony of City Hall that France's General de Gaulle cried out his famous *"Vive le Québec libre!"* ("Freedom for Québec!") in 1967, to the great delight of the crowd gathered in front of the building.

Head to the rear of the Hôtel de Ville, by way of the pretty Place Vauquelin, the continuation of Place Jacques-Cartier.

The statue of Admiral Jean Vauquelin, defender of Louisbourg at the end of the French Regime, was probably put here to counterbalance the monument to Nelson, a symbol of British control over Canada. Go down the staircase leading to the **Champ-de-Mars**, modified in 1991 in order to reveal some vestiges of the fortifications that once surrounded Montréal. Gaspard Chaussegros de Léry designed Montréal's ramparts, erected between 1717 and 1745, as well as those of Québec City. The walls of Montréal, however, never saw war, as the city's commercial calling and its location ruled out such rash acts. The large, tree-lined lawns are reminders of the Champ-de-Mars' former vocation as a parade ground for military manoeuvres up until 1924. A view of the downtown area's skyscrapers opens up through the clearing.

Head back to Rue Notre-Dame.

The humblest of all the "châteaux" built in Montréal, the **Château Ramezay ★★ (25)** *($5; summer, every day 10am to 6pm; rest of the year, Tue to Sun 10am to 4:30pm; schedule subject to change; 280 Rue Notre-Dame Est, ☎861-3708)*, is the only one still standing. It was built in 1705 for the governor of Montréal,

Claude de Ramezay, and his family. In 1745, it fell into the hands of the Compagnie des Indes Occidentales (The French West India Company), which made it its North American headquarters. Precious Canadian furs were stored in its vaults awaiting shipment to France. After the conquest (1760), the British occupied the house, before being temporarily removed by American insurgents, who wanted Québec to join the nascent United States. Benjamin Franklin even came to stay at the château for a few months in 1775, in an attempt to convince Montrealers to become American citizens.

In 1896, after serving as the first building of the Montréal branch of the Université Laval in Québec City, the château was converted into a museum, under the patronage of the Société d'Histoire et de Numismatique de Montréal (Montréal Numismatic and Antiquarian Society), founded by Jacques Viger. Visitors will still find a rich collection of furniture, clothing and everyday objects from the 18th and 19th centuries here, as well as a large number of native artefacts. The Salle de Nantes is decorated with beautiful Louis XV-style mahogany panelling, designed by Germain Boffrand and imported from the Nantes office of the Compagnie des Indes (circa 1750).

Walk along Rue Notre-Dame to Rue Berri.

At the corner of Rue Berri lies the **George-Étienne-Cartier National Historic Site ★ (26)** *($3.25; Apr to Dec, Wed to Sun 10am to noon and 1pm to 5pm; summer hours may vary; closed Dec to late Mar; 458 Rue Notre-Dame Est, ☎283-2282)*, composed of twin houses inhabited successively by George-Étienne Cartier, one of the Fathers of Canadian Confederation. Inside, visitors will find a reconstructed mid-19th-century French-Canadian bourgeois home, complete with sound effects. Temporary exhibitions top off a tour of the premises. The neighbouring building, at number 452, is the former **Cathédrale Schismatique Grecque Saint-Nicolas**, built around 1910 in the Romanesque-Byzantine Revival style.

Rue Berri marks the eastern border of Old Montréal, and thus the fortified city of the French Regime, beyond which extended the Faubourg Québec, excavated in the 19th century to make way for railroad lines, which explains the sharp difference in height between the hill known as Coteau Saint-Louis and the Viger and Dalhousie stations. **Gare Viger (27)**, visible on the left, was inaugurated by Canadian Pacific in 1895 in order to serve the eastern part of the country. Its resemblance to the Château Frontenac in Québec City is not merely coincidental; both buildings were designed for the same railroad company and by the same architect, an American named Bruce Price. The Château-style station, closed in 1935, also included a prestigious hotel and large stained-glass train shed that has been destroyed.

Smaller **Gare Dalhousie (28)**, located near the Maison Cartier *(514 Rue Notre-Dame)* was the first railway station built by Canadian Pacific, a company established for the purpose of building a Canadian transcontinental railroad. The station was the starting point of the first transcontinental train headed for Vancouver on June 28, 1886. Canadian Pacific seems to have had a weakness for foreign architects, since it was Thomas C. Sorby, Director of Public Works in England, who drew up the plans for this humble structure. Today, it is used by the École Nationale du Cirque, the National Circus School. From the top of Rue Notre-Dame, the port's former refrigerated warehouse, made of brown brick, is visible, as well as Île Sainte-Hélène, in the middle of the river. This island, along with Île Notre-Dame, was the site of the Expo '67.

Turn right on Rue Berri, and right again on Rue Saint-Paul, which offers a lovely view of the dome of the Marché Bonsecours. Continue straight ahead to Chapelle No-tre-Dame-de-Bonsecours.

This site was originally occupied by another chapel, built in 1657 upon the recommendation of Saint Marguerite Bourgeoys, founder of the congregation of Notre-Dame. The present **Chapelle Notre-Dame-de-Bonsecours ★ (29)** *(400 Rue Saint-Paul Est, ☎845-9991)* dates back to 1771, when the Sulpicians wanted to establish a branch of the main parish in the eastern part of the fortified city. In 1890, the chapel was modified to suit contemporary tastes, and the present stone façade was added, along with the "aerial" chapel looking out on the port. Parishioners asked God's blessing on ships and their crews bound for Europe from this chapel. The interior, redone at the same time, contains a large number of votive offerings from sailors saved from shipwrecks. Some are in the form of model ships, hung from the ceiling of the nave. At the back of the chapel, the little **Musée Marguerite-Bourgeoys** *($2; May to Oct, Tue to Sun 9am to 4:30pm; Nov to Apr 10:30am to 4:30pm)*

displays mementos of the saint. From there, visitors can reach a platform adjoining the "aerial" chapel, which offers an interesting view of the old port.

The **Maison Pierre-du-Calvet**, at the corner of Rue Bonsecours (number 401), is representative of 18th-century, French urban architecture adapted to the local setting, with thick walls made of fieldstone embedded in mortar, storm windows doubling the casement windows with their little squares of glass imported from France, and high firebreak walls, then required by local regulations as a means of limiting the spread of fire from one building to the next.

A little higher on Rue Bonsecours, visitors will find the **Maison Papineau (30)** *(440 Rue Bonsecours)* inhabited long ago by Louis-Joseph Papineau (1786-1871), lawyer, politician and head of the French-Canadian nationalist movement up until the insurrection of 1837. Built in 1785 and covered with a wooden facing made to look like cut stone, it was one of the first buildings in Old Montréal to be restored (1962).

The **Marché Bonsecours ★★ (31)** *(350 Rue Saint-Paul Est, ☎872-7730)* was erected between 1845 and 1850. The lovely grey stone neoclassical edifice with sash windows, was erected on **Rue Saint-Paul**, for many years Montréal's main commercial artery. The building is adorned with a portico supported by cast iron columns moulded in England, and topped by a silvery dome, which for many years served as the symbol of the city at the entrance to the port. The public market, closed since the early sixties following the advent of the supermarket, was transformed into municipal offices then an exhibition hall before finally reopening partially in 1996. The building originally housed both the city hall and a concert hall upstairs. The market's old storehouses, recently renovated, can be seen on Rue Saint-Paul, while from the large balcony on Rue de la Commune you can see the partly reconstructed **Bonsecours dock**, where paddle-wheelers full of farmers come to sell their produce in the city used to moor.

The **Tour de l'Horloge ★ (32)** *(at the end of the Quai de l'Horloge; May to Oct)* is visible to the east from the end of Quai Jacques-Cartier. Painted a pale yellow, the structure is actually a monument erected in 1922 in memory of merchant marine sailors who died during WWI. It was inaugurated by the Prince of Wales (the future Edward VIII) during one of his many visits to Montréal. An observatory at the top of the tower provides a clear view of Île Sainte-Hélène, the Jacques-Cartier bridge and the eastern part of Old Montréal. Standing on Place Belvédère at the base of the tower, one has the impression of standing on the deck of ship as it glides slowly down the St. Lawrence and out to the Atlantic Ocean.

To return to the Métro, walk back up Place Jacques-Cartier, cross Rue Notre-Dame, Place Vauquelin and lastly Champ-de-Mars, to the station of the same name.

Tour B: Downtown ★★★
(two days)

The downtown skyscrapers give Montréal a typically North American look. Nevertheless, unlike most other cities on the continent, there is a certain Latin spirit here, which seeps in between the towering buildings, livening up this part of Montréal both day and night. Bars, cafés, department stores, shops and head offices, along with two universities and numerous colleges, all lie clustered within a limited area at the foot of Mont Royal.

At the beginning of the 20th century, Montréal's central business district gradually shifted from the old city to what was up until then a posh residential neighbourhood known as The Golden Square Mile, inhabited by upper-class Canadians. Wide arterial streets such as Boulevard René-Lévesque were then lined with palatial residences surrounded by shady gardens. The city centre underwent a radical transformation in a very short time (1960-1967), marked by the construction of Place Ville-Marie, the Métro, the underground city, Place des Arts, and various other infrastructures which still exert an influence on the area's development.

Walk up on Rue Guy from the exit of the Guy-Concordia Métro station, then turn right on Rue Sherbrooke.

The numbers following the names of attractions refer to the map of Downtown.

In addition to being invaded by the business world, the Golden Square Mile also underwent profound social changes that altered its character — the exodus of the Scottish population, the shortage of servants, income taxes, World War I, during which the sons of

many of these families were killed, and above all the stock market crash of 1929, which ruined many businessmen. Consequently, numerous mansions were demolished and the remaining population had to adjust to more modest living conditions. **The Linton ★ (1)** *(1509 Rue Sherbrooke Ouest)*, a prestigious apartment building erected in 1907, provided an interesting alternative. It was built on the grounds of the house of the same name still visible in the back, on little Rue Simpson. The façade of the Linton is adorned with lavish Beaux-Arts details made of terra cotta and a beautiful cast-iron marquee.

The lovely presbyterian **Church of St. Andrew and St. Paul ★★ (2)** *(at the corner of Rue Redpath)* was one of the most important institutions of the Scottish elite in Montréal. Built in 1932 according to plans by architect Harold Lea Fetherstonaugh, as the community's third place of worship, it illustrates the endurance of the medieval style in religious architecture. The stone interior is graced with magnificent commemorative stained-glass windows. Those along the aisles came from the second church and are for the most part significant British pieces, such as the windows of Andrew Allan and his wife, produced by the workshop of William Morris after sketches by the famous English Pre-Raphaelite painter, Edward Burne-Jones. The Scottish-Canadian Black Watch Regiment has been affiliated with the church ever since it was created in 1862.

The **Musée des Beaux-Arts de Montréal ★★★ (3)** *(free admission for permanent collection; $10, students $5 for temporary exhibits, half-price Wed 5:30pm to 9pm; Tue to Sun 11am to 6pm, Wed until 9pm; 1380 Rue Sherbrooke Ouest, ☎285-1600)*, Montréal's Museum of Fine Arts, the oldest and most important museum in Québec, was founded in 1860 by the Art Association of Montreal, a group of Anglo-Saxon art lovers. The Pavillon Beniah-Gibb, on the north side of Rue Sherbrooke *(1379 Rue Sherbrooke Ouest)*, opened its doors in 1912. Its façade, made of white Vermont marble, is the work of the Scottish merchants' favourite architects, the prolific Edward and William Sutherland Maxwell. The building became too small for the museum's collection, and was enlarged towards the back on three different occasions. Finally, in 1991, architect Moshe Safdie designed the Pavillon Jean-Noël-Desmarais, just opposite on the south side of Rue Sherbrooke. This new wing includes the red brick façade of a former apartment building, and is linked to the original building by tunnels under Rue Sherbrooke. The museum's main entrance is now in the new wing, at the corner of Rue Crescent.

At Montréals **Musée des Arts Décoratifs (4)** *(4$; Tue to Sun 11am to 6pm, Wed 11am to 9pm; 2200 Rue Crescent, ☎259-2575)*, visitors can see International-style (1935 to the present day) furniture and decorative objects from the Liliane and David Stewart collection, as well as travelling exhibitions on glass, textiles, etc.

Erected in 1892, the **Erskine & American United Church ★ (5)** *(at the corner of Avenue du Musée)* is an excellent example of the Romanesque Revival style as interpreted by American architect Henry Hobson Richardson. The textured sandstone, large arches flanked by either squat or disproportionately elongated columns, and sequences of small, arched openings are typical of the style. The auditorium-shaped interior was remodelled in the style of the Chicago School in 1937. The lower chapel (along Avenue du Musée), contains lovely, brilliantly coloured, Tiffany stained-glass windows.

Rue Crescent ★ (6), located immediately east of the museum, has a split personality. To the north of Boulevard de Maisonneuve, the street is lined with old row houses, which now accommodate antique shops and luxury boutiques, while to the south, it is crowded with night clubs, restaurants and bars, most with sunny terraces lining the sidewalks. For many years, Rue Crescent was known as the English counterpart of Rue Saint-Denis. Though it is still a favourite among American visitors, its clientele is more diversified now.

A symbol of its era, **Le Château ★ (7)** *(1321 Rue Sherbrooke Ouest)*, a handsome Château-style building, was erected in 1925 for a French-Canadian businessman by the name of Pamphile du Tremblay, owner of the French-language newspaper *La Presse*. Architects Ross and Macdonald designed what was at the time the largest apartment building in Canada. The Royal Institute awarded these same architects a prize for the design of the fashionable **Holt-Renfrew** store which stands across the street *(1300 Rue Sherbrooke Ouest)* in 1937. With its rounded, horizontal lines, the store is a fine example of the streamline Deco.

The last of Montréal's old hotels, the **Ritz-Carlton Kempinski ★ (8)** *(1228 Rue Sherbrooke Ouest)* was inaugurated in 1911 by César Ritz himself. For many years, it was the favourite gathering place of the Montréal bourgeoisie. Some people even stayed here year-round, living a life of luxury among the drawing rooms, garden and ballroom. The building was designed by Warren and Wetmore of New York City, the well-known architects of Grand Central Station on New York's Park Avenue. Many celebrities have stayed at this sophisticated luxury hotel over the years, including Richard Burton and Elizabeth Taylor, who were married here in 1964.

Continue along Rue Sherbrooke to the entrance of Maison Alcan. Three noteworthy buildings lie across the street. **Maison Baxter** *(1201 Rue Sherbrooke Ouest)*, on the left, boasts a beautiful stairway. **Maison Forget** *(1195 Rue Sherbrooke Ouest)*, in the centre, was built in 1882 for Louis-Joseph Forget, one of the only French-Canadian magnates to live in this neighbourhood during the 19th century. The building on the right is the **Mount Royal Club**, a private club frequented essentially by business people. Built in 1905, it is the work of Stanford White of the famous New York firm McKim, Mead and White, architects of the head office of the Bank of Montréal on Place d'Armes (see p 90).

Maison Alcan ★ (9) *(1188 Rue Sherbrooke Ouest)*, head office of the Alcan aluminum company, is a fine example of historical preservation and inventive urban restructuring. Five buildings along Rue Sherbrooke, including the lovely **Maison Atholstan** *(1172 Rue Sherbrooke Ouest)*, the first Beaux-Arts-style structure erected in Montréal (1894), have been carefully restored, and then joined in the back to an atrium, which is linked to a modern aluminum building. The garden running along the south wall of the modern part provides a little-known passageway between Rue Drummond and Rue Stanley.

Enter the atrium through the Sherbrooke entrance, which used to lead into the lobby of the Berkeley Hotel. Exit through the garden, go to the left and head south on Rue Stanley. Turn left on Boulevard de Maisonneuve, then right on Rue Peel.

Montréal has the most extensive **underground city** in the world (see p 158). Greatly appreciated in bad weather, it provides access to over 2,000 shops and restaurants, as well as movie theatres, apartment and office buildings, hotels, parking lots, the train station, the bus station, Place des Arts and even the Université

● ATTRACTIONS

1. Le Linton
2. St.Andrew and St.Paul Church
3. Musée des Beaux-Arts
4. Musée des arts décoratifs de Montréal
5. Erskine & American Church
6. Rue Crescent
7. Le Château
8. Hôtel Ritz-Carlton
9. Maison Alcan
10. Les Cours Mont-Royal
11. Centre Infotouriste
12. Square Dorchester
13. Le Windsor
14. Édifice Sun Life
15. Place du Canada
16. St.George Anglican Church
17. Tour IBM-Marathon
18. Gare Windsor
19. Centre Molson
20. Hôtel Château Champlain (Marriott)
21. Planétarium Dow
22. Tour 1000
23. Cathédrale Marie-Reine-du-Monde
24. Place Bonaventure
25. Place Ville-Marie
26. Place Montréal Trust
27. Tour BNP
28. McGill University
29. Musée McCord d'Histoire Canadienne
30. Centre Eaton
31. Eaton
32. Christ Church Cathedral
33. Promenades de la Cathédrale
34. Square Phillips
35. La Baie
36. St. James United Church
37. Église du Gesù
38. St.Patrick's Basilica
39. Musée d'Art Contemporain
40. Place des Arts
41. Complexe Desjardins
42. Théâtre du Nouveau Monde
43. Musée Juste pour Rire
44. Monument National
45. Chinatown
46. Palais des Congrès

○ ACCOMMODATIONS

1. Auberge de Jeunesse/Youth Hostel
2. Benaventure Hilton
3. Casa Bella
4. Centre Sheraton
5. Delta Montréal
6. Holiday Inn Select Montréal Centre-Ville
7. Hôtel de la Montagne
8. Hôtel du Complexe Desjardins
9. Hôtel du Nouveau Forum
10. Hôtel du Parc
11. Loews Hôtel Vogue
12. Manoir Ambrose
13. Marriott Château Champlain
14. Marriott Residence Inn-Montréal
15. Novotel
16. Reine-Élizabeth
17. Ritz Carlton Kempinski Montréal
18. Université Concordia
19. Université de Montréal
20. Université McGill
21. Westin Mont-Royal
22. YMCA Centre-Ville

◇ RESTAURANTS

1. Ben's Delicatessen
2. Biddle's Jazz
3. Café Société
4. Club Lounge
5. Da Vinci
6. Eaton, le 9e
7. Julien
8. Katsura
9. L'Actuel
10. L'Élysée Mandarin
11. La Mère Tucker
12. Le Café de Paris
13. Le Caveau
14. Le Commensal
15. Le Grand Comptoir
16. Le Jardin du Ritz
17. Le Lutétia
18. Le Parchemin
19. Le Paris
20. Le Théâtre du Nouveau Monde
21. Maison George Stephen
22. Moe's Deli & Bar
23. Wienstein 'n' Gavino Pasta Bar Factory Co.

◆ CAFÉS

1. Café Starbuck's
2. Café Toman
3. La Brûlerie Saint-Denis
4. Second Cup
5. Second Cup
6. Van Houtte
7. Van Houtte

du Québec à Montréal (UQAM) via tunnels, atriums and indoor plazas. The **Cours Mont-Royal ★★ (10)** *(1455 Rue Peel)* are duly linked to this sprawling network, which centres around the various Métro stations. A multipurpose complex, the Cours consist of four levels of stores, offices and apartments laid out inside the former Mount Royal Hotel. With its 1,100 rooms, this Jazz Age palace, inaugurated in 1922, was the largest hotel in the British Empire. Aside from the exterior, all that was preserved during the 1987 remodelling was a portion of the ceiling of the lobby, from which the former chandelier of the Monte Carlo casino is suspended. The four 10-story *cours* (inner courts) are definitely worth a visit, as is a stroll through what may be the most well-designed shopping centre in the downtown area. The building that looks like a small Scottish manor across the street is in fact the head office of the Seagram Company (Barton & Guestier wines).

Head south on Rue Peel to Square Dorchester.

At Montreal's tourist office, the **Centre Infotouriste (11)** *(1001 Rue du Square-Dorchester, Métro Peel)*, visitors will find representatives from a number of tourist-related enterprises, such as tourist offices, Tours Royal

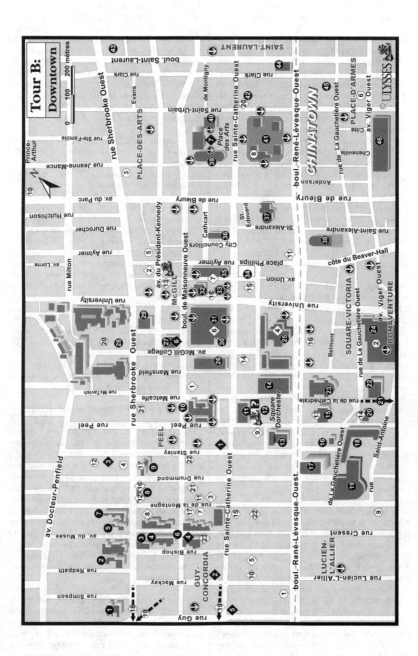

Tour B: Downtown

MONTRÉAL

Bus Lines, the Le Réseau hotel-reservation service and Ulysses Travel Bookshop.

From 1799 to 1854, **Square Dorchester ★ (12)** was occupied by Montréal's Catholic cemetery, which was then moved to Mont Royal, where it is still located. In 1872, the city turned the free space into two squares, one on either side of Dorchester Street (now Boulevard René-Lévesque). The northern portion is called Square Dorchester, while the southern part was renamed Place du Canada to commemorate the 100th anniversary of Confederation (1967). A number of monuments adorn Square Dorchester. In the centre, there is an equestrian statue dedicated to Canadian soldiers who died during the Boer War in South Africa, while a handsome statue of Scottish poet Robert Burns styled after Bartholdi's Roaring Lion, donated by the Sun Life insurance company, and Émile Brunet's monument to Sir Wilfrid Laurier, Prime Minister of Canada from 1896 to 1911, stand around the perimeter. The square also serves as the starting point for guided bus tours.

The **Windsor ★ (13)** *(1170 Rue Peel)*, the hotel where members of the royal family used to stay during their visits to Canada, no longer exists. The prestigious Second-Empire-style edifice, built in 1878 by architect W. W. Boyinton of Chicago, was claimed by fire in 1957. All that remains of it is an annex erected in 1906, which was converted into an office building in 1986. The ballrooms and lovely Peacock Alley have, however, been preserved. An impressive atrium, visible from the upper floors, has been constructed for the building's tenants. The handsome **Tour CIBC**, designed by Peter Dickinson (1962), stands on the site of the old hotel. Its walls are faced with green slate, which blends harmoniously with the dominant colours of the buildings around the square, namely the greyish beige of stone and the green of oxidized copper.

The **Édifice Sun Life ★★ (14)** *(1155 Rue Metcalfe)*, erected between 1913 and 1933 for the powerful Sun Life insurance company, was for many years the largest building in the British Empire. It was in this "fortress" of the Anglo-Saxon establishment, with its colonnades reminiscent of ancient mythology, that the British Crown Jewels were hidden during World War II. In 1977, the company's head office was moved to Toronto, in protest against provincial language laws excluding English. Fortunately, the chimes that ring at 5pm every day are still in place and remain an integral part of the neighbourhood's spirit.

Place du Canada ★ (15), the southern portion of Square Dorchester, is the setting for the annual Remembrance Day ceremony (November 11th), which honours Canadian soldiers killed in the two World Wars and in the Korean War. Veterans reunite around the War Memorial, which occupies the place of honour in the centre of the square. A more imposing monument to Sir John A. Macdonald, Canada's first Prime Minister, elected in 1867, stands alongside Boulevard René-Lévesque.

A number of churches clustered around Square Dorchester before it was even laid out in 1872. Unfortunately, only two of the eight churches built in the area between 1865 and 1875 have survived. One of these is the beautiful Gothic-Revival-style **St. George's Anglican Church ★★ (16)** *(at the corner of Rue de la Gauchetière and Rue Peel)*. Its delicately sculpted sandstone exterior conceals an interior covered with lovely, dark woodwork. Particularly noteworthy are the remarkable ceiling, with its exposed framework, the woodwork in the chancel, and the tapestry from Westminster Abbey, used during the coronation of Elizabeth II.

The elegant 47-story **Tour IBM-Marathon ★ (17)** *(1250 Boulevard René-Lévesque Ouest)*, forming part of the backdrop of St. George's, was completed in 1991 according to a design by the famous New York architects Kohn, Pedersen and Fox. Its winter bamboo garden is open to the public.

In 1887, the head of Canadian Pacific, William Cornelius Van Horne, asked his New York friend Bruce Price (1845-1903) to draw up the plans for **Gare Windsor ★ (18)** *(at the corner of Rue de la Gauchetière and Rue Peel)*, a modern train station, which would serve as the terminus of the transcontinental railroad, completed the previous year. At the time, Price was one of the most prominent architects in the eastern United States, where he worked on residential projects for high-society clients, as well as skyscrapers like the American Surety Building in Manhattan. Later, he was put in charge of building the Château Frontenac in Québec City, thus establishing the Château style in Canada.

Massive-looking Windsor Station, with its corner buttresses, Roman arches outlined in the stone, and series of arcades, is Montréal's best example of the Romanesque Revival style as interpreted by American architect Henry Hobson Richardson. Its construction established the city as the country's railway centre and initiated the shift of commercial and financial activity from the old town to the Golden Square Mile. Abandoned in favour of the Gare Centrale after World War II, Windsor Station was used only for commuter trains up until 1993.

The **Centre Molson (19)** *(7$; guided tours in English 11am and 2pm, guided tours in French 10:30am and 1:30pm, duration 1 hr. 15 min.; 1250 Rue de la Gauchetière, Métro Bonaventure)*, or Molson Centre, built on the platforms of Windsor Station, now blocks all train access to the venerable old station. Opened in March 1996, this immense building with its odd shape succeeds the Forum on Sainte-Catherine as the home ice of the National Hockey League's Montréal Canadiens, which are owned by the Molson Brewery. The amphitheatre can seat 21,247 people, and boasts 138 glassed-in private boxes sold to Montréal companies for hefty sums. The National Hockey League's regular season runs from October to April, and the play-offs can carry on into June. Two-thousand tickets are put on sale at the Molson Centre ticket booth the day of a game, making it possible to get good seats even at the last minute. Popular music concerts are also often held at the Centre. **Guided tours** *($7, seniors and students $5, children under 5 free; English tour at 11am and 2pm, 90 minutes; ☎989-2841)* of the Centre are available. These include, when possible, a visit to the Canadiens' dressing room and a chance to see the team practise.

Built in 1966, the **Hôtel Château Champlain ★ (20)** *(1 Place du Canada)*, nicknamed the "cheese grater" by Montrealers due to its many arched, convex openings, was designed by Québec architects Jean-Paul Pothier and Roger D'Astou. The latter is a disciple of American architect Frank Lloyd Wright, with whom he studied for several years. The hotel is not unlike some of the master's late works, characterized by rounded, fluid lines.

The **Planétarium Dow (21)** *($5.50; Jun to Sep, open every day; Sep to Jun, Tue to Sun 8:30am to noon and 1pm to 4pm; 45 min presentation from Mon to Fri at 1:30pm and 8:30pm; Sat, Sun. and holidays at 3:30pm; 1000 Rue Saint-Jacques Ouest, ☎872-4530)* projects astronomy films onto a 20-metre hemispheric dome. The universe and its mysteries are explained in a way that makes this marvellous, often poorly understood world

accessible to all. Guest lecturers provide commentaries on the presentations. The show lasts more than an hour.

Tour 1000 (22) *(1000 Rue de la Gauchetière)*, a 50-story skyscraper, was completed in 1992. It houses the terminus for buses linking Montréal to the South Shore, as well as the **Amphithéâtre Bell** an indoor skating rink open year-round *($5, skate rentals $4; schedule changes frequently, call ☎395-0555)*. The architects wanted to set the building apart from its neighbours by crowning it with a copper-covered point. Its total height is the maximum allowed by the city, namely the height of Mont Royal. The ultimate symbol of Montréal, the mountain may not surpassed under any circumstances.

Cathédrale Marie-Reine-du-Monde ★★ (23) *(Boulevard René-Lévesque Ouest at the corner of Mansfield)* is the seat of the archdiocese of Montréal and a reminder of the tremendous power wielded by the clergy up until the Quiet Revolution. It is exactly one third the size of St. Peter's in Rome. In 1852, a terrible fire destroyed the Catholic cathedral on Rue Saint-Denis. The ambitious Monseigneur Ignace Bourget (1799-1885), who was bishop of Montréal at the time, seized the opportunity to work out a grandiose scheme to outshine the Sulpicians' Basilique Notre-Dame and ensure the supremacy of the Catholic Church in Montréal. What could accomplish these goals better than a replica of Rome's St. Peter's, right in the middle of the Protestant neighbourhood? Despite reservations on the part of architect Victor Bourgeau, the plan was carried out. The bishop even made Bourgeau go to Rome to measure the venerable building. Construction began in 1870 and was finally completed in 1894. Copper statues of the 13 patron saints of Montréal's parishes were installed in 1900.

Modernized during the 1950s, the interior of the cathedral is no longer as harmonious as it once was. Nevertheless, there is a lovely replica of Bernini's baldaquin, executed by sculptor Victor Vincent. The bishops and archbishops of Montréal are interred in the mortuary chapel on the left, where the place of honour is occupied by the recumbent statue of Monseigneur Bourget. A monument outside reminds visitors yet again of this individual, who did so much to strengthen the bonds between France and Canada.

MONTRÉAL

An immense, grooved concrete block with no façade, **Place Bonaventure ★ (24)** *(1 Place Bonaventure)*, which was completed in 1966, is one of the most revolutionary works of modern architecture of its time. Designed by Montrealer Raymond Affleck, it is a multi-purpose complex built on top of the railway lines leading into the Gare Centrale. It contains a parking area, a two-level shopping centre linked to the Métro and the underground city, two large exhibition halls, wholesalers, offices, and an intimate 400-room hotel laid out around a charming hanging garden, worth a short visit.

Place Bonaventure is linked to the Métro station of the same name, designed by architect Victor Prus (1964). With its brown-brick facing and bare concrete vaults, the station looks like an early Christian basilica. The **Montréal Métro** system has a total of 65 stations divided up among four lines used by trains running on rubber wheels (see map of Métro, p 48). Each station has a different design, some very elaborate.

A railway tunnel leading under Mont Royal to the downtown area was built in 1913. The tracks ran under Avenue McGill College, then multiplied at the bottom of a deep trench, which stretched between Rue Mansfield and Rue University. In 1938, the subterranean **Gare Centrale** was built, marking the true starting point of the underground city. Camouflaged since 1957 by the **Hôtel Reine-Elizabeth**, the Queen Elizabeth hotel, it has an interesting, streamline-Deco waiting hall. **Place Ville-Marie ★★★ (25)** *(1 Place Ville-Marie, Métro Bonaventure)*, was erected above the northern part of the formerly open-air trench in 1959. The famous Chinese-American architect Ieoh Ming Pei (Louvre Pyramid, Paris; East Building of the National Gallery, Washington, D.C.) designed the multipurpose complex built over the railway tracks and containing vast shopping arcades now linked to most of the surrounding edifices. It also encompasses a number of office buildings, including the famous cruciform aluminum tower, whose unusual shape enables natural light to penetrate all the way into the centre of the structure, while at the same time symbolizing Montréal, a Catholic city dedicated to the Virgin Mary.

In the middle of the public area, a granite compass card indicates true north, while **Avenue McGill College**, which leads straight toward the mountain, indicates "north" as perceived by Montrealers in their everyday life. This artery, lined with multicoloured skyscrapers, was still a narrow residential street in 1950. It now offers a wide view of Mont Royal, crowned by a metallic cross erected in 1927 to commemorate the gesture of Paul Chomedey de Maisonneuve, founder of Montréal, who climbed the mountain in January 1643 and placed a wooden cross at its summit to thank the Virgin Mary for having spared Fort Ville-Marie from a devastating flood.

Cross Place Ville-Marie and take Avenue McGill College.

Avenue McGill College was widened and entirely redesigned during the 1980s. Walking along it, visitors will see several examples of eclectic, polychromatic postmodern architecture composed largely of granite and reflective glass. **Place Montréal Trust (26)** *(at the corner of Rue Sainte-Catherine)* is one of a number of Montréal shopping centres topped by an office building and linked to the underground city and the Métro by corridors and private plazas. Children often visualize huge robots from outer space in the building's pink and green façade.

The **Tour BNP ★ (27)** *(1981 Avenue McGill College)*, certainly the best designed building on Avenue McGill College, was built for the Banque Nationale de Paris in 1981, by the architectural firm Webb, Zerafa, Menkès, Housden Partnership (Tour Elf-Aquitaine, Paris; Royal Bank, Toronto). Its bluish glass walls set off a sculpture entitled *La Foule Illuminée* (The Illuminated Crowd), by the Franco-British artist Raymond Mason.

McGill University ★★ (28) *(805 Rue Sherbrooke Ouest, McGill Métro)* was founded in 1821, thanks to a donation by fur-trader James McGill. It is the oldest of Montréal's four universities. Throughout the 19th century, the institution was one of the finest jewels of the Golden Square Mile's Scottish bourgeoisie. The university's main campus lies nestled in greenery at the foot of Mont Royal. The entrance is located at the northernmost end of Avenue McGill College, at the Roddick Gates, which contain the university's clock and chimes. On the right are two Romanesque-Revival-style buildings, designed by Sir Andrew Taylor to house the physics (1893) and chemistry (1896) departments. The Faculty of Architecture now occupies the second building. A little farther along, visitors will see the Macdonald Engineering Building, a fine example of the English baroque-Revival style, with a broken pediment adorning its rusticated portal

(Percy Nobbs, 1908). At the end of the drive stands the oldest building on campus, the Arts Building (1839). For three decades, this austere neoclassical structure by architect John Ostell was McGill University's only building. It houses Moyse Hall, a lovely theatre dating back to 1926, with a design inspired by antiquity (Harold Lea Fetherstonaugh, architect).

The **Musée McCord d'Histoire Canadienne** ★★ **(29)** *($8, free on Sat 10am to noon; Jun to mid-Oct, every day 10am to 6pm; mid-Oct to May, Tue to Fri 10am to 6pm, Sat and Sun 10am to 5pm; 690 Rue Sherbrooke Ouest, McGill Métro, ☎398-7100)*, the McCord Museum of Canadian History, occupies a building formerly used by the McGill University Students' Association. Designed by architect Percy Nobbs (1906), this handsome building of English baroque inspiration was enlarged toward the back in 1991. Along Rue Victoria, visitors can see an interesting sculpture by Pierre Granche entitled *Totem Urbain/Histoire en Dentelle* (Urban totem/History in lace). For anyone interested in Amerindians and daily life in Canada in the 18th and 19th centuries, this is *the* museum to see in Montréal. It houses a large ethnographic collection, as well as collections of costumes, decorative arts, paintings, prints and photographs, including the famous Notman collection, composed of 700,000 glass plates and constituting a veritable portrait of Canada at the end of the 19th century.

Return to Rue Sainte-Catherine Ouest.

Rue Sainte-Catherine is Montréal's main commercial artery. It stretches 15 km, changing in appearance several times along the way. Around 1870, it was still lined with row houses; by 1920, however, it had already become an integral part of life in Montréal. Since the 1960s, a number of shopping centres linking the street to the adjacent Métro lines have sprouted up among the local businesses. The **Centre Eaton (30)** *(Rue Sainte-Catherine Ouest)* is the most recent of these. It is composed of a long, old-fashioned gallery lined with five levels of shops, restaurants and movie theatres, and is now linked to Place Ville-Marie by a pedestrian tunnel.

The **Eaton** department store ★★ **(31)** *(677 Rue Sainte-Catherine Ouest)* is one of the main "institutions" on Rue Sainte-Catherine. The Art Deco dining room on the 9th floor is well worth a visit. It is the work of Jacques Carlu, who designed the Palais de Chaillot in Paris, as well as the decor of a number of ocean liners. The restaurant, for that matter, is reminiscent of a first-class dining room on the French Line ships. Miraculously, the place has been kept fully intact since its opening in 1931, from the furniture, lights, utensils and wall lamps by Denis Gélin to the frescoes by Anne Carlu, entitled *Amazones* (Amazons) and *Dans un Parc* (In a Park).

The first Anglican cathedral in Montréal stood on Rue Notre-Dame, not far from Place d'Armes. After a fire in 1856, **Christ Church Cathedral** ★★ **(32)** *(at the corner of Rue University)* was relocated nearer the community it served, in the heart of the nascent Golden Square Mile. Using the cathedral of his hometown, Salisbury, as his model, architect Frank Wills designed a flamboyant structure, with a single steeple rising above the transepts. The soberness of the interior contrasts with the rich ornamentation of the Catholic churches included in this walking tour. A few beautiful stained-glass windows from the workshops of William Morris provide the only bit of colour.

The steeple's stone spire was destroyed in 1927 and replaced by an aluminum replica; otherwise, it would have eventually caused the building to sink. The problem, linked to the instability of the foundation, was not resolved, however, until a shopping centre, the **Promenades de la Cathédrale** ★★ **(33)**, was constructed under the building in 1987. Christ Church Anglican Cathedral thus rests on the roof of a shopping mall. On the same occasion, a postmodern glass skyscraper topped by a "crown of thorns" was erected behind the cathedral. There is a pleasant little garden at its base.

It was around **Square Phillips** ★ **(34)** *(at the corner of Rue Union, on either side of Rue Sainte-Catherine)* that the first stores appeared along Rue Sainte-Catherine, which was once strictly residential. Henry Morgan moved Morgan's Colonial House, now **La Baie** (The Bay) **(35)**, here after the floods of 1886 in the old city. Henry Birks, descendant of a long line of English jewellers, arrived soon after, establishing his famous shop in a handsome beige sandstone building on the west side of the square. In 1914, a monument to King Edward VII, sculpted by Philippe Hébert, was erected in the centre of Square Phillips. Downtown shoppers and employees alike enjoy relaxing here.

MONTRÉAL

A former Methodist church designed in the shape of an auditorium, **St. James United Church (36)** *(463 Rue Sainte-Catherine Ouest)* originally had a complete façade looking out onto a garden. In 1926, in an effort to counter the decrease in its revenue, the community built a group of stores and offices along the front of the building on Rue Sainte-Catherine, leaving only a narrow passageway into the church. Visitors can still see the two Gothic-Revival-style steeples set back from Rue Sainte-Catherine.

Turn right on Rue de Bleury.

After a 40-year absence, the Jesuits returned to Montréal in 1842 at Monseigneur Ignace Bourget's invitation. Six years later, they founded Collège Sainte-Marie, where several generations of boys would receive an outstanding education. **Église du Gesù ★★ (37)** *(1202 Rue de Bleury)* was originally designed as the college chapel. The grandiose project begun in 1864 according to plans drawn up by architect Patrick C. Keely of Brooklyn, New York was never completed, due to lack of funds. Consequently, the church's Renaissance-Revival-style towers remain unfinished. The *trompe-l'œil* decor inside was executed by artist Damien Müller. Of particular interest are the seven main altars and surrounding parquetry, all fine examples of cabinet work. The large paintings hanging from the walls were commissioned from the Gagliardi brothers of Rome. The Jesuit college, erected to the south of the church, was demolished in 1975, but the church was fortunately saved, and then restored in 1983.

Visitors can take a short side-trip to St. Patrick's Basilica. To do so, head south on Rue de Bleury. Turn right on Boulevard René-Lévesque, then left on little Rue Saint-Alexandre. Go into the church through one of the side entrances.

Fleeing misery and potato blight, a large number of Irish immigrants came to Montréal between 1820 and 1860, and helped construct the Lachine canal and the Victoria bridge. **St. Patrick's Basilica ★★ (38)** *(Rue Saint-Alexandre)*, was thus built to meet a pressing new demand for a church to serve the Irish Catholic community. When it was inaugurated in 1847, St. Patrick's dominated the city below. Today, it is well hidden by the skyscrapers of the business centre. Architect Pierre-Louis Morin and Père Félix Martin, the Jesuit superior, designed the plans for the

edifice, built in the Gothic Revival style favoured by the Sulpicians, who financed the project. One of the many paradoxes surrounding St. Patrick's is that it is more representative of French than Anglo-Saxon Gothic architecture. The high, dark interior encourages prayer. Each of the pine columns that divide the nave into three sections is a whole tree trunk, carved in one piece.

Head back to Rue Sainte-Catherine Ouest.

Formerly located at Cité du Havre, the **Musée d'Art Contemporain ★★ (39)** *($6; Tue to Sun 11am to 6pm, half-price on Wed 6pm to 9pm; 185 Rue Sainte-Catherine Ouest, at the corner of Rue Jeanne-Mance, ☎847-6212)*, Montréal's modern art museum, was moved to this site in 1992. The long, low building, erected on top of the Place des Arts parking lot, contains eight rooms, where post-1940 works of art from both Québec and abroad are exhibited. The interior, which has a decidedly better design than the exterior, is laid out around a circular hall. On the lower level, an amusing metal sculpture by Pierre Granche entitled *Comme si le temps... de la rue* (As if time... from the street), shows Montréal's network of streets crowded with helmeted birds, in a sort of semicircular theatre.

During the rush of the Quiet Revolution, the government of Québec, inspired by cultural complexes like New York's Lincoln Center, built **Place des Arts ★ (40)** *(260 Boulevard de Maisonneuve Ouest, through to Rue Sainte-Catherine Ouest, Métro Place-des-Arts)*, a collection of five halls for the performing arts. Salle Wilfrid Pelletier, in the centre, was inaugurated in 1963 (2,982 seats). It accommodates both the Montreal Symphony Orchestra and the Opéra de Montréal. The cube-shaped Théâtre Maisonneuve, on the right, contains three theatres, Théâtre Maisonneuve (1,460 seats), Théâtre Jean-Duceppe (755 seats) and the intimate little Café de la Place (138 seats). The Cinquième Salle (350 seats) was built in 1992 in the course of the construction of the Musée d'Art Contemporain. Place des Arts is linked to the governmental section of the underground city, which stretches from the Palais des Congrès convention centre to Avenue du Président-Kennedy. Developed by the various levels of government, this portion of the underground network distinguishes itself from the private section, centred around Place Ville-Marie, further west.

Since 1976, the head office of the Fédération des Caisses Populaires Desjardins, the credit union, has been located in the vast **Complexe Desjardins ★ (41)** *(Rue Sainte-Catherine Ouest)*, which houses a large number of government offices as well. The building's large atrium, surrounded by shops and movie theatres, is very popular during the winter months. A variety of shows are presented in this space, also used for recording television programmes.

The former Gaiety Theatre, in which the most famous North-American stripper of all time, Lili Saint-Cyr, would perform, was turned into the respectable **Théatre du Nouveau Monde (42)** *(84 rue Ste-Catherine Ouest, ☎866-8668)* in the beginning of the 1960s. The "TNM", which is located beside Complexe Desjardins, presents both French and Québecois classic plays. In 1996, the theatre was given a major facelift by architect Dan Hanganu; the foyer was completely reconstructed in an unbridled fashion, combining metal, glass and red brick.

The tour now leaves the former Golden Square Mile and enters the area around **Boulevard Saint-Laurent**. At the end of the 18th century, the Faubourg Saint-Laurent grew up along the street of the same name, which led inland from the river. In 1792, the city was officially divided into east and west sections, with this artery marking the boundary. Then, in the early 20th century, the addresses of east-west streets were re-assigned so that they all began at Boulevard Saint-Laurent. Meanwhile, around 1880, French-Canadian high society came up with the idea of turning the boulevard into the "Champs-Élysées" of Montréal. The west side was destroyed in order to make the street wider and to reconstruct new buildings in Richardson's Romanesque Revival style, which was in fashion at the end of the 19th century. Populated by the successive waves of immigrants, who arrived at the port, Boulevard Saint-Laurent never attained the heights of glory anticipated by its developers. The section between Boulevard René-Lévesque and Boulevard de Maisonneuve did, however, become the hub of Montréal nightlife in the early 20th century. The city's big theatres, like the Français, where Sarah Bernhardt performed, were located around here. During the Prohibition era (1919-1930), the area became run-down. Every week, thousands of Americans came here to frequent the cabarets and brothels, which abounded in this neighbourhood up until the end of the 1950s.

Turn right on Boulevard Saint-Laurent.

Set up inside the former buildings of the Ekers brewery, the **Nouveau Musée Juste Pour Rire ★★ (43)** *(opens in Jun, call for schedule and exhibition information; 2111 Boulevard Saint-Laurent, Saint-Laurent Métro, ☎845-4000)*, or Just for Laughs Museum, opened in 1993. This museum, the only one of its kind in the world, explores the different facets of humour, using a variety of film clips and sets. Visitors are equipped with infrared headphones, which enable them to follow the presentation. The building itself was renovated and redesigned by architect Luc Laporte, and has some 3,000 square meters of exhibition space.

Erected in 1893 for the Société Saint-Jean-Baptiste, which is devoted to protecting the rights of French-speakers, the **Monument National ★ (44)** *(1182 Boulevard Saint-Laurent)* was intended to be a cultural centre dedicated to the French-Canadian cause. It offered business courses, became the favourite platform of political orators and presented shows of a religious nature. However, during the 1940s, it also hosted cabaret shows and plays, launching the careers of a number of Québec performers, including Olivier Guimond Senior and Junior. The building was sold to the National Theatre School of Canada in 1971. As Canada's oldest theatre, it was artfully restored on its 100th anniversary.

Cross Boulevard René-Lévesque, then turn right on Rue de la Gauchetière.

Montréal's **Chinatown ★ (45)** may be rather small, but it is nonetheless a pleasant place to walk around. A large number of the Chinese who came to Canada to help build the transcontinental railroad, completed in 1886, settled here at the end of the 19th century. Though they no longer live in the neighbourhood, they still come here on weekends to stroll about and stock up on traditional products. Rue de la Gauchetière has been converted into a pedestrian street lined with restaurants and framed by lovely Chinese-style gates.

To the west of Rue Saint-Urbain lies Montreal's convention centre, the **Palais des Congrès (46)** *(201 Rue Viger Ouest, ☎871-3170, Métro Place-d'Armes)*, a forbidding mass of concrete erected over the Autoroute Ville-Marie highway, which contributes to the isolation of the old city from downtown. A small entrance on Rue de La Gauchetière leads into the long, windowed main hall in the centre. The conference rooms (16,700 square metres) can hold up to 5000 convention-goers at a time. Relocation and enlargement projects are being studied.

To return to the starting point of the tour, walk back up Boulevard Saint-Laurent to the Place-des-Arts Métro station (at the corner of Boulevard de Maisonneuve). Take the subway west to the Guy-Concordia station.

Tour C: Village Shaughnessy ★★
(one day)

When the Sulpicians took possession of the island of Montréal in 1663, they kept a portion of the best land for themselves, then set up a farm and a native village there in 1676. Following a fire, the Amerindian village was relocated several times before being permanently established in Oka. A part of the farm, corresponding to the area now known as Westmount, was then granted to French settlers. The Sulpicians planted an orchard and a vineyard on the remaining portion. Starting around 1870, the land was separated into lots. Part of it was used for the construction of mansions, while large plots were awarded to Catholic communities allied with the Sulpicians. It was at this time that Shaughnessy House was built — hence the name of the neighbourhood. During the 1970s, the number of local inhabitants increased considerably, making Shaughnessy Village the most densely populated area in Québec.

From Rue Guy (Guy-Concordia Métro) turn left on Rue Sherbrooke.

The numbers following names of attractions refer to the map of Shaughnessy Village.

Masonic lodges, which had already existed in New France, increased in scale with British immigration. These associations of free-thinkers were not favoured by the Canadian clergy, who denounced their liberal views. Ironically, the **Masonic Temple ★ (1)** *(1850 Rue Sherbrooke Ouest)* of the Scottish lodges of Montréal stands opposite the Grand Séminaire, where Catholic priests are trained. The edifice, built in 1928, enhances the secret, mystical character of Freemasonry with its impenetrable, windowless façade, equipped with antique vessels and double-headed lamps.

The Sulpicians' farmhouse was surrounded by a wall linked to four stone corner towers, earning it the name Fort des Messieurs. The house was destroyed when the **Grand Séminaire ★★ (2)** (1854-1860) *(2065 Rue Sherbrooke Ouest)* was built, but two towers, erected in the 17th century according to plans by François Vachon de Belmont, superior of the Montréal Sulpicians, can still be found in the institution's shady gardens. It was in one of these that Saint Marguerite Bourgeoys taught young native girls. Around 1880, the long neoclassical buildings of the Grand Séminaire, designed by architect John Ostell, were topped by a mansard roof by Henri-Maurice Perrault. Information panels, set up on Rue Sherbrooke, directly in line with Rue du Fort, provide precise details about the farm buildings.

It is well worth entering the Seminary to see the lovely Romanesque-Revival-style chapel, designed by Jean Omer Marchand in 1905. The ceiling beams are made of cedar from British Columbia, while the walls are covered with stones from Caen. The nave, which stretches 80 metres, is lined with 300 hand-carved oak pews. Sulpicians who have died in Montréal since the 18th century are interred beneath it. The Sulpician order was founded in Paris by Jean-Jacques Olier in 1641, and its main church is Saint-Sulpice in Paris, which stands on the square of the same name.

The Congrégation de Notre-Dame, founded by Saint Marguerite Bourgeoys in 1671, owned a convent and a school in Old Montréal. Reconstructed in the 18th century, these buildings were expropriated by the city at the beginning of the 20th century as part of a plan to extend Boulevard Saint-Laurent all the way to the port. The nuns had to resign themselves to leaving the premises and settling into a new convent. The congregation thus arranged for a convent to be built on Rue Sherbrooke, according to a design by Jean Omer Marchand (1873-1936), the first French-Canadian architect to graduate from the École des Beaux-Arts in Paris. The immense complex now bears witness to the vitality of religious communities in Québec before the Quiet Revolution of 1960.

The decline of religious practices and lack of new vocations forced the community to move into more modest buildings. **Collège Dawson ★ (3)** *(3040 Rue Sherbrooke Ouest)*, an English-language CÉGEP (*collège d'enseignement général et professionnel, a post-secondary college*), has been located in the

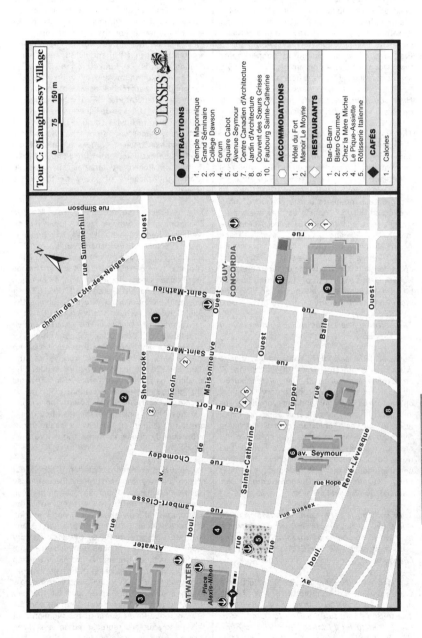

Tour C: Shaughnessy Village

0   75   150 m

© ULYSSES

ATTRACTIONS

1. Temple Maçonnique
2. Grand Séminaire
3. Collège Dawson
4. Forum
5. Square Cabot
6. Avenue Seymour
7. Centre Canadien d'Architecture
8. Jardin d'Architecture
9. Couvent des Soeurs Grises
10. Faubourg Sainte-Catherine

ACCOMMODATIONS

1. Hôtel du Fort
2. Manoir Le Moyne

RESTAURANTS

1. Bar-B-Barn
2. Bistro Gourmet
3. Chez la Mère Michel
4. Le Pique-Assiette
5. Rôtisserie Italienne

CAFÉS

1. Calories

MONTRÉAL

original convent since 1987. The yellow-brick building, set on luxuriant grounds, is probably the most beautiful CÉGEP in Québec. It is now directly linked to the subway and underground city. The Romanesque-Revival-style chapel in the centre has an elongated copper dome reminiscent of Byzantine architecture. It now serves as a library and has been barely altered.

Head south on Avenue Atwater, then turn left on Rue Sainte-Catherine Ouest.

The **Forum (4)** *(2313 Rue Sainte-Catherine Ouest, Métro Atwater)*, a large building with something of a heavily-modified airplane hangar look about it, was home to the Montréal Canadiens hockey team from 1924 until its closure in March 1996 (see p 105). Some of the greatest moments in the history of both hockey and of the "Habs", as they are known by their fans, occurred in this arena. Across the street, on Avenue Atwater, stands **Place Alexis-Nihon**, a multi-purpose complex containing a shopping mall, offices and apartments. It is linked to the underground city. **Square Cabot (5)**, south of the Forum, used to be the terminal for all buses serving the western part of the city.

Turn right on Rue Lambert-Closse, then left on Rue Tupper.

Between 1965 and 1975, Shaughnessy Village witnessed a massive wave of demolition. A great many Victorian row houses were replaced by high-rises, whose rudimentary designs, characterized by an endless repetition of identical glass or concrete balconies, are often referred to as "chicken coops". **Avenue Seymour ★ (6)** is one of the only streets in the area to have escaped this wave, which has now been curbed. Here, visitors will find charming houses made of brick and grey stone, with Queen-Anne, Second-Empire or Romanesque-Revival details.

Turn right on Rue Fort and then left on small Rue Baile (be careful of the fast-moving traffic heading to the highway on-ramp). Follow the path east alongside the CCA to reach René-Lévesque.

Founded in 1979 by Phyllis Lambert, the **Centre Canadien d'Architecture ★★★ (7)** *($5, students $3, free Thu 6pm to 8pm; Jun to Sep, Tue to Sun 11am to 6pm, Thu to 9pm; Oct to May, Wed to Fri 11am to 6pm, Thu to 8pm; Sat and Sun 11am to 5pm; address, ☎939-7026)*, or Canadian Centre for Architecture, is both a museum and a centre for the study of world architecture. Its collections of plans, drawings, models, books and photographs are the most important of their kind in the entire world. The Centre, erected between 1985 and 1989, has six exhibition rooms, a bookstore, a library, a 217-seat auditorium and a wing specially designed for researchers, as well as vaults and restoration laboratories. The main building, shaped like a "U," was designed by Peter Rose, with the help of Phyllis Lambert. It is covered with grey limestone from the Saint-Marc quarries near Québec City. This material, which used to be extracted from the Plateau Mont-Royal and Rosemont quarries in Montréal, adorns the façades of many of the city's houses.

The centre surrounds the **Maison Shaughnessy ★**, whose façade looks out on Boulevard René-Lévesque Ouest. This house is in fact a pair of residences, built in 1874 according to a design by architect William Tutin Thomas. It is representative of the mansions that once lined Boulevard René-Lévesque (formerly Boulevard Dorchester). In 1974, it was at the centre of an effort to salvage the neighbourhood, which had been torn down in a number of places. The house, itself threatened with demolition, was purchased at the last moment by Phyllis Lambert. She set up the offices and reception rooms of the Canadian Centre for Architecture inside. The building was named after Sir Thomas Shaughnessy, a former president of Canadian Pacific, who lived in the house for several decades. The inhabitants of the neighbourhood, grouped together in an association, subsequently chose to name the entire area after him.

The amusing **architecture garden (8)**, by artist Melvin Charney, lies across from Shaughnessy House, between two highway on-ramps. It illustrates the different stages of the neighbourhood's development, using a portion of the Sulpicians' orchard on the left, stone lines to indicate borders of 19th-century properties and rose bushes reminiscent of the gardens of those houses. A promenade along the cliff that once separated the wealthy neighbourhood from the working-class sector below offers a view of the lower part of the city (Little Burgundy, Saint-Henri, Verdun) and the St. Lawrence River. Some of the highlights of this panorama are represented in a stylized manner, atop concrete posts.

Walk along Boulevard René-Lévesque and turn left on Rue Saint-Mathieu.

Like the Congrégation de Notre-Dame, the Sœurs Grises had to relocate their convent and hospital, which used to be situated on Rue Saint-Pierre in Old Montréal (see p 95). They obtained part the Sulpicians' farm, where a vast convent, designed by Victor Bourgeau, was erected between 1869 and 1874. The **Couvent des Sœurs Grises ★★ (9)** *(1185 Rue Saint-Mathieu)* is the product of an architectural tradition developed over the centuries in Québec. The chapel alone reveals a foreign influence, namely the Romanesque Revival style favoured by the Sulpicians, as opposed to the Renaissance and baroque Revival styles preferred by the church.

In the northwest wing, visitors will find the **Musée Marguerite-d'Youville** *(free admission; Wed to Sun 1:30 to 4:30; ☎937-9501)*, named after the founder of the community, which displays objects relating to the daily life of the nuns, as well as paintings, furniture, Indian, Inuit and missionary art, and some beautiful liturgical clothing. Upon request, it is possible to enter the Chapelle de l'Invention-de-la--Sainte-Croix, in the centre of the convent. Its stained-glass windows come from the Maison Champigneule in Bar-le-Duc, France. In 1974, the convent was supposed to be demolished and replaced by high-rises. Fortunately, Montrealers protested, and the buildings were saved. Today, the convent is listed as a historical monument.

Turn right on Rue Sainte-Catherine Ouest.

At the **Faubourg Sainte-Catherine ★ (10)** *(1616 Rue Sainte-Catherine Ouest)*, a converted, glass-roofed garage, visitors will find movie theatres, a market made up of small specialty shops selling local and foreign products, and a fast-food area.

To return to the Guy-Concordia Métro station, head north on Rue Guy.

Tour D: Mont Royal and Westmount ★★ (one day)

Montréal's central neighbourhoods are distributed around Mont Royal, an important landmark in the cityscape. Known simply as "the mountain" by Montrealers, this squat mass, measuring 234 metres at its highest point, is composed of intrusive rock. It is in fact one of the seven hills studding the St. Lawrence plain in the Montérégie region. A "green lung" rising up at the far end of downtown streets, it exerts a positive influence on Montrealers, who, as a result, never lose touch with nature. The mountain actually has three summits; the first is occupied by Parc du Mont-Royal, the second by the Université de Montréal, and the third by Westmount, an independent city with lovely English-style homes. In addition to these areas, there are the Catholic, Protestant and Jewish cemeteries, which, considered as a whole, form the largest necropolis in North America.

To reach the starting point of the tour, take bus #11 from the Mont-Royal Métro station, located on the Plateau Mont-Royal, and get off at the Belvédère Camilien-Houde.

The numbers following attractions refer to the map of Mont Royal and Westmount.

From the **Belvédère Camilien-Houde ★★ (1)** *(Voie Camilien-Houde)*, a lovely scenic viewpoint, visitors can look out over the entire eastern portion of Montréal. The Plateau Mont--Royal lies in the foreground, a uniform mass of duplexes and triplexes, pierced in a few places by the oxidized copper bell towers of parish churches, while the Rosemont and Maisonneuve quarters lie in the background, with the Olympic Stadium towering over them. In clear weather, the oil refineries in the east end can be seen in the distance. The St. Lawrence River, visible on the right, is actually 1.5 km wide at its narrowest point. The Belvédère Camilien-Houde is Montréal's version of Inspiration Point and a favourite gathering place of sweethearts with cars.

Climb the staircase at the south end of the parking lot, and follow Chemin Olmsted on the left, which leads to the chalet and main lookout. You will pass the mountain's cross on the way.

Pressured by the residents of the Golden Square Mile (see tour p 100), who saw their favourite playground being deforested by various firewood companies, the City of Montréal created **Parc du Mont-Royal ★★★** in 1870. Frederick Law Olmsted (1822-1903), the celebrated designer of New York's Central Park, was commissioned to design the park. He decided to preserve the site's natural character, limiting himself to a few lookout points linked by winding paths. Inaugurated in 1876, the park, which covers 101 ha on the southern

MONTRÉAL

part of the mountain, is cherished by Montrealers as a place to enjoy the fresh air (see also p 134).

The **Chalet du Mont Royal** ★★★ (2) *(Mon to Fri 9:30am to 8pm; Parc du Mont-Royal, ☎844-4928)*, located in the centre of the park, was designed by Aristide Beaugrand-Champagne in 1932, as a replacement for the original structure, which was threatening to collapse. During the 1930s and 1940s, big bands gave moonlit concerts on the steps of the building. The interior is decorated with remounted paintings depicting scenes from Canadian history. These were commissioned from some of Québec's great painters, such as Marc-Aurèle Fortin and Paul-Émile Borduas. Nevertheless, people go to the chalet mainly to stroll along the lookout and take in the exceptional view of downtown, best in the late afternoon and in the evening, when the skyscrapers light up the darkening sky.

Take the gravel road leading to the parking lot of the chalet and Voie Camilien-Houde. One of the entrances to the Mount Royal Cemetery lies on the right.

The **Mount Royal Cemetery** ★★ (3) *(Voie Camilien Houde)*, is a Protestant cemetery that ranks among the most beautiful parks in the city. Designed as an Eden for the living visiting the deceased, it is laid out like a landscape garden in an isolated valley, giving visitors the impression that they are a thousand miles from the city, though they are in fact right in the centre of it. The wide variety of hardwood and fruit trees attract species of birds found nowhere else in Québec. Founded by the Anglican, Presbyterian, Unitarian and Baptist churches, the cemetery opened in 1852. Some of its monuments are true works of art, executed by celebrated artists.

The families and eminent personalities buried here include the Molson brewers, who have the most impressive and imposing mausoleum, shipowner Sir Hugh Allan, and numerous other figures from the footnotes and headlines of history, such as Anna Leonowens, governess of the King of Siam in the 19th century and inspiration for the play *The King and I*. On the left, on the way to Lac aux Castors, visitors will see the last of the mountain's former farmhouses.

Continue along Voie Camilien Houde, then head west on Chemin Remembrance. Take the road leading to Lac aux Castors (see map).

Small **Lac aux Castors (4)** *(alongside Chemin Remembrance)*, also known as Beaver Lake, was created in 1958 in what used to be a swamp. In winter, it becomes a pleasant skating rink. This part of the park also has grassy areas and a sculpture garden. It is laid out in a more conventional manner than the rest, violating Olmsted's purist directives.

The **Cimetière Notre-Dame-des-Neiges** ★★ (5), Montréal's largest cemetery, is a veritable city of the dead, as more than a million people have been buried here since its inauguration in 1854. It replaced the cemetery in Square Dominion, which was deemed too close to the neighbouring houses. Unlike the Protestant cemetery, it has a conspicuously religious character, clearly identifying it with the Catholic faith. Accordingly, two heavenly angels flanking a crucifix greet visitors at the main entrance on Chemin de la Côte-des-Neiges. The "two solitudes" (Canadians of French Catholic and Anglo-Saxon Protestant extraction) thus remain separated even in death. The tombstones read like a Who's Who in the fields of business, arts, politics and science in Québec. An obelisk dedicated to the Patriotes of the rebellion of 1837-38 and numerous monuments executed by renowned sculptors lie scattered alongside the 55 kilometres of roads and paths that crisscross the cemetery.

Both the cemetery and the roads leading to it offer a number of views of the **Oratoire Saint-Joseph** ★★ (6) *(free admission; every day 9am to 5pm, mass between 6:30 am and 9:30pm, nativity scene Nov 15 to Dec 15; 3800 Chemin Queen Mary, ☎733-8211 for information)*. The enormous building topped by a copper dome, the second largest dome in the world after that of St. Peter's in Rome, stands on a hillside, accentuating its mystical aura. From the gate at the entrance, there are over 300 steps to climb to reach the oratory. Small buses are also available for worshippers who do not want to climb the steps. It was built between 1924 and 1956, thanks to the efforts of the blessed Frère André, porter of Collège Notre-Dame (across the street), to whom many miracles are attributed. A veritable religious complex, the oratory is dedicated to both Saint Joseph and its humble creator. It includes the lower and upper basilicas, the crypt of Frère André and two museums, one dedicated to Frère André's life, the other to sacred art. Visitors will also find the porter's first chapel, built in 1910, a cafeteria, a hostelry and a store selling devotional articles.

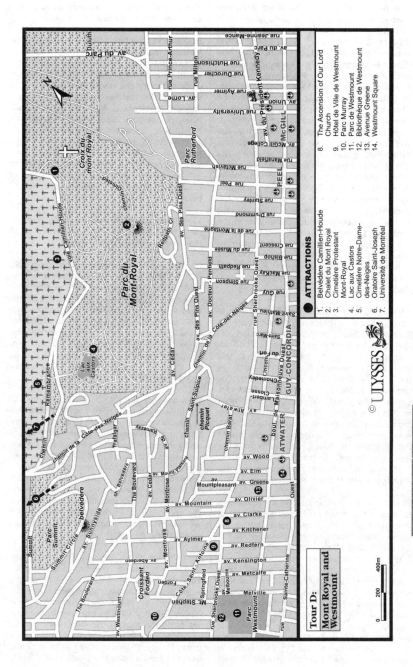

ATTRACTIONS

1. Belvédère Camillien-Houde
2. Chalet du Mont Royal
3. Cimetière Protestant Mont-Royal
4. Lac aux Castors
5. Cimetière Notre-Dame-des-Neiges
6. Oratoire Saint-Joseph
7. Université de Montréal

8. The Ascension of Our Lord Church
9. Hôtel de Ville de Westmount
10. Parc Murray
11. Parc de Westmount
12. Bibliothèque de Westmount
13. Avenue Greene
14. Westmount Square

© ULYSSES

Tour D:
Mont Royal and Westmount

0 200 400m

The oratory is one of the most important centres of worship and pilgrimage in North America. Every year, it attracts some 2,000,000 visitors. The building's neoclassical exterior was designed by Dalbé Viau and Alphonse Venne, while the essentially modern interior is the work of Lucien Parent and French Benedictine monk Dom Paul Bellot, the author from Saint-Benoît-du-Lac in the Cantons de l'Est, or Eastern Townships. It is well worth visiting the upper basilica to see the stained-glass windows by Marius Plamondon, the altar and crucifix by Henri Charlier, and the astonishing gilded chapel at the back. The oratory has an imposing Beckerath style organ, which can be heard on Wednesday evenings during the summer. Outside, visitors can also see the chimes, made by Paccard et Frères and originally intended for the Eiffel Tower, as well as the beautiful Chemin de Croix (Way of the Cross) by Louis Parent and Ercolo Barbieri, in the gardens on the side of the mountain. Measuring 263 metres, the Oratory's observatory, which commands a sweeping view of the entire city, is the highest point on the island.

After many attempts, Québec City's Université Laval, aiming to preserve its monopoly on French-language university education in Québec, finally opened a branch of its institution in the Château Ramezay. A few years later, it moved to Rue Saint-Denis, giving birth to the Quartier Latin (see p 127). The **Université de Montréal ★ (7)** *(2900 Boulevard Édouard-Montpetit)* finally became autonomous in 1920, enabling its directors to develop grandiose plans. Ernest Cormier (1885-1980) was approached about designing a campus on the north side of Mont Royal. The architect, a graduate of the École des Beaux-Arts in Paris, was one of the first to acquaint North Americans with the Art Deco style.

The plans for the main building evolved into a refined, symmetrical Art Deco structure faced with pale yellow bricks and topped by a central tower, visible from Chemin Remembrance and Cimetière Notre-Dame-des-Neiges. Begun in 1929, construction on the building was interrupted by the stock market crash, and it wasn't until 1943 that the first students entered the main building on the mountain. Since then, a whole host of pavilions has been added, making the Université de Montréal the second largest French-language university in the world, with a student body of over 58,000. Since the entrance to the university is somewhat removed from the present route, a visit to the campus constitutes an additional excursion, and takes about an hour.

Back on the mountain, follow the trails through Parc du Mont-Royal to the exit leading to Westmount (see map of this tour). This wealthy residential city of 20,239 inhabitants, enclosed within the city of Montréal, has long been regarded as the bastion of the Anglo-Saxon elite in Québec. After the Golden Square Mile was invaded by the business centre, Westmount assumed its role. Its shady, winding roads, on the southwest side of the mountain, are lined with Neo-Tudor and Neo-Georgian residences, most of which were built between 1910 and 1930. The heights of Westmount offer some lovely views of the city below.

Take The Boulevard to Avenue Clarke (near the small triangular park), then turn left to reach Rue Sherbrooke Ouest.

Erected in 1928, Westmount's English Catholic church, **The Church of the Ascension of Our Lord ★ (8)** *(at the corner of Avenue Kitchener)* is evidence of the staying power of the Gothic Revival style in North American architecture and the historical accuracy, ever more apparent in the 20th century, of buildings patterned after ancient models. With its rough stone facing, elongated lines and delicate sculptures, it looks like an authentic church from a 14th-century English village.

Westmount is like a piece of Great Britain in North America. Its **City Hall ★ (9)** *(4333 Rue Sherbrooke Ouest)* was built in the Neo-Tudor style, inspired by the architecture of the age of Henry VIII and Elizabeth I, which was regarded during the 1920s as the national style of England, because it issued exclusively from the British Isles. The style is characterized, in part, by horizontal openings with multiple stone transoms, bay windows and flattened arches. The impeccable green of a lawn-bowling club lies at the back, frequented by members wearing their regulation whites.

Take Chemin de la Côte-Saint-Antoine to Parc Murray. In Québec, the term *côte*, which translates literally as "hill," usually has nothing to do with the slope of the land, but is a leftover of the seigneurial system of New France. The roads linking one farm to the next ran along the tops of the long rectangles of land distributed to colonists. As a result, these plots of land gradually became known as *côtes*, from the French word for "side," *côté*. Côte

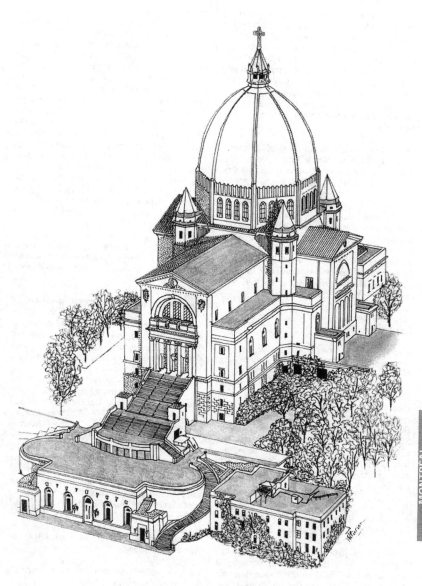

Oratoire Saint-Joseph

Saint-Antoine is one of the oldest roads on the island of Montréal. Laid out in 1684 by the Sulpicians on a former native trail, it is lined with some of Westmount's oldest houses. At the corner of Avenue Forden is a **milestone** dating back to the 17th century, discreetly identified by the pattern of the sidewalk, which radiates out from it. This is all that remains of the system of road signs developed by the Sulpicians for their seigneury on the island of Montréal.

For those who would like to immerse themselves in a Mid-Atlantic atmosphere, composed of a blend of England and America, **Parc Murray (10)** *(north of Avenue Mount Stephen)* offers the perfect combination — a football field and tennis courts in a country setting. Here, visitors will find the remains of a natural grouping of acacias, an extremely rare species at this latitude, due to the harsh climate. The tree's presence is an indication that this area has the mildest climate in Québec. This mildness is a result of both the southwest slant of the land and the beneficial influence of the nearby Lachine rapids.

Go down Avenue Mount Stephen to return to Rue Sherbrooke Ouest.

Parc Westmount ★ (11) and the **Westmount Library ★ (12)** *(4575 Rue Sherbrooke Ouest)*. The park was laid out on swampy land in 1895. Four years later, Québec's first public library was erected on the same site. Up until then, religious communities had been the only ones to develop this type of cultural facility, and the province was therefore somewhat behind in this area. The red-brick building is the product of the trends toward eclecticism, picturesqueness and polychromy that characterized the last two decades of the 19th century.

From the park, head east on Avenue Melbourne, where there are some fine examples of Queen-Anne-style houses. Turn right on Avenue Metcalfe, then left on Boulevard de Maisonneuve Ouest. At the corner of Avenue Clarke stands **Église Saint-Léon ★**, the only French-language Catholic parish in Westmount. The sober, elegant Romanesque Revival façade conceals an exceptionally rich interior decor begun in 1928 by artist Guido Nincheri, who also painted the frescoes in Château Dufresne (see Maisonneuve tour, p 120). Nincheri was provided with a large sum of money to decorate the church using no substitutes and

no tricks. Accordingly, the floor and the base of the walls are covered with the most beautiful Italian and French marble available, while the upper portion of the nave is made of Savonnières stone and the chancel, of the most precious Honduran walnut, hand-carved by Alviero Marchi. The complex stained-glass windows depict various scenes from the life of Jesus Christ, including a few personages from the time of the church's construction, whom visitors will be amused to discover among the Biblical figures. Finally, the entire Christian pantheon is represented in the chancel and on the vault, in vibrantly coloured frescoes, executed in the traditional manner, using an egg-wash. This technique (used, notably, by Michelangelo) consists in making pigment stick to a wet surface with a coating made of egg, which becomes very hard and resistant when dry.

Continue along Boulevard de Maisonneuve, which leads through the former French section of Westmount before intersecting with Avenue Greene.

On **Avenue Greene (13)**, a small street with a typically English-Canadian character, visitors will find several of Westmount's fashionable shops. In addition to service-oriented businesses, there are art galleries, antique shops and bookstores filled with lovely things.

Architect Ludwig Mies van der Rohe (1886-1969), one of the leading masters of the modernist movement and the head of Bauhaus in Germany, designed **Westmount Square ★★ (14)** *(at the corner of Avenue Wood and Boulevard de Maisonneuve Ouest)* in 1964. The complex is typical of the architect's North American work, characterized by the use of black metal and tinted glass. It includes an underground shopping centre, topped by three towers containing offices and apartments. The public areas were originally covered with veined white travertine, one of Mies's favourite materials, which was replaced by a layer of granite, more resistant to the harsh effects of freezing and thawing.

An underground corridor leads from Westmount Square to the Atwater Métro station.

Tour E: Maisonneuve ★★
(one day)

In 1883, the city of Maisonneuve was founded in the east part of Montréal thanks to the

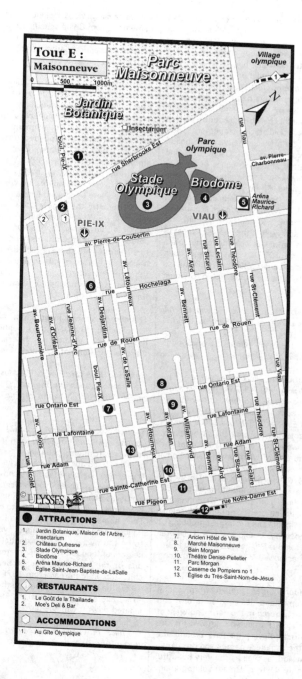

Tour E :
Maisonneuve

0   500   1000m

Parc Maisonneuve

Jardin Botanique

Insectarium

Village olympique

Parc olympique

Stade Olympique

Biodôme

Aréna Maurice-Richard

PIE-IX

VIAU

boul. Pie-IX

rue Sherbrooke Est

rue Viau

av. Pierre-Charbonneau

av. Pierre-de-Coubertin

av. Létourneux

rue Hochelaga

av. Aird

rue Sicard

rue Leclaire

rue Théodore

av. Bennett

rue de Rouen

rue St-Clément

av. Bourbonnière

av. d'Orléans

rue Jeanne-d'Arc

av. Desjardins

boul. Pie-IX

av. de LaSalle

rue de Rouen

rue Ontario Est

rue Viau

rue Ontario Est

rue Lafontaine

av. Valois

rue Lafontaine

av. Létourneux

av. Morgan

av. William-David

av. Bennett

rue Théodore

rue Adam

rue Sicard

rue Leclaire

rue St-Clément

rue Nicolet

rue Adam

rue Sainte-Catherine Est

rue Pigeon

rue Notre-Dame Est

rue Aird

© ULYSSES

MONTRÉAL

● ATTRACTIONS

1. Jardin Botanique, Maison de l'Arbre, Insectarium
2. Château Dufresne
3. Stade Olympique
4. Biodôme
5. Aréna Maurice-Richard
6. Église Saint-Jean-Baptiste-de-LaSalle

7. Ancien Hôtel de Ville
8. Marché Maisonneuve
9. Bain Morgan
10. Théâtre Denise-Pelletier
11. Parc Morgan
12. Caserne de Pompiers no 1
13. Église du Très-Saint-Nom-de-Jésus

◇ RESTAURANTS

1. Le Goût de la Thaïlande
2. Moe's Deli & Bar

○ ACCOMMODATIONS

1. Au Gîte Olympique

initiative of farmers and French-Canadian merchants; port facilities expanded into the area and the city's development picked up. Then, in 1918, the formerly autonomous city was annexed to Montréal, becoming one of its major working-class neighbourhoods, with a 90% francophone population. In the course of its history, Maisonneuve has been profoundly influenced by men with grand ideas, who wanted to make this part of the country a place where people could thrive together. Upon taking office at the Maisonneuve town hall in 1910, brothers Marius and Oscar Dufresne instituted a rather ambitious policy of building prestigious Beaux-Arts-style public buildings intended to make "their" city a model of development for French Québec. Then, in 1931, Frère Marie-Victorin founded Montréal's Jardin Botanique (botanical garden) in Maisonneuve; today, it is the second largest in the world. The last major episode in the area's history was in 1971, when Mayor Jean Drapeau initiated construction on the immense sports complex used for the 1976 Olympic Games.

From the Pie-IX Métro station, climb the hill leading to the corner of Rue Sherbrooke Est.

The numbers following names of attractions refer to the map of Maisonneuve.

The **Jardin Botanique, Maison de l'Arbre** and **Insectarium** ★★★ (1) *(8.75$ high season, 6.50$ low season; Sep to late Jun, every day 9am to 5pm, summer 9am to 7pm; 4101 Rue Sherbrooke Est, ☎872-1400).* The Jardin Botanique, covering an area of 73 hectares, was begun during the economic crisis of the 1930s on the site of Mont-de-La-Salle, home base of the brothers of the Écoles Chrétiennes. Behind the Art Deco building occupied by the Université de Montréal's institute of biology, visitors will find a stretch of 10 connected greenhouses, which shelter, notably, a precious collection of orchids and the largest grouping of bonsais and *penjings* outside of Asia. The latter includes the famous Wu collection, given to the garden by master Wu Yee-Sun of Hong Kong in 1984.

Thirty outdoor gardens, open from spring through autumn, and designed to inform and amaze visitors, stretch to the north and west of the greenhouses. Particularly noteworthy are the symmetrical display gardens around the restaurant, the Japanese garden and its *sukiya*-style tea pavilion, as well as the very beautiful Chinese Lac de Rêve, or Dream Lake, garden, whose pavilions were designed by artisans who came here from China specifically for the task. Since Montréal is twinned with Shanghai, it was deemed appropriate that it should have the largest such garden outside of Asia.

The northern part of the botanical garden is occupied by an arboretum. The **Maison de l'Arbre**, literally the tree house, was established in this area to familiarize people with the life of a tree. The interactive, permanent exhibit is actually set up in an old tree trunk. There are displays on the yellow birch, Québec's emblematic tree since 1993. The building's structure, consisting of beams of different types of wood, reminds us how leafy forests really are. Note the play of light and shade from the frame onto the large white wall, meant to resemble trunks and branches. A terrace in the back is an ideal spot from which to contemplate the arboretum's pond; it also leads to a charming little bonsai garden. To reach the Maison de l'Arbre, climb on board the Balade, the shuttle which regularly tours the garden, or use the garden's northern entrance located on Boulevard Rosemont.

The complementary **Insectarium** *(☎872-8753)* is located to the east of the greenhouses. This innovative, living museum invites visitors to discover the fascinating world of insects.

Return to Boulevard Pie-IX. The Musée des Arts Décoratifs stands on the west side of the street, immediately south of Rue Sherbrooke Est.

The **Château Dufresne** ★★ (2) *(2929 Rue Jeanne-d'Arc, métro Pie-IX)* is, in fact, two 22-room private mansions behind the same façade, built in 1916 for brothers Marius and Oscar Dufresne, shoe-manufacturers and authors of a grandiose plan to develop Maisonneuve. The plan was abandoned after the onset of World War I, causing the municipality to go bankrupt. Their home, designed by Marius Dufresne and Parisian architect Jules Renard, was supposed to be the nucleus of a residential upper-class neighbourhood, which never materialized. It is one of the best examples of Beaux-Arts architecture in Montréal. From 1979 to March of 1997, the château was home to the Musée des Arts Décoratifs de Montréal *(☎259-2575)* now located downtown (see p 101).

Go back downhill on Boulevard Pie-IX, then turn left on Avenue Pierre-de-Coubertin.

Stade Olympique

The **Stade Olympique** ★★★ (3) *(guided tour $5.25, package with tour and funicular $10.25; guided tours in French at 11am and 2pm, and in English at 12:40pm and 3:40pm; closed mid-Jan to mid-Feb; 4141 Avenue Pierre-de-Coubertin, ☎252-8687)* is also known as the Olympic Stadium and the "Big O". Jean Drapeau was mayor of Montréal from 1954 to 1957, and from 1960 to 1986. He dreamed of great things for "his" city. Endowed with exceptional powers of persuasion and unfailing determination, he saw a number of important projects through to a successful conclusion, including the construction of Place des Arts and the Métro, Montréal's hosting of the World's Fair in 1967 and, of course, the 1976 Summer Olympics. For this last international event, however, it was necessary to equip the city with the appropriate facilities. In spite of the controversy this caused, the city sought out a Parisian visionary to design something completely original. A billion dollars later, the major work of architect Roger Taillibert, who also designed the stadium of the Parc des Princes in Paris, stunned everyone with his curving, organic concrete shapes. The 56,000-seat oval stadium is covered with a kevlar roof supported by cables stretching from the 190-metre leaning tower. In the distance, visitors will see the two pyramid shaped towers of the **Olympic Village**, where the athletes were housed in 1976. Every year, the stadium hosts different events, such as the Salon de l'Auto (Car Show) and the Salon National de l'Habitation (National Home Show). From April to September, Montréal's National League baseball team, the Expos, plays its home games here.

The stadium's tower, which is the tallest leaning tower in the world, was rebaptised the **Tour de Montréal**. A funicular *($7.25; schedule changes frequently, please call for information ☎252-8687)* climbs the structure to an interior observation deck which commands a view of the eastern part of Montreal. Exhibits on the Olympics are presented on the upper levels. There is also a rest area with a bar.

The foot of the tower houses the swimming pools of the Olympic Complex, while the former cycling track, known as the Vélodrome, located nearby, has been converted into an artificial habitat for plants and animals called the **Biodôme** ★★★ (4) *($9.50; every day 9am to 5pm; mid-Jun to early Sep, to 7pm; 4777 Avenue Pierre de Coubertin; ☎868-3000)*. This new type of museum, associated with the Jardin Botanique, contains four very different ecosystems — the Tropical Rainforest, the Laurentian Forest, the St. Lawrence Marine Ecosystem and the Polar World — within a space of 10,000 square metres. These are complete microcosms, including vegetation, mammals and free-flying birds, and close to real climatic conditions. Be careful not to catch a cold!

Ice hockey holds a special place in the hearts of Quebecers. Many consider Maurice "the

MONTRÉAL

Rocket" Richard as the greatest hockey player of all time. **L'Univers Maurice "Rocket" Richard (5)** *(free admission; Tue to Sun noon to 8pm; 2800 Rue Viau, ☎251-9930, Métro Viau)* is a small museum in his honour. Located in the arena that carries his name next to the Olympic facilities, the museum contains equipment, trophies and other significant memorabilia that once belonged to this hero of hockey who played for the Canadiens from 1942 to 1960. The museum also has a small boutique with hockey paraphernalia, as well as a skate-sharpening service.

As for the **Aréna Maurice-Richard (5)** *(2800 Rue Viau, ☎872-6666, Métro Viau)*, it precedes by 20 years the Olympic Village, with which it is now affiliated. Its rink is the only one in Eastern Canada whose area respects international norms. Canada's Olympic speed-skating team practises here, as do several figure-skating champions.

Return to Boulevard Pie-IX, and head south.

Église Saint-Jean-Baptiste-de-LaSalle (6) *(at the corner of Rue Hochelaga)* was built in 1964 within the context of the Vatican II liturgical revival. In an effort to maintain its following, members of the Catholic clergy cast aside traditions and introduced an audacious style of architecture, which still, however, did not enable them to accomplish their goal. The evocative mitre-like exterior conceals a depressing interior made of bare concrete, which seems to be falling onto the congregation.

Continue south on Boulevard Pie-IX, then turn left on Rue Ontario.

The **Ancien Hôtel de Ville ★ (7)** *(4120 Rue Ontario Est)*. In 1911, the Dufresne administration kicked off its policy of grandeur by building a city hall, designed by architect Cajetan Dufort. From 1926 to 1967, the building was occupied by the Institut du Radium, which specialized in cancer research. Since 1981, the edifice has served as the Maison de la Culture Maisonneuve, one of the City of Montréal's neighbourhood cultural centres. On the second floor, a 1915 bird's-eye view drawing of Maisonneuve shows the prestigious buildings completed at the time, as well as those that remained only on paper.

Built directly in line with Avenue Morgan in 1914, the **Marché Maisonneuve ★ (8)** *(Place du Marché)* is in keeping with a concept of urban design inherited from the teachings of the École des Beaux-Arts in Paris, known as the City Beautiful movement in North America. It is a mixture of parks, classical perspectives and civic and sanitary facilities. Designed by Cajetan Dufort, the market was the most ambitious of Dufresne's projects to be completed. The centre of Place du Marché is adorned with an important work by sculptor Alfred Laliberté, entitled *La Fermière* (The Woman Farmer). The market closed in 1962, then partially reopened in 1980.

Follow Avenue Morgan.

Although it is small, the **Bain Morgan ★ (9)** *(1875 Avenue Morgan)*, a bath house, has an imposing appearance, due to its Beaux-Arts elements — a monumental staircase, twin columns, a balustrade on the top and sculptures by Maurice Dubert from France. A bronze entitled *Les Petits Baigneurs* (The Little Bathers) is another piece by Alfred Laliberté. Originally, people came to the public baths not only to relax and enjoy the water, but also to wash, since not all houses in working-class neighbourhoods such as this were equipped with bathrooms.

In 1977, the former Cinéma Granada was converted into a theatre, and renamed **Théâtre Denise Pelletier (10)** *(4353 Rue Sainte-Catherine Est)* after one of the great actresses of the Quiet Revolution, who died prematurely. The terra cotta façade is decorated in the Italian Renaissance style. The original interior (1928), designed by Emmanuel Briffa, is of the atmospheric type, and has been partially preserved. Above the colonnade of the mythical palace encircling the room is a black vault that used to be studded with thousands of stars, making the audience feel as if they were attending an outdoor presentation. A projector was used to create images of moving clouds and even airplanes flying through the night.

Parc Morgan (11) *(at the southernmost end of Avenue Morgan)* was laid out in 1933 on the site of the country house of Henry Morgan, owner of the stores of the same name. From the cottage in the centre there is an interesting perspective on the Marché Maisonneuve silhouetted by the enormous Olympic Stadium.

Follow Rue Sainte-Catherine Est west to Avenue Létourneux, and turn left.

Maisonneuve boasted two firehouses, one of which had an altogether original design by Marius Dufresne. He was trained as an engineer and businessman, but also took a great interest in architecture. Impressed by the work of Frank Lloyd Wright, he designed the **Caserne de Pompiers no 1** ★ **(12)** *(on the south side of Rue Notre-Dame)*, or fire station, as an adaptation of the Unity Temple in Oak Park, on the outskirts of Chicago (1906). The building was therefore one of the first works of modern architecture erected in Canada.

Turn right on Avenue Desjardins. Due to the unstable ground in this part of the city, some of the houses tilt to an alarming degree.

Behind the somewhat drab Romanesque Revival façade of the **Église du Très-Saint-Nom-de-Jésus** ★ **(13)** *(at the corner of Rue Adam)*, built in 1906, visitors will discover a rich, polychromatic decor, created in part by artist Guido Nincheri, whose studio was located in Maisonneuve. Particularly noteworthy are the large organs built by the Casavant brothers, divided up between the rear jube and the chancel, very unusual in a Catholic church. Since this building stands on the same shifting ground as the neighbouring houses, its vault is supported by metal shafts.

Tour F: Île Sainte-Hélène
and Île Notre-Dame ★★ (one day)

When Samuel de Champlain reached the island of Montréal in 1611, he found a small rocky archipelago located in front of it. He named the largest of these islands in the channel after his wife, Hélène Boulé. Île Sainte-Hélène later became part of the seigneury of Longueuil. Around 1720, the Baroness of Longueuil chose the island as the site for a country house surrounded by a garden. It is also worth noting that in 1760, the island was the last foothold of French troops in New France, commanded by Chevalier François de Lévis. Recognizing Île Saint-Hélène's strategic importance, the British army built a fort on the eastern part of the island at the beginning of the 19th century. The threat of armed conflict with the Americans having diminished, the Canadian government rented Île Sainte-Hélène to the City of Montréal in 1874, at which time the island was turned into a park and linked to Old Montréal by ferry, and, from 1930 on, by the Jacques-Cartier bridge.

In the early 1960s, Montréal was chosen as the location of the 1967 World's Fair (Expo '67). The city wanted to set up the event on a large, attractive site near the downtown area; a site such as this, however, did not exist. It was thus necessary to build one: using earth excavated during the construction of the Métro tunnel, Île Notre-Dame was created, doubling the area of Île Sainte-Hélène. From April to November 1967, 45 million visitors passed through Cité du Havre, the gateway to the fairground, and crisscrossed both islands. Expo, as Montrealers still refer to it, was more than a jumble of assorted objects; it was Montréal's awakening, during which the city opened itself to the world, and visitors from all over discovered a new art of living, including miniskirts, colour television, hippies, flower power and protest rock.

It is not easy to reach Cité du Havre from downtown. The best way is to take Rue Mill, then Chemin des Moulins, which runs under Autoroute Bonaventure to Avenue Pierre-Dupuy. This last road leads to Pont de la Concorde and then over the St. Lawrence to the islands. It is also possible to take bus number 168 from the McGill Métro station, or the taxi-boat from Quai Jacques-Cartier, in the old port.

The numbers following names of attractions refer to the map of Île Sainte-Hélène and Île Notre-Dame.

The **Tropique Nord (1)**, **Habitat '67 (2)** and the **Parc de la Cité du Havre (3)** ★★ were all built on a spit of land created to protect the port of Montréal from ice and currents. This point of land also offers some lovely views of the city and the water. The administrative offices of the port are located at the entrance to the area, along with a group of buildings that once housed the Expo-Théâtre and Musée d'Art Contemporain (see p 108). A little further on, visitors will spot the large glass wall of the Tropique Nord, a residential complex composed of apartments with a view of the outdoors on one side, and an interior tropical garden on the other.

Next, visitors will see Habitat '67, an experimental housing development built for Expo '67 in order to illustrate construction techniques using prefabricated concrete slabs and to herald a new art of living. The architect, Moshe Safdie, was only 23 years old when he drew up the plans. Habitat '67 looks like a gigantic cluster of cubes, each containing one

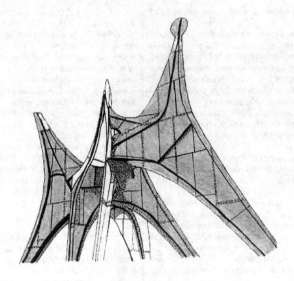

L'Homme

or two rooms. The apartments are as highly prized as ever, and are lived in by a number of notable Quebecers.

At the Parc de la Cité du Havre, visitors will find 12 panels containing a brief description of the history of the St. Lawrence River. A section of the bicycle path leading to Île Notre-Dame and Île Sainte-Hélène passes through the park.

Cross Pont de la Concorde.

Parc Hélène-de-Champlain ★★ (4) lies on Île Sainte-Hélène, which originally covered an area of 50 hectares, but was enlarged to over 120 hectares for Expo '67. The original portion corresponds to the raised area studded with boulders made of breccia. Peculiar to the island, breccia is a very hard, ferrous stone that takes on an orange colour when exposed to air for a long time. In 1992, the western part of the island was transformed into a vast open-air amphitheatre, where large-scale shows are presented. On a lovely park bordering the river, across from Montréal, visitors will find *L'Homme* (Man), a large metal sculpture by Alexandre Calder, created for Expo '67.

A little further, close to the entrance to the Île-Sainte-Hélène Métro station, is a work by the Mexican artist Sebastian entitled *La porte de*

l'amitié (The Door to Friendship). This sculpture was given to the City of Montréal by Mexico City in 1992 and erected on this site three years later to commemorate the signing of the free-trade agreement between Canada, the United States and Mexico (NAFTA).

Follow the trails leading toward the heart of the island. The pool house, faced with breccia stone, and outdoor swimming pools, built during the crisis of the 1930s, lie at the edge of the original park. This island, with its varied contours, is dominated by the **Tour Lévis**, a simple water tower built in 1936, which looks like a dungeon, and by the blockhouse, a wooden observation post erected in 1849.

Follow the signs for the Fort de l'Île Sainte-Hélène.

After the War of 1812 between the United States and Great Britain, the **Fort de l'Île Sainte-Hélène ★★ (5)** was built so that Montréal could be properly defended if ever a new conflict were to erupt. The construction, supervised by military engineer Elias Walker Durnford, was completed in 1825. Built of breccia stone, the fort is in the shape of a jagged "U", surrounding a drill ground, used today by the Compagnie Franche de la Marine and the 78th Regiment of the Fraser High

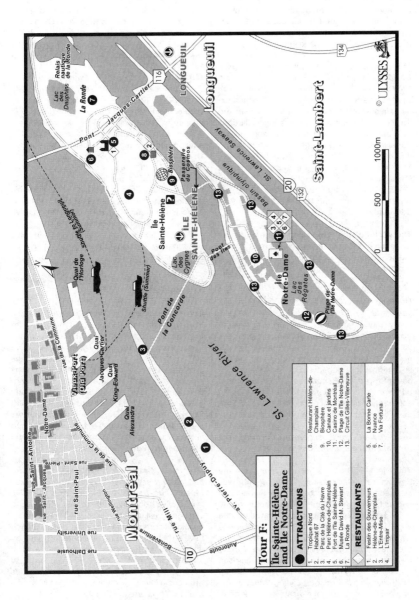

Tour F:
Île Sainte-Hélène
and Île Notre-Dame

● **ATTRACTIONS**

1. Tropique Nord
2. Habitat 67
3. Parc de la Cité du Havre
4. Parc Hélène-de-Champlain
5. Fort de l'Île Sainte-Hélène
6. Musée David M. Stewart
7. La Ronde

8. Restaurant Hélène-de-Champlain
9. Biosphère
10. Canaux et jardins
11. Casino de Montréal
12. Plage de l'Île Notre-Dame
13. Circuit Gilles-Villeneuve

◇ **RESTAURANTS**

1. Festin des Gouverneurs
2. Hélène-de-Champlain
3. L'Entre-Mise
4. L'Impair

5. La Bonne Carte
6. Nuance
7. Via Fortuna

© ULYSSES

MONTRÉAL

landers as a parade ground. These two costumed mock regiments delight visitors by reviving Canada's French and Scottish military traditions. The drill ground also offers a lovely view of both the port and **Pont Jacques-Cartier**, inaugurated in 1930, which straddles the island, separating the park from La Ronde.

The arsenal is now occupied by the **Musée David-M.-Stewart** ★★ **(6)** *($5; Sep to May, Wed to Mon 10am to 5pm; Jun to Aug, Wed to Mon 10am to 6pm;* ☎*861-6701)*, which exhibits a collection of objects from the 17th and 18th centuries, including interesting collections of maps, firearms, and scientific and navigational instruments put together by Montréal industrialist David Stewart and his wife Liliane. The latter heads both the museum and the Macdonald-Stewart Foundation, which also manages the Château Ramezay and the Château Dufresne (the former Musée des Arts Décoratifs).

The vaults of the former barracks now house **Le Festin des Gouverneurs**, a restaurant geared mainly toward large groups. Each evening, it recreates the atmosphere of a New France feast (see p 149).

La Ronde ★ **(7)** *($17.30, children 3 to 12 years old $8.55, families $40; Jun to Sep, every day 11am to 11pm, Fri and Sat to midnight.;* ☎*872-6222)*, an amusement park set up for Expo '67 on the former Île Ronde, opens its doors to both the young and the not so young every summer. For Montrealers, an annual trip to La Ronde has almost become a pilgrimage. An international fireworks competition is held here on Saturdays or Sundays during the months of June and July.

Head toward the Biosphere on the road that runs along the south shore of the island.

Built in 1938 as a sports pavilion, the **Restaurant Hélène-de-Champlain** ★ **(8)** was inspired by the architecture of New France, and is thus reminiscent of the summer house of the Baroness of Longueuil, once located in the area. Behind the restaurant is a lovely rose garden planted for Expo '67, which embellishes the view from the dining room. The **former military cemetery** of the British garrison stationed on Île Sainte-Hélène from 1828 to 1870 lies in front of the building. Most of the original tombstones have disappeared. A commemorative monument, erected in 1937, stands in their place.

Very few of the pavilions built for Expo '67 have survived the destructive effects of the weather and the changes in the islands' roles. One that has is the former American pavilion, a veritable monument to modern architecture. The first complete geodesic dome to be taken beyond the stage of a model, it was created by the celebrated engineer Richard Buckminster Fuller (1895-1983). The **Biosphere** ★★ **(9)** *($6.50; Jun. 24 to Sep. 1, every day 10am to 6pm; off-season, Tue to Sun, 10am to 5pm;* ☎*283-5000, Métro Île-Sainte-Hélène)*, built of tubular aluminum and measuring 80 metres in diameter, unfortunately lost its translucent acrylic skin in a fire back in 1978. An environmental interpretive centre on the St. Lawrence River, the Great Lakes and the different Canadian ecosystems, is now located in the dome. The permanent exhibit aims to sensitize the public on issues of sustainable development and the conservation of water as a precious resource. There are four interactive galleries with giant screens and hands-on displays to explore and delight in. A terrace restaurant with a panoramic view of the islands complete the museum.

Cross over to Île Notre-Dame on the Passerelle du Cosmos.

Île Notre-Dame emerged from the waters of the St. Lawrence in no less than 10 months, with the help of 15 million tons of rocks and soil transported here from the Métro construction site. Because it is an artificial island, its creators were able to give it a fanciful shape by playing with both soil and water. The island, therefore, is traversed by pleasant **canals and gardens** ★★ **(10)**, laid out for the 1980 Floralies Internationales, an international flower show. Boats are available for rent, enabling visitors to ply the canals and admire the flowers mirrored in their waters.

Montréal's **Casino** ★ **(11)** *(free admission, parking and coat check; every day 24 hours; Métro Île-Sainte-Hélène, bus #167;* ☎*392-2746)* occupies the former French and Québec pavilions of Expo '67. The main building corresponds to the old **French Pavilion** ★, an aluminum structure designed by architect Jean Faugeron. It was renovated in 1993 at a cost of $92.4 million in order to accommodate the Casino. The upper galleries offer some lovely views of downtown Montréal and the St. Lawrence Seaway.

Immediately to the west of the former French pavilion, the building shaped like a truncated pyramid is the former **Québec pavilion ★** *(every day 9am to 3am)*. It was incorporated into the Casino after being raised and recovered with gold-tinted glass in 1996.

Visitors will find all sorts of things to do at the Casino, and all this in a very festive atmosphere among some of the 15,000 people that visit the casino each day. With 2,700 slot machines and 107 gaming tables, this is one of the 10 largest casinos in the world. This is also a popular spot thanks to its bars and cabaret (see "Entertainment" chapter p 158), along with its four restaurants, including Nuances (see "Restaurants" chapter, p 149), which is rated as one of the best in Canada. Entrance is reserved for 18 and over. Dress code.

Nearby, visitors will find the entrance to the **Plage de l'Île Notre-Dame (12)**, a beach enabling Montrealers to lounge on real sand right in the middle of the St. Lawrence. A natural filtering system keeps the water in the small lake clean, with no need for chemical additives. The number of swimmers allowed on the beach is strictly regulated, however, so as not to disrupt the balance of the system.

There are other recreational facilities here as well, namely the Olympic Basin created for the rowing competitions of the 1976 Olympics and the **Circuit Gilles-Villeneuve (13)**, where Formula One drivers compete every year in the Grand Prix Player's du Canada, part of the international racing circuit.

To return to downtown Montréal, take the Métro from the Île-Sainte-Hélène station.

Tour G: Quartier Latin ★★
(three hours)

People come to this university neighbourhood, centred around Rue Saint-Denis, for its theatres, cinemas and countless outdoor cafés, which offer a glimpse of the heterogeneous crowd of students and revellers. The area's origins date back to 1823, when Montréal's first Catholic cathedral, Église Saint-Jacques, was inaugurated on Rue Saint-Denis. This prestigious edifice quickly attracted the cream of French-Canadian society, mainly old noble families who had remained in Canada after the conquest — to the area. In 1852, a fire ravaged the neighbourhood, destroying the cathedral and Monseigneur Bourget's bishop's palace in the process. Painfully reconstructed in the second half of the 19th century, the area

remained residential until the Université de Montréal was established here in 1893, marking the beginning of a period of cultural turmoil that would eventually lead to the Quiet Revolution of the 1960s. The Université du Québec, founded in 1974, has since taken over from the Université de Montréal, now located on the north side of Mont Royal. The prosperity of the quarter has thus been ensured.

This tour starts at the west exit of the Sherbrooke Métro station.

The numbers following names of attractions refer to the map of the Quartier Latin.

The **Institut de Tourisme et d'Hôtellerie du Québec (1)** *(3535 Rue Saint-Denis)*, a school devoted to the tourism and hotel industries, ironically occupies what many people consider the ugliest building in Montréal. Set on the east side of Square Saint-Louis, on Rue Saint-Denis, it is part of an uninspiring group of buildings designed between 1972 and 1976, on the eve of the Olympics. The institute's courses in cooking, tourism and hotel management are nevertheless excellent.

Go across Rue Saint-Denis to Square Saint-Louis.

After the great fire of 1852, a reservoir was built at the top of the hill known as Côte-à-Barron. In 1879, it was dismantled and the site was converted into a park by the name of **Square Saint-Louis ★★ (2)**. Developers built beautiful Second-Empire- style residences around the square, making it the nucleus of the French-Canadian bourgeois neighbourhood. These groups of houses give the area a certain harmonious quality rarely found in Montréal's urban landscape. To the west, **Rue Prince-Arthur** extends west from the square. In the 1960s, this pedestrian mall (between Boulevard Saint-Laurent and Avenue Laval) was the centre of the counterculture and the hippie movement in Montréal. Today, it is lined with numerous restaurants and terraces. On summer evenings, street performers liven up the atmosphere.

Turn left onto **Avenue Laval**, one of the only streets in the city where the Belle Époque atmosphere is still very tangible. Abandoned by the French-Canadian bourgeoisie from 1920 on, the houses were converted into rooming houses before attracting the attention of local artists, who began restoring them one by one. Poet Émile Nelligan (1879-1941) lived at

MONTRÉAL

number 3688 with his family at the turn of the century. The Union des Écrivains Québécois (Québec Writers' Association) occupies number 3492, the former home of film-maker Claude Jutra, who directed such films as *Mon Oncle Antoine* (Uncle Antoine). A number of other artists, including singer Pauline Julien, writers Michel Tremblay and Yves Navarre and pianist André Gagnon, live or have lived in the area around Square Saint-Louis and Avenue Laval.

Mont-Saint-Louis ★ (3) *(244 Rue Sherbrooke Est)*, a former boys' school run by the brothers of the Écoles Chrétiennes, was built facing straight up Avenue Laval in 1887. The long façade punctuated with pavilions, grey stone walls, openings with segmental arches and mansard roof make this building one of the most characteristic examples of the Second Empire style as adapted to suit Montréal's big institutions. The school closed its doors in 1970, and the edifice was converted into an apartment building in 1987, at which time an unobtrusive parking lot was built under the garden.

Maison Fréchette (4) *(306 Rue Sherbrooke Est)*. Journalist, poet and deputy Louis Fréchette (1839-1908) lived in this Second-Empire-style house. Sarah Bernhardt stayed here on several occasions during her North American tours.

Turn right on Rue Saint-Denis and walk down "Côte-à-Barron" toward the Université du Québec à Montréal.

Montée du Zouave, the hill on the right known today as **Terrasse Saint-Denis**, was the favourite meeting place of Québec's poets and writers at the turn of the century. The group of houses was built on the site of the home of Sieur de Montigny, a proud papal Zouave.

Montréal architect Joseph-Arthur Godin's work was one of the precursors of modern architecture in North America. In 1914, he began construction on three apartment buildings with visible reinforced concrete frames in the Quartier Latin area. One of these is the **Saint-Jacques ★ (5)** *(1704 Rue Saint-Denis)*. Godin blended this avant-garde concept with subtle Art-Nouveau curves, giving the buildings a light, graceful appearance. The venture was a commercial failure, however, leading Godin to bankruptcy and ending his career as an architect.

The **Bibliothèque Nationale ★ (6)** *(1700 Rue Saint-Denis)*, the national library, was originally built for the Sulpicians, who looked unfavourably on the construction of a public library on Rue Sherbrooke. Even though many works were still on the *Index*, and thus forbidden reading for the clergy, the new library was seen as unfair competition. Known in the past as Bibliothèque Saint-Sulpice, this branch of the Bibliothèque Nationale du Québec was designed in the Beaux-Arts style by architect Eugène Payette in 1914. This style, a synthesis of classicism and French Renaissance architecture, was taught at the Paris École des Beaux-Arts, hence its name in North America. The interior is graced with lovely stained-glass windows created by Henri Perdriau in 1915.

The **Théâtre Saint-Denis (7)** *(1594 Rue Saint-Denis)* is made up of two theatres, among the most popular in the city. During summer, the Festival Juste pour Rire, also known as the Just for Laughs Festival, is presented here. The theatre opened in 1914, and has since welcomed big names in show business from the world over. Modernized several times over the years, it was completely renovated yet again in 1989. As visitors can see, the top of the original theatre is higher than the recently added pink-granite façade.

The screening room and rental service of the **Office National du Film du Canada (ONF) (National Film Board of Canada)** *(1564 Rue St-Denis)* are located at the corner of Boulevard de Maisonneuve. The ONF-NFB has the world's only *cinérobothèque ($5 for two hours, 3$ for one hour; Tue to Sun noon to 9pm; ☎496-6887)*, enabling about 100 people to watch different films at once. The complex also has a movie theatre *($5; every day, monthly schedule)* where various documentaries and NFB films are screened. Movie lovers can also visit the **Cinémathèque Québécoise** *(335 Boulevard de Maisonneuve Est)*, a little further west, which has a collection of 25,000 Canadian, Québec and foreign films, as well as hundreds of pieces of equipment dating back to the early history of film (see also Entertainment, p 156). The Cinémathèque recently re-opened after extensive renovations. UQAM's new concert hall, **Salle Pierre-Mercure**, is across the street.

Unlike most North American universities, with buildings contained within a specific campus, the campus of the **Université du Québec à Montréal (UQAM) ★ (8)** *(405 Rue Sainte-Catherine Est, at the corner of rue Saint-Denis)* is integrated into the city fabric like French and

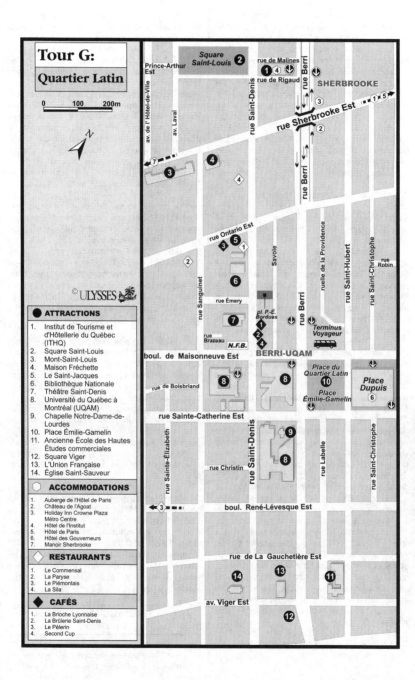

German universities built during the Renaissance. It is also linked to the underground city and the Métro. The university is located on the site once occupied by the buildings of the Université de Montréal and the Église Saint-Jacques, which was reconstructed after the fire of 1852. Only the wall of the right transept and the Gothic-Revival steeple were integrated into Pavillon Judith-Jasmin (1979), and have since become the symbol of the university. UQAM is part of the Université du Québec, founded in 1969 and established in different cities across the province. Every year, over 40,000 students attend this flourishing institution of higher learning.

Turn left on Rue Sainte-Catherine Est.

Artist Napoléon Bourassa lived in a large house on Rue Saint-Denis. **Chapelle Notre-Dame-de-Lourdes ★ (9)** *(430 Rue Sainte-Catherine Est)*, erected in 1876, was his greatest achievement. It was commissioned by the Sulpicians, who wanted to secure their presence in this part of the city. Its Roman-Byzantine style is in some way a summary of its author's travels. The little chapel's recently restored interior, adorned with Bourassa's vibrantly coloured frescoes, is a must-see.

Place Émilie-Gamelin ★ (10) *(at the corner of Rue Berri and Rue Sainte-Catherine, Métro Berri-UQAM)*, laid out in 1992 for Montréal's 350th anniversary, is the city's newest large public space. In 1994, the area along Rue Sainte-Catherine was renamed **Esplanade Émilie-Gamelin**, while the northern section was renamed **Place du Quartier Latin**. At the far end, visitors will find some curious metal sculptures by Melvin Charney, who also designed the garden of the Centre Canadien d'Architecture (see p 112). Across the street lies the bus terminal (Terminus Voyageur), built on top of the Berri-UQAM Métro station, where three of the city's four metro lines converge. To the east, the Galeries Dupuis and the Atriums, two shopping centres containing a total of about 100 stores, are located on the site of the former Dupuis Frères department store. A few businesses dear to Montrealers, such as the Archambault record shop, still grace Rue Sainte-Catherine Est. The part of this street between Rue Saint-Hubert and Avenue Papineau is regarded as Montréal's **"gay village"**.

Turn right on Rue Saint-Hubert, then right again on Avenue Viger.

A symbol of the social ascent of a certain class of French-Canadian businessmen in the early 20th century, the former business school, the **École des Hautes Études Commerciales ★ (11)** *(535 Avenue Viger)*, profoundly altered Montréal's managerial and financial circles. Prior to the school's existence, these circles were dominated by Canadians of British extraction. This imposing building's (1908) very Parisian Beaux-Arts architecture, characterized by twin columns, balustrades, a monumental staircase and sculptures, bears witness to the Francophile leaning of those who built it. In 1970, this business school, known as HEC, joined the campus of the Université de Montréal on the north side of Mont Royal.

Before moving to the Square Saint-Louis area around 1880, members of the French-Canadian bourgeoisie settled around **Square Viger (12)** *(Avenue Viger)* during the 1850's. Marred by the underground construction of Autoroute Ville-Marie (1977-79), the square was redesigned in three sections by as many artists, who opted for an elaborate design, as opposed to the sober style of the original 19th-century square. In the background, visitors will see the castle-like former Gare Viger (see p 98).

The **Union Française (13)** *(429 Avenue Viger Est)*, Montréal's French cultural association, has occupied this old, aristocratic residence since 1909. Lectures and exhibitions on France and its various regions are held here. Every year, Bastille Day (July 14) is celebrated in Square Viger, across the street. The house, attributed to architect Henri-Maurice Perrault, was built in 1867 for shipowner Jacques-Félix Sincennes, founder of the Richelieu and Ontario Navigation Company. It is one of the oldest examples of Second Empire architecture in Montréal.

At the corner of Rue Saint-Denis is the **Église Saint-Sauveur (14)** *(329 Avenue Viger)*, a Gothic-Revival church built in 1865, according to a design by architects Lawford and Nelson. From 1922 to 1995, it was the seat of Montréal's Syrian Catholic community. The church has a semicircular chancel, adorned with lovely stained-glass windows by artist Guido Nincheri.

Tour H: Plateau Mont-Royal ★
(three hours)

If there is one neighbourhood typical of Montréal, it is definitely this one. Thrown into the spotlight by writer Michel Tremblay, one of its illustrious sons, the "Plateau," as its inhabitants refer to it, is a neighbourhood of penniless intellectuals, young professionals and old francophone working-class families. Its long streets are lined with duplexes and triplexes adorned with amusingly contorted exterior staircases leading up to the long, narrow apartments that are so typical of Montréal. Flower-decked balconies made of wood or wrought iron provide box-seats for the spectacle on the street below. The Plateau is bounded by the mountain to the west, the Canadian Pacific railway tracks to the north and east, and Rue Sherbrooke to the south. It is traversed by a few major streets lined with cafés and theatres, such as Rue Saint-Denis and Avenue Papineau, but is a tranquil area on the whole. A visit to Montréal would not be complete without a stroll through this area to truly grasp the spirit of Montréal. This tour starts at the exit of the Mont-Royal Métro station. Turn right on Avenue du Mont-Royal, the neighbourhood's main commercial artery.

The numbers following names of attractions refer to the map of Plateau Mont-Royal.

The **Monastère des Pères du Très-Saint-Sacrement ★ (1)** *(500 Avenue du Mont-Royal Est)* and its church, Église Notre-Dame-du-Très-Saint-Sacrement, were built at the end of the 19th century for the community of priests *(Père* is the French word for Father) of the same name. The somewhat austere façade of the church conceals an extremely colourful interior with an Italian-style decor designed by Jean-Zéphirin Resther. This sanctuary, dedicated to the "eternal Exhibition and Adoration of the Eucharist", is open for prayer and contemplation every day of the week. Concerts of baroque music are occasionally presented here.

Continue heading east on Avenue du Mont-Royal Est, blending in with the neighbourhood's widely varied inhabitants on their way in and out of an assortment of businesses, ranging from the chic "Pâtisserie Bruxelloise" (a Belgian pastry shop) to shops selling knickknacks for a dollar and used records.

Turn right on Rue Fabre for some good examples of Montréal-style housing. Built between 1900 and 1925, the houses contain between two and five apartments, all with a private entry from outside. Decorative details vary from one building to the next. Visitors will

see Art-Nouveau stained glass, parapets, cornices made of brick or sheet metal, balconies with Tuscan columns, and ornamental ironwork shaped in ringlets and cables.

Turn left on Rue Rachel Est.

At the end of Rue Fabre, visitors will find **Parc Lafontaine (2)**, the Plateau's main green space, laid out in 1908 on the site of an old military shooting range. Monuments to Sir Louis-Hippolyte Lafontaine, Félix Leclerc and Dollard des Ormeaux have been erected here. The park covers an area of 40 hectares, and is embellished with two artificial lakes and shady paths for pedestrians and bicyclists. There are tennis courts and bowling greens for summer sports enthusiasts, and in the winter, the frozen lakes form a large rink, which is illuminated at night. The Théâtre de Verdure (Outdoor Theatre) is also located here. Every weekend, the park is crowded with people from the neighbourhood, who come here to make the most of beautiful sunny or snowy days.

The parish churches on Plateau Mont-Royal, designed to accommodate large French-Canadian working-class families, are enormous. The Romanesque-Revival-style **Église de l'Immaculée-Conception (3)** *(at the corner of Avenue Papineau)*, designed by Émile Tanguay, was built in 1895. The interior, decorated with plaster statues and remounted paintings, is typical of that period. The stained-glass windows come from the Maison Vermont in France.

Turn right on Avenue Papineau, and right again on Rue Sherbrooke Est.

An obelisk dedicated to General de Gaulle, by French artist Olivier Debré, towers over the long **Place Charles-de-Gaulle (4)** *(at the corner of Avenue Émile-Duployé)*, located alongside Rue Sherbrooke. The monument, made of blue granite from the quarries of Saint-Michel-de-Montjoie in Normandy, stands 17 metres high. It was given to the City of Montréal by the City of Paris in 1992, on the occasion of Montréal's 350th anniversary.

Hôpital Notre-Dame, one of the city's major hospitals, lies across the street. The attractive **École Le Plateau** (1930) is located a little further west, at 3700 Avenue Calixa-Lavallée. This Art Deco building, designed by architects Perrault and Gadbois, also houses the hall used by the Montréal Symphony Orchestra in its

MONTRÉAL

early days. A trail to the north of the school provides access to the lakes in Parc Lafontaine. Back on Rue Sherbrooke Est, visitors will find the **Bibliothèque Municipale de Montréal**, the city's public library, inaugurated in 1917 by Maréchal Joffre *(1210 Rue Sherbrooke Est)*. Even back in the early 20th century, the edifice was of modest size, given the number of people it was intended to serve, a result of the clergy's reservations about a non-religious library being opened in Montréal. Today, fortunately, the library has a network of 27 neighbourhood branches. Inside, an entire room is devoted to the genealogy of French-Canadian families (Salle Gagnon, in the basement).

The monument to Sir Louis-Hippolyte Lafontaine (1807-1864), after whom the park was named, is located on the other side of the street. Regarded as the father of responsible government in Canada, Lafontaine was also one of the main defenders of the French language in the country's institutions. Take **Rue Cherrier**, which branches off from Rue Sherbrooke Est across from the monument. This street, along with Square Saint-Louis, located at its west end, once formed the nucleus of the French Canadian bourgeois neighbourhood. At number 840, visitors will find the **Agora de la Danse**, where the studios

of a variety of dance companies are located. The red-brick building, completed in 1919, originally served as the Palestre Nationale, a sports centre for the neighbourhood youth and the scene of many tumultuous public gatherings during the 1930s. *Turn right on Rue Saint-Hubert, lined with fine examples of vernacular architecture. Turn left on Rue Roy to see Église Saint-Louis-de-France, built in 1936 as a replacement for the original church, destroyed by fire in 1933.*

At the corner of **Rue Saint-Denis** stands the former **Institut des Sourdes-Muettes (5)** *(3725 Rue Saint-Denis)*, a large, grey stone building made up of numerous wings and erected in stages between 1881 and 1900. Built in the Second Empire style, it covers an entire block, and is typical of institutional architecture of that period in Québec. It once took in the region's deaf-mutes. The strange chapel with cast-iron columns, as well as the sacristy, with its tall wardrobes and surprising spiral staircase, may be visited upon request from the entrance on Rue Berri.

Head north on Rue Saint-Denis. Between Rue Sainte-Catherine, to the south, and Boulevard Saint-Joseph, to the north, this long artery is

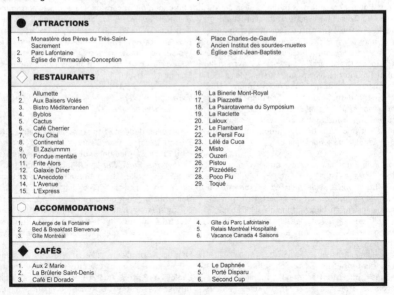

ATTRACTIONS

1. Monastère des Pères du Très-Saint-Sacrement
2. Parc Lafontaine
3. Église de l'Immaculée-Conception
4. Place Charles-de-Gaulle
5. Ancien Institut des sourdes-muettes
6. Église Saint-Jean-Baptiste

RESTAURANTS

1. Allumette
2. Aux Baisers Volés
3. Bistro Méditerranéen
4. Byblos
5. Cactus
6. Café Cherrier
7. Chu Chai
8. Continental
9. El Zaziummm
10. Fondue mentale
11. Frite Alors
12. Galaxie Diner
13. L'Anecdote
14. L'Avenue
15. L'Express
16. La Binerie Mont-Royal
17. La Piazzetta
18. La Psarotaverna du Symposium
19. La Raclette
20. Laloux
21. Le Flambard
22. Le Persil Fou
23. Lélé da Cuca
24. Misto
25. Ouzeri
26. Pistou
27. Pizzédélic
28. Poco Più
29. Toqué

ACCOMMODATIONS

1. Auberge de la Fontaine
2. Bed & Breakfast Bienvenue
3. Gîte Montréal
4. Gîte du Parc Lafontaine
5. Relais Montréal Hospitalité
6. Vacance Canada 4 Saisons

CAFÉS

1. Aux 2 Marie
2. La Brûlerie Saint-Denis
3. Café El Dorado
4. Le Daphnée
5. Porté Disparu
6. Second Cup

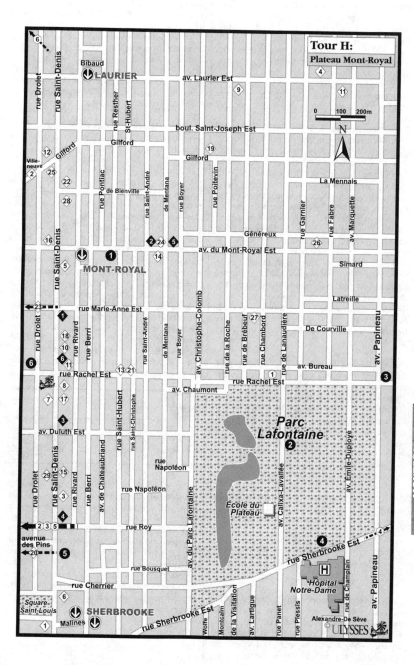

Tour H:
Plateau Mont-Royal

0   100   200m

N

MONTRÉAL

lined with numerous outdoor cafés and beautiful shops, established inside Second-Empire-style former residences built during the second half of the 19th century. Visitors will also find many bookstores, tea rooms and restaurants, that have become veritable Montréal institutions over the years.

*Take a brief detour left onto Rue Rachel Est in order to see Église Saint-Jean-Baptiste and the institutional buildings around it.***Église Saint-Jean-Baptiste ★★ (6)** *(309 Rue Rachel Est)*, dedicated to the patron saint of French Canadians, is a gigantic symbol of the solid faith of Catholic working-class inhabitants of the Plateau Mont-Royal at the turn of the 20th century, who, despite their poverty and large families, managed to amass considerable amounts of money for the construction of sumptuous churches. The exterior was built in 1901, according to a design by architect Émile Vanier. The interior was redone after a fire, and is now a veritable Baroque Revival masterpiece designed by Casimir Saint-Jean that is not to be missed. The pink-marble and gilded wood baldaquin in the chancel (1915) shelters the altar, made of white Italian marble, which faces the large Casavant organs — among the most powerful in the city — in the jube. Concerts are frequently given at this church. It can seat up to 3,000 people.

Collège Rachel, built in 1876 in the Second Empire style, stands across the street from the church. Finally, west of Avenue Henri-Julien, visitors will find the **former Hospice Auclair** (1894), with its semi-circular entrance on Rue Rachel. On Rue Drolet, south of Rue Rachel, are several good examples of the working-class architecture of the 1870s and 1880s on the Plateau, before the advent of vernacular housing, namely duplexes and triplexes with exterior staircases like those found on Rue Fabre.

Go back to Rue Saint-Denis, and continue walking up it to Avenue du Mont-Royal. Turn right in order to return to the Mont-Royal Métro station.

Tour I: Laval

Laval, Québec's second largest city, is located on a large island north of Montréal called Île Jésus. The island is surrounded by three bodies of water, Lac des Deux-Montagnes to the east, Rivière des Prairies to the south and Rivière des Mille-Îles to the north. French settlers were attracted to Île Jésus very early on by its fertile soil. Saint-François-de-Sales, the first village on Île Jésus, was founded in 1706 after a peace treaty with the Amerindians was signed. Laval is now a residential and industrial suburb, but it has managed to preserve some of its architectural heritage and farmland, and also has set aside several large spaces for outdoor activities. Laval is easily accessible from Montréal by car.

The **Cosmodôme** *($9.50; Jun 24 to Sep 4, every day 10am to 6pm; Sep 5 to Jun 23, Tue to Sun 10am to 6pm; 2150 Highway 15, St-Martin Ouest Exit, ☎ 978-3600)* is a space museum. A tour of the premises starts with a fascinating multimedia presentation on the history of man's discovery of outer space. The second part is devoted to means of space travel and explains the laws of physics that govern life in outer space using all sorts of high-tech interactive displays. The third part deals with telecommunications and the "global village"; the fourth, devoted to Earth, explains the principal terrestrial phenomena, such as the changing of the seasons and geology. Section five contains the museum's *pièce de résistance*, a piece of lunar rock. This sample was donated by NASA, thus granting this Laval museum international recognition. A look at the solar system winds things up; there are scale reproductions of all the planets, showing how very small Earth is when compared to the solar system as a whole.

PARKS

Tour D: Mount-Royal and Westmount

All year round, Montrealers flock to **Parc du Mont-Royal**, a huge green expanse in the middle of the city, to enjoy a wide range of athletic activities. During summer, footpaths and mountain bike trails are maintained. Bird feeders have been set up along one trail for the benefit of bird-watchers. During winter, the paths serve as cross-country ski trails, leading across the snowy slopes of the mountain, and Lac aux Castors becomes a big, beautiful skating rink, where people of all ages come to enjoy themselves.

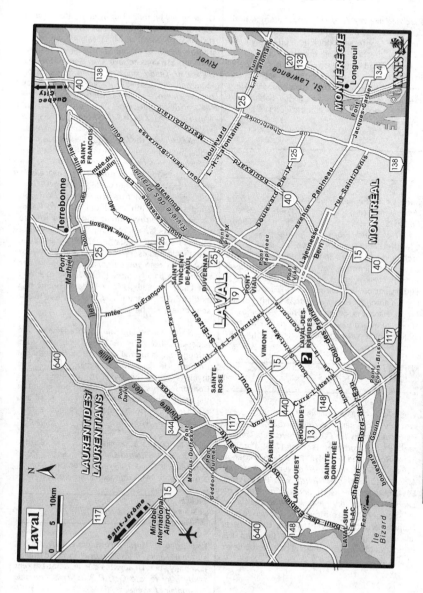

Laval

Tour F: Île Sainte-Hélène and Île Notre-Dame

Parc des Îles *(☎872-4537)* encompasses both Île Sainte-Hélène and Île Notre-Dame. In summer, Montrealers flock here on sunny days to enjoy the beach and the swimming pools. Footpaths and bicycle trails crisscross the park. In wintertime, a whole host of activities is organized here, including cross-country skiing (14 kilometres), tobogganing, ice fishing and skating on the two-kilometre-long Olympic rowing basin.

Tour I: Laval

Parc de la Rivière-des-Mille-Îles *(May 15 to Jun. 4, 9am to 5pm; Jun. 5 to Sep. 4, 9am to 8pm; Sep. 5 to Oct. 9, 9am to 5pm; 345 Boulevard Ste-Rose, ☎ 664-4242)* is a beautiful and verdant place to stop. The archipelago's plants and wildlife are accessible along several paths. You can also enjoy several activities like kayaking and pedal-boating. Equipment can be rented on site. The park's is known amongst hikers and cross-country skiers for its **Parcours du Héron**. This is a series of short paths on various islands. The hike includes observation points that reveal this self-contained environment.

 OUTDOORS

The island of Montréal is strewn with parks where visitors can enjoy all sorts of activities. **Parc Angrignon** *(3400 Boulevard des Trinitaires)*, **Parc Lafontaine** (see p 131), **Parc du Mont-Royal** (see p 134), **Parc Jeanne-Mance** *(Avenue de l'Esplanade, between Avenue du Mont-Royal and rue Duluth)* and **Parc René-Lévesque** *(at the west end of the Canal de Lachine)* are all very pleasant places to relax in a peaceful atmosphere. Year-round, Montrealers take advantage of these small islands of greenery to unwind far from the urban tumult, while remaining right in the heart of the city.

 Cycling

Cyclists will be thrilled to discover the close to 400 kilometres of interesting bicycle paths that traverse the island of Montréal. A map of the paths is available at tourist information offices, or visitors can purchase the *Great Montréal Bike Path-Guide* map in travel bookstores. Except during rush hour, bicycles can be taken on the metro. For more information visit the Maison des Cyclistes *(1251 Rue Rachel Est, Montréal, H2J 2J9, ☎521-8356, ↔521-5711)*.

The area around the **Canal de Lachine** has been redesigned in an effort to highlight this communication route, so important during the 19th and early 20th centuries. A pleasant bike path was laid out alongside the canal. Very popular with Montrealers, especially on Sundays, the path leads out to **Parc René-Lévesque**, a narrow strip of land jutting out into Lac Saint-Louis, and offering splendid views of the lake and surroundings. There are benches and picnic tables in the park and plenty of seagulls to keep you company. The path leads around the park, returning beside the river and the Lachine rapids. Many birds frequent this side of the park, and if you are lucky you might see some great herons.

Île Notre-Dame and **Île Sainte-Hélène** are accessible from Old Montréal. The path runs through an industrial area, then through the Cité du Havre before reaching the islands (cyclists cross the river on the Pont de la Concorde). It is easy to ride from one island to the other. The islands are well maintained and are a great place to relax, stroll and admire Montréal's skyline.

Bike rentals are available at **La Cordée** *(2159 Rue Sainte-Catherine Est, Métro Papineau, ☎524-1515)* and are around $18 for a full day (a $400 deposit is required).

 Rafting

Looking for a refreshing outdoor activity for hot summer days? The young and dynamic company, **Les Descentes sur le Saint-Laurent** *(early May to late Oct; C.P. 511, Succursale Champlain, LaSalle, ☎767-2230, ↔767-6396)*, offers various types of river rides in inflatable boats down the Lachine rapids, and are located only minutes from downtown. Lots of laughter and splashing are guaranteed while rafting down the river in a group, and the guides will recount the history and ecology of the rapids. For those who prefer something calmer, they also offer cruises that last an hour or so. A free shuttle service is provided between the Centre Infotouristie *(1001 du Square-Dorchester)* and the departure point in Lasalle. Bring a change of clothes.

 Adventure Packages

If you are vacationing in Montréal and feel like going on an escapade in the great outdoors, **Globe-Trotteur Aventure Canada** *(1619 Rue St-Hubert, métro Berri-UQAM,* ☎*598-7688 or 888-598-7688,* ⌂*598-7687)* offers different adventure packages for both summer and winter activities including canoeing, camping, snowmobiling, etc., in different areas on the island. Packages include transportation and equipment rental. Excursions are led by experienced guides and last from half a day to several days. In summer they have a schedule of different activities, so you can plan your own adventures.

 Skating

During the winter, a number of public skating rinks are set up. Among the nicest ones are **Lac aux Castors** *(Parc du Mont-Royal)*, the rink at **Parc Lafontaine** *(between Sherbrooke and Rachel, and Papineau and Lafontaine)*, the rink at the **Vieux-Port** *(333 Rue de la Commune Ouest,* ☎*496-PORT)*, the one at **Parc Maisonneuve** *(4601 Rue Sherbrooke Ouest,* ☎*872-5558)* and the one at **Parc des Îles** *(on the Olympic rowing basin on Île Notre-Dame)*. This last rink is the longest in Montréal at 1,6 kilometres.

The **Amphithéatre Bell** *($5; every day 11:30am to 10pm; 1000 Rue De La Gauchetière Ouest,* ☎*395-0555)* located in 1000 de la Gauchetière (the tallest office building in Montréal), houses a large skating rink with a surface area of 900 square metres. The rink is surrounded by food stands and rest areas, and overlooked by a mezzanine. Above the skating rink is a superb glass dome that lets the sun shine in. Ice skates can be rented at the rink for $4.

 ACCOMMODATIONS

Travellers will discover a large variety of hotels and inns in all categories in Montréal. Rates vary greatly from one season to the next, and are much higher during the summer. Rates are usually lower on the weekends than during the week, however. Finally, remember that the weeks of the Grand Prix Automobile de Formule 1 (mid-July) and of the Jazz Festival (late June, early July) are the busiest of the year; we recommend that reservations be made long in advance if you plan to be in Montréal during these events. In the off-season, it is often possible to obtain better rates than the ones quoted in this guide.

Montreal is one of those places where it is difficult to see everything in one day. We therefore suggest a variety of lodging possibilities so that you might enjoy a longer visit. The following addresses are organized in the same order as the walking tours and according to price, starting with the least expensive.

The Fédération des Agricotours produces an annual guide entitled *Affordable Bed & Breakfasts in Québec*, which lists the names and telephone numbers of all of its members who provide rooms for travellers. The rooms offered have been selected according to the federation's standards of quality. They are also fairly economical. The book is available in bookstores.

Gîte Montréal *($45-$55 per person, $65 for two people; 3458 Avenue Laval, H2X 3C8,* ☎*289-9749 or 1-800-267-5180,* ⌂*287-7386)* is an association of nearly 100 bed & breakfasts (*gîtes*), mostly Victorian houses in the Latin Quarter. In order to make sure that all rooms offered are comfortable, the organization visits each one. Reservations required.

About 30 bed & breakfasts are also registered with the **Relais Montréal Hospitalité** *($35 single and double to $55 double; 3977 Avenue Laval, H2W 2H9,* ☎*287-9635 or 1-800-363-9635,* ⌂*287-1007)*. All have been carefully inspected, and the rooms are clean and comfortable. The establishments are located throughout Montreal, though many are on on Rue Laval.

MONTRÉAL

Tour A: Vieux-Montréal

The **Auberge Alternative** *($15-$45; 358 Rue Saint-Pierre, H2Y 2M1, ☎282-8069; http://odyssee.net/eber/intro.html)*, located in Old Montréal, opened in April 1996. Run by a young couple, it is a renovated building dating from 1875. The 34 beds in the rooms and dormitories are rudimentary but comfortable, and the bathrooms are very clean. Brightly coloured walls, lots of space and a large common room and kitchenette with stone walls and old wooden floors complete the facilities. A blanket costs $2 per night, and guests have laundry machines at their disposal. Twenty-four hour access.

Even though Old Montréal is visited by thousands of tourists, it has little to offer in the way of accommodation. There is, however, set in the heart of the old city, the **Passants du Sans-Soucy** *($95 to $120 bkfst incl.; 9 rooms; 171 Rue Saint-Paul Ouest, ☎842-2634, ⁼842-2912, Métro Place d'Armes)*, an extremely pleasant inn whose charming rooms are furnished with antiques. Built in 1723, the building was renovated eight years ago. Reservations required.

The **Hôtel du Vieux-Port** *($110-$165; bkfst incl.; ≡, tv, ℝ, ⊚; 97 Rue de la Commune O., H2Y 1J1, ☎514-876-0081, ⁼876-8923)*, which stands right in front of the old Port, opened in 1996. This place is a real gem. It occupies an historic building dating from 1882, whose stone walls have been left exposed in the chic, attractively decorated lobby. All the rooms have been decorated in way that shows respect for the past, with outstanding results. Each has a telephone with voice mail. There is a French restaurant in the basement, where you can see a segment of the fortifications of the old city. No smoking in the rooms. Parking $7.50 per day.

Except for one of its wings, the **Hôtel Inter-Continental** *($139-$230 bkfst incl.; 357 rooms, ≈, ⊙, △, ℝ, 𝒫; 360 Rue Saint-Antoine Ouest, H2Y 3X4, ☎987-9900 or 1-800-327-0200, ⁼847-8550, www.interconti.com)*, located on the edge of Old Montréal, is a fairly new building (1991) that is linked to the Centre de Commerce Mondial (World Trade Centre) and several shops. The Palais des Congrès (convention centre) is right nearby. It has an original appearance, due to its turret with multiple windows, where the living rooms of the suites are located. The rooms are tastefully decorated with simple furniture. Each one is equipped with a spacious bathroom, among other nice touches. Guests are courteously and attentively welcomed. Business people will enjoy all the necessary services, such as computer hook-ups, fax machines and photocopiers.

Built in 1725, the **Maison Pierre-du-Calvet** *($165-$195 bkfst incl.; 6 rooms, pb, ℜ; 405 Rue Bonsecours, ☎282-1725, ⁼282-0456, Métro Champ-de-Mars)* is one of Montréal's oldest homes, discretely tucked away at the intersection of Bonsecours and Saint-Paul streets. It has recently been entirely renovated, as have many other older houses in the neighbourhood. The rooms and suites, each different from the next and each with its own fireplace, exude an irresistible charm, with lovely antique wood panelling accentuated by oriental rugs, stained glass and beautiful antiques; the ancestral yet refined setting gives visitors the illusion of travelling back in time. Moreover, the bathrooms are immaculately clean and tiled in Italian marble. A pretty indoor courtyard and day room allow guests to escape from the swarming crowds. Breakfast is served in a lovely Victorian dining room. The service is attentive and meticulous. In short, this inn, located in the heart of the city's historic district is a real gem, and will make your stay absolutely unforgettable.

Tour B: Downtown

The **Auberge de Jeunesse** *($18-$21 per person for members, $24-$40 per person for non-members; 1030 Rue Mackay, H3G 2H1, ☎843-3317 or 1-800-663-3317, ⁼934-3251)*, or youth hostel, located a stone's throw from the downtown area, is one of the least expensive places to sleep in Montréal. Two-hundred and fifty beds occupy rooms that can accommodate from four to ten people as well as fifteen private rooms. Breakfast is served in the café, which opened in 1996. Guests have access to a laundry room, a tv room, a pool table and a kitchen. Finally, a variety of reasonably priced activities and excursions are organized by the hostel; these can include anything from trips to a sugar-shack or guided tours of the city. This is a non-smoking hostel.

Ulysses' Favourites

A classic:
Le Reine-Élizabeth (p 141) and the Ritz-Carlton Kempinski (p 141).

For history buffs:
Hôtel de Vieux-Port (p 138) and Maison Pierre-du-Calvet (p 138).

For the reception:
Auberge de la Fontaine (p 143).

For business people:
Westin Mont-Royal (p 141), Loews Hôtel Vogue (p 141), Bonaventure Hilton (p 141), Hôtel Intercontinental (p 138), Novotel (p 140), Centre Sheraton (p 140), Marriott Château Champlain (p 141).

For the swimming pool:
Hôtel de la Montagne (p 140) and the Bonaventure Hilton (p 141).

During summer, it is possible to rent a room in one of the student residences of the city's universities. Comfort here is basic; the rooms are equipped with a single bed and a small chest of drawers, and all bathrooms are communal. Nevertheless, this is an economical way to stay in the city. Reservations are recommended. The student residences at the **Université de Montréal** *($23 per person, $33 for two people; mid-May to late Aug; 2350 Boulevard Édouard-Montpetit, H3T 1J4, ☎514-343-6531, ⁓343-2353)* stand at the foot of Mont Royal, in a quiet neighbourhood. They are located a few kilometres from downtown, which is easily accessible. Monthly and weekly stays are also possible.

The student residences of **Concordia University** *($32 per person, $38 for two people; 7141 Rue Sherbrooke Ouest, H4B 1R6; e-mail: foretim@vax2.concordia.com, ☎848-4757, ⁓848-4780)*, located 15 minutes by bus from the Vendôme Métro station, have 144 beds. Open from mid-May to mid-August. Weekly and monthly rentals available.

There is a total of about 1,100 rooms, each containing one or two beds, in the six residence halls of **McGill University** *($37 per person, $54 for two people; sb; 550 Rue Sherbrooke Ouest, West Tower, Suite 490, H3A 1B9, McGill Métro, ☎398-3637, ⁓398-4854, Reserve@Residences.lan.Mcgill.ca)* located on the side of the mountain. The rooms are small, but each has a large chest of drawers and a desk, and some offer magnificent views of Mont Royal. Most are equipped with a miniature refrigerator, and all the windows open. There are two kitchenettes and two large bathrooms on each floor. For an additional charge, guests can use the university pool, gym and tennis courts. Open May 15 to August 15.

The downtown **YMCA** *($40-$56; tv, ≈, ☉, △; 1450 Rue Stanley, H3A 2W6, Peel Métro, ☎849-8393, ⁓849-8017)*, the oldest YMCA in North America, was built in 1851 and has 331 basic but comfortable rooms with one or two beds each. Men, women and children are welcome. Most of the rooms are equipped with a telephone and a television; some have a sink or a bathroom. The cafeteria on the ground floor serves morning and evening meals *($3-$6)*. Guests enjoy free access to the YMCA's swimming pool, fully equipped gym and locker room. The Young Men's Christian Association (YMCA) was founded in London in 1844 for the purpose of helping young English workers.

Located near Place des Arts on Rue Sherbrooke, beside an abandoned lot, the **Casa Bella** *($42-$85, bkfst incl.; ≡, tv, ☎; 264 Rue Sherbrooke Ouest, H2X 1X9, ☎849-2777, ⁓849-3650)* is a charming hotel set in a hundred-year-old house. The rooms are pretty, and reflect the care that has gone into decorating them. There are free laundry service and free parking. The friendly welcome makes guests feel quickly at ease. This hotel offers good value for the money.

Manoir Ambrose *($45-$75, bkfst incl.; 22 rooms, sb or pb, tv, ☎; 3422 Rue Stanley,*

MONTRÉAL

H3A 1R8, ☎288-6922, ⊷288-5757, http://interresa.ca/hotel/mambrose.htm) is set in two big, beautiful Victorian houses made of hewn stone, side by side on a peaceful street. It has several little rooms, scattered all over the house. The outdated decor will amuse some guests, but the rooms are well-kept and the service is friendly. Laundry service for a fee ($5).

Located right next to the Molson Centre and not far from Old Montréal, the **Hôtel du Nouveau Forum** ($55 bkfst incl.; pb, ≡, tv; 1320 Rue Saint-Antoine Ouest, H3C 1C2, ☎514-989-0300, ⊷514-989-3090, e-mail: hdforum@globale.net) opened in June 1996, and has about 40 small, modest but decent rooms. It occupies an historic house, whose stone façade has been restored, and whose interior was completely redone. Fortunately, the friendly staff add a little warmth to the sterile atmosphere of the hallways and the dining room, where you can enjoy a very hearty breakfast. There is a public telephone on each floor, and guests can communicate with the reception desk by intercom. The rooms do not have bathtubs. Parking.

Novotel ($98-$180; ⊘, △, ⊛, ℜ; 1180 Rue de la Montagne, H3G 1Z1, ☎861-6000 or 1-800-668-6835, ⊷ 861-0992) is a French hotel chain. The pleasant rooms in its downtown Montréal hotel are equipped with numerous extras, including a large desk and outlets for computers. Special packages are available for guests travelling with children. The emphasis seems to be on security, as there is no access to the upper floors after 10pm without your room key.

Tourists and business people stay in the fully-equipped rooms of the **Hôtel du Parc** ($99-$180; 449 rooms, ℜ, ≈, ⊘; 3625 Avenue du Parc; H2X 3P8, ☎288-6666 or 1-800-363-0735, ⊷288-2469, http://www.duparc.com). The hotel has a new exercise centre, and guests have access to the pool at the Université de Montréal's athletic centre. There is a coffee maker in each room.

The **Delta Montréal** ($99-$235; 435 rooms, ≈, ⊘, ⊛, △, ℜ; 450 Rue Sherbrooke Ouest, H3A 2T4, ☎286-1986 or 1-800-463-1133, ⊷284-4342 or 284-4306, http://www.deltahotels.com/properties/montreal.html) is a recently built hotel with two entrances, one on Rue Sherbrooke and the other on Avenue du Président-Kennedy. Recent renovations included a new decor, new carpeting, new beds, new paint, etc. It has pleasant rooms, which are attractively decorated with dark wooden furniture. Each room has a voice mailbox.

The **Hôtel du Complexe Desjardins** ($99-$170, less expensive packages available on weekends with bkfst $129; 572 rooms, ≈, △, ⊘, ℜ; 4 Complexe Desjardins, H5B 1E5, ☎285-1450 or 1-800-361-8234, ⊷514-285-1243), formerly the Meridien, is part of Complexe Desjardins. Consequently, on the main floor, there is a series of shops, movie theatres and restaurants. Located a step away from Place des Arts and the Musée d'Art Contemporain, the hotel has a prime downtown location right next to all the action of the Jazz Festival along Rue Ste-Catherine. The large, comfortable rooms correspond with what one would expect from a hotel in this category.

Standing over 30 stories high, the **Centre Sheraton** ($119-$295; ≈, ⊘, ℜ; 1201 Boulevard René-Lévesque, H3B 2L7, ☎878-2000 or 1-800-325-3535, ⊷878-3958) has 824 rooms. A number of little extras (coffee maker, hair dryer, iron and ironing board, non-smoking floors) are evidence of the meticulous service provided here. Some rooms are equipped for businesspeople with fax machines, modem hook-ups, voice mailboxes, etc. The rooms are pretty without being luxurious. Take some time to admire the beautiful lobby, decorated with picture windows and tropical plants. Several renovations were completed in 1996.

Besides its 134 rooms spread over 19 floors, the **Hôtel de la Montagne** ($129-$195; ℜ, ≈, ≡; 1430 Rue de la Montagne, H3G 1Z5, ☎288-5656 or 1-800-361-6262, ⊷288-9658) also offers a pool, an excellent restaurant and a bar, as well as friendly and courteous staff. The pool is found outside, on the roof, and is only open in the summer.

Located between Old Montréal and downtown, the **Holiday Inn Select Centre-Ville** ($123 to $180; 235 rooms, ℜ, ≈, ⊛; 99 Avenue Viger Ouest, H2Z 1E9, ☎878-9888, 1-888-878-9888, ⊷878-6341, Métro Place d'Armes), built in 1992, offers all the comfort you'd expect from a superior quality hotel. It is located in the heart of Chinatown, and its oriental decor is its distinguishing feature. All of the rooms are spacious and spotlessly clean, and the staff is courteous and attentive. Partial wheelchair access. Indoor pool, exercise room, whirlpool, sauna and massage service are all available to guests.

The **Marriott Château-Champlain** *($110-$226; 611 rooms, ≈, ☉, ◊, ℜ, ⅋; 1 Place du Canada, H3B 4C9, ☎878-9000 or 1-800-228-9290, ≈878-6761, http://www.marriott.com/ marriott/cana-321.htm)* is a very original-looking white building with semicircular windows, much resembling a cheese-grater. Unfortunately, this renowned hotel has small rooms, which are less attractive than one might expect from an establishment in this class. Guests nevertheless enjoy a slew of services, including a masseuse. Direct access to the underground city (see p 158).

The **Marriott - Résidence Inn Montréal** *($125-$175; ☉, ≈, ≡, K, ℜ; 2045 Rue Peel, H3A 1T6, Peel Métro, ☎982-6064 or 1-800-999-9494, ≈844-8361)* was completely renovated before re-opening at the beginning of 1997. A library with a fireplace is available to guests. It has 189 suites, each with a kitchenette complete with stove, microwave oven, refrigerator and dishwasher. These may be rented for a single night or for months at a time. Twenty-four-hour laundry service, free parking, large outdoor terrace and a roof-top swimming pool are all available to guests.

The **Queen Elizabeth** *($149-$275; 1022 rooms, ≈, ℜ, ◊; 900 Boulevard René-Lévesque Ouest, H3B 4A5, www.cphotels.ca/qehindex.htm, ☎861-3511 or 1-800-441-1414, ≈954-2256)* is one Montréal hotel that has set itself apart over the years. Its lobby, decorated with fine wood panelling, is magnificent. Visitors will find a number of shops on the main floor. Two of the hotel's floors, designated "Entrée Or", boast luxurious suites and are like a hotel within the hotel. Numerous renovations were completed in 1996. The hotel has the advantage of being located in the heart of downtown, and its underground corridors, furthermore, provide easy access to the train station and the underground city.

The **Ritz Carlton Kempinski Montréal** *($205 to $235; ☉, ℜ; 1228 Rue Sherbrooke Ouest, H3G 1H6, ☎842-4212 or 1-800-363-0366, ≈842-4907, http://ritz-carlton-montreal.com)* was inaugurated in 1912. Renovated over the years in order to continue offering its clientele exceptional comfort, it has managed to preserve its original elegance. The rooms are decorated with superb antique furniture. The marble bathrooms, moreover, add to the charm of this outstanding establishment.

One of the most renowned hotels in Montréal, the **Westin Mont-Royal** *($195 to $275; 300 rooms, ≈, ☉, ◊, ℜ; 1050 Rue Sherbrooke Ouest, H3A 2R6, ☎514-284-1110 or 1-800-228-3000, ≈845-3025, www.westin.com/listings/text/montreal.html)* offers comfortable, spacious accommodations. Nevertheless, the standard rooms are decorated in an unoriginal fashion and the bathrooms are small for such a prestigious establishment. The lobby, however, is large and elegant, and the hotel is famous for its restaurants. The outdoor pool is heated and open year-round.

Guests of the **Bonaventure Hilton** *($214-$302; 367 rooms, ≈, ☉, tv, ℜ; 1 Place Bonaventure, H5A 1E4, ☎878-2332 or 1-800-267-2575, ≈878-3881 or 878-1442)*, located on the boundary between downtown and Old Montréal, enjoy a number of little extras that make this hotel a perfect place to relax; these include, among other things, a massage service. The rooms are decorated in a simple manner, without a hint of extravagance, and the bathrooms are small. The hotel has a heated outdoor swimming pool, where guests can swim all year round, as well as a lovely garden and access to the underground city (see p 158).

At first sight, the **Loews Hôtel Vogue** *($240-$285; 126 rooms, 16 suites, ≈, ⊛, ℜ; 1425 Rue de la Montagne, H3G 1Z3, ☎285-5555 or 1-800-465-6654, ≈849-8903, http://www.loewshotels.com/vogue.html)*, a glass and concrete building with no ornamentation, looks bare. The lobby, embellished with warm-coloured woodwork, gives a more accurate idea of the luxury and elegance of this establishment. The large rooms, with their elegant furniture, reveal how comfortable this hotel is. Each room has a whirlpool bath and two suites have a sauna.

Tour C: Village Shaughnessy

The **Hôtel du Fort** *($80-$300; K, ℜ, ☉; 1390 Rue du Fort, H3H 2R7, Atwater Métro, ☎938-8333 or 800-565-6333, ≈938-3123)* offers comfort, security and personalized service. All 127 rooms have a kitchenette equipped with a microwave oven, a refrigerator, a coffee maker, as well as a hair dryer and a mini-bar. The deluxe rooms and suites also have a modem hook-up. All the windows in the rooms open.

Manoir LeMoyne All Suite Hotel *($94-$110; 266 suites, ◉, ☺, ◌, ℜ, K; 2100 Boulevard de Maisonneuve Ouest, H3H 1K6, ☎931-8861 or 1-800-361-7191, ⋯931-7726)* is located on a busy street near downtown. A cold atmosphere pervades the lobby, which is decorated with mirrors and gilded chandeliers. The rooms, equipped with a kitchenette, are nevertheless decent.

Tour E: Maisonneuve

Despite it's location on busy Boulevard Pie IX, the **Gîte Olympique** *($65-$80; ℙ; 2752 Boulevard Pie IX, H1V 2E9, ☎254-5423 or 1-888-254-5423)* benefits from five tranquil rooms and stunning views of the Stade Olympique. Two rooms have been set up for guests to relax and converse with their fellow travellers. Along the back of the house, there is a large terrasse where breakfast is served in summer. The Pie IX metro station is just steps away, and major attractions in the eastern part of the city are nearby.

Tour G: Quartier Latin

In 1995, the Hôtel de Paris (see below) opened the **Auberge de l'Hôtel de Paris** *($16 per person; 901 Rue Sherbrooke Est, H2L 1L3, Sherbrooke Métro, ☎522-6861 or 1-800-567-7217, ⋯522-1387, http://interresa.ca/hotel/hotparis.htm)*, a house across the street with 10 big rooms and a 40-bed hostel divided into dormitories for four, eight or 14 people. Blanket, sheets and pillow are provided. The common kitchen is small but has everything you'll need to prepare meals, and there's an outdoor seating area with an attractive view. The place has four showers and toilets, and there's a laundromat right nearby. No curfew.

The **Manoir Sherbrooke** *($46-$99, bkfst incl.; 38 rooms; 157 Rue Sherbrooke Est, H2X 1C7, ☎285-0895 or 1-800-203-5485, ⋯284-1126)* is an old stone house. The rooms are modest, while the staff are polite and efficient.

The very simple façade of the **Château de l'Argoat** *($50-$120 bkfst incl.; 26 rooms, ◉, tv, ℙ, ≡, ☎, 524 Rue Sherbrooke Est, H2L 1K1, ☎842-2046, ⋯286-2791, Métro Sherbrooke)* is not at all luxurious, and the entrance is not very inviting. The rooms are decorated with old-fashioned furniture, which looks as if it came from another era. Nevertheless, the room where breakfast is served is adorable.

The **Hôtel de Paris** *($55-$95; ≡, tv, pb; 901 Rue Sherbrooke Est, H2L 1L3, Sherbrooke Métro, ☎522-6861 or 1-800-567-7217, ⋯522-1387, http://interresa.ca/hotel/hotparis.htm)*, a lovely house built in 1870, has 29 rooms. Recently renovated, the house has retained its distinctive character, thanks to the magnificent woodwork in the entryway. The rooms are comfortable. In 1995, the hotel annexed a house across the street, which has 10 larger dormitory rooms with hardwood floors, each equipped with a microwave oven (see above).

The **Hôtel de l'Institut** occupies the upper floors of the Institut de Tourisme et d'Hôtellerie du Québec (ITHQ) *($99-$140 bkfst incl.; ≡, ℜ; 3535 Rue Saint-Denis, H2X 3P1, Sherbrooke Métro, www.ithq.qc.ca, ☎282-5120 or 1-800-361-5111, ⋯873-9893)*, a renowned post-secondary college devoted to the tourism and hotel industries. The hotel is run by students enrolled in practical classes at the ITHQ or who are undergoing on-the-job training there. Their work is closely monitored by the professors charged with grooming them for the finest hotels in the world; the result is very comfortable rooms and quality service, including full concierge service. The hotel is located right on Rue Saint-Denis, with its scores of restaurant terraces, shops and cafés, and right near the pedestrian mall on Rue Prince-Arthur, which is packed with good restaurants. Parking is an additional $10.

The 320 spacious rooms of the **Holiday Inn Crowne Plaza Métro Centre** *($115-$129; ℜ, ☺, ≡, ◉, ≡, ◌, tv; 505 Rue Sherbrooke Est, H2L 1K2, Sherbrooke Métro, ☎842-8581 or 1-800-2CROWNE, ⋯842-8910, http://crowneplaza.com/hotels/yulrh)* have a modern decor and are all equipped with a coffee maker, colour television and two telephones. The hotel is located right near the Quartier Latin, steps away from numerous restaurants, bars and shops. It offers a large number of services for businesspeople, including voice mail and a secretarial service.

The **Hôtel des Gouverneurs Place Dupuis**
*($155; ≈, tv, △, ℜ, &; 1415 Rue Saint-Hubert,
H2L 2Y9, Berri-UQAM Métro, ☎842-4881 or
1-800-463-2820, ⌨842-1584)* has an elegant
lobby and 352 recently renovated rooms with
all the modern comforts. It is located right in
the heart of the Quartier Latin, a stone's throw
away from the outdoor cafés on Rue Saint-
Denis, and is linked to both Place Dupuis, with
its many shops, and the Université du Québec
à Montréal. Parking lot and direct underground
access (by way of the Métro) to points all over
the city.

Tour H: Plateau Mont-Royal

Unlike those in the university residences, the
rooms at **Vacances Canada 4 Saisons** *(Collège
Français)* *($11.50-$15.50; 550 beds in
summer, 220 in winter; ⊙; 5155 de Gaspé,
H2T 2A1, Laurier Métro; ☎495-2581,
⌨278-7508)* are available year-round. In
addition, studios with private bath and
kitchenette may be rented for $300 a month.

The **Gîte du Parc Lafontaine** *($19 shared
rooms, $45 double rooms, continental bkfst
incl.; 1250 Rue Sherbrooke Est, H2L 1M1,
☎522-3910)* is a sort of youth hostel that is
also a cosy inn for young travellers. Guests
have access to furnished rooms, a kitchen, a
living room and a small laundry room. The
hostel is ideally located next to Parc Lafontaine
and close to Rue Saint-Denis. The owners of
this hundred-year-old rooming house have built
a terrace with a magnificent view of Montreal's
central library.

The seventeen charming rooms of **Le Bed &
Breakfast Bienvenue** *($55-$85; sb or pb;
3950 Avenue Laval, H2W 2J2, ☎844-5897 or
1-800-227-5897, ⌨844-5894,
bbvenue@mlink.net)* have welcomed guests for
about 10 years now. A peaceful atmosphere
pervades the beautifully maintained house,
making it an ideal place to relax and meet
people. The B&B is particularly popular with
French tourists.

 The **Auberge de la Fontaine** *($109-$175
bkfst and parking included; 21 rooms, tv, pb;
1301 Rue Rachel Est, H2J 2K1, ☎597-0166,
⌨597-0496)* lies opposite lovely Parc
Lafontaine. Designed with a great deal of care,
it has a lot of style. A feeling of calm and
relaxation emanates from the rooms, all of

which are nicely decorated. Guests are offered
a complimentary snack during the day. All
these attractive features have made this a
popular place — so much so that it is best to
make reservations.

Near the Airports

Mirabel Airport

Directly accessible from Mirabel Airport, the
Château de l'Aéroport-Mirabel *($89-$115, suite
for $175; ⊙, ≈, △, ℜ; 12555 Rue Commerce,
A4, J7N 1E3, ☎476-1611 or 1-800-361-0924,
⌨476-0873, www.châteaumirabel.com)* was
built to accommodate travellers with early
morning flights. Unlike its downtown cousins,
this hotel's high season is from November to
May. A massage service is particularly
appreciated by nervous flyers. The rooms are
very functional and comfortable.

Dorval Airport

Entirely renovated in 1996, the rooms in the
Best Western Hôtel International *($79-$99; ⊙,
®, △, ≈, ℜ; 13000 Chemin Côte-de-Liesse,
☎514-631-4811 or 1-800-361-2254,
⌨631-7305)* are pleasant and affordable. The
hotel also offers an interesting service: after
passing the night here, guests can park their
car here for up to a month, free of charge.

The **Hilton International** *($158-$202, weekends
$109-$129, bkfst incl.; 482 rooms, ⊙, ®, ≈, △,
ℜ; 12505 Côte-de-Liesse, H9P 1B7,
☎631-2411 or 1-800-268-9275, ⌨631-0192)*
has pleasant rooms. Its main advantage is its
proximity to the airport.

✗ RESTAURANTS

Montréal's reputation as far as food is
concerned is enviable, to say the least; it is
also well-deserved. The culinary traditions of
countries around the world are represented
here by restaurants of all different sizes. The
best thing is that no matter what your budget,
a memorable meal is always possible! Find
those hidden treasures while you are exploring
a particular area!

MONTRÉAL

Tour A: Vieux-Montréal

The little café located on the ground floor of the **Maison Pierre-du-Calvet** *($; 405 Rue Bonsecours, ☎282-1725)* welcomes localshopkeepers as well as explorers in search of coffee, home-made soup or a sandwich.

For health food, **Bio Train** *($; 410 Rue Saint-Jacques, ☎842-9184)* is a favourite self-serve restaurant. At lunchtime, things move very quickly.

Only open in the summertime, the **Crémerie Saint-Vincent** *($; 153 Rue St-Paul Est, at the corner of Rue St-Vincent)* is one of the rare spots in Montreal to enjoy excellent maple-syrup soft ice cream. The menu lists a wide selection of ice cream flavours.

The sumptuous, modern, northern-Italian decor of the wine bistro **L'Altro** *($$; closed Sun; 205 Avenue Viger Ouest, ☎393-3456)* welcomes a clientele composed mainly of businesspeople and convention-goers. Wine has the place of honour, and there is a large variety of good vintages to choose from, by the glass or bottle. The Italian food is delicious.

The varied menu of the French restaurant **Bonaparte** *($$; 443 Rue Saint-François-Xavier, ☎844-4368)* always includes some delicious surprises. The tables on the mezzanine offer a lovely view of Old Montréal.

The unique **Café Electronique** *($$; 405 Rue St-Sulpice, corner Rue St-Paul, ☎849-1612)* allows everyone the chance to discover the joys of computing while at the same time sipping a coffee or having a bite to eat. You will obviously have to pay for your time on the computers. Expect to shell out about $5 for half an hour on the Internet or $4 to use the CD-ROM. Classes are offered to demystify accessing the Internet and CD-ROM.

Simple, no-fuss, yet delicious, Italian cuisine is what you will find at the **Café Parigi** *($$; 95 Rue de la Commune, ☎878-0031)*. Ligurian *focaccia* garnished with oh-so Mediterranean treats like ricotta, olives and pesto, as well as fresh pastas that also honour the boot will surely please. And finally the decor, a creative combination of many styles, but nevertheless very Italian.

The specialty of **Chez Delmo** *($$; close Sat noon and Sun; 211 Rue Notre-Dame Ouest, ☎849-4061)* is seafood and fish. The outstanding bouillabaisse is not to be missed. The first room, with its two long oyster bars, is the most pleasant one.

Le Petit Moulinsart *($$; closed Sat noon and Sun; 139 Rue St-Paul Ouest, ☎843-7432)* is a friendly Belgian bistro that could easily pass for a small museum devoted to the characters of the Tintin comic books by Georges Rémi, a.k.a. dit Hergé. All sorts of knick-knacks and posters related to the Tintin books decorate the walls, menus and tables of the establishment. Service is friendly, but slow. Besides the traditional dish of mussels and French fries, don't miss Colonel Sponz's sorbet and Capitaine Haddock's salad.

Stash's Café Bazar *($$; 200 Rue St-Paul Ouest, ☎845-6611)* was forced to move a street corner away from its original location in the shadow of Notre-Dame basilica after a terrible fire. With a simple decor, this charming little Polish restaurant is the ideal choice for delicious cheese-stuffed pirogues, sausage and sauerkraut. The vodka is also excellent.

Gibby's restaurant *($$$; closed at noon; 298 Place d'Youville, ☎282-1837)* is located in a lovely, renovated old stable and its menu offers generous servings of beef or veal steaks served at antique wooden tables set around a glowing fire and surrounded by low brick and stone walls. In the summer months, patrons can eat comfortably outdoors in a large inner courtyard. All in all, an extraordinary decor, which is reflected in the rather high prices. Vegetarians beware.

The attraction of the **Vieux Saint-Gabriel** *($$$; 426 Rue Saint-Gabriel, ☎878-3561)* lies above all in its enchanting decor reminiscent of the first years of New France; the restaurant is set in an old house that served as an inn in 1754 (see p 96). The French and Italian selections from the somewhat predictble menu are adequate.

Ideally located in Old Montréal and overlooking Place Jacques-Cartier, **Chez Queux** *($$$-$$$$; 158 Rue Saint-Paul, ☎866-5194)* serves classic French cuisine in the finest tradition. Refined service in a refined setting guarantee a positive culinary experience.

Claude Postel *($$$-$$$$; closed Sat noon and Sun; 443 Rue Saint-Vincent, ☎875-5067)*

Ulysses' Favourites

Montréal's finest tables:
> Claude Postel (p 144), Beaver Club (p 147), Nuances (p 149), Toqué (p 152) and Chez la Mère Michel (p 148).

For the decor:
> Eaton, le 9e (p 146)

For history buffs:
> Le Festin des Gouverneurs (p 149), Gibby's (p 144), Le Vieux Saint-Gabriel (p 144), Maison Pierre-du-Calvet (p 144, 145) and Maison George Stephen (p 147).

For the view:
> Club Lounge 737 (p 147) and Nuances (p 149)

For the terrace:
> Café Cherrier (p 151)

For the location:
> Hélène-de-Champlain (p 149)

For Quebec cuisine:
> Nuances (p 149) and Festin des Gouverneurs (p 149)

For the romantic atmosphere:
> Aux Baisers Volés (p 151)

To see and be seen:
> L'Express (p 152), le Continental (p 151) and Pizzedelic (p 151)

---

enjoys an established reputation in the old part of town. An extensive menu boasts some true triumphs of French cuisine that are rather pricey; the *table d'hôte* is just as tasty, and much more reasonable. The decor is simple and refined. The chef and owner also runs a pastry shop next door, so save some room for dessert.

Following a disagreement, the Filles du Roi restaurant closed its doors to reopen under the name **Maison Pierre-du-Calvet** *($$$$; closed Sun and Mon; 405 Rue Bonsecours, ☎282-1725)*. This jewel among Montréal restaurants has given way to a magnificent inn (see "Accommodations" chapter, p 138) boasting one of the best dining rooms in the city. The new establishment is to be particularly recommended for its delicious and imaginative French cuisine. Its menu, based on game, poultry, fish and beef, changes every two weeks. The elegant surroundings, antiques, ornamental plants and discrete service further add to the pleasure of an evening meal here.

Located on bustling Place Jacques-Cartier, **La Marée** *($$$$; closed Sat and Sun noon; 404 Place Jacques-Cartier, ☎861-9794)* has managed to maintain an excellent reputation over the years. The chef prepares fish and seafood to perfection. The dining room is spacious, so everyone is comfortable.

Tour B: Downtown

At the beginning of the century, a Lithuanian immigrant modified a recipe from his native country to suit the needs of workers, and thus introduced the smoked meat sandwich to Montréal, and in the process created **Ben's Delicatessen** *($; 900 Boulevard de Maisonneuve Ouest, ☎844-1000)*. Over the years, the restaurant has become a Montréal institution, attracting a motley crowd from 7am to 3:30am. The worn, Formica tables and photographs yellowed by time give the restaurant an austere appearance.

MONTRÉAL

🍴 **Le Commensal** *($; 1204 McGill College,* ☎*871-1480)* is a buffet-style restaurant. The food, all vegetarian, is sold by weight. Le Commensal is open every day until 11pm. The inviting modern decor and big windows looking out on the downtown streets make it a pleasant place to be. See also p 149, 150.

At lunchtime, the place to be is the **Grand Comptoir** *($; closed Sun and Mon evenings during the winter; 1225 Place Phillips,* ☎*393-3295)*, not for its decor, which is rather nondescript, but for the bistro menu at unbeatable prices.

Jazz musician Charlie Biddle's haunt, **Biddle's Jazz & Ribs** *($-$$; closed Sat and Sun noon; 2060 Rue Aylmer,* ☎*842-8656)* presents live music on a regular basis. Business people and hungry jazz fans come here to savour the delicious ribs and chicken wings, while enjoying music at just the right volume so as not to preclude conversation. It's terrasse allows you to take advantage of Montréal's short-lived summers.

L'Actuel *($$; closed Sun; 1194 Rue Peel,* ☎*866-1537)*, the most typically Belgian restaurant in Montréal, is always full for both lunch and dinner. It has two large, fairly noisy and very lively dining rooms, where affable waiters hurry about among the clientele of business people. The restaurant serves mussels, of course, as well as a number of other specialties.

Café du TNM *($$; 84 Rue Ste-Catherine Ouest,* ☎*866-8668)* is a wonderful addition to this somewhat rundown area. You can enjoy a simple drink, coffee or dessert in the deconstructionist decor on the ground floor or a good meal upstairs, where the atmosphere is like a Parisian *brasserie*. The menu goes with the decor: classic French bistro cuisine. Impeccable service, attractive presentation and flawless food, what more could you ask for?

🍴 The superb dining room at **Eaton, le 9ᵉ** *($$; 677 Rue Sainte-Catherine,* ☎*284-8421)* is worth a brief visit, if only to experience the sensation of stepping back into another era. The restaurant is open for lunch and, on Thursdays and Fridays, for dinner. it is located on the ninth floor. Unfortunately, the cuisine is nothing to rave about.

The **Élysée Mandarin** *($$; close Sat and Sun noon; 1221 Rue Mackay,* ☎*866-5975)* is definitely one of the most beautiful Chinese restaurants in Montréal, tastefully decorated in a style suited to the old Victorian residence it occupies. The *menu dégustation* enables guests to taste a number of house specialties, including Peking duck, shrimp with basil and frogs' legs, and also lists a wide range of appetizers. This is a good place to keep in mind for fine exotic cuisine.

The **Jardin du Ritz** *($$; 1228 Rue Sherbrooke Ouest,* ☎*842-4212)* is the perfect escape from the summer heat and the incessant downtown bustle. Classic French cuisine is featured on the menu, with tea served on a patio surrounded by flowers and greenery, next to the pond with its splashing ducks. Only open during the summer months, the Jardin is an extension of the hotel's other restaurant, Le Café de Paris (see p 147).

Made up of several large dining rooms, the restaurant **La Mère Tucker** *($$; 1175 Place du Frère André,* ☎*866-5525)* is ideal for families and large groups. The all-you-can-eat roast beef has developed a solid reputation with big eaters. The atmosphere is relaxed.

Moe's Deli & Bar *($$; 1050 Rue de la Montagne,* ☎*931-6637)* opened its doors on Rue de la Montagne just months before the new Molson Centre was inaugurated across the street and has since cashed in on the increased attention to the area. Smoked meat, burgers and the like have made the reputation of this chain of restaurants. This particular one could even be termed a "sports deli and bar".

For fans of *boudin, foie de veau* or mackerel in white wine, **Le Paris** *($$; closed Sun; 1812 Rue Sainte-Catherine Ouest,* ☎*937-4898)* is the place to enjoy such French delicacies in a friendly and relaxed ambiance. As for the decor, well, it hasn't changed in years, besides a fresh coat of paint (the same colour of course) when and where required! The wine list is, however, quite respectable and up to date.

Da Vinci *($$-$$$; closed Sun; 1180 Rue Bishop,* ☎*874-2001)* is an established family restaurant that caters to an upscale crowd (a crowd that incidentally often includes a few hockey stars, past and present). The menu is classic Italian and though you won't find too many surprises on it, everything served is well-prepared with the finest of ingredients. The extensive wine list contains just the bottle to complement any meal. Rich, subdued lighting and beautifully laid tables create a refined and inviting atmosphere.

Wienstein 'n' Gavino's Pasta Bar Factory Co. *($$-$$$; 1434 Rue Crescent, ☎288-2231)* occupies a brand-new building that visitors and locals alike might swear had been part of the streetscape for years. Each table receives a loaf of fresh French bread along with olive oil for dipping and roasted garlic for rubbing. The honour code is in place when it comes to the wine — you drink as much as want from the jug on the table and tell the waiter how many glasses you had when it is time to add up the bill. Among the menu offerings, the pizzas are respectable, if a little bland, but the pasta dishes are delicious, especially the Gorgonzola with dill. Red snapper in foil is another treat. Though the decor here might seem a bit plastic fantastic, this place is worth a try; you may just find yourself pleasantly surprised.

The **Café de Paris** *($$$; 1228 Sherbrooke Ouest, ☎842-4212)* is the renowned restaurant of the magnificent Ritz-Carlton Hotel (see p 141). Its sumptuous blue and ochre decor is refined and beautiful. The carefully thought-out menu offers delicious dishes.

The restaurant and bar of **Café Société** *($$$; 1415 Rue de la Montagne, ☎987-8168)*, located inside the very stylish Vogue Hôtel (see p 141), both have a remarkable, 1960s-style decor. The menu is composed of exquisite Eurasian dishes.

Le Caveau *($$$; closed Sat and Sun noon; 2063 Rue Victoria, ☎844-1624)* occupies a charming white house nestled against the downtown skyscrapers. The restaurant serves skilfully prepared, refined French cuisine.

Located on the 42nd floor of Place Ville-Marie, the **Club Lounge 737** restaurant *($$$; closed Sat and Sun noon; 1 Place Ville-Marie, ☎397-0737)* boasts large windows allowing for an unobstructed view of Montreal and its surroundings. It's buffet consists of a variety of French-inspired creations. Be warned that the prices here are as high as the restaurant is.

Julien *($$$; closed Sat and Sun; 1191 Rue Union, ☎871-1581)* is a Montreal classic, thanks largely to its *bavette à l'échalote* or steak with shallots, which is one of the best in the city. But it isn't just the *bavette* that attracts patrons, as each dish is more succulent than the last. For that matter, everything here

is impeccable, from the service to the decor and even the wine list.

At **Katsura** *($$$; 2170 Rue de la Montagne, ☎849-1172)*, located in the heart of downtown, visitors can savour refined Japanese cuisine. The main dining room is furnished with long tables, making this a perfect place for groups. Smaller, more intimate rooms are also available.

The chic Victorian decor on display at the Hotel de la Montagne's restaurant, **Le Lutétia** *($$$; 1430 Rue de la Montagne, ☎288-5656)* cannot fail to impress, nor can its menu, with all the classics of French cuisine: lamb chops, rib steak and filet mignon.

The **Maison George Stephen** *($$$; 1440 Rue Drummond, ☎849-7338)* houses the Mount Stephen Club, founded in 1884, which recently opened its restaurant to the public on Sundays, when it serves a musical brunch. The decor is from another time, with superb panelled walls adorned with 19th-century stained glass. You will have the privilege of treating both your palate and your ears to a feast, as classical music interpreted by Conservatory students wafts through the air.

In the former rectory of the Christ Church Cathedral, the **Parchemin** *($$$; closed Sun; 1333 Rue University, ☎844-1619)* is distinguished by its stylish decor and velvety atmosphere. Guests enjoy carefully prepared French cuisine, suitable for the finest of palates. For those with a well-lined purse, the six-course *ménu dégustation* is a real feast ($43 per person), while the four-course *table d'hôte*, with its wide range of choices, is also a treat.

Beautiful wood-panelling lend an atmosphere of refinement to the internationally renowned **Beaver Club** *($$$$; 900 Boulevard René-Lévesque Ouest, in the Queen Elizabeth Hotel, ☎861-3511)*, which elevates the hotel dining room to a whole new level. A changing *table d'hôte* can feature anything from fresh lobster to fine cuts of beef or wild game. Everything is prepared with the utmost attention to detail, right down to the exquisite presentation. Knowledgeable wine steward. There is music and dancing on Saturday evenings.

MONTREAL

148   Montréal

Cafés

The **Brûlerie Saint-Denis** *($; 2100 Rue Stanley, in the Maison Alcan,* ☎985-9159) serves the same delicious coffee blends, simple meals and sinful desserts as the other two Brûleries. Though the coffee is not roasted on the premises, it does come fresh from the roasters on Saint-Denis (see also p 150, 152).

The **Café Starbuck's** *($; 1171 Rue Ste-Catherine, Chapters bookstore, 2nd floor,* ☎843-4418) set in a corner of the downtown branch of Chapters has a lot going for it: excellent coffee – and books! What better way to pass the time before the shops open or after they close than to find a good book or magazine (the magazine section is right next to the café) and savour a good cup of Jo? A selection of cakes, muffins and pre-made sandwiches are also available.

Café Toman *($; 1421 Rue Mackay,* ☎844-1605) is popular among students from the neighbouring universities. The menu features delicious Czech specialties, including cakes, soups and salads. Unfortunately, the restaurant closes early (5pm) and is open on neither Sunday nor Monday.

The friendly **Second Cup** café franchise *($; 1465 Rue Crescent, corner Boulevard Maisonneuve)* is open 24 hours a day and offers an exceptional choice of coffees, pastries and desserts. **Second Cup** *($; 1616 Rue Sainte-Catherine Ouest, in the Faubourg Sainte-Catherine,* ☎939-3237) serves the same great coffee as the others, is open 24 hours a day and is completely non-smoking.

Besides a great selection of draught beers and Viennese breads, **Van Houtte** *($; 1255 Avenue McGill College,* ☎861-5260), offers a beautiful, comfortable decor. There is table service as well as, but the prices are a bit higher. The **Van Houtte** *($; Place des Arts)* at Place des Arts has a modern decor that is well adapted to its surroundings. It is the ideal spot to grab a bite to eat before the show. Croissants, coffees and muffins make up the menu.

Tour C: Village Shaughnessy

The **Bar-B-Barn** *($; 1201 Rue Guy,* ☎931-3811) serves sweet, delicious pork ribs cooked just right. The food is hardly refined, especially seeing as you have to eat it with your hands,

but it appeals to many Montrealers. Those planning to come here on the weekend should prepare to be patient, since there is often a long wait.

The **Pique Assiette** *($; 2051 Rue Sainte-Catherine Ouest,* ☎932-7141) has an Indian-style decor and a quiet atmosphere. The lunchtime Indian buffet is well worth the trip. The menu lists excellent curries and Tandoori specialties. Guests can have as much *nan* bread as they please. Anyone with a weak stomach should stay away, because the food is very spicy. English beer washes these dishes down nicely.

The **Rôtisserie Italienne** *($; closed Sun; 1933 Rue Sainte-Catherine Ouest,* ☎935-4436) is a self-serve restaurant where visitors can enjoy a quick, delicious plate of pasta. The place is pleasant, but the rustic decor lacks charm.

Le **Bistro Gourmet** *($$$; 2100 Rue Saint-Mathieu,* ☎846-1553) is a pleasant little French restaurant where visitors can savour delicious dishes, always prepared with fresh ingredients and carefully served.

Arguably one of Montreal's best restaurants, **Chez la Mère Michel** *($$$$; closed Sat noon, Sun, Mon noon; 1209 Rue Guy,* ☎934-0473) is the definition of fine French dining. Inside the lovely old house on Guy Street lie three exquisitely decorated, intimate dining rooms. At the front, banquettes and chairs covered in richly printed fabrics welcome patrons to their elegantly laid tables, while in the back a cosy fireplace and profusion of plants set the mood. Market-fresh ingredients are combined with excellence by Chef Micheline to create delightful French regional specialties as well as a changing five-course seasonal *table d'hôte*. The service is friendly and attentive. The impressive wine cellar boasts some of the finest bottles in the city.

Cafés

Calories *($; 4114 Rue Sainte-Catherine Ouest,* ☎933-8186), which welcomes a noisy clientele late into the night, features delicious cakes served in generous portions.

Tour D: Mount Royal and Westmount

The **Commensal** *($; 3715 Chemin Queen Mary, ☎733-9755)* is located in the building that housed a former wax museum. see also p 146 and p 150.

Upon entering **Pizzafiore** *($; 3518 Lacombe, ☎735-1555)*, visitors will see the cook standing beside the wood-burning oven in which the pizzas are baked. He makes pizza for every taste, with every different kind of sauce, topped with the widest range of ingredients imaginable. This pleasant restaurant is often filled with locals and people from the university.

The kitchen of the French restaurant **Aux Deux Gauloises** *($$; 5195 Chemin de la Côte-des-Neiges, ☎737-5755)* churns out a wide variety of crepes, each more delicious than the last. Pleasant ambience and friendly service.

A fairly recent addition to the restaurant scene in this area, the **Claremont** *($$; 5032 Rue Sherbrooke Ouest, ☎483-1557)* is a lively place, to say the least. A fine menu offers a wide range of choices from one of the best and freshest pestos around to a delicious and savoury mulligatawny soup. You might also prefer, as many here do, just to enjoy a drink and a platter of nachos with fresh salsa. The loud music rules this place out as a spot for a quiet dinner, but if you don't mind a little excitement, you won't be disappointed. The decor is enhanced by changing exhibits of works by local artists and photographers.

Mess Hall *($$; 4858 Rue Sherbrooke Ouest, ☎482-2167)* boasts a striking decor, the *pièce de résistance* being an exquisite starburst chandelier in the centre of the room. The menu is both original and standard with great salads, burgers and pasta dishes as well as a few more refined dishes. Westmount's young professionals come here to see and be seen.

The Italian bistro **La Transition** *($$; closed Mon; 4785 Rue Sherbrooke Ouest, ☎486-2742)* has been catering to a local clientele for over ten years. Pleasant lighting and the sounds of jazz create a relaxing atmosphere, which is unfortunately marred at times by fairly high noise levels. The menu is classic Italian with a few innovative touches.

Cafés

Franni *($; closed Mon; 5528 Rue Monkland, ☎486-2033)*, a café decorated with woodwork, ceramic tiles and plants, is unfortunately too small for its many customers who flock here for the delicious cheesecakes.

Tour F: Île Sainte-Hélène and Île Notre-Dame

Festin des Gouverneurs *($$$; ☎879-1141)*, recreates feasts like those prepared in New France at the beginning of colonization. Characters in period costumes and traditional Québec dishes bring patrons back in time to these celebrations. The restaurant only serves groups and reservations are necessary.

On Île Sainte-Hélène, the restaurant **Hélène-de-Champlain** *($$$; closed noon; ☎395-2424)* lies in an enchanting setting, without question one of the loveliest in Montréal. The large dining room, with its fireplace and view of the city and the river, is extremely pleasant. Each corner has its own unique charm, overlooking the ever-changing surrounding landscape. Though the restaurant does not serve the fanciest of gastronomic cuisine, the food is good. The service is courteous and attentive.

Ensconced on the fifth floor of Montréal's Casino, **Nuances** *($$$$; every day 5:30pm to 11pm; Casino de Montréal, Île Notre-Dame, ☎392-2708 or 1-800-665-2274, ext 4322)* is one of the best dining establishments in the city, perhaps even the country. Refined and imaginative cuisine is served in a decor rich in mahogany, brass, leather and views of the city's lights. Of particular note on the menu are the creamy lobster *brandade* in flaky pastry (*brandade crémeuse de homard en millefeuille*), brochette of grilled quail (*brochette de caille grillée*), roast cutlet of duck (*magret de canard rôti*), tenderloin of Québec lamb (*longe d'agneau du Québec*) or striped polenta with grilled tuna (*polenta rayée entourée d'une grillade mi-cuite de thon*). The delectable desserts are each presented exquisitely. The plush and classic ambiance of this award-winning restaurant is perfect for business meals and special occasions. The casino also has four less expensive restaurants: **Via Fortuna** *($$)*, an Italian restaurant, **L'Impair** *($)*, a buffet, **La**

MONTRÉAL

Bonne Carte *($$$)*, a buffet with *à la carte* service and **L'Entre-Mise** *($)*, a snack bar.

Tour G: Quartier Latin

Le Commensal *($; 1720 Saint-Denis, ☎845-2627)* just moved into its new location, the former Grand Café. See description p 146.

Tiny **La Paryse** *($; 302 Rue Ontario Est, ☎842-2040)* is often crowded with students, for a very simple reason: it serves delicious hamburgers and home-made French fries in generous portions.

All true lovers of Italian cuisine know and adore **Le Piémontais** *($$; closed Sun; 1145-A Rue de Bullion, ☎861-8122)*. The dining room is narrow and the tables are close together, making this place very noisy, but the soft, primarily pink decor, the kind, good humoured and efficient staff, and the works of culinary art on the menu make dining here an unforgettable experience.

La Sila *($$$-$$$$; closed Sat noon and Sun; 2040 Rue Saint-Denis, ☎844-5083)* serves traditional Italian cuisine in an elegant setting, which includes an inviting bar and an outdoor terrace for warm summer evenings. Fresh pastas cooked just right are topped with flawless sauces. The wine list boasts the finest Italian vintages. Free parking.

Cafés

The **Brioche Lyonnaise** *($; 1593 Rue Saint-Denis, ☎842-7017)* is a pastry shop and café offering an extremely wide selection of pastries, cakes and sweetmeats, all the more appealing because everything really is as delicious as it looks!

The **Brûlerie Saint-Denis** *($; 1587 Rue Saint-Denis, ☎286-9159)* see description p 152, 148.

Located near Rue Saint-Denis, **Le Pèlerin** *($; 330 Rue Ontario Est, ☎845-0909)* is a pleasant, unpretentious café. The wooden furniture, made to look like mahogany, and the works of modern art on exhibit create a friendly atmosphere, which attracts a diverse clientele. This is a perfect place to grab a bite and chat with a friend. The service is attentive and friendly.

Second Cup *($; 1551 Rue Saint-Denis, ☎285-4468)* is a café that serves sandwiches and coffee all day long. It is often full of students from the neighbouring university, who come to enjoy the relaxed and completely non-smoking atmosphere.

Tour H: Plateau Mont-Royal

L'Anecdote *($; 801 Rue Rachel Est, ☎526-7967)* serves hamburgers and vegetarian club sandwiches made with quality ingredients. The place has a 1950s-style decor, with movie posters and old Coke ads on the walls.

With its decor made up of four tables and a counter, the **Binerie Mont-Royal** *($; 367 Avenue Mont-Royal Est, ☎285-9078)* looks like a modest little neighbourhood restaurant. It is known for its specialty, baked beans (*fèves au lard* or "*binnes*") and also as the backdrop of Yves Beauchemin's novel, *Le Matou* (*The Alley Cat*).

The cozy decor of the **Bistro Méditerranéen** *($; 3857 Rue Saint-Denis, ☎843-5028)* conjures up images of Maghreb. The menu consists of North African specialties, such as couscous and kebabs. The food is good and the prices are unbeatable.

A small, very modest-looking restaurant whose walls are decorated with Persian handicrafts, **Byblos** *($; closed Mon; 1499 Rue Laurier est, ☎523-9396)* appears both simple and exotic. The light, refined dishes are marvels of Iranian cuisine. The service is attentive and guests are always greeted with a smile.

An aluminum structure decorated with neon lights, the **Galaxie Diner** *($; 4801 Rue Saint-Denis, ☎499-9711)* can seem somewhat surprising in this quiet neighbourhood. Admittedly, however, it does have a certain charm. People come to this 1950s-style diner for quick, simple food. Breakfast served.

The **Lélé da Cuca** *($; bring your own wine; 70 Rue Marie-Anne Est, ☎849-6649)* restaurant serves Mexican and Brazilian dishes. The cramped dining room can only accommodate about 30 people, but exudes a relaxed and laid-back ambience.

Piazzetta *($; 4097 Rue Saint-Denis, ☎847-0184)* serves pizza made in the true Italian style, with a thin, crisp crust. The *proscuitto* and melon salad is worth a try. And all this in beautiful surroundings.

Pizzédélic *($; 1250 Avenue Mont-Royal Est, ☎522-2286)* serves delicious thin-crust pizza with a delicious selection of toppings. The large windows open up in the summer to let in a nice breeze.

Aux Baisers Volés *($$; closed Sun and Mon; 371 Rue Villeneuve Est, ☎289-9921)*, which means stolen kisses, truly lives up to its name. This cosy little restaurant is the ideal place for an intimate tête-à-tête over simply prepared dishes.

L'Avenue *($$; 922 Avenue Mont-Royal Est, ☎523-8780)* has become a sanctuary for the beautiful people in search of hearty meals. Arrive early to avoid the line-up. The service is attentive and polite.

Bistro Saint-André *($$; 3807 Rue St-André, ☎525-1624)* servers bistro-style food in a pleasant environment.

Cactus *($$; 4461 Rue Saint-Denis, ☎849-0349)* prepares refined Mexican food. Though servings are small the ambiance is cosy and very pleasant. Unfortunately, the service isn't as friendly as before.The restaurant's little terrace is very popular during summer.

The meeting place of an entire contingent of thirty-something yuppies, the terrace and dining room at the **Café Cherrier** *($$; 3635 Rue Saint-Denis, ☎843-4308)* is always packed. The bustling French *brasserie* ambiance is enjoyable. The menu features respectable bistro-style cuisine. A brunch is served on weekends.

Chu Chai *($$; 4088 Rue St-Denis, ☎843-4194)* dares to be innovative and you have to congratulate them for it. So many restaurants are just like so many others! Here, the Thai vegetarian menu they've come up with is quite a pastiche: vegetarian shrimp, vegetarian fish and even vegetarian beef and pork. The resemblance to the real thing is so extraordinary that you will spend the evening wondering how they do it! The chef affirms that they really do consist of vegetable-based products like seitan, wheat, etc. The results are delicious and delight the mixed clientele that squeezes into the modest dining room or onto the terrace. They offer economical lunch specials.

The staging is very subtle at the **Continental** *($$; closed noon; 4169 Saint-Denis, ☎845-6842)*. Some evenings, the restaurant is positively charming, with its attentive, courteous staff, stylish clientele and updated 1950s-style decor. The varied menu includes a few surprises such as crispy oriental noodles. The cuisine is sublime at times and the presentation is always most carefully presented.

El Zaziummm *($$; 1276 Laurier Est, ☎598-0344; 4525 Avenue du Parc, ☎499-3675; 51 Rue Roy Est, ☎844-0893)* is unlike any other Mexican restaurant in Montréal. The decor is highly eccentric and includes, for example, an old bathtub used as a table and glass-top tables through which post cards and plane tickets half-buried in sand can be seen. The toilet paper rolls at each table and the countless knick-knacks placed haphazardly here and there confer an undeniable, though unusual, charm to the restaurant. The menu proposes a long list of typical Mexican dishes prepared in new and original ways. Unfortunatley, the service is one of the slowest in the city.

Fondue Mentale *($$; closed noon; 4325 Rue Saint-Denis ☎499-1446)* occupies an old house, which, with its superb woodwork, is typical of Plateau Mont-Royal. As the restaurant's name suggests, fondue is the specialty here — and what a choice, each one more appetizing than the last! The Swiss fondue with pink pepper is particularly delicious.

La Gaudriole *($$; 825 Rue Laurier Est, ☎276-1580)*. Although this somewhat cramped restaurant leaves something to be desired in terms of comfort, it offers excellent "cross-bred" food, recreating French cuisine that has drawn from sources throughout the world. The menu changes constantly, so the food is always fresh and clients can take advantage of chef Marc Vézina's creativity.

Misto *($$; 929 Avenue Mont-Royal Est, ☎526-5043)* is an Italian restaurant patronized by a hip clientele, who come here to savour delicious and imaginative Italian cooking. The decor features exposed brick walls and shades of green, and the noisy atmosphere and crowded tables only add to the ambience and the attentive and friendly service.

MONTRÉAL

Ouzeri *($$; 4690 Rue Saint-Denis, ☎845-1336)* set out on a mission to offer its clientele refined Mediterranean cuisine, and succeeded. The food is excellent, and the menu includes several surprises, such as vegetarian moussaka and scallops with melted cheese. With its high ceilings and long windows, this is a pleasant place, where you'll be tempted to linger on and on, especially when the Greek music sets your mind wandering.

Facing the Théâtre du Rideau Vert, the friendly little French restaurant **Persil Fou** *($$; closed Mon; 4669 Rue Saint-Denis, ☎284-3130)* boasts an excellent and well-priced *table d'hôte*.

Pistou's *($$; closed Sat and Sun noon; 1453 Rue Mont-Royal Est, ☎528-7242)* large, high-ceilinged dining room, with its modern decor, is certainly not cosy, not to mention that it is usually so packed that quiet conversation is virtually impossible. All this excitement does have its advantages, however, especially for a night out with friends, when conversation levels tend to be high. The menu lists some classics like salad with warm goat cheese and honey (*salade de chèvre chaud au miel*), absolutely delicious, and steak tartar. Another good choice is the daily *table d'hôte*.

🦞 Upon entering **Poco Piu** *($$; closed Sun and Mon; 4621 Rue Saint-Denis, ☎843-8928)* you will be seduced by the plush yet relaxed atmosphere. The choice of dishes will certainly satisfy, all the while allowing a delicious voyage through the wonders of Italian cuisine.

The blue and white decor and warm, island spirit of the service at **La Psarotaverna du Symposium** *($$; closed Sat and Sun noon; 4293 Rue Saint-Denis, ☎842-0867)* transports guests instantly to the Aegean Sea. Fish (sea bream) and seafood are the specialties here. Try the delicious moussaka and *saganaki*. For dessert, make sure to sample the delicious, milk-based *galatoboureco*.

La Raclette *($$; 1059 Rue Gilford, ☎524-8118)* is a popular neighbourhood restaurant on warm summer evenings, thanks to its attractive terrace. Menu choices like raclette (of course), salmon with *Meaux* mustard and cherry clafoutis are some other draws. Those with a big appetite can opt for the *menu dégustation*, which includes appetizer, soup, main dish, dessert and coffee.

🦞 The yuppie gathering place during the mid-eighties, **L'Express** *($$-$$$; 3927 Rue Saint-Denis, ☎845-5333)* is still highly rated for its dining-car decor, lively Parisian bistro atmosphere, which few restaurants have managed to recreate, and consistently appealing menu. Over the years, this restaurant has developed a solid reputation.

A pleasant bistro decorated with woodwork and mirrors, **Le Flambard** *($$; 5064 Avenue Papineau, ☎596-1280)* excels in the preparation of quality French cuisine. Though the place is charming, the narrow dining room and closely set tables offer little room for intimacy.

Set up inside a superb residence, **Laloux** *($$-$$; closed noon; 250 Avenue des Pins Est, ☎287-9127)* resembles a chic and elegant Parisian-style bistro. People come here to enjoy nouvelle cuisine of consistently high quality. A reasonably priced *menu théâtre,* which includes three light courses is offered.

🦞 If you're looking for a new culinary experience, **Toqué** *($$$; 3842 Rue Saint-Denis, ☎499-2084)* is without a doubt the address to remember when in Montréal. The chef, Normand Laprise, insists on having the freshest ingredients and oversees the kitchen, where dishes are always prepared with great care, and beautifully presented. Not to mention the desserts, which are veritable modern sculptures. The service is exceptional, the wine list good, the new decor elegant, and the high prices do not seem to deter anyone. One of the most original dining establishments in Montréal.

Cafés

Typical Plateau wildlife hang out at the charming small café **Aux 2 Marie** *($; 4329 Rue Saint-Denis, ☎844-7246)*. Besides an impressive selection of coffees roasted on the premises, they also serve excellent and unpretentious meals at affordable prices. The new terrace upstairs is quite pleasant in the summer. Slow service.

The **Brûlerie Saint-Denis** *($; 3967 Rue Saint-Denis, ☎286-9158)* imports its coffees from all over the world and offers one of the widest selections in Montréal. The coffee is roasted on the premises, filling the place with a very distinctive aroma. The menu offers light meals and desserts. See also p 148, 150.

Café El Dorado *(921 Avenue du Mont-Royal Est, ☎278-3333)*, where the Plateau's new trendy crowd hangs out for a coffee or a quick simple meal, boasts a decor of curves. The El Dorado's desserts deserve particular recognition.

At the charming **Le Daphnée** tea room *($; closed Mon; 3803 Rue Saint-Denis, ☎849-3042)*, visitors can enjoy dainty little treats of the sweet or salty variety. During summer, the balcony offers a choice view of Rue Saint-Denis. The staff is sometimes a bit pretentious.

The **Porté Disparu** *($; 957 Avenue Mont-Royal Est, ☎524-0271)* is a friendly café-bistro that welcomes a clientele of intellectuals intent on conversation into opulent surroundings, where they can also sit and read books off the shelves for hours on end. Besides shows on the weekends, Monday nights are animated by poetry readings that range from the conventional to the humorous.

The **Second Cup** café franchise *($; 4287 Rue Saint-Denis, ☎289-9501)* offers an interesting choice of coffees 24 hours a day. Muffins and croissants are also available at any hour. Warm ambiance and lively terrasse.

  ENTERTAINMENT

Bars and Nightclubs

From sundown until early morning, Montréal is alive with the sometimes boisterous, other times more romantic rhythm of its bars. Crowded with people of all ages, there are bars designed to suit everyone's tastes, from the sidewalk bars along Rue Saint-Denis to the underground bars of Boulevard Saint-Laurent; from the most fashionable bars on Rue Crescent to the gay bars in the "Village"; there are whole other worlds to discover.

L'Air du Temps *(194 Rue Saint-Paul Ouest)* ranks among the most famous jazz bars in Montréal. Set in the heart of Old Montréal, it

has a fantastic interior decorated with scores of antiques. As the place is often packed, it is necessary to arrive early to get a good seat. The cover charge varies according to the show. Call for information on upcoming acts.

Next door to Disalvio's, the private salons and velvet curtains of the **Allegra** *(3523A Boulevard Saint-Laurent)* are a veritable haven for those who prefer a quiet evening with a vintage cigar, available here for anywhere between $3 and $30. Jean- and sneaker-clad wanna-bes will be turned away.

Dark, smoky, jam-packed, hot, hectic and noisy, **Le Balattou** *(4372 Boulevard Saint-Laurent)* is without a doubt the most popular African nightclub in Montréal. On weekends, the cover charge is $7 (including one drink). Shows are presented only during the week, when the cost of admission varies.

A bar with a modest decor, **Les Beaux Esprits** *(2073 Rue Saint-Denis)* presents good jazz and blues shows.

A clientele composed mainly of junior executives crowds into the **Belmont sur le Boulevard** *(4483 Boulevard Saint-Laurent)*. On weekends, the place is literally overrun with customers. Cover charge: 3$ Thursdays, 4$ Fridays and Saturdays.

Obliged to move from its location in front of the Université de Montréal, **Café Campus** *(57 Prince Arthur)* has settled into a large place on Rue Prince Arthur. Over the years, it had become a Montréal institution, and had to prove itself all over again. The decor is still quite plain. Good musicians frequently give shows here.

Le Cheval Blanc *(809 Rue Ontario Est)* is a Montréal tavern that does not appear to have been renovated since the 1940s; hence its unique style! A few beers are brewed on the premises, and vary depending on the season.

Di Salvio's *(3519 Boulevard Saint-Laurent)* art deco interior and fifties-style furniture create a unique and original setting. Patrons lucky enough to get picked from the line-up (it can be difficult to get in) dance to acid-jazz music.

MONTRÉAL

The **Dogue** *(4177 Rue Saint-Denis)* is the ideal place to dance, dance, dance. The music, which ranges from Elvis classics to the latest Rage Against the Machine hit, gratifies a rather young, high-spirited crowd thirsting for cheap beer. There are two pool tables, which are a bit in the way, but keep the pool sharks entertained. The place is jam-packed seven days a week, so you are strongly advised to get there early.

Les Foufs *(87 Rue Sainte-Catherine Est)* is a fantastic, one-of-a-kind bar-discotheque pick-up joint. The best bar in Québec for dancing to alternative music, it attracts a motley crowd of young Montrealers, ranging from punks to medical students. The decor, consisting of graffiti and strange sculptures, is wacky, to say the least. Don't come here for a quiet night.

Discreetly tucked away south of Rue Sainte-Catherine among the innumerable Crescent street restaurants and bars, **Hurley's Irish Pub** *(1225 Rue Crescent)* succeeds in recreating an atmosphere worthy of the most traditional of Irish pubs, thanks largely to the excellent amateur Irish folk musicians and the world-famous Guinnessstout.

The **Île Noire** *(342 Rue Ontario Est)* is a beautiful bar in the purest Scottish tradition. The abundance of precious wood used for the decor gives the place a cosy charm and sophisticated atmosphere. The learned staff guide guests through the impressive list of whiskeys. The bar also has a good selection of imported draught beer. Unfortunately, the prices are high.

The **Jello Bar**'s *(151 Rue Ontario Est)* premises are strewn with an unusual mix of furniture and knick-knacks straight out of the suburban living rooms of the sixties and seventies. The bar serves a selection of 32 different martini cocktails to be sipped to the mellow sounds of jazz or blues. Great musical acts are regularly booked.

The **Loft**'s *(1405 Boulevard Saint-Laurent)* austere techno interior, accented in mauve, and alternative music attract a varied clientele between the ages of 18 and 30. Interesting exhibits are occasionally presented. Pool tables provide some diversion, and the roof-top terrace is pleasant.

Right opposite Square Saint-Louis, the **P'tit Bar** *(3451 Rue Saint-Denis)* is the perfect place to discuss literature, philosophy, photography, etc. The former hangout of the late lamented Gérald Godin, a celebrated Québec poet, this place will appeal to fans of French music. Photo exhibits make up the sober decor.

Le Pub... de Londres à Berlin *(4557 Rue Saint-Denis)* has a somewhat austere decor with the added bonus of popcorn and a wide selection of draught beers.

The **Pub le Vieux-Dublin** *(1219 A Rue University)* is an Irish pub with live Celtic music and an impressive selection of draught beer.

The **Quartier Latin Pub** *(318 Rue Ontario Est)* serves a variety of draught and bottled beers. Decorated with photographs of Montréal, this pub is a pleasant place to kick back and relax to the sounds of acid-jazz and soul. A thirty-something clientele comes here to chat about business, music, etc. The place was completely renovated in the summer of 1996, and its elegant new look is sure to please even the most sophisticated visitors.

The **Saint-Sulpice** *(1682 Rue Saint-Denis)* occupies all three floors of an old house and is tastefully decorated. Its front and back terraces are perfect places to make the most of summer evenings.

Le Sherlock *(1010 Rue Sainte-Catherine Ouest)* has a very lovely decor, reminiscent of an English pub, including busts of Sherlock Holmes. It also has the advantage of being very big and very popular! Everything, however, is quite expensive, and the restaurant is not recommended. About 15 pool tables are also at the disposal of customers.

The **Sir Winston Churchill Pub** *(1455 Rue Crescent)*, an English-style bistro, attracts crowds of singles, who come here to cruise and meet people. It has pool tables and a small dance floor.

The entrance to **Swimming** *(3643 Boulevard Saint-Laurent)* leads through the dilapidated vestibule of a building dating back to the beginning of the century, making the view from the third floor of this gigantic pool room even more striking. The large rectangular bar and endless rows of pool tables and players are surrounded by glazed concrete columns, deliberately emphasized and topped by strange polyhedrons. The old tin ceiling is a reminder of both the industrial city of the early 20th century and the building's original purpose.

Thursday's *(1449 Rue Crescent)* bar is very popular, especially among the city's English-speaking population. It is a favourite meeting place for business people and professionals.

Located in the heart of downtown Montréal, **Upstairs** *(1254 Rue Mackay)* hosts jazz and blues shows seven days a week. During summer, the walled terrace behind the bar is a wonderful place to take in the sunset.

The **Whisky Café** *(5800 Boulevard Saint-Laurent)* has been so conscientiously decorated that even the men's bathrooms are on their way to becoming a tourist attraction. The warm colours used in a modern setting, the tall columns covered with woodwork and pre-1950s-style chairs all create a sense of comfort and elegance. The well-off, well-bred clientele consists of a gilded youth between the ages of 20 and 35.

Looking for a good place to talk about everything and nothing while enjoying a *picon bière*? The **Zinc Café Bar Montréal** *(1148 Avenue Mont-Royal Est)* is an inviting place that serves a variety of unusual drinks.

Gay and Lesbian Bars

The **Cabaret l'Entre-Peau** *(1115 Rue Sainte-Catherine Est,* ☎*525-7566)* puts on transvestite shows. The place attracts a lively, mixed clientele.

The **O'Side** *(4075 A Rue Saint-Denis,* ☎*849-7126)* is for women only (men will be politely turned away at the door). The atmosphere is relaxed, making this a good place for a drink and some conversation. There are pool tables.

Sisters *(1450 Rue Sainte-Catherine Est,* ☎*523-0064)* is for lesbians. The latest mainstream hits get things moving and shaking on the dance floor.

With its four dance floors that each play a different type of music: alternative, commercial, techno, retro, etc., the two-storey **Sky Pub** *(1474 Rue Sainte-Catherine Est,* ☎*529-6969)*, is the biggest gay club in Montreal. Obviously, in such an immense place, there is more than one atmosphere. The crowd is mostly young. The only disappointment is that the cover charge frequently changes.

La Track *(1584 Rue Sainte-Catherine Est)* is a lively men's gay bar.

Theatres

Montréal has a distinct cultural scene. All year round, there are shows and exhibitions, which enable Montrealers to discover different aspects of the arts. Accordingly, shows and films from all over the world, exhibitions of art of all different styles, and festivals for all tastes and ages are presented here. The free weekly newspapers *Voir*, *The Mirror* and *Hour* summarize the main events taking place in Montréal.

Prices vary greatly from one theatre to the next. Most of the time, however, there are student rates.

Club Soda *(5240 Avenue du Parc,* ☎*270-7848)*, presents great shows, particularly during the Just for Laughs Festival and the Jazz Festival. During the latter festival, the shows are free after 11pm.

Place des Arts *(260 Boulevard de Maisonneuve Ouest,* ☎*285-4200, box office* ☎*842-2112, Métro Place-des-Arts)*.The complex contains five theatres: Salle Wilfrid-Pelletier, Théâtre Maisonneuve, Théâtre Jean-Duceppe, Théâtre du Café de la Place and the Cinquième Salle, opened in 1992. The **Orchestre Symphonique de Montréal** *(for subscription information call* ☎*849-0269, otherwise call the Place des Arts box office)* and **Grands Ballets Canadiens** *(for subscription information call* ☎*842-9951, otherwise call the Place des Arts box office)* both perform in this venerable hall.

Centaur Theatre *(453 Rue Saint-François,* ☎*288-3161)* presents musicals.

Saidye Bronfman Centre *(5170 Côte Sainte-Catherine,* ☎*739-7944)* exhibits artworks by local and internationally renowned names and hosts theatrical performances such as Yiddish plays. Fine-arts courses are also given, and there is a drama camp for children in summer.

Théâtre Saint-Denis *(1594 Rue Saint-Denis,* ☎*849-4211 Métro Berri-UQAM)*

Shows at the **Spectrum** *(318 Rue Sainte-Catherine Ouest,* ☎*861-5851, Métro Place-des-Arts)* usually begin around 11pm. Count on at least $10 to get in. As with Club

MONTRÉAL

Soda, shows after 11pm are usually free during the Festival de Jazz.

Théâtre du Nouveau Monde *(84, rue Ste-Catherine Ouest, ☎861-0563)*. See p 109, 146

Ticket Sales

There are three major ticket agencies in Montréal, which sell tickets for shows, concerts and other events over the telephone. Service charges, which vary according to the show, are added to the price of the ticket. Credit cards are accepted.

Admission
☎(514) 790-1245
☎1-800-361-4595

Telspec
☎(514) 790-2222

Billetterie Articulée (an *Admission* ticket outlet)
☎(514) 844-2172

Information on the Arts

Info-Arts (Bell): ☎790-ARTS. This service's operators provide information on current cultural and artistic events in the city.

Movie Theatres

Montréal has many movie theatres; here is a list of the major downtown theatres. Special rates are offered on Tuesdays and for matinees. The regular price of a ticket is $8 (except at repertory theatres).

The following show films in French:

Berri *(1280 Rue Berri, ☎849-3456, Métro Berri-UQAM)*.

Complexe Desjardins *(Rue Sainte-Catherine Ouest, between Jeanne-Mance and Saint-Urbain, ☎849-3456, Métro Place-des-Arts)*.

Le Parisien *(480 Rue Sainte-Catherine Ouest, ☎866-3856, Métro McGill)*.

Quartier Latin *(350 Rue Émery, ☎849-4422)*.

The following show films in English:

Égyptien *(Cours Mont-Royal, 1455 Rue Peel, ☎849-3456, Métro Peel)*.

Loews *(954 Rue Sainte-Catherine Ouest, ☎861-7437, Métro Peel)*.

Palace *(698 Rue Sainte-Catherine Ouest, ☎866-6991, Métro McGill)*.

The following are repertory theatres:

La Cinémathèque Québécoise *(335 Boulevard de Maisonneuve Est, ☎842-9763, Métro Berri-UQAM)* is a French theatre that is the most technologically advanced for the projection quality is always outstanding. Repertory and art films are shown here.

Le Cinéma Parallèle *(3682 Boulevard Saint-Laurent, ☎843-6001)*, shows films in French and English.

Impérial *(1430 Rue de Bleury, ☎848-0300, Métro Place-des-Arts)*. This is the oldest movie theatre in Montréal.

Cinéma du Parc *(3575 Avenue du Parc, ☎287-7272, Métro Place-des-Arts, bus 80)* shows English-language films or films dubbed or subtitled in English.

Office National du Film (National Film Board) *(1564 Rue Saint-Denis, ☎496-6301)*. A *cinérobothèque* allows several people to watch NFB films at once. A robot, the only one like it in the world, loads each machine. The complex is dedicated to Québec and Canadian cinema.

You can also see large-screen productions at:

Le Cinéma Imax *(Vieux-Port de Montréal, Rue de la Commune corner Boulevard Saint-Laurent, ☎496-4629)*. Films are presented on a giant screen (see p 96).

Festivals and Cultural Events

During summer, festival fever takes hold of Montréal. From May to September, the city hosts a whole series of festivals, each with a different theme. One thing is for certain—there is something for everyone. As the summer season draws to a close, these events become less frequent.

The **Tour de l'Île** takes place in early June. The event can accommodate a maximum of 45,000 cyclists, who ride together for some 65 km around the island of Montréal. Registration begins in April, and costs $21 for adults and half-price for children under 11 and senior citizens. Registration forms are available at Canadian Tire stores (in Québec) and from *Tour de l'Île de Montréal*, 1251 Rue Rachel Est, H2J 2J9, ☎514-847-8356).

June is marked by an international event that captivates a large number of fans from all over North America—the **Grand Prix Players du Canada** *(to reserve seats, call ☎514-392-0000)*, which takes place at the Circuit Gilles Villeneuve on l'Île Notre-Dame during the second week of June. This is without question one of the most popular events of the summer. During these three days, it is possible to attend a variety of car races, including the roaring, spectacular Formula One competition.

In 1998, the **Concours International d'Art Pyrotechnique** (International Fireworks Competition) *(☎872-6222)* starts in mid-June and runs until mid-July. The world's top pyrotechnists present high-quality pyro-musical shows every Saturday in June and every Sunday in July. Montrealers crowd to the La Ronde amusement park *(tickets cost $28, $29 or $30; call ☎790-1245)*, on the Pont Jacques-Cartier or alongside the river (both at no cost) to admire the spectacular blossoms of flame that colour the sky above the city for over half an hour.

During the **Festival International de Jazz de Montréal** *(☎871-1881)*, hundreds of shows set to the rhythm of jazz and its variations are presented on stages erected around Place des Arts. From late June to the second week in July, this part of the city and a fair number of theatres are buzzing with activity. The event offers people an opportunity to take to the streets and be carried away by the festive atmosphere of the fantastic, free outdoor shows that attract Montrealers and visitors in large numbers. You have to pay for indoor shows, except for late night performances at the Spectrum or at Club Soda.

Humour and creativity are highlighted during the **Festival Juste pour Rire - Just for Laughs Festival** *(☎845-3155 or 790-HAHA)*, held the last two weeks of July. Theatres host

comedians from a variety of countries for the occasion. Théâtre Saint-Denis presents shows consisting of short performances by a number of different comedians. Given the growing numbers of spectators, all outdoor activities will now take place at the Vieux-Port. Outdoor shows will take place on Quai Jacques-Cartier and the two small islands adjacent. An admission fee of $2 for adults and $1 for children will be charged to help finance the festival.

The **FrancoFolies** *(☎871-1881)* are organized to promote French-language music and song. During the last two weeks of June, all francophone countries (Europe, Africa, French Antilles, Québec and French Canada) give shows, providing spectators with a unique glimpse of the world's French musical talent.

During the last week of August, the **Festival International des Films du Monde** (World Film Festival) *(☎848-3883)* is held in various Montréal movie theatres. During this competition, films from different countries are presented to Montréal audiences. At the end of the competition, prizes are awarded to the most praiseworthy films. The most prestigious category is the *Grand Prix des Amériques*. During the festival, films are shown from 9am to midnight, to the delight of movie-goers across the city.

Winter's cold does not preclude the festival spirit, it merely provides an opportunity to organize another festival in Montréal, this time to celebrate the pleasures and activities of this frosty season. The **Fête des Neiges** takes place on Île Notre-Dame, from the late January to mid-February. Skating rinks and giant toboggans are available for the enjoyment of Montréal families. The ice-sculpture competition also attracts a number of curious onlookers.

Spectator Sports

Sports enthusiasts will be pleased to learn that Montreal hosts professional hockey and baseball games as well as international sporting events.

The **Centre Molson** *(1250 Rue de la Gauchetière, ☎989-2841)*. In the fall, the hockey games of the famous Montreal Canadiens hockey team start in the new Centre Molson. There are 42 games during the regular season. The play-offs follow, at the end of which the winning team walks away with the legendary Stanley Cup.

Spring signals the beginning of baseball season at the **Stade Olympique** *(4141 Avenue Pierre-de-Courbertin, ☎846-3976)*.The Expos play against the various teams of the National Baseball League at the Olympic Stadium.

Casino

With 2,700 slot machines and one hundred gaming tables (blackjack, roulette, baccarat, poker, etc.), the **Casino de Montréal** *(free admission, every day 9am to 5am, Métro île Sainte-Hélène and Bus 167, ☎392-2746)* is without a doubt a major player in the city's nightlife. Following the addition of a new wing in 1996 in the former Québec pavilion, the casino is now one of the 10 biggest casinos in the world in terms of its gaming equipment. A cabaret show, also added in 1996, has seen the likes of Liza Minelli, André-Philippe Gagnon and Jean-Pierre Ferland to name but a few, and has brought a new vitality to the place.

 SHOPPING

Whether it be original Québec creations or imported articles, Montréal's shops sell all sorts of merchandise, each item more interesting than the last. To assist visitors in their shopping, we have prepared a list of shops with exceptionally high-quality, original or inexpensive products.

"En vente" and *"en solde"* both mean on sale, therefore the price is reduced.

The Underground City

The 1962 construction of Place Ville-Marie, with its underground shopping mall, marked the origins of what is known today as the underground city. The development of this "city under the city" was accelerated by the construction of the Métro, which opened in 1966. Soon, most downtown businesses and office buildings, as well as a few hotels, were strategically linked to the underground pedestrian network and, by extension, to the Métro.

Today, the underground city, now the largest in the world, has five distinct sections. The first lies at the very heart of the Métro system, around the Berri-UQAM station, and is connected to the buildings of the Université du Québec à Montréal (UQAM), the Galeries Dupuis and the bus station. The second stretches between the Place-des-Arts and Place-d'Armes stations, and is linked to Place des Arts, the Musée d'Art Contemporain, Complexe Desjardins, Complexe Guy Favreau and the Palais des Congrès, forming an exceptional cultural ensemble. The third, at the Square-Victoria station, serves the business centre. The fourth, which is the busiest and most important one, is identified with the McGill, Peel and Bonaventure stations. It encompasses the La Baie and Eaton department stores; the Promenades de la Cathédrale, Place Montréal Trust and Cours Mont-Royal shopping centres, as well as Place Bonaventure, 1000 de la Gauchetière, the train station and Place Ville-Marie. The fifth and final area is located in the commercial section around the Atwater station; it is linked to Westmount Square, Collège Dawson and Place Alexis Nihon (see detailed map of underground city).

Shopping Centres and Department Stores

Several downtown shopping centres and department stores offer a good selection of clothing by well-known fashion designers, including Jean-Claude Chacok, Cacharel, Guy Laroche, Lily Simon, Adrienne Vittadini, Mondi, Ralph Lauren and many others.

Holt Renfrew
1300 Rue Sherbrooke Ouest, ☎842-5111

Ogilvy
1307 Rue Sainte-Catherine Ouest, ☎842-7711

Place Montréal Trust
1600 Avenue McGill College, ☎843-8000

Place Ville-Marie
5 Place Ville-Marie, ☎861-9393

Westmount Square
4 Westmount Square, ☎932-0211

The Bay
Square Phillips (on Rue Sainte-Catherine Ouest), ☎281-4422

Eaton
677 Rue Sainte-Catherine Ouest, ☎284-8411

Québec Designs

The boutique **Revenge** *(3852 Rue Saint-Denis, ☎843-4379)* promotes the top creations of Québécois couturiers. The store always has the new lines of high-quality fashion. If you like clothing that's a little different, you will find it here.

Hats

For hats, **Chapofolie** *(3944 Rue Saint-Denis, ☎982-0036)* offers a great selection that will satisfy all tastes.

Fur

Mink, leopard, muskrat, silver fox...**Desjardins Fourrure** *(325 Boulevard René-Lévesque Est, ☎288-4151)* and **McComber** *(440 Boulevard de Maisonneuve Ouest, ☎845-1167)* count among Montreal's most elegant fur boutiques.

Jeans

Paris-Texas *(4201B Rue St-Denis, ☎281-6686)* sells jeans and an interesting collection of suede and leather jackets.

Sports and Outdoor Gear

Those who are going on an expedition in the great outdoors should make their first stop at **La Cordée** *(2159 Rue Sainte-Catherine Est, ☎524-1106)*.

For warm, fashionable clothing that is perfectly suited to the outdoors, see the creations at **Kanuk** *(485 Rue Rachel, ☎527-4494)*

Bookstores

There are francophone as well as anglophone bookstores in Montréal. American, Canadian and Quebecois books are sold at reasonable prices. Visitors interested in literature from Québec will find a large selection in bookstores in Montréal, so now is the time to stock those library shelves! Books imported from Europe are generally a bit more expensive, due to shipping costs.

General

Champigny (French)
4380 Rue Saint-Denis, ☎844-2587

Chapters (French and English)
1171 Rue Sainte-Catherine Ouest, ☎849-8825

Librairie Gallimard (French)
3700 Boulevard Saint-Laurent, ☎499-2012

Paragraphe Books and Café (English)
2220 McGill College, ☎845-5811

Librairie Renaud-Bray (French)
5252 Chemin de la Côte-des-Neiges, ☎342-1515
4301 Rue Saint-Denis, ☎499-3656
5117 Avenue du Parc, ☎276-7651

WH Smith (French and English)
Place Ville-Marie, ☎861-1736
Promenades de la Cathédrale, ☎289-8737

Specialized

Librairie Allemande (German books)
3434 Chemin de la Côte-des-Neiges, ☎933-1919

Librairie Las Americas (Spanish books)
10 Rue Saint-Norbert, ☎844-5994

Librairie l'Androgyne (gay and feminist literature)
3636 Boulevard Saint-Laurent, ☎842-4765

Librairie C.E.C. Michel Fortin (education, languages)
3714 Rue Saint-Denis, ☎849-5719

Librairie du Musée des Beaux-Arts (art)
1368 Rue Sherbrooke Ouest, ☎285-1600, ext 350

Librairie Olivieri (contemporary art)
185 Rue Sainte-Catherine Ouest, ☎847-6903

MONTRÉAL

Librairie Olivieri (foreign literature, art)
5200 Rue Gatineau, ☎739-3639

Librairie Renaud-Bray (children)
5219 Chemin de la Côte-des-Neiges,
☎342-1515

Librairie Ulysse (travel)
4176 Rue Saint-Denis, ☎843-9447
560 Avenue du Président-Kennedy, ☎843-7222

Music

In Quebec, CDs are less expensive than in Europe. Music stores offer a wides selection of popular and classical music, jazz and Francophone and Anglophone artists.

Archambault Musique
500 Rue Sainte-Catherine Est, ☎849-6201
175 Rue Sainte-Catherine Ouest, Place des Arts, ☎281-0367

HMV
1020 Rue Sainte-Catherine Ouest, ☎875-0765
Annexe at 1035 Rue Ste-Catherine Ouest, ☎987-1809 (sale-priced merchandise)

Sam the Record Man
399 Rue Sainte-Catherine Ouest, corner Rue Saint-Alexandre, ☎281-9877

Québec Crafts

Craft shops, known as *boutiques d'artisanat* in French, offer an impressive selection of pieces illustrating the work and specific themes dear to artisans from here and abroad.

Local crafts include Canadian, Native and Inuit, as well as Québec works. Each year during the month of December, the *Salon des Métiers d'Art du Québec* (Québec Art and Crafts show) is held at Place Bonaventure *(901 Rue de la Gauchetière Ouest)*. The show lasts about 10 days and provides Québec artists the opportunity to display and sell their work.

Throughout the year, it is also possible to purchase several beautifully crafted items by

Quebec artists and on of the **Le Rouet** boutiques *(136 Rue Saint-Paul Est, ☎875-2333; 4201 Rue Saint-Denis, ☎842-4306; 1500 Avenue McGill College in Place Montréal-Trust, ☎843-5235 or 289-0803).*

Le Chariot *(446, Place Jacques-Cartier, ☎875-6134)* offers a good selection of Inuit and Native art and crafts.

Guilde Canadienne des Métiers d'Arts *(2025 Rue Peel, ☎849-6091)* is a small boutique sells pieces of Canadian and Quebecois art, and two small galleries exhibit Inuit and Native art and crafts.

The **Galerie d'Objets d'Art du Marché Bonsecours** *(350 Rue St-Paul E., ☎878-2787)* is another great place to buy Quebec art.

Jewellery and Accessories

If beautiful jewelery is more important to you than price, stop by **Birks** *(1240 Square Phillips, ☎397-2511)*. For those who prefer reasonably priced costume jewellery, choose **Agatha** *(1054 Avenue Laurier Ouest, ☎272-9313)*.

Two other boutiques display modern-designed, sliver and gold original and elegant pieces: **Oz Bijoux** *(3955 Rue Saint-Denis, ☎845-9568)* and **Suk Kwan Design** *(5141 Boulevard St-Laurent, ☎278-4079)*.

Gifts and Gadgets

Boutique du Musée d'Art Contemporain *(185 Rue Sainte-Catherine Ouest, ☎847-6226)* and **Boutique du Musée des Beaux-Arts de Montréal** *(1390 Rue Sherbrooke Ouest, ☎285-1600)* have a whole store of splendid reproductions and trinkets of all kinds: t-shirts, decorative objects and more. A great find for beautiful souvenirs.

La Mouette Rieuse *(4418 Rue St-Denis, ☎843-4851)* will surpirse comic fans of Tintin, de Gaston Lagaffe, des Bidochon and Asterix.

At **Valet de Cœur** *(4408 Rue Saint-Denis, ☎499-9970)*, you will find parlour games, puzzles and chess and checker boards among other things.

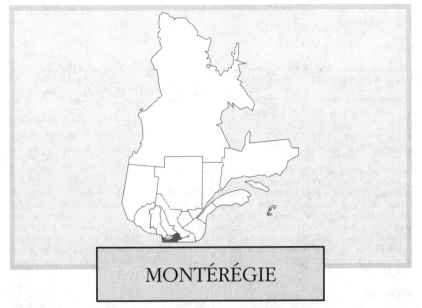

MONTÉRÉGIE

The six hills in Montérégie, Mont Saint-Bruno, Mont Saint-Hilaire, Mont Yamaska, Mont Rigaud, Mont Saint-Grégoire and Mont Rougemont, are the only large hills in this flat region. The hills, which do not rise much over 500 metres, are spread out and were long considered ancient volcanoes. Actually, they are metamorphic rocks that did not break through the upper layer of the earth's crust, and became visible as the neighbouring land eroded over a long period of time.

The Montérégie area is a beautiful plain, rich in history and agriculture, located between Ontario, New England and the foothills of the Appalachians in the Eastern Townships. Located just south of Montréal, with many natural communication routes such as the majestic Rivière Richelieu, Montérégie has always played an important military and strategic role. The many fortifications that can now be visited in the area were once outposts that served to protect the colony from the Iroquois, the British and the Americans respectively. It was also in Montérégie that the American nation experienced its first military defeat, in 1812. The *Patriotes* and the British confronted each other in Saint-Charles-sur-Richelieu and Saint-Denis, during the 1837 rebellion.

Although the towns surrounding the island of Montréal have become the southern suburbs of the this large city, most of Montérégie has managed to preserve its pastoral charm. Medium-sized towns such as Saint-Jean-sur-Richelieu and Saint-Hyacinthe (farm produce capital of Québec), continue to preserve their own institutions and identities, while a large part of the region's economy is still connected to agriculture and livestock. To visit Montérégie is to explore the hills and the superb Vallée du Richelieu, to experience the area's rich historical heritage and to breathe the fresh country air. Apple picking in the Rougemont orchards is also very popular during the fall.

 FINDING YOUR WAY AROUND

Tour A: Forts on the Richelieu

By car

From Montréal, take Pont Champlain, then Highway 10 to Chambly, on the western shore of the Richelieu, to the Boulevard Fréchette exit. From Chambly, take Highway 223 S., then follow Highways 202 and 221 to complete the tour.

Ferry

St-Paul-de-l'île-aux-Noix – Île-aux-Noix
☎514-291-5700, seasonal

Bus Station

Saint-Jean-sur-Richelieu: 600 Boulevard Pierre-Caisse, ☎514-359-6024.

Tour B: Chemin des Patriotes

By car

From Montréal, take the Pont Champlain, then Highway 10 until you've crossed the Rivière Richelieu, then take Route 133 North, also called "Chemin des patriotes". Then drive along the eastern shore of the Richelieu, from St-Mathias to Mont-St-Hilaire. From here take Route 116 and then Route 231 to St-Hyacinthe. At this point, Route 137 N. leads to St-Denis and Route 133 to Sorel.

Bus Station

Saint-Hyacinthe: 1330 Rue Calixa-Lavallée, ☎514-778-6090.
Sorel: 191 Rue du Roi, ☎514-743-4411.

Ferry

St-Denis – St-Antoine-sur-Richelieu: ☎514-787-2759, seasonal.
St-Marc-sur-Richelieu – St-Antoine-sur-Richelieu: ☎514-584-2813, seasonal.
St-Roch-de-Richelieu – St-Ours: ☎514-785-2161, seasonal.
Sorel – St-Ignace-de-Loyola: ☎514-743-3258, open all year.

Tour C: Shore of the St. Lawrence

By Car

From Montréal, take the Pont Mercier toward La Prairie, then Route 132 E., the main road for this tour. When you reach Ste-Catherine, drive along the river until Contrecœur. You can also make a detour to St-Bruno and Calixa-Lavallée.

Bus Station

Longueuil: bus terminal: 1001 Rue de Sévigny, ☎514-670-3422.
STRSM (Métro terminal, Longueuil station): 100 Place-Charles-Lemoyne, ☎514-463-0131.

Ferry

Ferry Longueuil - Île Charron: ☎514-442-9575, seasonal.
River shuttle Longueuil - Montréal: ☎514-281-8000, seasonal.

Tour D: Vaudreuil-Soulanges

By Car

From Montréal, take Highway 20 W. to Vaudreuil-Dorion, the start of the tour. By taking Route 342, you can reach Como, Hudson, Rigaud and Pointe-Fortune. Take either Route 342 or Highway 40 to Route 201 to Coteau-du-Lac. From here head east along the St-Lawrence River to Pointe-des-Cascades, then north to Île Perrot.

By Ferry

Hudson - Oka: ☎514-458-4732, seasonal.

Tour E: The Southwest

By Car

From Montréal, cross the Pont Mercier and take Route 138 to the intersection of Route 132. Take Route 132 to St-Timothée (Salaberry-de-Valleyfield is a few kilometres further). Then go south on Route 132, cross the Canal de Beaharnois, and continue to Rivière Châteauguay. Drive south along the river to Ormstown, from where Route 201 follows Route 202 and will lead you through to the end of the tour.

 PRACTICAL INFORMATION

The area code for Montérégie is **450**, except for Île Perrot, which is **514**.

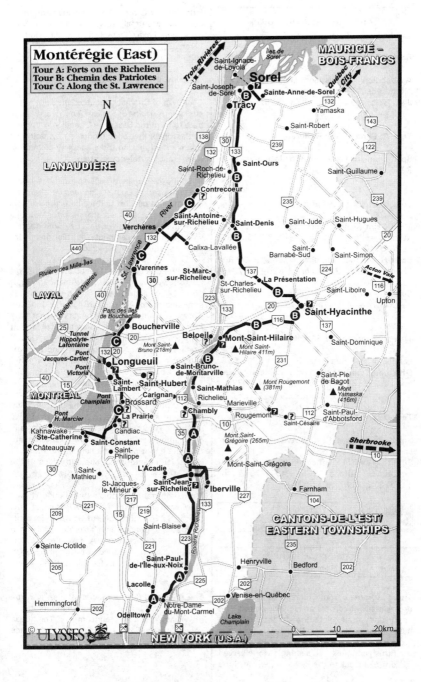

Tourist Information Offices

Regional Office

Association Touristique Régional de la Montérégie: 989, Rue Pierre-Dupuy, Longeuil, J4K 1A1, ☎674-5555, ⬩463-2876.

Tour A: Forts on the Richelieu

Saint-Jean-sur-Richelieu: 315 Macdonald, suite 225, J3B 8J3, ☎358-4849.

Tour B: Chemin des Patriotes

Mont-Saint-Hilaire: 1080 Chemin des Patriotes Nord, ☎536-0395 or 1-888-748-3783, ⬩536-3147
Saint-Hyacinthe: Parc des Patriotes, 2090 Rue Cherrier, ☎774-7276 or 1-800-849-7276, ⬩774-9000.
Sorel: 92 Chemin des Patriotes, ☎746-9441 or 1-800-474-9441, ⬩780-5737

Tour C: Shore of the St. Lawrence

Longueuil: 989 Rue Pierre-Dupuy, ☎674-5555.
Office du Tourisme de la Rive-Sud (convention bureau) 205 Chemin Chambly, ☎674-2977.

Tour D: The Southwest

Salaberry-de-Valleyfield: 980 Boulevard Mgr-Langlois, ☎377-7676.
Sûroit Tourism Office: 30 Avenue du Centenaire, office 126, ☎377-7676 or 1-800-378-7648, ⬩377-3727

 EXPLORING

Tour A: Forts on the Richelieu ★★
(two days)

This tour moves from Chambly all the way to the American border, and gives visitors the opportunity to explore the defence network built along the Rivière Richelieu under the French Regime, which was reinforced following the British conquest. This string of forts served to control access to the Richelieu, which, for a long time, was the main communication route between Montréal, New England and New York, via Lake Champlain and the Hudson River.

Chambly ★★ (pop. 16,834)

The town of Chambly is located on a privileged site alongside the Richelieu. The river widens here to form the Bassin de Chambly at the end of the rapids that once hindered navigation on the river and making the area a key element in New France's defence system.

In 1665, the Carignan-Salières regiment, under the command of Captain Jacques de Chambly, built the first pile fort to drive back the Iroquois who made frequent incursions into Montréal from the Mohawk River. In 1672, the captain was granted a seigneury in his name for services rendered to the colony.

The town that gradually formed around the fort flourished during the Canadian-American war of 1812-14, while a sizeable British garrison was stationed there. Then, in 1843, the Canal de Chambly opened, allowing boats to bypass the Richelieu Rapids and thereby facilitating commerce between Canada and the United States. Many transportation and import-export companies opened in the area at this time. Today, Chambly is both a suburb of Montréal and a getaway and leisure spot.

Follow Rue Bourgogne to the narrow **Rue Richelieu ★**, which leads to the fort. Travel along the Parc des Rapides, where the Barrage de Chambly can be admired from up close and then the imposing homes built in the first half of the 19th century that line both sides of the road.

The comfortable palladian-style house known as **Maison John-Yule** *(27 Rue Richelieu)* was built in 1816. John Yule, of Scottish descent, emigrated to Canada with his brother William in the late 18th century. A few years later, William became seigneur of Chambly. John Yule prospered from his local flour and carding mills.

The **Atelier du Peintre Maurice Cullen** *(28 Rue Richelieu)* was built in 1920 on the foundations of William Yule's seigneurial manor. The house served as a studio for Canadian painter Maurice Cullen (1866-1934).

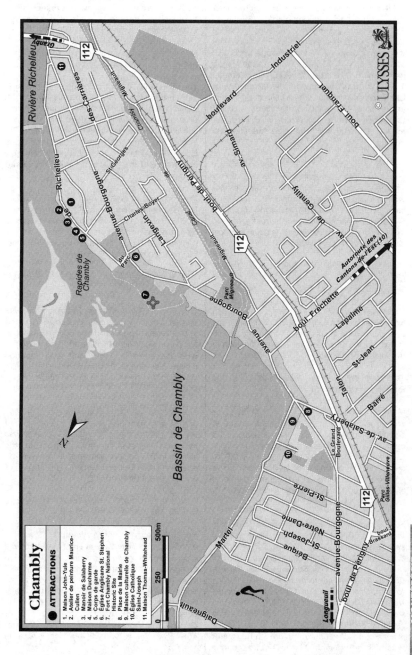

Chambly

● **ATTRACTIONS**

1. Maison John-Yule
2. Atelier de peinture Maurice-Cullen
3. Manoir de Salaberry
4. Maison Ducharme
5. Corps de garde
6. Église Anglicane St. Stephen
7. Fort Chambly National Historic Site
8. Place de la Mairie
9. Maison culturelle de Chambly
10. Église Catholique Saint-Joseph
11. Maison Thomas-Whitehead

Colonel Charles-Michel d'Irumberry de Salaberry is known for his decisive victory over the American army during the War of 1812-1814. Salaberry and his wife, Julie Hertel de Rouville, were descendants of French nobility who chose to stay in Canada despite the British conquest of 1760. They moved into the **Manoir de Salaberry** *(18 Rue Richelieu)*, built around 1814, in order to govern the seigneury of Chambly, one third of which belonged to them at that time. The Manoir de Salaberry is one of the most elegant properties in the region, mixing French and Palladian architectural styles.

Following the War of 1812-14, several military infrastructures were built in the vicinity of Fort Chambly. Many have since been demolished, while others have been renovated. This is the case with the **Maison Ducharme** *(10 Rue Richelieu)*, a former soldiers' barracks, built in 1814 and transformed into a residence at the end of the 19th century.

The former **Corps de Garde** (guardhouse) *(8 Rue Richelieu)*, built in 1814, is next to the Maison Ducharme to the north. It is adorned with a wooden Palladian-style portico, the only element that truly distinguishes it from French Regime architecture. It houses an exhibit on the British presence in Chambly. At the end of Rue Richelieu, the Fort de Chambly can be seen in the middle of a park.

Turn left on Rue du Parc, and take Rue Bourgogne to the right.

Many British people, civilian and military, as well as American Loyalist refugees settled in Chambly during the first half of the 19th century. The **St. Stephen Anglican Church ★** *(2004 Rue Bourgogne)* was built in 1820 to serve this community as well as the fort's garrison. The exterior, designed by local entrepreneur François Valade, is reminiscent of the Catholic churches of that era.

Fort Chambly National Historic Site ★★★ *(adults $3.50; Feb, Sat and Sun 10am to 5pm; early Mar to mid-May, Wed to Sun 10am to 5pm; mid-May to late Jun, every day 9am to 5pm; late Jun to early Sep, every day 9:30 to 6pm; Sep, Mon 1pm to 5pm, Tue to Sun 10am to 5pm; Oct, Wed to Sun 10am to 5pm; closed from late Oct to early Feb; 2 Rue Richelieu, ☎658-1585)*. Also called Lieu Historique National du Fort Chambly, this is the largest remaining fortification of the French Regime. It was built between 1709 and 1711 according

to plans drawn by engineer Josué Boisberthelot de Beaucours at the request of the marquis of Vaudreuil. The fort, defended by the *Compagnies Franches de la Marine*, had to protect New France against a possible British invasion. It replaced the two pile forts that had occupied this site since 1665.

The military complex is located in a spectacular setting along the Bassin de Chambly, where the rapids begin. It is a rectangular-shaped building of rubble stone, with fortified bastions and completed by small wooden watchtowers. The interior of the fort houses an interesting interpretation centre describing the strategic importance of the Rivière Richelieu throughout history.

The **Place de la Mairie**, built in 1912, can be found at the intersection of Rue Bourgogne and Rue Martel. In front of it stands a bronze statue by Louis-Philippe Hébert commemorating the hero of the battle of Châteauguay, Charles-Michel d'Irumberry de Salaberry.

Take Rue Martel, which runs along the Bassin de Chambly.

The **Maison Culturelle de Chambly** *(56 Rue Martel)*. Chambly's community centre is located in this former convent of the Congrégation de Notre-Dame, erected in 1885. The building, with its two-sided roof and long wooden gallery, is typical of the convents that sit imposingly in the heart of most Québec cities and towns.

The **Église Catholique Saint-Joseph** *(164 Rue Martel)* was built in 1881 from the remains of the walls of the first church (1784) after it was seriously damaged by fire. In front of the church is the last known piece of artwork by sculptor Louis-Philippe Hébert, the statue of parish priest Migneault.

Return to Rue Martel, then take Rue Bourgogne toward Saint-Jean-sur-Richelieu.

When leaving Chambly, you'll spot a blue wooden house. The **Maison Thomas-Whitehead** *(2592 Rue Bourgogne)* was built in 1815 for an employee of the fort barracks. Few of these wooden houses, once very popular in villages and suburbs of large cities, survived the many fires that ravaged Québec during the 19th century. A 1934 painting by Robert Pilot showing the Thomas-Whitehead home in winter *(The Blue House*, Musée des Beaux-Arts de

Montréal) served as a reference during its restoration in 1985.

Follow Route 223 South to Saint-Jean-sur-Richelieu.

Saint-Jean-sur-Richelieu ★ (pop. 39,724)

This industrial city was, for a long time, an important gateway into Canada from the United States, as well as an essential rest stop on the road from Montréal. Three features made this city important: its port on the Richelieu, active from the end of the 18th century onwards; its railway, the first in Canada, and which linked it to La Prairie as of 1836; and the opening of the Canal de Chambly in 1843. In the mid-19th century, many businesses in Saint-Jean-sur-Richelieu related to these communication routes prospered, such as pottery and earthenware manufacturers (teapots, jugs and plates were to become the region's specialties). The city's architecture reflects its industrial past, with its factories, commercial buildings, working-class areas and beautiful Victorian homes.

Saint-Jean, however, has older roots than this. It developed around Fort Saint-Jean, built in 1666. In 1775, it was attacked many times by the American rebel army, who finally had to beat a retreat upon the arrival of British troops. The fort has been rebuilt many times and is now home to the Collège Militaire Royal de Saint-Jean.

Take **Rue Richelieu**, the main commercial road, to enter Saint-Jean. The street was devastated by fire on two occasions during the course of its history. It was rebuilt immediately after the last fire of 1876, giving it an architectural homogeneity unusual in Québec.

With the exception of the Musée du Fort Saint-Jean, the city's tourist attractions are located in a limited area that can be covered on foot from Rue Richelieu. Return to Rue Saint-Jacques and continue to the corner of Rue de Longueuil.

The body of the **Cathédrale Saint-Jean-L'Évangéliste** (*corner Saint-Jacques and Longueuil*) dates back to 1827, but the exterior was completely redone in 1861, when the façade and the chevet were switched. The current façade, with its copper bell, dates from the early 20th century.

The neoclassical style **Palais de Justice**, is located at the north end of Rue de Longueuil, and was built in 1854 in a grey limestone model very popular at the time. Take Rue de Longueuil south to Place du Marché.

The **Musée Régional du Haut-Richelieu ★** (*$2; late Jun to early Sep, Tue to Sat 9:30am to 5pm, Sun 12:30pm to 5pm; 182 Rue Jacques-Cartier Nord, ☎347-0649*) is located inside the former public market, built in 1859. The museum holds, apart from various objects relating to the history of *Haut-Richelieu*, the upper-Richelieu, an interesting collection of pottery and earthenware produced in the region during the 19th century, including beautiful pieces from the Farrar and St. Johns Stone Chinaware companies.

The construction date of the bourgeois building, the **Maison Macdonald** (*166 Rue Jacques-Cartier Nord*), is not known, but it appeared on maps for the first time in 1841. What is known, however, is that its current decor is the result of the addition of a mansard roof and Second-Empire styling around 1875. At that time the house belonged to Duncan Macdonald, owner of the St. Johns Stone Chinaware Company. He held many receptions here until the collapse of his business.

The **St. James Church** (*corner Jacques-Cartier and Saint-Georges*), built in 1817 is one of the oldest Anglican churches in Montérégie. Its American-inspired architecture reminds us that, during this period, Saint-Jean was home to a large community of Loyalist refugees from the United States.

The **Musée du Fort Saint-Jean ★** (*$2; late Jun to early Sep, Tue to Sun 10am to 5pm; ☎358-6500*) is located in the former guardhouse (1850) of Fort Saint-Jean. Because most of the fort's buildings were reconstructed after the 1837-38 rebellion, only a few installations of the French forts of 1666 and 1748 remain. The museum houses collections of weapons as well as clothing and maps. The fort buildings now make up the centre of the large Collège Militaire Royal de Saint-Jean, where francophone officers trained for the Canadian army from 1952 to 1994. It is now part of the Fort-Saint-Jean university campus.

A visit to Saint-Jean-sur-Richelieu can be completed with a walk along the river, on the strip of land that demarcates the mouth of the Canal de Chambly.

MONTÉRÉGIE

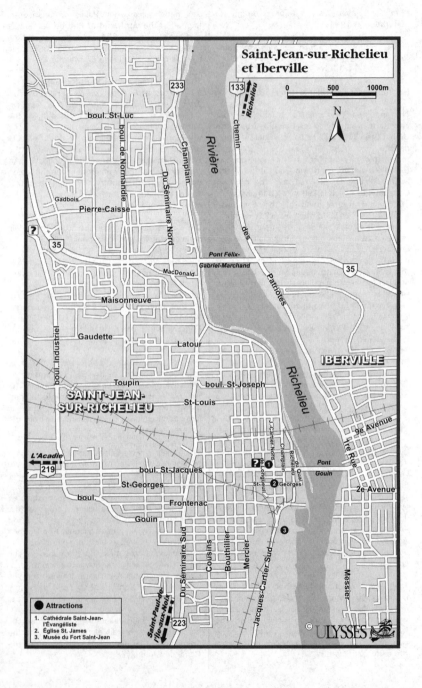

Iberville (pop. 9,882)

Across from Saint-Jean, on the other bank of the Richelieu, is Iberville, accessible via the Pont Gouin. The land that makes up the municipality, once known as Mille Roches, was granted to brothers Charles and Clément Sabrevois de Bleury in 1733. In 1770, following the conquest, the French owners withdrew, and the seigneury passed into the hands of Gabriel Christie and Moses Hazen. In 1815, the village of Christieville came into being. The village was the beginning of the municipality of Iberville, a tranquil community many of whose inhabitants work or study in Saint-Jean.

This optional excursion begins at the exit from the Pont Gouin. Turn left on 1ʳᵉ Rue which runs along the Richelieu.

The Saint-Athanase-de-Bleury Catholic parish, founded in 1822, had **Église Saint-Athanase** (*1ʳᵉ Rue*), their third church, built in 1914. The presbytery, however, is older as its construction dates back to 1836. There is a panoramic view of Saint-Jean-sur-Richelieu from the front steps of the church.

In 1835, William Plenderleath Christie inherited the family seigneury. During the same year, he began construction on the imposing **Manoir Christie** ★ (*375 1ʳᵉ Rue*), done in a Georgian style, and visible through the trees. It is a large stone house, whose roof is topped with an elegant lantern. The Christies only lived in their Iberville property sporadically, as they found themselves in London, then in Bath. Their former home remains one of the most evocative of the seigneurial regime (*not open to visitors*).

The **Maison Provinciale des Frères Maristes** (*1ʳᵉ Rue*). A monument in the memory of Marcellin Champagnat, founder of the Mariste brothers community, was erected in front of the orders' country house, built during the twenties. In the middle of summer, residents of Iberville hold a traditional eel fishing event on the Richelieu, across from the monastery.

Return toward Saint-Jean-sur-Richelieu by the Pont Gouin, then take Route 223 Sud, which runs along the Richelieu.

Saint-Paul-de-l'Île-aux-Noix (pop. 1,864)

This village is known for its fort, built on Île aux Noix (literally, island of nuts) in the middle of the Richelieu. Farmer Pierre Joudernet was the first occupant of the island, and he payed his seigneurial rent in the form of a bag of nuts, hence the island's name. Towards the end of the French Regime, the island became strategically important because of its proximity to Lake Champlain and the American colonies. The French began to fortify the island in 1759, but had such poor resources that the fort was taken by the British without difficulty. In 1775, the island became the headquarters for the American revolutionary forces, who attempted to invade Canada. Then, during the war of 1812-14, the reconstructed fort served as a base for the attack on Plattsburg (New York State) by the British.

Visitors must leave their cars at the information centre (61ᵉ Avenue) to take the ferry to the island.

Fort Lennox National Historic Site ★★ (*$5; mid-May to late Jun, Mon to Fri 10am to 5pm, Sat and Sun 10am to 6pm; late Jun to early Sep, Mon noon to 6pm, Tue to Sun 10am to 6pm; 1 61e Avenue, J0J 1G0, Saint-Paul-de-l'Île-aux-Noix, ☎291-5700*), also called Lieu Historique National du Fort Lennox. Taking up two-thirds of Île aux Noix and significantly altering its face, Fort Lennox was built on the ruins of previous forts between 1819 and 1829 by the British, prompting the construction of Fort Montgomery by the Americans just south of the border. Behind the wall of earth and surrounded by large ditches are a powder keg, two warehouses, the guardhouse, the officers' residences, two barracks and 19 blockhouses. This charming cut-stone ensemble, built according to the plans of engineer Gother Mann, is a good example of the colonial neoclassical architectural style of the British Empire.

Return to Route 223 S. toward Lacolle.

The two-story **Blockhaus de Lacolle** ★, a squared wooden building with loopholes (*free admission; late May to late Aug every day 9am to 5pm; early Sep to early Oct, Sat and Sun 9am to 5pm; 1 Rue Principale, ☎246-3227*), is found at the southernmost point of the Saint-Paul-de-l'Île-aux-Noix municipality. Its construction dates back to 1782, making it one of the oldest wooden structures in Montérégie. It

MONTÉRÉGIE

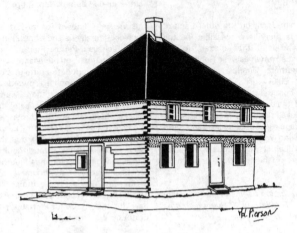

Blockhaus de Lacolle

is also one of the few buildings of this type to survive in Québec.

From here, it is only about 10 kilometres to the American border. Although Canada-United States relations have been very cordial for many decades now, this was not always the case. The blockhouse acted as a sentry at the forefront of the Richelieu's defence system in the late 18th century. The occupants had to warn soldiers in neighbouring forts of the imminent arrival of troops from the other side of the border.

Turn right on Route 202 W. to connect with Highway 15 N. Two short optional excursions can be taken to the village of Lacolle (Route 221 N.) and the Église d'Odelltown in Notre-Dame-du-Mont-Carmel (Route 221 S.).

Lacolle (pop. 1,392)

Lacolle was once part of the Beaujeu seigneury, property of Daniel Hyacinthe Liénard de Beaujeu. During the American Revolution, a few Dutch families living in northern New York State, came to settle in the region, which explains the many Dutch-style red-brick homes.

Behind the village is the former Napierville Junction Railway station (Canadian National), the **Gare de Lacolle**, built in 1930 in the style of French provincial manor. As the first stop on the Canadian side of the border, the station

became more important than the size of the town might have merited.

Odelltown

This small hamlet with only a few dozen inhabitants is now part of the Notre-Dame-du-Mont-Carmel municipality. Odelltown was the scene of a decisive episode during the rebellion of 1837-38, when the *Patriotes*, who took refuge in the nearby United States, attempted to make a breakthrough by taking the region of Lacolle by storm. They declared the area the République du Bas-Canada (Republic of Lower Canada). This lasted only seven days however, since the *Patriotes* were forced to retreat when faced with the arrival of British troops commanded by Colborne. The *Patriotes* attacked the Loyalist community of Odelltown before recrossing the border. The inhabitants of the hamlet, who took refuge in their church, defended themselves fiercely until the arrival of the troops.

The many Dutch Loyalist families who settled in the area became Methodists on their arrival in Canada. The small Methodist **Odelltown Church** *(243 Route 221)* was built in 1823, making it one of the oldest Methodist churches in Québec.

Return to Route 202 W., which leads to Highway 15 N., toward Montréal.

Tour B: Chemin des Patriotes ★★
(three days)

The Vallée du Richelieu was the second area of settlement in New France after the banks of the St. Lawrence and many traces remain of the former seigneuries granted along the river in the 17th and 18th centuries. In the early 19th century it was one of the most populous regions in Québec, as such, the aftershocks of the 1837-1838 armed rebellion were keenly felt in the area. Meaningful testimonies of these events, among the most tragic in the history of Québec, are numerous throughout the valley.

Saint-Mathias (pop. 3,729)

This municipality, once an important port on the Richelieu, is now a calm residential suburb. There are beautiful homes and a church with one of the most interesting interior decors in the region.

Saint-Mathias was the site of significant events during the American War of Independence, as Ethan Allen and his Green Mountain Boys from Vermont took over the village in order to convince the inhabitants to join the United States. Finally, Saint-Mathias experienced a new period of intense activity during the 1837-38 rebellion, when the *Patriotes'* militia established their headquarters here.

The **Magasin Franchère** (*254 Chemin des Patriotes*) is the only remaining evidence of commercial activity in Saint-Mathias during the 19th century. The store was built in 1822 for brothers Joseph and Timothée Franchère. Timothée was jailed in 1838 for participating in the rebellion. The store originally housed two apartments where many *Patriotes* meetings took place.

Noted for its outstanding interior decor and its stone cemetery enclosure, the **Église Saint-Mathias** ★★ (*279 Chemin des Patriotes*) also boasts a charming exterior that reflects traditional Québec architecture. It was built in 1784 by mason François Châteauneuf.

Continue heading north along Chemin des Patriotes. The silhouette of Mont Saint-Hilaire, the highest hill in Montérégie (411 m), comes into view as you approach.

Mont-Saint-Hilaire ★ (pop. 12,995)

This small town, located at the foot of Mont Saint-Hilaire, was originally part of the seigneury of Rouville, granted to Jean-Baptiste Hertel in 1694. It remained in the hands of the Hertel family until 1844, when it was sold to Major Thomas Edmund Campbell, secretary to the British governor, who operated an experimental farm, which remained in operation until 1942.

Mont-Saint-Hilaire has two urban centres, one along the Richelieu, where the parish church is located, and the other on the southeast side of the mountain, an area that enjoys a mild microclimate and is home to orchards and maple groves.

Though recently scarred by the addition of parking lots and an ostentatious gate, the **Manoir Rouville-Campbell** ★ (*125 Chemin des Patriotes Sud*) remains one of the most magnificent seigneurial residences in Québec. It was built in 1854 according to the plans of British architect Frederick Lawford, who also contributed to the interior decor of the Église de Saint-Hilaire. During the eighties, the house and the stables were transformed into an inn (see p 193). Facing the Manoir Rouville-Campbell, stands Mont-Saint-Hilaire's **Monument aux Patriotes**.

The **Église Saint-Hilaire** ★★ (*260 Chemin des Patriotes Nord*) was originally supposed to have two façade towers topped with spires. As a result of internal arguments, only the bases of the towers were erected in 1830, and a steeple, placed in the centre of the façade, was later installed. The interior decor, done in the Gothic-Revival style, was completed over a long period of time, between 1838 and 1928. The masterpiece of this interior is the work of painter Ozias Leduc (1864-1955), completed at the end of the 19th century.

The presbytery (1798) is north of the church, while the **Couvent des Sœurs des Saints Noms de Jésus et de Marie**, with its odd rounded wing, is located behind the church. From the square of the Église Saint-Hilaire, visitors can see the Église de Saint-Mathieu-de-Belœil on the other side of the Richelieu.

The **Musée d'Art de Mont-Saint-Hilaire** ★ (*$2; Tue to Sat 10am to 5pm, Sun 1pm to 5pm; 150 Rue du Centre Civique, ☎536-3033*) promotes the development of contemporary visual arts and highlights the works of famous

MONTÉRÉGIE

Manoir Rouville-Campbell

artists that have lived in Mont-Saint-Hilaire including Ozias Leduc, Paul-Émile Borduas and Jordi Bonet among others.

Follow Route 133 N. Turn right onto Route 116 E. (follow the directions for the Centre de Conservation de la Nature du Mont Saint-Hilaire). Take Rue Fortier to the right, which turns into Chemin Ozias-Leduc. Finally, turn left onto the Chemin de la Montagne, then again on Chemin des Moulins. The pretty Chemin de la Montagne is lined with apple orchards. The owners sell apples, juice, cider, and apple sauce when in season (September and October) at small roadside stands.

The **Centre de Conservation de la Nature du Mont Saint-Hilaire ★★** (see p 190).

The tour leaves the Vallée du Richelieu for a short while in order to pass through Saint-Hyacinthe, nicknamed the "farm-produce capital of Québec". To get there, return to Route 116 E. for approximately 20 kilometres. Enter the city by Rue Girouard, passing under the Porte des Anciens Maires, a medieval style monument located along the Rivière Yamaska.

Saint-Hyacinthe ★★ (pop. 41,063)

Saint-Hyacinthe's main attraction is the vitality of the city and its inhabitants. The city is divided into the upper part of town, which is more administrative, religious, and middle-class, and the lower part of town, more working-class and commercial. Rarely in rural Québec have the liveliness of a town centre and the monuments that dominate its landscape been so successfully preserved as here. It is best to explore downtown Saint-Hyacinthe on foot.

Saint-Hyacinthe was settled in the late 18th century, around the mills on the Rivière Yamaska and the estate of Jacques-Hyacinthe Delorme, seigneur of Maska. The surrounding fertile soil helped the town expand rapidly, attracting several religious institutions, businesses and industries. The processing and distribution of agricultural products still play a leading role in the town's economy. Saint-Hyacinthe also has the only French-language veterinary medicine program in North America as well as farm-produce research and insemination institutes. A large regional agricultural fair is held here every July.

The town also specializes in the construction of large pipe organs. The Casavant brothers set up their famous organ factory outside the city in 1879 *(900 Rue Girouard Est)*. Approximately 15 electro-pneumatic organs are made here every year and are installed throughout the world by the house experts. Guided tours are sometimes organized. Guilbault-Thérien organ-builders have been building mechanical traction organs since 1946 according to French and German models of the 18th century *(2430 Rue*

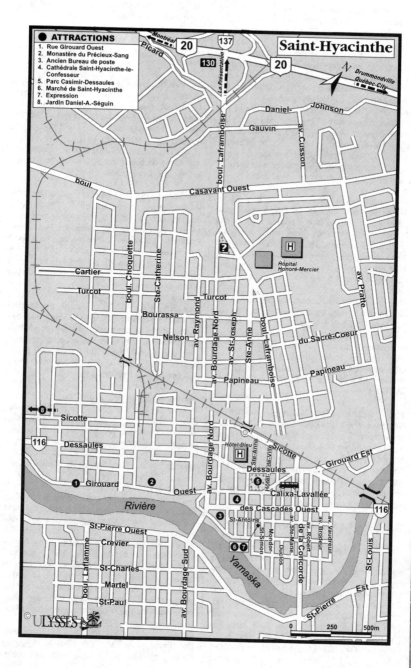

ATTRACTIONS
1. Rue Girouard Ouest
2. Monastère du Précieux-Sang
3. Ancien Bureau de poste
4. Cathédrale Saint-Hyacinthe-le-Confesseur
5. Parc Casimir-Dessaules
6. Marché de Saint-Hyacinthe
7. Expression
8. Jardin Daniel-A.-Séguin

Saint-Hyacinthe

Crevier). Saint-Hyacinthe also has a music bookstore dedicated solely to the organ and the harpsichord (Ex Arte, 12790 Rue Yamaska).

Rue Girouard Ouest ★ is the main street in the upper part of Saint-Hyacinthe. This opulent residential neighbourhood reflects the success of local entrepreneurs, it runs between the gates known as the Portes des Anciens Maires, erected in 1927 to honour the memory of the 11 first magistrates of the city, and the Église Notre-Dame-du-Rosaire. There are examples of Victorian architecture, such as the house at number 2790, designed in the Queen Anne style, distinguished by its turret and setting-sun-motif carved into the central gable.

The large white house at number 2500, decorated with dormer windows and a bell turret (circa 1860), is the original part of the **Monastère du Précieux-Sang**, which houses a community of nuns. The monastery, enlarged many times, has red- and white-painted brick wings that contrast oddly with the style of the building.

The two rusticated-stone buildings that for many years housed the Saint-Hyacinthe **Bureau de Poste** (1915 Rue Girouard Ouest) as well as the former **Douane** (1995 Rue Girouard Ouest), or customs, are two of the rare buildings of this type to have survived the wave of modernization that took place during the sixties. The buildings are now used for offices and housing.

The **Cathédrale Saint-Hyacinthe-le-Confesseur ★** (1900 Rue Girouard Ouest) is a squat building despite its 50-metre-high spires. It was built in 1880 and modified in 1906 according to designs by Montréal architects Perrault and Venne. They contributed the Romanesque Revival style and interesting rococo interior, reminiscent of some of the subway stations in Moscow.

Continue along Rue Girouard heading east.

The **Parc Casimir-Dessaulles** (Rue Girouard Ouest at the corner of Avenue du Palais), named after an important mayor of Saint-Hyacinthe, was laid-out in 1876 on the ruins of the seigneurial estate. It quickly became the favourite place of the local bourgeois class, who had many imposing homes built near here. Today, it hosts various outdoor activities (contests, concerts, etc.). To the east is the **Hôtel de Ville** (700 Avenue de l'Hôtel-de-Ville), located in the former Hôtel Yamaska,

remodelled and enlarged in 1923, and to the north is the new **Palais de Justice**.

Go to the lower part of town via Avenue Mondor. Turn right on Rue des Cascades Ouest.

Rue des Cascades ★ is the main commercial artery in Saint-Hyacinthe. It fell victim to fire in 1876, but was quickly rebuilt. The street is lined with many pleasant shops and cafés. The **Place du Marché**, demarcated in 1796 by the seigneur of Maska, can be found at number 1555. The market building (1877) remains the real heart of town, as agriculture is still the largest industry in town.

The **Allée du Marché**, west of Place du Marché, is a modern reconstruction built after a devastating fire in 1970, which destroyed several dozen buildings between Rue Saint-François and Rue Sainte-Anne. Architects Courchesne and Bergeron created a multipurpose group of buildings linked by a pedestrian walkway, helping to revitalize the downtown area.

A testimony to the 19th century, the **Marché de Saint-Hyacinthe** (1555 Rue des Cascades Ouest) is the oldest market in Québec and the symbol of the city's farm-producing industry. Market-gardeners bring their produce here in the summer and, inside, there are some specialty shops that are open year round.

Expression (open year round, Tue to Fri 10am to 5pm Sat and Sun 1pm to 5pm; 495 Rue St-Simon, 3rd floor, ☎773-4209), an organization whose mission is to promote contemporary art, is located above the Marché Central de Saint Hyacinthe. The gallery, considered one of the most beautiful in Québec, hosts approximately ten exhibitions each year.

Originally created for scholastic purposes (a practice site for landscape management students of the Institut Agroalimentaire is just across the street), the **Jardin Daniel-A.-Séguin ★** ($5; late Jun to early Sep, Tue to Sun 11am to 6:30pm; 3215 Rue Sicotte, ☎778-0372 or 778-6504), has been open to the public since 1995. With the help of guided tours, information panels and workshops, amateur horticulturalists can improve their knowledge to better tend their own gardens.

Continue on Rue Sicotte to Boulevard Choquette, turn left. On Choquette go to Boulevard Casavant Ouest and turn right.

Continue to Boulevard Laframboise (Route 137), turn left and head to La Présentation and Saint-Denis.

La Présentation (1,855 inhab.)

The beautiful church in this modest village was built shortly after the La Présentation parish was created, following the division of part of Saint-Hyacinthe in 1804.

The **Église de La Présentation** ★★ *(551 Chemin de L'Église)* is unique among other temples built in Montérégie during the same era because of its finely sculpted stone façade, completed in 1819. Note the inscriptions written in Old French above the entrances. The vast presbytery, hidden in the greenery, as well as the modest sexton house, complete this landscape typical of Québec rural parishes.

Follow Route 137 N. to Saint-Denis. Turn left on Chemin des Patriotes, which runs along the Richelieu (Route 133 S.).

Saint-Denis ★ (pop. 2,110)

Throughout the 1830s, Saint-Denis was home to large political gatherings as well as the headquarters of the *Fils de la Liberté* (Sons of Freedom), a group of young French Canadians who wanted Lower Canada (Québec) to become an independent country. But even more important, Saint-Denis was the site of the only *Patriotes* victory over the British during the 1837-38 rebellion. On November 23, 1837, General Gore's troops were forced to withdraw to Sorel after a fierce battle against the *Patriotes*, who were poorly equipped but determined to defeat the enemy. The British troops took revenge a few weeks later, however, by surprising the inhabitants while they slept, pillaging and burning the houses, businesses and industries of Saint-Denis.

The town of Saint-Denis, founded in 1758, experienced an intense period of industrialization in the early 19th century. Canada's largest hat industry was located here, where the famous beaver pelt top hats worn by men throughout Europe and America, were made. Other local industries in Saint-Denis included pottery and earthenware. The repression that followed the rebellion put an end to this economic expansion, and from then on, the town became a small agricultural village.

A monument was unveiled in 1913 in **Parc des Patriotes** to honour the memory of the Saint-Denis *Patriotes*. It is located in the middle of the square that was once known as Place Royale before becoming Place du Marché, a market place, and then a public park in the early 20th century.

The **Maison Nationale des Patriotes** ★ *($3.50; early May to early Jun and early Sep to late Nov, Tue to Sun 10am to 5pm; early Jun to late Aug, Tue to Sun 11am to 6pm; 610 Chemin des Patriotes, ☎787-3623).* To the south of the park stands a former stone inn built for Jean-Baptiste Mâsse, in 1810. The building's irregular shape is characteristic of urban homes of the late 18th century (firebreak walls with corbels, veranda on the main floor, optimum usage of the land). It is one of the rare examples of this type found outside of Montréal and Québec City.

Since 1988, the building has housed an informative interpretation centre dealing with the 1837-38 rebellion and the history of the *Patriotes*. The main battles of the rebellion are described as well as the causes of these revolts, which had a great impact on the Richelieu region and the entire province of Québec. Two interesting festivals take place here: the **Fête du Vieux Marché** *(early Aug, ☎787-2401 or 787-3229)*, a re-creation of an old public market with approximately 100 craftspeople in historical costume, who visitors get to see at work; and the **Fête des Patriotes** *(late Nov)*, a popular gathering in commemoration of the 1837 Patriotes victory.

Across from the church stands the **Maison Cherrier** *(639 Chemin des Patriotes)*, a comfortable home that François Cherrier, parish priest of Saint-Denis from 1763 to 1809, had built when he retired. He unfortunately did not have the opportunity to enjoy it, as he passed away before the roof was completed in 1810.

Return to Route 133 North *(Chemin des Patriotes)* heading toward Saint-Ours. The battlefield of the 1837 battle at Saint-Denis is located near Rue Phaneuf, at the edge of town. The Maison Pagé at 553 Chemin des Patriotes was the scene of the first skirmishes between the *Patriotes* and the British troops. Six wounded British soldiers were treated by the young Dormicour women at the **Maison Dormicour** *(549 Chemin des Patriotes)*.

MONTÉRÉGIE

Saint-Ours (pop. 1,620)

Descendants of the Saint-Ours seigneurs still inhabit the seigneurial manor on land granted by Louis XIV in 1672 to their ancestor Pierre de Saint-Ours, captain in the Carignan-Salières regiment. The small village that neighbours the seigneur's house was once an active port on the Richelieu. The only current reminder of this activity is the lock, rebuilt in 1933.

The **Écluse de Saint-Ours** *($2; mid-May to mid-Jun and early Sep to mid-Oct, Mon to Fri 8:30am to 4pm, Sat and Sun 8:30am to 6pm; mid-Jun to mid-Aug, every day 8:30 to 8pm; mid-Aug to early Sep 8:30am to 6pm; ☎658-0681).* For a long time, the Richelieu was a vital communication route between Montréal and New York, via Lake Champlain and the Hudson. The river was held in awe until the beginning of the 19th century because it allowed the enemy to enter Québec territory. However, with long-lasting peace achieved following the War of 1812-14 between Great Britain and the United States, the Richelieu became an important economic link for the import of American products and the export of Canadian goods. The first lock, built in 1849, was refurbished in the 20th century. Today picnic tables and viewing areas add to the site.

The **Manoir de Saint-Ours** *(2500 Rue de l'Immaculée-Conception)* stands amidst a wooded area on the outskirts of town, and is sometimes hard to see in the summer. A bust of Pierre de Saint-Ours stands on the side of the road and is the only indication of the manoir's presence. Essentially, it is a quarried stone house surrounded by a large wooden gallery with views of the garden and Richelieu valley. The manor was built in 1792 for Charles de Saint-Ours, fourth seigneur of the property, and was updated to the current style in 1870.

Continue along Route 133 North (Chemin des Patriotes) to Sorel, where it turns into Chemin Saint-Ours, then into Rue de la Reine.

Sorel (pop. 24,964)

In Sorel, the Richelieu flows into the St. Lawrence. Heavy industry and naval construction are still the town's main economic activities. It got its name from Pierre de Saurel, captain of the Carignan-Salières regiment, to whom the land was granted in 1672. The town itself owes its current layout to British governor Frederick Haldimand, who wanted to make a model town populated by Anglo-Saxons. He tried to attract American Loyalists to Sorel (once named William-Henry) in several different ways. First, the town joined the Domaine Royal in 1781, then adopted a checkerboard plan in 1783, the streets were named in honour of members of the British royal family at that time (Augusta, Charlotte, George, etc.), and an Anglican mission was opened in 1784. Despite all this, his plan was a resounding failure.

During the 1860s, Sorel experienced phenomenal growth with the opening of several naval building sites that are still in operation. At the same time, the town adopted its original name, but changed the spelling.

The white stucco **Maison des Gouverneurs** *(90 Chemin Saint-Ours)* was built in 1781 to accommodate the Brunswick regiment's major, who was stationed in Sorel to counter the threat of an American invasion. The regiment, made up of German and Swiss mercenaries, was under the command of General von Riedesel, who immediately enlarged the house to make it more comfortable. For Christmas 1781 Riedesel and his family set up the first Christmas tree in America, in the Maison des Gouverneurs. A sculpture in the shape of a Christmas tree now stands in front of the home to commemorate the event.

From 1784 to 1860, the house served as a summer residence for the Governor Generals of Canada. During these years, it accommodated many famous people such as Lord Dorchester, the Duke of Kent (father of Queen Victoria) and Prince William-Henry (future William IV).

Continue along Rue de la Reine toward the downtown area.

The **Carré Royal** *(corner Charlotte and de la Reine)* is a pleasant green space in the centre of Sorel, incorrectly named "Carré Royal", an improper translation of the Royal Square. It was demarcated in 1791 and landscaped out following the lines of the British Union Jack.

To the east of the square is the Anglican **Christ Church** and its presbytery done in the Gothic Revival style, both built in 1842 *(79 Rue du Prince)*. The Sorel mission, whose foundation dates back to 1784, is the dean of the Anglican churches of Québec. For a long time, it was placed under the patronage of the Crown, which meant that its minister was named directly by the British sovereign.

The **Place du Marché** *(at the end of Rue de la Reine)* includes the original market (rebuilt in 1937 in the Art Deco style) in its centre, and several interesting shops and cafés on the periphery. The neighbourhood has a strange port atmosphere with cranes, sheds and ships. The Richelieu and the St. Lawrence are visible from several lookout points between these buildings, as well as to the east, from a park located along Rue Augusta.

The Sorel Catholic parish was created in 1678 by Monseigneur de Laval. Construction of the **Église Saint-Pierre ★** *(170 Rue George)* began in 1826, but the building has been considerably modified over the years. Among the original elements are the cut stone portals of the façade and, inside, the division of the nave into three vessels, supported by beautiful Corinthian pillars, an unusual sight during this era. Also of interest are the choir stalls, taken from the old Église Notre-Dame in Montréal, demolished in 1830.

An optional excursion is possible to Sainte-Anne and the islands of Sorel to explore the Pays du Survenant (named after a novel). From Rue George, take Boulevard Fiset heading south. Turn left onto Rue de l'Hôtel-Dieu, which becomes Rue de la Rive. Take Chemin du Chenal-du-Moine, through Sainte-Anne-de-Sorel.

Sainte-Anne-de-Sorel ★ (pop. 2,955)

This village is oriented more towards hunting and fishing than other communities in Montérégie because of its proximity to the Sorel islands. Writer Germaine Guèvremont (1893-1968), who lived on one of these islands, introduced this archipelago located in the middle of the St. Lawrence to the literary world in her novel *Le Survenant*.

The best way to explore the **Îles de Sorel ★** is by taking one of the cruise boats that crosses the archipelago of approximately 20 islands *(two types of cruises are offered: Croisière des Îles de Sorel, 1665 Chemin du Chenal-du-Moine, and Excursions et Expéditions de Canots, ☎743-7227 or 743-7807).* The hour and a half-long cruises begin at the Chenal du Moine. This large waterway was named in the 17th century following the discovery of the frozen body of a Recollet monk *(moine)* who had been travelling from Trois-Rivières to Sorel along the channel *(chenal).*

The islands are an excellent place to observe aquatic birds, especially during the spring and fall. A few houses on piles with individual piers dot the flat landscape, which offers views of the vast expanse of Lac Saint-Pierre downstream. There are two restaurants at the end of the Île d'Embarras (accessible by car) that serve *gibelotte*, a fish fricassee typical of this region.

Return to Sorel. To reach Montréal, take Rue de l'Hôtel-Dieu heading west. Turn left on Rue du Roi, then right onto Chemin Saint-Ours which leads to Highway 30; follow it to Montréal.

Tour C: Shore of the St. Lawrence ★
(two days)

The shores of the St. Lawrence surrounding the island of Montreal have become bedroom communities of the metropolis. Once farming villages or small industrial towns, they have experienced tremendous growth over the past 40 years with the exodus of urban populations to the suburbs. In some cases these towns have preserved their interesting urban cores, where churches, museums and old houses can be found. Throughout this tour, Montréal looms across the river, and can be admired from many different perspectives.

Saint-Constant (pop. 19,535)

This municipality has a large railway museum, the Musée Ferroviaire Canadien, as well as an ecomuseum, considered a forerunner in its field.

The **Musée Ferroviaire Canadien ★★** *($5.75; early May to early Sep, every day 9am to 5pm; early Sep to mid-Oct, Sat and Sun 9am to 5pm; 120 Rue Saint-Pierre, ☎632-2410)* displays an impressive collection of railway memorabilia, locomotives, freight cars, and maintenance vehicles. The famous *Dorchester* locomotive, put into service in 1836 on the country's first railway between Saint-Jean-sur-Richelieu and La Prairie, is worth noting, as well as many luxurious passenger cars of the 19th century that belonged to Canadian Pacific. Also on display are foreign locomotives such as the powerful *Châteaubriand* from the SNCF (French Railway System), put into service in 1884.

MONTÉRÉGIE

The **Écomusée de Saint-Constant** *($3; early May to early Sep, Tue to Fri 9am to 5pm, Sat and Sun 10am to 7pm; Sep to May, Sat and Sun noon to 4pm; 66 Rue Maçon, ☎632-3656)* is more of a natural- and constructed-environment awareness centre for the local population than a museum for the general public. However, visitors interested in the traditional tools, work, local customs, genealogy and ecology of the region will find plenty of interesting information.

*Return toward Sainte-Catherine. Take Boulevard Marie-Victorin east. You will travel along the seaway and cross the town of **Candiac** before reaching La Prairie. Take Boulevard Salaberry, and turn left onto Rue Desjardins, which turns into Rue Saint-Laurent in Vieux-La Prairie. Turn left on Chemin de Saint-Jean.*

La Prairie ★ (pop. 15,839)

The seigneury of La Prairie was granted to the Jesuits in 1647, who turned the land into a retreat for their missionaries and a village for converted Iroquois. More and more French settlers began populating the surrounding area, forcing the Jesuits to move their mission in order to shield their protégés from the bad influence of Europeans. La Prairie's strategic location led the authorities to fortify the village in 1684. Very little remains today of the stone and wood enclosure that was dismantled by the Americans during the 1775 invasion.

La Prairie experienced a new era of prosperity in the early 19th century when it became an important link in the transportation route that brought merchandise to the United States, and in particular, to the American port of Portland, ice-free during the winters. A pier was built in 1835, where steamships linking the South Shore to Montréal docked. The following year saw the inauguration of Canada's first railway, linking Saint-Jean-sur-Richelieu to La Prairie. Unfortunately in 1864, a fire started in a locomotive destroyed the village and obliterated almost all traces of the French Regime buildings. It was to put an end to a promising future. However, the economy recovered with the opening of the brickyards, and of a new working-class neighbourhood created in 1880 in the Rue Sainte-Rose area. It was called *Fort Neuf* (new fort), to distinguish it from the old fortified village.

It is best to visit Vieux-La Prairie on foot, given the narrowness of the streets and the small size of the historical district. There is parking on Chemin de Saint-Jean near the Église de la Nativité de la Sainte Vierge.

The first church of La Prairie, built in 1687, is long gone. Construction of the **Église de la Nativité de la Sainte Vierge ★** *(155 Chemin de Saint-Jean)*, began in 1840. It has a high neoclassical façade, designed by architect Victor Bourgeau, and is topped with an elegant peristyle steeple that dominates the surrounding area.

The corner building across from the church *(120 Chemin de Saint-Jean)* and the **Maison Aubin**, built in 1824, *(150 Chemin de Saint-Jean)* are good examples of the persistence of French Regime architecture following the British conquest of 1760.

The **Musée du Vieux-Marché** *(free admission; late Jun to late Aug, Mon to Fri 9am to 5pm, closed Sat, Sun noon to 4pm; early Sep to late Jun, Mon to Fri 9am to 5pm; 249 Rue Sainte-Marie, ☎659-1393)*. An interpretive trail across from the church leads behind the old market building (1863). In addition to the market, this brick building originally housed the fire department on the main floor and a theatre upstairs. An interesting museum dealing with the history of La Prairie now occupies the building.

The **streets of Vieux-La Prairie ★★** have an urban character rarely found in Québec villages during the 19th century. Several houses were carefully restored after the Québec government declared the area an historical district in 1975. A stroll along Saint-Ignace, Sainte-Marie, Saint-Jacques and Saint-Georges streets reveals this distinctive flavour. Some of the wood houses are reminiscent of those once found in Montréal districts *(240 and 274 Rue Saint-Jacques)*. Other homes draw their inspiration from French Regime architecture (two sided roofs, firebreak walls, dormer windows), except for the fact that they are partially or totally built of brick instead of stone *(234 and 237 Rue Saint-Ignace, 166 Rue Saint-Georges)*. Lastly, the stone house covered with wood at number 238 Rue Saint-Ignace is the only surviving testimony of the French Regime in Vieux-La Prairie.

Return to Chemin de Saint-Jean.

At the end of the streets on the left is a square with a bandstand and a plaque commemorating the battle of La Prairie (1691), which pitted

French settlers against Native bands, who were loyal to the British army. The square, known as Square Foch and then Square La Mennais, once directly overlooked the river. The soft sound of lapping waves was drowned out in 1960 by the sound of traffic on a six-laned highway built between the village and the seaway.

Return to Chemin de Saint-Jean but head in the opposite direction. Turn right onto Rue Saint-Laurent, then right again onto Rue Saint-Henri. Take Highway 15 (Route 132), which passes through Brossard before reaching Saint-Lambert (exit Boulevard Simard). Turn left onto Chemin Riverside (also called Riverside Drive).

Saint-Lambert (pop. 22,148)

The development of Saint-Lambert was closely linked to the construction of the Pont Victoria during the 19th century. The railway attracted a large anglophone community, which imparted a British flavour to the town. There are a few old farm houses spread along the St. Lawrence, well restored by sensitive owners. Unfortunately, Saint-Lambert lost much of its charm when the highway was built, isolating the town from the river.

Pont Victoria ★ is the oldest bridge linking the island of Montréal to the mainland. It was built with difficulty by hundreds of Irish and French-Canadian workers between 1854 and 1860 for the Grand Trunk railway company. It started out as a tubular bridge, designed by famous British engineer Robert Stephenson, known for the Menai Strait bridge in Wales. He is the son of George Stephenson, inventor of steam traction on railways. The bridge has since been modified several times, mainly to allow for automobile traffic. The only remaining original structures are the pointed pillars, for breaking up the ice. The bridge's 2,742-metre length was exceptional for the time—journalists called it the eighth wonder of the world!

The **Écluse de Saint-Lambert ★** *(free admission; mid-Apr to late Sep, every day sunrise to sunset; at the late Boulevard Sir-Wilfrid-Laurier).* These locks act as a front door onto the seaway, which begins here and ends 3,800 kilometres downstream, at the tip of the Great Lakes. The seaway allows ships to overcome the natural obstacles posed by the St. Lawrence and to supply the American and Canadian Midwest directly. Its opening in 1959 led to the closing of the Canal de Lachine and contributed to the economic decline of southwestern Montréal. The sophisticated mechanisms and the view of Montréal make the locks at Saint-Lambert the most interesting of the Montérégie locks.

The **Musée Marsil** *($2; Tue to Fri 11am to 4pm, Sat and Sun 1pm to 4pm; 349 Chemin Riverside, ☎465-3357)* presents temporary art and history exhibits, as well as an interesting collection of costumes and textiles. It is located in the Marsil house, whose stone foundation probably dates back to 1750.

Other similar houses can still be seen along Chemin Riverside, buried amongst suburban cottages. At number 405, the **Maison Auclair** (circa 1750), has undergone fewer changes than the Maison Marsil, and better illustrates the humble rural architecture of the French Regime. The **Maison Mercille**, at number 789 (circa 1775), is more imposing than its neighbours of the same era. The dairy adjoining the main building has a window protected by rather ominous looking bars called *étripe-chats* (cat-gut) in French.

An optional excursion to the municipality of Saint-Bruno-de-Montarville further inland explores Mont Saint-Bruno, one of the ten hills in Montérégie. To get there, take Boulevard Sir-Wilfrid-Laurier and turn left onto Chemin de la Rabastalière. If you do not want to take this excursion, continue toward Longueuil on Chemin Riverside, which turns into Rue Saint-Charles Ouest. For a full kilometre before arriving downtown, the road runs through overpasses leading to the Pont Jacques-Cartier, as well as a neighbourhood of modern highrises grouped around the Longueuil Métro station.

Parc du Mont-Saint-Bruno ★
(330, Chemin des 25 Est) see p 190.

Longueuil ★ (pop. 137,134)

Located across from Montréal, this city is the most populous in Montérégie. It once belonged to the Longueuil seigneury, granted to Charles Le Moyne (1624-1685) in 1657. He headed a dynasty that played a key role in developing New France. Many of his 14 children are famous, such as Pierre Le Moyne d'Iberville (1661-1706), first governor of Louisiana, Jean-Baptiste Le Moyne de Bienville (1680-1768), founder of New Orleans, and Antoine Le Moyne de Châteauguay (1683-1747), governor of Guyana.

MONTÉRÉGIE

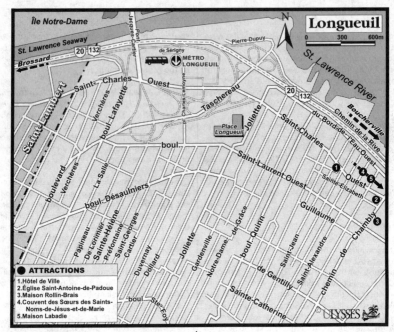

Île Notre-Dame

Longueuil

0   300   600m

St. Lawrence Seaway

Brossard

20 132

Pont Jacques-Cartier

de Sérigny

MÉTRO LONGUEUIL

Pierre-Dupuy

N

St. Lawrence River

Saint—Charles——Ouest

Saint-Lambert

Verchères

boul-Lafayette

Pl. Charles-Lemoyne

Taschereau

Place Longueuil

20 132

Saint-Charles

Chemin du-Bord-de-l'Eau-Ouest

Boucharville

boul.

Joliette

Saint-Laurent-Ouest

1

Ouest

4 5

Sainte-Élizabeth

2

3

boulevard Verchères

La-Salle

boul.-Désaulniers

Guillaume

de-Chambly

Papineau

De-Lorimier

Sainte-Hélène

Préfontaine

Saint-Georges

Cartier

Duvernay

Dollard

Joliette

Gardenville

Notre-Dame-de-Grâce

boul.-Quinn

Saint-Jean

Saint-Alexandre

chemin—de—Chambly

de Gentilly

boul.-Ste-Foy

Sainte-Catherine

© ULYSSES

● **ATTRACTIONS**

1. Hôtel de Ville
2. Église Saint-Antoine-de-Padoue
3. Maison Rollin-Brais
4. Couvent des Sœurs des Saints-Noms-de-Jésus-et-de-Marie
5. Maison Labadie

The eldest son, Charles Le Moyne de Longueuil, inherited the seigneury upon the death of his father. Between 1685 and 1690, he had a fortified castle built on the site of the current Église Saint-Antoine-de-Padoue. The castle had four corner towers, a church and many wings. In 1700, Longueuil was raised to the rank of barony by Louis XIV, the only such case in the history of New France. The baron of Longueuil saw to the development of his land, which continued to grow until it reached the banks of the Richelieu.

Longueuil experienced continuous growth during the 19th century with the introduction of the railway (1846) and the arrival of many summer vacationers who built beautiful villas along the river banks. At the beginning of the 20th century, the town welcomed a small Pratt and Whitney factory which created an important industrial centre specializing in engineering and airplane technology. The construction of the Pont Jacques-Cartier between Montréal and the south shore, inaugurated during the thirties, made Longueuil one of Montréal's first suburbs. Many examples of cottages built between the two World Wars can still be seen south of Rue Saint-Charles. Today, the embankments of the nearby seaway and the lakeside highway deprive Longueuil of all direct contact with water. The town remedied the situation by setting up a marina and a cycling path along the river, both accessible by footbridges.

Rue Saint-Charles is Longueuil's main commercial artery. Many pleasant cafés and restaurants can be found east of the **town hall** *(300 Rue Saint-Charles Ouest)*. Near the Catholic church, the former **Foyer Saint-Antoine des Sœurs Grises**, designed in 1877 by Victor Bourgeau, now houses artistic and social organizations.

The site of the **Église Saint-Antoine-de-Padoue** ★★ *(Rue Saint-Charles, at the corner of Chemin de Chambly)* was once occupied by a 17th-century castle known as the Château de Longueuil. After being besieged by American rebels during the 1775 invasion, it was requisitioned by the British army. In 1792, while a garrison was stationed here, a fire broke out, destroying a good part of the building. In 1810, the ruins were used as a quarry during the building of a second Catholic church. A few years later, Rue Saint-Charles was built right through the rest of the site, forcing the complete destruction of this unique North American building. Archeological excavations took place during the seventies, tracing the castle's exact site and unearthing part of its foundations, visible to the east of the church.

The 1810 church, was demolished in 1884 to make room for the present building, the largest church in Montérégie. The exterior is inspired by flamboyant Gothic art, but remains close to Victorian eclecticism.

The Longueuil tourist information centre is located in the **Maison Rollin-Brais** *(205 Chemin de Chambly)*, an 18th century stone house. Throughout its history, the house has accommodated an inn and a forge. The imposing building at number 225 once housed the Collège de Longueuil. Straight down Chemin de Chambly is an interesting view of the leaning tower of Montréal's Olympic Stadium.

The **Couvent des Sœurs des Saints-Noms-de-Jésus-et-de-Marie** ★ *(tours by appointment; 80 Rue Saint-Charles Est, ☎651-8104)*, has been beautifully restored and is still inhabited by the Saints-Noms-de-Jésus-et-de-Marie nuns, a religious community founded in Longueuil in 1843 by the blessed Mother Marie-Rose. The building includes a residence built in 1769, but the main construction work was carried out between 1844 and 1851.

East of the convent is the **Maison Labadie**, built in 1812 on land that was once part of the seigneurial estate *(90 Rue Saint-Charles Est)*. The Saints-Noms-de-Jésus-et-de-Marie religious order devoted to the education of young girls was founded in this house. The neighbouring house *(100 Rue Saint-Charles Est)* was built in 1749.

Continue heading east towards Boucherville along Rue Saint-Charles Est, which turns into Boulevard Marie-Victorin. Breathtaking views of the port of Montréal can be seen along the way.

Boucherville ★ (pop. 36,198)

Unlike many seigneuries in New France that were granted to servicemen or tradesmen, the Boucherville seigneury was handed over by Intendant Talon to a settler from Trois-Rivières, Pierre Boucher, in 1672. Rather than speculate or use it as a hunting reserve, Boucher made sustained efforts to develop his seigneury, an act that earned him a title of nobility from the King. By the end of the 17th century, Boucherville already consisted of a fortified village, a couple of mills and a church. Few buildings of this period survived the major fire

in 1843 which destroyed a large part of the town.

The seigneury of Boucherville remained in the hands of the Boucher family until the abolition of the seigneurial regime in 1854. More recently, residents of this municipality fought successfully to have Highway 15 skirt around the old village and run further inland, thereby preserving the beauty and tranquillity found by the water's edge.

Parc des Îles-de-Boucherville, see p 190.

Like its two neighbours, the **Maison Louis-Hippolyte-Lafontaine** *(free admission; Thu and Fri 7pm to 9pm, Sat and Sun 1pm to 5pm; 314 Boulevard Marie-Victorin, ☎449-8347)* was moved to the Parc de la Brocquerie in 1964. It was previously located in the heart of the village of Boucherville. Louis-Hippolyte Lafontaine, an ardent defender of French Canadians and Prime Minister of United-Canada in 1842 and from 1848 to 1850, grew up here. The building, whose construction dates back to 1766, now houses an exhibition centre with a section dedicated to the house's history. The park was once part of the Sabrevois de Bleury family estate, and surrounded the La Brocquerie villa which was built around 1735 but unfortunately destroyed by fire in 1971.

The **Manoir de Boucherville** ★ *(468 Boulevard Marie-Victorin)* is one of the rare manors dating back to the French Regime to have survived in the Montréal area. The large stone house was built in 1741 for François-Pierre Boucher of Boucherville, the third seigneur. The Boucherville family lived in the manor until the end of the 19th century. Especially interesting are the purely decorative firebreak walls that slope slightly steeper than the roof.

The harmonious ensemble of the **Église Sainte-Famille** ★★ *(560 Boulevard Marie-Victorin)*, the convent (1890) and the presbytery (1896), surrounds a public square, created during the 17th century. The church is an important piece of vernacular architectural work in Québec. It was built in 1801, according to plans by parish priest Pierre Conefroy. He was not content with sketching the outlines, so he drew up a detailed plan. Thus, the Boucherville church, with three portals at the front and its large latin cross layout, served as a model for religious architecture in Québec villages up until 1830. Damaged during the fire of 1843, it was restored the same year.

MONTÉRÉGIE

Varennes ★ (pop. 15,809)

This town has always been a small, isolated agricultural community, specializing in market gardening. Since the fifties however, many chemical and petroleum industries have moved in just east of the old part of town. Hydro-Québec also opened a research centre in 1967, known as IREQ.

Located at the entrance to the old village, the wooden **Calvary** *(2511 Rue Sainte-Anne)* is one of the oldest monuments of this type to survive in Québec. In 1829 the current cross replaced an 18th century cross, though some of the original statues were salvaged.

The **Basilique** and **Chapelles Votives** ★ *(Rue Sainte-Anne)*. The votive chapels serve mainly as altars of repose during Corpus Christi processions. At one time, many of them lined the roads of Québec, but several disappeared following a decline in religion. The chapels in Varennes are still visited by pilgrims, and are open for worship during the summer. The oldest one, done in a neoclassical style, was built in 1832 to replace a building from the early 18th century. The second one was erected in 1862 according to plans by Victor Bourgeau in the Gothic Revival style, identifiable by its spire and its pointed arch apertures. It has very elaborate ornamentation for this type of building. The vast Romanesque Revival style church that dominates the village was elevated to the rank of minor basilica by Rome in 1993. Through its high façade with two steeples, visitors will discover a richly decorated interior. Many traditional Québec houses can be seen along **Rue Sainte-Anne**, in pleasant surroundings facing the river.

Verchères (pop. 5,125)

In 1692, heroine Madeleine de Verchères took charge of the pile fort and village, defending it against the Iroquois attacking from all sides. News of her brilliant victory resonated throughout the colony and lifted the settlers' spirits during a time of war and food shortages. After this, the town of Verchères developed slowly following the ups and downs of the harvest. However, like Varennes, it has experienced massive industrialization over the past few decades.

The **Moulin** *(Rue Madeleine)*. Up until the mid-19th century, Verchères boasted seven windmills to grind its grain. Today, only two remain, including this one, built in 1730, transformed by the municipality into an exhibition centre. It served as a lighthouse from 1913 to 1949, which explains its appearance.

The imposing **Monument à la Mémoire de Madeleine de Verchères**, cast in bronze by Louis-Philippe Hébert, stands proudly facing the river beside the mill, commemorating this figure. The statue is a testimony to the feelings of Verchères residents for this frail but courageous adolescent of the 17th century who has become an almost mythic figure over the years.

The **Église Saint-François-Xavier** *(Rue Madeleine)* was built in 1787 on the site of the first church of 1724. The façade was updated in the late 19th century, giving it a Romanesque Revival style. The interior, decorated by Louis-Amable Quévillon, is more interesting, including the flat-bottomed chancel with a flat backdrop and adorned with a triumphal arch (1808), as well as French paintings from the 18th century, sold off by Parisian churches during the French Revolution.

Contrecœur (pop. 5,891)

Steel industry giants, Sidbec-Dosco and Stelco, haunt the landscape of this town located in the heart of "the steel region". The downtown area has luckily managed to preserve some interesting rural buildings.

Maison Le Noblet-Duplessis *(late Jun to early Sep, every day 10am to 6pm; 4752 Boulevard Marie-Victorin, ☎587-5750)*. This 1794 house was extensively transformed in the late 19th century to give it a Victorian feeling. For a long time it belonged to lawyer Alexis Le Noblet-Duplessis (1780-1840). He welcomed Patriotes during many secret meetings which led to the armed rebellion of 1837-38. The insurrection was very active in the Richelieu Valley, located not far from the rear guard post of Contrecœur.

Today the house has become municipal property and accommodates a museum that retraces the history of both the building and the town. It is located in the middle of the pretty **Parc Cartier-Richard**, where a walkway and lookout provide great views of the St. Lawrence.

To reach Montréal, take Highway 30. Then head towards the Pont-Tunnel Louis-Hippolyte-Lafontaine, Pont Jacques-Cartier or Pont

Champlain. On the way, you can stop at the Hydro-Québec *Électrium*, located inside the city limits of Sainte-Julie (Exit 128).

The **Électrium d'Hydro-Québec ★** *(early Jun to late Aug, every day 9:30am to 4pm; the rest of the year, Mon to Fri 9:30am to 4pm and Sun 1pm to 4pm; Highway 30, ☎658-8977 or 1-800-267-4558)* is especially interesting for younger visitors. It offers computer games as well as different examples of the use of electricity.

Tour D: Vaudreuil-Soulanges ★
(one day)

This region forms a triangular point of land isolated from the rest of Montérégie. It is demarcated to the west by the Ontario border, to the north and east by the Ottawa River and by the beautiful Lac des Deux-Montagnes and Lac Saint-Louis, both areas known for excellent water sports, and lastly, to the south, by the St. Lawrence, which widens here to form Lac Saint-François. Don't be surprised if you here the name Suroît mentioned – the region is sometimes referred to by this name for a wind from the southwest. Weekend strollers can see beautiful properties in the distant Montréal suburbs as well as many lakeside landscapes.

Vaudreuil-Dorion (pop. 18,000 inhab.)

The western tip of the region was once part of the network of old seigneuries under the French Regime. As a result it was considered part of Québec, rather than the neighbouring province of Ontario during the creation of Upper and Lower Canada (1791). The seigneuries of Vaudreuil and of Soulanges, granted in 1702, developed with difficulty, since they were located upstream from the impassable Lachine Rapids. Thus, despite the proximity to Montréal, the area was sparsely populated until the end of the 18th century. **Dorion**, once an integral part of the Vaudreuil seigneury, developed with the help of tradesmen of German descent. The seigneury of **Vaudreuil** was granted to François de Rigaud, marquis of Vaudreuil, in the early 18th century. As governor of Montréal, he was too busy to run his seigneury. He sold it along with his estate on Rue Saint-Paul to Michel Chartier de Lotbinière before leaving for France in 1763. Lotbinière worked hard to develop the estate. Through marriage, the seigneury passed into the hands of Robert Unwin Harwood, who

attracted British settlers to the region. They settled mostly in the villages of Como and Hudson, which have retained a certain British flavour. Dorion and Vaudreuil merged to become one municipality in 1996.

The **Maison Trestler ★** *($3.50; Mon to Fri 9am to 5pm, Sun 1pm to 4pm; concerts Mon 8pm; 85 Chemin de la Commune, ☎455-6290)* is ideally located on the shores of Lac des Deux-Montagnes. This unusual stone house is 44 metres long and was built in stages between 1798 and 1806. The owner of the house, Jean-Joseph Trestler, a mercenary in the Hesse-Hanau regiment, arrived in Canada in 1776. Ten years later, he settled in Dorion and became involved in the fur trade. In 1976 the house was partially converted into a cultural centre by the current owners. Many concerts and conferences are now held here.

Return to Boulevard Saint-Henri. Turn right in the direction of Vaudreuil, where the road turns into Boulevard Roche.

Built between 1783 and 1789, the **Église Saint-Michel ★★** *(414 Avenue St-Charles)* was given a new Gothic-Revival-style façade in 1856 in an effort to modernize it. The Latin cross layout and apse with cut-off corners are similar to the first churches of the French Regime. The most complete collection of liturgical furniture sculpted by Philippe Liébert in the 18th century (pulpit, high altar, candelabra, statues) is located inside. Also of particular note because they were eliminated from most other Québec churches during the restorations that took place in the sixties, are the seigneurial bench and the polychromatic decor painted in trompe-l'œil by F. E. Meloche in 1883. Other interesting elements include the 1871 organ and the striking paintings, including one entitled *Saint Louis* painted in 1792 by Louis-Chrétien de Heer.

The **Musée Régional de Vaudreuil-Soulanges ★** *($3; year round, Tue to Fri 10am to 5pm, Sat and Sun 1pm to 5pm; 431 Avenue St-Charles, ☎455-2092)*, founded in 1953, is one of Québec's oldest regional museums, and a testimony to Vaudreuil's cultural vitality at the time. It is located in the former Collège Saint-Michel (1857), once run by the clerics of Saint-Viateur. The beautiful building, covered with a mansard roof, houses collections of everyday items, craft tools of the 18th and 19th century, as well as interesting religious art, antique paintings and carvings.

MONTÉRÉGIE

Como

Visitors to this charming village can enjoy beautiful views of Oka (p 248), located on the other side of the lake. A ferry links Oka to Como.

Hudson ★ (pop. 5,249)

Hudson is a pretty, mostly English-speaking town. The well-off residents live in comfortable homes, modern and old. Many enjoy the rural landscape and then commute to work in downtown Montréal by commuter train (Rigaud-Montréal) during the week. In the summer, residents of this lakeside community practise their favourite water sports on Lac des Deux-Montagnes. The **St. James of Hudson Anglican Church** was founded in 1841 at the instigation of Seigneur Harwood de Vaudreuil. The structure is a good example of a stone Gothic Revival village church. Whatever the season, exploring this small town with its many shops, charming little restaurants and small, tree-lined streets, is a pleasure.

Rigaud (pop. 6,276)

The sons of the Marquis of Vaudreuil were granted the Rigaud seigneury in 1732. However, the village did not develop until after the arrival of the clerics of Saint-Viateur, who opened **Collège Bourget** in 1850. In addition to its educational vocation, Rigaud welcomes pilgrims to its hilltop sanctuary.

Follow Rue Saint-Jean-Baptiste (Route 342). Turn left onto Rue Saint-Pierre. Follow the directions for the sanctuary.

The **Sanctuaire Notre-Dame-de-Lourdes** ★ *(early May to late Sep, every day 9am to 9pm, 20 Rue Bourget, ☎451-4631)*. Suffering from illness in 1874, brother Ludger Pauzé c.s.v. carved a small hole in a rock and he placed a statuette of the Virgin Mary there as a demonstration of his faith. And so Marian worship began in Rigaud. A first eight-sided chapel, from which visitors can enjoy a beautiful view of the region, was built in 1887. Later various additions were made so outdoor celebrations for large crowds could be organized. These included a new chapel, where mass has been celebrated since 1954. Not far from the sanctuary is a strange pile of stones left on this site after the ebb of the Champlain Sea during glaciation. Legend has it that this bed of stones was once a potato field. God,

appalled to see its owner working on a Sunday, changed it to a field of stones now known as the "devil's field".

Return to Highway 40 E. until Exit 17. Follow Route 201 S. passing through Saint-Clet to arrive in Coteau-du-Lac, located on the edge of the St. Lawrence. Turn right onto Chemin du Fleuve.

Coteau-du-Lac ★ (pop. 4,559)

A narrowing of the river combined with a series of rapids makes all sailing impossible here. The St. Lawrence reaches its lowest level after a change in altitude of 25 metres over just 12.8 kilometres. Coteau-du-Lac therefore became a rallying and portage point even before the arrival of the Europeans. Many vestiges of aboriginal civilization have been found here, namely three skeletons some 6,000 years old. At the end of the French Regime (1759), authorities set up a sort of channel at the end of a small point, a simple reinforced dyke made with piles of rocks and parallel to the shore. Through this first canal, boatmen pulled flat-bottomed boats filled with furs. In 1779, the British built the first lock in North America here. A fort built by military engineer William Twiss was added to the canal in 1812.

The **Maison du Tourisme** *(visits by appointment only; 308 Chemin du Fleuve, ☎763-1840)*. The name of this place, which translates to tourism house, is misleading because this building is actually a former mill (1858) restored in 1992 to house reception rooms.

The **Coteau-du-Lac National Historic Site** ★ *($2.50; mid-May to late Jun, every day 9am to 5pm; late Jun to late Aug every day 10am to 6pm; early Sep to mid-Oct, Wed to Sun 10am to 5pm, off-season by appointment; 308 Chemin du Fleuve, ☎763-5631)*, also called Lieu Hisorique National de Coteau-du-Lac. Relics of the British and French canals can be seen from here, as well as ruins of the fort erected to defend this important passageway. Visitors first come across the welcome centre, where an instructive model fort represents the area at the peak of its activity. Then, a trail through the site provides a closer look at the ruins of the facilities as well as an exterior reconstruction of the blockhouse, built by the British at the end of the point. There is also a beautiful view of the St. Lawrence's rapids from here.

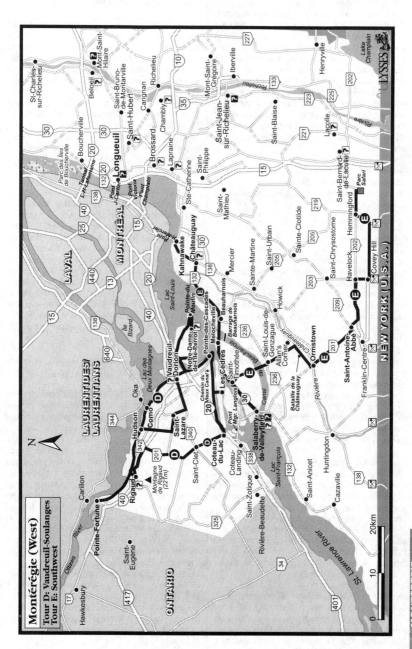

Return to Chemin du Fleuve heading east (direction Les Cèdres and Pointe-des-Cascades). Three kilometres from Coteau-du-Lac, a hydroelectric power station designed to resemble a German castle can be seen to the left, set back from the road; it has now been transformed into a residence (not open to the public). This rare building, erected in 1899, supplied electricity to the Canal de Soulanges workings. The canal stretches along the north bank of the river between Coteau-Landing and Pointe-des-Cascades. Québec sculptor Armand Vaillancourt had his workshop here for many years.

Follow Chemin du Fleuve to Pointe-des-Cascades. Turn left onto Rue Centrale, then make an immediate right onto Chemin du Canal.

Pointe-des-Cascades (pop. 750)

Located at the mouth of the Ottawa River, this town owes its existence to the Canal de Soulanges, which is now closed. Pointe-des-Cascades was visited as early as 1684 by the Baron of Lahontan, while a bloody war between the French and the Iroquois raged in the area. A first channel was set up by the French in 1749, followed by a small lock in 1805, named Canal Cascades. This canal and the Canal de Coteau-du-Lac were replaced by the first Canal de Beauharnois, inaugurated in 1845 on the south side of the St. Lawrence. The Canal de Soulanges, set up on the site of the Canal Cascades, succeeded the Canal de Beauharnois in 1899; it ceased operating when the St. Lawrence Seaway opened (current Canal de Beauharnois) in 1959.

Pointe des Cascades ★ *($2.75, parking $1; at the eastern late Chemin du Canal).* A campground and a summer theatre in a lumber warehouse now occupy the former command station of the Canal de Soulanges. Beautiful brick buildings designed by engineer Thomas Monroe in 1900 can be seen throughout the site as well as two lighthouses and three of the five locks. There are also lovely views of the Ottawa River, Lac Saint-Louis and Île Perrot from the entrance of the canal.

Return to Rue Centrale. Turn right onto Route 338 E., then right again onto Highway 20. Cross the bridge over the Ottawa River to arrive on Île Perrot (Exit Boulevard Don-Quichotte). Follow Boulevard Perrot and turn left onto Boulevard Don-Quichotte.

Notre-Dame-de-l'Île-Perrot (pop. 5,841)

In 1672 the seigneury of Île Perrot was granted to the governor of Montréal François-Marie Perrot, who set up a fur-trading post at the fief of Brucy. The seigneury then passed into the hands of Charles Le Moyne, before being sold in 1703 to Joseph Trottier Desruisseaux, who set up a farm on the point near the Mill. His widow began construction of Île Perrot's first church in 1740. Because it is closer to Montréal and not isolated by the rapids that hamper river traffic, the seigneury of Île Perrot experienced more extensive development than the other land of the area granted under the French Regime.

The **Parc Historique de la Pointe-du-Moulin** ★ *(free admission; mid-May to early Sep, every day from sunrise to sunset; early Sep to mid-Oct Sat, Sun.; 2500 Boulevard Don-Quichotte, ☎453-5936).* Beyond the modern reception area, visitors can reach the wooded park, where on clear days, there are beautiful views of downtown Montréal across Lac Saint-Louis. The windmill, built in 1708, and the miller's house are located at the end of the point. Guides explain how the mill works (it is still in working order today), and the history of the area. A heritage information centre and picnic areas are also set up on site.

Return to Boulevard Perrot. Turn left, then left again onto Rue de l'Église.

The **Église Sainte-Jeanne-de-Chantal** ★★ *(1 Rue de l'Église)* is often described as the perfect example of a French-Canadian church in the Montréal region. In fact, its modest dimensions, reminiscent of the first churches of the French Regime, as well as its interior decor in the Louis-XV and Louis-XVI styles, make the church an excellent example of traditional Québec architecture. The building was completed in 1786, and embellished between 1812 and 1830 under the direction of Joseph Turcault and Louis-Xavier Leprohon. A commemorative chapel, with its back to the river, was built in 1953, using the stones from the first church of Pointe-du-Moulin (1753). The chapel walls contain the Intendant Hocquart's plaque which gave the seigneur of Île Perrot permission to establish a parish on this land (1740), as well as strange red sandstone mascarons brought over from France around 1945 by Colonel Roger Maillet. The chapel towers above a terraced cemetery, unique in Québec.

Md. Pierson

Parc Historique de la Pointe-du-Moulin

Return to Highway 20 to reach Montréal.

Tour E: The Southwest ★
(one-and-a-half days)

This tour covers the southwestern part of Montérégie. It winds through the region along the shores of Lac Saint-Louis, through the foothills of the Appalachians along the New York State border, and into the valley of the Rivière Châteauguay. The southwest is an agricultural region, perfect for autumn strolls, fruit-picking and market perusing. The old seigneuries established along the lake and the Rivière Chateauguay are mostly French speaking, while the townships that developed in the interior at the beginning of the 19th century are still mostly English speaking.

Kahnawake (pop. 6,500)

In 1667, the Jesuits set up a mission for the converted Iroquois at La Prairie. After moving four times, the mission settled permanently in Sault-Saint-Louis in 1716. The Saint-François-Xavier mission has now become Kahnawake, a name that means "where the rapids are". Over the years, Iroquois Mohawks from the State of New York joined the mission's first inhabitants, so that English is now the first language on the reserve, even though most inhabitants stilll use the French names given to them by the Jesuits. In 1990, Mohawk Warriors demonstrated by blocking the Pont Mercier for months in a show of support for the demands made by the Mohawks of Kanesatake (Oka). Tension between Québec authorities and the natives still exists in the area surrounding the reserve, but visitors need not worry as they are generally warmly welcomed in Kahnawake.

MONTÉRÉGIE

The **Enceinte, Musée** and **Église Saint-François-Xavier** ★★ *(Main Street)* Saint-François-Xavier wall, museum and church. Villages and missions were required under the French Regime to surround themselves with fortifications. Very few of these walls have survived. The wall of the Kahnawake mission, still partially standing, is the kind of ruin rarely found north of Mexico. It was built in 1720, according to plans of the King's engineer, Gaspard Chaussegros de Léry, to protect the church and the Jesuit convent, built in 1717. The guardroom, powder magazine and officers' residences (1754) are also still standing. From the platform behind the Jesuit convent, visitors can enjoy spectacular views of the seaway, Lachine and Montréal.

The church was modified in 1845 according to the plans of Jesuit Félix Martin, and redecorated by Vincent Chartrand (1845-47), who also made some of the furniture. Guido Nincheri designed the polychromatic vaulted ceiling in the 20th century. Also found here is the tomb of Kateri Tekakwitha, a young native. The convent houses the museum of the Saint-François-Xavier mission, where visitors can see some of the objects that belonged to the Jesuits, still leading the parish. The village around the church offers one of the largest concentrations of rubble masonry homes in Québec. However, following the example of the fortification walls, these homes are not shown off to their full advantage, many of them have been defaced, covered up with more modern materials, or simply abandoned.

Take Chemin Saint-Bernard towards Châteauguay (near the metallic cross and the school). Turn left onto Chemin Christ-Roi (after the water purification plant), then right onto Rue Dupont. Turn left onto Boulevard Salaberry Nord, follow the Rivière Châteauguay until the Pont Laberge. Cross the bridge to get to the Église Saint-Joachim. Turn right onto Boulevard Youville behind the church, where the parking lot is located.

Châteauguay (pop. 42,246)

The Châteauguay seigneury was granted to Charles Le Moyne in 1673. He immediately had Château de Guay built on Île Saint-Bernard, at the mouth of the Rivière Châteauguay. One hundred years later, a village stood out around the Église Saint-Joachim. The roads and Boulevards that run along the river and Lac Saint-Louis are still dotted with pretty farm homes built between 1780 and 1840, when the seigneury belonged to the Sœurs Grises (the Grey Nuns). The municipality has developed considerably since 1950, making it a large component of the Montréal suburbs.

When the first church in Châteauguay was built in 1735 it was the westernmost parish on the south shore of the St. Lawrence. Work on the present **Église Saint-Joachim** ★★ *(1 Boulevard Youville)* began in 1775 in order to more easily serve a growing number of parishioners. The **Hôtel de Ville** neighbours the church to the north. It is located in the former convent of the Congrégation de Notre-Dame (1886).

Continue along Boulevard Youville and travel along the river to Lac Saint-Louis.

Route de Léry ★ *(Chemin du Lac-Saint-Louis)*. **Île Saint-Bernard**, which still belongs to the Sœurs Grises, can be seen on the right; it is not open to visitors. The large stone house sitting on the shore is the seigneurial estate, the **Manoir d'Youville**, built by the nuns in 1774 on the site of the Château de Guay.

Chemin du Lac-Saint-Louis joins up with Route 132 W. at Maple Grove. Follow this road in the direction of Beauharnois.

Beauharnois (pop. 6,665)

The seigneury of Villechauve was granted to the Marquis of Beauharnois, fifteenth governor of New France, in 1729. At the end of the 18th century, tradesman Alexander Ellice announced his intention to purchase it. He then had a saw mill built on the Rivière Saint-Louis, vestiges of which still remain. In 1863, the Kilgour family opened a large furniture factory in Beauharnois, turning the village into a small industrial city. The large brick buildings still dominate the river's west bank. Today, Beauharnois is known mostly for its hydroelectric power plant, the third-largest in Québec.

The **Église Saint-Clément** ★ *(at the top of the hill on Chemin Saint-Louis)* is very picturesque when seen from the Rivière Saint-Louis. Its Romanesque Revival-style façade, attributed to Victor Bourgeau, is built in front of a simple nave, completed in 1845.

Melocheville (2,366 inhab.)

The locks that control the Beauharnois canal and hydroelectric station (the third most important in Québec) are located here.

The **Centrale Hydro-Électrique de Beauharnois ★★** *(free admission; late May to late Jun, Mon to Fri; late Jun to early Sep, Wed to Sun; guided tours 9:30am, 11:15am, 1pm and 2:45pm; 80 Boulevard Edgar-Hébert, ☎429-6481).* The Beauharnois hydro station was once the jewel of the large Montréal Light, Heat and Power Electric Company, owned by the uncompromising Sir Herbert Holt. Built in stages between 1929 and 1956, the power plant is a sprawling 864 metres long. The electricity produced in Beauharnois is distributed throughout Québec and to the United States during the summer, when local needs are not as high. The power plant now belongs to Hydro-Québec. It is open to visitors, guided tours *(departures every hour)* show visitors the very long turbine room as well as the computers used in the control room.

Route 132 runs in front of the power plant before disappearing under the Canal de Beauharnois, inaugurated in 1959. It is the last in a series of canals set up along the St. Lawrence. The canals are used to bypass the many rapids found in the area, and resolve the navigational problem posed by a 25-metre drop between Lac Saint-Louis and Lac Saint-François.

The **Parc Archéologique de la Pointe-du-Buisson ★** *($4; mid-May to early Sep, Mon to Fri 10am to 5pm, Sat and Sun 10am to 6pm; early Sep to mid-Oct, Sat and Sun noon to 5pm; 333 Rue Émond, ☎429-7857).* The Buisson headland was inhabited sporadically for thousands of years by aboriginals, leaving the area rich with native relics (arrow heads, cooking pots, harpoons, etc). During the summer, different areas of the archeological park can be visited, such as an excavation site active since 1977, an information centre and a reconstructed prehistoric fishing camp. Ecological paths and picnic areas are also set up.

The **Parc Régional des Îles de Saint-Timothée** see p 191.

Take Highway 30 E. to Salaberry-de-Valleyfield.

Salaberry-de-Valleyfield (pop. 28,500)

This industrial city came into being in 1845 around a saw and paper mill purchased a few years later by the Montréal Cotton Company. This growing industry led to an era of prosperity in the late 19th century in Salaberry-de-Valleyfield, making it one of Québec's main cities at the time. The old commercial and institutional centre on Rue Victoria recalls this prosperous period, and gives the city more of an urban atmosphere than Châteauguay whose population is higher. The city is cut in half by the old Canal de Beauharnois, in operation from 1845 to 1900 (not to be confused with the current Canal de Beauharnois located to the south of the city.)

A diocese since 1892, Salaberry-de-Valleyfield was graced with the current **Cathédrale Sainte-Cécile ★** *(31 Rue de la Fabrique)* in 1934, following a fire in the previous church. The cathedral is a colossal piece of work. Architect Henri Labelle designed it in the late Gothic Revival style, narrower and closer to the historical models, and combined the result with elements of Art Deco. The façade is adorned with a statue of Sainte Cécile, patron saint of musicians, and the bronze entrance doors are decorated with many bas-reliefs done by Albert Gilles, depicting the life of Jesus.

The Pont Monseigneur-Langlois, west of Salaberry-de-Valleyfield, connects the Southwest tour to the Vaudreuil-Soulanges tour. To continue on the Southwest tour, return to Saint-Timothée. Turn right and head towards the Village de Saint-Louis-de-Gonzague to get to the banks of the Rivière Châteauguay.

The **Battle of the Châteauguay National Historic Site ★** *($2.50; late Jun to late Aug, every day 10am to 6pm; Sep and Oct, Wed to Sun 9am to 5pmk; 2371 Chemin Rivière-Châteauguay Nord),* also called the Lieu Historique National de la Bataille de la Châteauguay. During the American War of Independence (1775-76), the Americans attempted their first take-over of Canada, a British colony since 1760. They were forced back by the majority French population. In 1812-13, the Americans tried once again to take over Canada. This time, it was loyalty to the Crown of England and decisive battle of Châteauguay that bungled the Americans' attempt. In October 1813, troops of American General Hampton, 2,000-men strong, gathered at the border. They entered Canadian territory during the night along the Rivière Châteauguay. But Charles

MONTÉRÉGIE

Michel d'Irumberry de Salaberry, seigneur of Chambly, was waiting for them along with 300 militiamen and a few dozen natives. On October 26, the battle began. Salaberry's tactics got the better of the Americans, who retreated, putting an end to a series of conflicts and inaugurating a lasting friendship between the two countries.

Travel along the Rivière Châteauguay until Ormstown.

Ormstown ★ (pop. 1,575)

Founded by British settlers, Ormstown was named in honour of one of the sons of Seigneur Alexander Ellice de Beauharnois. It is, without a doubt, one of the prettiest villages of Montérégie. Many churches of various denominations are found here, such as the stone **St. James Anglican Church** (1837). Note the colourful homes on the west shore with their red bricks, white wooden accents, and the green (or black) shutters. Ormstown specializes in horse-breeding. There is a **racetrack** here as well as a few riding schools (breeding and boarding), owned by long-standing Anlgo-Saxon families.

Hemmingford

Highway 15 leads to the town of Hemmingford near the American border. **Parc Safari** ★ is located here *($19; $66 per car; early May to early Sep, every day 10am to 5pm; 850 Route 202, ☎247-2727)*. The park is an interesting zoological garden, where animals from Africa, Europe and America, wander freely, as visitors tour the grounds in their cars.

 PARKS

Centre de Conservation de la Nature du Mont Saint-Hilaire ★★ *($4; every day 8am until sundown; 422 Rue des Moulins, Mont-Saint-Hilaire, J3G 4S6, ☎467-1755)*. Situated on the upper half of Mont Saint-Hilaire, this nature conservation centre is a former estate that brigadier Andrew Hamilton Gault passed on to Montréal's McGill University in 1958. Scientific research is conducted here and recreational activities (hiking, cross-country skiing) are permitted throughout the year on half of the estate, which covers 11 square kilometres. The Centre was also recognized as a Biosphere

Reserve by UNESCO in 1978, because it is covered by a mature forest that has remained virtually untouched over the centuries. An information centre on the formation of the Montérégie hills and a garden of indigenous plants can be found at the park's entrance.

The small Lac Hertel, visited by migrating birds, is located at the bottom of a valley. The surrounding peaks are criss-crossed by a 24-kilometre long network of paths. One of these peaks, called Pain du Sucre or Sugarloaf, offers an exceptional panoramic view of the Richelieu valley. On clear days, visitors can also see Montréal to the west (before noon) and the Appalachians to the southeast (during the afternoon).

Tour C: Shore of the St. Lawrence

Parc du Mont Saint-Bruno ★ *($3 between Nov and Apr, free admission between Apr and Nov; every day 8am until sundown; 330 Chemin des 25 Est, St-Bruno-de-Montarville, ☎653-7544)* was once a holiday resort frequented by upper-class, English-speaking Montrealers. Many families, such as the Birks, the Drummonds and the Merediths, had beautiful second homes built here in what is now a park. There are two lakes at the top of the mountain, Lac Seigneurial and Lac du Moulin, next to 19th-century water mill. The park is a pleasant place to walk and relax. Self-guided trails and guided walks help familiarize visitors with the park. Cross-country skiing is possible during the winter, with almost 27 kilometres of trails set up and small heated cabins along the way.

To get to the **Parc de Récréation des Îles-de-Boucherville** *(year round, every day 8am to sundown; 55 Île Sainte Marguerite, Boucherville, J4B 5J6, ☎928-5088)* take Highway 20, Exit 89, or take the ferry from Longueuil *(Promenade René-Lévesque)*. Some of the islands are still farmland, but the archipelago, linked by cable-ferries, is accessible to visitors. The park is devoted to outdoor activities, mainly cycling and hiking in the summer. There is also a golf course and a picnic area. Rich with birds of all kinds, the park is a favourite among ornithologists. You can also get a completely different perspective on the park by exploring it in a canoe; there are four tours totalling 28 kilometres.

Tour D: Vaudreuil-Soulanges

Take Route 132 West and follow the signs starting at St-Anicet to **Lac Saint-François National Wildlife Area** ★★ *(Dundee, ☎370-6954 or 264-5908)*, also called Réserve Nationale de Faune du Lac St-François. On the south shore of the St. Lawrence River, this park is a wetland recognized by the Ramsar Convention (a world-wide list of protected sites). Visitors can observe 220 species of birds, 600 plants and over 40 species of mammals. From May to October, excursions in Rabaska canoes and hikes, both with guides, are offered.

Tour E: The Southwest

On the banks of the St. Lawrence, close to the town of Salaberry-de-Valleyfield is the tourist-recreation complex on the **beach** of the **Parc Régional des Îles de Saint-Timothée** *($5; Jun to Aug, every day 10am to 5pm, Sat and Sun until 7pm; 240 Rue St-Laurent, ☎377-1117)*. Popular for a number of years, this spot offers all sorts of activities: swimming, in-line skating, kayaking lessons, a volleyball competition, canoe and pedal-boat rental, etc. It's an interesting place for families and groups but not recommended for those seeking peace and quiet.

OUTDOORS

Hiking

The Montérégie region includes six hills that were, for a long time, thought to be old volcanos. They actually consist of metamorphic rock that didn't break the surface of the earth's crust. These hills are great for day hikers, and most are accessible from the highways. Here's a list of some of the best places:

Parc des Îles-de-Boucherville *(55 Île Ste-Marguerite, Louis-Hyppolite-Lafontaine tunnel, Exit 89, ☎928-5088)*, located on an island in the middle of the St. Lawrence River, has a lot to offer in terms of flora and fauna. Over 170 species of fish and 40 species of birds have been spotted here.

Parc de Conservation du Mont-Saint-Bruno *(330 Chemin des 25 Est, ☎653-7544)*, nestled in the middle of the charming municipality of Saint-Bruno, offers a network of pleasant trails that lead to a number of lakes. Many picnic and rest areas have been set up to accommodate hikers.

The **Centre de Conservation de la Nature Mont-Saint-Hilaire** *(422 Chemin des Moulins, ☎467-1755)* in Mont Saint-Hilaire is 400 metres high, has many trails that offer great hiking possibilities, and rewards your efforts with fantastic views notably along the Pain de Sucre trail.

Mont Saint-Grégoire *(☎346-0406)* offers wonderful hiking in maple groves and orchards.

Lac Saint-François National Wildlife Area *(☎264-4519)*, also called Réserve Nationale de Faune du Lac Saint-François, on the south shore of the St. Lawrence, close to Valleyfield, is not to be missed. The marsh environment, canals and ponds are home to unique vegetation and wildlife; certain species aren't found anywhere else in the country.

Cycling

Cycling has become a lot more popular over the last few years. For this reason, Montérégie, along with the Eastern Townships, established an amazing network of bicycle trails. La **Montérégiade** trail, inaugurated in 1993, links the two regions and is the first step in the creation of a far-reaching corridor which, when finished, will extend to the Appalachian Trail in Maine.

Here are a few other suggestions for paths in the region:

Tour A: Forts on the Richelieu

Canal de Chambly *(☎658-0321; 39 km from Chambly to St-Jean)*. While riding alongside historic Chambly Canal and Richelieu River, you'll see lock-keepers at work, daysailors and magnificent views of the Richelieu. If you're lucky, you might even spot a mallard or a heron.

The **Circuits des Pommes** *(☎469-3600, 49 km)*, which means apple route, couldn't have a more appropriate name. The wonderful thing about

MONTÉRÉGIE

this trail is the many tasty, refreshing discoveries that can be made all along the way; they also provide great excuses to catch your breath. Be careful about wine and cider sampling: drinking and driving don't go well together.

Circuit de la Covey Hill (☎674-5555; 90.7 km), a route shared with motor vehicles, loops through the lovely Covey Hill valley and crosses fields, orchards and charming little towns. Residents say that the area benefits from a microclimate; the sun shines more here than anywhere else in the country.

 Cross-country Skiing

Although Montérégie is obviously neither the Laurentians nor the Eastern Townships, there is still an interesting network of cross-country ski trails here. It is close to the city and the trails are easier. The following parks have trails:

Centre de Conservation de la Nature du Mont-Saint-Hilaire ($4; rental; 422 Chemin des Moulins, ☎467-1755, 4 trails - 7.5 km)

Parc de Conservation du Mont Saint-Bruno ($3.25 per car, $6.25 per person; rental; 330 Chemin des 25 Est, ☎653-7544, 9 trails - 27 km)

Centre de Plein Air Les Forestiers ($7; rental; 1677 Chemin St-Dominique, ☎455-6771 or 452-4736, 9 trails - 33 km)

 Fruit-Picking

Fruit picking! What better way to spend some time than outdoors and in fine company! It's also economical since you can stock up on your favourite fruits at unbeatable prices. For a list of pick-your-own orchards call ☎674-5555; the towns of Saint Hilaire, Rougemont and Saint Grégoire are famous for their apples. Beware though, in season, that is on weekends in September and October when traffic on the small roads, especially in the St-Hilaire area, is a nightmare. If you can, go during the week.

 Kayaking

Tour A: Forts on the Richelieu

Kayak et cetera (56 Rue Martel, Chambly, behind the Maison Culturelle, ☎658-2031); kayak and canoe rental. Classes are available for young people, 12 years old and up, and for adults of all levels.

 ACCOMMODATIONS

Tour A: Forts on the Richelieu

Chambly

L'Air du Temps ($65 bkfst incl.; 124 Rue Martel, ☎658-1642 or 888-658-1642). This charming house right across from Bassin de Chambly, has been tastefully decorated despite the slight overabundance of pastels. There is one large bedroom on the ground floor and four others in the old attic. Friendly reception.

La Maison Ducharme ($90-$110 bkfst incl.; ≈; 124 Rue Martel, ☎447-1220, ↵447-1018). This pleasant B&B occupies an old 19th-century barracks (see p 166), right near Fort Chambly. Tastefully decorated, the house is steeped in the antique luxury of an era, when people took the time make every detail in the house immaculate. A lovely English garden and pool add to this large property next to the Rivière Richelieu rapids.

Saint-Jean-sur-Richelieu

The **Auberge des Trois Rives** ($55, ℜ; 297 Rue Richelieu, J3B 6Y3, ☎358-8077, ↵358-8077) is a pleasant B&B set up in a rustic home. A restaurant and a terrace offer a pretty view of the water. There are 10 modestly-decorated but comfy rooms spread over two floors. Take note that prices may be higher during the hot-air balloon festival.

The **Best Western Vallée des Forts** ($64-117; tv, ≈, ℜ, ◯; 725 Boulevard du Séminaire, J3B 8H1, ☎348-7376 or 1-800-667-3815, ↵348-9778) stands at the entrance to the city, along the Richelieu. The rooms are spacious

Ulysses' Favourites

Hotels

For tranquillity:
Hostellerie des Trois Tilleuls (p 194)

For history buffs:
Manoir Rouville-Campbell (p 193) and Maison Ducharme (p 192)

For a friendly reception:
Auberge des Trois Rives (p 192)

Restaurants

Montérégie's finest tables:
Au Tournant de la Rivière (p 194), Hostellerie des Trois Tilleuls (p 196), Clémentine (p 197) and Le Champagne (p 196)

For Québec cuisine:
Le Samuel II (p 195), Sucrerie de la Montagne (p 196) and Clémentine (p 197)

For the terrace:
Ostéria (p 195), Trait d'Union (p 195), Chez Noesser (p 195), Crêperie du Fort Chambly (p 194) and Manneken Pis (p 195)

For the view:
Le Samuel II (p 195)

and bright. Facilities include an indoor swimming pool, a bar, and a non-smoking floor. Service is courteous.

Tour B: Chemin des Patriotes

Beloeil

The **Hostellerie Rive Gauche** *($85, tv, ≈, ℜ; 1810 Boulevard Richelieu, J3G 4S4, ☎467-4477, ≈467-0525)* is located off Highway 20 (Exit 112), along the edge of the Rivière Richelieu. This inn has 22 rooms decorated in warm tones and linens, and offers a view of the water. Two tennis courts are available for guests. There is also a cosy dining room.

Mont-Saint-Hilaire

The **Auberge Montagnard** *($57-$150; 439 Boulevard Laurier, J3H 3P2, ☎467-0201 or 1-800-363-9109, ≈467-0628)* is located on a noisy boulevard, across from Mont Saint-

Hilaire. It offers old-fashioned but comfortable rooms, with a friendly staff.

The **Manoir Rouville Campbell** *($105; ≡, ≈, ℜ; 125 Chemin des Patriotes, ☎446-6060, ≈446-4878)* has a certain mystical air about it; as you enter the manor it's as though time has stopped or even gone back a century. This place, now 200 years old, has seen many chapters of Québec history unfold. It was converted into a luxury hotel in 1987 and is now owned by Québec comedian Yvon Deschamps. The dining room, bar and gardens overlooking the Richelieu complement this lordly manor.

Saint-Hyacinthe

In a building next to the highway, the **Auberge des Seigneurs** *($70-$120, ≈, ☉, △, ℜ; 1200 Daniel-Johnson, J2S 7K7, ☎774-3810 and 1-800-363-0110, ≈774-6955)* offers pretty rooms as well as other services, to ensure its visitors a pleasant stay. Tennis and

MONTÉRÉGIE

squash courts are available, and the peaceful lobby is decorated with plants and a fountain.

Saint-Marc-sur-Richelieu

Located in a beautiful home across from the Richelieu, the **Auberge Handfield** *($70-$175; ≈, ℜ, △, ☉, tv; 555 Chemin du Prince, J0L 2E0, ☎584-2226 or 1-800-667-1087, ⇒584-3650)* is a true escape. It offers its guests many services including a health spa and the *Escale* boat-theatre. The garden is well kept and offers a great view. The rooms are modest, but nevertheless comfortable.

The **Hostellerie les Trois Tilleuls** *($90-$390; ≈, tv, ℜ; 290 Rue Richelieu J0L 2E0, ☎584-2231 or 1-800-263-2230, ⇒584-3146)* is a member of the prestigious Relais et Châteaux association. Built next to the Richelieu, it enjoys a tranquil rural setting. The name of the establishment comes from the three grand linden trees, called *tilleul* in French, that shade the property. The rooms are decorated with rustic furniture and they each have a balcony overlooking the river. Outside, guests have access to gardens, a lookout and a heated pool.

Tour D: Vaudreuil-Soulanges

Vaudreuil-Dorion

Château Vaudreuil *($117; ≡, ≈, ℜ; 21700 Highway 40, J7V 8P3, ☎455-0955 or 1-800-363-7896, ⇒455-6617)*. Located on Lac des Deux-Montagnes, this modern, imposing-looking hotel, which has very comfortable rooms, is a good choice in this region.

Hudson

The **Auberge Willow Place** *($85 bkfst incl.; 208 Main Road, J0P 1H0, ☎458-7006, ⇒458-4615)* is pleasantly located on the shores of Lac des Deux-Montagnes. Old-fashioned charm and a hushed atmosphere.

RESTAURANTS

Tour A: Forts on the Richelieu

Carignan

The restaurant **Au Tournant de la Rivière** *($$$; closed Mon And Tue; 5070 Rue Salaberry, ☎658-7372)* has a critically acclaimed gourmet menu. In business for more than 20 years, the establishment's succulent French cuisine has helped it maintain its standing among the best restaurants in Quebec. A must for gourmet palates.

Chambly

The snack bar **Chez Marius** *($-$$; 1737 Rue Bourgogne, ☎658-6092)* is a local favourite. While savouring a delicious hamburger and poutine combo, you can examine old photographs documenting the history of the restaurant, as well as that of Chambly. During summer, you can eat outdoors on the riverside terrace.

Crêperie du Fort Chambly *($$; 1717 Rue Bougogne, ☎447-7474)*, on the edge of Bassin de Chambly, occupies a wooden house that recalls the sea. They serve crêpes, of course, but also cheese fondues. Waterfront terrace and friendly service.

Les Fous de Bassin *($$-$$$; 1574 Rue Bourgogne, ☎447-6945)* serves mouthwatering, innovative French cuisine in a pleasant, unpretentious atmosphere.

La Maison Bleu *($$$; 2592 Rue Bourgogne ☎658-6426)*. What was once the large, wooden house of Thomas Whitehead, (see p 166), now houses a luxurious restaurant with a country feel: large fireplaces, creaky floors and antiques. Upstairs, private rooms can be reserved for family gatherings or business meetings. Classic French cuisine and a warm reception.

Richelieu

Aux Chutes du Richelieu *($$$-$$$$; 486 Rue Richelieu, ☎658-6689)* prepares excellent

French and Italian cuisine. Their crepes Suzette are truly sinful. What's more, you can admire the Richelieu falls while you eat.

Saint-Jean-sur-Richelieu

Le Manneken Pis *($; every day 9am to 9pm; 320 Rue Champlain,* ☎348-3254*)*. With a name like that, Belgian waffles are sure to be nearby – and what delicious waffles they are, and with such fine chocolate! The coffees, roasted on site, are also excellent. A pleasant terrace faces a little marina. They also serve bread with various spreads and salads.

Much loved by the locals, **Le Samuel II** *($$-$$$; 291 Rue Richelieu,* ☎347-4353*)* has always had a faithful following of connoisseurs. Large bay windows overlooking the canal, offer a view of the boats going by. Always a delight.

Chez Noeser *($$$;* ♥*, wine; 236 Rue Champlain,* ☎346-0811*)*. A few years ago, Denis and Ginette Noeser left Montréal and their Rue Saint-Denis restaurant to settle in Saint-Jean-sur-Richelieu. Their latest restaurant offers particularly courteous service and delicious classic French cuisine. There is a terrace during the summer months.

Lacolle

The **Brochetterie Pharos** *($$; 7 Rue de l'Église,* ☎246-3897*)* would be a Greek restaurant like any other were it not located in a church. Many old Québec churches are being turned into restaurants, luxury apartments, etc.

Tour B: Chemin des Patriotes

Saint-Bruno-de-Montarville

The menu at the **Bistro Le Béguin** *($$-$$$; 1485 Montarville,* ☎441-5500*)* lists French specialties and a good selection of fresh fish and imported beer.

La Rabastalière *($$-$$$; closed Mon and for lunch Sat and Sun, 125 De La Rabastalière,* ☎461-0173*)* is in a warm hundred-year-old home; the restaurant offers classic French cuisine plus a gourmet six-course menu that varies each week. There is a sun room for quiet meals. The staff is friendly and the food, excellent.

Saint-Hyacinthe

In Saint-Hyacinthe there are two restaurants that everyone knows about, and they both have the same owner. Although it's not *haute cuisine*, **Chez Pépé** *($$; 1705 Rue Girouard Ouest,* ☎773-8004*)* and **Grillade Rose** *($$; 494 Rue Saint-Simon,* ☎771-0069*)* both offer simple tasty meals in a pleasant decor and both places have terraces. Each restaurant is based on a different theme; Pépé's is Italian and offers a selection of pastas, and Grillade Rose is Santa Fe-style with grill dishes and nachos.

The **Auvergne** *($$-$$$; closed Mon; 610 Rue Mondor;* ☎774-1881*)* has long offered one of the best French cuisines in the region. Brunch is served on Sundays from 10am.

Beloeil

Le Trait d'Union *($; 919 Rue Laurier,* ☎446-5740*)* is an unpretentious, hip little bistro where local residents come to meet. With its relaxed atmosphere and charming terrace, you're sure to have a pleasant time. They serve healthy little dishes at affordable prices. Open for breakfast on weekends.

The Crêperie du Vieux-Beloeil *($$; closed Monday, 940 Richelieu,* ☎464-1726*)* offers generous portions of their house crêpes, made of white flour or buckwhat, and served with seafood, ham or cheese.

L'Ostéria *($$; 914 Rue Laurier,* ☎467-4477 or 464-7491*)*, located in the old part of town is a charming little restaurant that serves fine Italian cuisine, veal and game meats, as well as copious Sunday brunches. The adjoining terrace is inviting, and they offer a children's menu.

Hidden in Beloeil's commercial district, the **Danvito** *($$; closed Sunday, 154 Boulevard Laurier,* ☎464-5166*)* attracts a business clientele with its fine Italian cuisine and Mediterranean character. They serve the traditional spaghetti *carbonara* and a succulent *manicotti fiorentina*. The decor is simple and airy.

Saint-Marc-sur-Richelieu

🦐 The **Auberge Handfield** *($$$;* ♥; *555 Chemin du Prince,* ☎*584-2226)* houses a vast dining room decorated with wooden beams and a chimney. The country atmosphere and delicious Quebecois cuisine go well together. In the spring you can also sample the sweets of the sugar shack.

The restaurant in the **Hostellerie des Trois Tilleuls** *($$$$; 290 Rue Richelieu,* ☎*584-2231)*, serves up some gems of fine French gastronomy. The artfully prepared menu offers traditional and sophisticated meals, and the dining room has a nice view of the river. The beautiful terrace is open to guests during the summer.

Saint-Antoine-sur Richelieu

🦐 A friendly little family-owned restaurant in the heart of this small town, **La Fournée du Village** *($; 1096 Chemin Du Rivage,* ☎*496-3883)* is a quick and inexpensive alternative to Champagne just across the street. In the garden, the youngest daughters serve their mother's delicious home-made food. The atmosphere is relaxed.

🦐 **Le Champagne** *($$$$; closed Sun to Tue, 1000 du Rivage,* ☎ *787-2966)* looks like an old Moroccan castle. The interior is magnificently decorated with panelling, while the tables are laid with silverware, fine glassware, signed dishes and embroidered tablecloths. Delicious French cuisine.

Tour C: Shore of the St. Lawrence

Saint-Lambert

Café-Passion *($; 476 Rue Victoria,* ☎*671-1405)* is located in the heart of Saint-Lambert. Although it hasn't been open for long, it already has quite a following. It's a pleasant place though the food does not quite live up to all the fuss.

Au Vrai Chablis *($$-$$$; 52 Rue Aberdeen,* ☎*465-2795)*. The food-service professionals here invite you to partake of a fabulous fine-dining experience. The menu changes daily and

contains French specialties, superbly prepared by renown chef Bernard Jacquin

Longueuil

For a good sandwich, the **Charcuterie du Vieux Longueuil** *($; 177 Rue St-Charles Ouest,* ☎*670-0643)* is an excellent choice, despite the slightly rushed service.

L'Incrédule *($$; 288 Rue St-Charles Ouest,* ☎*674-0946)* offers an interesting choice of bistro-style meals, as well as an excellent selection of imported beer and scotch.

The **Bœuf en Folie** *($$; 357 Rue St-Charles Ouest,* ☎*677-8743)*, set up inside an ordinary, old-fashioned little house, offers continental French cuisine and an excellent selection of grilled dishes.

Saint-Hubert

The **Bistro des Bières Belges** *($-$$; 2088 Montcalm,* ☎*465-0669)*, as its name poetically reveals, has a selection of about sixty Belgian beers. The menu is also in the Flemish tradition.

Tour D: Vaudreuil-Soulanges

Rigaud

The **Sucrerie de la Montagne** *($$$$; 300 Chemin St-Georges,* ☎*451-5204)* is practically an attraction in itself. It serves traditional sugaring-off dishes, such as those perennial favourites *oreilles de Christ* (literally Christ's ears, but actually deep-fried lard) and *œufs dans le sirop* (eggs in syrup). A folk group livens up the atmosphere with rigadoons and quadrille tunes. Open year-round, this place might not appeal to those familiar with the *cabane à sucre* routine.

Hudson

🚢 On the shores of Lac des Deux-Montagnes, the **Auberge Willow Place** *($$-$$$; 208 Main Road,* ☎*458-7006)* serves steaks and grilled specialties. With its English-style decor and cosy atmosphere, this place is irresistible.

Courteous young staff and a lovely lakefront location add to its charm.

 The **Chez Clémentine** *($$$-$$$$; closed Mon, 398 Rue Principale, ☎458-8181)* is easily one of the finest restaurants in Quebec. A member of Toques Blanches Internationales, this small restaurant located in the heart of town, in a magnificent little country house, serves innovative cuisine. The service is courteous and friendly.

 ENTERTAINMENT

Bars and Nightclubs

Saint-Bruno-de-Montarville

The bar **12/50** *(1250 Roberval)*, equipped with three pool tables, attracts a young, unpretentious clientele. The preference is for good old rock 'n' roll on Wednesdays and Thursdays, and top-40 hits on the Fridays and weekends

Chambly

The **Bistro Le Vieux Bourgogne** *(1718 Bourgogne, ☎447-9306)* attracts a young crowd with traditional French and Québec tunes.

Richelieu

Super 9 *(60 Chemin des Patriotes)*. This place is recommended for two reasons: it's not every day that you come across a dance club in an old barn, and it's been a popular weekend spot for young people from all over the region for many generations. Essentially this place is a typical, small-town disco with lasers, sports cars and all the other hoopla. Nonetheless, there's no lack of ambience here.

St-Hyacinthe

Le Biboquet *(1850 Rue des Cascades Ouest)* is a comfortable spot. It's a microbrewery (they brew Métayer Blonde, Brune and Rousse), a fun place for a meal with friends, and also a centre for the promotion of the arts. They invite musicians to play, decorate the premises with works by local artists, present plays and poetry readings and host literary discussions.

Festivals and Cultural Events

Upton

Unique in North America, the concept of **La Dame de Coeur** *(Jun to late Aug; 611 Rang de la Carrière, ☎549-5828)* is sure to fascinate both young and old alike. Located in a magnificent historical site, the "Queen of Hearts" puts on terrific marionette shows complete with striking visual effects. The outdoor theatre has an immense roof and pivoting seats that are heated on chilly evenings.

Saint-Jean-sur-Richelieu

The **Festival de Montgolfières**, a hot-air-balloon festival *(☎346-6000)*, fills the sky over Saint-Jean-sur-Richelieu with approximately one hundred multicoloured hot-air balloons. Departures take place every day from 6am to 6pm, weather permitting. Exhibitions and shows make up some of the other activities that take place during the festival.

Chambly

The **Fête de Saint-Louis** *(late Aug; ☎658-1585)* at Fort Chambly recreates old military encampments and an old-style market. Military manoeuvres by the Compagnie Franche de la Marine are part of the show. Restaurants in the area prepare special colonial-inspired menus of game, chervil chicken, and fish soup. An excellent way to immerse yourself in the colonial way of life, without the misery.

Chambly is home to Unibroue, one of the biggest micro-breweries in the province. The brewery is behind **Festi-Bière** *(early Sep; ☎447-0426)*, a beer festival. The popularity of this event has exceeded all expectations with attendance records rising year after year. Beers from all over the world can be sampled at Fort Chambly. With an entrance fee of $8 and the price of coupons ($10 for five, and beers cost from one to four coupons) it is a bit pricy, and your money tends to disappear quickly.

Saint-Denis

The **Fête des Patriotes** *(third Sunday in Nov,* ☎*787-3229)* is a popular gathering that takes place in Saint-Denis to commemorate the Patriotes' victory of 1837-1838.

Valleyfield

In early July, Valleyfield hosts the **Régates de Valleyfield** *($15 before Jun 24, $19.50 afterward,* ☎*371-6144)*. The competition involves several categories of hydroplane races, with speeds reaching 240 km/h. The regattas always attract a large number of visitors.

Kahnawake

Various traditional aboriginal events (dances, songs, etc.) are organized as a part of the **Pow Wow** *(*☎*632-8667)*, held in Kahnawake every year during the second weekend of July. Most of the activities are held on Île Kateri Tekakwitha.

 SHOPPING

Chambly

Une Histoire d'Amour *(1878 Rue Bourgogne,* ☎*658-9222)* sells a lovely collection of authentic Québec arts and crafts. Located across from Fort Chambly.

Iberville

Les Jardins de Versaille *(Jun 24 to Dec 24 every day 9am to 5pm; Jan 15 to Jun 23, Wed to Sun; 399 Rang Versailles, Route 227,* ☎*346-6775)* specializes in beautiful dried-flower arrangements. Workshops offered.

La Maison sous les Arbres *(2024 Route 133 Sud,* ☎*347-1639)*. Imagine an art gallery set up in someone's house; you can shop for your bathroom articles in the bathroom, kitchen articles in the kitchen, and so on. Great for people who love to poke around in other people's houses.

Vignoble Dietrich-Jooss *(year round 9am to 6pm; 407 Grande Ligne,* ☎*347-6857)*. Friendly owners, Victor, Christiane and their daughter Stéphanie, originally from Alsace, have owned this vineyard since 1986 and their wines have already earned many prizes in various prestigious competitions – 38 international medals to be precise. Connoisseurs consider the white *cuvé spécial* to be the most Alsation in character. Wine tasting available.

Hudson

Finnigan's Market *(shop open all week, market Sat only May to Nov; 775 Rue Principale,* ☎*458-4377)*. This famous outdoor antique market also has loads of other great finds and is one place in the region not to be missed. It's a joy to wander around all these treasures which, for the most part, are sold at affordable prices! A hot spot for collectors!

Saint-Antoine-Abbé

Vin Mustier Gerzer, Hydromel *(3299 Route 209,* ☎*826-4609)*. Light and fresh, mead is the perfect drink for those wonderful summer days and Vins Mustier, in the splendid St-Antoine-Abbé region, is an expert in the field. This place is also devoted to bee-keeping and offers a wide variety of honey-based products. Sampling available.

Otterburn Park

Chocolaterie La Cabosse d'Or *(summer, every day 9am to 9pm; rest of the year Sat to Wed 9am to 6pm, Thu and Fri 9am to 9pm, 973 Chemin Ozias-Leduc,* ☎*464-6937)*. This place has earned its reputation by not only for selling Belgian chocolate of the finest quality but also for its enchanting fairy-tale-like ambiance. It's a splendid house with a shop, a terrace and a tearoom. Lovely little hostesses greet you with a smile. There is even a mini-golf course with a chocolate theme. Fairly simple you say, but it definitely took some thought!

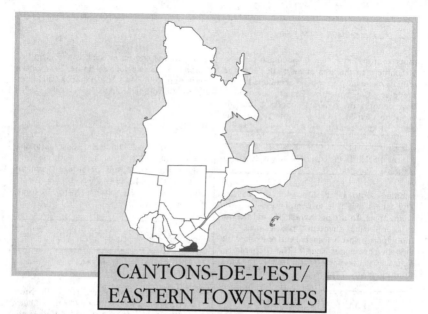

CANTONS-DE-L'EST/ EASTERN TOWNSHIPS

The Eastern Townships is a beautiful region in the Appalachian foothills, in the southernmost part of Québec. Its rich architectural heritage and mountainous countryside give it a distinctive character reminiscent in many ways of New England. Picturesque villages marked by what is often typically Anglo-Saxon architecture, lie nestled between mountains with rounded summits and lovely little valleys.

As may be gathered from many place names, such as Massawippi and Coaticook, this vast region was originally explored and inhabited by natives of the Abenaki tribe. Later, when New France came under English control and the United States declared its independence, many American colonists still loyal to the British monarchy (known as Loyalists) settled in the Eastern Townships. Throughout the 19th century, these settlers were followed by waves of immigrants from the British Isles, mainly Ireland, and French colonists from the overpopulated St. Lawrence lowlands. Though the local population is now over 90% French-speaking, the area still bears obvious traces of its Anglo-Saxon past, most notably in its architecture. Many towns and villages are graced with majestic Anglican churches surrounded by beautiful 19th-century Victorian or vernacular American-style homes. The Townships are still home to a handful of prestigious local institutions, like Bishop's University in Lennoxville.

Though dairy farms still grace the countryside, the Eastern Townships is now a dynamic region with two universities and a number of high technology enterprises. Located about an hour's drive from Montréal, this is cottage country and vacation land for many. The mountains are great for winter skiing, and the lakes and rivers perfect for summer water sports. But visitors also come to the Eastern Townships for its fine food and wineries, or simply to take part in one of its various festivals or family activities.

In terms of territory, the townships (*cantons*) are different from seigneuries. Not only are they more or less square, rather than oblong, but their administrative system was based on a British model. Instead of being granted to a single individual, a township was established at the request of the community wishing to settle there. Most were founded in the 19th century, filling spaces left vacant by the French seigneurial system, usually mountainous sites removed from the already populated banks of the St. Lawrence and its tributaries, which at the time were the colony's main communication routes. Nowhere in Québec was this means of populating the territory more widespread that in the Eastern Townships.

In 1966, following the division of Quebec into administrative regions, the Eastern Townships region took on the name "Estrie". Thirty years later, however, the region's tourist association decided to return to the original appellation. For that matter, the local populace's deep attachment to the area made it such that the original name had never been abandoned in the first place. Consequently, "Eastern Townships" now denotes the region's important touristic vocation while "Estrie" refers to the administrative region.

 FINDING YOUR WAY AROUND

Located southeast of Montréal, the Eastern Townships region is in competition with the Laurentians, to the northwest, for the honour of Montrealers' favourite "playground". The three tours below will enable you to explore the Eastern Townships: **Tour A: The Orchards ★**, **Tour B: The Lakes ★★★** and **Tour C: The Back Country ★**.

Tour A: The Orchards

By Car

From Montréal, cross the Pont Champlain and take Highway 10 (the Autoroute des Cantons de l'Est) to Exit 29, then head south on the 133. Near Philipsburg and the American border, keep left in order to turn onto the small road leading to Saint-Armand-Ouest and Frelighsburg.

Bus Station

Bromont: 624 Rue Shefford (dépanneur Shefford), ☎ (450) 534-2116.

Tour B: The Lakes

By Car

From Montréal, take the Autoroute des Cantons de l'Est (10) to Exit 90, then head south on Route 243. Make sure to turn left towards Knowlton in order to follow the eastern shore of Lac Brome. In Knowlton, Route 104 leads to the intersection with Route 215. Turn left towards Brome and Sutton. By following Route 139 then Route 243 from here, you will reach Bolton Sud, where you can pick up Route 245 to Saint-Benoît-du-Lac. By continuing around the northern tip of Lac Memphrémagog on Route

247 you will end up in Rock Island. The last portion of the tour follows Route 143, with a detour on Route 141 to Coaticook, and then Route 208 to Sherbrooke.

Bus Stations

Sutton: 28 Rue Principale (Esso station), ☎(450) 538-2452.
Magog-Orford: 67A Rue Sherbrooke (Terminus Café), ☎(450) 843-4617.
Sherbrooke: 20 Rue King Ouest, ☎(450) 569-3656.

Tour C: The Back Country

By Car

From Sherbrooke, take Route 108 to Birchton. From Cookshire, follow Route 212 to Wolburn. From here head north on Route 161 along the eastern shore of Lac Memphrémagog to Ham-Nord from where Route 216 and then Route 255 lead to Danville.

Bus Station

Lac-Mégantic: 6630 Rue Salaberry (Dépanneur 6630 Fatima), ☎819-583-2717.

 PRACTICAL INFORMATION

There are two area codes in the Eastern Townships, **819** and **450**. To avoid confusion, the area codes have been included in this chapter; you do not need to dial the three-digit area code for local calls.

Tourist Information Offices

Regional Office

Tourisme Cantons de l'Est 20 Rue Don-Bosco S., Sherbrooke, J1L 1W4, ☎(819) 820-2020 or 1-800-355-5755, ⊷566-4445, www.tourisme-estrie.qc.ca.

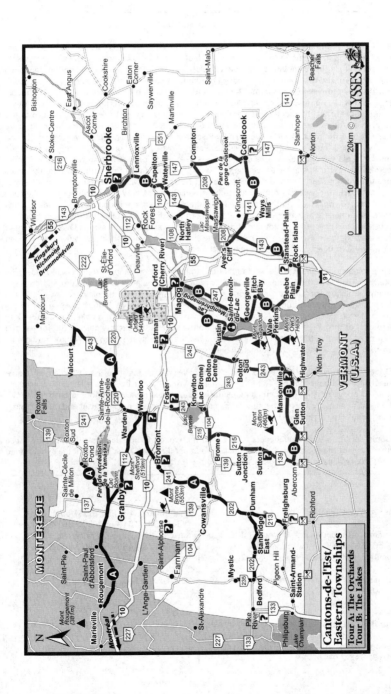

**Cantons-de-l'Est/
Eastern Townships**

**Tour A: The Orchards
Tour B: The Lakes**

20km © ULYSSES

0   10   20km

Maple Syrup

By the time the first colonists arrived in America, the various indigenous cultures had already been enjoying maple syrup for a long time. In fact, it is impossible to determine when exactly the aboriginals first discovered the sweet liquid. According to an Iroquois legend, it happened like this: Woksis, the Great Chief, headed out hunting one morning. The night had been cold, but the day promised to be warm. The day before, he had left his tomahawk stuck in a maple tree, and when he removed it, sap began to flow from the crack in the wood. The sap flowed into a bucket that happened to be sitting under the hole. Later, Woksis' wife needed water to prepare the evening meal. Upon seeing the bucket full of sap, she thought it would spare her a trip to the river. An intelligent and conscientious woman who hated waste, she tasted the water and found it a bit on the sweet side, but nevertheless good, and used it to make the meal. On his way home, Woksis smelled the sweet scent of maple from far away and knew something extra special was cooking. The sap had turned into syrup, making the meal positively succulent. And thus was born one of North America's sweetest traditions. Natives did not have the necessary materials to heat a cauldron at very high temperatures, so they used heated rocks, which they dropped into the water to make it boil. Another method was to let the maple water freeze overnight, then remove the layer of ice the following morning, repeating this process until nothing remained but a thick syrup. Maple syrup played a prominent role in aboriginal diet, culture and religion. The syrup-making methods used today were handed down by Europeans, who taught them to the natives.

Technological advances have led to great changes in the way maple products are made. The sugar season is in the spring, when nighttime temperatures are still below zero and days are warm, enabling the sap to flow more easily. The temperature thus plays a key role in the production of maple syrup. The first step is to carve a hole about 2.5 cm deep in the maple trees, 1 m from the ground. A spout is then inserted in the hole and the sap flows either into a bucket or through a series of pipes leading to the sugar shack. In the case of the former, the sap must be collected every morning. Of course, the latter system is more common, and only small outfits still use the traditional bucket method.

Once it reaches the sugar shack, the sap is boiled to reduce it to syrup. When the liquid reaches 7°C above boiling, it becomes maple syrup. If it is boiled longer, until it reaches 14.5°C above boiling, it becomes maple taffy (*tire*), a real treat when poured onto the snow. It is also possible to make other products, such as maple sugar, maple butter and maple candy, but these all require more careful preparation.

Come springtime, the Quebecers head off to the woods to go sugaring-off and enjoy those mainstays of the sugar shack menu, *oreilles de Christ* (literally Christ's ears, actually deep-fried lard), *œufs dans le sirop* (eggs in syrup) and *tire* (taffy) on snow.

Tour A: The Orchards

Bromont: 83 Boulevard Bromont, J0E 1L0, ☎(450) 534-2006.
Granby: 650 Rue Principale, J2G 8L4, ☎(450) 372-7273.
Rougemont: 11 Chemin Marieville, J0L 1M0, ☎(450) 469-3600

Tour B: The Lakes

Magog-Orford: 55 Rue Cabana, J1X 2C4, ☎(819) 843-2744.

Sherbrooke: 48 Rue du Dépôt, J1H 5G1, ☎(819) 821-1919 or 1-800-561-8331.
Sutton: 11 Rue Principale, J0E 2K0, ☎(514) 538-8455 or 1-800-565-8455.

Tour C: The Back Country

Lac-Mégantic: 3295 Rue Laval N., G6B 2S6, ☎(819) 583-5515.

★ EXPLORING

Tour A: The Orchards ★ (one day)

There are three clusters of orchards in the countryside surrounding Montréal, one in the Saint-Joseph-du-Lac region, another in the Saint-Antoine-Abbé region, and a third, which is both larger and more spread out, in the western part of the Eastern Townships. In recent years vineyards have grown up alongside the traditional apple orchards, turning a part of this tour into a sort of miniature wine route. In the fall, city dwellers come here on Sundays to admire the brilliant foliage, watch the grape harvest and pick their own MacIntosh apples in one of the many pick-your-own orchards. Apple growers also sell their products (apple butter, cider, juice, pies) by the side of the road, while viticulturists, wine growers, offer guided tours of their properties, and provide visitors with an opportunity to taste and purchase their wine.

Frelighsburg ★ (pop. 1,066)

Eastern Townships' architecture differs from that of the rest of Québec, due to its Anglo-American origins, which account for the frequent use of red brick and white clapboard and the predominance of sash windows, composed of two vertically sliding panels. In houses built prior to 1860, the windowpanes are usually separated into little squares (three or four squares wide and four to eight squares high), while windows in the more recent Victorian houses contain large, undivided plates of glass.

The village of Frelighsburg grew up around its stone **mill** *(private, no visitors allowed; 12 Route 237 N.)*, built in 1790 by two Loyalist pioneers. In 1839, the structure was enlarged by its new owner, Abram Freligh of New York State, for whom the village was named. The mill, which was converted into a residence in 1967, is visible through the trees on the left.

Frelighsburg's **Anglican Church ★** is very well situated atop a hill overlooking the village. Both its oblong structure and its steeple, which is at the side of the nave and marks the main entrance, are uncommon architectural features

in the Eastern Townships. The church was built in 1884 in the Gothic-Revival style advocated by the Church of England. Its red brick walls, yellow brick door, window frames and slate roof create a polychromatic effect not unlike that of village churches in Ontario.

Take Route 213 N. toward Dunham.

Dunham ★ (pop. 3,430)

Traditionally a single, somewhat imposing church lies at the centre of towns founded by Catholic French Canadians. As villages in the Eastern Townships are often inhabited by Anglicans, Presbyterians, Methodists, Baptists and Lutherans, little churches of various denominations abound. Accordingly, a number of churches are sprinkled among the well-kept residences lining Dunham's main street *(Rue Principale)*. The oldest township in Lower Canada, Dunham is home to some of the first houses ever built in the Eastern Townships. **All Saints Anglican Church**, built of stone between 1847 and 1851, faces straight down the center of Route 202, nicknamed the wine route.

Turn left on Route 202 W. to start the wine route. It is also possible to visit Stanbridge East, Bedford and Mystic from this road. Afterward, continue on the 213 N. towards Cowansville.

The Wine Route ★

European visitors might consider it quite presumptuous to call the road between Dunham and Stanbridge East *(Route 202 W.)* the "Wine Route", but the concentration of vineyards in this region is unique in the province, and Québec's attempts at wine-making have been so surprisingly successful that people have been swept away by their enthusiasm. There are no châteaux or distinguished old counts here, only growers who sometimes have to go as far as renting helicopters to save their vines from freezing. The rotor blades cause the air to circulate, preventing frost from forming on the ground during crucial periods in May. The region is, however, blessed with a microclimate and soil favourable for grape growing (slate). The various wines are sold only at the vineyards where they are produced.

You can visit the **L'Orpailleur** *(1086 Route 202, JOE 1M0, Dunham,* ☎*450-295-2763,* ☎ *295-3112)* winery, whose products include a dry white wine and Apéridor, an apéritif similar to Pineau des Charentes.

The **Domaine des Côtes d'Ardoises** *(879 Route 202, Dunham, JOE 1M0,* ☎*450-295-2020)* is one of the few Québec vineyards that produces red wine. Here, as at other wineries, the owner will give you a warm welcome.

Les Blancs Coteaux *(1046 Route 202, Dunham, JOE 1M0,* ☎*450-294-3503)* not only makes quality wine but also has a lovely craft shop.

Stanbridge East (pop. 860)

This charming village is known mainly for its regional museum. Along its shady streets, visitors can also see large houses surrounded by gardens. **St. James the Apostle** (circa 1880), an Anglican church made of multicoloured brick, is particularly noteworthy, as its cruciform structure is somewhat unusual in Québec.

The **Musée de Missisquoi ★** *($3; late May to mid-Oct, every day 10am to 5pm; 2 Rue Rivière;* ☎*514-248-3153)* is devoted to preserving the region's essentially Loyalist heritage. The 12,000 objects displayed are in three period buildings, the **Cornell Mill** (1832), **Bill's Barn**, which houses antique cars and ploughing implements, and the **Magasin Général Hodge**, a general store whose counters date back to the beginning of the 20th century.

Continue on Route 202 W. to Bedford.

Bedford (pop. 2,788)

Another little town with Anglo-Saxon characteristics, Bedford is renowned for its grey and green slate extracted from surrounding quarries. Visitors can see lovely red brick houses surrounded by greenery, as well as the pretty **St. James Anglican Church** (circa 1840), also made of brick. The **Pont des Rivières**, to the northwest, is a 41-metre covered bridge, built in 1884. One of a few rare examples of the wooden Howe style of bridge to be found in Québec, it is characterized by girders, assembled in the shape of a cross.

To go to Mystic, turn right on Route 235 N. The village is located off the main road.

Mystic ★

Mystic is like a little piece of New England in Québec. Its population, still mainly Anglo-Saxon, is very patriotic, so many houses fly Canadian or American flags. The handsome round barn and wooden churches are very picturesque.

Head back towards Dunham in order to continue the main tour.

Cowansville (pop. 12,500)

Another Loyalist community, Cowansville has lovely Victorian homes made of wood and brick, as well as a few interesting public and commercial buildings, which bear witness to the town's prosperous past. Especially interesting is the former **Eastern Townships Bank** *(225 Rue Principale)*, built in 1889, which has been converted into a community centre. The edifice's mansard roof is characteristic of the Second Empire style, which was popular in the English and French cultures. Not far away lies the small, Anglican **Trinity Church**, a Gothic Revival structure erected in 1854, and surrounded by a cemetery.

Take Route 241 N., located east of Cowansville.

Bromont (pop. 3,601)

Developed in the 1960s, Bromont has become a favourite resort area among Montrealers. It is renowned for its downhill ski resort, its sports facilities, and also for having hosted the 1976 Olympic equestrian competitions.

Visiting the **Musée du Chocolat** *(Tue and Wed 10am to 6pm, Thu and Fri 10am to 7pm, Sat and Sun 10am to 5:30pm, summer every day; 679 Rue Shefford,* ☎*514-534-3893)* is a golden opportunity for gourmands with discriminating palates to indulge in sinfully delicious chocolate. The museum presents the history of chocolate since the coming of the Spanish to South America, the process of changing cocoa beans into powder and a few art works featuring... chocolate, of course! If your taste buds become overly sated, you can purchase

January 1998: Ice Storm

Southern Québec was hit by the worst ice storm in history in January, 1998. More than one million homes were without electricity, many for more than a week. Downtown Montréal was completely paralyzed by ice for nearly five days. The metro, which runs on electricity, stopped working. The bridges connecting the south shore were closed because of dangerous falling ice.

The most severely affected regions were in the Eastern Townships, Outaouais and especially Montérégie; an area dubbed the triangle of darkness. Virtually buried beneath the ice, these areas were thrown into darkness and the cold; outside communication was almost impossible. A hundred or so shelters were created to help the population. Neighbours, friends, relatives and strangers from Québec and Canada provided badly needed shelter and basic necessities. Firewood, candles, carburators and generators were particularly scarce.

Heavy ice, almost 25 centimetres thick in some places, toppled some sixty electric pylons, leaving Hydro-Québec little choice but to virtually reconstruct its network in these regions. Headless trees, devastated orchards, ravaged maples – the landscape has been changed permanently. The broken branches and felled trees are impossible to miss. Residents, with their own story of the big storm, have also been changed. Undoubtedly, residents will be quick to tell you about their experiences, since everyone, from far away and nearby, was affected in some way by this event.

all kinds of delicious sweets made right on the premises. Light meals are also served here.

The **Centre Équestre**, riding school, see p 218.

The **Station de Ski Bromont**, ski resort, see p 218.

From here, visitors can make an optional detour to Valcourt, the village where Joseph-Armand Bombardier developed and began marketing the snowmobile.

To get there, take Route 241 to Warden. Turn right on Route 220, in the direction of Sainte-Anne-de-la-Rochelle, then left on Route 243, and follow the signs for Valcourt.

Valcourt (pop. 2,349)

Bombardier was not the only mechanic in Québec to develop a motor vehicle for use on snow-covered surfaces. Residents had to come up with something, since many roads in the province were not cleared of snow until the beginning of the 1950s. As automobiles were, for all practical purposes, somewhat unreliable, people had to depend on the same means of transportation as their ancestors, namely, the horse-drawn sleigh. Bombardier, however, was the only individual to succeed in making a profit from his invention, most notably because of a lucrative contract with the army during World War II. Though the company later

diversified and underwent considerable expansion, it never left the village of Valcourt—to this day the site of its head office.

The **Musée J.-Armand-Bombardier** ★ *($5; mid-Jun to late Apr, Tue to Sun 10am to 5pm; 1001 Avenue Joseph-Armand-Bombardier; ☎450-532-5300)* is a museum that traces the development of the snowmobile, and explains how Bombardier's invention was marketed all over the world. Different prototypes are displayed, along with a few examples of various snowmobiles produced since 1960. Group tours of the factory are also available.

From Waterloo, take Route 112 West to Granby.

Granby (pop. 45,194)

A few kilometres from the verdant Parc de la Yamaska, **Granby**, the "princess of the Eastern Townships", basks in the surrounding countryside's fresh air. In addition to its Victorian-style houses, this city boasts grand avenues and parks graced with fountains and sculptures. Transected by the Yamaska Nord river, it is also the point at which the Montérégiade and Estriade bicycle trails converge. The city's youth and dynamism are reflected through its multiple festivals, notably the celebratory Festival International de la Chanson, an international song festival that has exposed the French-speaking world to a number of excellent performers.

Visitors to the **Granby Zoo** ★★ *($15; mid-May to early Sep, every day 10am to 6pm; take Exit 68 or 74 from Hwy 10 and follow the signs; ☎450-372-9113)* can see some 250 animal species from various different countries, in particular North America and Africa. This is an old-style zoo, so most of the animals are in cages and there are few areas where they can roam freely. It is nevertheless an interesting place to visit.

The **Parc de Récréation de la Yamaska**, see p 217.

The **Centre d'Interprétation de la Nature du Lac Boivin**, see p 217.

Continue on Route 112 W. towards Rougemont.

Rougemont (pop. 1,219)

Though it is located outside of the Eastern Townships's tourist area, Rougemont attracts visitors because of its status as Québec's apple capital. The village lies at the base of the smallest hill in the Montérégie region, Mont Rougemont.

The **Centre d'Interprétation de la Pomme du Québec** *($2.25; Jun to Oct, every day 9am to 5pm; 11 Chemin Marieville; ☎450-469-3600)* reveals the fascinating ins and outs of apple-growing.

The **Cidrerie Artisanale Michel Jodoin** *(1130 Rang de la Petite Caroline, Rougemont, J0L 1M0; ☎450-469-2676)*, produces high-quality cider. The secret lies in the aging process, which takes place in oak barrels, with delicious results. Unfortunately, the cider factory is only open to the public upon reservation. Visitors have the opportunity to taste, and of course buy, the various ciders produced on site.

This is the end of the Orchards Tour. To return to Montréal, take Route 112 W. until it intersects with Route 227 S., then turn left to reach Highway 10.

Tour B : The Lakes ★★★
(two days)

This tour winds around the three most popular lakes in the Eastern Townships and includes sweeping views, more charming villages, and friendly inns. It is an ideal excursion just a short distance from Montréal. In the summer, visitors can enjoy a variety of water sports, go rock-climbing, hiking, skiing or snowshoeing.

Knowlton ★★ (pop. 5,048)

When the Townships are compared to New England, Knolton is often given as an example. Quaint shops and restaurants welcome visitors strolling through this well-to-do little village. In contrast to traditional French-Canadian villages, where the accent is on the parish church and its presbytery, civic buildings are the highlight in Knowlton. A notable example is the **Bureau d'Enregistrement** *(15 Rue St. Paul)*, the registration office designed by Timothy E. Chamberlain. Built in 1857, it was once the local courthouse. All around, visitors will see examples of Loyalist architecture, characterized by red brick, white trim and dark green shutters.

Lac Brome ★, a circular body of water, is popular among windsurfers, who can use a parking lot and a little beach on the side of the road near Knowlton. The duck from this lake is known for its flavour and is featured on the menus of local inns and restaurants when in season.

The **Musée Historique du Comté de Brome** ★ *($3; mid-May to mid-Sep, Mon to Sat 10am to 4:30pm, Sun 11am to 4:30pm; 130 Rue Lakeside; ☎450-243-6782)*, the historical museum of Brome County, occupying five Loyalist buildings, traces the lives and history of the region's inhabitants. In addition to the usual furniture and photographs, visitors can see a reconstructed general store, a 19th-century court of justice and, what's more unusual, a collection of military equipment, including a World War I airplane.

The village of Knowlton is now part of the municipality of Lac-Brome, which encircles the lake. To reach Sutton, turn right onto Route 104 W. at the end of Chemin Lakeside, and then left onto Route 215 S. in the direction of Brome and Sutton Junction.

Sutton ★ (pop. 1,610)

Sutton, which is located at the base of the mountain of the same name, is one of the major winter resorts in the Eastern Townships. The area also has several well-designed golf courses Among the local houses of worship, the Gothic Revival Anglican **Grace Church**, built out of stone in 1850, is the most noteworthy. Unfortunately, though, its steeple no longer has its pointed arch.

Take Route 139 S. towards the tiny village of Abercorn, located less than 3 km from the American border (Vermont). From there, turn left on the secondary road that runs along the beautiful valley of the Rivière Missisquoi and passes through Glen Sutton, Highwater and Mansonville before reaching Vale Perkins.

Mont Sutton ★ see p 218.

Vale Perkins

From Vale Perkins itself, **Owl's Head** is visible on the right. A charming little Ukrainian chapel lies further along. The scenic road then runs alongside **Sugar Loaf** and **Mont Éléphant**. Near the latter, there are heaps of stones known as cairns, as well as a large flat stone engraved with hieroglyphics of enigmatic origins. Some people associate these archeological relics with the Loyalist colonists, others to the local natives, and still others even to the Phoenicians, who, it would seem, left their mark in the very distant past. From the top of the hill overlooking **Knowlton's Landing**, there is a delightful view of **Lac Memphrémagog**, the pride of the Eastern Townships. The little village at the foot of the hill is where vacationning Montrealers used to board the ferryboat to go to the eastern shore of the lake.

Owl's Head ★ see p 219.

Lac Memphrémagog ★★

Lac Memphrémagog, which is 40 kilometres long and only one to two kilometres wide, will remind some visitors of a Scottish loch. It even has its own equivalent of the Loch Ness monster, named "Memphre"; sightings go back to 1798! The southern portion of the lake, which cannot be seen from Magog, is located in the United States. The name Memphrémagog, like Massawippi and Missisquoi, is an Abenaki word. Sailing enthusiasts will be happy to learn that the lake is one of the best places in Québec to enjoy this sport.

Turn right on Route d'Austin, and right again on Chemin Fisher, which leads to the Abbaye de Saint-Benoît-du-Lac.

Saint-Benoît-du-Lac ★★

This municipality consists solely of the estate of the **Abbaye de Saint-Benoît-du-Lac**, an abbey founded in 1913 by Benedictine monks who were driven away from the Abbaye de Saint-Wandrille-de-Fontenelle in Normandy. Aside from the monastery itself, there are the guest quarters, the abbey chapel and the farm buildings. However, only the chapel and a few corridors are open to the public. Visitors will not want to miss the Gregorian chants sung at vespers at 5pm every day.

Anyone who needs to meditate may stay in the guest quarters, where men and women are separated. The monks also raise Charolais cattle, run a dairy (where they make Ermite and Mont-Saint-Benoît cheeses) and have two orchards, which are used for producing cider.

Backtracking along Chemin Fisher, a little road on the left leads to a handsome **round barn**, built in 1907 by Damase Amédée Dufresne. It is not open to the public, but its exterior qualifies it all the same as one of the province's best examples of this style of barn, developed in the United States to withstand strong winds (and also to prevent the devil from hiding in a corner).

Austin's **Église Saint-Augustin-de-Cantorbéry**, formerly an Anglican church, stands at the intersection, along with a monument honouring the hamlet's most famous citizen, Reginald Aubrey Fessenden, who worked out the principle behind the transmission of the human voice by radio waves.

Turn right on the road leading to Magog. Between the houses, there are some lovely views of the lake and the abbey. Turn right on Route 112.

Magog ★ (pop. 14,669)

Equipped with more facilities than any other town between Granby and Sherbrooke, Magog has a lot to offer sports lovers. It is extremely well situated on the northernmost shore of Lac

Memphrémagog, but has unfortunately been subjected to unbridled development for several years now. The town's cultural scene is worth noting. Visitors can go to the theatre or the music complex, set in the natural mountain surroundings. The textile industry, once of great importance in the lives of local residents, has declined, giving way to tourism. Visitors will enjoy strolling down Rue Principale, which is lined with shops and restaurants.

The **Théâtre du Vieux-Clocher** see p 227.

The **Parc de Récréation du Mont-Orford** ★★ see p 217.

The **Centre d'Arts Orford** ★ see p 227.

To get to Georgeville, take Route 247 S., which runs along the east coast of Lac Memphrémagog.

Georgeville ★ (pop. 910)

Most of director Denys Arcand's *Le Déclin de l'Empire américain (The Decline of the American Empire)* was shot in the heart of this area's rolling countryside, evocative of relaxing vacations. For a long time now, the little village of Georgeville has been a favourite resort area among English-speaking families. The Molsons, for example, own an island in the vicinity. Various celebrities in search of seclusion have also purchased houses on the lake. In the 19th century, ferryboats from Newport, on the southernmost American part of the lake, and from Knowlton's Landing, on the western shore, would all stop at Georgeville, where a number of large wooden hotels once stood. All of these unfortunately burned to the ground; only the modest, but extremely pleasant **Auberge Georgeville** remains. The **Vieille École** (Old School), the **Centre Culturel** (Cultural Centre) and **St. George's Church** (1866) are other buildings of significant historical interest. The quay, furthermore, offers a lovely view of the Abbaye de Saint-Benoît-du-Lac.

Fitch Bay

The **Covered Bridge Narrows** lie further along on Route 247 (turn right on Chemin Merri, then left on Chemin Ridgewood). Though more expensive to build, covered bridges lasted much longer because they were protected from the elements. Consequently, there are a number of them in Québec. This particular one, built in 1881, spans 28 metres across Fitch Bay. Just next to it, there is a small park with picnic tables.

The surrounding roads are pleasant to explore, especially **Magoon Point Road**, which offers sweeping views of the lake, and **Route de Tomifobia**, which could be straight out of a painting by Grant Wood or one of his fellow American Regionalists. Route 247 South leads to **Beebe Plain**, a town known for its granite quarries, which have enjoyed a revival in popularity in recent years, as granite, either bluish or pinkish, has been used for the facing of many postmodern skyscrapers all over North America.

Rock Island ★ (pop. 1,110)

Straddling the American border, Rock Island is one of the strangest villages in the province. Walking down its streets, you will find themselves in the United States in certain spots and in Canada in others. Notices written in French give way suddenly to signs in English. The flagpole on Monsieur Thériault's lawn flies the Canadian maple leaf, while the Stars and Stripes unfurls in a patriotic and peaceable manner right next door. Its many beautiful stone, brick and wooden buildings make Rock Island a pleasant place to explore on foot.

The **Haskell Free Library and Opera House** ★ (*at the corner of Church and Caswell*), inaugurated in 1904, is both a library and a theatre. Sitting on the Canadian-American border, it was built as a symbol of the friendship between the two nations. The architect, James Ball, drew his inspiration from Boston's opera house, which is no longer standing. A black line running diagonally across the interior of the building marks the exact location of the border, which corresponds to the 45th parallel.

Head north to Stanstead Plain on Route 143 N. (Rue Main, then Rue Dufferin).

Stanstead Plain ★ (pop. 883)

Some of the most beautiful houses in the Eastern Townships are located in this prosperous community. The distilleries of the 1820s, and later, the granite quarries, enabled a number of the area's inhabitants to amass large fortunes in the 19th century. Particularly noteworthy is the Renaissance Revival **Maison**

Butters (1866), in the style of a Tuscan villa, and the **Maison Colby**, which is described below. The **Collège de Stanstead** (1930), the **Couvent des Ursulines** (a French-Canadian order of nuns from Québec City and an unusual institution in these parts), and the Methodist and Anglican churches all merit a leisurely visit.

The **Musée Colby-Curtis** ★ *($4; late Jun to mid-Sep, Tue to Sun 10am to 5pm; rest of the year, Tue to Fri 10am to noon and 1pm to 5pm, closed mid-Dec to mid-Jan; 35 Rue Dufferin; ☎819-876-7322)*, located in a house complete with all of its original furnishings, provides an excellent indication of how the local bourgeoisie lived during the second half of the 19th century. The residence, which has a grey granite façade, was built in 1859 for a lawyer named James Carroll Colby, who called it Carrollcroft.

Continue on Route 143 N. Those who would like to make an optional detour to Coaticook and Compton may do so by continuing east on the 141.

Coaticook (pop. 6,942)

Coaticook, which means "River of the Land of Pines" in the language of the Abenakis, is a small industrial town. It is surrounded by a large number of dairy farms, making it Québec's dairy capital. Its old railroad station is quite interesting.

Located in the heart of Coaticook's residential area, the **Musée Beaulne** ★ *($3; mid-May to mid-Sep, every day 11am to 5pm; mid-Sep to mid-May, Wed to Sun 1pm to 4pm; 96 Rue Union; ☎819-849-6560)* is located in a large wooden mansion built in 1912 for the Norton family. The house was designed in a mixture of Queen Anne and Shingle Styles, then popular in the United States. It stands amidst a large English garden. Some of its rooms have been kept in the style typical of bourgeois homes at the dawn of the 20th century, while others contain textile and costume displays.

The **Parc de la Gorge de Coaticook** ★ see p 217.

Head back toward Compton on Route 147 N.

Compton (pop. 899)

This village's main attraction is the birthplace of Louis-Stephen Saint-Laurent, Prime Minister of Canada from 1948 to 1957. He is remembered above all for his role in establishing NATO.

Louis S. Saint-Laurent National Historic Site *($2.50; mid-May to mid-Oct, every day 10am to 5pm; 6 Rue Principale Sud; ☎819-835-5448)*, is also called the Lieu Historique Nationale Louis-S.-St-Laurent. In terms of references to Saint-Laurent as a politician this National Historic Site will only be of interest to ardent fans of political history. The house where Saint-Laurent was born and the general store alongside it, which belonged to his father, contain nothing other than early 20th century furnishings and everyday objects, similar to those on display in every little museum in the region.

To return to the main tour, take Route 208 to Massawippi, then turn right on Route 243, which leads to North Hatley.

North Hatley ★★ (pop. 705)

Attracted by North Hatley's enchanting countryside, wealthy American vacationers built luxurious villas here between 1890 and 1930. Most of these still line the northern part of Lac Massawippi, which, like Lac Memphrémagog, resembles a Scottish loch. Beautiful inns and gourmet restaurants add to the charm of the place, ensuring its reputation as a vacation spot of the utmost sophistication. In the centre of the village, visitors will notice the tiny Shingle-style **United Church**, which appears more Catholic than Protestant.

Manoir Hovey ★ *(Chemin Hovey)*, a large villa built in 1900, was modelled on Mount Vernon, George Washington's home in Virginia. It used to be the summer residence of an American named Henry Atkinson, who entertained American artists and politicians here every summer. The house has since been converted into an inn.

Continue on Route 108 to Lennoxville.

A former copper mine, the **Mine Capelton** *($10.95; 800 Route 108, ☎819-346-9545)* was, around the 1880s, one of the most impressive and technologically advanced mining complexes in Canada and in the

Commonwealth. Dug by hand, it runs 135 metres below the surface of Stoke mountain. Besides its geological interest, the visit stretches over 1.7 kilometres and reveals the fascinating way in which miners lived and the first industrial revolution. With temperatures fluctuating around 9°C, wear warm clothing.

Lennoxville ★ (pop. 4,209)

This little town, whose population is still mainly English-speaking, is home to two prestigious English-language educational institutions, Bishop's University and Bishop's College. Established alongside the road linking Trois-Rivières to the American border, it was named after Charles Lennox, the fourth Duke of Richmond, who was governor of Upper and Lower Canada in 1818. Once off the main road (Route 143) explore the town's side streets to see the institutional buildings and lovely Second Empire and Queen Anne houses nestled in greenery.

Thanks to changes made to it between 1847 and 1896, **St. George's Anglican Church** (*Rue Queen*) has a picturesque appearance that makes it one of the most charming churches in the Eastern Townships.

Jefferson Davis, President of the Confederacy and one of the leading figures behind the southern states' secession from the Union in 1861, enjoyed staying with his family in the **Maison Cummings** (*33 Rue Belvedere*), a brick house erected in 1864.

Since 1988, the Maison Speid, built in 1862, has housed the **Musée Uplands** (*$1.50; Jun to mid-Sep, Tue to Fri 10am to noon and 1pm to 5pm, Sat and Sun 1pm to 5pm; mid-Sep to May, Tue to Sun 1pm to 5pm; 50 Rue Park; ☎819-564-0409*), a museum where visitors can see different exhibits evoking the richness of the region's past.

Bishop's University ★ (*College Road*), one of three English-language universities in Québec, offers 1,300 students from all over Canada a personalized education in an enchanting setting. It was founded in 1843, through the efforts of a minister named Lucius Doolittle. Upon arriving at the university, visitors will see **McGreer Hall**, built in 1876 according to a design by architect James Nelson and later modified by Taylor and Gordon of Montréal to give it a medieval look. **St. Mark's Anglican Chapel**, which stands to its left, was rebuilt in

1891 after a fire. Its long, narrow interior has lovely oak trim, as well as stained-glass windows by Spence and Sons of Montréal.

The **Bishop-Champlain Art Gallery** (*free admission; Sep to Apr, Tue to Sat noon to 4pm; on campus, ☎819-822-9600, ext. 2687*) has a permanent collection of over 150 works of art, including paintings by 19th-century Canadian landscape artists, and also organizes multidisciplinary exhibitions between September and April.

Head back towards Route 143, which leads to Sherbrooke.

Sherbrooke ★★ (pop. 79,432)

Sherbrooke, the Eastern Townships' main urban area, is nicknamed the Queen of the Eastern Townships. It spreads over a series of hills on both sides of the Rivière Saint-François, accentuating its disorderly appearance. The city nevertheless has a number of interesting buildings, the majority of which are located on the west bank. Sherbrooke's origins date back to the beginning of the 19th century; like so many other villages in the region, it grew up around a mill and a small market. However, in 1823, it was designated as the site of a courthouse intended to serve the entire region, which set it apart from the neighbouring communities. The arrival of the railroad here in 1852, as well as the downtown concentration of institutions, such as the head office of the Eastern Township Bank, led to the construction of prestigious Victorian edifices thereby transforming Sherbrooke's appearance. Today, the city is home to an important French-language university, founded in 1952 in order to counterbalance Bishop's University in Lennoxville. Despite the city's name, chosen in honour of Sir John Coape Sherbrooke, governor of British North America at the time it was founded, the city's population has been almost entirely French-speaking (95 %) for a long time.

Route 143 leads to Rue Queen, inside the Sherbrooke city limits. Turn left on Rue King Ouest, then right on Rue Wellington, where we recommend parking in order to continue the tour of the city on foot.

The **Hôtel de Ville** ★ (*145 Rue Wellington Nord*), occupying the former Courthouse (the city's third), a granite building dating from 1904, was designed by Elzéar Charest, head architect of the Department of Public Works. It

CANTONS-DE-L'EST

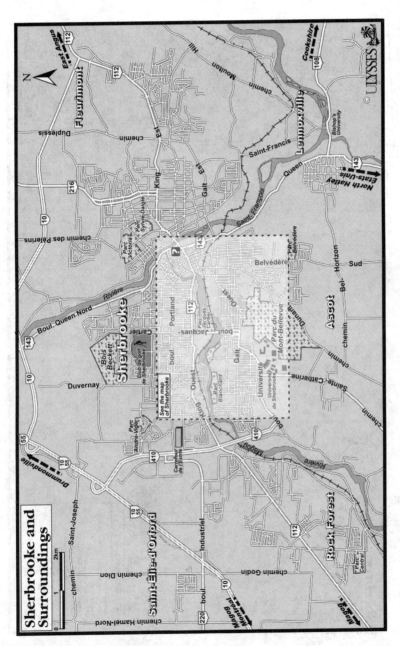

Sherbrooke and Surroundings

© ULYSSES

N

0   1   2km

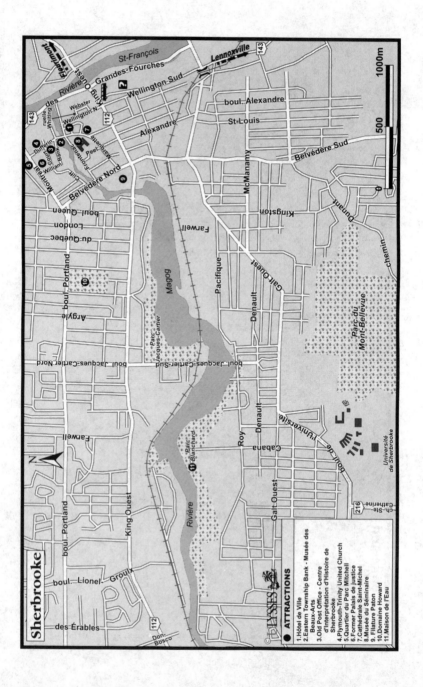

Sherbrooke

Lennoxville

St-François

des Rivière Ouest

Grandes-Fourches

Wellington-Sud

boul. Alexandre

St-Louis

Alexandre

Webster

Wellington N.

ruelle Whiting

Dufferin

Frontenac

Marquette

Peel

Belvédère Sud

Court

William

Bank

Montreal

Cliff

Belvédère Nord

boul. Queen

London

du Québec

boul. Portland

Argyle

McManamy

Kingston

Belvédère Sud

Dunant

Magog

Farwell

Pacifique

Denault

Gait-Ouest

chemin

Parc du Mont-Bellevue

Parc Jacques-Cartier

boul. Jacques-Cartier Nord

boul. Jacques-Cartier-Sud

Roy

Denault

Cabana

boul. de l'Université

Université de Sherbrooke

ch. Ste-Catherine

Parc Blanchard

Rivière

King Ouest

Gait-Ouest

boul. Portland

boul. Portland

Farwell

boul. Lionel-Groulx

des Érables

Don-Bosco

N

© ULYSSES

● ATTRACTIONS

1. Hôtel de Ville
2. Eastern Township Bank - Musée des Beaux-Arts
3. Old Post Office - Centre d'interprétation d'Histoire de Sherbrooke
4. Plymouth-Trinity United Church
5. Quartier du Parc Mitchell
6. Former Palais de justice
7. Cathédrale Saint-Michel
8. Musée du Séminaire
9. Filature Paton
10. Domaine Howard
11. Maison de l'Eau

1000m

500

0

is an example of Quebecers' enduring fondness for Second Empire architecture, with its French spirit. Visitors will recognize the segmental arches, the corner pavillions topped by false mansard roofs with wrought-iron cresting and the bull's-eye characteristic of the style. Strathcona Square, the garden in front of the Hôtel de Ville, marks the exact site of the market square that played such an important role in Sherbrooke's early development.

Turn left on Rue Frontenac, then right on Rue Dufferin, which leads over the frothy rapids of Rivière Magog, whose force was harnessed in the 19th century in order to provide power for the many mills located along the river.

An important financial institution in the last century, now merged with the CIBC (Canadian Imperial Bank of Commerce), the former **Eastern Townships Bank ★★** *(241 Rue Dufferin)* was established by the region's upper class, who were unable to obtain financing for local projects from the banks in Montréal. Its Sherbrooke head office, erected in 1877, was designed by Montréal architect James Nelson, involved at the time in building Bishop's University. It is considered the finest Second Empire building in Québec outside of Montréal and Québec City. Following a donation from the Canadian Imperial Bank of Commerce (CIBC) and major renovations, the building now houses the **Musée des Beaux-Arts** *($2.50; mid-Jun to Aug, Tue to Sun 11am to 5pm; Sep to mid-Jun, 1pm to 5pm; 241 Rue Dufferin, ☎819-821-2115)*. Gérard Gendron's work, which greets visitors in the main hall, parallels the building's former tenants and its present vocation. Besides the museum's large collection of naive art, there are several works by local contemporary artists. Volunteers are available to answer questions on the exhibitions, which usually change every two months.

The bank and the **former post office** *(275 Rue Dufferin)* next door, designed by François-Xavier Berlinguet (1885), form a fine architectural ensemble. The post office houses the offices of the **Centre d'Interprétation de l'Histoire de Sherbrooke** *($3; Tue to Fri 9am to noon and 1pm to 5pm; ☎819-821-5406)*, an interpretation centre on Sherbrooke's history. The centre organizes architectural and historical tours of the city, and rents audio tapes *($6)* for walking or driving tours.

Designed in 1851 by William Footner, the **Plymouth-Trinity United Church** *(380 Rue Dufferin)*, seems to come straight out of a New England village, due to its size as well as the building materials (red brick and wood painted white). Originally used by the Congregationalists, it was given its present name after several Protestant denominations joined together to form the United Church in 1925.

Continue on to Parc Mitchell.

Some of the loveliest houses in Sherbrooke are located on **Parc Mitchell ★★**, which is adorned with a fountain by sculptor George Hill (1921). **Maison Morey** *(not open to visitors; 428 Rue Dufferin)*, is an example of the bourgeois Victorian style favoured by merchants and industrialists from the British Isles and the United States. It was built in 1873 for Thomas Morey.

Walk around the park, then down Rue Montréal, and turn left on Rue Williams.

Facing straight down the center of Rue Court, the **former Palais de Justice ★** *(Rue Williams)*, Sherbrooke's second courthouse, was converted into a drill hall for the city's Hussards regiment at the end of the 19th century. Built in 1839 according to a design by William Footner, the edifice has a lovely neoclassical façade similar to another of Footner's designs, the Marché Bonsecours (see p 99) in Montréal.

Head back toward Rue Dufferin on Rue Bank. Turn right on Rue Marquette and climb the hill in the direction of the seminary and the cathedral.

Seen from a certain distance, the **Cathédrale Saint-Michel** *(Rue Marquette)* looks like a European abbey church perched on a promontory. The cathedral's medieval air contrasts with the city's neoclassical past. Up close, however, it becomes apparent that the structure was built very recently and never completed. Begun by the architect Louis-Napoléon Audet in 1917, this Gothic Revival cathedral wasn't consecrated until 1958.

The Séminaire Saint-Charles, built in 1898, now houses the **Musée du Séminaire de Sherbrooke ★** *($3.25; Sep to mid-Jun, Tue to Sun 12:30pm to 4:30pm; mid-Jun to early Sep, every day 10am to 5pm; 195 Rue Marquette and 222 Rue Frontenac; ☎819-564-3200)*, where visitors can see bird, plant and mineral collections, as well as interesting oil paintings, watercolours, sculptures and handmade native objects. The museum is associated with the Centre d'Exposition Léo-Marcotte, which presents travelling multidisciplinary exhibitions.

Continue on Rue Marquette towards the former Filature Paton, located on Rue Belvedere.

Sherbrooke's former textile industry started up in the second half of the 19th century, and was very profitable, as in many New England towns. The **Filature Paton** ★ *(at the end of Rue Marquette)*, once the most important textile mill in the Eastern Townships, was in operation from 1866 to 1977. It was scheduled for demolition the year it closed, but after a few visits over the border, where many such factories have been converted into housing and businesses, the municipal authorities decided to preserve a number of the buildings for a multi-functional complex. Today, the mill is not only a model of how an area's industrial heritage may be preserved and such spaces trans-formed, but also a new focus for downtown Sherbrooke.

To return to Montréal, take Route 143 N. to Highway 10 and head west.

Tour C: The Back Country ★ (2 days)

This most isolated part of the Eastern Townships is composed of an alternating series of mountains and plains. Long, deserted stretches of road link the local Loyalist villages. Far from the urban centres, these communities have in many cases remained primarily English-speaking and have retained their old-fashioned charm. The area around Mont Mégantic was colonized in the early 19th century by Scottish settlers from the Hebrides, and Celtic was commonly spoken here 100 years ago. French Canadians from the Rivière Chaudière valley (Beauce) began arriving at the end of the 19th century.

In Cookshire pick up Route 212 E., which leads through the villages of Island Brook, West Ditton and La Patrie, offering beautiful views of Mont Mégantic. Continue on to Notre-Dame-des-Bois.

Notre-Dame-des-Bois (pop. 620)

Located in the heart of the Appalachians at an altitude of over 550 metres, this little community acts as a sort of gateway to Mont Mégantic and its observatory, as well as Mont Saint-Joseph and its sanctuary.

From Notre-Dame-des-Bois, take the road in front of the church toward Val Racine. After 3.3 kilometres, turn left (after the Rivière aux Saumons). On the left, before the road starts heading upward, there is a tourist information booth. Several kilometres further, you will reach a junction. The road on the left leads to the observatory.

The **Astrolab du Mont-Mégantic** ★★ *($10; mid-Jun to Sep, every day 10am to 6pm, 8pm to 11pm with reservations; 189 Route du Parc, ☎819-888-2941 or 1-888-881-2941)* is an interpretation centre on astronomy. The interactive museum's various rooms and multimedia show reveals the beginnings of astronomy with the latest technology. A guided tour to the summit of Mont Mégantic, lasting approximately 1 hour and 15 minutes, walks visitors through the facilities. Famous for its observatory, Mont Mégantic was chosen for its strategic position between the Universities of Montreal and Laval, as well as its distance from urban light sources. The second highest summit in the Eastern Townships, it stands at 1105 metres. During the **Festival d'Astronomie Populaire du Mont Mégantic**, a local astronomy festival held the second week of July, astronomy buffs can observe the heavens through the most powerful telescope in eastern North America. Otherwise, the latter is only available to researchers. In summer, however, basic celestial mechanics workshops are given. These begin at 8pm and include giant-screen presentations and observation of the sky. Reservations required.

Head back to Route 212 E. At Woburn, take Route 161 N., which runs along beautiful Lac Mégantic.

A vast expanse of crystal-clear water stretching 19 kilometres, **Lac Mégantic** ★★ is teeming with all sorts of fish, especially trout, and attracts a good many vacationers eager to go fishing or simply enjoy the local beaches. Five municipalities around the lake, Lac-Mégantic being the most well-known, welcome visitors lured by the lovely mountainous countryside.

Lac-Mégantic ★ (pop. 5,941)

The town of Lac-Mégantic was founded in 1885 by Scottish settlers from the Hebrides. Unable to make enough money from the

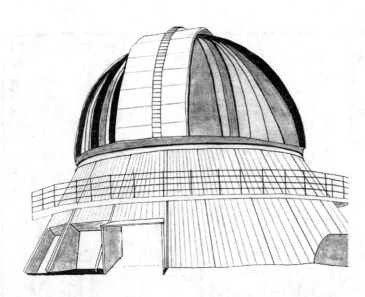

Astrolab du Mont-Mégantic

relatively poor soil, the residents soon turned to forestry. Today, thousands of people come to the region every year to enjoy a wide variety of sporting activities. The town is beautifully located on the shores of Lac Mégantic.

In the **Église Sainte-Agnès** ★ *(4872 Rue Laval)*, erected in 1913, visitors will discover a beautiful stained-glass window designed in 1849 for the Catholic Church of Immaculate Conception in Mayfair, London.

The road then leads through the villages of ***Nantes*** *and* ***Stornoway***, ***Stratford*** *and* ***Saint-Gérard***, *passing alongside the Parc de Récréation de Frontenac and skirting round Lac Aylmer before connecting with Route 216 and Route 255, which lead to Asbestos.*

The **Parc de Récréation de Frontenac** ★ see p 217.

Asbestos (pop. 6,674)

Asbestos, as its name indicates, is one of the foremost asbestos mining centres in the world. Asbestos releases harmful particles when improperly handled, leading to a ban by the United States on the use of it and a subsequent decline in mining activity in the town of Asbestos.

A bus excursion takes visitors to the **JM Asbestos Mine** *($8; mid-May to mid-Oct, Sat 1pm; Jul to Aug, Wed, Fri and Sun 1pm; Blvd. St. Luc,* ☎*819-839-2911)*. The most spectacular attraction here is without a doubt the gargantuan fleet of 125-ton CAT 789 trucks, whose wheels measure 2 metres in diameter.

The **Musée Minéralogique et d'Histoire Minière** *(free admission; late Jun to early Sep, Wed to Sun 10am to 5pm; 104 Rue Letendre;* ☎*819-879-6444)*, a museum outlining mineralogy and the history of mining includes samples of asbestos from different mines both in Québec and abroad.

Danville ★ (pop. 1,858)

This attractive, shady village has preserved a number of noteworthy Victorian and Edwardian residences, which bear witness to a time when wealthy Montréal families summered in Danville.

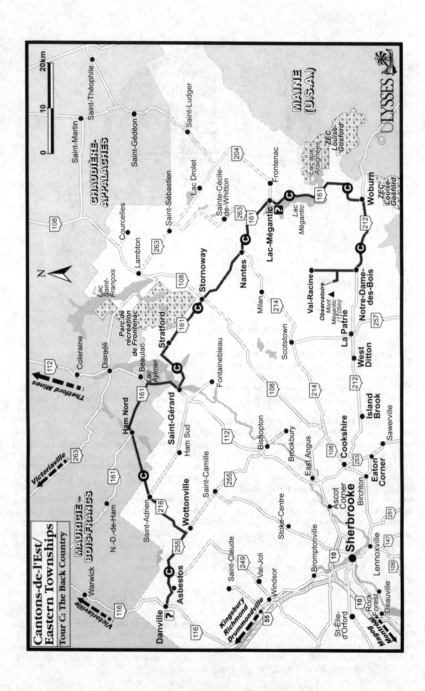

PARKS

Tour A: The Orchards

The **Parc de Récréation de la Yamaska** (*$3.50; every day 8am until sundown; 1780 8ᵉ Rang E., ☎450-776-7182*) was laid out around the Réservoir Choinière, now a pleasant swimming area. During winter, there are 40 km of cross-country ski trails available for public use.

Just a few kilometres from downtown Granby, the **Centre d'Interprétation de la Nature du Lac Boivin** (*free admission; every day 8:30am to 4:30pm; 700 Rue Drummond; ☎450-375-3861, ≈375-3736*) offers four trails along the marshy shores of the lake. An observation tower and blind offer good vantage points for aquatic plants and a variety of water birds. Mornings, when the trails are less busy, are the best time for birding. The paths are also open in the winter. There are temporary exhibits throughout the year in the information centre.

Tour B: The Lakes

The **Parc du Mont-Orford** ★★ (*C.P. 146, Magog, J1X 3W7; ☎819-843-6233*) stretches over 58 square kilometres and includes—in addition to the mountain—the area around Lac Stukely. During the summer, visitors can enjoy the beach, the magnificent golf course ($30 a round), back-country campsites, and some 50 kilometres of hiking trails (the most beautiful path leads to Mont Chauve). The park also attracts winter sports lovers with its cross-country ski trails and 33 downhill ski runs ($34 a day).

The **Parc de la Gorge de Coaticook** ★★ (*$6; May to Nov, every day 9am to 8pm; 135 Rue Michaud; ☎819-849-2331*) protects the part of the impressive 50-metre gorge created by the Rivière Coaticook. Trails wind across the entire area, enabling visitors to see the gorge from all different angles. Cross the suspension bridge over the gorge, if you dare!

Tour C: The Back Country

Known foremost for its famed observatory (see p 214), the **Parc de Conservation du Mont-Mégantic** (*189 Route du Parc, Notre-Dame-des-Bois, ☎819-888-2800*) covers an area of 58.8 square kilometres and is an example of the different types of mountainous vegetation characteristic of the Eastern Townships. Heavy infrastructure has not even been able to disturb the tranquillity of this park whose goal is an educational one. Hikers and skiers can take advantage of the Park's interpretive trails, cabins and campsites and, if lucky, observe up to 125 species of migrating birds. Snowshoeing in winter and mountain-biking in summer. Its summits, Mont Mégantic and Mont Saint-Joseph, are accessible by car.

The **Parc de Récréation de Frontenac** ★ (*9 R.R. 3, Thetford Mines; ☎418-486-7807*), offers a wide variety of outdoor activities. Located on the shores of Lac Saint-François, it boasts lovely beaches. Sports lovers can go canoeing, windsurfing and sailing (there is a school here). The park also has hiking trails. Visitors can stay in cottages for $23 per person per day. See also in Chaudière-Appalaches p 408.

OUTDOORS

Hiking

Tour A: The Orchards

The **Sentier de l'Estrie** (*☎819-868-3889*) network of trails winds over 150 kilometres through the Chapman, Kingsbury, Brompton, Orford, Bolton, Glen, Echo and Sutton areas. You can obtain a topographical guide of the trail and the membership card necessary to walk it for $20. Keep in mind that most of the trail runs across private property. The various landowners have accorded an exclusive right of way to members.

Tour B: The Lakes

Parc d'Environnenment Naturel de Sutton (*☎450-538-4085*) is just as popular in the summer as in winter. The **Roundtop** hike, with its spectacular panoramas, attracts hikers from far and wide.

Parc de Mont Orford *(☎819-843-6233)* is a prized hiking spot in the Townships. Several sections of the **Sentier de l'Estrie** traverse it. It is an excellent choice for hikers as it contains a network of over 60 kilometres of trails of varying degrees of difficulty. The **Mont Chauve** and **Mont Orford** hikes are particularly interesting.

Tour C: Back Country

Eight trails crisscross the **Parc du Mont-Mégantic**, totalling about 50 kilometres of hiking trails. The latest one, traversing Mont Mégantic and the crests of Monts Victoria and St. Joseph, is certainly among the most beautiful in the region.

 Biking

Tour A: The Orchards

The **Estriade** bicycle path runs along an old railway line. It covers 21 kilometres, linking Granby, Bromont and Waterloo.

The **Station de Vélo de Montagne de Bromont** *($8; 83 Boulevard Bromont, Bromont ☎514-538-8455)* has close to 100 kilometres of intermediate and expert level trails. Bikers can also use the chairlift.

Tour B: The Lakes

An 80-kilometre bicycle trail crisscrosses the Sutton region. A detailed map is available for $3.50. For more information, call ☎(450) 538-2646.

 Horseback Riding

The **Centre Équestre de Bromont** *(100 Rue Laprairie, ☎450-534-3255)* hosted the 1976 Olympic equestrian events, for which a variety of stables and rings, both exterior and interior, were built. Some of these facilities are now used for riding classes.

 Cruises

The **Croisières Memphrémagog** *(regular cruises: $12; mid-May to Jun 23, Fri to Sun noon, 2pm; Jun 24 to Aug, every day 10am, noon, 2pm, 4pm; one-day cruises: $45; Jun to Sep 9am; Quai Fédéral, ☎819-843-8068, ☎843-1200)* offer two-hour cruises on magnificent Lac Memphrémagog, whose shores form part of both the Quebec and American borders. At around 9am, a second, one-day cruise leaves the wharf for Vermont where it makes a brief call at Newport. These cruises are all the more spectacular in the fall when the colours are at their brightest. Fares include a light snack. Reservations required.

 Golf

Much Valued for its quality greens, the **Owl's Head** golf course *($37; 181 Chemin Owl's Head, Mansonville, ☎450-292-3666 or 1-800-363-3342)* is easily the favourite amongst local golfers. Moreover, it is endowed with a very posh club house and offers a superb view of the mountain after which it was named. Chances of teeing off are better on weekdays.

The **Dufferin Heights** golf course *($30; 4115 Route 143, Stanstead, ☎819-876-2113)*, which recently celebrated its 75th anniversary, puts even the staunchest of golfers to the test. Its undulating terrain offers splendid views of the Appalachian mountains and of Lakes Massawippi and Memphrémagog.

 Downhill Skiing

Tour A: The Orchards

The **Station de Ski Bromont** *($32; 150 Rue Champlain, ☎450-534-2200)* has 23 runs, 20 of which are lit until 11:30pm for night-skiing. The mountain has a vertical drop of over 400 metres.

Tour B: The Lakes

Mont Sutton ★ *($39; 671 Chemin Mapple; ☎450-866-2545, ☎538-2339 during summer)* has 53 downhill ski runs and a vertical drop of

460 metres. It is known for its magnificent glade runs.

Mont Orford ★ *($32.75; Magog, ☎819-843-6549)* is among the prettiest ski centres in Québec. It boasts 40 trails.

Owl's Head ★ *($30; Chemin du Mont Owl's Head, Mansonville, ☎450-292-3342)* is one of the most beautiful ski resorts in the Eastern Townships region, with sweeping views of Lac Memphrémagog and the surrounding mountains. There are 27 runs for skiers of all different levels.

Cross-country Skiing

Tour B: The Lakes

The Sutton region is not only ideal for downhill skiing and hiking, but is also home to a superb network of cross-country ski trails. The **Sutton-en-Haut** network *($6.95; 297 Rue Maple, Sutton en Haut, JOE 2KO, ☎450-538-2271)* includes 15 trails, which intertwine allowing skiers to switch tracks and levels of difficulty throughout the day.

Parc du Mont Orford *($8.50; Magog-Orford, ☎819-843-9855)* also has a network of cross-country trails with a good reputation. Twelve trails cover some 55 kilometres of terrain that will please all levels.

Tour C: The Back Country

The 82-kilometre long **Centre de Ski de Fond Bellevue** *($9; 70 Chemin Lay, Melbourne JOB 2BO, ☎819-826-3869)* is a pleasant surprise. Fifteen trails for all levels.

Besides its famed observatory and excellent snow conditions, Parc du Mont-Mégantic has eight cross-country skiing trails. The **Sentiers du Mont-Mégantic** *($5; Chemin de l'Observatoire, Rang 2, JOB 2EO, Notre-Dame-des-Bois, ☎819-888-2800)* offers one of the longest ski seasons in the province. Because of its altitude, skiing sometimes lasts into the month of May!

Dogsledding

Tour A: The Orchard

What could be more exotic than experiencing winter in Quebec behind a team of Siberian Huskies? **Safari Loowak** *($100/hr. for 2 people; 475 Blvd. Horizon, Waterloo, ☎450-539-0501)* offers just such unforgettable adventures.

Adventure Packages

Tour B: The Lakes

A young and dynamic enterprise, the **Adrénaline** outdoor-adventure school *(☎819-843-0045 or 1-888-475-3462, ≈843-0479)* boasts an experienced staff and offers diverse activities. In winter, regular departures are made for dogsledding expeditions, ice climbing, ice fishing and snowshoeing. In summer, proposed activities run from introduction to rock climbing and river kayaking to panoramic rafting. In short, a host of activities for thrill-seekers! Prices include instructors and the required equipment. Personalized activities are also available upon request. Reservations required.

ACCOMMODATIONS

Tour A: The Orchards

Dunham

With its 0.5 hectares of land, the **Pom-Art B&B** *($55, sb, $75 pb, bkfst incl.; 677 Chemin Hudson, ☎450-295-3514)*, built in 1820, is a real gem. Denis and Lise offer guests a warm welcome, not to mention an exceptional breakfast where apples from the region figure prominently. An ideal abode in which to seek refuge after a tiring day on the slopes of Mont Sutton, located 15 kilometres away. Indeed, the most luxurious of the three rooms boasts a fireplace and a window looking out on the surrounding mountains.

La Chanterelle *($70 bkfst incl.; 3721 Rue Principale, Route 202, JOE 1M0, ☎450-195-3542, ⌐273-7243),* located at the

edge of the village, is a magnificent *gîte*. The courteous service and copious breakfast at this peaceful, attractively decorated, period house, make for a memorable stay.

Cowansville

The **Camping Domaine Tournesol** *($14 to $18; 331 Chemin Brousseau, Cowansville, ☎450-263-9515)* is a rather cheerful campground with a swimming pool and canteen.

Bromont

The **Camping Bromont** *($19; 24 Rue Lafontaine, ☎450-534-2712 or 534-2669)* has every convenience, including showers, bathrooms, swimming pool – even miniature golf! Most sections are wooded, providing campers with a certain amount of privacy.

The **Motel le Menhir** *($89; ≈; 125 Boulevard Bromont, JOE 1L0, ☎450-534-3790, ⌐ 534-1933),* stretched out alongside the road leading to Mont Bromont, has some 41 decently furnished rooms. It offers package rates including breakfast and a day of skiing or golf, and has an indoor swimming pool.

The **Auberge Bromont** *($109; ≈, ℜ; 95 Montmorency, C.P. 510, JOE 1L0; ☎450-534-1199, ⌐ 534-1700)* is located near the town's sports facilities (golfing and Mont Bromont). The setting is lovely, with lots of trees, but the rooms are somewhat ordinary for the price.

Those looking for comfort can head to the **Château Bromont** *($140; ≈, △, ℜ; 90 Stanstead, JOE 1L0; ☎450-534-3433 or 1-800-304-3433, ⌐ 534-0514),* where both the main rooms and the bedrooms are elegantly decorated with antique furniture. It is located alongside Mont Bromont, providing skiers with easy access to the slopes.

Granby

A typical roadside motel for travellers on the move, **Le Granbyen** *($50; ≈, ℜ; 700 Rue Principale, J2G 2Y4; ☎450-378-8406)* has decent but nondescript rooms.

Tour B: The Lakes

Around Lac Brome

Devoid of trees, the entrance to **Camping de Brome** *($12; 552 Valley Road, Brome, ☎450-243-0196 or 742-5431)* proves disappointing. Nevertheless, camp sites at the far end offer greater privacy, and the river bordering the grounds is pleasant for swimming.

Located on the shores of Lac Brome, the well-kept **Camping Domaine des Érables** *($20; 688 Bondville, Route 215, Foster, ☎819-242-8888)* offers all the comforts of life with its laundromat, showers, convenience store, etc. In short, those who swear by wilderness camping should give this place a miss.

Joli Vent *($80 bkfst incl.; ≈; 667 Chemin Bondville, Foster, JOE 1R0; ☎450-243-4272, ⌐ 243-0202)* is a lovely inn within a pleasant setting, despite being alongside the road. The modestly furnished rooms have a rustic charm.

Knowlton

Ideally located near ski resorts and golf courses, the **Auberge Lakeview** *($125 bkfst incl. Fri to Sun, $88 bkfst incl. Mon to Thu; ⊛, ≈, ℜ, ⊛; 50 Rue Victoria, ☎450-243-6183 or 1-800-661-6183, ⌐243-0602)* offers an altogether Victorian atmosphere. Indeed, the 1986 renovations have restored some of the noble antiquity to this historic monument, built in the latter half of the 19th century. Rates for rooms, both comfortable and spacious, include the continental breakfast.

Sutton

La Paimpolaise *($76 bkfst incl.; ℜ; 615 Maple C.P. 548, JOE 2K0; ☎450-538-3213 ⌐ 538-3970)* inn near the ski slopes is set up in two separate buildings. The reception is in a

---

Ulysses' Favourites

Accommodations

For warm receptions:
Pom-Art B&B (p 219) and Aux Jardins Champêtres (p 221).

For luxury:
Manoir Hovey (p 223), Château Bromont (p 220) and Auberge Ripplecove (p 222).

For history buffs:
Auberge Lakeview (p 220).

For the views:
Aubergine Relais de Campagne (p 221).

Restaurants

The Eastern Townships' finest tables:
McHaffy (p 224), Auberge Ripplecove (p 225), Auberge Hatley (p 226) and Manoir Hovey (p 226)

For the romantic atmosphere:
Auberge Ripplecove (p 225)

For Québec cuisine:
Maison de Chez-Nous (p 224), Les Jardins (p 225) and Aux Berges de l'Aurore (p 227).

For terraces:
L'Orpailleur (p 224), Knowlton Pub (p 225), Il Duetto (p 225), Les Berges (p 225), Pub de Lion d'Or (p 226) and Da Toni (p 226).

---

small, wooden, Swiss chalet-style house, and the rooms are in a long concrete annex. These are somewhat austere. This is a very plain hotel with a clientele consisting mainly of skiers.

Vale Perkins (Knowlton's Landing)

The **Aubergine Relais de Campagne** *($75 bkfst incl., $125 ½b; beach; Chemin Mansonville, JOE 1X0; ☎450-292-3246)* occupies a former post house dating from 1816. Built out of red brick, it is graced with a long wooden veranda perfect for summer evenings. This inn is all the more pleasant for the gorgeous view it offers of Lac Memphrémagog.

Bolton Centre

Iris Bleue *($80 bkfst incl.; ℜ; Route 245, JOE 1G0, ☎450-292-3530)* is a charming bed and breakfast. The atmosphere is warm, thanks to the lace curtains, flowered wallpaper and antique furniture decorating the rooms. You will be welcomed by the friendly owners, who go out of their way to make your stay a pleasant one. A Mediterranean-style evening meal *($$)* is served in the adorable dining room.

Magog

Surrounded by wild flowers and cats, **Aux Jardins Champêtres** *($65 sb, $90 pb, $126 ½b; 1575 Chemin des Pères, ☎819-868-0665)* recalls summers spent at grandma's. Located a few minutes from Magog and l'Abbaye St-Benoit-du-Lac, this B & B boasts comfortable rooms as well as a swimming pool. The welcoming little farm also owes its reputation to its excellent and varied country cooking.

À **Tout Venant** *($70 bkfst incl.; 624 Bellevue Ouest, J1X 3H4; ☎819-868-0419)* is a quaint-looking bed and breakfast located on a quiet street in the heart of Magog. The house, fairly typical of local residences, has five guest rooms.

At the end of a long piece of land, stands the bed and breakfast **La Sauvagine** *($75 bkfst incl.; 975 Merry N., J1X 2G9; ☎819-843-9779)*, a lovely house attractively decorated with flower boxes. There are five spacious rooms.

The little **Motel de la Pente Douce** *($76 bkfst incl.; ≈, K; 1787 Rivière aux Cerises, R.R.2, J1X 3W3; ☎819-843-1234 or 1-800-567-3530)* is plain-looking, but well-located near Mont Orford. It also has the added advantage of offering decent rooms at attractive rates.

Mont-Orford

Situated near the Centre d'Arts d'Orford, the **Auberge La Grande Fugue** *($15/person; May to Oct; 3166 Chemin du Parc, ☎819-843-8595 or 1-800-567-6155)* consists of a series of small cottages surrounded by nature. A communal kitchen is available to guests. In the early afternoon, a shuttle service ($2 return trip) takes visitors from Magog to the Centre d'Arts. For information about timetables, contact the tourist office or call at ☎819-847-0151.

Located in Mont Orford park, the **Camping Stukley** *($22; via Hwy 10 or 55, Exit 118, heading toward Mont Orford, ☎819-843-9855)* is on the way to the lake of the same name. Dense forests surround the campground and mountain-biking trails are close by. At night, during summer, the community centre becomes a cinema. The campground also has a beach and leases small boats.

The **Village Mont-Orford** *($95; ≈, K; 5015 Chemin du Parc, J1X 3W8, ☎819-847-2662 or 1-800-567-7315, ≈847-2487)* is comprised of several buildings, each containing a few lovely, equipped condos. Approximately 200 metres from there, a quadruple chair lift takes skiers up to Mont Orford's runs.

Built near Mont Orford, **Auberge Estrimont** *($103/room, $110/condo; ≈, ⊖, △, ℜ, K;*

44 Avenue de l'Auberge, J1X 3W7, ☎819-843-1616 or 1-800-567-7320, ≈843-4909)* has rooms and small condos. Made entirely of wood, the condos are equipped with balconies and fireplaces. Woods border the property.

The **Étoile-sur-le-Lac** inn *($118; ≈, ℜ; 1150 Rue Principale, J1X 3B8, ☎819-843-6521 or 1-800-567-2727)* boasts charming rooms, each offering a beautiful view of Lac Memphrémagog. The inn has a lovely, relaxing terrace.

In the shadow of Mont Orford is the very opulent and modern **Manoir des Sables** *($119 to $134; ≈, ℜ, △, ⊖, ≈, tv; 90 Avenue des Jardins, ☎819-847-4747 or 1-800-567-3514, ≈847-3519)*. The hotel features a multitude of services and facilities such as indoor and outdoor swimming pools, an 18-hole golf course, tennis courts and a health spa. Several rooms boast fireplaces, and those on the top floor offer magnificent views of the lake and of the 60-hectare property. Rooms in the "Privilège" wing come with exemplary service and include continental breakfasts.

The **Auberge du Grand Lac** *($129 bkfst incl.; 40 Merry Sud, J1X 3L1, ☎819-847-4039)* is an uninspired brick and aluminum building. Guest rooms are nevertheless, well kept and modern.

Ayer's Cliff

Set on a natural, six-hectare property facing Lac Massawippi, the **Auberge Ripplecove** *($234 ½b; ≈, ⊛, ≈, ℜ; 700 Rue Ripplecove, ☎819-838-4296 or 1-800-668-4296, ≈819-838-5541)*, is wonderfully peaceful. Its elegant Victorian-style dining room and tasteful rooms ensure comfort in unparalleled, intimate surroundings. Moreover, the more luxurious rooms boast their own fireplaces and whirlpool baths. A variety of outdoor activities is offered. The place becomes absolutely magical in winter.

Coaticook

The *gîte* **La Brise des Nuits** *($50 bkfst incl.; 142 Cutting, J1A 2G5, ☎819-849-4667)* is a good place to keep in mind. The rooms are pleasantly decorated and the service is very friendly.

North Hatley

Simplicity and comfort are first and foremost at **La Rose des Vents** *($90 to $145 bkfst incl.; ≈, ℜ; 312 Chemin de la Rivière, ☎819-842-4530, ⋅⋅842-2610)*, an inn in the heart of the picturesque village of North Hatley. Originally from Marseilles, its proprietors have brought a bit of Provence to the Townships. Indeed, its restaurant specializes in Provençale cuisine.

La Raveaudière *($85 bkfst incl.; 11 Hatley Centre; ☎819-842-2554)* is a superb house which has been renovated yet retains its old-fashioned character. All the rooms are decorated with grace and good taste, and a few have their own bathroom. The discreet, attentive manner in which guests are welcomed will make them feel right at home.

The **Auberge Hatley** *($200 ½b; ≈, ℜ; Route 108, J0B 2C0; ☎819-842-2451, ⋅ 842-2907)* occupies a superb residence built in 1903. The spacious living room looking out on the lake is decorated with beautiful antiques. A vast garden surrounds the inn and its pool. A magical place to escape to.

Built in 1900, the **Manoir Hovey** *($250 ½b; ⊙, ≈, ℜ; Chemin Hovey, J0B 1C0; ☎819-842-2421, ⋅ 842-2248)* reflects the days when wealthy families spent their vacations in the beautiful country houses of the Townships (see p 209). Converted into an inn 40 years ago, it is still extremely comfortable. The 40 rooms are decorated with lovely antique furniture, and most offer a magnificent view of Lac Massawippi. The property retains much of the old, natural charm of the site.

Lennoxville

The pretty black and white building of the **La Paysanne** *($57; ≡, ≈; 42 Queen, J1M 1H9; ☎819-569-5585)* motel is attractive. It is also easily accessible on the way into town. There are 29 spacious, simply decorated rooms.

Sherbrooke

Recently converted into a B&B, **Le Vieux Presbytère** *($55 sb, $65 pb, bkfst incl.; 1162 Boulevard Portland, ☎819-346-1665)* has five tastefully decorated rooms. Several of the proprietors' finds will delight antique lovers, as will the beautiful lobby and reception on the ground floor. Moreover, safe storage is provided for bicycles.

The **Ermitage** *($56; ℗, ≈; 1888 Rue King Ouest, J1J 2E2; ☎819-569-5551, ⋅569-1446)*, a wood and brick motel located on the way into the city, is one of the prettiest in its category. The rooms are fairly comfortable, but starkly decorated.

It is hard to miss the **Hôtel des Gouverneurs** *($69; ≈, ℜ; 3131 Rue King Ouest, J1L 1C8, ☎819-565-0464, ⋅565-5505)* on the way into town. Careful attention has been paid t the decor: pretty prints and flowers adorn the long hallways, and the rooms feature modern and elegant furniture.

The pinkish **Delta Hotel** *($78; ≈, ⊙, △, ℜ; 2685 Rue King Ouest, J1L 1C1; ☎819-822-1989 or 1-800-268-1133)* is also on the way into town. Recently built, it offers its guests a wide range of facilities, including an indoor pool, a whirlpool and an exercise room.

Tour C: The Back Country

Notre-Dame-des-Bois (Mont-Mégantic)

Situated less than two kilometres from Mont Mégantic, the quiet **Camping Altitude** *($15; Route du Parc)* offers nature lovers about fifteen gravelled camp sites at some distance from each other. Rudimentary facilities: outhouses and spring water taps.

Aux Berges de l'Aurore *($185 ½b, $85 bkfst incl.; 51 Chemin de l'Observatoire, Notre-Dame-des-Bois, on the road leading to the observatory, right before the tourist information booth; ☎819-888-2715)* is a charming little house in a peaceful, natural setting, with four simple rooms. The inn is closed during winter.

Lac-Mégantic

The modest B&B, **La Maison de Philibert** *($50; 3502 Boulevard Agnès, G8B 1L3, ☎819-583-3515)* makes for a pleasant change from your typical hotel or motel. A warm welcome and beautiful home will make this a memorable stay.

RESTAURANTS

Tour A: The Orchards

Dunham

The restaurant at the **L'Orpailleur** *($$; early Jun to mid-Oct, closed Mon and Tue; 1086 Route 202; ☎450-295-3763)*, vineyard, open only in the summer, has a short, but high-quality menu. A pleasant terrace looking out on the vineyard enables guests to enjoy the lovely countryside while they eat. The service is extremely friendly.

The **Picolletto** *($$-$$$; closed Tue; 3698A Rue Principale, ☎450-295-2664)*, located along the Wine Route, is a cozy, rustic place that serves delicious French and Italian cuisine.

Frelighsburg

The bistro **Aux Deux Clochers** *($$; at the corner of Rue Principale and Rue l'Église, ☎450-298-5086)* has a pretty rural setting. Guests can enjoy consistently good classic cuisine or simply order a light meal. Breakfast is served on Saturdays and Sundays.

Granby

The name **Ben la Bédaine** *($; 599 Rue Principale; ☎450-378-2921)*, which means "Potbelly Ben" is certainly evocative; this place is a veritable shrine to the French fry.

The **Casa du Spaghetti** *($; 781 Rue Principale; ☎450-372-3848)* is a good place for an inexpensive meal of pasta or pizza cooked in a wood-burning oven.

Aubergade *($$$; closed Mon; 53 Drummond; ☎450-777-5797)* is apparently the trendiest restaurant in Granby. The atmosphere is relaxed in both dining rooms, which can accommodate about fifty patrons.

The owner of **Maison de Chez Nous** *($$$-$$$$; closed Mon and Tue; 847 Rue Mountain; ☎450-372-2991)* gave up his wine cellar so that his customers, who may now bring their own wine, could save a little money.

Furthermore, the menu offers the best and most refined of Québec cuisine.

Cowansville

A must in the region, the **McHaffy** restaurant *($$$; 351 Rue Principale, ☎450-266-7700)*, whose menu changes every two months, offers fine, international cuisine made with local ingredients and accompanied by a Blancs Coteaux wine chosen by Alain Bélanger, one of Quebec's best sommeliers. At lunch, patrons enjoy lighter meals on a pleasant terrace. Not to be missed is the duck festival, from mid-October to mid-November, when chef Pierre Johnston creates excellent dishes for the occasion.

Bromont

The **Picolo Café Terrasse** *($; 702 Shefford; ☎450-534-4868)* serves very good food at prices so reasonable you can bring the whole family.

The **Etrier Rest-O-Bar** *($$; closed Mon; 547 Shefford; ☎450-534-3562)* serves excellent cuisine to an established clientele. The restaurant is located a short distance outside the city in a pleasant, though unsophisticated setting.

Chez Simon *($$$; Wed to Sun 5:30pm to 9pm; 632 Rue Shefford, ☎450-534-4626)* is the perfect place for an intimate dinner. Located in a small country-style house, the restaurant's three dining rooms can only accommodate about ten people each. Chef Giovanni Costanzo, one of the initiators of the Lac Brome duck festival, prepares European dishes with regional products. Portions are generous and the menu is varied. Reservations required.

The chef at the **Jardinière** *($$$; Auberge Bromont, 95 Montmorency; ☎450-534-2200)* prepares French cuisine with regional ingredients, such as duck from the poultry farms of Lac Brome and lamb from Saint-Grégoire. In the summer, guests can enjoy the terrace, the grill and the magnificent views of Mont Bromont. Sunday brunch is about $15.

FAUNA

Québec's vast natural spaces are populated by a tremendously diverse collection of birds and mammals. A symbol of the colonization of the New World, the beaver, chomps his way through forests to create his abode; the mighty moose, which prefers the cover of a stand of firs, reigns over the forest with its velvety crown; in deciduous and coniferous forests listen and watch for the call of the blue jay and the flash of the robin's red breast. One of the most beautiful riches of the province is certainly this striking wildlife.

Snowy Owl

Unlike others, this great owl is diurnal. It is common to arctic tundras around the world, but can also be found in the southern United States. It feeds primarily on small mammals, its favourite are lemmings.

Snow Goose

Snow geese pause in the St. Lawrence valley every spring and fall during their migratory journey of several thousand kilometres, and literally cover the shoreline around Cap Tourmente.

Canada Goose

Found throughout Canada, the eponymous goose is easily identified by its long black neck, black head and the two conspicuous white cheek patches. This bird nests on small islets or on muskrat or beaver dams.

Northern Gannet

Northern gannets inhabit Île Bonaventure: and the sight of a whole colony taking flight is like a flurry of snowflakes on a sunny day. These birds are not shy and it is easy to observe them up close.

Great Cormorant

With its glistening black plumage, this bird can reach 1 m in height. An excellent diver, it can hold its breath for up to 30 seconds, time enough to catch some food.

Belted Kingfisher

This sturdy little bird is found throughout the Americas and in Australia. You might be lucky enough to spot it getting ready to plunge into waters teeming with fish in search of its next meal.

Great Blue Heron

This wader, which can reach 132 cm, can be found throughout southern Québec. Hunted for many years it is now protected by Canadian law. The great blue heron feeds by standing still in open water and waiting for its unsuspecting prey to approach.

Common Loon

Shortly after the spring thaw, this bird returns Québec to nest. They are usually seen in solita pairs on lakes.

American Robin

The robin's song announces the start of spring. This bird, which can be observed throughout Québec, pokes about grassy areas for its diet of small fruits, insects and worms.

Blue Jay

This crested bird is found across southern Canada. Practically carnivorous, the blue jay eats the eggs and chicks of other birds, fruits, seeds, acorns and insects.

Black-capped Chickadee

The chickadee is one of those cheerful little birds that flits about, even in winter, without a care for the cold. This bird is easily attracted to feeders. It eats insects, small fruits and seeds.

Northern Cardinal

The cardinal can be spotted year round in southern Québec. The male's brilliant red plumage makes him easy to spot.

Red-winged Blackbird

The red spots on each wing of the male are visible in flight. The blackbird nests in marshes where frogs and bulrushes are plentiful. Seen as a pest by farmers it consumes grain from cultivated fields.

Beaver

Known as a skilful and tireless dam builder, the beaver is Canada's national symbol. It has a stout body, short, webbed hind feet and a large flat scaly tail used as a rudder when it swims. Its powerful lower incisors allow it to cut down trees for its shelter.

Porcupine

Found in significant numbers in both deciduous and coniferous forests, the porcupine is famous for the way it defends itself. When threatened, the quills covering its body stand on end, turning the porcupine into a kind of unassailable pin cushion.

Skunk

This small mammal is known mostly for its defence mechanism: it sprays its attackers with a foul-smelling liquid. The first European settlers called it *bête puante* or stinking beast. The animal is common to eastern North America, even to some cities and, while it is attractive, it is a good idea to keep your distance.

Raccoon

The racoon is a nocturnal and particularly crafty animal found in southeastern Canada. It has a reputation for cleanliness because of its habit of plunging its food underwater before eating it.

Ungava Caribou
(arctic reindeer)

This large species of deer can weigh up to 250 kg when fully grown. It lives in the tundra, and its name comes from the Algonquian language.

White-tailed Deer

The white-tailed deer is the smallest species of deer in eastern North America, attaining a maximum weight of about 150 kg. This graceful creature lives at the forest's edge and is one of the most commonly hunted animals in Québec. The male's antlers fall off each winter and grow back in the spring.

Moose

This is the largest member of the deer family in the world; it can measure more than two metres in height and weigh up to 600 kg. The male is distinguished by its broad, flattened antlers, large head, rounded nose and by the hump on its back.

Black Bear

Most often found in forests, this is the most common species of bear in eastern Canada. It can weigh up to 150 kg when fully grown, yet is the smallest type of bear in Canada. Be careful – the black bear is unpredictable and dangerous.

Wolf

This predator lives in packs. It measures between 67 and 95 cm, and weighs no more than 50 kg. Wolves attack their prey (often deer) in packs, and their viciousness makes them rather unsympathetic creatures. Wolves keep their distance from humans.

Red Fox

This small animal has striking auburn fur and is found throughout the forests of eastern Canada. A cunning creature, it keeps its distance from humans and is rarely spotted. It hunts small animals and also feeds on nuts and berries.

Coyote

Smaller than the wolf, the coyote adapts easily to various surroundings; it can be spotted through southeastern Canada. Depending on what is available, this carnivore can survive as a vegetarian.

Tour B: The Lakes

Knowlton

The **Knowlton Pub** *($; 267 Knowlton Road, ☎450-534-1199)* is without question one of the most popular spots in the Eastern Townships. The loud music hardly suits the rural setting, but its a favourite nonetheless. During busy periods, the service is extremely slow. When business is slower, however, the English pub atmosphere and large terrace are pleasant.

Housed in an attractive building, **Le Nilsson** *($$-$$$; 70 Lakeside Road)* has a modern, slightly flashy decor. Located on the banks of the river in a pleasant rural setting, the restaurant serves unpretentious French cuisine. Weekends only during winter.

Sutton

The **Mocador** *($-$$; 17 Rue Principale; ☎450-538-2426)*, located on Rue Principale in a charming house with a picture window, serves simple fare, and is a perfect place to enjoy a quiet meal.

At **À la Fontaine** *($$-$$$; 30 Rue Principale, ☎450-538-3045)* visitors can enjoy succulent French cuisine seated on a pretty terrace.

Il Duetto *($$$; every day from 5pm; 227 Académie-Élie, ☎819-538-8239)* serves fine Italian cuisine in a quiet country setting in the hills around Sutton. The pasta is home-made and the main dishes are inspired by the regional cuisines of Italy. The five-course menu is a good sampling of the variety of Italian cooking.

Magog

A perfect place to enjoy a meal in a relaxed atmosphere, **La Merise** *($-$$; 2339 Chemin du Parc, Orford, Route 101 N., 4 km north of Magog; ☎819-843-6288)* is in a charming house made entirely of wood. In addition to the consistently delicious cuisine, guests will appreciate the extremely friendly, attentive service.

La Grosse Pomme *($$; 276 Principale Ouest, ☎819-843-9365)* is a friendly restaurant serving good bistro-style food. In the evening, the ambiance is livened up by chatty patrons both young and old.

The restaurant at the **Auberge Cheribourg** *($$-$$$; 2603 Chemin du Parc; ☎819-843-3308)* prepares excellent local dishes. Made up of a group of little cottages with red roofs, the inn is easy to spot.

Facing Lac Memphrémagog, the **Les Berges** "restaurant-bar-terrace" *($$-$$$; May to Oct; 251 Rue Merry Sud, ☎819-847-3695)* offers the warm and romantic atmosphere of a country cottage. Its veranda is the perfect place in which to enjoy fondues or mussels. The service is delightful.

Though it is located on a very busy street, **La Paimpolaise** *($$$; closed Mon; Route 112; ☎819-843-1502)* still has character. A friendly restaurant in a charming little house, it serves a wide selection of crepes and other French dishes. This is without question one of the best places to eat in the city.

Orford

With its modern decor, the restaurant at the Manoir des Sables, **Les Jardins** *($$$$; 90 Avenue des Jardins, ☎819-847-4747 or 1-800-567-3514, ⊷847-3519)* is somewhat lacking in character. Fortunately, its large windows look out on Mont Orford. The menu features gourmet cuisine, including a *"table estrienne"*, allowing guests to sample regional flavours.

Ayer's Cliff

Recognized as a four-diamond establishment, the **Auberge Ripplecove**'s restaurant *($$$$; 700 Rue Ripplecove, ☎819-838-4296 or 1-800-668-4296, ⊷838-5541)* offers fine gourmet cuisine of great distinction. Its Victorian atmosphere and elegant decor make it an excellent place for a romantic meal.

North Hatley

Located inside a large house on the shores of Lac Massawippi, the **Pilsen** *($$; 55 Rue Principal; ☎819-842-2971)* serves good, simple food, such as salads and hamburgers, in a warm, friendly atmosphere. Its attractive country decor gives it a very pleasant old-fashioned character.

The restaurant at the **Auberge Hatley** *($$$$; Route 108; ☎819-842-2451)*, which has received numerous awards, is without question one of the region's best places to eat. The skillfully prepared gourmet meals will please even the most delicate palate. Not to mention that the dining room is beautifully decorated and offers a magnificent view of Lac Massawippi.

Graced with antique furniture and a fireplace, the dining room of the **Manoir Hovey** *($$$$; ♥; 575 Chemin Hovey; ☎819-842-2421)* has a soft atmosphere which makes for a lovely evening. The cuisine, as refined as the Auberge Hatley's, has also earned a lot of praise.

Lennoxville

The terrace at **Pub le Lion d'Or** *($; 2 Rue du Collège, ☎819-565-1015)* is both pretty and noisy—especially when the students are celebrating! Three beers are brewed on site, a pale beer, a dark ale and a dark bitter. The food is simple, essentially the same as what is served in English pubs.

The **Café Fine Gueule** *($-$$; 170 Rue Queen, ☎819-346-0031)*, located inside a superb stone house, serves simple fare in a relaxed atmosphere.

Sherbrooke

A laid-back clientele frequents the **Presse Boutique Café** *($; 4 Rue Wellington Nord, ☎819-822-2133)*. In addition to visual-art exhibitions and shows by local and other musicians, patrons can enjoy a wide variety of imported beers, a simple menu (salads, *croque-monsieur*, sandwiches, etc.) and vegetarian dishes. Moreover, two Internet stations are available ($6/hour, $1/10 minutes).

Café Bla-Bla *($$; 2 Rue Wellington Sud; ☎819-565-1366)* has a varied menu and a wide selection of imported beers.

Located in the Le Baron complex, **Le Kaori** Japanese restaurant *($$; 3200 Rue King Ouest, ☎819-565-4515 or 1-800-329-7466)*

has an amusing kitschy decor. The cooks liven up the place as they prepare meals before you.

At **La Rose des Sables** *($$; 270 Rue Dufferin; ☎819-346-5571)* visitors can enjoy good Moroccan food. Eastern dance presentations liven up the atmosphere on Thursday evenings.

Sultan *($$; 205 Rue Dufferin; ☎819-821-9156)* also specializes in Middle Eastern cuisine, in this case Lebanese food. The grilled meats are excellent.

The specialty at **Andrew Steak House** *($$-$$$; 35 Belvedere Nord, at the corner of Rue King; ☎819-822-8919)* is charbroiled steak, served in generous portions.

Though rather unimpressive from the outside, **L'Arlequin** *($$-$$$; closed on Mon; 875 Belvédère Sud, ☎819-573-2818)* is a fine restaurant that boasts a simple decor inspired by medieval elements and, more importantly, original dishes.

Falaise Saint Michel *($$$; 100 Rue Webster; ☎819-346-6339)* is like a hidden treasure on a small, somewhat dreary street. Its specialty being refined regional cuisine, the restaurant serves a variety of excellent dishes, and also has a particularly well-stocked wine cellar.

The **Petit Sabot** *($$$; closed Sun; 1410 Rue King Ouest; ☎819-563-0262)* is located inside a pretty blue house, which is attractively decorated and has lots of character. The food is pleasantly different, game being the specialty.

Located right in the heart of the new downtown area, the opulent **Da Toni** restaurant *($$$-$$$$; 15 Belvédère Nord, Sherbrooke, ☎819-346-8441)* has a well-established reputation. Indeed, for 25 years now, patrons have been enjoying its fine French and Italian cuisine, served with a wide selection of wines in a classical decor. The table d'hôte features five excellent, reasonably priced main courses. Though somewhat noisy, a terrace allows guests to enjoy a drink outside during the summer.

Tour C: The Back Country

Notre-Dame-des-Bois

Located close to verdant Mont Mégantic, the intimate and very charming **Aux Berges de l'Aurore** restaurant *($$$-$$$$; May to Oct, Wed to Sun 6pm to 9pm; July and Aug everyday; 139 Route du Parc, ☎819-888-2715)* serves excellent Quebec cuisine. Seasoned with wild herbs gathered in the surrounding countryside, its dishes are most original. From the very first bite, guests will appreciate why it received the *Mérite de la Fine Cuisine Estrienne* award!

Danville

Le Temps des Cerises *($$-$$$; 79 Rue Carmel; ☎819-839-2818)* serves elegant and inventive cuisine in the distinctive and unique atmosphere of a former Protestant church.

ENTERTAINMENT

Bars and Nightclubs

North Hatley

The **Pilsen** *(55 Rue Principal)* is frequented by vacationers who come to chat and have a beer while gazing out at Lac Massawippi.

Knowlton

The **Knowlton Pub** *(267 Knowlton Road)* has earned itself such a reputation that even Montrealers in search of a change of scenery go there to while away an evening among friends.

Sherbrooke

Located in the old downtown area, the **Au Vieux Quartier** pub *(252 Rue Dufferin)* has a relaxed ambiance. The place remains faithful to classic rock, as evidenced by photographs of various rock stars covering the walls.

Moreover, every Sunday night, different local musicians perform here.

The favourite dance bar with vacationers is the **Bar au Café du Palais** *(every day until 3am; 184 Ruelle Whiting, Sherbrooke)*. Shows are presented on certain evenings.

King Hall *(286 King Ouest, Sherbrooke)* is a comfortable bar with an interesting selection of international beers.

Theatres

Sherbrooke

The Université de Sherbrooke's cultural centre houses the **Salle Maurice O'Bready**, *(2500 Boulevard Université, ☎819-820-1000)*, where concerts, be they classical or rock, are put on.

A former church converted into a concert hall, the **Vieux Clocher de Sherbrooke** *(1590 Galt Ouest, ☎819-822-2102)* now welcomes music lovers and entertainment-seekers. Taking on the same role as its predecessor in Magog, the new hall, accommodating approximately 500 spectators, offers "discovery-shows" featuring young Quebecers and well-established performers. Performance listings can be found in the Sherbrooke daily *La Tribune*.

Orford

The **Centre d'Arts Orford** *(3165 Chemin du Parc, ☎819-843-3981 or 1-800-567-6155)* provides advanced training courses to young musicians during summertime. An annual festival also takes place at the centre, which is made up of several buildings designed in the 1960s by Paul-Marie Côté. The exhibition room that completes the whole was originally the Man and Music *(l'Homme et la Musique)* pavilion at Expo 67, and was designed by Desgagné and Côté.

Magog

Located inside an old Protestant church built in 1887, the **Théâtre du Vieux-Clocher** *(64 Rue Merry Nord Magog-Orford; ☎819-847-0470)* staged many shows that later became very successful in both Québec and France. Those

CANTONS-DE-L'EST

interested in attending a show should reserve their seats well in advance. The theatre is attractive, but small.

Festivals and Cultural Events

Magog

A few days of festivities are organized as part of the **Traversée Internationale** *($5; mid-July; ☎819-843-5000, ⇒843-5621)*, including performances by Quebec theatrical artists, exhibits of all kinds and folk singers. The highlight of the celebrations is the arrival of swimmers from Newport, USA. The 42-kilometre swim is undertaken by athletes considered among the best in the world. In the summer of 1998, this event will be celebrating its 20th anniversary.

During the months of July and August, the **Festival Orford** *(3165 Chemin du Parc, ☎819-843-2405 or 1-888-310-3665, ⇒843-7274)* offers a series of concerts featuring ensembles and world-famous virtuosos. Several excellent free concerts are also presented by young musicians, here for the summer to hone their skills at the Centre d'Arts Orford. This high-calibre festival is an absolute must for all music lovers.

 SHOPPING

Tour A: The Orchard

Rougemont

The **Cidrerie Michel Jodoin** *(every day; 1130 Rang de la Petite-Caroline, ☎450-469-2676 or 1-888-469-2676)* is a family-run business that sells arguably the best cider in Québec. Michel Jodoin's studies in Champagne, Brittany and Normandy, along with the unique taste of Québec's variety of apples help him to create a delicious brew. On site, you can visit the facilities and learn about the minimum two-year, oak-barrel aging process of these fine ciders. Tastings available.

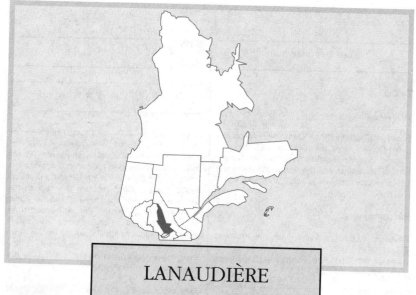

LANAUDIÈRE

The Lanaudière region extends north of Montréal, from the plains of the St. Lawrence to the Laurentian plateau. Except for the part of the region engulfed in the urban sprawl of Montréal, Lanaudière is a peaceful area of lakes, rivers, farmland, wild forests and huge open spaces. It is a great place to kick back and try your hand at the various sports and activities the area has to offer like skiing, canoeing, snowmobile rides, hiking, hunting and fishing. One of the first colonized areas in New France, your visit will most certainly also include a tour of the region's rich architectural heritage.

For a few years now the region has hosted an important event: le Festival Internatinoal de Lanaudière. Music-lovers from across Québec converge on the region for concerts of classical and popular music performed by artists from around the globe. Some concerts are given in the halls and churches of the region, while open-air concerts take place in a huge 2,000 seat amphitheatre, near Joliette. The city of Joliette is also home to one of Québec's most interesting regional museums, with an impressive collection of Québec and religious art.

 FINDING YOUR WAY AROUND

Once a countryside of seigneurial manors and farmland that stretched from the shores of the St. Lawrence to the wild, mountainous land of

the aboriginals, the Lanaudière region has today been engulfed by the Montréal urban area. In keeping with this split personality we suggest two very different routes from Montréal: **Tour A: La Plaine ★★** and **Tour B: La Matawinie ★**.

Tour A: La Plaine

By Car

Highway 25 is the extension of Boulevard Pie-IX and leads towards Terrebonne, the first stop on this tour. It continues east to Assomption on Route 344. Next take Route 343 N. to Joliette and Route 158 W. to Berthierville. To return to Montreal follow lovely Route 138 W., also known as the Chemin du Roy along the St. Lawrence River, with stops in Lanoraie, Saint-Sulpice and Repentigny.

Bus Stations

Terrebonne: Galeries de Terrebonne.
Joliette: 250 Rue Richard (at the Point d'Arrêt restaurant), ☎759-1524.
Repentigny: 435 Boulevard Iberville (at the *hôtel de ville*) ☎654-2315.

Train Station

Joliette: 470 Rue Champlain, ☎759-3252

Tour B: Matawinie

By Car

Highway 25 N., the extension of Boulevard Pie-IX, joins Route 125 N., which leads to Rawdon, Chertsey, Notre-Dame-de-la-Merci and Saint-Donat. From there Route 347 leads to Saint-Gabriel-de-Brandon. Access to Saint-Michel-des-Saints and the Rouge-Matawin and Mastigouche reserves is north on Route 131.

Bus stations

Rawdon: 3168 1re Avenue (at the Patate à Gogo) ☎834-2000
Saint-Donat: 751 Rue Principale (Dépanneur Boni-Soir) ☎(819) 424-1361

 PRACTICAL INFORMATION

Most of this region falls within the **450 area code** (except Saint-Donat, which is 819).

Tourist Information Offices

Regional Office

Tourisme Lanaudière 2643 Rue Queen, C.P. 1210, Rawdon, J0K 1S0, ☎843-2535 or 1-800-363-2788, ☞843-8100, http://tourisme-lanaudiere.qc.ca.

Tour A: La Plaine

Berthierville: 760 Rue Gadoury, ☎836-1621
Joliette: 500 Rue Dollard, ☎759-5013 or 1-800-363-1775
Terrebonne: 1091 Boulevard Moody, ☎964-0681

Tour B: La Matawinie

Rawdon: 3588 Rue Metcalfe, ☎834-2282.
Saint-Donat: 536 Rue Principale, ☎(819) 424-2883

 EXPLORING

Tour A : La Plaine ★★ (two days)

In 1813, Marie-Charlotte Tarieu Taillant de Lanaudière, daughter of the seigneur of Lavaltrie, married Barthélémy Joliette. These two figures were much more than a couple of newlyweds however, for their union left behind a precious heritage to the inhabitants of this region: the name of the region, Lanaudière, and the name of its main city, Joliette. But far beyond that, they also inspired an enterprising spirit rarely found amongst French Canadians at the time. This stimulated the creation of a manufacturing base, locally-controlled banks, and finally the development of specialized farming.

Take Highway 25, the extension of Boulevard Pie-IX. Turn right at the Terrebonne-Centreville Exit (22). Turn right immediately on Boulevard Moody then left on Rue Saint-Louis. Park on Rue des Braves, facing Île des Moulins.

Terrebonne ★★ (pop. 44,425)

Located along the banks of the rushing Rivière des Mille-Îles, this municipality gets its name from the fertile soil (*terre* meaning earth, and *bonne* meaning good) from which it grew. Today it is included in the ribbon of suburbia surrounding Montréal, yet the old town, divided into an *haute-ville* and *basse-ville* (upper and lower town), has preserved some of its residential and commercial buildings. Terrebonne is probably the best place in Québec to get an idea of what a prosperous 19th-century seigneury was really like.

The city was founded in 1707 and shortly thereafter the first flour and saw mills were built. In 1802 the seigneury of Terrebonne was purchased by Simon McTavish, director of the Northwest Company, which specialized in the fur trade. Terrebonne became a departure point for his lucrative commercial expeditions into northern Québec. Carding mills for wool were soon added to those built under the French Regime, creating a veritable pre-industrial complex. In 1832 the Masson family took over the running of the seigneury, and rebuilt most of the mills.

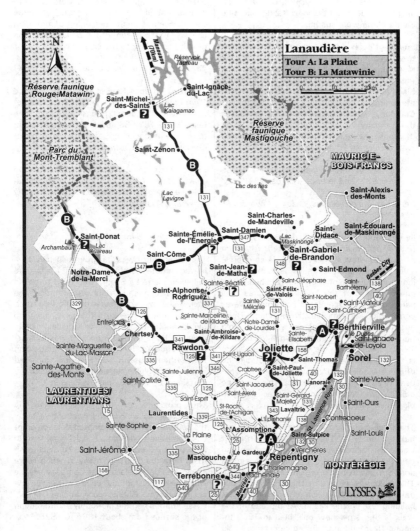

The 20th century began promisingly, until a large section of the lower town was destroyed by fire on December 1st 1922. Only the buildings on Rue Saint-François-Xavier and Rue Sainte-Marie were spared.

Rue Saint-Louis is the main artery of the upper-town, bourgeois area. Besides the Manoir Masson, several other stately residences line the streets, in particular the **home of Roderick MacKenzie** *(906 Rue Saint-Louis)*. As one of the principal shareholders in the Northwest Company, MacKenzie's home also served as the company's headquarters at one time. Built of stone covered with stucco, it is adorned with an elegant Doric wood portico. A bit further along Rue Saint-Louis are some fine examples of Victorian architecture in wood (number 938) and in brick (number 939).

Return to Rue des Braves, heading towards l'Île des Moulins.

Île des Moulins ★★ *(free admission; late Jun to early Sep, every day 1pm to 9pm; at the end of Rue des Braves, ☎471-0619)* is an impressive concentration of mills and other pre-industrial equipment from the Terrebonne seigneury. Most of the buildings, located in a park, have been renovated and now serve as community and administrative buildings. Upon entering, the first building on the left is the old flour mill (1846) then the saw mill (restored in 1986) which houses the municipal library. Next is the Centre d'Accueil et d'Interprétation de l'Île des Moulins (information centre) in what used to be the seigneurial office. This cut stone building was constructed in 1848 according to plans by Pierre-Louis Morin.

The three-story building on the left is the old bakery, built in 1803 for the Northwest Company, who used it to make cookies and *galettes* for the *voyageurs* collecting furs in the northern and western regions of the country. This bakery was one of the first large-scale bakeries in North America, it is also the oldest building left on the island. At the end of the walk is the larger new mill, built in 1850 for Sophie Raymond. It produced wool fabrics sold throughout the region. The Terrebonne cultural centre is now located there.

On your way back, follow the small Rue Saint-François-Xavier east of la Rue des Braves.

Along **Rue Saint-François-Xavier** are the picturesque homes that escaped the fire of 1922, now housing various restaurants and galleries. Some of these houses were built in the second half of the 18th century and have been painstakingly restored. They are similar to houses found on the outskirts of large Canadian cities at the beginning of the 19th century, made of wood and built low to the ground, and close to the sidewalk.

Turn left onto Rue Saint-Louis.

The twin **Maisons Roussil** *(870 and 886 Rue Saint-Louis)*, were built in 1825 by master carpenter Théodore Roussil. During the Rebellion of 1837-38, local rebels were held in the house before being transferred to the Pied-du-Courant prison in Montréal.

Leave Terrebonne via Route 344 E. (the continuation of Rue Saint-Louis) towards Lachenaie, then de Le Gardeur, to eventually arrive in L'Assomption.

L'Assomption ★ (pop. 12,341)

This small city owes its growth in part to a portage route established in 1717 by the Sulpician Pierre Le Sueur, who used to spend time paddling on the Rivière L'Assomption. The trail, used by voyageurs transporting their canoes from one river to the next, avoids a five-kilometre detour by water. Originally simply called Le Portage, the settlement was a cross-roads frequented by fur trappers and traders on the northern route. It was eventually included in the Saint-Sulpice seigneury, conceded to the Messieurs de Saint-Sulpice of Paris in 1647.

The proximity of the carding mills in Terrebonne, as well as the frequent visits by the *coureurs des bois*, prompted the women of L'Assomption to design a special wool sash to be worn by French Canadians, to distinguish them from the Scottish, many of whom were employees of the Northwest Company. Hence was born the famous *ceinture fléchée* (v-shaped-design sash), now a symbol of Québec. L'Assomption had the monopoly on production of the sashes from about 1805 to 1825.

Enter L'Assomption by Rue Saint-Étienne. Parking is permitted opposite the church.

The monumental façade of the **Église de L'Assomption-de-la-Sainte-Vierge ★** *(153 Rue du Portage)* was designed by Victor Bourgeau (1863). The chancel was undertaken in 1819 and contains the tabernacle, the altar and the Baroque pulpit by Urbain Brien dit Desrochers in

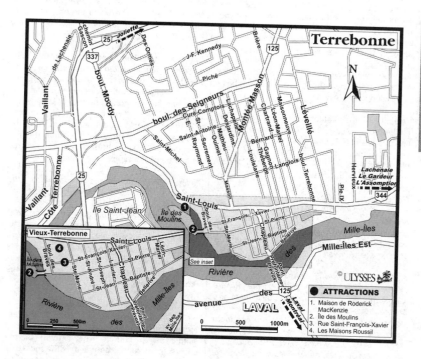

1834. The artistry of the vault is the work of Bourgeau, modeled after the one in La Prairie.

Take Rue du Portage, alongside the presbytery. This road follows Pierre le Sueur's original portage route. At the corner of Boulevard L'Ange-Gardien, stand the old seigneurial office of the Sulpiciens (402 Boulevard L'Ange-Gardien) and the building that once housed the store known as the Magasin Le Roux, specializing in the sale of the ceinture fléchée (sashes) (195 Rue du Portage). Turn right on Boulevard L'Ange-Gardien.

The **Maison Archambault** *(351 Boulevard L'Ange-Gardien)* is one of a few examples left around Montréal of this type of house where the main floor serves as a workshop and the second, accessible by a long staircase, is reserved as living quarters. This particular example, built in 1780, was the birthplace of Francis Ar-

chambault (1880-1915), opera star in London, New York and Boston at the turn of the century.

The **Collège de L'Assomption** ★ *(270 Boulevard L'Ange-Gardien)* for boys was founded in 1832 by the town's elite. The building is a fine example of 19th century institutional architecture in Québec, with its rubble masonry exterior (1869), mansard roof, and superb silver dome, added in 1882. The eclectic wing to the east was built in 1892. Among the notable personalities who attended the college is Sir Wilfrid Laurier, Prime Minister of Canada from 1896 to 1911.

Turn right onto Rue Sainte-Anne, then left on Rue Saint-Étienne.

The **Vieux Palais de Justice** *($2; late Jun to early Sep, every day 9am to 5pm; 255 Rue*

Saint-Étienne; ☎589-3266), or old courthouse, was originally three separate houses, constructed between 1811 and 1822. This rather long building housed a court of law and a registration office for many years. Victor Bourgeau, who designed the courtroom on the second floor, was not content with just modifying the openings, he also designed the furniture and woodwork. The courtroom remains intact, even though court has not been in session here since 1929.

The site of the first church in L'Assomption (1724), the remains of the seigneurial manor and the **Maison Séguin** *(284 Rue Saint-Étienne)*, a bourgeois residence in the Second Empire style built in 1880 are all located across from the old courthouse.

Get back on Rue Saint-Étienne heading west (towards the church). At number 349 is the **Maison Le Sanche** *(1812), an interesting example of a typical urban dwelling of the day with firebreak walls and location right up against the sidewalk.*

Follow Boulevard L'Ange-Gardien, then Route 343 N., which follows the Rivière L'Assomption. Alongside the road there are several houses with mansard roofs all oriented perpendicularly to the road, to protect them from the prevailing winds. Continue along Route 343 N., which becomes Boulevard Manseau in Joliette, and passes some beautiful Victorian residences. Park the car near the large Place Bourget in order to explore the streets of Joliette on foot. The downtown area extends around Boulevard Manseau.

Joliette ★ (pop. 18,308)

At the beginning of the 19th century, the notary Barthélémy Joliette (1789-1850) opened up logging camps in the northern section of the Lavaltrie seigneury, at the time, still undeveloped land. In 1823 he founded "his" town around the sawmills and called it "L'Industrie", a name synonymous with progress and prosperity. The settlement grew so rapidly that in just a few years it had eclipsed its two rivals, Berthier and L'Assomption. In 1864 it was renamed Joliette in honour of its founder. Barthélémy Joliette completed many other ambitious projects, most notably the construction of the first railroad belonging to French Canadians, and a bank where money bearing the Joliette-Lanaudière name was printed.

Today, Joliette is an important centre in the Lanaudière region. The city has a diocese, as well as two renowned cultural centres, the Musée d'Art de Joliette and the Amphithéâtre, where part of the famous music festival, the Festival International de Lanaudière, is held.

The market building and the Hôtel de Ville, both donated by Monsieur Joliette, used to stand in the middle of **Place Bourget**. Since their demolition, shops have been built and the area has been turned into a pedestrian mall. The **Palais de Justice**, at the far end, follows the neoclassical model proposed by the Minister of Public Works at the time. Its construction in 1862, confirmed Joliette's status as capital of the region.

Follow Boulevard Manseau towards the cathedral.

The interesting white building at number 400 was built in 1858 and used to house both the **Institut**, the first cultural centre in Québec to house the municipal library and a performance hall. The Greek-Revival style of the façade was chosen as a display of defiance against the British colonial power.

The **Cathédrale Saint-Charles-Borromée** *(2 Rue Saint-Charles-Borromée N.)*, with its modest façade and single steeple, was originally just a simple parish church. The exterior of the church, constructed between 1888 and 1892 is plain and impressive. The plans, drawn by architects Perrault and Mesnard, called for large proportions of the same scale as the Romanesque-Revival style churches built in Montréal at the time.

At the back of the cathedral is the **Palais Épiscopal**, an eloquent testament to the almighty power of the church in Québec before the Quiet Revolution. At 20 Rue Saint-Charles-Borromée Sud, is the old seminary, now used as a CÉGEP.

Joliette owes its cultural vibrance to the clerics of Saint-Viateur who established themselves at the **Maison Provinciale des Clercs de Saint-Viateur** ★ *(132 Rue Saint-Charles-Borromée N.)* in the mid-19th century. In 1939, they undertook the construction of their new house. The plans, by Montréal architect René Charbonneau, were inspired by a sketch done by Père Wilfrid Corbeil. The building's massive Romanesque Revival arches and heavy stone tower are reminiscent of medieval German

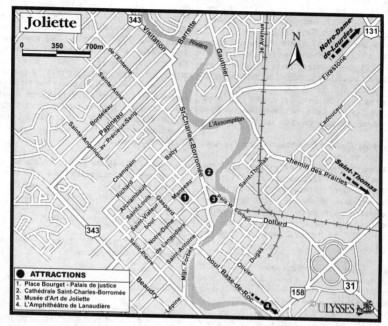

monasteries of the Middles Ages. The chapel at the centre is often described as a modern version of the German Church in Frielingsdorff. The magnificent stained-glass windows, designed by Marius Plamondon, the sculptures on the pews and the stations of the cross all create an ethereal atmosphere of mystery and contemplation.

Père Wilfrid Corbeil c.s.v. founded the exceptional **Musée d'Art de Joliette ★★** *($4; late Jun to early Sep, Tue to Sun 11am to 5pm; the rest of the year, Wed to Sun noon to 5pm; 145 Rue Wilfrid-Corbeil, ☎756-0311)* with works collected during the forties by the clerics of Saint-Viateur that show Québec's place in the world. This is the most important regional museum in Québec. Since 1976 it has been located in a rather menacing building on Rue Corbeil. On display are major pieces from Québec and Canadian artists like Marc-Aurèle de Foy Suzor-Côté, Jean-Paul Riopelle and Emily Carr, as well as works by European and American artists like Henry Moore and Karel Appel. One section of the museum is devoted to Québec religious art, while another section contains religious art of the Middle Ages and Renaissance periods, with some excellent examples from France, Italy and Germany.

L'Amphithéâtre de Lanaudière is on the outskirts of town. To get there follow Rue Saint-Charles Borromée Sud, then Rue Saint-Antoine, turn left on Chemin Base-de-Roc.

The Festival International de Lanaudière was begun by Père Fernand Lindsay c.s.v. Each year during the months of July and August, a variety of music concerts and opera singers are presented as part of the festival. In 1989 the 2,000-seat open-air **Amphithéâtre de Lanaudière** *(1575 Base-de-Roc, ☎759-7636 or 1-800-561-4343)* was constructed in order to increase the capacity and accessibility of the event, which up to that time was limited to the churches of the area. Artist Georges Dyens completed the interior design of the aisles and the exquisite sculptures.

Take the on-ramp to Route 158 E. close to the amphitheatre, and follow it toward Berthierville.

Berthierville ★ (pop. 4,183)

The modest Autray Seigneury was conceded to Jean Bourdon, an engineer of the King, in 1637. The land corresponds to the sector Berthier-en-bas, or Berthierville, along the shores of the St. Lawrence. The Berthier Seigneury, which was much more extensive, was conceded to Sieur de Berthier in 1672 before passing through several hands. It corresponds in part to Berthier-en-haut, or Berthier. In 1765 both these tracts of land were acquired by James Cuthbert, an aide de camp of General Wolf during the battle of the Plains of Abraham in Québec City, as well as a friend of the Duke of Kent. He developed the land mainly for use as a vacation spot.

The **Pont Couvert Grandchamps** *(on the right near Route 158)* crosses Rivière Bayonne. This covered wooden bridge was constructed in the Town style in 1883, making it one of the first of this kind of structure popularized in the United States in the 19th century. These bridges were built by town residents to reduce the cost, and were covered to avoid the deterioration of the structure supporting the road surface.

The **Église Sainte-Geneviève** ★★ *(780 Montcalm)* is a Lanaudière treasure. Constructed in 1781 it is one of the oldest churches in the region. The interior's Louis-XVI styling was designed by Amable Gauthier and Alexis Millette between 1821 and 1830. Many elements in the decor combine to make this building truly exceptional. The decor has a richness rarely seen at that time, comprising elements such as the original high altar, crafted by Gilles Bolvin in 1759, the shell-shaped retable and the diamond-pattern ornamenting the vault. There are also several paintings, including one of Sainte-Geneviève (a French canvas from the 19th century hanging over the high altar), and six paintings by Louis Dulongré, painted in 1797.

The seigneurial **Chapelle des Cuthbert** *(entrance on Rue de Bienville)* of the Cuthbert family (1786), known officially as St. Andrew's, was the first Protestant church built in Québec. In the years following the British Conquest of 1760, French-inspired architecture remained the reigning style, as there were few British architects and workers. This explains the Catholic configuration of the church, designed by mason Antoine Selton and carpenter Vadeboncœur. Many members of the Cuthbert family were buried in the chapel, however their remains were moved in 1866. Since 1978, the building has served as a cultural centre for the residents of Berthierville.

Gilles Villeneuve, the championship race car driver who was killed tragically during the qualifying trials for the 1982 Grand-Prix of Belgium, was from Berthierville. The **Musée Gilles-Villeneuve** *($6; Mar to Oct, every day 10am to 4pm; 960 Avenue Gilles Villeneuve, ☎836-2714)* is dedicated to the illustrious career of the Ferrari Formula 1 driver, his prizes, his souvenirs and his cars. In the last few years, Gilles' son Jacques, has taken up where his father left off and become a top-ranked Formula 1 driver, at the heart of the British Williams-Renault team. The museum now devotes a new section to the career of Jacques Villeneuve.

Farther on, take Route 158 to Île Dupras and the village of **Saint-Ignace-de-Loyola**, from which a ferry leads to Sorel on the south shore of the St. Lawrence *(in summer departures every half hour between 5:30am and 3pm, the crossing takes 10 min; ☎836-4600)*.

Follow Route 138 W. towards Lanoraie, Lavaltrie and Saint-Sulpice.

Lanoraie (pop. 1,942)

Route 138 follows the original Chemin du Roy, laid out in 1734 between Montréal and Québec City. Before then, people had to travel by canoe along the St. Lawrence. Several old houses still stand along the road between Berthierville and Lavaltrie.

At **Coteau-du-Sable**, located to the northeast of the village of Lanoraie, is an important aboriginal archeological site. The foundations of a longhouse built by Iroquois in the 19th century were discovered. Numerous crafted artifacts have also been found at the site since the beginning of the 20th century.

Continue on Route 138 to Repentigny

Repentigny (pop. 56,555)

The city of Repentigny was named after its first seigneur, Pierre Le Gardeur de Repentigny. It is pleasantly located at the confluence of the Rivière L'Assomption and the mighty St. Lawrence. Unfortunately, the three buildings of interest in Repentigny have almost been swallowed up by the urban chaos along Rue Notre-Dame. No longer in their original context, these buildings have to admired as individual examples of a bygone era.

Construction of the **Église de la Purification-de-la-Bienheureuse-Vierge-Marie** ★ *(445 Rue Notre-Dame Est)* began in 1723, making it the oldest church in the diocese of Montréal. It has many characteristics of New France churches, such as the apse with the corners cut off and the orientation of the building parallel to the river. The façade was redone in 1850 with two towers instead of the original one steeple. The interior was restored to its original simplicity in 1984 following a fire which almost destroyed the whole church. The beautiful Louis-XV-style high altar was designed by Philippe Liébert in 1761.

The **Moulins à Vent** *(numbers 460 and 861 Rue Notre-Dame Est)*, are quite a sight. These two windmills seem out of place amidst the gas stations and post-war bungalows of modern-day Repentigny. The Moulin du Sieur Antoine Jetté, at number 861, was built in 1823 and served as a grain mill until 1915. The Moulin de François Grenier was built in 1819, and is empty today. Both buildings have lost their mechanisms and sails.

To return to Montréal, follow Rue Notre-Dame de Repentigny, which is actually the continuation of the Montréal street of the same name.

Tour B : La Matawinie ★ (four days)

The colonization of the hinterland of Lanaudière was undertaken around 1860 by Catholic missionaries concerned about the mass exodus of French-Canadian farmers to the cotton textile mills of New England. Matawinie is not only well-supplied with forests but also has an abundance of lakes, mountains and rivers, which attract hunters, fishers and vacationers. The northern part of the region has long been inhabited by the Attikamekw Nation, a small native tribe, who used to be nomadic but are now settled around the village of Manawan.

This tour is long and rugged. A vehicle in good condition and camping equipment are strongly recommended since hotels and service stations are rare or nonexistent along the gravel roads around and beyond Saint-Michel-des-Saints.

Rawdon ★ (pop. 3,820)

After the conquest of 1760, the British established a more familiar means of dividing the territory, namely the township. Governed by residents, townships were established to accommodate American loyalists and British immigrants. These townships were usually located on the perimeter of land already conceded as seigneuries under the French Regime. The townships of Lanaudière were established in the foothills of the Laurentians, between the 19th-century seigneuries and the new territories opened up by the clergy after 1860. The township of Rawdon, at the centre of which is the town of Rawdon, was created in 1799.

The **Centre d'Interprétation Multiethnique de Rawdon** *(free admission, donations welcome; Fri to Sun 1pm to 4pm; 3588 Rue Metcalfe, ☎834-3334)* describes the short history of the many ethnic groups which have settled in the region since the establishment of the township. The centre is located in a wood house painted in the typical style of the region. A stroll through the neighbouring streets to see the different community churches is a pleasant way to complete a tour of the centre. The Anglican Church and the Russian Orthodox Church are the most interesting.

The other spot of interest in the vicinity is **Parc des Cascades** ★ *($6 per car; mid-May to mid-Oct, every day; ☎834-4149)*, which can be reached on Route 341, the extension of Boulevard Pontbriand. Also on the bank of Rivière Ouareau, which runs in lovely cascades over the rocky riverbed here, this park includes a picnic area where sunbathers stretch out during the hot months of summer.

Saint-Donat ★ (pop. 3,176)

Minutes away from Mont-Tremblant, tucked between mountains reaching up to 900 metres and the shores of Lac Archambault, the small town of Saint-Donat extends east to the shores of Lac Ouareau. Saint-Donat is also a departure point for the **Parc du Mont-Tremblant** (see p 257).

*Though Saint-Michel-des-Saints is accessible via a long trip through Parc du Mont-Tremblant, it is best to retrace your steps on Route 125 to **Notre-Dame-de-la-Merci**. Once there, follow Route 347 towards Sainte-Émilie-de-l'Énergie and then Route 131 N. towards Saint-Michel-des-Saints. Continue on Route 347 to reach Saint-Gabriel-de-Brandon.*

Saint-Gabriel-de-Brandon (pop. 2,338)

The town of Saint-Gabriel-de Brandon borders magnificent Lac Maskinongé. In fact, this 10-square-kilometre lake is pretty much the town's only attraction; its beautiful **municipal beach**, which apparently can accommodate up to 5,000 swimmers, is very popular (see below).

Saint-Michel-des-Saints (pop. 2,455)

Saint-Michel-des-Saints grew up along the shores of Lac Kaiagamac, and is surrounded by the **Réserve Faunique Rouge-Matawin** (see p 257 and below) and the **Réserve Faunique Mastigouche** (see p 314).

 PARKS

Tour B: La Matawinie

The **Réserve Faunique Rouge-Matawin** *(26 km west of Saint-Michel-des-Saints; ☎819-424-3026 in Saint-Donat or 833-5530 in Saint-Michel-des-Saints)* is 1,394 square kilometres of greenery, through which flow about 450 lakes and waterways. It is home to an abundant and fertile wildlife. There is no lack of things to do, from hiking, hunting, fishing, canoe-camping tripping and wild-berry-picking, all the way to snowmobiling in the winter.

Saint-Donat is one of the entry points to **Parc du Mont-Tremblant ★★** (see p 257), which is generally thought of as part of the Laurentians region.

 OUTDOORS

 Hiking

Tour B: La Matawinie

Hiking trails run through 5.8 kilometres of exceptional countryside before ending up at **Sept-Chutes** *($3; mid-May to Oct 9am to 5pm, Route 131; ☎884-0484)* with its tremendous diversity of the local plant and animal life. All seven falls are accessible to the public, they are usually dried up in the summer. However, during the spring thaws when flooding is common, water levels can reach an impressive 60 metres.

The **Sentier de la Matawinie** *(about 5 km from the town along Route 131 N.)* provides the opportunity to observe the Sept-Chutes from the Rivière Noire as well as some of the other sights of the region. The trail zigzags between various lookout points and reaches an altitude of 565 metres before leading along a steep section of trail to the Sept-Chutes in Saint-Zénon.

Parc Régional des Chutes-Monte-à-Peine-et-des-Dalles *(admission; accessible from Routes 131, 337 and 343, ☎883-2245)* is jointly managed by the municipalities of Saint-Jean-de-Matha, Sainte-Béatrix and Sainte-Mélanie. Many walking trails, totalling 12 kilometres, have been laid out in this 300-hectare park inaugurated in 1987. Among other sights along these are three beautiful waterfalls on Rivière L'Assomption.

Just near Chertsey is **Secteur Grande Vallée** *(☎252-7812)*, with 30 kilometres of hiking trails. Among these is a linear trail of 13.5 kilometres that runs the length of the valley.

 Swimming

Tour B: La Matawinie

The **Rawdon municipal beach** *(admission; ☎834-8121)*, on the lake of the same name, is very popular during the summertime. Picnic area, fast-food stand, private parking, and windsurfer rental are available.

On the shores of superb Lac Maskinongé, the **Saint-Gabriel-de-Brandon municipal beach** *(free; ☎835-2212)* constitutes the main attraction in this little town. This large, beautiful beach can accommodate up to 5,000 bathers. Amenities include a picnic area, a fast-food stand, private parking, and pedal-boat, canoe, windsurfer and jetski rentals.

Golf

Tour A: La Plaine

Terrebonne's **Centre de Golf Le Versant** *($10-$34.50; 2075 Côte Terrebonne, ☎964-2251)* has three 18-hole courses that are rated par 54, 71 and 72.

Club de Golf Base-de-Roc *($30-$33; 2870 Bd. Base-de-Roc, ☎759-1818)* in Joliette offers a par-72, 18-hole course.

Tour B: La Matawinie

Among the many golf courses in the area, two that stand out are the 18-hole, par-73 course at **Club de Golf de Rawdon** *($19-$24.50; 3999 Lakeshore Dr., ☎834-2320)* and the 18-hole, par-72 course at **Club de Golf Saint-Jean-de-Matha** *($31-$37; 945 Route 131 N., ☎886-9321)*.

 Cross-country Skiing

Tour B: La Matawinie

The **Montagne Coupée** *(204 Rue de la Montagne-Coupée, ☎886-3845)* tourist information centre can suggest outdoor activities year-round. In winter there are 80 kilometres of cross-country ski trails, with 43 kilometres of wider trails designed for practising "skating" techniques. There are skis available for rent on site. In the summer, trails exist for horseback riding and hiking.

There are many cross-country skiing trails in the Saint-Donat area, in **Secteur La Donatienne** of **Parc des Pionniers** *(Chemin Hector-Bilodeau)*, in **Montagne Noire** and in **Secteur La Pimbina** of **Parc du Mont-Tremblant**.

 Downhill Skiing

Tour B: La Matawinie

Station Touristique de Val Saint-Côme *($23.50-$30; Mon and Tue 9am to 5pm, Wed to Sun 9am to 10:30pm; 501 Ch. Val St-Côme, ☎883-0701)* is one of the largest downhill ski centres in the Lanaudière region. It has 21

trails, some of which are lit for night skiing, and a vertical drop of 300 metres. Accommodation is also available.

 Snowmobiling

Tour B: La Matawinie

La Cuillère à Pot, in Saint-Donat, is a favourite rest stop for snowmobilers; it offers various packages and snowmobile rental *(every day 8:30am to 5pm; 67 Route 329, ☎819-424-4761)*.

In Saint-Michel-des-Saints, **Location de Motoneiges Haute-Matawinie** has a fleet of approximately 125 snowmobiles for rent *(Mon to Fri 8:30am to 8:30pm, Sat and Sun 8:30am to 5pm; 180 Rue Brassard, ☎833-1355)*.

 Dogsledding

Tour B: La Matawinie

Nature et Chiens de Traîneau Entrelacs *(Oct to Jun, every day 9am to 5pm; 790 Bd. Montcalm, Entrelacs, ☎228-8944)*, organizes dogsledding excursions and also runs a small interpretive centre.

 ACCOMMODATIONS

Tour A: La Plaine

Joliette

In a large red brick building by the river, the **Château Joliette** *($75; ℜ; 450 Rue St-Thomas, J6E 3R1, ☎752-2525 or 1-800-361-0572, ⌐752-2520)* is the largest hotel in town. Though the long corridors are cold and bare, the modern rooms are large and comfortable.

Repentigny

Located on the outskirts of Montréal, where a maple grove once stood, **La Villa des Fleurs** *($50 sb, $60 pb, bkfst incl.; 45 Rue Gaudreault, J6A 1M3, ☎654-9209)* has four attractively decorated rooms. Friendly service and generous breakfasts.

Ulysses' Favourites

Accommodations

For businesspeople:
Château Joliette (p 239).

For tranquillity:
Auberge sur la Falaise (p 240), Auberge de la Montagne Coupée (p 240) and Auberge Havre du Parc (p 241).

For the lively atmosphere:
Manoir des Laurentides (p 241).

Restaurants

Lanaudière's finest tables:
Étang des Moulins (p 241), Auberge sur la Falaise (p 242) and Auberge de la Montagne Coupée (p 242).

For the terrasse:
Le Folichon (p 241).

For the romantic atmophere:
Le Folichon (p 241) and Étang des Moulins (p 241).

For the views:
Auberge de la Montagne Coupée (p 242).

For Québec cuisine:
Le Prieuré (p 241), Auberge sur la Falaise (p 242) and Auberge de la Montagne Coupée (p 242).

Tour B: La Matawinie

Rawdon

The owners of a lovely Victorian house on Rue Queen have converted their home into a bed and breakfast, **Le Gîte du Catalpa** *($50-$65 bkfst incl.; sb; 3730 Rue Queen, C.P. 1639, JOK 1SO, ☎834-5253)*. Five rooms are available to guests. In good weather, a five-course breakfast is served on the terrace or in the garden.

Saint-Alphonse-Rodriguez

Ten kilometres from the village of Saint-Alphonse-Rodriguez, after a long climb past peaceful Lac Long and into what seems like another world, is the marvellous **Auberge sur la Falaise** *($89-154; ≡, ≈, ℜ, △; 324 Av. Du Lac*

Long Sud, JOK 1WO, ☎883-2269 or 1-888-325-2437, ⊶883-0143). The inn, perched on a promontory, dominates this serene landscape, reserving exceptional views for its guests. The 25 rooms in this modern building are luxurious, some of them with whirlpool baths and fireplaces. The hotel does double duty as a spa and offers many sports activities. Finally, the cuisine served in the dining room is among the best in the area (see p 242).

Saint-Jean-de-Matha

Another exceptional establishment, **Auberge de la Montagne Coupée** *($110-$195; ≡, ≈, ℜ, △; 1000 Ch. de la Montagne-Coupée, JOK 2SO, ☎886-3891 or 1-800-363-8614, ⊶886-5401)* appears after what seems like an interminable climb. Reward is at hand though in this immense white building with huge bay windows. The hotel has 50 comfortable, modern rooms bathed in natural light, some of which have fireplaces. In the dining room and the lounge, large windows reveal a breathtaking panorama. There is an equestrian centre and a summer theatre at the bottom of the grounds, and the hotel has a remarkable restaurant (see p 242).

Saint-Donat

The Pimbina section of **Parc du Mont-Tremblant** *($18; 2951 Route 125 Nord, C.P. 1169, JOT 2C0, ☎819-424-7012, ≈424-2413)*, near Saint-Donat and accessible via Route 125, includes 341 campsites.

The **Manoir des Laurentides** *($70; 290 Rue Principale, JOT 2C0, ☎819-424-2121 or 1-800-567-6717, ≈424-2621)*, well located by the water's edge, offers good value for your money. The rooms in the three-story main building are comfortable but boring, though each has its own balcony. There are also two rows of motel rooms that stretch to the lakefront and about forty cottages equipped with kitchenettes. Since this spot is often quite lively, visitors who value peace and quiet should opt for motel rooms or cottages. A beach and a small marina at the water's edge are available to guests.

The **Auberge Havre du Parc** *($140 ½b; 2788 Route 125 N., Lac-Provost, JOT 2C0, ☎819-424-7686, ≈424-3432)* is a haven of tranquillity. The magnificent location, on the shores of Lac Provost, and the comfort of the accommodations make it easy to relax and forget the daily grind.

Saint-Gabriel-de-Brandon

Le Relais de l'Amitié *($50 bkfst incl.; 71 Chemin Arthur, JOK 2N0, ☎835-1003)* has decent rooms, and guests are warmly received.

Auberge Aile-En-Ciel *($50-$110; ≡, ≈, ℝ, K; 376 Rue Maskinongé-Route 347, C.P. 1807, JOK 2N0, ☎835-3775, ≈835-1115)* is an inn in name only. It is actually more of a "condotel", offering about twenty apartments each of which can accommodate two to six people. Some of these are equipped with fireplaces and whirlpool baths. The rooms are large enough, although some of them are quite plain; the apartments feature fully-equipped kitchenettes. Guests have access to an outdoor pool, a little

beach on Lac Maskinongé, and a terrace with a grill.

RESTAURANTS

Tour A: La Plaine

Terrebonne

Terrebonne's **Le Jardin des Fondues** *($$; 186 Sainte-Marie, ☎492-2048)*, where the chic ambience adds to a delicious assortment of fondues and traditional French dishes, is sure to please fondue-lovers from far and wide.

Le Folichon *($$$-$$$$; closed Mon; 804 Saint-François-Xavier, ☎492-1863)* which means playful and lighthearted, lives up to its name in the historic quarter of Terrebonne. In the summer, the shaded terrace is the best place to relax. The five course table d'hôte menu has a solid reputation. Particularly tasty are the escargot and grilled duck. Impressive wine list.

L'Étang des Moulins *($$$-$$$$; closed Mon; 888 Rue St-Louis, ☎471-4018)* occupies a magnificent stone house. The inventive French menu oozes refinement from the lobster Thermidore to the frog's legs in puff pastry. Without doubt, one of the best restaurants in Lanaudière.

L'Assomption

Le Prieuré *($$$; 402 Bd. L'Ange-Gardien, ☎589-6739)* has developed an excellent reputation over the years. In an historic 18th-century building, the chef concocts savoury French cuisine with local products. The tempting dishes include trout filet in an apple and maple marinade and duck cutlet in blueberry wine.

Joliette

Chez Henri le Kentucky *($; 30 Visitation, Saint-Charles-Borromée; ☎759-1113)* offers everything you would expect from a place open 24 hours a day, come hell or high water! A good place for travellers on a small budget.

Amongst the many fine restaurants, **Antre Jean** *($$$; closed Mon; 385 St-Viateur; ☎756-0412)* seems to be the undeclared favourite with the locals. French cuisine specialties, as they are prepared in France are served as part of a table d'hôte menu. The decor is warm and inviting and the atmosphere is unpretentious.

Tour B: La Matawinie

Rawdon

Auberge Steward *($$; 4333 Ch. du Lac Brennen, ☎834-8210)* occupies a rustic log building and serves succulent French and Québec cuisine. Escargots, Coquille Saint-Jacques, frog's legs, apple pie and other classics figure on the menu. This establishment offers excellent value with set menus for between $10.95 and $18.95.

Saint-Alphonse-Rodriguez

At the extraordinary **Auberge sur la Falaise** *($$$-$$$$; 324 Av. Du Lac Long Sud, ☎883-2269)*, meals are served in a setting of perfect tranquillity. Nestled in the deep forest, overlooking the calm surface of a lake, this establishment is a perfect retreat from the hectic rhythm of modern life (even if it is just for a meal). With a great deal of skill, the chef adapts French cuisine with Québec flavours – *médaillon de caribou aux bleuets du Lac* (caribou with blueberries), loin of lamb, pike *mousseline*, maple custard, etc. The obvious choice for epicureans is the five-course gourmet menu – a memorable experience indeed!

Saint-Jean-de-Matha

Auberge de la Montagne Coupée *($$$$; 1000 Ch. de la Montagne-Coupée, ☎886-3891)*, another spot famous for its peaceful setting, offers an exciting menu of innovative Québecois cuisine. The dining room is surrounded by two-story bay windows that look out on an absolutely breathtaking scene. And this is just the beginning – the best part of the evening (the meal!) is yet to come. To imaginatively presented game dishes are added succulent treasures such as grain-fed poultry with leeks, Oka cheese in *dijonnaise* sauce and crispy lamb with goat cheese. The service is

doting; the wine list is excellent. Very copious breakfasts are also served.

Saint-Donat

La Petite Michèle *($; 327 Rue St-Donat, ☎819-424-3131)* is just the place for travellers looking for a good family restaurant. The atmosphere is relaxed, the service, friendly and the menu, traditional Québecois.

The food is always delicious at the **Maison Blanche** *($$; 515 Rue Principale, ☎819-424-2222)*. The house specialty, a divine juicy, rare steak, is known far and wide.

The **Auberge Havre du Parc** *($$$; 2788 Route 125, Lac-Provost, ☎819-424-7686)* not only boasts an exceptionally peaceful setting, but also has an excellent selection of French specialties.

   ENTERTAINMENT

Theatres

Terrebonne

Tiny but cozy **Théâtre du Vieux-Terrebonne** *(867 St-Pierre, ☎492-4777)* has earned the respect of the Québec artistic community over the years and now draws some of the biggest names in song and comedy, who use it as a sort of testing ground before they bring their acts to Montreal. Touring theatre troupes also stop in regularly.

Joliette

There is nothing more pleasant that attending an open-air concert at **Amphithéâtre de Lanaudière** *(1575 Bd. Base-de-Roc, ☎759-2999 or 1-800-561-4343)*, perfectly situated in a little, tree-ringed valley. The best of this acoustically privileged site's summer program is presented during the Festival International de Lanaudière.

Saint-Jean-de-Matha

Auberge de la Montagne Coupée (see p 240) possesses its very own 250-seat summer theatre, **Cabaret-Théâtre de la Montagne Coupée** *(204 Rue Montagne-Coupée, ☎886-3845 or 886-3847).*

Festivals and Cultural Events

Joliette

The most important event on the regional calendar is the **Festival International de Lanaudière** *(early Jul to early Aug; ☎759-4343 or 1-800-561-4343).* During the most beautiful weeks of the summer, dozens of classical, contemporary and popular music concerts are presented in the churches of the area and outdoors at the superb Amphithéâtre de Lanaudière.

Repentigny

The annual **Internationaux de Tennis Junior du Canada** *(Aug 29 to Sep 6, 1998; ☎654-2411)* lets tennis fans discover tomorrow's Monica Selles's and John McEnroes.

Saint-Donat

When autumn arrives, the forests of the Saint-Donat region turn into a multicoloured natural extravaganza. To celebrate this spectacular burst of colour, various family activities are organized during **Week-ends des Couleurs** *(Sep and Oct; ☎819-424-2833 or 1-888-783-6628).*

LANAUDIÈRE

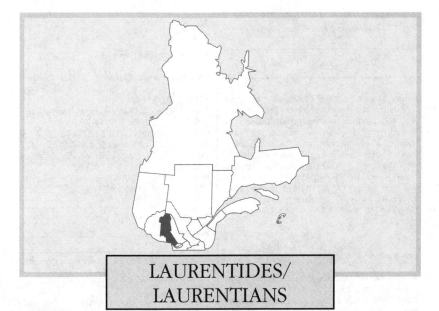

LAURENTIDES/
LAURENTIANS

 ithout question the most renowned resort area in Québec, the beautiful Laurentides region, also called the Laurentians attracts a great many visitors all year round. For generations now, people have been "going up north" to relax and enjoy the beauty of the Laurentian landscape. The lakes, mountains and forests provide a particularly good setting for a variety of physical activities or outings. As the region boasts the highest concentration of ski resorts in North America, skiing gets top billing here when winter rolls around. The villages scattered at the foot of the mountains are often both charming and friendly.

The southern part of the region, known as the Basses-Laurentides, was settled early on by French colonists, who came here to cultivate the rich farmland. A number of local villages reveal this history through their architectural heritage. The settling of the Laurentian plateau, engineered by the now legendary Curé Labelle, began much later, toward the middle of the 19th century. The development of the Pays d'En Haut, or highlands, was part of an ambitious plan to colonize the outlying areas of Québec in an effort to counter the exodus of French Canadians to industrial towns in the northeastern United States. Given the poor soil, farming here was hardly profitable, but Curé Labelle nevertheless succeeded in founding about twenty villages and attracting a good number of French-Canadian colonists to the region.

 FINDING YOUR WAY AROUND

Vacationers of all types have been coming to this region since the beginning of the century, making tourism the most important local industry. The following two tours have been laid out to discover this vast area. **Tour A: Lac des Deux-Montagnes** ★ and **Tour B. Cottage Country** ★★.

Tour A: Lac des Deux-Montagnes

By Car

From Montréal follow Highway 13 N. Take the exit for Route 344 W. towards Saint-Eustache. This road continues to Oka. A ferry from Oka leads to Hudson (see p 162) in the Montérégie region.

Bus Station

Saint-Eustache: 550 Arthur Sauvé, ☎(514) 472-9911.

Tour B: Cottage Country

From Montréal, take Highway 15 (the *Autoroute des Laurentides*) to Saint-Jérôme (Exit 43). Landmarks along the way include the imposing Collège de Sainte-Thérèse (1881) and its church, on the right, and the only General Motors automobile assembly plant in Québec, on the left. A little further, before Saint-Jérôme, is Mirabel Airport. Highway 15 and then Route 117 lead to Saint-Jovite. Mont-Tremblant is north of here on Route 327, Continue on the 117 to reach Labelle and Mont-Laurier.

Bus Stations

Saint-Sauveur: 166 Rue Principale (in front of the municipal garage).
Sainte-Adèle: 1208 Rue Valiquette (Pharmacie Brunet) ☎(514) 229-6609.
Mont-Tremblant: Chalet des Chutes, ☎(819) 425-2738.
Mont-Laurier: 555 Boulevard Paquette (Dépanneur Provi-Soir) ☎(819) 623-5538.

 PRACTICAL INFORMATION

Two **area codes** are used in the Laurentians, **450** up to Sainte-Adèle and **819** beyond. To avoid confusion, the area codes have been included in this chapter; you do not need to dial the three-digit area code for local calls.

Tourist Information

Regional Office

Maison du Tourisme des Laurentides 14142 Rue de la Chapelle, R.R. 1, Sainte-Antoine, J7Z 5T4, ☎(450) 436-8532, ⊷(450) 436-5309.

Tour A: Lac des Deux-Montagnes

Saint-Eustache: 600 Rue Dubois, J7P 5L2, ☎(450) 472-5825 (summer only).

Tour B: Cottage Country

Saint-Sauveur-des-Monts: 100 Rue Guindon, Local M, 3e Étage, J0R 1R6, ☎(450) 227-2564.
Sainte-Adèle: 333 Boulevard Sainte-Adèle, J0R 1L0, ☎(450) 229-5399.
Mont-Tremblant: C.P. 248, 140 Rue du Couvent, J0T 1Z0, ☎(819) 425-2434.
Labelle: 7404 Boulevard du Curé-Labelle, ☎(819) 686-2606
Mont-Laurier: 177 Boulevard Paquette, J0T 1H0, ☎(819) 623-4544.

 EXPLORING

Tour A: Lac des Deux-Montagnes ★
(one day)

The priests of the Sulpician order were instrumental to the colonization of this part of the Laurentians right from the early days of the French Regime. Vestiges of the seigneurial era may still be found on the shores of Lac des Deux-Montagnes, where nearly half the stops on this tour are located. Highlights of this short excursion through the lower Laurentians, just a half-hour from Montréal, are beautiful views of the lake and the opportunity to sample a wide variety of fresh produce at road-side stands along the way during the summer and fall.

Saint-Eustache (pop. 38,000)

In the early 19th century, Saint-Eustache, was a prosperous farming community that had produced a French-Canadian intellectual and political elite. These individuals played a major role in the Patriote Rebellion of 1837-38, making Saint-Eustache one of the main arenas of the tragic events that took place at the time. The village used to be the centre of the Mille-Îles seigneury, which was granted to Michel Sidrac du Gué of Boisbriand in 1683. It was the Lambert-Dumont family, however, that undertook the development of the seigneury in the middle of the 18th century. From 1960 on, Saint-Eustache became one of the most important suburbs on the Rive-Nord.

The **Église Saint-Eustache** ★★ *(123 Rue Saint-Louis)* is remarkable mainly for its high Palladian façade built out of cut stone between 1831 and 1836. Its two bell towers bear witness to the prosperity of local residents in

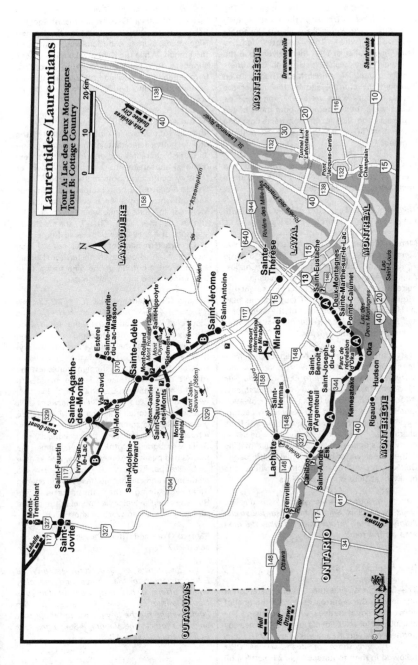

the years leading up to the rebellion. The church still bears traces of the harsh fighting that took place within its walls on December 19, 1837, when 150 Patriotes led, by Jean-Olivier Chénier shut themselves up in the building while resisting General Colborne's British troops. The British leader had his men bombard the church, and by the end of the battle, only its walls were left standing. The troops were then ordered to burn most of the houses in the village. It took Saint-Eustache more than 30 years to recover from these events.

Beside the church, visitors will find the presbytery, the convent (1898) and a monument to the Patriotes.

Take Rue Saint-Eustache, directly in line with the centre of the church, to Moulin Légaré.

Manoir Globensky *(free admission; 235 Rue Saint-Eustache, ☎450-974-5055)* is a large white house that once belonged to Charles-Auguste-Maximilien Globensky, husband of the heiress of the Saint-Eustache seigneury, Virginie Lambert-Dumont. Though it was built in 1862 after the abolition of the seigneurial system (1854), local residents have always referred to it as the "manor."

The stone walls of the **Moulin Légaré** *(free admission; late Apr to late Nov, Mon to Fri 8am to 5pm; early May to late Oct, Sat and Sun 12:30pm to 4:30pm; 236 Rue St-Eustache, ☎450-472-9529)* date back to 1762. However, modifications made in the early 20th century have robbed the building of some of its character. This flour mill has been in continuous operation since it was built, making it the oldest water-powered mill still in use in Canada. Visitors can purchase wheat and buckwheat flour on the premises.

Return to Route 344 W., which leads through Deux-Montagnes, Sainte-Marthe-sur-le-Lac and Pointe-Calumet before reaching Oka, the next stop on the tour.

Oka ★ (pop. 3,836)

The Sulpicians, like the Jesuits, established missions in the Montréal area with the goal of converting local natives to Catholicism. The disciples of Ignatius Loyola installed themselves permanently in Kahnawake in 1716 (see p 187), and those of Jean-Jacques Olier followed in their footsteps in 1721, settling on

the shores of Lac des Deux-Montagnes in a lovely spot named Oka, which means "golden fish". Here, the Sulpicians welcomed Algonquins, Hurons and Mohawks, all allies of the French. While the Kahnawake mission was supposed to remain isolated from European-born inhabitants, a village of French colonists developed simultaneously around the Sulpician church.

At the end of the 18th century, a number of Iroquois from New York State supplanted the original native inhabitants of the mission, giving an English character and, more recently, a new name (Kanesatake) to a whole section of territory located upriver from the village. Today, Oka is a centre for both recreational activities and tourism, as well as a distant suburb of Montréal. In 1990, during what has come to be known as the "Oka Crisis", the Mohawk Warriors of Kanesatake barricaded Route 344 at the western edge of Oka for several long months in an effort to affirm territorial rights and prevent a portion of the pine forest from being developed into a golf course.

Abbaye Cistercienne d'Oka ★ *(1600 Chemin d'Oka, ☎450-479-8361)* is run by the Cistercian order, founded at the Abbaye de Cîteaux by Robert de Molesme, Albéric and Étienne Harding at the end of the 11th century. It is a reformed branch of the Benedictine order. In 1881, a few Cistercian monks left the Abbaye de Bellefontaine in France in order to found a new abbey in Canada. The Sulpicians, who had already donated several pieces of their extensive territorial holdings in Montréal to various religious communities, granted the new arrivals a hillside in the seigneury of Deux-Montagnes. Within a few years, the monks had built the Abbaye d'Oka, also known as La Trappe. The famous Oka cheese is still made here, and can be purchased in the cheese dairy adjoining the monastery. The Romanesque Revival style chapel in the centre of the abbey is also worth a short visit.

Parc d'Oka and the Calvaire d'Oka ★, see p 257.

From the centre of Oka, turn left on Rue L'Annonciation to the church and the pier, which offers a beautiful view of Lac des Deux-Montagnes. The pier serves as the landing stage for the tiny private ferryboat that links this tour to the Vaudreuil-Soulanges tour in Montérégie (see p 183).

The **Église d'Oka** ★ *(181 Rue des Anges)*, an eclectic church built in 1878 in the Romanesque-Revival style, stands in front of the lake, on the same site once occupied by the church of the Sulpician mission (1733). It houses paintings belonging to the 18th century French school, commissioned in Paris by Sulpician priests to adorn the stations of the cross (Calvaire) in Oka (1742). In 1776, these oil paintings were replaced by wooden bas-reliefs executed by François Guernon, which were better able to withstand the harsh Canadian climate. The bas-reliefs were severely damaged by vandals in 1970 before being removed from the oratories and chapels and hung in the Chapelle Kateri Tekakwitha, adjacent to the Église d'Oka.

Continue along Rue des Anges, then turn right on Rue Sainte-Anne before taking a left back on to Route 344 and heading towards Saint-André-d'Argenteuil.

The road then leads through **The Pines**, planted in 1886 to counter the erosion of the sandy soil. It was here, in this forest of 50,000 pine trees, that tensions peaked during the 1990 "Oka crisis", when the provincial police force, the Sûreté du Québec, and then the Canadian Army, faced the Mohawk Warriors in an armed stand-off.

On the edge of the village of Saint-Placide, further to the west, is the **Maison Routhier** *(3320 Route 344)*, childhood home of Basile Routhier, author of the lyrics to Canada's national anthem.

Turn left on Rue Saint-André which leads to Carillon (Route 344).

Carillon (pop. 300)

Charged with defending the colony against attacks from native tribes allied with the Dutch and then the English, Dollard des Ormeaux and 17 fellow soldiers were killed during a battle with the Iroquois in 1660. Their deaths prevented the Iroquois from taking Montréal. A plaque and a monument commemorate this bloody episode in the early history of New France. Known for many years as Long-Sault, Carillon is a peaceful village, which was populated by Loyalists in the early 19th century. Visitors will find a hydroelectric dam here, as well as a vast park with a pleasant picnic area. Every year, thousands of amateur sailors pass through Carillon's lock on their way to Ottawa.

The **Musée Regional d'Argenteuil** *($2.50; mid-May to mid-Oct, Tue to Sun 11am to 5pm; 50 Rue Principale, ☎450-537-3861)* exhibits local antiques as well as a collection of 19th-century clothing in a handsome Georgian-style stone building erected in 1836. Originally intended to serve as an inn, it was converted the following year into a military barracks for the British troops who had come to put down the Patriote Rebellion in the Saint-Eustache region.

To return to Montréal, take Route 640 E., then Route 13 S. and finally Route 20 E.

Tour B: Cottage Country ★★
(one to three days)

This part of the Laurentians has been the favourite playground of Montrealers since the thirties. Located less than an hour and a half from the big city, it encompasses a multitude of lakes, wooded mountains and villages equipped to accommodate visitors. Montrealers "go up north" to their cottage in the summer to relax, go canoeing—in short, to enjoy the natural surroundings. In winter, visitors from Ontario, New York or Atlanta join the numbers of Montrealers in the charming local inns and luxury hotels. They come here not only to go downhill skiing, but also to snowshoe, cross-country ski or snowmobile across the white snow, and spend pleasant evenings by the fireside. The Laurentians boast the largest concentration of ski runs in North America.

Saint-Jérôme (pop. 23,384)

This administrative and industrial town is nicknamed La Porte du Nord (The Gateway to the North), because it marks the passage from the St. Lawrence valley into the mountainous region that stretches north of Montréal and Québec City. The Laurentians are one of the oldest mountain ranges on earth. Compressed by successive glaciations, the mountains are low, rounded, and composed of sandy soil. Colonization of this region began in the second half of the 19th century, with Saint-Jérôme as the starting point.

In the years following the rebellion of 1837-38, French Canadians began to feel cramped on their old, overpopulated seigneuries. There was

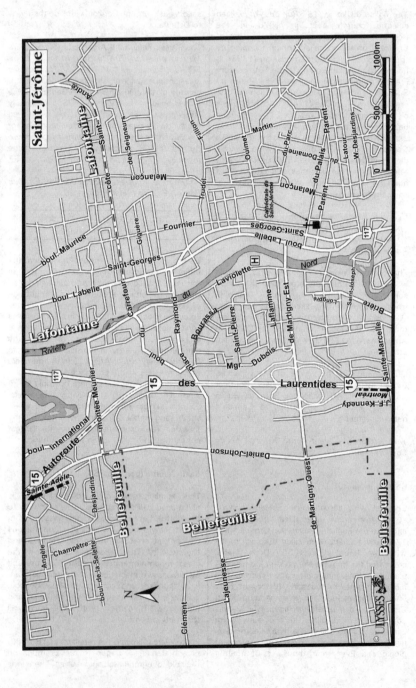

Saint-Jérôme

so little regional industry that families were forced to subdivide their farmlands in order to provide work for the new generations. These efforts, however, were decidedly insufficient. Thus began a mass exodus, during which several tens of thousands of Quebecers headed for the spinning mills of New England in the hopes of a better future. To this day, much of the population of that region is of French-Canadian extraction. The all-powerful clergy of Québec tried a number of tactics to halt this exodus to the United States, the most important being the colonization of the Upper Laurentians between 1880 and 1895, led by Curé Antoine Labelle of Saint-Jérôme. This unproductive land, hardly suitable for farming, was the source of many headaches for the colonists, who had to earn extra income cutting wood. Farmers became lumberjacks when winter rolled around. It was only thanks to sports-oriented tourism that the Upper Laurentians finally began to enjoy a certain degree of prosperity after 1945.

The **Cathédrale de Saint-Jérôme ★** *(every day 8:30am to 4:30pm; in front of Parc Labelle)*, a simple parish church when it was erected in 1899, is a large Roman-Byzantine style edifice reflecting Saint-Jérôme's prestigious status as the "headquarters" of the colonization of the Laurentians. A bronze statue of Curé Labelle, sculpted by Alfred Laliberté, stands in front of the cathedral.

In 1997, an **open-air amphitheatre** was inaugurated in front of the church, in Parc Labelle. Behind it lies the **Promenade de la Rivière Nord** a pleasant riverside trail studded with information panels about the history of Saint-Jérôme.

Saint-Jérôme is also the starting point of the **Parc Linéaire le P'tit Train du Nord ★★**. This extraordinary bike path, which becomes a cross-country ski trail in winter, stretches 200 kilometres, from Saint-Jérôme to Mont-Laurier, along the same route once followed by the Laurentian railroad.

This railroad was built between 1891 and 1909 and played a crucial role in the colonization of the Laurentians. It came to be known as the P'tit Train du Nord, a nickname immortalized in a song by Félix Leclerc. Later, right up until the 1940s, the railroad fostered the development of the region's tourist industry by providing access to all sorts of summer and winter resort areas.

Roads and then highways eventually made the Laurentians more and more accessible, rendering the P'tit Train du Nord obsolete by the 1980s. The railroad was dismantled in 1991, and the park was laid out a few years later. The park has since become one of the Laurentians' major attractions. It is punctuated from one end to the other with information panels, enabling visitors to learn more about the region's rich history, particularly the original train stations (Saint-Jérôme, Prévost, Mont-Rolland, Val-Morin, Sainte-Agathe-des-Monts, Saint-Faustin—Lac-Carré, Mont-Tremblant, Labelle, L'Annociation and Mont-Laurier), which are still standing. Some have even been restored, as is the case with the **Saint-Jérôme station**, which was not only overhauled in the fall of 1997, but now has a pretty square next to it as well, the **Place de la Gare**.

*Continue along Highway 15 N. toward Saint-Sauveur-des-Monts. On the way, the road runs alongside the village of **Prévost**, where the Laurentians' first downhill ski trails were opened in 1932. The following year, the first mechanical chairlift in North America was installed here. Take the Piedmont Exit (58).*

Piedmont (pop. 2,360)

Unlike other villages in the vicinity, Piedmont has not undergone much large-scale development. Mostly residential, it is a jumping-off point for fun waterslides and downhill skiing.

Glissades des Pays-d'en-Haut, see p 260

Station de Ski du Mont-Olympia, see p 260

Station de Ski du Mont-Avila, see p 260

Follow the signs for Route 364 and Saint-Sauveur-des-Monts, located right nearby, west of Highway 15.

Saint-Sauveur-des-Monts ★ (pop. 5,864)

Located perhaps a little too close to Montréal, Saint-Sauveur-des-Monts has been over-developed in recent years, and condominiums, restaurants and art galleries have sprung up like mushrooms. Rue Principale is very busy and is the best place in the Laurentians to mingle with the crowds. This resort is a favourite among entertainers, who own luxurious secondary residences on the mountainside. The Église

LAURENTIDES

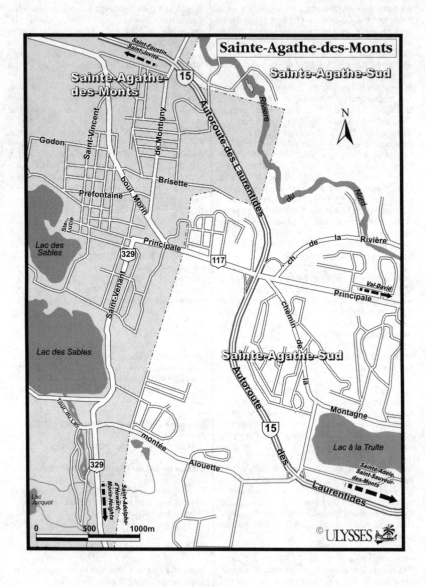

Jack Rabbit

Born in Norway in 1875, Herman Smith-Johannsen emigrated to Canada in 1901. An engineer by profession, he started selling railroad equipment, which enabled him to visit a number of remote areas. He would ski to these places, meeting many natives along the way, who dubbed him "*Wapoos*", or Jack Rabbit. This nickname was then picked up by Smith-Johannsen's friends at the Montréal Ski Club.

Jack Rabbit Johannsen explored the Laurentians throughout the twenties and thirties. He even set up residence here and managed to develop an excellent network of cross-country ski trails. It took him four years to clear a 128-kilometre trail known as the Maple Leaf, which stretches between the towns of Prévost and Labelle. Unfortunately, this lovely trail has since been segmented by Highway 15 (Autoroute des Laurentides).

By founding a number of cross-country ski centres and opening numerous trails, Jack Rabbit Johannsen is remembered as a pioneer of sorts. This living legend hung up his skis, so to speak, at the age of 106 and passed away in 1987, at the age of 111. His legacy is the history of cross-country skiing in Québec.

LAURENTIDES

Saint-Sauveur is also very popular with future couples, who have to put their namesdown on a long waiting list in order to be married there.

Station de Ski du Mont-Saint-Sauveur, see p 260.

Station de Ski du Mont-Habitant, see p 260.

Parc Aquatique du Mont-Saint-Sauveur, see p 260.

*From Saint-Sauveur-des-Monts, you can make a loop through charming **Morin-Heights**, with its two small white churches, one Catholic and the other Anglican, and pretty **Saint-Adolphe-d'Howard**. Route 364 O. and Route 329 N. lead ultimately to Saint-Agathe. Alternatively, get back on Highway 15 N., then take the exit for Sainte-Adèle and Sainte-Marguerite-du-Lac-Masson (69).*

Sainte-Adèle ★ (pop. 7,800)

The Laurentians were nicknamed the Pays-d'En-Haut (the Highlands) by 19th century colonists heading for these northern lands, far from the St-Laurent valley. Writer and journalist Claude-Henri Grignon, born in Sainte-Adèle in 1894, used the region as the setting for his books. His famous novel, *Un homme et son péché* (A Man and his Sin), depicts the wretchedness of life in the Laurentians back in those days. Grignon asked his good friend, architect Lucien Parent, to design the village church, which graces Rue Principale to this

day. On August 27, 1997, the villages of Mont-Rolland and Sainte-Adèle merged to form the new municipality of Sainte-Adèle.

Musée-Village de Séraphin ★ *($9; mid-Jun to mid-Oct, every day from 10am to 6pm; Montée à Séraphin, ☎514-229-4777).* Séraphin Poudrier is the main character of Claude-Henri Grignon's novel, *Un homme et son péché.* Miserly and unlikable, Séraphin has supreme control over his village. The film and television series (*Les Belles Histoires des Pays-d'en-Haut*) based on the novel proved so successful that a village was built to recreate the era of colonization in the Laurentians. In all, about 20 furnished buildings are open to the public. This is an interesting place to visit, even for those unfamiliar with Grignon's work.

Au Pays des Merveilles *($8; Jun to Aug, every day 10am to 6pm; 3595 Chemin de la Savane, ☎229-3141)* is a small, modest amusement park that will appeal mainly to small children. Slides, a wading pool, a miniature golf course, a maze, etc. have all been laid out in a setting reminiscent of Alice's Adventures in Wonderland (*Alice au Pays des Merveilles* in French). At $8 per person, children included, the admission charge is a bit steep, though.

Station de Ski du Chanteclerc, see p 261.

Station de Ski du Mont-Gabriel, see p 260.

Take Route 370 to Sainte-Marguerite-du-Lac-Masson. On the way, you'll see the charming Pavillon des Arts de Sainte-Adèle (see p 270).

Sainte-Marguerite-du-Lac-Masson (pop. 2,000)

All year round, vacationers come to the lovely rolling countryside of the Lac Masson area to unwind far from the hustle and bustle of Montréal. Two villages have grown up on the shores of the lake, the elegant L'Estérel and the more modest, but more populated Sainte-Marguerite-du-Lac-Masson, which is located on the westernmost part of the lake.

Route 370 will take you to Sainte-Marguerite, on the shores of Lac Masson. A little square next to the church, in front of the renowned Bistro à Champlain (see p 267) offers a good view of the lake. The road then turns right, skirting around the lake on its way to Ville d'Estérel.

Ville d'Estérel ★ (pop. 124)

In Belgium, the name Empain is synonymous with financial success. Baron Louis Empain, who inherited the family fortune in the early 20th century, was an important builder, just like his father, who was responsible for the construction of Heliopolis, a new section of Cairo (Egypt). During a trip to Canada in 1935, Baron Louis purchased Pointe Bleue, a strip of land that extends out into Lac Masson. In two years, from 1936 to 1938, he erected about 20 buildings on the site, all designed by Belgian architect Antoine Courtens, to whom we also owe the Palais de la Folle Chanson and the façade of the Église du Gésu in Brussels, as well as the Grande Poste in Kinshasa, Zaïre. Empain named this entire development **Domaine de l'Estérel**. The onset of World War II thwarted his plans, however, and after the war, the land was divided up. In 1958, a portion of it was purchased by a Québec businessman named Fridolin Simard, who began construction of the present **Hôtel L'Estérel** alongside Route 370, and then divided the rest of the property into lots. On these pieces of land, visitors will find lovely modern houses made of stone and wood, designed by architect Roger D'Astou.

Head back to Highway 15 N., take Exit 76 to Val-David.

Val-David (pop. 3,225)

Val David attracts visitors not only because it is located near the Laurentian ski resorts, but also because of its craft shops, where local artisans display their work. The village, made up of pretty houses, has managed to retain its own unique charm.

Every year, the **Village-du-Père-Noël** *($8; early Jun to late Aug, every day 10am to 6pm; Route 117, ☎819-322-2146 or 1-800-287-NOEL)*, or Santa's Village, attracts children eager to meet Saint Nicholas at his summer retreat. A number of activities are organized, ensuring memorable days for the kids.

From Highway 15 (Exit 86), turn right onto Route 117 N. Keep left and turn onto Route 329 S. (Rue Principale).

Sainte-Agathe-des-Monts ★ (pop. 9,307)

Set in the heart of the Laurentians, this is a business and tourist oriented town, which sprang up around a sawmill in 1849. When the railway was introduced into the region in 1892, Sainte-Agathe-des-Monts became the first resort area in the Laurentians. Located at the meeting point of two waves of colonization, the Anglo-Saxon settling of the county of Argenteuil and the French-Canadian settling of Saint-Jérôme, the town succeeded in attracting wealthy vacationers, who, lured by Lac des Sables, built several beautiful villas around the lake and in the vicinity of the Anglican church. The region was once deemed a first-class resort by important Jewish families of Montréal and New York. In 1909, the Jewish community founded Mount Sinai Sanitarium (the present building was erected in 1930) and in the following years, built synagogues in Sainte-Agathe-des-Monts and Val-Morin.

Lac des Sables can be toured **by land or by water ★**. The Chemin du Lac (11 km) can be followed by bicycle or by car, another option is to climb aboard one of the boats run by **Croisières Alouettes** *($11; mid-May to late Oct, every day, departures at 10:30am, 11:30am, 1:30pm, 2:30pm and 3:30pm, summer also at 5pm and 7pm; Quai de la Rue Principale, ☎819-326-3656)* for a short cruise. Besides being out on the water, you can see the magnificent lakeside homes, including the former residence of American millionaire Lorne McGibbon. This house has unfortunately been considerably altered by missionaries, who have added three floors to the central portion.

Take the winding Route de Saint-Faustin through the mountains and around the lakes.

Turn left on to Route 117 (caution: dangerous intersection), which leads to Saint-Jovite.

Saint-Jovite (pop. 4,118)

Visitors will enjoy strolling down Rue Ouimet lined with restaurants, tea rooms, antique shops and boutiques. Particularly notable buildings include a pretty little Victorian-style shopping centre and the village's original railway station which has been moved to the side of the road and converted into a restaurant. At the end of a country road east of Saint-Jovite, lies the enormous **Monastère des Apôtres de l'Amour Infini**. The monastery is crowned with a statue of the Sacred Heart. This schismatic sect has named its own pope, whose seat of power is Saint-Jovite.

The **Musée de la Faune** *(free admission; every day 9am to 5pm; 635 Rue Limoges, ☎819-425-9179)* displays a small collection of stuffed and mounted wild animals.

Near the church, turn down Rue Limoges (327) in the direction of Mont Tremblant, which is already visible on the horizon. The road passes through Mont-Tremblant Village before reaching the Mont-Tremblant resort (open year-round).

Mont-Tremblant Resort ★★★ (pop. 707)

Some of the largest sports and tourist complexes in the Laurentians were built by wealthy American families with a passion for downhill skiing. They chose this region for the beauty of the landscape, the province's French charm and above all for the northern climate which makes for a longer ski season than in the United States. The Station de Ski du Mont-Tremblant was founded by Philadelphia millionaire Joseph Ryan in 1938. The resort is now owned by Intrawest, which also owns Whistler Resort in British Columbia, and which has invested a considerable amount of money in Tremblant in order to put it on a par with the huge resorts of western Canada and the United States. At the height of the season, 74 trails, including several new ones, attract downhill skiers to Tremblant's slopes (914 m), in the summer the magnificent new golf course is just as popular. Not only does this place have the longest and most difficult vertical drops in the region, it also boasts a brand-new resort complex set in a cute little village of traditional Quebecois-style buildings at the base of the mountain. The Disney-ish appearance of these colourful units is not for everyone, but there is

certainly lots to keep you busy... The ultimate goal, to create a one-of-a-kind vacation spot, was achieved.

Place Saint-Bernard is surrounded by the new hotel complexes (the **Saint-Bernard**, the **Deslauriers** and the **Johannsen**) as well as about 50 shops, 15 restaurants and nearly a dozen bars. Vieux-Tremblant preserves a more authentic feel; several of the original and more traditional buildings have been renovated. No motor vehicles are permitted anywhere in the village, so you'll have to get around on foot, skis or snowshoes.

This all-season resort area is still growing. The **AquaClub**, a year-round water park, was completed at the end of 1997, and Intrawest has announced that it will invest another half a billion dollars in the resort by the year 2001 in order to add 1,200 more accommodation units to the 1000 already in existence, as well as new ski runs on both sides of the mountain, two new golf courses, riding stables, an amphitheatre, etc.

Charming **Chapelle Saint Bernard** (1942), a replica of Église Saint-Laurent that once stood on Île d'Orléans greets visitors on the way into the village, beside Lac Tremblant. A road on the right leads to the public parking lot, the **Panoramic Chairlift** and, 10 kilometres further north, to the entrance of **Parc du Mont-Tremblant** ★★ (see p 257).

Mont-Tremblant Village ★ (pop. 764)

On the other side of Lac Tremblant lies the charming Mont-Tremblant Village, not to be confused with the resort area that Intrawest started developing in 1993. Here, in a more authentic setting, visitors will find attractive shops and restaurants, as well as a number of other places to stay, including the famous Club Tremblant (see p 266).

Labelle (pop. 2,134)

Tourism in the densely forested northern portion of the Laurentians, commonly known as the Hautes-Laurentides, is largely devoted to a wide range of outdoor activities (observing plant and animal life, hunting, fishing, camping, cross-country skiing, etc.). The traditional local industry, lumber, is currently on the decline. The region developed between 1870 and 1890, thanks to Saint-Jérôme's parish priest, Antoine

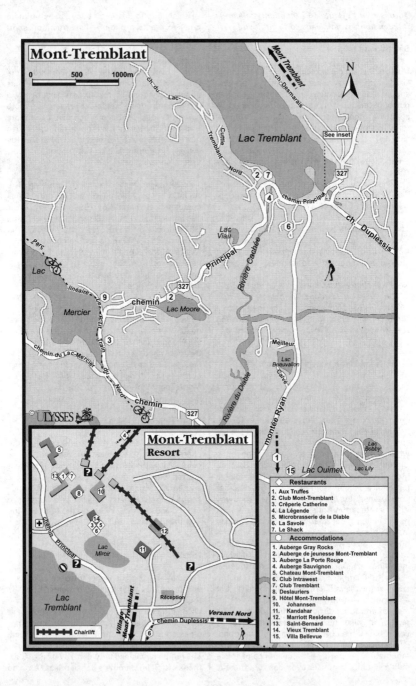

Mont-Tremblant

0   500   1000m

N

ch. du Lac

Mont-Tremblant

ch. Desmarais

Lac Tremblant

Cuttle Tremblant Nord

See inset

2 7

327

4

chemin Principal

ch. Duplessis

6

Lac Viau

Rivière Cachée

Parc

Lac

linéaire Le P'tit Train du Nord

9

chemin

2

327

Mercier

Lac Moore

3

chemin du Lac-Mercier

Meilleur

Lac Beauvallon

chemin

327

Rivière du Diable

Cachée

montée Ryan

ULYSSE

1

Lac Bobby

15 Lac Ouimet

Lac Lily

Mont-Tremblant Resort

4

5

13 1 7

?

8

10

14
3 5
6

12

+ chemin Principal

Lac Miroir

11

?

Lac Tremblant

?

?

Village Mont-Tremblant

Réception

Versant Nord

Chairlift

chemin Duplessis

6

◇ Restaurants
1. Aux Truffes
2. Club Mont-Tremblant
3. Crêperie Catherine
4. La Légende
5. Microbrasserie de la Diable
6. La Savoie
7. Le Shack

○ Accommodations
1. Auberge Gray Rocks
2. Auberge de jeunesse Mont-Tremblant
3. Auberge La Porte Rouge
4. Auberge Sauvignon
5. Chateau Mont-Tremblant
6. Club Intrawest
7. Club Tremblant
8. Deslauriers
9. Hôtel Mont-Tremblant
10. Johannsen
11. Kandahar
12. Marriott Residence
13. Saint-Bernard
14. Vieux Tremblant
15. Villa Bellevue

Labelle, who did his utmost to open up new lands in order to attract farmers from the congested plain of the St. Lawrence to the Hautes-Laurentides. To do so, he converted the former lumberjack camps in the Rouge and Lièvre valleys, known as *fermes forestières* (forest farms), into villages for the colonists. This explains why certain municipalities in the Hautes-Laurentides still bear the name "ferme."

The town of Labelle is the main jumping-off point into Parc du Mont-Tremblant.

Réserve Faunique Papineau-Labelle, see p 281

Réserve Faunique Rouge-Matawin, see below.

| PARKS |

Tour A: Lac des Deux-Montagnes

The **Parc d'Oka and the Calvaire d'Oka ★** *(2020 Chemin d'Oka,* ☎*450-479-8337)* encompasses about 45 kilometres of trails for hikers in the summer and cross-country skiers in the winter. Most of the trails lie south of Route 344, crisscrossing a relatively flat area. North of Route 344, there are two other trails, which lead to the top of the Colline d'Oka (168 m), where visitors can drink in a view of the entire region. The longer trail (7.5 km) ends at a panoramic viewing area, while the shorter one (5.5 km) guides visitors past the oldest stations of the cross in the Americas. This calvary was set up by the Sulpicians back in 1740, in an effort to stimulate the faith of natives recently converted to Catholicism. Humble and dignified at the same time, the calvary is made up of four trapezoidal oratories and three rectangular chapels built of whitewashed stone. These little buildings, now empty, once housed wooden bas-reliefs depicting the Passion of Christ. The park also has campsites *($18.75 per day,* ☎*450-479-8337)* and an information centre.

Tour B: Cottage Country

Parc du Mont-Tremblant ★★ *(Chemin du Lac Tremblant,* ☎*819-688-2281 or 1-800-461-8711),* created in 1894, was originally known as Parc de la Montagne Tremblante (Trembling Mountain Park) in

reference to an Algonquian legend. It covers an area of 1,250 square kilometres, encompassing the mountain, seven rivers and some 500 lakes. The ski resort opened in 1938, and has been welcoming skiers ever since. Today, it has modern facilities and 45 trails, with a vertical drop of up to 710 metres. A day of skiing costs $44. The park also includes nine cross-country ski trails, which stretch over 50 kilometres. The resort caters to sports enthusiasts all year round. Hiking buffs, can explore up to 100 kilometres of trails here. Two of these, La Roche and La Corniche, have been rated among the most beautiful in Québec. The park also has bicycle paths, mountain bike circuits, and offers water sports like canoeing and windsurfing.

The **Réserve Faunique Rouge-Matawin** *(accessible via Route 117 and Route 321,* ☎*819-424-2981 or 1-800-665-6527)* is a wildlife preserve and home to a number of different species of animals, including the highest concentration of moose in the province. Bridle paths and hiking trails have been laid out. The rivers running through the park are suitable for canoeing.

Réserve Faunique Papineau-Labelle, see p 281.

| OUTDOORS |

| Hiking |

Tour A: Lac des Deux-Montagnes

Parc d'Oka has 40 kilometres of hiking trails, see above.

Tour B: Cottage Country

The 0.4-kilometre **promenade** along the **Rivière du Nord** *(between Rue Martigny and Rue Saint-Joseph)* is studded with thematic signposts, which enable visitors to learn about the region's history while enjoying a lovely view of the river.

Near Saint-Faustin, the **Centre Touristique et Éducatif des Laurentides** *(admission charge; May to Oct, every day; Lac Cordon,* ☎*819-326-1606)* has eight trails, which range in length from one to 10 kilometres, covering a total of 25. Among these, Le Panoramique

(3 km) offers the loveliest views of the area. L'Aventurier, the longest trail (10 km), leads to the top of a 530-metre-high mountain.

At the Mont-Tremblant resort, the Tremblant Express chairlift will take you up to the new ÉcoZone (☎819-681-2000) centre, which has trails designed specifically for families (Le Manitou, Le 360°, Le Montagnard and Les Ruisseaux), as well as others for more seasoned hikers (Les Caps, Le Grand Brûlé, Les Sommets, Le Parben and Le Johannsen). All along the trails, there are markers containing information on the Laurentian wildlife.

Parc du Mont-Tremblant is an excellent place for hiking, as it has trails of all levels of difficulty. La Roche and La Corniche are both short, delightful hikes, while the 45-kilometre Diable trail is sure to satisfy even the most fanatical hiking buffs.

Rock-climbing

Tour B: Cottage Country

The **Val-David** area is renowned for its rock faces. A number of mountains here are fully equipped to accommodate climbers' needs; **Mont King**, **Mont Condor** and **Mont Césaire** are among the most popular. For more information, equipment rentals or guide services, contact **Passe Montagne** (1760 Montée 2e Rang, Val-David, JOT 2N0, ☎819-322-2948), a trailblazing rock-climbing outfit in the Val-David region. Their team of experts offer excellent advice.

Swimming

Tour A: Lac des Deux-Montagnes

The **Park d'Oka** (☎450-479-8337) has a very popular beach, where canoes, sailboards and pedalboats are all available for rent. Picnic area, snack bar and restrooms.

Tour B: Cottage Country

Among the region's other public beaches, we should mention the one in **Sainte-Adèle** ($4; Chemin Chanteclerc, ☎450-229-2921), which is small but pleasant; the one in **Saint-Adophe-d'Howard** (Chemin du Village,

☎450-327-2626); the one in **Sainte-Agathe-des-Monts** ($4; Lac des Sables); the one in **Sainte-Marguerite-du-Lac-Masson** ($4; ☎514-228-2543) and the one in **Mont-Tremblant** (Chemin Principal, ☎819-425-8671), as well as the **Club Plage et Tennis de la Station Touristique du Mont-Tremblant** (☎819-681-5643), which rents out canoes, kayaks, rowboats, sailboards and pedalboats.

Biking

Tour B: Cottage Country

The former railway line of the **P'tit Train du Nord** (300 Rue Longpré, Bureau 110, St-Jérôme, J7T 3B9, ☎450-436-4051, ≈436-2277), which carried Montrealers up North for many years, has been transformed into a superb 200-kilometre bike path from Saint-Jérôme to Mont-Laurier. It leads through a number of little villages where accommodations and restaurants in all price ranges can be found.

The **Station Touristique du Mont-Tremblant** (☎819-681-2000 or 1-800-461-8711) has about 20 mountain bike trails. To reach them, you and your bike take a specially designed chairlift. There are several trails: La Cachée (novice); Le Labyrinthe (intermediate); La Nord-Sud, La Chouette and La Grand Nord (advanced); and La Sasquatch (expert).

Parc du Mont-Tremblant (☎819-688-2281) maintains some 100 kilometres of bike paths.

Rafting

Thanks to the thrilling Rivière Rouge, the Laurentians offer excellent conditions for whitewater rafting — among the best in Canada, according to some experts. Of course, there is no better time to enjoy this activity than during the spring thaw. Rafting during this period can prove quite a challenge, however, so previous experience is recommended. The best season for novices is summer, when the river is not too high and the weather is milder. For further information, contact **Nouveau Monde, Expéditions en Rivière** ($85 per person; 100 Chemin de la Rivière Rouge, Calumet, JOV 1B0, ☎819-242-7238 or 1-800-361-5033, ≈242-0207), which offers group outings every day.

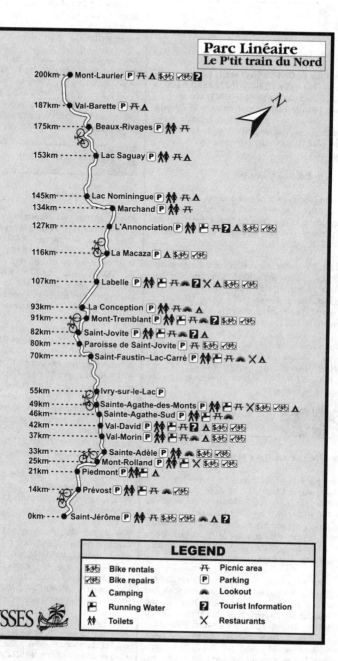

Golf

Tour A: Lac des Deux-Montagnes

The **Club de Golf Carling Lake** *($42; Route 327 Nord, Pine Hill, ☎450-476-1212 or 533-5333)*, established near Lachute in 1961, is one of the most beautiful public golf courses in Canada, according to *Golf Digest* magazine. Furthermore, the elegant Hôtel du Lac Carling (see p 262) is located right near by.

Tour B: Cottage Country

Among the dozens of golf courses scattered all over the Laurentians, one of the more renowned is the **Club de Golf L'Estérel** *($35; Boulevard Fridolin-Simard, Ville d'Estérel, ☎450-228-2571)*.

Mont-Tremblant resort also boasts a good golf course, **Le Géant** *(3005 Chemin Principal, Mont-Tremblant, ☎1-800-461-8711)*, which experts have ranked among the 10 best in Canada. The resort plans to add a second golf course in 1998.

The same goes for the nearby **Club de Golf Gray Rocks** *(525 Chemin Principal, Mont-Tremblant, ☎819-425-2771 or 1-800-567-6744)*, which has one 18-hole course at present.

Waterslides and Toboganning

Tour A: Lac des Deux Montagnes

There are no fewer than 45 water slides at the **Super Aqua Club** *($11 to $20; Jun to Aug, 10am to 7pm; 322 Montée de la Baie, ☎450-473-1013)* in Pointe-Calumet, as well as a wave pool and inner tube "rivers". The water park is on the shores of Lac des Deux Montagnes and has a pretty sandy beach. Pedalboat and canoe rentals available.

During the winter, those who are interested in spending a pleasant day in the fresh air but don't want to ski, can head over to the **Glissades des Pays-d'en-Haut** *($19; mid-Dec to late Mar, Mon to Thu, 9am to 4pm, Fri and Sat 9am to 10pm; 440 Chemin Avila, ☎450-224-4014)*, and try the 19 different slides. In the summer, visitors can opt for the

Cascades d'Eau *($16; early Jun to late Aug, open every day 10am to 7pm; Exit 58 off Highway 15, ☎450-227-3353)*, which has 17 water slides.

Another waterslide option is the **Parc Aquatique du Mont-Saint-Sauveur** *($14-$18; mid-Jun to early Sep, every day 10am to 7pm; Exit 58 off Highway 15, ☎514-227-4671 or 1-800-363-2426)*, with a wave pool and six slides, four of which are in a spiral, plus three more especially designed for children.

Downhiill Skiing

Tour B: Cottage Country

There are two ski resorts in the mountains around Piedmont, **Station Mont-Olympia** *($29; Rue de la Montagne, ☎450-227-3523 or 1-800-363-3696)*, which has 21 slopes and a total vertical drop of 192 metres, and **Station du Mont-Avila** *($27; Chemin Avila, ☎450-227-4671 or 1-800-363-2426)*, where visitors will find about 10 slopes, the longest of which stretches 1,050 metres.

A small mountain with a vertical drop of only 210 metres, **Mont Saint-Sauveur** *($34; 350 Rue Saint Denis, ☎514-227-4671)* attracts a large clientele because of its proximity to Montréal. It offers 26 downhill ski trails, a few of which are lit for night-skiing.

As Mont-Saint-Sauveur is often overcrowded, some might prefer the slopes of the neighbouring mountains, which have fewer trails, but shorter lift lines. The **Station de Ski du Mont-Habitant** *($25; 12 Boulevard des Skieurs, ☎450-227-2637)*, with 8 runs, is one of these. There is also **Mont-Christie** *($22; Côte Saint-Gabriel Est, ☎450-226-2412)*, which has 12 trails shared by skiers and snowboarders.

We should also mention **Ski Morin-Heights** *($29; Chemin Bennett, ☎450-227-2020)*, which has 22 trails, 16 of which are lit for night-skiing; and the modest (eight trails) **L'Avalanche** *($20; 1657 Chemin de l'Avalanche, ☎450-327-3232)* ski centre, located near Saint-Adolphe-d'Howard.

The Sainte-Adèle region also attracts skiers with its two good-sized ski resorts. The **Station de Ski du Mont-Gabriel** *($29; Montée Mont-Gabriel, Mont-Rolland; ☎450-229-3547)* has 21 trails (10 lit for night-skiing) for skiers of all different levels. The handsome Chanteclerc tourist complex was built near the **Station de Ski du Chanteclerc** *($30, Chemin Chanteclerc, ☎450-229-3555)*, with 22 trails, including 13 that are lit in the evening.

In Val-Morin, skiers can head to **Belle Neige** *($26; Route 117, ☎819-322-3311)*, which has 14 trails of all different levels of difficulty. In the Val-David area, you'll find **Mont-Alta** *($19.50; Route 117, ☎819-322-3206)* and the **Station de Ski Vallée-Bleue** *($22; 1418 Chemin Vallée-Bleue, ☎819-322-3427)*, with 22 and 16 trails respectively.

The **Station de Ski Mont-Blanc** *($30; Route 117, ☎819-688-2444 or 1-800-567-6715)*, in Saint-Faustin, has 54 runs and the second highest vertical drop in the Laurentians (300 metres).

Station de Ski Mont-Tremblant see p 257.

Gray Rocks *($25; Route 327, ☎819-425-2771 or 1-800-567-6767)* is another resort in the region. It has about 20 trails, with a vertical drop of 191 metres (much lower than at Mont-Tremblant). A major overhaul of the facilities is scheduled for the spring of 1998. New accommodations (apartments and chalets) will be added, along with a new golf course.

Cross-country Skiing

Tour A: Lac des Deux-Montagnes

Park d'Oka *($6.75; Chemin d'Oka, ☎450-479-8337)* has eight trails covering a total of about 70 kilometres. Three are ranked easy, three difficult and two very difficult. Those who prefer snowshoes to skis will be pleased to learn that the park also has two snowshoe trails (5 km in all).

Tour B: Cottage Country

The **Parc Linéaire du P'tit Train du Nord** *($3; 300 Rue Longpré, Bureau 110, St-Jérôme, J7T 3B9, ☎450-436-4051, ⊷436-2277)*, which stretches some 200 kilometres, becomes a wonderful cross-country and snowmobile trail in the winter. The section from Saint-Jérôme to Sainte-Agathe is reserved for skiers; the rest, as far as Mont-Laurier, is snowmobile territory.

The **Centre de Ski de Fond Morin-Heights** *($4; 612 Rue du Village, Morin-Heights, J0R 1H0, ☎450-226-3232)* is one of the oldest cross-country ski resorts in Canada. It's the perfect place for "adventure skiing", that is, taking longer trips on ungroomed, back-country trails.

The **Centre de Ski de Fond L'Estérel** *($6; 39 Boulevard Fridolin-Simard, Ville d'Estérel, J0T 1E0, ☎450-228-2571 or 1-800-363-3623, ⊷228-4977)* is one of the best organized cross-country resorts in the region. It is located at an altitude of 330 metres, so the snow conditions are excellent. Furthermore, this is truly a resort for skiers of all levels of experience. Most of the trails are short, though not necessarily easy. There are 14 in all, six of which are easy, four difficult and four very difficult.

In winter, the **Centre Far Hills** *($5; Chemin Far Hills, Val-Morin, ☎819-322-2014)* maintains over 125 kilometres of cross-country trails. These run through a hilly, forested region, enabling skiers to drink in some lovely scenery. This is where you'll find the famous **Maple Leaf Trail**, cleared by none other than Jack Rabbit Johanssen.

Snowmobiling

Tour B: Cottage Country

Scores of snowmobile trails crisscross the Laurentians. Snowmobile rentals are available at the following places:

Sport Action 2000 717 Chemin du Village, Saint-Adolphe-d'Howard, ☎450-226-2000.
Randonnée Québec 25 Rue Brisette, Sainte-Agathe-des-Monts, ☎819-326-0642 or 1-800-326-0642.
Location Constantineau 1117 Boulevard Albiny-Paquette, Mont-Laurier, ☎819-623-1724 or 1-800-567-4574.
Hôtel L'Estérel Chemin Fridolin-Simard, ☎450-866-8224.

LAURENTIDES

ACCOMMODATIONS

Tour A: Lac des Deux-Montagnes

Oka

The **Park d'Oka** *($24;* ☎*450-479-8369)* boasts a magnificent campground with about 800 sites laid out in the middle of the forest.

La Maison Dumoulin *($55 bkfst incl.; sb; 53 Rue St-Sulpice, C.P. 1072, JON 1E0,* ☎*450-479-6753)* has comfortable rooms, friendly service and a wonderful location on the shores of Lac des Deux-Montagnes.

Lachute

Hidden away on the shores of a lake just northwest of Lachute lies the remarkable but little-known **Hôtel du Lac Carling** *($170-$195; pb, tv, ≡, ≈, ⊛, ℜ, ⊘, △; Route 327 Nord, Pine Hill, J0V 1A0,* ☎*450-533-9211,* ⬄*533-9197).* A rangy building made of stone and pale wood and graced with tall windows, this luxurious hotel cuts a fine figure. Inside, a sumptuous decor set off by numerous works of art and antiques awaits. The huge guest rooms, for their part, are bathed in natural light. Some have a whirlpool bath, a patio or a fireplace. The hotel also has a sports centre complete with indoor tennis courts, a workout room, an indoor pool and a sauna. The renowned Club de Golf Carling Lake tops off the amenities (see p 260).

Tour B: Cottage Country

Saint-Sauveur-des-Monts

From the outside, the **Motel Jolibourg** *($75; ≈, ≡, tv; 60 Rue Principale, JOR 1R0,* ☎*450-227-4651)* is fairly typical of motels in this category, with the parking lot occupying the place of honour. The management has, however, tried to make the rooms comfortable, equipping each of them with a fireplace.

The **Auberge Sous l'Édredon** *($85 bkfst incl.; 777 Rue Principale, JOR 1R2,* ☎*450-227-3131)* stands on a hillside, offering a lovely view of the mountain. Not unlike a B&B, it has only seven rooms, all nicely decorated, five of which include a private bathroom. Special efforts ensure that guests have a pleasant stay and feel at home. Extremely courteous reception.

A beautiful row of fir trees graces the garden of the **Hôtel Châteaumont** *($85;≡, tv, ⊘; 50 Rue Principale, JOR 1R6,* ☎*450-227-1821,* ⬄*227-1483),* forming an attractive entranceway. The rooms have modern furnishings, and all but two are equipped with a fireplace, a real plus after a day of skiing.

The long green and white building of the **Relais Saint-Denis** *($84; ≈, ≡, tv, ℜ; 61 Rue Saint-Denis, JOR 1R4,* ☎*450-227-4602,* ⬄*227-8504)* is modern-looking for a country inn. Fortunately, the attractively decorated rooms are more inviting. Behind the building is a pleasant garden with a swimming pool.

The **Manoir Saint-Sauveur** *($129; ≈, ≡, ⊘, △, tv, ℜ, ♿; 246 Chemin du Lac Millette, JOR 1R3;* ☎*450-227-1811 or 1-800-361-0505,* ⬄*227-8512),* with some 200 rooms, focuses on athletic activities, offering lots of summer and winter packages with downhill skiing, golf or horseback riding, as well as a wide variety of facilities including tennis and squash courts. It has the advantage of being within walking distance of the town of Saint-Sauveur.

Morin-Heights

Located in an enchanting setting outside the village, the **Auberge le Clos Joli** *($160 bkfst incl.; ≈, ℜ; 19 Chemin Watchorn, JOR 1H0,* ☎/⬄*450-226-5401)* is a pleasant place to stay. The service is personalized, the rooms are comfortable and the food is delicious. As there are only nine rooms, reservations are recommended.

Sainte-Adèle

The **Motel Chantolac** *($49; ≡, ≈, ℝ; 156 Rue Morin, JOR 1L0,* ☎*450-229-3593 or 1-800-561-8875)* is a comfortable, well-located place with reasonable rates. The rooms may not be spectacular, but they're a real bargain. Furthermore, the place boasts a lovely location on the street leading to the Chanteclerc, near lots of pleasant restaurants and just steps away from Lac Rond and its little beach.

Ulysses' Favourites

Accommodations

For businesspeople:
Hôtel du Lac Carling (p 262) and Château Mont-Tremblant (p 265).

For romantics:
Auberge La Caravelle (p 264).

For outdoors-enthusiasts:
Base de Plein Air le P'tit Bonheur (p 265), Manoir Saint-Sauveur (p 262), Chanteclerc (p 263), Hôtel l'Estérel (p 264) and Hôtel Far Hills (p 264).

For luxury:
Hôtel du Lac Carling (p 262) and Hôtel L'Eau à la Bouche (p 263).

For the views:
Hôtel L'Eau à la Bouche (p 263) and Club Tremblant (p 266).

Restaurants

The Laurentians' finest tables:
L'Eau à la Bouche (p 267), Bistro à Champlain (p 267), La Clef des Champs (p 267) and La Sapinière (p 268).

For a romantic atmopshere:
Hôtel du Lac Carling (p 266) and Auberge La Biche au Bois (p 267).

For Québec cuisine:
Auberge La Biche au Bois (p 267), Bistro à Champlain (p 267), La Sapinière (p 268) and La Table Enchantée (p 269).

For the views:
La Légende (p 269) and Club Tremblant (p 269).

For the terrace:
Jardin d'Agnès (p 266), Le Chrysanthème (p 266), La Scala (p 267), Le Shack (p 269) and Microbrasserie de la Diable (p 269).

For wine connoisseurs:
Bistro à Champlain (p 267), Eau à la Bouche (p 267), La Sapinière (p 268) and Clef des Champs (p 267).

LAURENTIDES

At **Le Chanteclerc** (*$89 bkfst incl., $170 ½b; ≈, ≡, tv, △, ⊙, &; 1474 Chemin du Chanteclerc, JOR 1L0; ☎450-229-3555, ⇒229-5593*), whose name and emblem (a rooster) were inspired by Edmond Rostand's play, guests can enjoy a multitude of activities in an pristine lakeside setting at the foot of Mont Chanteclerc. The golf course is picturesque, with mountains on either side. The sizeable sports complex and the handsome stone building with its 300 or so rooms attracts quite a crowd.

A member of the prestigious Association des Relais et Châteaux, the hotel **L'Eau à la Bouche** (*$125, $255 ½b; ≈, ≡, tv, ℜ, &; 3003 Boulevard Sainte-Adèle, JOR 1L0, ☎450-229-2991, ⇒229-7573*) is known for its excellent gourmet restaurant and extremely comfortable rooms. Don't be fooled by the building's rustic appearance, the rooms are elegantly furnished. The hotel itself dates from the mid-1980s and is set back from the road. It offers a splendid view of the ski slopes of Mont Chanteclerc. The restaurant, for its part, is in a separate building. The complex is located on Route 117, a fair distance north of the village of Sainte-Adèle.

Ville d'Estérel

At the **Hôtel l'Estérel** *($238 ½b; ≈, ⊝, ◇, ℜ, ㅅ; Boulevard Fridolin-Simard, J0T 1E0; ☎450-228-2571 or 1-888-378-3735, ⌐228-4977)*, a large complex located on the shores of Lac Masson, guests can enjoy a variety of water sports and diverse athletic activities such as tennis, golf and cross-country skiing. The accent is placed mainly on these activities; the rooms, although comfortable, are decorated with outmoded colours.

Val-Morin

Making the most of its extensive grounds, the **Far Hills** *($200 ½b; ≈, ◇, ℜ, ㅅ; Far Hills; ☎819-866-2219 or from Montréal 990-4409, ⌐322-1995)* has an extremely peaceful country setting. Its clientele includes cross-country skiers, who come to enjoy over 100 kilometres of trails. Not only are the rooms adorable, but the hotel also has a very good restaurant.

Val-David

The **Chalet Beaumont** *($23 per person sb, $26 per person pb; K; 1451 Beaumont, J0T 2N0, ☎819-322-1972; from the bus stop, take Rue de l'Eglise across the village to Rue Beaumont and turn left; it's about a 2-km walk)*, located in a peaceful mountain setting, is one of only two youth hostels in the Laurentians. A log building with two fireplaces, it's a very appealing, comfortable place. The Chalet Beaumont is an excellent option for outdoor enthusiasts on a tight budget. It is wise to ask who you'll be sharing a room with, as groups of young students often stay here on field trips to Val-David.

The *gîte* **Le Temps des Cerises** *($53 sb, $64 pb, bkfst incl.; Chemin de la Sapinière, ☎819-322-1751, ⌐322-3279)* is a good choice for travellers. The people who run it are very friendly, which makes for a pleasant stay. The rooms are beautifully decorated, and each has a distinctive charm about it.

The comfortable **Auberge du Vieux Foyer** *($194 ½b; ⊛, ℜ, ≈, ㅅ; 3167 R.R. 1, J0T 2N0, ☎819-322-2686 or 1-800-567-8327, ⌐322-2687)* is ideal for travellers looking for a peaceful getaway. The service is impeccable, the rooms are comfortable and the food is highly rated. Guests can borrow bicycles.

La Sapinière *($250 ½b; ≈, ≡, tv, ℜ, ㅅ; 1244 Chemin de la Sapinière, J0T 2N0, ☎819-322-2020 or 1-800-567-6635, ⌐322-6510)*, in a rustic log building, is far from luxurious. The rooms have nevertheless been entirely renovated. The hotel is therefore a comfortable place to stop during a tour of the region, especially thanks to its beautiful location.

Sainte-Agathe-des-Monts

The **Auberge La Caravelle** *($65-$125 bkfst incl.; pb, tv, ≈; 92 Rue Major, J8C 1G1, ☎819-326-4272 or 800-661-4272, ⌐819-326-0818)*, a pretty blue and red house, defines itself as a "small, romantic inn". Appropriately, it is surrounded by a lovely garden full of flowers. Furthermore, half of its 16 rooms, including the bridal suite, are equipped with a whirlpool bath. The inn also has bicycles for its guests.

The **Auberge La Saint-Venant** *($85-130 bkfst incl.; pb, tv; 234 Rue Saint-Venant, J8C 2Z7, ☎819-326-7937, 1-800-697-7937 or 819-326-4848)* is one of the best-kept secrets in Sainte-Agathe. A big, beautiful, yellow house perched atop a hill, it has nine large, tastefully decorated rooms whose big windows let lots of light flood in. The service is friendly yet discreet.

The **Auberge La Calèche** *($110-$240; pb, ≈, ℜ; 125 Rue du Tour du Lac, J8C 1B4, ☎819-326-3753 or 1-800-567-6700)* has built itself a solid reputation over the years. A large inn with some 70 comfortable rooms, it is located a short distance from the village, on Lac des Sables.

Lac-Supérieur

There is a good B&B in Lac-Supérieur: **Chez Nor-Lou** *($50-$60 bkfst incl.; 803 Chemin Lac à l'Équerre, J0T 1J0, ☎819-688-3128)*, a lovely house with a pretty little river winding across its grounds. Three rooms are available.

A peaceful atmosphere and a warm welcome are guaranteed here.

The **Base de Plein Air le P'tit Bonheur** *($314 fb for 2 nights; ℜ; 1400 Chemin du Lac Quenouille, Lac-Supérieur, JOT 1P0, ☎819-326-4281, ⋍326-9516)* is nothing less than an institution in the Laurentians. Once a children's summer camp, it now caters to families looking to take an "outdoor vacation". Set on a vast piece of property on the shores of a lake, right in the heart of the forest, there are four buildings containing a total of nearly 450 beds, most in dormitories. About 20 of the beds are in separate rooms, each equipped with a private bathroom and able to accommodate up to four people. Of course, this is the perfect place to enjoy all sorts of outdoor activities: sailing, hiking, cross-country skiing, skating, etc.

Mont-Tremblant Resort

The prestigious, international Marriot chain has also joined the action at Tremblant, with its **Marriott Residence Inn** *($109-$229; pb, ≡, ≈, ℜ, ☺, tv, K; 170 Chemin Curé-Deslauriers, JOT 1Z0, ☎819-681-4000, ⋍681-4099)*, a large building located right at the start of the village. The place rents out studios and one- or two-bedroom apartments, each equipped with a kitchenette. Some units even have a fireplace.

Overlooking the village, the Mont-Tremblant, the **Château Mont Tremblant** *($135-$199; pb, ≡, ≈, ℜ, ◻, ☺, tv; 3045 Chemin Principal, JOT 1Z0, ☎819-681-7000, ⋍681-7099)* is one of only two additions to have been made to the prestigious Canadian Pacific hotel chain in a century, the other being located in Whistler, British Columbia. This imposing 316-room hotel manages to combine a genuine rustic warmth, well-suited to the surroundings, with all the comforts one expects from a top-flight establishment. It also houses a large convention centre and numerous conference rooms.

The **Station Touristique du Mont-Tremblant** *($99-$279; ☎819-681-3000 or 1-800-461-8711, ⋍681-5999)* manages a whole assortment of lodgings directly. Visitors may rent a room or an apartment in the **Kandahar** complex *($99-$238; pb, ≡, ≈, ◻, tv, K)*, located near a pond in the "Vieux-

Tremblant" area, or in the luxurious **Deslauriers**, **Saint-Bernard** and **Johanssen** *($99-$279; pb, tv, ≡, K)* complexes, which all face onto Place Saint-Bernard. Families will be better off with a fully equipped condo in **La Chouette** *($92-$130)*. These units are small but flooded with natural light. What's more, they offer excellent value for the money, making them an option well worth considering in this area.

Mont-Tremblant Village

The **Auberge de Jeunesse Mont-Tremblant** *($15.50; sb, ℜ; 2213 Chemin Principal, P.O. Box 1001, JOT 1Z0, ☎819-425-6008, ⋍425-3760)* youth hostel opened in the fall of 1997. Formerly the L'Escapade hotel, it has 84 beds in dormitories. The common areas include a kitchen, a café/bar/restaurant and a living room with a fireplace.

There are nearly 600 campsites in the Diable sector of **Parc du Mont-Tremblant** *($21; ☎819-688-2281)*. Restrooms and showers.

On the first floor of the **Hôtel Mont Tremblant** *($60, $90 with ≡, bkfst incl.; 1900 Chemin Principale, JOT 1Z0, ☎819-425-3232, ⋍425-9755)*, visitors will find a bar; and on the second, rooms that are modest but satisfactory given the price and the location—all in the heart of the village, near the ski resort.

The **Auberge Sauvignon** *($80 bkfst incl.; ≡; 2723 Chemin Principal, JOT 1Z0, ☎819-425-5466, ⋍425-9260)* is a refreshing alternative to the gigantic hotels of Mont-Tremblant. Its seven rooms are attractively decorated, and the service is highly personalized.

The **Auberge de la Porte Rouge** *($82, $124 ½b; tv, ℜ, ≡; C.P., JOT 1Z0, ☎819-425-3505)* is a motel-style outfit. The rooms are simple but comfortable and offer a pretty view of the lake.

The **Villa Bellevue** *($49, $120 ½b; ≈, ≡, ◻, ☺, ℜ, ♿; 845 Chemin Principal, Lac Ouimet, JOT 1Z0; ☎819-425-2734 or 1-800-567-6763, ≡425-9360)* is a vast hotel complex with over 100 rooms. A pleasant place to relax, where guests can enjoy all sorts of athletic activities, it has extensive facilities and offers skiing and golf packages. The Villa places more of an emphasis on the activities than the decor, which is a little austere.

The **Auberge Gray Rocks** *($240 ½b; ≈, =, ℛ, △, ☉, tv, ♿; Route 327, J0T 2H0, ☎819-425-2771 or 1-800-567-6767, ◷425-3474)* also offers a range of activities and facilities, aiming to satisfy vacationers' every desire. Particular care has been taken to provide guests with the widest range of activities possible.

 At the **Club Mont-Tremblant** *($300; ≈, =, △, ☉, tv, ℛ, ♿, K; Avenue Cuttles, J0T 1Z0, ☎819-425-2731 or 1-800-567-8341, ◷425-5617)*, guests are offered the choice of renting a very functional, well-equipped condo or a conventional room. The vast peaceful site is perfect for outdoorsy types (Parc du Mont-Tremblant is right nearby), as well as those who prefer to relax far from the city in a beautiful natural setting.

Labelle

La Cloche de Vert *($55 sb, $65 pb, bkfst incl.; 1080 Chemin Saindon, J0T 1H0, ☎819-686-5850)* is an excellent choice compared to the local motels. Located in the heart of the countryside, it is just the place for travellers looking for a peaceful atmosphere and attentive service at affordable rates.

✕ RESTAURANTS

Tour A: Lac des Deux-Montagnes

Deux-Montagnes

Les Petits Fils d'Alice *($$$; closed Mon and Tue; 1506 Chemin d'Oka, ☎450-491-0653)* serves fine French cuisine in a pleasant, intimate setting. During summer, you can eat outside on the terrace.

Oka

La Petite Maison d'Oka *($$$-$$$$; closed Mon and Tue; 85 Rue Notre-Dame, ☎450-479-6882)* is an excellent choice for anyone looking for fine French cuisine and an unpretentious atmosphere.

The brand-new **Restaurant Chez Régnier** *($$$-$$$$; closed Mon and Tue; 261 Rue des Anges, ☎450-479-9957)*, which specializes in regional cuisine, surprises a lot of people. The atmosphere is somewhat cold, but the service is worthy of the finest dining establishments.

Lachute

 The splendid **Hôtel du Lac Carling** *($$$$; Route 327 Nord, Pine Hill, ☎450-533-9211 or 1-800-661-9211)* (see p 262) has a remarkable restaurant, L'If, located in the rotunda of the main building, looking out onto the lake. Start off your gastronomic experience with a pheasant terrine *en croûte*, served with an apple and cranberry chutney, then continue with a vegetarian specialty like curried rice sautéd in olive oil or boneless free-range quail stuffed with pears and green peppercorns. Luxurious decor. Romantic atmosphere.

Tour B: Cottage Country

Saint-Jérôme

Nestled in a peaceful residential neighbourhood, **La Champenoise** *($$; closed Sun and Mon; 444 Rue du Palais, ☎450-438-2678)* occupies a big, beautiful, white house with a green awning stretching out over its front walk. It serves succulent French cuisine at very reasonable prices. The pastry selection is particularly impressive.

Le Jardin d'Agnès *($$$; 401 Rue Laviolette, ☎450-431-2575)* is set up inside a pretty stone house overlooking the Rivière du Nord. Its four-course table d'hôte is $59.95 for two and includes such promising dishes as breast of chicken with old-fashioned mustard and filet of lamb with basil cream. Waterfront terrace out back.

Saint-Sauveur-des-Monts

Always packed with regulars, the **Vieux Four** *($-$$; 252 Rue Principale, ☎450-227-6060)* owes its popularity to its pasta dishes and delicious pizzas baked in a wood-burning oven. Its pleasant decor makes it a cozy place to go after a day of skiing.

Le Chrysanthème *($$; 173 Rue Principale, ☎450-227-8888)* has a beautiful, spacious outdoor seating area, a wonderful place to dine on a fine summer evening. The restaurant serves authentic Chinese cuisine, making for a nice change of pace in this area.

Moe's *($$; 21 de la Gare, ☎450-227-8803)* is a delicatessen-style restaurant with a varied menu. Big eaters will love the generous portions. The atmosphere is noisy, but extremely pleasant, making this a good place to enjoy a friendly get-together. The service is occasionally brusque.

The restaurant **La Marmite** *($$-$$$; 314 Rue Principale, ☎450-227-1554)* serves succulent dishes in an extremely pleasant setting. It also has a lovely terrace, which you can enjoy during the summer.

The **Bistro Saint-Sauveur** *($$-$$$; 146 Rue Principale, ☎450-227-1144)* offers its guests delicious bistro-style French cuisine. The attractive decor creates a warm atmosphere perfect for a good meal among friends.

The menu at **Papa Luigi** *($$$; 155 Rue Principale, ☎450-227-5311)* is made up of – you guessed it – Italian specialties, as well as seafood and grill. Set up inside a lovely, blue, wooden house, this restaurant draws big crowds, especially on weekends. Reservations strongly recommended.

Near by, on the other side of the street, you'll see the green house that is home to **Le Mousqueton** *($$$; closed Mon and Tue; 120 Rue Principale, ☎450-227-4330)*. Innovative, contemporary Québec cuisine is served here in a warm, unpretentious atmosphere. Game, fish and even ostrich appear on the menu.

Mont-Rolland

The enchanting natural setting of the **Auberge La Biche au Bois** *($$$$; closed Sun and Mon in winter, Mon in summer; 1806 Route 117, ☎450-229-8064)* on the banks of the Rivière Simon is sure to give you an appetite. The menu is made up of Québec and French specialties like duck with Québec blueberries, veal Roquefort and smoked salmon with eggplant. Romantic ambiance.

Sainte-Adèle

There are several small restaurants on the little road leading to the Chanteclerc. The most appealing is **La Scala** *($$; closed Mon and Tue; 1241 Chemin Chanteclerc, ☎450-229-7453)*. Guests can sit in the cozy, inviting dining room or, weather permitting, outside on the shady terrace, which offers a lovely view of Lac Rond. The menu is made up of Italian and French specialties. The lamb tenderloin is a tried and true favourite.

At **La Chitarra** *($$-$$$; 140 Rue Morin, on the south side, at the corner of Rue Ouimet, at the top of the hill; ☎450-229-6904)*, guests can savour French and Italian specialties. The pasta, meat and fish dishes are always excellent. However, the desserts are occasionally disappointing. This is a good restaurant to keep in mind when visiting Sainte-Adèle. Reservations are recommended.

The **Clef des Champs** *($$$$; 875 Chemin Sainte-Marguerite; ☎450-229-2857)* serves French cuisine fit for even the most delicate palate. The warmly decorated dining room is just right for an intimate dinner for two. The wine cellar is excellent.

One of the finest restaurants not only in the Laurentians but in all of Québec can be found at the hotel **L'Eau à la Bouche** *($$$$; 3003 Boulevard Sainte-Adèle, ☎450-229-2991)*. Chef Anne Desjardins takes pride in outdoing herself day after day, serving her clientele outstanding French cuisine made with local ingredients. Her Abitibi trout, Atlantic salmon and Far North caribou all bear witness to her exceptional finesse. Two menus, one with three courses, the other with six, are offered each evening. Excellent wine list. An unforgettable gastronomic experience!

Sainte-Marguerite-du-Lac-Masson

Don't be put off by the uninspired exterior of the **Bistro à Champlain** *($$$$; closed Fri and Sat in winter; 75 Chemin Masson, ☎450-228-4988)*, in Sainte-Marguerite-du-Lac-Masson. The place is actually one of the best restaurants in the Laurentians. It serves excellent nouvelle cuisine made with fresh local ingredients. The interior is absolutely extraordinary – a veritable art gallery, where you can admire a number of paintings by Jean-Paul Riopelle, a close friend of the owner's, as well as works by other artists like Joan Mitchell and Louise Prescott. The restaurant also boasts one of the province's most highly reputed wine cellars, which may be toured by appointment. Everyone can sample some of the wines in this impressive stock, since even the finest are available by the glass.

Val-Morin

The **Hôtel Far Hills** *($$$$; Rue Far Hills, ☎819-322-2014 or from Montréal 990-4409)* still has one of the finest restaurants in the Laurentians. The gourmet cuisine is positively world-class. Make sure to try the salmon *aux herbes folles du jardin* (with homegrown wild grasses), a sheer delight.

Val-David

Le Nouveau Continent *($-$$; 2301 Rue de l'Église; ☎819-322-6702)* serves simple, inexpensive food. The restaurant doubles as an exhibition space, so the interior is decorated with works of art. It is a meeting place for artists.

The French restaurant **Le Grand Pa** *($$; 2481 Rue de l'Église, ☎819-322-3104)* is a very simple place with a homey atmosphere. On some evenings, the owner takes the time to play a few tunes on his guitar.

The restaurant in **La Sapinière** *($$$; 1244 Chemin La Sapinière, ☎819-322-2020)* (see p 264) has been striving for over 60 years now to concoct creative dishes inspired by the culinary repertoires of both Québec and France. Among the house specialties, the *lapereau* (young rabbit), *porcelet* (piglet) and the gingerbread are particularly noteworthy, and the *tarte au sucre à la crème* (sugar pie) is an absolute must. Very good wine list.

Sainte-Agathe-des-Monts

The **Intimi-Thé** *($; 84 Rue Principale, ☎819-326-7055)* is a charming little tea room with a small terrace perfect for relaxing and people-watching.

At the restaurant **Le Havre des Poètes** *($$; 55 Rue Vincent, ☎819-326-8731)*, singers perform French and Québec classics. The food is well-rated, but people come here mainly for the ambiance.

Installed in a little building, the **Quimperlaise** *($$; 11 Tour du Lac, ☎819-326-1776)* specializes in Breton dishes, especially crepes filled with a wide variety of ingredients. The decor is charming; the atmosphere relaxed.

Chatel Vienna *($$-$$$; closed Tue; 6 Sainte-Lucie; ☎819-326-1485)* occupies a lovely period residence set on a little hill in front of Lac des Sables. While taking in the lovely view, guests savour Austrian dishes that are nourishing without being heavy. In the summer, the meal starts with a short cruise and cocktails on the lake.

At the restaurant **Chez Girard** *($$$-$$$$; 18 Rue Principale Ouest; ☎819-326-0922)*, set back a little from the road and not far from Lac des Sables, guests can enjoy delicious French cuisine in an extremely pleasant setting. It has two floors, the first being the noisiest.

Sauvagine *($$$$; 1592 Route 329 Nord, ☎819-326-7673)* is a French restaurant cleverly set up inside what used to be the chapel of a convent. Extremely well thought out, it is decorated with large pieces of period furniture.

Saint-Jovite

Le Brunch Café *($; 816 Rue Ouimet; ☎819-425-8233)* serves simple cuisine and mouth-watering desserts. The atmosphere is pleasant, despite the noisy radio, which would be better off forgotten in these enchanting surroundings.

Le Montagnard *($; 816 Rue Ouimet, Le Petit Hameau, ☎819-425-8987)* is just the spot for a tasty pastry and a good cup of tea. The service is courteous and the ambiance, charming.

The **Bagatelle Saloon** *($$; 852 Rue Ouimet, ☎819-425-5323)* is the place to go for a good steak or seafood in Saint-Jovite. As you may have guessed by the name, the decor will transport you straight to the Far West.

Antipasto *($$-$$$; 855 Rue Ouimet, ☎819-425-7580)*, set up inside a former train station, is a good place to stop for a bite. The walls are adorned with pictures and signs that bear witness to the building's original purpose. The mouthwatering menu consists mainly of pizza, pasta and veal dishes.

🦫 **La Table Enchantée** *($$-$$$; from 5pm on, closed Mon; 600 Route 117 Nord, ☎819-425-7113)*, an inviting place with an understated decor, serves delectable Québec specialties. The chef does wonders with the *cipaille* and venison, among others.

Mont-Tremblant Resort

At the **Crêperie Catherine** *($-$$; 3005 Chemin Principal, Vieux-Tremblant, ☎819-681-4888)*, you can savour an excellent selection of crêpes, which the chef prepares right before your eyes. During summer, you can sit outside on the pretty terrace.

During summer, you can take in the action on the pedestrian street from the lovely outdoor seating area of the **Microbrasserie de la Diable** *($$; 3005 Chemin Principal, ☎819-681-4546)*. The interior, with tables set up on two floors, is a lot bigger than you'd think. Here, people tuck into spare ribs, sausages and smoked meats, washed down with one of the beers brewed on the premises, such as Extrême Onction, which has an 8.5% alcohol content.

The overloaded decor of **Le Shack** *($$; 3035 Chemin Principal, ☎819-681-4700)*, which parodies a traditional sugar shack with its rustic furniture, artificial maple trees with the red leaves of an Indian summer, and wild geese hanging from the ceiling, is sure to bring a smile to your face. The place is located at the top of the village in the resort near the Château Mont-Tremblant. Its big outdoor seating area, which is very popular in the summertime, looks out onto Place Saint-Bernard. The menu features simple fare like steak, roast chicken and burgers. Le Shack also has a morning buffet, where you can concoct a copious breakfast for yourself.

In an old U-shaped house in Vieux-Tremblant, slightly removed from all the hubbub, **La Savoie** *($$$; Vieux-Tremblant, ☎819-681-4573)* serves *raclettes*, *pierrades*, fondues and other Alpine specialties. Small outdoor seating area. Simple, pleasant atmosphere.

Aux Truffes *($$$$; 3035 Chemin Principal, ☎819-425-4544)* is the best restaurant in the Mont-Tremblant resort. In an inviting modern decor, guests dine on succulent nouvelle cuisine. Truffles, foie gras and game are among the predominant ingredients.

🦫 **La Légende** *($$$$; closed May and from Oct 15 to Nov 15; Mont Tremblant, ☎819-681-3000 or 1-800-461-8711, ext. 5500)* is a gourmet restaurant located at the top of Mont Tremblant in the Grand-Manitou complex, which also has a cafeteria. Of course, the spectacular view of the area is the main attraction. Don't underestimate the restaurant's Québec cuisine, though; game, fish, veal, beef and pork are all prepared with a great deal of finesse here. Outdoor seating available.

Mont-Tremblant Village

🦫 The magnificent dining room of the **Club Tremblant** *($$$$; Avenue Cuttles, ☎819-425-2731)* (see p 266) offers a panoramic view of the lake and Mont Tremblant. The chef prepares traditional French gastronomic cuisine. On Thursday and Saturday nights, the restaurant serves a lavish buffet. The Sunday brunch is also very popular. Reservations strongly recommended.

ENTERTAINMENT

Bars and Nightclubs

Saint-Sauveur-des-Monts

The bar **Les Vieilles Portes** *(Rue Principale)* is a nice place to get together with friends for a drink. It has a pleasant outdoor terrace which is open during the summer.

Bentley's *(235 Rue Principale)* is often full of young people, who come here to have a drink before going out dancing.

Mont-Rolland

Bourbon Street *(Route 117, Mont-Rolland)* hosts good live music and is frequented by a relatively young clientele.

Mont-Tremblant Resort

The **Petit Caribou** is a young, energetic bar that really fills up after a good day of skiing.

LAURENTIDES

Theatres

There is a real tradition of summer theatre in the Laurentians. A number of well-known, well-loved theatres present quality productions throughout the season. These include the **Théâtre Saint-Sauveur** *(22 Rue Claude, ☎450-227-8466)*, the **Théâtre le Chanteclerc** *(1474 Chemin du Chanteclerc, Saint-Adèle, ☎450-229-3591)*, **Le Patriote de Sainte-Agathe** *(Rue Saint-Venant, ☎819-326-3655)* and the **Théâtre Sainte-Adèle** *(1069 Boulevard Sainte-Adèle, ☎450-229-7611)*.

Sainte-Adèle

Pavillon des Arts de Sainte-Adèle *(1364 Chemin Sainte-Marguerite, ☎450-229-2586)* is a 210-seat concert hall in a former chapel. Twenty-five classical concerts are presented here annually. Each is followed by a music lover's wine and cheese in the adjoining gallery.

Festivals and Cultural Events

The **Festival des Couleurs** *(☎450-436-8532)* takes place from mid-September to the beginning of October, when the landscape is ablaze with flamboyant colours. Countless family activities are organized in Saint-Sauveur, Sainte-Adèle, Sainte-Marguerite-du-Lac-Masson, Sainte-Adolphe-d'Howard, Sainte-Agathe and Mont-Tremblant to celebrate this time of the year.

Val-Morin

Each year, on the third Sunday in September, the village of Val-Morin is closed off to automobile traffic, and cycling buffs flood into the area. The event in question, known as **Les Couleurs en Vélo** *($13 per person $40 for families of five; participants receive a souvenir t-shirt; in Val-Morin ☎819-322-2150, in Montréal ☎514-279-0060; entry fees go up three weeks prior to event, so register as soon as possible)*, offers a chance to explore this magnificent region while it's decked out in all its autumn finery. There are five routes ranging in length from 25 to 40 kilometres and covering various types of terrain, from flat stretches suitable for beginners and families to mountainous areas for more athletic types looking for a good challenge. The cycling event itself starts at 12:30pm, but scores of other activities are held throughout the day.

Mont-Tremblant Resort

At the beginning of August, blues greats gather at the Mont-Tremblant resort for the **Festival de Blues de Tremblant** *(☎819-681-2000)*. The shows are presented outdoors, as well as in local bars and restaurants.

The **Fête de la Musique** *(☎819-681-2000)*, a classical music festival run by Angèle Dubeau, is held at the Mont-Tremblant resort at the end of August. The concerts are held outdoors and in the Chapelle Saint-Bernard (see p 255).

 SHOPPING

Tour B: Cottage Country

Saint-Sauveur-des-Monts

Visitors will find all sorts of treasures at **La Petite École** *(153 Rue Principale)*, ranging from Christmas decorations to dried flowers, not to mention kitchen utensils and beauty products.

Those in search of all kinds of souvenirs will find just what they're looking for at **L'Art du Souvenir** *(191A Rue Principale)*.

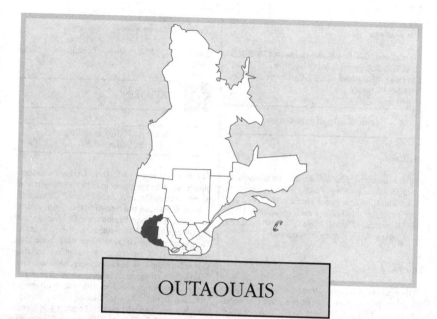

OUTAOUAIS

The Outaouais region, discovered early on by explorers and trappers, was not settled by whites until the arrival of Loyalists from the United States in the early 19th century. Forestry was long the region's main economic activity. Of particular importance to the industry were red and white pine; trees used in ship building. The logs were sent down the Ottawa River and the St-Lawrence to Québec City, where they were loaded onto ships headed for Great Britain. Forestry still plays an important role here, but service industries and government offices are also a major source of jobs, a situation resulting from the proximity of Canada's capital region.

Directly north of the cities of Hull, Gatineau and Aylmer, lies an expanse of rolling hills, lakes and rivers, which includes the magnificent Parc de la Gatineau. The park is the location of the official summer residence of the Canadian Prime Minister and is a wonderful area for bicycling, canoeing and cross-country skiing. The city of Hull, which borders Canada's capital city of Ottawa, has one of the best museums in the country: the Musée Canadien des Civilisations. For its part, Ottawa, just across the river, is home to Canada's beautiful Parliament Buildings and a plethora of excellent museums.

 FINDING YOUR WAY AROUND

Two tours of the region, following Ottawa and Gatineau rivers, respectively are outlined below, Tour A: Ottawa Valley ★ and Tour B: Gatineau Valley ★ (see p 272).

Tour A: Ottawa Valley

By Car

From Montréal, there are two options for reaching the departure point of the tour; one through the valley of the Ottawa River, and a faster way through Ontario.

1. Take Highway 13 N., then Route 344 W., which corresponds to part of the Lac des Deux-Montagnes ★ tour (see p 245). Finally take Route 148 W. toward Ottawa.

2. Take Highway 40 W., which becomes Route 17 W. over the Ontario border. In Hawkesbury, cross the Ottawa River to return to Québec. Turn left on Route 148 W., toward Montebello and Ottawa.

Bus Stations

Montebello: 570 Rue Notre-Dame, ☎423-6900.
Hull: 238 Boulevard Saint-Joseph, ☎771-2442.
Ottawa (Ontario): 265 Catherine Street,
☎613-238-5900.

Tour B: Gatineau Valley

By Car

By car or by bicycle remain the best ways to
tour the whole valley. Follow Pormenade de la
Gatineau from Boulevard Taché in Hull. You will
enter the Parc de la Gatineau, created in 1938
by Canadian Prime Minister William Lyon
Mackenzie King, almost immediately.

By Train

The small Hull-Chelsea-Wakefield steam train is
a great way to see part of the rural Gatineau
valley. The 32-kilometre trip takes
approximately five hours and stops for two
hours in Wakefield. In general however, the
best ways to explore the valley are by car and
bicycle.

 PRACTICAL INFORMATION

Area code: 819

Tourist Information Offices

Regional Office

Association Touristique de l'Outaouais 103 Rue
Laurier, Hull, J8X 3V8, ☎778-2222 or
1-800-265-7822, ☎778-7758,
www.achilles.net/~ato/

Tour A: Ottawa Valley

Montebello: 502-A   Rue   Notre-Dame,
☎423-5602.
Hull: 103 Rue Laurier, ☎778-2222.
Ottawa (Ontario):   14   Rue   Metcalfe,
☎613-239-5000   or   toll   free   at
1-800-465-1867.

Tour B: Gatineau Valley

Maniwaki: 156   Rue   Principale   Sud,
☎449-6291.

 EXPLORING

Tour A: Ottawa Valley
(one to three days)

All that remains of the Ottawa nation,
slaughtered by the Iroquois in the 17th century,
is their name. Ottawa, or in French, Outaouais
is used to denote the beautiful river that forms
the border between Québec and Ontario, a vast
region of lakes and forests, as well as Canada's
capital city. The Ottawa River was once the
main route of fur-trappers travelling to the
Canadian shield. These *voyageurs*, who worked
for large trading companies, used this river
each spring, returning in the fall with their
precious cargo of pelts (beaver, seal, mink),
which were then shipped to London and Paris
from Montréal. This tour includes "National
Capital Region", most of which consists of the
city of Ottawa, in Ontario.

Montebello ★ (pop. 1,050)

The Outaouais region did not experience
significant development under the French
Regime. Located upstream from the Lachine
Rapids, the area was not easily accessible by
water, and was thus left to hunters and
trappers until the early 19th century and the
beginning of the forestry operations. The
Petite-Nation seigneury, granted to
Monseigneur de Laval in 1674, was the only
attempt at colonization in this vast region. Not
until 1801, when the seigneury passed into the
hands of notary Joseph Papineau, was the
town of Montebello established. Papineau's
son, Louis-Joseph Papineau (1786-1871), head
of the French-Canadian nationalist movement in
Montréal, inherited the Petite-Nation seigneury
in 1817. Returning from an eight-year exile in
the United States and France following the
rebellion of 1837-38, disillusioned and
disappointed by the stand taken by the Catholic
clergy during the rebellion, Papineau retired in
Montebello, where he built an impressive
manor.

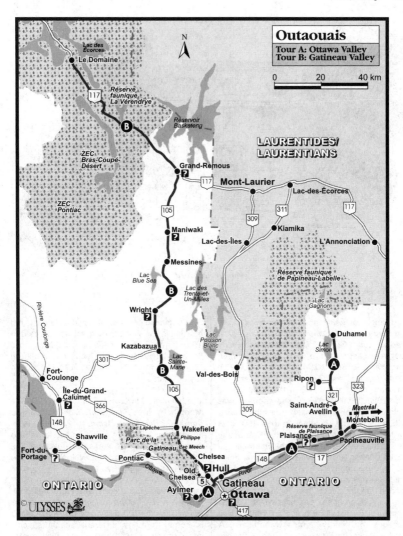

Manoir Papineau

The **Manoir Louis-Joseph-Papineau** ★★ *($3.50; mid-May to mid-Jun and early Sep to mid-Oct, Wed to Sun 10am to 5pm; mid-Jun to early Sep, every day 10am to 6pm; mid-Oct to mid-Nov, Sat and Sun 10am to 5pm; 500 Rue Notre-Dame, ☎423-6965)* was erected between 1846 and 1849 in the monumental neoclassical villa style. The house was designed by Louis Aubertin, a visiting French architect. The towers added in the 1850s give the house a medieval appearance. One of the towers houses a precious library that Papineau placed here to protect it from fire. The house has approximately 20 staterooms, through which visitors can now stroll, and features rich Second Empire decor. It is located on lovely tree-shaded grounds, and is owned by the Canadian Pacific hotel chain, which also manages the nearby Château Montebello. A small wooden walkway leads to the **Chapelle Funéraire des Papineau** (1853), where 11 members of the family are buried. Note that this is an Anglican chapel. Papineau's son joined the Church of England when his father died and was refused a Catholic burial. A bust of the elder Papineau by Napoléon Bourassa made from the funeral mask of the deceased, is one of the interesting objects found in the chapel.

The **Château Montebello** ★★ *(392 Rue Notre-Dame; ☎423-6341)* is a large resort hotel on the Papineau estate. It is the largest log building in the world. The hotel was erected in 1929 (Lawson and Little, architects) in a record 90 days. The impressive lobby has a central fireplace with six-hearths, each facing one of the building's six wings. See also p 282.

The **Centre d'Interprétation de la Gare de Montebello** *(free admission; every day 9am to 6pm; 502 Rue Notre-Dame, ☎423-5602)* is an information centre in the former Montebello train station (1931). A display describes the role of the railway in the development of the Petite-Nation seigneury.

Spread over 1,500 acres, the **Parc Oméga** ★ *($8; every day 10 am to 1 hour before sunset; Route 323, ☎/≈423-5487 or 1-888-423-5487)* is home to many different animal species including bison, wild sheep, elk, wild goats, wild boar and deer.

Route 321 heads north from Papineauville to Duhamel providing access to the Sentier d'Interprétation du Cerf de Virginie see p 280 and the Réserve Faunique Papineau-Labelle see p 281. Continuing east of Papineauville on Route 148, you'll soon reach the Réserve Faunique de Plaisance ★ see p 281 and the Chutes de Plaisance (Rang Malo), see p 281. Continue east on the 148 to Hull.

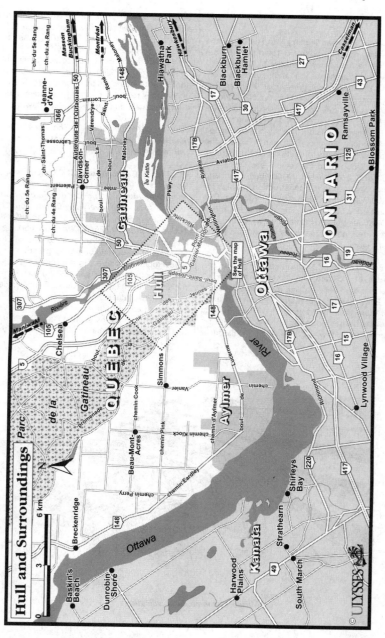

Hull (pop. 65,764)

Although the road leading into Hull is named after an important post-war town planner, the city is certainly not a model of enlightened urban development. It's architecture is very unlike that of Ottawa, just across the river. Hull is a mixture of old factories, typical working-class houses, tall, modern government office buildings, and barren land awaiting future government expansion. The town was founded by American Loyalist Philemon Wright, who introduced forestry operations to the Ottawa Valley. Wood from the region was cut, made into rafts and floated to Québec City, and eventually used in the construction of ships for the British Navy. By 1850, Hull was an important wood processing centre. For many generations the Eddy Company, which is based in the area, has been supplying matches to the entire world.

The modest wood-frame houses that line the streets of Hull are nicknamed "matchboxes" because they once housed many employees of the Eddy match factory, and because they have had more than their fair share of fires. In fact, Hull has burned so many times throughout its history that few of the town's historical buildings remain. The former town hall and beautiful Catholic church burned down in 1971 and 1972, respectively. Ottawa has the reputation of being a quiet city, while Hull is considered more of a fun town, essentially because legal drinking age is a year younger and the bars stay open later in Québec. It is not uncommon to see crowds of Ontarians along the **Promenade du Portage** on Saturday nights.

Turn left onto Rue Papineau. The parking lot of the Musée Canadien des Civilisations is at the end of this street.

The **Musée Canadien des Civilisations** ★★★ *(adults $5, free admission on Sun 9am to noon; May to mid-Oct, every day 9am to 6pm; mid-Oct to late Apr, every day 9am to 5pm; Jul to Sep, Fri to 9pm; open Thu until 9pm all year; 100 Rue Laurier, ☎776-7000)*. Many parks and museums were established along this section of the Québec-Ontario border as part of a large redevelopment program in the National Capital Region between 1983 and 1989. Hull became the site of the magnificent Musée Canadien des Civilisations, dedicated to the history of Canada's various cultural groups. If there is one museum that must be seen in Canada it is this one. Douglas Cardinal of Alberta drew up the

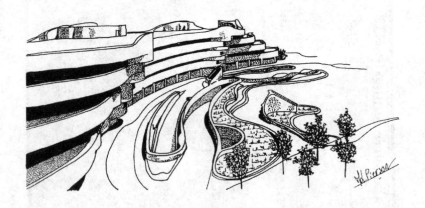

Musée Canadien des Civilisations

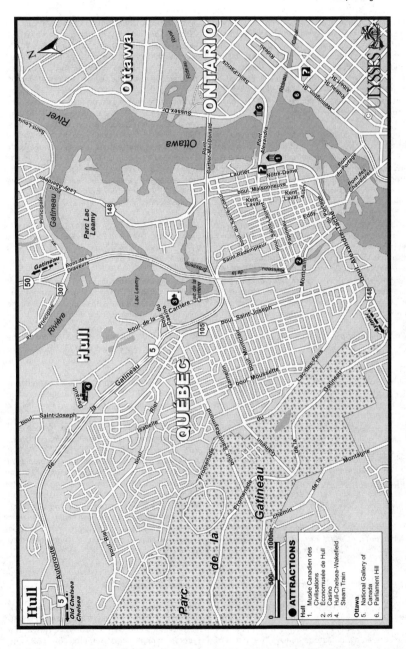

ATTRACTIONS

Hull
1. Musée Canadien des Civilisations
2. Économusée de Hull
3. Casino
4. Hull-Chelsea-Wakefield Steam Train

Ottawa
5. National Gallery of Canada
6. Parliament Hill

plans for the museum's two striking curved buildings, one housing the administrative offices and restoration laboratories, and the other the museum's collections. Their undulating design brings to mind rock formations of the Canadian shield, shaped by wind and glaciers. There is a beautiful view of Ottawa River and Parliament Hill from the grounds behind the museum.

The Grande Gallerie (Great Hall) houses the most extensive collection of native totem poles in the world. Another collection brilliantly recreates different periods in Canadian history, from the arrival of the vikings around 1000 AD to life in rural Ontario in the 19th century and French Acadia in the 17th century. Contemporary native art, as well as popular arts and traditional crafts are also on display. In the Musée des Enfants (Children's Museum), young visitors choose a theme before being led through an extraordinary adventure. Screening rooms have been equipped with OMNIMAX technology, a new system developed by the creators of the large-screen IMAX. Most of the movies shown here deal with Canadian geography.

Continue south on Rue Laurier. At Rue Montcalm, turn right.

The mission of the **Écomusée de Hull** *($5; Apr to Oct 10am to 6pm, Nov to Mar 10am to 4pm; Rue Montcalm, ☎595-7790)* is to make people more aware of ecological issues, and to achieve this goal, it presents various exhibits on themes such as the origin of the solar system and the evolution of planet Earth. This institution, however, goes beyond tracing the origins of life on earth, because it is also home to an insectarium with no less than 4,000 different species of insects. Finally, you can also take a look at a small exhibit on the industrial history of the city.

Take Highway 50, then Highway 5 north to the Boulevard du Casino Exit. Then take Rue Saint-Raymond, which becomes Boulevard du Casino.

The **Casino de Hull** ★★ *(11am to 3am; 1 Boulevard du Casino, ☎1-800-665-2274 or 772-2100)* has an impressive location between two lakes; Leamy Lake, in the park of the same name, and Lac de la Carrière, which is in the basin of an old limestone quarry. The theme of water is omnipresent all around the superb building, inaugurated in 1996. The magnificent walkway leading to the main entrance is dotted

with towering fountains, and the harbour has 20 slips for boaters. The gambling area, which is 2,741 square metres in size, includes 1,300 slot machines and 58 playing tables spread around a simulated tropical forest. Quebec painter Jean-Paul Riopelle's famous 40-metre-long painting, **Hommage à Rosa Luxembourg** ★★★, dominates the room. The artist created this immense triptych in honour of Joan Mitchell, his partner of many years. The opening of the casino also marked the first annual fireworks festival, **Les Grands Feux du Casino** *(☎771-FEUX or 800-771-FEUX)*, which takes place every year in August. The casino has excellent restaurants, including Baccara (see p 284), and two bars (see p 285). The casino opened a heliport in 1997.

If you wish to go to Ottawa, turn right onto Rue Laurier, and head to the Alexandra Bridge, visible from the grounds of the Musée des Civilisations.

Crossing the Ottawa River, visitors enter English-speaking Ontario, the most populous province in Canada, with approximately nine million inhabitants.

You can also continue driving south of the Ottawa River. Take Boulevard de la Carrière to Rue Deveault.

Imagine contemplating the magnificent landscape of Parc de la Gatineau, comfortably seated aboard a steam engine dating back to 1907: **Train à Vapeur Hull-Chelsea-Wakefield** ★ *($26; late May to late Oct, departures Sat to Thu 1:30pm, Fri 10am; 165 Rue Deveault, ☎778-7246, ≈778-5007)*. As well as giving you a chance to see beautiful natural sites, this half-day excursion takes you to Wakefield, a charming little English town, where you have two hours to explore and shop. If you're interested in the trip but don't want to take the train both ways, you can cross Gatineau park on bicycle and return by train. Packages including a meal are also available.

Ottawa (Ontario) ★★★

Canada has one federal capital and 12 provincial or territorial capitals corresponding to 10 provinces and two territories. Ottawa, the federal capital, was founded in 1827 by Colonel By, who first named the city Bytown. Following the 1849 Montreal riots and the lack of consensus on a location for a permanent capital for the British colony, Queen Victoria decided in 1857 to place the seat of the colonial government on the border of anglophone Upper Canada and francophone Lower Canada. Specifically, she chose the small Ontario city of Ottawa, on the Ottawa River. Ten years later, in 1867, the agreement that created the independent Dominion of Canada was finally signed, and the House of Commons sat for the first time in the new Parliament Buildings.

Ottawa has several interesting museums, including the **National Gallery of Canada**, located on the left when coming off the Alexandra Bridge. Also of interest in the city are the Gothic-Revival style buildings on **Parliament Hill** *(Wellington St.)*, and the **Parliament Buildings** dominated by the **Peace Tower**. For more detailed information, consult the *Ulysses Travel Guide Ontario* or the *Ulysses Guide Ottawa*.

Return to Québec over the Pont du Portage, a continuation of Wellington Street. Turn left onto Boulevard Alexandre-Taché toward Aylmer (Route 148 W.). The Eddy factory can be seen on the left. Further down on the right is Promenade de la Gatineau, the starting point for the Gatineau Valley tour (see below).

Aylmer ★ (pop. 34,927)

Aylmer was once the administrative centre of the Outaouais region. The city was founded by Charles Symmes, an American from Boston who arrived in Canada in 1814. The Hudson's Bay Company, then a major player in the fur trade, centered its activities in this region. Today, Aylmer, with its residential streets lined with middle-class homes, is a suburb of Ottawa.

Prompted by his uncle, Philemon Wright, Charles Symmes settled in the Aylmer region in 1824. In 1830, he built the **old Symmes inn ★** *(1 Rue Front, ☎685-5033)*, which became very popular with fur-trappers heading out on the Canadian Shield. The building, which has been completely restored, shows how widespread the urban architectural styles of the French Regime had become, even among Americans like Symmes. The inn thus features a raised ground floor, a covered porch, extended drip mouldings on the roof, imposing chimney stacks and the fieldstone walls and casement windows typical of traditional Québec houses. Perhaps Symmes had the inn built this way for

purely commercial reasons, to appeal to a predominantly French Canadian clientele.

Tour B: Gatineau Valley ★ (one day)

The Gatineau Valley runs perpendicular to the Ottawa Valley. The Algonquins who once lived in the region were heavily involved in the fur trade with the French and later the English of the Hudson's Bay Company, before being driven out of the area by increasing development in the 19th century. Today the valley is a peaceful rural region dotted with villages founded by American Loyalists and Scottish settlers. The architecture, influenced by that of nearby Ontario, is characterized by simple neoclassical buildings built between 1830-1860. The forestry industry plays a significant role in the valley's economy, particularly farther north. At one time, wood was sent floating to Hull on the Rivière Gatineau.

Parc de la Gatineau

Parc de la Gatineau ★ (see p 281) is the starting point for this tour. The park, established in 1934, is an area of rolling hills, lakes and rivers, that measures more than 35,000 hectares.

To get to the Parc de la Gatineau Visitor Centre from Hull, take Highway 5 N. to Exit 12. Turn left and follow the road signs. For the Domaine Mackenzie King, take Chemin Kingsmere heading west, and turn left onto Rue Barnes.

The **Domaine Mackenzie-King ★★** *($6 for parking; mid-May to mid-Jun, Wed to Sun 11am to 5pm; mid-Jun to mid-Oct, 11am to 5pm; Rue Barnes in Kingsmere, Parc de la Gatineau, ☎613-239-5000 and 827-2020)*. William Lyon Mackenzie King was Prime Minister of Canada from 1921 to 1930, and again from 1935 to 1948. His love of art and horticulture rivalled his interest in politics and he was always happy to get away to his summer residence near Lac Kingsmere, which today is part of Parc de la Gatineau. The estate consists of two houses (one of which is now a charming tea room), a landscaped garden and follies, false ruins that were popular at the time. However unlike most follies, which were designed to imitate ruins, those on the Mackenzie-King estate are authentic building fragments. For the most part, they were

OUTAOUAIS

The *Coureurs des Bois*

The *coureur des bois* is a legendary figure in Québec culture. When the colony was first established, Champlain left a young man named Étienne Brûlé here. Brûlé learned the language of the Algonquins and travelled inland. In those days, men like him — who were in some way a gauge of the impact, be it positive or negative, that the French had on the natives — were known as *truchements*. Upon his return, Champlain found Brûlé dressed like the natives and completely sold on their way of life. The *truchements* originally adopted the native lifestyle for economic reasons, as they did not want to offend their hosts and thus imperil the fur trade. However, as the months went by, they discovered that the natives' daily routines were in direct response to the environment. They thus learned to eat corn, wear snowshoes and use bark canoes. They also started using toboggans to carry their cargo. Removed from Church and State as they were, however, these *truchements* did have a tendency to let themselves go altogether, and their unfettered liberty led to some rather dubious practices. This side of their life is clearly exemplified by Étienne Brûlé's death; he was killed and eaten by the Hurons, with whom he had lived for a long time.

With time, the *truchements*' reputation improved, thanks in large part to the wisdom of a number of men who played a crucial role in the development of the new colony. *Truchements* became *coureurs des bois*. The two most illustrious figures of this new generation were Médard Chouart, Sieur Des Groseillers, and Pierre-Esprit Radisson. Thanks to their bravery and ingenuity, these men managed to establish ties with the natives. Radisson learned the ropes by being captured, tortured and then finally adopted by the Iroquois. He even joined them on an expedition, wielding a tomahawk and returning with scalps and prisoners in the purest Iroquois tradition.

Des Groseilliers and Radisson extended the fur-trading routes as far as Lakes Michigan and Superior, where they set up trading posts. In 1654, the governor established a permit system for the fur trade, thus putting an end to their plans to push on past the Great Lakes, where the natives hunted. In 1661, Des Groseilliers and Radisson were unable to reach an agreement with the governor and ran off without an official permit. They returned two years later with a sizeable load of furs, having learned of a land route to Hudson Bay. They were expecting to be welcomed as pioneers, but instead found themselves faced with a fine. Refusing to hang their heads, these two proud he-men switched over to the English camp and helped found the Hudson's Bay Company, a move that revived the negative image of the *coureurs des bois*.

Be that as it may, these *truchements*-turned-*coureurs-des-bois* were the still the first Europeans to adopt and understand the traditional native way of life. They chose this lifestyle because it corresponded to the geographic, climatic, economic and sociological conditions in the New World. Their behaviour may not always have been exemplary, and some of them were veritable sex fiends, but they nevertheless played a crucial role in Canada's development by serving as link between the European and native cultures.

---

taken from the original Canadian House of Parliament, destroyed by fire in 1916, and from Westminister Palace, damaged by German bombs in 1941.

Return to Chemin Kinsmere and head east to Old Chelsea, where the Parc de la Gatineau Visitor Centre is located.

Beyond the park, Route 105 cuts a path through mountains and forests all the way to the 117 at Grand-Remous. The 117 leads eventually to the **Réserve Faunique La Vérendrye ★***, see p below.*

 PARKS

Tour A: Ottawa Valley

The 26-kilometre long **Sentier d'Interprétation du Cerf de Virginie** *(Dec 1st to Mar 31st; Route 321, ☎428-7089)* is a trail that crosses an area frequented by white-tailed deer, called *cerf de Virginie* in French, during the winter. The trails are open to hikers, snowshoers and cross-country skiers and allows visitors to observe these graceful animals. Fed by the inhabitants of Duhamel, the deer come here every year. The herd is estimated to number approximately 3,000.

Located in both the Laurentians and Outaouais regions, the **Réserve Faunique Papineau-Labelle** *(mid may to Nov; 443 Route 309, Val-des-Bois; accessible from Route 311 coming from Kiamika, from Route 321 coming from Lac-Nominingue, or from Route 117 coming from La Minerve;* ☎454-2013*)* stretches over almost 1,600 square kilometres of land and is home to a multitude of animals, including deer and moose. Hunting and fishing are permitted, and the hiking trails are well maintained. Canoe-camping enthusiasts can plan long trips here, though these usually require many portages. Long cross country ski trails (100 kilometres) are also maintained, and skiers can stay in the huts along the way *($17.50 per person per day)*. Approximately 120 kilometres of snowmobile trails crisscross the reserve.

The **Réserve Faunique de Plaisance** ★ *(Route 148, Chemin de la Presqu'île,* ☎772-3434*)* is one of the smallest reserves in Québec. It borders the Ottawa River for some 27 kilometres and has a mandate to introduce visitors to the animal and plant life of the region. To better observe birds and aquatic plants, wooden footbridges have been built above the marshes along the river. The reserve can also be explored by canoe, bicycle or hiking trails. Excursions guided by naturalists are also organized.

During the eighties, the former village of North Nation Mills was the site of several archeological digs. Nearby are the magnificent **Chutes de Plaisance** *($2.50 summer 10am to 6pm; spring and fall, weekends; free admission at other times; Rang Malo,* ☎427-6400*)*. This is a perfect area for picnics and hikes.

Tour B: Gatineau Valley

Parc de la Gatineau ★ *(visitor centre is located in Chelsea, also accessible via Boulevard Taché in Hull;* ☎827-2020*)* is not far from downtown Hull. The 35,000 hectare park was founded during the Depression in 1934 in order to protect the forests from people looking for firewood. It is crossed by a 34 kilometre long road dotted with panoramic lookout points, including as **Belvédère Champlain**, which offer superb views of the lakes, rivers and hills of the region. Outdoor activities can be enjoyed here throughout the year. Hiking and mountain biking trails are open during the summer. There are many lakes in the park, including Lac Meech, which was also the name of a Canadian constitutional agreement drawn up nearby but never ratified. Watersports such as windsurfing, canoeing and swimming are also very popular and the park rents small boats and camp sites. **Lusk Cave**, formed some 12,500 years ago by water flowing from melting glaciers can be explored. During the winter, approximately 190 kilometres of cross-country skiing trails are maintained *(approx. $7 per day)*. **Camp Fortune** *(*☎827-1717*)* has 19 downhill skiing runs, 14 are open at night. It costs $24 during the day and $20 at night.

To the north of the Outaouais is the **Réserve Faunique La Vérendrye** ★ *(Route 117,* ☎438-2017*)*, a vast area measuring more than 13,000 square kilometres. The many rivers threading their way through the region are popular canoe-camping destinations. However, the area is flat, so the scenery can sometimes become monotonous. Hiking trails have been cleared and abundant wildlife makes the reserve a paradise for hunters and fishers. The park is open only during the summer.

 OUTDOORS

 Hiking

Parc de la **Gatineau** *(*☎827-2020*)* offers a great number of hiking trails, over 125 kilometres in all, and just as many chances to discover its beauty. You can explore Lac Pink, a beautiful but polluted lake (you can't swim in it), on a 1.4-kilometres-trail. If you prefer splendid panoramic views, choose Mont-King, a 2.5-kilometre-long trail that leads you to the summit and to gorgeous views of the Ottawa River Valley. And finally, if you have a bit more time and are interested in a fascinating excursion, the Lusk Cave trail is 10.5 kilometres long and leads to 12,500-year-old marble cave.

At 1,628 square kilometres, the immense **Réserve Faunique Papineau-Labelle** *(Route 309, Val-des-Bois,* ☎454-2013*)* is a veritable outdoor paradise. To allow you to appreciate the beauty of this untamed territory, there are hiking trails that lead into the depths of the forest.

Walking tours through marshlands have been arranged at **Réserve Faunique de Plaisance** (☎427-5334) (see p 281) to help people understand the significant role that these wetlands play in maintaining an ecological balance. The one-kilometre-long path, La zizanie des Marais, is fully accessible and particularly captivating. It leads to the heart of the marsh, by way of wooden footbridges that pass over Baie de la Petite Presqu'île. In addition to being located in an extremely captivating landscape, the route is instructive; signs with a wealth of information on various aspects of the wildlife have been posted along the way. Many species of birds can be observed, including notably, wild geese that stop here in great numbers during spring migration. Mammals, such as beavers and muskrats also inhabit the region.

Canoeing

Canoeing is both a unique and pleasant way to contemplate the magnificent landscape of the Outaouais. **Trailhead** (1960 Rue Scott, ☎613-722-4229 or 1-800-574-8375), a company located in Ottawa, organizes single-day canoe trips and longer excursions in Gatineau park. These tours are guided, thereby allowing you to head deep into the forest in complete safety.

Expédition Eau Vive (868 Route 105, Chelsea, ☎827-4341, www.orbit.qc.ca/canoe) organizes trips on the rivers of the Outaouais for people who are completely inexperienced but still dream of canoe-tripping. More accomplished canoeists can choose a seven- to fifteen-day trips.

Cross-country Skiing

In winter, when there's a thick layer of snow, **Parc de la Gatineau** maintains no less than 200 kilometres of cross-country ski trails. These trails, 47 in all, are sure to delight skiers of all levels.

Bolder skiers who dream of going deep into the woods, far away from any signs of civilization, will find what they're looking for at the **Réserve Faunique Papineau-Labelle** ($5 per day; $8 for overnite cabins; ☎454-2013): namely a hundred-kilometre-long ski trail. There are heated cabins all along the route. Definitely a memorable adventure but only for experienced skiers.

Snowmobiling

In Duhamel, at **Marine Sport Duhamel** (☎428-3366), you can rent snowmobiles and find the necessary accessories for snowmobile trips through the Réserve Faunique Papineau-Labelle.

Dogsledding

To experience the exhilaration of mushing a team of dogs through the Gatineau woods contact **Activec** ($25; ☎771-8500). Although somewhat physically demanding, the experience is sure to be memorable.

ACCOMMODATIONS

Tour A: Ottawa Valley

Montebello

If the idea of staying in an ancestral home (1853) tickles your fancy, the B&B **Au Fil des Ans** ($55 sb, $65 pb, bkfst incl.; 228 Duquette, Papineauville, J0V 1R0, ☎427-5167) is the best option in this area - for both you and your wallet! This wooden house, which has been renovated in keeping with the style of days gone by, has five rooms, including one with a private bath. Guests also have access to a sitting room, the only place where smoking is permitted. The generous breakfasts are served in a solarium flooded with light.

Christened the **Château Montebello** ($145; ℜ, ≈, ⊙, △, ⅙; 392 Rue Notre-Dame; ☎423-6341 or 1-800-268-9411, ⌐423-5283), this beautiful pine and cedar building stands next to Ottawa River. It is the largest log building in the world and is equipped with several facilities including an indoor and outdoor swimming pool, squash courts and an exercise room.

Ulysses' Favourites

Accommodations

For tranquillity:
Château Montebello (p 282)

Restaurants

The region's grand tables:
Baccara (p 284), Café Henry Burger (p 284), Orée du Bois (p 284) and Table de Pierre Delahaye (p 284).

For the terrace:
Twist (p 283)

For Québec cuisine:
Soupière (p 283), Baccara (p 284)

Hull

The **Auberge de la Gare** *($74 bkfst incl.; 205 Boulevard St-Joseph, J8Y 3X3, ☎778-8085 or 773-4273, ≈595-2021)* is a simple, conventional hotel that offers good value for your money. The service is both courteous and friendly, and the rooms are clean and well kept, albeit nondescript.

The small, austere lobby of the **Hôtel Best Western** *($79; ≈, ℜ; 131 Rue Laurier, J8X 3W3, ☎770-8550 or 1-800-265-8550)* is hardly inviting. The rooms, decorated with modern furniture, are neither cozy nor luxurious but nonetheless comfortable.

The **Hôtel Ramada Plaza** *($83; ℜ, ≈, ♿; 35 Rue Laurier, J9Y 4E9, ☎778-6111 or 1-800-567-9607, ≈778-8548)* is located opposite the Musée des Civilisations. It is a simple-looking building in the typical chain-hotel style, and the rooms are stocked with nondescript, functional furnishings. During the low season, you can take advantage of the hotel's economical package rates.

Tour B: Gatineau Valley

Gatineau Park

Without a doubt one of the most beautiful places in the area to camp, **Parc de la Gatineau**

($18 Camping du Lac Philippe, Route 366, ☎456-3016; $15 Camping du Lac La Pêche, Route 366, ☎456-3494), with over 350 campsites, has everything for people who want to sleep in the great outdoors. There are also facilities for recreational vehicles.

RESTAURANTS

Tour A: Ottawa Valley

Hull

A pleasant café/restaurant/bar/gallery/movie theatre/terrace with a very laid-back atmosphere, **Aux Quatre Jeudis** *($; 44 Rue Laval, ☎771-9557)* is patronized by a young, slightly bohemian clientele. It shows movies, and its pretty terrace is very popular in the summertime.

At **Pi-za'za** *($; 36 Rue Laval, ☎771-0565)*, you can sample an excellent variety of fine pizzas in a pleasant, relaxed atmosphere.

Le Twist *($$; 88 Rue Montcalm, ☎777-8886)* provides a terrific setting in which to satisfy your cravings for a good burger and home-made fries; especially since that's about all they serve here, though there are other tasty offerings as well. During summer, you can sit outside on a large, completely private terrace. In short, this place has lots of atmosphere and attracts a fun crowd.

A little restaurant specializing in French cuisine, **Le Panaché** *($$$; closed Sun and Mon; 201 Rue Eddy, ☎777-7771)* has a relaxed, intimate ambiance.

If you're looking for a good, unpretentious place to eat, head to **Le Pied Cochon** *($$$; closed Sun and Mon; 248 Montcalm, ☎777-5808)*, where the food is as varied as it is delicious, and the service is impeccable.

A former private house, **La Soupière** *($$$; closed Sun and Mon; 53 Kent, ☎771-6256)* offers excellent regional cuisine in large portions. As the restaurant is small, accommodating only 40 people, it is best to make reservations.

Le Tartuffe *($$$; closed Sun; 133 Rue Notre Dame, ☎776-6424)* is a marvelous little gourmet French restaurant located just steps from the Musée Canadien des Civilisations. With its friendly, courteous service and delightful, intimate ambiance, this place is sure to win your heart.

Le Sans-Pareil *($$$-$$$$; closed Sun and Mon; 71 Boulevard St-Raymond, ☎771-1471, closed Sun)* is located 5 minutes from Hull's new casino, and right near the shopping centres. This is a Belgian restaurant, so it's only normal that chef Luc Gielen offers a two for one special on mussels (prepared in twelve different ways) on Tuesday nights. The sinfully good menu usually changes every three weeks, and the focus is on fresh products from various parts of Québec. The chef has a flair for combining ingredients in innovative ways, so don't hesitate to opt for the *menu gourmand*, which includes several courses, complete with the appropriate wines to wash them down. This place may be small, but it's truly charming. Check it out!

The Casino has all the facilities for your gambling pleasures – two restaurants serve excellent meals away from all the betting: **Banco** *($$)* offers a reasonably priced, quality buffet and various menu items; the more chic and expensive **Baccara** *($$$$; closed for lunch; 1 Boulevard du Casino, ☎772-6210)* has won itself a place among the best restaurants of the region. The set menu always consists of superb dishes that you can enjoy along with spectacular views of the lake. The well-stocked wine cellar and impeccable service round out this memorable culinary experience.

The stylish **Café Henry Burger** *($$$$; 69 Laurier, ☎777-5646)* specializes in fine French cuisine. The menu changes according to the availability of the freshest ingredients, and always offers dishes to please the most discerning palate. The restaurant has long maintained an excellent reputation.

Chelsea

It would be unheard of to visit the Outaouais without going to the Parc de la Gatineau — if only for a meal. **L'Orée du Bois** *($$$; closed Sun and Mon in winter; 15 Kingsmere Road, Old Chelsea, ☎827-0332)* is set up inside a rustic house in the country. The crocheted curtains, wood and brick inside add to the ambiance. This is the kind of family business that you find all over France. For 17

years now, gentle, cheerful Manon has been welcoming guests and overseeing the dining rooms, while Guy focuses his expertise on the food. Guy has developed a French cuisine featuring ingredients from the various regions of Québec. The menu thus lists dishes made with wood mushrooms, fresh goat cheese, Lac Brome duck, venison and fish smoked on the premises, using maple wood. The prices are very reasonable, and the portions generous. A pleasant evening is guaranteed for all!

Papineauville

La Table de Pierre Delahaye *($$$-$$$$; closed Mon and Tue; 247 Papineau; ☎427-5027)* is worth a stop. Forget Montebello! This restaurant is sure to linger in your memory. It's run by a couple — Madame greets the guests and Monsieur takes care of the food. The welcome is always warm and cordial, the Norman-style cuisine succulent. If the thought of sweetbreads makes your mouth water, look no farther. The rooms in this historic house (1880) are oozing with atmosphere. Parties of eight or more can even have one all to themselves.

ENTERTAINMENT

Bars and Nightclubs

Hull

Everyone knows about the bars along the Promenade du Portage, including Ontarians, who come here to top off the night when they've been out partying. The crowd is relatively young.

For many years now, **Aux Quatre Jeudis** *(44 Laval)* has been *the* place for the café crowd. It has lots of atmosphere, and there's a big, attractive terrace to hang out on in the summer.

Le Bop *(5 Aubry)* is a pleasant little place in old Hull. You can kick off your evening with a reasonably priced, decent meal. The music ranges from techno and disco to soft rock and even a little hard rock.

Le Fou du Roi *(253 Boulevard St-Joseph)* is where the thirty-something crowd hangs out. There's a dance floor, and the windows open onto a little terrace in the summertime. This place is also a popular after-work gathering place.

The Casino de Hull has two beautiful bars: the **777** and the **Marina** *(1 Boulevard du Casino)* which serve no less than 70 Canadian microbrews.

Theatres

Gatineau

Throughout the year, the **Maison de la Culture de Gatineau** *(855 Boulevard de la Gappe, Gatineau,* ☎*243-2525)* presents good-quality shows.

Hull

If you're interested in theatre, go to **Théâtre de l'Île** *(1 Rue Wellington, Hull,* ☎*595-7455)*. In the summer they offer dinner-theatre packages.

Festivals and Cultural Events

Hull-Ottawa

The **Ottawa et de Hull International Jazz Festival** *(late July,* ☎*613-594-3580)* presents many shows in Hull and offers the chance to hear various contemporary jazz artists for a reasonable price (a pass costs less than $30 and allows entry to all performances).

Winterlude is the largest winter carnival in North America. Various activities are organized on the world's longest skating rink, the Rideau Canal, in Ottawa, as well as in other locations. For further information: ☎(613) 239-5000 or 1-800-465-1867.

Aylmer

The **Fête de l''Été d'Aylmer** (formerly the Festivoile) *(*☎*684-9406)* is mainly centred around the Aylmer marina. For a few days in August, you can watch or take part in various competitions and activities out on the water. In the evening, well-known Québec singers take turns entertaining the crowd.

Gatineau

During the **Festival des Montgolfières** *(*☎*243-2330)*, held in Gatineau on Labour Day weekend, in early September, the sky is filled with colourful hot-air balloons, a real feast for the eyes. This well organized event has earned itself an enviable reputation in just a few years. A number of prominent singers perform here in the evening.

Casino

If you want to have fun and possibly win some money, the **Casino de Hull** *(11am to 3am; 1 Boulevard du Casino,* ☎*1-800-665-2274 or 772-2100)* has what you're looking for. This huge casino has slot machines, Keno, blackjack and roulette tables, as well as two restaurants (see p 284).

 ## SHOPPING

Hull

The **boutique of the Musée Canadien des Civilizations** *(100 Rue Laurier)* is, in a way, part of the exhibit. Although the Canadian and native craft pieces aren't of the same quality of those exhibited at the museum, you'll find all sorts of reasonably priced treasures and lots of great little curios.

The museum also has a **bookstore** with a wonderful collection on the history of crafts in many different cultures.

OUTAOUAIS

ABITIBI-TÉMISCAMINGUE

 bitibi-Témiscamingue, together with Nouveau-Québec and the James Bay region, form Québec's last frontier. While the rich fertile land bordering Lac Témiscamingue and the Ottawa River was cleared in the 19th century, agricultural development in the rest of the region, where the soil is not as good, did not begin in earnest until the 1930s. The discovery of gold deposits in the twenties provoked a second wave of migration, a true gold rush. The region has preserved its boom town atmosphere as the mining industry still employs a fifth of the local workforce. Forestry and farming are also important to the regional economy.

Abitibi-Témiscamingue is traversed by an invisible line which divides the drainage of the land, to one side rainfall drains into James Bay and to the other side, into the St-Lawrence; the land is, however, quite flat. Nowadays, people come here to relive the great adventure of the gold rush, but most of all to enjoy the vast spaces and explore the huge forests and countless lakes, which are a hunter's, fisherman's and snowmobiler's paradise.

FINDING YOUR WAY AROUND

Although Abitibi and Témiscamingue are considered part of the same general region, both are areas with unique identities, thus, two

separate tours are suggested: **Tour A: Abitibi ★** and **Tour B: Témiscamingue ★**.

Tour A: Abitibi

By Car

Since Abitibi is located approximately 500 kilometres from Montréal, it is best to plan an overnight stop along the way. Take Highway 15 N. from Montréal, which turns into Route 117 at Sainte-Agathe. The Abitibi tour can be combined with the "Cottage Country" tour in the Laurentians tourist region (see p 249) and the Témiscamingue tour (see p 292).

Bus Stations

Val d'Or: 851 4ᵉ Avenue, ☎824-3635
Amos: 132 10ᵉ Avenue Ouest, ☎732-2821
Rouyn-Noranda: 52 Rue Horne, ☎762-0735

Train Station

Amos: 100 Avenue de la Gare, ☎727-2510.

Tour B: Témiscamingue

By Car

Témiscamingue can be reached from either Abitibi or various places in the province of Ontario. In the first case, follow Route 391 S. from Rouyn-Noranda. From Ontario, take Routes 17, 533 or 63 (on the south shore of the Ottawa River) to Témiscaming and follow the tour in reverse.

Bus Station

Ville-Marie: 19 Rue Sainte-Anne (in Cajibi), ☎629-2166.

By Boat

Another way to reach Témiscamingue is via the **Voie Navigable du Témiscamingue et de l'Outaouais**. This water route runs along the Ottawa River and ends at Lac Témiscamingue, the same route once used to float wood down to the sawmills and pulp and paper factories in Hull. For more information, contact the regional tourist information offices.

 PRACTICAL INFORMATION

Area code: 819

Tourist Information Offices

Regional Office

Association Touristique Régionale de L'Abitibi-Témiscamingue 170 Avenue Principale, Bureau 103, Roun-Noranda, J9X 4P7, ☎762-8181 or 1-800-808-0706, ⁼762-5212, www.tourisme.abitemis.qc.ca

Tour A: Abitibi

Val d'Or: 20, 3ᵉ Avenue Est, J9P 5Y8, ☎824-9648
Amos: 892 Rue Principale Sud, J9T 2K4, ☎727-1242 or 1-800-670-0499
Rouyn-Noranda: 191 Avenue du Lac, J9X 5C3, ☎797-3195.

Tour B: Témiscamingue

Ville-Marie: 21 Rue Notre-Dame-de-Lourdes, J0Z 3W0, ☎629-3355. Summer: 1 Rue Industrielle, ☎629-2959

 EXPLORING

Tour A: Abitibi ★ (two days)

The development of the Abitibi region began in 1912 with the arrival of the railroad. Because the region is isolated from the rest of Québec by the Cadillac fault (which demarcates the northern limit of the St-Lawrence River basin), it was virtually impossible to reach via water. At one time Abitibi was thought of as a promised land by the Catholic clergy, who began to direct farmers from the overdeveloped St-Lawrence Valley into the area to stop emigration to the United States. Discovery of copper and gold deposits in the early twenties sped up the development of towns such as Val d'Or, but the rest of the region has remained sparsely inhabited. During the Depression, developing Abitibi for agriculture became a way of reducing the desperate unemployment situation in large cities to the south. Measures taken by the Québec government between 1932 and 1939 resulted in a doubling of Abitibi's population and the creation of 40 new villages and towns.

The rolling countryside of Abitibi has countless lakes and rivers and is blanketed by extensive forests, making it ideal for hunting and fishing. In the Algonquin language, the word "Abitibi" means "area of high lands".

Val-d'Or (pop. 24,476)

The search for gold in Québec under the French Regime ended after explorers who believed they had discovered the precious metal in the colony sent samples of their exciting find back to King François I. As it turned out, they had uncovered a worthless deposit of fool's gold. Following this embarrassing incident, further processing was abandoned as a waste of time. In 1922, however, prospectors discovered a tremendous gold deposit along the Cadillac fault. Shortly afterward, the town of Val d'Or, literally Valley of Gold, quickly sprang to life. Throughout the thirties, Val-d'Or was the first

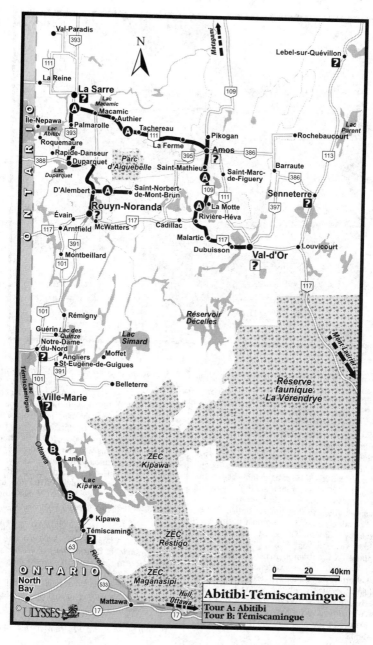

Abitibi-Témiscamingue

Tour A: Abitibi
Tour B: Témiscamingue

ABITIBI-TÉMISCAMINGUE

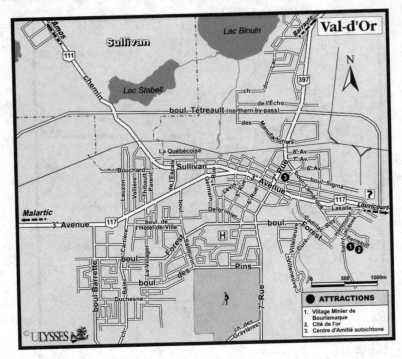

gold mining town in the world, and today, it is still an important mining centre.

The Canadian-American company Teck-Hughes Gold Mines began exploiting the Lamaque mine in 1933, a welcome initiative during a period of significant unemployment. The **Village Minier de Bourlamaque** ★ *($2.50; late Jun to early Sep, every day 9am to 9pm; 123 Avenue Perreault, ☎825-7616)* was established in the spring of 1935 to accommodate the miners and their families. This gold rush town has been preserved down to the smallest detail, first by the Lamaque company, who built it, and then by the town of Val-d'Or, which has had control of the town since 1965. This village is composed of authentic mining houses built from unhewn timber, which exemplify the typical rugged Canadian log cabin. The buildings are well maintained and still inhabited. The house at 123 Avenue Perrault has been converted into an information centre devoted to the history of Val-d'Or and the mining industry in Abitibi.

At **La Cité de l'Or** ★★ *($15, students and seniors $12.50, families $45; mid-May to early Sep, 9:40am to 3:40pm; Sep to May, Mon to Wed 10am to 5pm, closed Thu and Fri, Sat 9am to 6pm, Sun 1pm to 6pm; 123 Avenue Perrault, ☎825-7616)*, you head 80 metres underground into an old mine and learn about various gold-mining techniques. The tour, which lasts nearly two hours, offers a chance to see the incredible working conditions of the miners. Temperatures at the bottom of a mine are completely different from those outside, so bring along a warm sweater. After the tour, you can take a look at the above-ground facilities of the old Lamaque mine. A must.

Native culture, including an annual Cree hockey tournament, is important in Val-d'Or and the **Native Friendship Centre** *(free admission; year round, Mon to Sat, during business hours; 7e Rue, ☎825-6857)* offers special access to the history, legends and traditions of local first nations. At the shop you can see works by native craftspeople.

Continue along Route 117 to Malartic.

Malartic (pop. 4,394)

The mining of gold is no longer an important economic activity in Malartic, but the buildings from the gold rush era have survived, giving the town an interesting Old West appearance.

The **Musée Régional des Mines** ★ *($4; early Jun to mid-Sep, every day 9am to 5pm, mid-Sep to late May, Mon to Fri 9am to noon and 1pm to 5pm; 650 Rue de la Paix, ☎757-4677)* was founded by a group of miners who wanted to share their experiences with the public. Don't let the museum's forbidding exterior discourage you, for a visit to its three exhibition rooms is very informative. The process that led to the creation of Earth, and the uses of its minerals in our everyday lives is dealt with.

At Rivière-Héva take Route 109 to Amos.

Amos (pop. 13,996)

After an exhausting voyage the first settlers arrived in Abitibi in the summer of 1912. They set up camp along the banks of the Rivière Harricana, founding the village of Amos, named after the wife of Québec's Premier at the time, Sir Lomer Gouin. The original village, with its rustic cabins built from the trees that were cut to clear the site, quickly gave way to a modern town. Amos was the first settlement in Abitibi, and is still the administrative and religious centre of the region.

The **Cathédrale Sainte-Thérèse-d'Avila** ★ *(11 Boulevard Mgr-Dudemaine)*, raised to the rank of cathedral in 1939, was built in 1923 from a design by Montréal architect Aristide Beaugrand-Champagne. Its unusual circular structure, large dome and Roman Byzantine appearance are reminiscent of the Église Saint-Michel-Archange in Montréal, designed by the same architect. The interior is decorated with Italian marble, beautiful mosaics and French stained-glass windows.

The **Refuge Pageau** ★★ *($6; late Jun to late Aug, Tue to Fri 1pm to 5pm, Sat and Sun 1pm to 8pm; late Aug to late Sep, Sat and Sun 1pm to 4pm; 3981 Rang Croteau, ☎732-6875 or 732-8999)* takes in wounded animals, treats their injuries, then sets them free again. Unfortunately, not all these animals can safely return to the wilderness, so they stay on the reserve and amuse visitors. In autumn, you can take in the magnificent spectacle presented by the migratory birds who stop here. You'll even see a barnacle goose who protects a cow! With a little luck, you'll spot Michel Pageau playing with these wild animals, which no other person can approach, in their cages. It is always impressive to see a man getting his face licked by a wolf or struggling with a bear. Aside from bears and wolves, there are foxes, raccoons, owls and various other members of Québec's animal population.

Route 109 then passes through Pikogan, and the 620 kilometres further reaches James Bay and its massive hydroelectric installations (see Nouveau-Québec p 534). To continue the Abitibi tour, take Route 111 from Amos. And then Route 393 N. to La Sarre.

La Sarre (pop. 8,660)

The village of La Sarre is located in a remote area crossed by long straight roads and where buying a litre of milk often requires a 20-kilometre drive. Forestry, an industry developed during the economic crisis of the 1930s, is still the main source of income in the region.

The **Centre d'Interprétation de la Foresterie** *(free admission; early Jun to early Sep, every day 9am to 9pm; 600 Rue Principale, ☎333-3318)*, at the local tourist information centre, describes the development of La Sarre's forestry industry.

There's more to La Sarre than just wood. Cultural expression finds its home at the **Maison de la Culture** *(year round visits, Mon to Fri 8:30am to noon, 1pm to 5pm and 7pm to 9pm, Sat and Sun 1pm to 5pm; 195 Rue Principale; ☎333-2294)* where you'll find both the Richelieu municipal library and the Centre d'Art Rotary which offer travelling and permanent exhibits by artists from the Abitibi-Témiscamingue region and elsewhere. Notice the **fresco** in the entrance of the Maison; if you look closer, you'll be able to read about 70 years of local history!

*Retrace your steps south on Route 393 and continue to Duparquet, the site of an abandoned gold mine. Turn left onto Route 388 E., then right onto Route 101 S. to D'Alembert. At D'Alembert, turn left toward Saint-Norbert-de-Mont-Brun, where the entrance to **Parc d'Aiguebelle** ★★ is located (see p 295).*

Take Route 101 S. to Rouyn-Noranda

ABITIBI-TÉMISCAMINGUE

Rouyn-Noranda (pop. 29,774)

Rouyn-Noranda was once made up of two separate towns, Rouyn and Noranda, respectively located on the south and north shores of Lac Osisko (also called Trémoy). The town was established following the discovery of large gold and copper deposits in the region. In 1921 there was only forest and rock here. Five years later, however, a town, complete with churches, factories and houses had developed. Historically, Rouyn has been the more commercial and industrial of the two cities. In contrast, the Noranda mining company carefully developed the village of Noranda as a predominately residential and institutional settlement. Even though the Rouyn-Noranda mines are now depleted, the town remains an important ore-processing centre.

The **Maison Dumulon** *($2.50; late Jun to early Sep, every day 9am to 6pm, early Sep to late Jun, Mon to Fri 9am to noon and 1pm to 5pm; 191 Avenue du Lac, ☎797-7125)* is a house of unhewn-timber, built by shopkeeper Joseph Dumulon in 1924; the property includes an adjoining general store. The Dumulon family played a central role in the development of Rouyn by opening a store, an inn and a local post office. The building, made of spruce blocks, now houses a tourist information centre and a small information centre on the history of Rouyn-Noranda.

The **Musée Religieux** *($1; late Jun to early Sep, every day, 9am to 5pm; 201 Rue Tachereau Ouest, ☎797-7125)*, in a former Russian Orthodox church, pays homage to the many Eastern European immigrants who played an important role in the development of Abitibi mining towns in the thirties and forties. While the communities they established have declined in recent years, vestiges such as synagogues and other temples remain, though most are being used for other purposes.

Tour B: Témiscamingue ★
(one and a half days)

Beautiful Lac Témiscamingue, the namesake of the entire region, feeds the Ottawa River. Témiscamingue, which means "place of deep waters", was once the heart of Algonquin territory. For 200 years before the region started to become an important forestry area, the only non-natives in Témiscamingue were French trappers. By 1850, lumberjacks from the Outaouais region began travelling the area to cut a seemingly endless supply of wood. In 1863, priests of the Oblate religious order settled in the region and helped found Ville-Marie in 1888, the first town in Témiscamingue.

Ville-Marie (pop. 2,655)

Due to its strategic location between southern Québec and Hudson Bay, Lac Témiscamingue entered into regional colonial history in the 17th century. In 1686, the French Knight of Troyes stopped here briefly on an expedition to rid the British from the Hudson Bay region. During the same year, a trading post was set up along the lake. The opening of lumber camps in Témiscamingue during the 19th century brought a seasonal population to the area. Soon, permanent settlers and priests from an Oblate mission established the town of Ville-Marie. The town has a beautiful lakeside location that is highlighted by surrounding parkland.

The **Fort Témiscamingue National Historic Site ★** *(late May to late Jun, Mon 1pm to 5pm, Tue to Sun 9am to 5pm; late Jun to mid-Aug, Mon 1pm to 8pm, Tue to Sun 9am to 8pm; mid-Aug to mid-Sep, every day 9am to 5pm; Route 101, ☎629-3222)*, also called Lieu Historique National du Fort-Témiscamingue. The last of three fur-trading posts established on Lac Témiscamingue by the Northwest Company stood here. Each was named Fort-Témiscamingue. The property, which has been named a historic site by the Canadian government, was abandoned in 1902. Today it is little more than a beautiful green park by the lake, since most of the old wooden trading post structures are gone. Nearby, visitors can see the enchanted forest, a wooded area with thuja trees, distinguished by their strangely twisted trunks.

Follow Route 101 S. to Témiscaming.

Témiscaming (pop. 2,390)

This one-industry town was founded in 1917 by the Riordon paper company. The result was a "new town" along the lines of the British garden cities. The pretty homes are mostly Arts & Crafts in style; note the attractive, but somewhat out of place, marble fountain in the residential area.

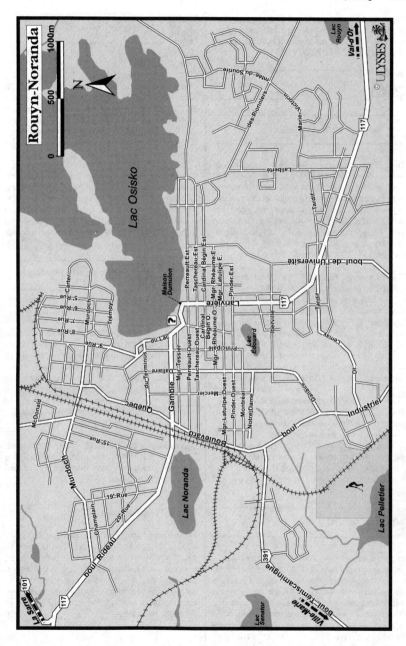

Paper and carboard production are demystified at the **Tembec** factory ★ *(free admission; Mon to Fri 9am to 3pm, reservations required; Route Georges Petty, ☎627-3321).*

 PARKS

Tour A: Abitibi

The **Parc d'Aiguebelle** ★★ *(Saint-Norbert-de-Mont-Brun, ☎637-7322 or 762-8154)* covers 243 square kilometres. In addition to many lakes and rivers, the park has the region's highest hills. Several outdoor activities are possible including canoeing, fishing, bike riding and hiking during the summer, and cross-country skiing and snowshoeing during the winter.

The **Réserve Faunique La Vérendrye** ★ *(reception at northern entrance; ☎736-7431 or 825-2392; you can also get information from the Société des Établissement de Plein Air du Québec, C.P. 1330, 42 Place Hammond, bureau 102, Val-d'Or, J9P 4P8 ☎825-2392).* At 13,615 square kilometres, this wildlife reserve is the second largest natural area in Québec. There are three entrances: the north entrance, which is 60 kilometres south of Val-d'Or, the Domaine, which is indicated on the TransCanada Highway, and an entrance at the south. At the Domaine there is a gas station, garage, convenience store, restaurant, and a place to rent boats and cottages. Picnic tables are set up on the side of the road and many people take advantage of them since there is no parking lot. Every summer they flock here: enthusiasts of canoeing, camping, fishing and cycling.

 OUTDOORS

In terms of tourism, Abitibi-Témiscamingue is still unchartered territory! Modern explorers will discover incredible richness, unspoiled places in abundance and waterways leading to infinity! Although hunters and fishers, already aware of the fertile forests and waters, have been coming here for years, there's a lot more here than game and fish. Countless adventures await, from gentle to extreme, in the untamed spaces and on the rivers and lakes.

 Cross-country Skiing

Tour A: Abitibi

Camp Dudemaine *($7; every day, 10am to 5pm; Route 395, Amos; ☎732-8453)* offers 22 kilometres of trails, a waxing room, ski rental and a restaurant. Both the skating and standard techniques are practised here. In the summer the trails are used for hiking and mountain-biking.

The **Club de Ski de Fond de Val-d'Or** *($6; Mon to Fri noon to 9pm, Sat and Sun 10am to 9pm; Chemin de l'Aéroport, Val-d'Or; ☎825-4398)* has 50 kilometres of trails including one international trail with lights! There's a waxing room, a rental shop, a heated hut and a snack bar.

  Fishing and Hunting

Tour A: Abitibi

Hunting and fishing rule in this realm of lakes and rivers, wide open spaces and endless forests. The **Pourvoirie du Domaine Balbuzard Sauvage** *(Lac Trévet, C.P. 100, Senneterre, J0Y 2M0, ☎/≈737-8681),* an outfitter, was awarded a Québec tourism prize for the excellence of its restaurant and the comfort of its facilities. The rates depend on the season and activity.

The **Pourvoirie Lac Faillon** *(C.P. 95, Senneterre, J0Y 2M0, ☎737-4429)* is another very popular outfitter offering hunting and fishing. It also boasts a pretty beach.

Tour B: Témiscamingue

The internationally renowned **Réserve Beachêne** *(C.P. 910, Témiscamingue, J0Z 3R0, ☎627-3865)* offers sport fishing with a twist: the fish must be thrown back into the water. The quality of the fishing is thus guaranteed to be superior. The rooms, furthermore, are very comfortable, and the restaurant has an excellent reputation.

Adventure Packages

A few companies offer many different types of expeditions in Abitibi-Témiscamingue to challenge explorers, enthusiasts and beginners that want to experience some real wilderness.

Tour A: Abitibi

The **Ordre des Conquérants du Nord** *(350 Principale, La Sarre, J9Z 1Z5; ☎339-3300; e-mail: voy.ricard@sympatico.ca)* promotes the nature capital of the north by organizing events like the Traversée du Lac Abitibi (seven-day lake crossing on skis) and the Raid des Conquérants (mountain bike trek).

New in La Sarre, but not in the field, **Lune Hiver Abitibi** *(46 5ᵉ Avenue Est, La Sarre, J9Z 1K9; ☎339-5639, ⊨339-2148)* offers adventure packages in the James Bay and Abitibi-Ouest areas including trips that reveal the Cree and Abitibi culture.

Croissance Plein Air *(125 Chemin Lac Sauvage, C.P. 203, La Sarre, J9Z 3H8; ☎333-1199)* offers an introduction to sea kayaking, sea-kayak expeditions, mountain biking, hiking, orienteering and cross-country skiing.

Dogsledding

Tour A: Abitibi

For dogsledding excursions, **Croinor Aventure** *(61 Chemin Croinor, C.P. 151, Senneterre, J0Y 2M0; ☎737-8606)* offers custom-designed tours in the area.

Snowmobiling

This region is a veritable paradise for snowmobilers in winter. The 3,000 kilometres of trails accessible to snowmobiles cover the most beautiful areas of Abitibi-Témiscamingue. With the abundant snow, mild weather (cold but never humid) and the warm welcome from the people in the area, those who appreciate enchanting landscapes and nordic adventures are sure to be satisfied.

The routes in Abitibi join up with many other Quebec tourist regions. From the Trans-Québec trails you can reach Senneterre, Lebel-sur-Quévillon and Belleterre. From Ontario, trails pass through Temiscaming, Notre-Dame-du-Nord, Arntfield and La Reine. A number of businesses offer snowmobile and clothing rental. Be aware that certain companies impose restrictions such as a minimum age requirement and a valid driver's license.

Excursion Québec/Canada Harricana: Clément Girard, C.P. 1076, Val-d'Or, J9P 5Y9, ☎825-4360. Five-day tours including visits to many interesting sites in the region. ATV tours also offered.

Location Blais: 280 Avenue Larivière, Rouyn-Noranda, H9X 4H4, ☎797-9292.

Moto Sport du Cuivre: 175 Boulevard Évain, Évain, J0Z 1Y0, ☎768-5611.

ACCOMMODATIONS

Tour A: Abitibi

Amos

Despite its rather uninviting exterior, the **Château d'Amos** *($45-150; ≡, ℜ, tv; 201 Avenue Authier, J9T 1W1, ☎732-5386 or 1-800-361-6162)* has over 75 comfortable rooms where visitors can enjoy a pleasant stay.

The **Hôtel-Motel Amosphère** *($54-$144; ≡, tv, ⊛, ℜ; 1031 Route 111 Est, J9T 1N2; ☎732-7777 or 1-800-567-7777, ⊨732-5555)* is a hotel complex that offers high-class accommodation; in the evening the dining room offers specialties of house steak and seafood. The Amoshère is also a stopover for snowmobilers in the winter offering heated garages for snowmobiles. There's a lively dance club frequented by Abitibi-Témiscamingue's night owls.

La Sarre

The biggest hotel in the La Sarre area, the **Motel Villa Mon Repos** *($52; ≡, tv, ⊛; 32 Route Est, J9R 1R7; ☎333-2224)* offers a variety of rooms close to the centre of town.

Ulysses' Favourites

Accommodations

For history buffs:
Auberge de l'Orpailleur (p 296).

Restaurants

Abitibi-Témiscamingue's grand tables:
Douce Heure (p 297) and
Restaurant Rossy (p 297).

For the terrasse:
Renaissance (p 297).

Located on the way into La Sarre, the **Motel Le Bivouac** *($55; tv, ⊛; 637 2ᵉ Rue Est, J9Z 2S7; ☎333-2241)* has an unusual character: the rooms are dedicated to the soldiers of the Montcalm army who have had townships and certain Abitibi-Temiscamingue municipalities named after them. Extremely pleasant.

Rouyn-Noranda

L'Autre Chez-Soi *($45 bkfst incl.; sb, K, ℝ; 784 Av. Murdoch, J9X 1H8, ☎762-3187)* is a pleasant guesthouse where you'll be made to feel like one of the family.

There are a few motels along Avenue Larivière, including a **Journey's End** *($55; 1295 Avenue Larivière, ☎797-1313 or 1-800-668-4200)*.

The **Hôtel Albert** *($75; ≡, tv; 84 Avenue Principale, J9X 4P2, ☎762-3545)*, located downtown, is a real bargain. Its convenient location, impeccable service and simple yet comfortable rooms make this a reliable option in Rouyn.

Val-d'Or

In Val-d'Or there are two full-service campgrounds, **Camping du Lac Lemoyne Inc.** *($20; 451 Chemin Plage Lemoyne; ☎874-3066)* that has over one hundred sites and **Centre de Plein Air Arc-en-Ciel** *($10; 600 Chemin des Scouts, J9P 4N7; ☎/⊶824-4152)*, with some 70 sites. Set up in a forest of jackpine, eastern white pine, spruce, birch and poplar trees, the Arc-en-Ciel offers fishing in a pond with cultivated rainbow trout, a nature trail, a pool, a wading pool, a domestic

zoo (chickens, rabbits, cows, ponies) as well as child-care services and tent rental (for 4 to 12 people, with reservation) on a daily, weekly or monthly basis.

The **Auberge de l'Orpailleur** *($48 bkfst incl.; 104 Avenue Perreault, J9P 2G3, ☎825-9518, ⊶825-8275)*, located in the mining village of Bourlamaque, was once a bunk house for unmarried miners. Not only is the place of historical interest, but its rooms are also attractively decorated, each in its own style. The warm welcome and generous breakfasts make for an unforgettable stay. The owner of the inn also runs an outfit that offers adventure packages and his groups stay here, so reservations are necessary.

L'Escale *($57, renovated rooms $67; ≡, tv; 1100 Rue de l'Escale, J9P 1T3, ☎824-2711, ⊶825-2145)* is a comfortable place with lots of atmosphere. Ask for one of the renovated rooms, which are considerably more attractive.

At the east edge of town is the **Hôtel Confortel Val-d'Or** *($72; ≡, tv, ⊛, ≈, ℜ; 1001 3ᵉ Avenue Est, J9P 1T3; ☎825-5660 or 1-800-567-6599)*, a three-star hotel. Confortel also houses the Centre des Congrès de Val-d'Or (conference centre). The restaurant serves regional and French cuisine and offers imported and Quebec beers as well as an elaborate wine list.

Tour B: Témiscamingue

Ville-Marie

The **Motel Caroline** *($40-$60; ≡, tv; 2 Route 101 Sud, J0Z 3W0, ☎629-2965)* has 16 simple rooms, some with a lovely view of Lac Témiscamingue. Good value.

Témiscaming

The **Auberge Témiscaming** *($80; ≡, tv, ⊛, ℜ; 1431 Chemin Kipawa, J0Z 3R0, ☎627-3476)* has a solid reputation in these parts. Its modern and courteous service have earned it regional prizes. Avoid the rooms near the staircases, they can be noisy.

RESTAURANTS

Tour A: Abitibi

Amos

 The restaurant **La Douce Heure** *($$ or $ in the bistro; 21 10e Avenue Ouest, ☎732-2335)* serves delicious seafood and equally praiseworthy French cuisine. Coffee lovers take note: this place probably serves the best cup of jo in town.

 The most surprising of all the restaurants in Abitibi-Témiscamingue, hidden behind an anonymous and unattractive façade, is the **Restaurant Rossy** *($$; 416 6ᵉ Rue Sud; ☎732-8271)* They serve French cuisine worthy of the finest gourmets. It's one of the region's best kept secrets.

Rouyn-Noranda

La Renaissance *($$; 199 Avenue Principale; ☎764-4422)* offers delicious, innovative and creative regional cuisine and an interesting selection of wines. This family restaurant, headed by chef Gino Côté, is decorated in a regionally inspired fashion; one of the dining rooms is called l'Anode, which is the name of a copper plaque moulded in a very distinctive shape. La Renaissance is also the only restaurant in the area with a lounge where guests can sample spirits (14 kinds of scotch, many renowned cognacs, Port and others) and cigars (Montecristo, Cuban cigars, Honduras and Dominican Republic)... quite a hip place.

At **Les Trois-Fourchettes** *($$$; 41 6e Rue, ☎762-2341)*, you can enjoy an excellent meal in a very pleasant atmosphere.

Val-d'Or

Fans of Belgian food and top-quality pizza will love **La Fiesta** *($; 636 3e Avenue,* ☎825-0469)*. The beer list and relaxed, efficient service are noteworthy bonuses.

L'Amadeus *($$; 166 Avenue Perreault, ☎825-7204)* serves excellent French cuisine. The service is impeccable; the decor, as pleasant as can be.

Tour B: Témiscamingue

Ville-Marie

La Seigneurie *($$; 25 Chemin de Guigues, ☎622-0062)* is an unpretentious restaurant. The menu, a combination of French, regional and homestyle cuisine, offers nice surprises.

Laniel

The three charming cottages of **Chalets de la Pointe-aux-Pins** *($$; 1955 Chemin du Ski; ☎634-5211)* are located at the end of Chemin du Ski in a forest. The main cottage, where the restaurant is located, overlooks Lac Kipawa. The hostess, Madame Perreault offers an original menu of fine cuisine: caviar blinis and vodka, morsels of wild boar with pine jelly, suckling pig with spicy blueberry sauce, stewed grain-fed veal with candied lemon.

ENTERTAINMENT

Festivals and Cultural Events

Rouyn-Noranda

During the non-competitive **Festival du Cinéma International en Abitibi-Témiscamingue** *(late Oct; ☎762-6212)*, films from various countries are given their North-American (and sometimes even world) premiere.

ABITIBI-TÉMISCAMINGUE

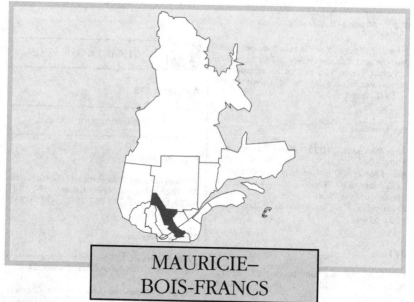

MAURICIE–BOIS-FRANCS

T he Mauricie–Bois-Francs region is an amalgam of diverse regions on either side of the St. Lawrence. Located about halfway between Montréal and Québec City, this large region runs from north to south and includes terrain of the three types that make up the province: the Canadian Shield, the St. Lawrence plains, and part of the Appalachian mountain range. The city of Trois-Rivières is generally considered the heart of this region. Trois-Rivières was the second city founded in New France (1634). First a fur-trading post, it became an industrial centre with the founding of the Saint-Maurice ironworks in 1730. Since the end of the 19th century, the exploitation of the surrounding forests has made Trois-Rivières the hub of the provincial pulp and paper industry. Further up the Rivière Saint-Maurice, the towns of Shawinigan and Grand-Mère, also major industrial sites, serve as centres for the production of hydro-electric power, as well as a centre for the major industries that consume that power. To the north lies a vast untamed expanse of lakes, rivers and forest. This land of hunting and fishing also contains the magnificent Mauricie National Park, reserved for outdoor activities such as canoeing and camping. To the south lie the rural zones on either side of the St. Lawrence. Opened up very early to colonization, the land is still divided according to the lines of the old seigneurial system. Finally, in the extreme south of the region lies the area known as "Bois-Francs". The gently rolling hills of this countryside herald the mountains of the Appalachians. There are interesting annual festivals in the area including an international music festival in Victoriaville and an international folklore festival in Drummondville.

 FINDING YOUR WAY AROUND

To get to know the Mauricie–Bois-Francs region, two tours are suggested, one for the north shore of the St. Lawrence, the other for the south: **Tour A: Mauricie ★★ Tour B: Bois-Francs ★**.

Tour A: Mauricie

By Car

From Montréal, take Highway 40 (Félix Leclerc), followed by Highway 55 S. for a short while, and then turn onto Route 138 E. as far as Trois-Rivières. Take Boulevard Royal and continue along Rue Notre-Dame to the downtown area. This part of town is best visited on foot. Next, you'll drive inland to Saint-Tite on Route 159 then head to Grand-Mère on Route 153. Once at Grand-Mère, those wishing to explore Haute-Mauricie can make a detour to La Tuque on the 155. To continue the main tour, stay on the 153, which leads through the Shawinigan region, among others. The portion of the tour between Trois-Rivières and Sainte-Anne-de-la-Pérade, which run along Route 138 E., can be incorporated into an excursion along the St. Lawrence and up to Québec City.

Bus terminals

Trois-Rivières: 1075 Rue Champflour, ☎374-2944
Grand-Mère: 800 6ᵉ Avenue, ☎533-5565.
La Tuque: 530 Rue St-Louis, ☎523-2121, Dépanneur Provi-Soir.
Shawinigan: 1563 Boulevard Saint-Sacrement, ☎539-5144

By Ferry

La Tuque: 550 Rue Saint-Louis, ☎523-3257.
Shawinigan: 1560 Rue de la Station, ☎537-9007.

Tour B: Bois-Francs

By Car

This tour focuses on the St. Lawrence plains, where the main towns of the area are located. From Montréal or from Québec City, take Highway 40 and then Highway 55 S. Cross the Pont Laviolette at Trois-Rivières. Opened in 1967, this bridge is the only one that links the two shores between Montréal and Québec City. Once across, take Route 132 E. to Beschaillons. From there, follow Route 256 to Plessisville, then Route 116 to Victoriaville. Complete the loop by taking Routes 255, 226 and then 132 Est.

Bus Terminals

Victoriaville: 64 Boulevard Carignan, ☎752-5400.
Drummondville: 330 Rue Hériot, ☎477-2111.

By Ferry

Drummondville: 263 Rue Lindsay, ☎472-5383.

 PRACTICAL INFORMATION

Area code: 819

Tourist Information Offices

Regional Office

Tourism Mauricie-Bois-Francs 1180 Rue Royale, 3ʳᵈ floor, Trois-Rivières Ouest, G9A 4J1, ☎375-1222 or 1-800-567-7603, ⊷375-0301.

Tour A: Mauricie

Trois-Rivières: 168 Rue Bonaventure, ☎375-9628; 1457 Rue Notre-Dame, G9A 4X4, ☎375-1122.
Cap-de-la-Madeleine: 170 Rue des Chenaux, ☎375-5346.

Tour B: Bois-Francs

Victoriaville: 122 Rue Aqueduc, P.C. 641, ☎758-6371.
Drummondville: 1350 Rue Michaud, ☎477-5529.
Nicolet: 30 Rue Notre-Dame, ☎293-4537.

 EXPLORING

Tour A : Mauricie ★★ (three days)

The Valley of the Rivière Saint-Maurice is located half-way between Montréal and Québec City, on the north shore of the St. Lawrence River. The cradle of Canada's first major industry, Mauricie has always been an industrial region. Its towns feature fine examples of architecture of the industrial revolution. Nevertheless, the vast countryside surrounding the towns remains primarily an area of mountain wilderness covered in dense forest, perfect for hunting, fishing, camping and hiking.

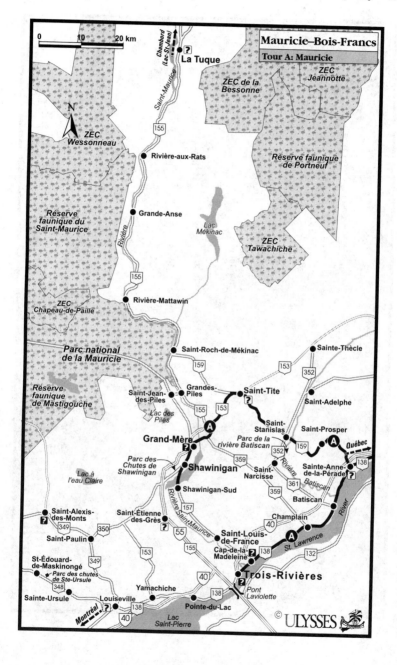

Mauricie–Bois-Francs

Tour A: Mauricie

0   10   20 km

Chambord (Lac-St-Jean)

La Tuque

ZEC de la Bessonne

ZEC Jeannotte

Saint-Maurice

N

ZEC Wessonneau

155

Réserve faunique de Portneuf

Rivière-aux-Rats

Grande-Anse

Lac Mékinac

Réserve faunique du Saint-Maurice

Rivière

155

ZEC Tawachiche

Rivière-Mattawin

ZEC Chapeau-de-Paille

Parc national de la Mauricie

Saint-Roch-de-Mékinac

Sainte-Thècle

159

153

352

Réserve faunique de Mastigouche

Saint-Jean-des-Piles

Grandes-Piles

Saint-Tite

Saint-Adelphe

155

153

Lac des Piles

A

Saint-Stanislas

Saint-Prosper

A

Québec

Grand-Mère

Parc de la rivière Batiscan

352

159

138

Parc des Chutes de Shawinigan

Shawinigan

Saint-Narcisse

359

Rivière Batiscan

Sainte-Anne-de-Pérade

Lac à l'eau Claire

Shawinigan-Sud

359

361

Batiscan

Saint-Alexis-des-Monts

Saint-Étienne-des-Grès

157

Champlain

Rivière Saint-Maurice

40

349

350

55

Saint-Louis-de-France

A

St. Lawrence River

Saint-Paulin

153

155

132

St-Édouard-de-Maskinongé

349

Cap-de-la-Madeleine

138

Parc des chutes de Ste-Ursule

40

Trois-Rivières

Sainte-Ursule

348

Yamachiche

138

Pont Laviolette

Louiseville

138

Montréal

40

Pointe-du-Lac

Lac Saint-Pierre

© ULYSSES

MAURICIE-BOIS-FRANCS

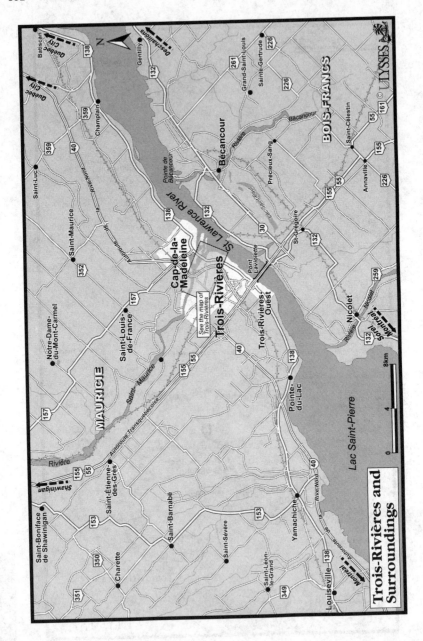

Trois-Rivières and Surroundings

Trois-Rivières ★★ (pop. 51,412)

The aspect of the town, once similar to Vieux-Québec, was completely changed by a fire in June 1908. Now, it more resembles a town of the American Midwest. However, Trois-Rivières remains a city redolent of Old-World charm with its many cafés, restaurants and bars on Rue des Forges, and the terrace overlooking the St. Lawrence. Halfway between Montréal and Québec City, this urban centre is home to 100 000 people.

Located at the confluence of the St. Lawrence and Saint-Maurice rivers, where the latter divides into three branches, giving the town its name, Trois-Rivières was founded in 1634 by Sieur de Laviolette. From the outset, the town was surrounded by a stone wall which now marks the city's historic area. In the 17th century, there were three regional governments in the St. Lawrence valley apart from the Governor of New France: Québec City's, Montréal's, and Trois-Rivières's. More modest than its two sister cities, the latter boasted a population of a mere 600 and a total of 110 houses. The real boom took place in the middle of the 19th century with the creation of the pulp and paper industry. For a time, Trois-Rivières was the world's leading paper producer.

Park near the intersection of Notre-Dame and Laviolette. Walk up Rue Bonaventure (one street west of Laviolette) as far as the old Manoir de Boucher-de-Niverville, now the Tourist Information Centre.

The **Manoir Boucher-de-Niverville ★** *(free admission; Mon to Fri, 9am to 5pm; 168 Rue Bonaventure, ☎375-9628)* was fortunately spared during the 1908 fire. It is a unique example of 17th-century architecture, with few adaptations to the local environment. Inside the manor are a display of antique furniture and a diorama on local history.

A statue of Maurice Le Noblet Duplessis (1890-1959), Premier of Québec from 1936 to 1939, and from 1944 to 1959, stands in front of the manor. Duplessis was a conservative whose power was closely linked with the Catholic clergy of the time. His term of office is often referred to as the great darkness that preceded the Quiet Revolution.

Cross Rue Hart and walk along Parc Champlain as far as the cathedral.

The **Cathédrale de l'Assomption ★** *(every day 7am to 11:30am and 2pm to 5:30pm, Sun open at 8:30am; 362 Rue Bonaventure ☎374-2409)* was built in 1858 according to the plans of architect Victor Bourgeau, well known for the many churches he designed in the Montréal area. The cathedral's massive Gothic-Revival style is vaguely reminiscent of London's Westminster Abbey, also designed in the mid-19th century. Guido Nincheri's stained-glass windows, executed between 1923 and 1934, are certainly the most interesting element in what is otherwise an austere interior.

Retrace your steps down Rue Bonaventure and turn left on Rue Hart.

The **Musée des Arts et Traditions Populaires du Québec** *($6; guided tours; Jul and Aug, every day 10am to 7pm; Sep to Jun, Tue to Sun 10am to 5pm; 200 Rue Laviolette, ☎372-0406 or 1-800-461-0406)*, south of Rue Hart, was inaugurated in 1996. The town's old prison, a handsome neoclassical building erected in 1822 according to plans by François Baillargé, is incorporated into the post-modern structure. The museum presents exhibitions on the customs and daily life of Quebecers over the centuries. In addition to traditional quilts, it displays old toys, whale bones and a 17th-century aboriginal dugout canoe, as well as a number of small buildings from the collection of Robert-Lionel Séguin, one of the pioneers of Québec ethnology.

Turn right on Rue Saint-Pierre and then left at Place Pierre-Boucher. Walk up Rue des Ursulines, the only street to have been spared from the fire of 1908.

Standing in Place Pierre-Boucher is the **Monument du Flambeau**, built in 1934 as part of the tricentennial celebrations of the town.

The **Manoir de Tonnancour** *(Tue to Fri 10am to noon and 1:30pm to 5pm, Fri 7pm to 9:30pm, Sat and Sun 1pm to 5pm; 864 Rue des Ursulines, ☎374-2355)* was built in 1725 for René Godefroy de Tonnancour, Lord of Pointe-du-Lac and the King's Prosecutor. After successive 19th-century incarnations as a fire station, a presbytery and a school, it is today an art gallery. On the Place d'Armes, opposite, is a cannon from the Crimean war.

The former **Couvent des Récollets ★** *(811 Rue des Ursulines)* is the only Récollet convent still standing in Québec. The building no doubt owes its continued existence to the fact that it

MAURICIE-BOIS-FRANCS

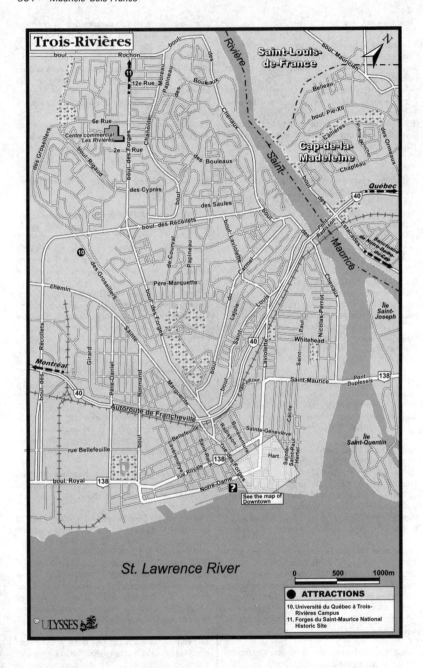

Trois-Rivières

Saint-Louis-de-France

Cap-de-la-Madeleine

Québec

Montréal

St. Lawrence River

Île Saint-Joseph

Île Saint-Quentin

0   500   1000m

● **ATTRACTIONS**

10. Université du Québec à Trois-Rivières Campus
11. Forges du Saint-Maurice National Historic Site

© ULYSSES

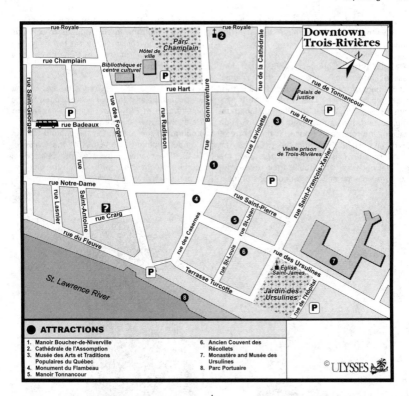

ATTRACTIONS

1. Manoir Boucher-de-Niverville
2. Cathédrale de l'Assomption
3. Musée des Arts et Traditions Populaires du Québec
4. Monument du Flambeau
5. Manoir Tonnancour

6. Ancien Couvent des Récollets
7. Monastère and Musée des Ursulines
8. Parc Portuaire

© ULYSSES

was turned into an Anglican church following the demise of the last member of the Trois-Rivières branch of the Récollet Order in 1776.

The **Monastère and Musée des Ursulines** ★ *($2.50; early May to early Nov, Tue to Fri 9am to 5pm, Sat and Sun 1:30pm to 5pm; Nov to Feb by appointment only; Mar and Apr, Wed to Sun 2pm to 5pm; 734 Rue des Ursulines, ☎375-7922).* The Ursulines first settled in 1697 in the house of Claude de Ramezay who left Trois-Rivières after being named Governor of Montréal. The museum presents thematic displays featuring items from the collection of the Ursulines (paintings, liturgical garments, needlework, etc.). The displays are arranged so as to lead the visitor towards the chapel. It was redecorated and given a dome in 1897.

Walk across the pretty park in front of the Monastère des Ursulines to get to Terrasse Turcotte and Parc Portuaire.

In the port area **Parc Portuaire** *(along the St. Lawrence River)*, formerly known as Terrasse

Turcotte was, until the twenties, the favourite meeting place of the local upper class. It later fell into disrepair, and was replaced by a new, tiered terrace between 1986 and 1990. Now the starting point for mini-cruises on the St. Lawrence, it also features a café and an exhibit on the pulp and paper industry.

The Forges Saint-Maurice are 10 kilometres from downtown along Boulevard des Forges.

The **Forges du Saint-Maurice National Historic Site** ★★ *($4, May to mid-Oct, every day 9am to 5pm; 10000 Boulevard des Forges, ☎378-5116)* is also called Lieu Historique National Les Forges du Saint-Maurice. These ironworks began in 1730, when Louis XV granted permission to François Poulin de Francheville to work the rich veins of iron-ore that lay under his land. The presence of dense wood lots from which to make charcoal, of limestone, and of a swift-running waterway favoured the production of iron. The workers of this first Canadian ironworks came for the most part from Burgundy and Franche-Comté in

MAURICIE-BOIS-FRANCS

France. They were kept busy making cannons for the King and wood-burning stoves for his subjects in New France.

After the British Conquest (1760), the plant passed into the hands of the colonial government of the British, who ceded it in turn to private enterprise. The works were in use until 1883. At that time, the plant included the smelter and forges, as well as the Grande Maison, the foreman's house, at the centre of a worker's village. Following the 1908 fire, the residents of Trois-Rivières recuperated the material necessary to rebuild their town from the forge, leaving only the foundations of most

buildings. In 1973, Parks Canada acquired the site and rebuilt the foreman house to serve as an information centre. They set up a second, very interesting centre on the site of the smelting forge.

A visit begins at the foreman's house, a huge white building said to have been inspired by the architecture of Burgundy. Various aspects of life at the ironworks are presented, as are the products of the works. On the second floor is a model depicting the layout of the works in 1845. The model is used as the basis of a sound and light show, after which the site can be perused by walking along various footpaths.

Sanctuaire Notre-Dame-du-Cap

Go back toward Trois-Rivières along Boulevard des Forges. Turn left on Boulevard des Récollets which then becomes Boulevard des Chenaux. Turn left again on Route 138 E., cross the Rivière Saint-Maurice and turn right onto Rue Notre-Dame at Cap-de-la-Madeleine, one of the suburbs of Trois-Rivières.

Cap-de-la-Madeleine (pop. 35,070)

As the heartland of Catholicism in North America, Québec is home to a number of major pilgrimage destinations visited by millions every year from all over the world. The **Sanctuaire Notre-Dame-du-Cap** ★★ *(626 Rue Notre-Dame, ☎374-2441)*, a shrine under the auspices of the Oblate Missionaries of the Virgin Mary, is consecrated to the worship of the Virgin.

The history of this sanctuary began in 1879 when it was decided a new parish church in Cap-de-la-Madeleine was needed. It was the month of March, and the stones for the new church had to be transported from the south side of the river. Strangely, the river had not yet frozen. Following the prayers and rosaries addressed to the statue of the Virgin presented to the parish in 1854, an ice-bridge formed "as if by miracle", allowing the necessary stones to be transported in one week. The parish priest, Father Désilet, decided to preserve the old church and to turn it into a sanctuary devoted to the Virgin. Built between 1714 and 1717, the sanctuary is one of the oldest churches in Canada. Visitors meditate before the statue of the Virgin. It is recounted that in 1888, the statue opened its eyes in front of several witnesses.

The miraculous ice-bridge is today symbolized by the **Pont des Chapelets** (1924), visible in the garden of the sanctuary. A stations of the cross, a calvary, a holy sepulchre and a small lake complete this riverside garden. Surrounded by an expanse of asphalt and looking like something from the set of a Cecil B. DeMille epic is the enormous **Basilique Notre-Dame-du-Rosaire**. Work on the basilica was begun in 1955, according to the plans of the architect Adrien Dufresne, a disciple of Dom Bellot. The Dutch master glazier Jan Tillemans created three sets of windows depicting the history of the sanctuary, that of Canada, and the mysteries of the rosary.

Take Notre-Dame Est to Route 138 (Boulevard Sainte-Madeleine). Along the way are the villages of Champlain, and then Batiscan, the site of an old presbytery.

Parc de l'Île de Saint-Quentin, see p 314.

Sainte-Anne-de-la-Pérade ★ (pop. 2,299)

In the winter, this pretty farming village hosts a second village that springs up in the middle of the Rivière Sainte-Anne running through the village. Hundreds of multicoloured shacks, heated and lit by electricity, shelter families that come from all over the world to fish for tomcod, also known as *petit poisson des chenaux*, which means "little channel fish". Ice-fishing in Sainte-Anne has become part of Québecois folklore over the years, along with the trips to the sugar shack and corn-roasts. The village is dominated by an imposing Gothic-Revival church (1855) based on the basilica of Notre-Dame de Montréal.

Take Route 159 inland toward Saint-Prosper, Saint-Stanislas and Grand-Mère.

Grand-Mère ★ (pop. 14,841)

The town was named after a rock bearing a strong resemblance to the profile of an old woman. Found on an island in the middle of the Saint-Maurice, the rock was transported piece by piece to a park in downtown Grand-Mère when the hydro-electric dam was constructed in 1913. The town and its neighbour Shawinigan are good examples of "company towns" where life revolves around one or two factories. The omnipresence of the factories extends to the residential patterns, the towns being divided into two distinct sections, one for management (mostly anglophone in the beginning) and one for workers (almost exclusively francophone). The town features many well thought-out industrial buildings designed by talented architects brought in from outside the area.

Grand-Mère came into being at the end of the 19th century as a result of the forestry industry. Pulp and paper factories processed trees cut down in the logging camps of Haute-Mauricie. The town was developed in 1897 by the Laurentide Pulp and Paper Company, the property of John Foreman, Sir William Van Horne and Russell Alger, hero of the American War of Secession. After the 1929 stock market crash, the town's economy diversified and

MAURICIE-BOIS-FRANCS

moved away from the pulp and paper industry which had helped it grow.

The **Pont de Grand-Mère** ★ across the swift-running Rivière Saint-Maurice was built in 1928 by American engineers Robinson and Steinman, who would become famous in the fifties for their reconstruction of the Brooklyn Bridge in New York and the Mackinac Bridge in Michigan. On the left are the facilities of the Stone Consolidated Company, the descendant of Laurentide Pulp and Paper. The hydro-electric centre of the vast industrial complex straddles the Saint-Maurice. It was designed in 1914 by the New York architect George F. Hardy, who looked to the Cathedral of Albi in France for inspiration. On the right of the bridge is the Auberge Grand-Mère, a former inn designed by Edward Maxwell in 1897. The inn houses part of the splendid collection of *art nouveau* furniture from the Château Menier on the island of Anticosti.

Chemin Riverside leads to an exclusive residential neighbourhood and an attractive municipal golf course designed by Frederick de Peyster Townsend in 1912. The sod for the course was taken from the renowned St. Andrews golf course in Scotland. A left on 3ᵉ Avenue leads up a street with charming houses designed for the executives of the paper companies in the early 20th century. At the corner of 4ᵉ and 1ʳᵉ is the picturesque Anglican Church of St. Stephen by Le Boutillier and Ripley of Boston (1924). Opposite, between 5ᵉ and 6ᵉ Avenues, is the Rocher de Grand-Mère with its famous profile of an old woman.

The **Église Catholique Saint-Paul de Grand-Mère** ★ *(on the corner of 6ᵉ Avenue and 4ᵉ Rue)* has an Italian-style false façade put up in 1908. The colourful interior is adorned with both remounted paintings executed by the Montréal artist Monty during the twenties and a Guido Nincheri fresco depicting the apotheosis of S.Paul. The high altar as well as the side altars are marble. Behind the church is an Ursuline convent affiliated with the one in Trois-Rivières.

The television miniseries *Les Filles de Caleb* (*Émilie* in English), based on Arlette Cousture's novel, was immensely successful across Canada. **Le Village d'Émilie** ★ *($8.95; mid-May to late Sep, every day 10am to 6pm; Route 55 Exit 226, ☎538-1716 or 1-800-667-4136)* is a showcase for the sets used in the shooting of the series *Shehaweh, Les Filles de Caleb*

(Émilie) and *Blanche*. It features, among other things, the Ovila log house, the Bourdais schoolhouse, the Shehaweh native village, the Caleb farms and Desjardins hall. There is a park for children and carriage rides are also available.

La Mauricie National Park ★, see p 314.

Réserve Faunique Saint-Maurice ★, see p 314.

Shawinigan (pop. 20,723)

In 1899, Shawinigan became the first city in Québec to be laid out according to the principles of urban planning, thanks to the powerful Shawinigan Water and Power Company, which supplied electricity to all of Montréal. The name of this hilly town means "portage at the peak" in Algonquian. The town itself was hard hit by the recession of 1989-93, which left indelible marks on its urban landscape: abandoned factories, burnt-out buildings, empty lots and so on. Nevertheless, Shawinigan boasts many architecturally interesting buildings from the first third of the 20th century. Some of its residential streets resemble those of interwar English suburbs.

Inaugurated in the spring of 1997, the **Cité de l'Énergie** *($10; late Jun to mid-Sep, every day 10am to 7pm; mid-Sep to late Jun, Tue to Sun 10am to 5pm; 1000 Avenue Melville, G9N 6T9, ☎536-4992, 536-2982 or 1-800-383-2483)* promises to acquaint many a visitor, child and adult alike, with the history of industrial development in Québec, in general, and in Mauricie, in particular. The hub of this development is the town of Shawinigan, singled out by aluminum factories and electric companies at the beginning of the century thanks to the strong currents in the Rivière Saint-Maurice and the 50-metre-high falls nearby. A huge theme park, the Cité de l'Énergie features several attractions: two hydroelectric power stations, one of which, the Centrale Shawinigan 2, is still in operation; a science pavilion and a 115-metre-high observation tower, which needless to say offers a sweeping view of the area, including the frothy Chutes Shawinigan Waterfronts.

The Cité de l'Énergie provides transportation (by trolley bus and by boat) to make it easier to visit these attractions. A multimedia show is also presented. During your tour of the Cité, you will learn how various regional industries, such as hydroelectricity, pulp and paper,

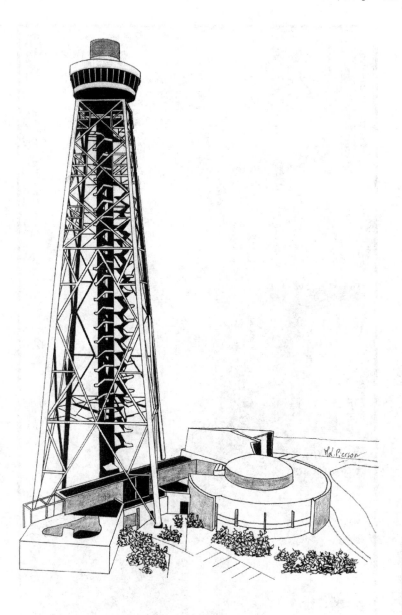

Cité de l'Énergie

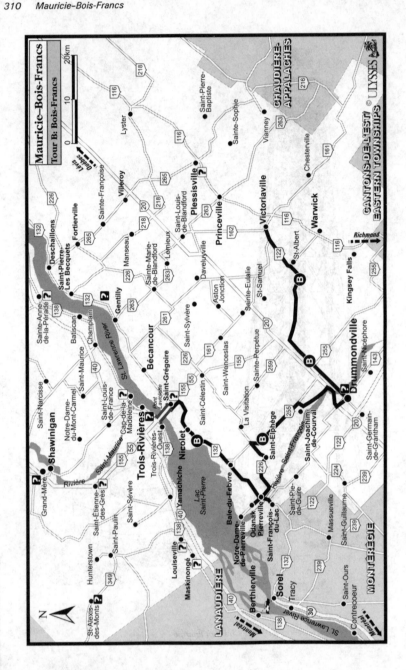

aluminum, etc., have evolved over the past hundred years. The development of innovations that led to scientific advances in these fields is explained step by step. Interactive exhibitions are presented in the Centre des Sciences, which also has a restaurant and a shop.

Parc des Chutes ★, see p 314.

Réserve Faunique Mastigouche, see p 314

Tour B : Bois-Francs ★ (two days)

The region takes its name from the hardwood, *(bois-francs)*, forests that made the reputation of cabinet-making businesses in the surrounding villages. The population of the area is a mix of French, British, Acadian and Loyalist colonists. Up until the mid-19th century, there was not much going on here. However, the arrival of the Grand Trunk Railway began a process of industrialization that has yet to taper off. In the course of the last twenty years, some of Canada's largest and most modern factories have been built here. Paradoxically, there remains nothing of the railway but the strip of land it occupied. Plans are underway to turn the rail bed into a cycling path that will link the Eastern Townships to Québec City.

Victoriaville (pop. 38,191)

The economic heartland of the Bois-Francs, Victoriaville owes its development to the forestry and steel industries. Named after Queen Victoria, who reigned at the time of the town's establishment (1861), Victoriaville now incorporates the surrounding municipalities of Arthabaska et Sainte-Victoire-d'Arthabaska.

Arthabaska ★, the southern portion of Victoriaville, means "place of bulrushes and reeds" in the native language. It has produced or welcomed more than its share of prominent figures in the worlds of art and politics. Its residential sectors have always boasted a refined architecture, notably in the European and American styles. The town is especially known for its Victorian houses, particularly those along Avenue Laurier Ouest. In 1859, Arthabaska became the judicial district of the township. Construction of the courthouse, the prison and the registry office, that would make the fortune of the town, followed. Arthabaska was superseded by Victoriaville at the turn of the century, and though these buildings have

now been demolished it still retains a good part of its Belle Époque charm.

The **Maison Suzor-Côté** *(846 Boulevard Bois-Francs Sud)* is the birthplace of landscape painter Marc-Aurèle de Foy Suzor-Côté (1869-1937). His father had built the humble home 10 years earlier. One of Canada's foremost artists, Suzor-Côté began his career decorating churches, including Arthabaska's, before leaving to study at Paris' École des Beaux-Arts in 1891. After taking first prize at both the Julian and Colarossi academies, he worked in Paris before moving to Montréal in 1907. From then on, he returned annually to the family house, gradually turning it into a studio. His impressionist winter scenes and July sunsets are well known. The house is still a private residence *(not open to the public)*.

Turn left on Rue Laurier Ouest (Route 161).
The **Musée Laurier ★** *($3.50; Jul to Aug, Mon to Fri 9am to 6pm, Sat and Sun 1pm to 5pm; Sep to May, Mon to Fri 9am to noon and 1pm to 5pm, Sat and Sun 1pm to 5pm; 16 Rue Laurier Ouest, ☎357-8655)* occupies the house of the first French-Canadian Prime Minister (1896 to 1911). Sir Wilfrid Laurier (1841-1919) was born in Saint-Lin in the Basses-Laurentides but moved to Arthabaska as soon as he finished his legal studies. His house was turned into a museum in 1929 by two admirers. The ground floor rooms retain their Victorian furniture, while the second floor is partly devoted to exhibits. Paintings and sculptures by Québec artists encouraged by the Lauriers are on view throughout the house. Of particular interest are the portrait of Lady Laurier by Suzor-Côté and the bust of Sir Wilfrid Laurier by Alfred Laliberté.

The **Église Saint-Christophe ★** *(40 Rue Laurier Ouest, ☎357-2376)* was designed in 1871 by Joseph-Ferdinand Peachy from Québec City. It is best known for its polychromatic interior, completed by architects Perrault et Mesnard in 1887, and for its decoration by painters Marc-Aurèle de Foy Suzor-Côté and J. O. Rousseau from Saint-Hyacinthe.

Drummondville (pop. 45,554)

Drummondville was founded in the wake of the War of 1812 by Frederick George Heriot, who gave it the name of the British Governor of the time, Sir Gordon Drummond. The colony was at first a military outpost on the Rivière Saint-

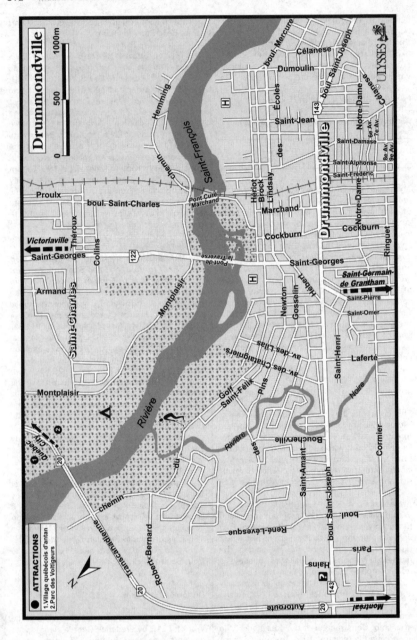

François, but the building of mills and factories soon made it a major industrial centre.

Turn right on Rue Montplaisir.

The **Village Québécois d'Antan ★★** (*$10; early Jun to early Sep, every day 10am to 5pm; Sep, Sat and Sun; 1425 Rue Montplaisir, ☎478-1441*) traces 100 years of history. Some 70 colonial-era buildings have been reproduced to evoke the atmosphere of village life from 1810 to 1910. People in period costume make *ceintures fléchées* (v-design sashes), candles and bread. Many historical television shows are shot on location here.

Continue along Montplaisir following the signs for Parc des Voltigeurs.

The **Parc des Voltigeurs ★** has recently been undergoing a facelift. The only heritage building between Montréal and Québec, which happens to be visible from Highway 20, lies in the southern part of the park. The **Manoir Trent**, built in 1848 for retired British Navy officer George Norris Trent, is not really a manor, but a large farmhouse. It was acquired by the Compagnons de l'École Hotelière, a hostel school, which turned it into the **Centre Québécois des Vins et Fromages**. A reference centre and training school, this unusual information centre is the site of wine and cheese tastings.

Continue along the east shore of Rivière Saint-François toward Saint-Joachim-de-Courval. Continue toward Pierreville and the nearby Odanak reserve.

Odanak (pop. 300)

Marguerite Hertel, the owner of the Saint-François seigneury at the beginning of the 18th century, ceded to the government of Trois-Rivières a portion of her land on the east bank of the Saint-François for the creation of an aboriginal village. The goal of regrouping and settling the Abenaki nation of Maine, allies of the French, was attained in 1700. Subsequently, at the time of the British Conquest in 1759, the village was laid waste by the British in reprisal. Odanak is still a reserve.

The **Musée des Abénakis ★** (*$4; early May to late Oct, Mon to Wed 10am to 5pm, Sat and Sun 1pm to 5pm; 108 Rue Waban-Aki, ☎514-568-2600*) was founded in 1962, and allows the visitor to explore Abenaki culture. A permanent exhibit depicts the ancestral way of life of the Abenaki and their relations with the French. The museum's animators bring to life the artifacts on display with traditional songs, legends and dances. The village church with its native carvings is also well worth a visit.

Nicolet (pop. 5,100)

The St. Lawrence valley shelters some towns and villages that were founded by the Acadians after their deportation from the Maritimes by the British army in 1755. Nicolet is one of these towns. It has been a bishopric since 1877. In 1955, a major landslide destroyed a part of the town's centre (the clay and marshy soil around Lac Saint-Pierre precludes settlement on its banks).

The **Cathédrale Saint-Jean-Baptiste ★** (*every day 9am to 4pm; 671 Boulevard Louis-Fréchette, ☎293-4696*) replaced the one destroyed by the landslide of 1955. The curved shape of the reinforced concrete building, designed by Gérard Malouin in 1962 evokes a ship's sail. Jean-Paul Charland's gigantic stained-glass window (21 m by 50 m) for the church's façade is best appreciated from the inside.

Several religions are represented in Nicolet, a fact that surely influenced the founders of its **Musée des Religions ★** (*$3.50; every day 10am to 5pm; 900 Boulevard Louis-Fréchette, ☎293-6148*). This museum presents interesting thematic exhibits on the different religious traditions of the world.

The **Ancien Séminaire ★** (*350 Rue d'Youville*) of Nicolet was founded in 1803 by the Bishop of Québec, who wanted future priests to receive their training far from the temptations of the city. The third-oldest seminary in Québec, Nicolet Seminary was also for a long time one of the province's most prestigious colleges. The imposing building was designed by Thomas Baillargé and built between 1827 and 1836. The Seminary was closed in the course of the Quiet Revolution and the building now houses the Institut de Police du Québec (Police Academy). Unfortunately, part of the building was damaged by fire in 1973 and is still awaiting restoration.

The **Maison Rodolphe-Duguay** (*$3.50; early Jun to mid-Sep, Tue and Wed, 10am to 5pm; 195 Rang Saint-Alexis at Nicolet-Sud,*

☎293-4103) was the home of Québécois painter Rodolphe Duguay (1891-1973). He was devoted to the Bois-Francs landscape and painted its rural scenes throughout his 60-year career. He began his studies at Montréal's Monument National, before spending seven years in Paris. When he returned to Québec, he moved back home to Nicolet and remained there for the rest of his life. In 1929, next to his house he set up a studio whose interior is similar to the one he had in Paris. This vast space is now open to the public and houses a retrospective of the artist's work.

Continue along Route 132 E. to Bécancour.

Saint-Grégoire (Bécancour)

The **Église Saint-Grégoire** ★ ★ (*4200 Boulevard Port-Royal, Bécancour*) is in the middle of the old village of Saint-Grégoire de Nicolet, founded in 1757 by a group of Acadians originally from Beaubassin. The parishioners began the construction of the present church in 1803. Since then the church has been touched up by two famous Québécois architects, Thomas Baillargé, who designed the 1851 neoclassical façade, and Victor Bourgeau, who remodelled the bell-towers before decorating the arch of the nave.

In 1811, the church council acquired the precious retable and tabernacle from the Récollet church in Montréal that used to stand at the corner of Sainte-Hélène and Notre-Dame. Well-placed at Saint-Grégoire, the retable is the oldest in Québec, dating from 1713, and made by Jean-Jacques Bloem, dit Le Blond. The Louis-XIII style tabernacle is a major work executed by the carver Charles Chaboulié in 1703. The paintings by Parisian artist Joseph Uberti are much more recent (circa 1910).

 PARKS

Tour A: La Mauricie

Situated at the mouth of the Rivière Saint-Maurice is the **Parc de l'île Saint-Quentin** (*$2; May to Oct 9am to 8pm, Nov to Apr 9am to 5pm; ☎373-8151*). This island of tranquillity and nature is ideal for strolling or swimming. There are also picnic grounds.

The **Parc de la Rivière-Batiscan** ★ (*$3.50 per person, up to $12 per car, free for children; early May to late Oct, every day 9am to 9pm; 200 Route du Barrage à Saint-Narcisse, ☎418-328-3599*) is devoted to the conservation of the wildlife and habitat. Still, it remains a pleasant place for all kinds of activities, from walking and mountain-biking to camping and fishing. The park also offers ecological and historical tours. In the middle of the park stands one of Québec's first hydro-electric plants. Constructed in 1897, the Saint-Narcisse station still provides power to Trois-Rivières.

The **Mauricie National Park** ★ (*$3.50 per person for one day; Grand-Mère; ☎538-3232*) is also known as Parc national de La Mauricie. It was created in 1970 to preserve a part of the Laurentians. It is a perfect setting for outdoor activities such as canoeing, hiking, mountain biking, snowshoeing and cross-country skiing. Hidden among the woods are several lakes and rivers, as well as natural wonders of all kinds. Visitors can stay in dormitories year-round for $21 per person. Reservations can be made at ☎537-4555.

The **Réserve Faunique du Saint-Maurice** ★ (*Route 155, 109 km north of Trois-Rivières, for reservations, bed and breakfasts and camping: ☎646-5680*) is reached by boat on the Rivière Saint-Maurice. Covering more than 750 square kilometres, it includes several hiking trails equipped with huts. In the fall, moose- and game-hunting are allowed.

The **Parc des Chutes de Shawinigan et Shawinigan-Sud** ★ (*free admission; ☎536-7155*) is well equipped to receive cross-country skiers and snowshoers throughout the winter. In the summer, it is a pleasant spot for a leisurely row on the Rivière Saint-Maurice. There is also an enclosure with over a dozen white-tailed deer. The waterfalls are spectacular all year round, but especially right after the spring thaw.

The **Réserve Faunique Mastigouche** (*Route 349, St-Alexis-des-Monts, ☎265-2098*) covers 1,600 square kilometres. Dotted with lakes and rivers, it is a prized canoe-camping spot. Hunting and fishing are also allowed. In winter, 180 kilometres of cross-country-ski trails and 130 kilometres of snowmobile trails are maintained. You can sleep in the shelters for $17 per person (*reservations ☎265-3925*). Small chalets for four to eight people can also be rented for \$25 per person *(reservations ☎1-800-665-6527)*.

OUTDOORS

Ice-fishing

Tour A: La Mauricie

From December to February, thousands of devotees of **ice-fishing**, converge on the Rivière Sainte-Anne to fish for tomcod. The river is covered with fishing huts in the winter. These can be rented, along with the necessary equipment, from the Comité de Gestion de la Rivière Sainte- Anne, the river's management committee *(Ste-Anne-de-la-Pérade, ☎418-325-2475)*. The price is \$15 per person per day (four per cabin, maximum), \$18 on the weekend.

Canoeing

The **Mauricie National Park** (see above) is perfect for canoe trips. Strewn with lakes of all sizes, as well as a number of rivers, it has long been renowned among canoe-campers. Let yourself glide down narrow channels from one lake to another beneath luxuriant vegetation, accompanied by friendly water birds. You can rent a boat at the park and plan your own itinerary.

The region's two wildlife reserves, the **Réserve Faunique du Saint-Maurice** (see p 314) and the **Réserve Faunique Mastigouche** (see p 314), are also good places to explore by canoe.

Cross-country Skiing

During winter, the **Réserve Faunique Mastigouche** (see p 314) has 200 kilometres of well-maintained trails. The **Réserve Faunique du Saint-Maurice** (see p 314) and the **La Mauricie National Park** (see p 314) are also pleasant places to go cross-country skiing.

Biking

In Québec, more and more bike paths are being laid out where railway lines used to be. One of these is the 60-kilometre **Parc Linéaire des Bois-Francs** *(231 Rue Notre-Dame Est, Victoriaville, ☎758-6414)*, which runs between Warwick and Lyster.

Snowmobiling

During winter, the **Réserve Faunique de Mastigouche** (see p 314) is a playground for snowmobilers, with 130 kilometres of marked trails studded with heated shelters.

Dogsledding

At the **Réserve Faunique du Saint-Maurice** (see p 314), you can experience the thrill of racing along a snowy trail with a team of dogs at your command. All winter long, this park maintains nearly 270 kilometres of marked trails laid out expressly for dogsledding.

ACCOMMODATIONS

Tour A: La Mauricie

Trois-Rivières

The **Auberge de Jeunesse la Flotille** *(\$18 for dormitories, \$36 for private rooms; 497 Rue Radisson, G9A 2C7, ☎378-8010)*, the youth hostel, is right downtown. There are some 40 beds in the summer season, this number dwindles to 30 in the winter.

The high tower of the **Hôtel Delta** *(84 \$, ≈, ⊙, ⌂, ℜ; 1620 Notre-Dame, G9A 6E5, ☎376-1991, ⊷372-5975)* is easy to spot next to the downtown area. The rooms are spacious. The hotel also has sports facilities.

Ulysses' Favourites

Accommodations

For a friendly reception:
Auberge Le Bôme (p 316)

For the views:
Auberge du Lac-Saint-Pierre
(p 316)

For outdoors-enthusiasts:
Le Baluchon (p 316)

Restaurants

Mauricie–Bois Francs grand tables:
Chez Claude (p 317), Auberge du
Lac-Saint-Pierre (p 317) and
Auberge Godefroy (p 318)

For Québec cuisine:
Le Baluchon (p 317)

Grand-Mère

The **Auberge Le Florès** (*$45 in the old wing,
$60 in the new wing; tv, ≈, ≡, ℜ; 4291 50e
Avenue, G9T 6S5, ☎538-9340, ≈538-1884)* is
a superb period house. Though not spectacular,
the rooms are quite comfortable.

The **Auberge St-Exupéry** (*$50 bkfst incl.;
3520 50e Avenue, G9T 1A7, ☎538-2505)* is a
pretty, inviting little *gîte* with spacious,
comfortable rooms.

Saint-Jean-des-Piles

The **Maison Cadorette** (*$55 bkfst incl.;
1701 Principale, G0X 2V0, ☎538-9883)*
accommodates guests just a few minutes from
the entrance to the La Mauricie National Park.
The rooms are attractively decorated and the
service is impeccable.

Grandes-Piles

The **Auberge Le Bôme** (*$70; 720 2e
Avenue, G0X 1H0, ☎538-2805)* is an excellent
option in this region. The rooms are beautifully
decorated, and the friendly service makes for a
very inviting atmosphere. There is also a superb

sitting room, for fascinating discussions with
other travellers.

Shawinigan

A well-kept place on the way into town, the
Auberge l'Escapade (*$58; ℜ; 3383 Rue
Garnier, G9N 6R4, ☎539-6911 or 539-7669)*
has several different personalities. The choice
of accommodations here ranges from basic,
inexpensive rooms (*$48*) to luxurious rooms
decorated with period furniture (*$145*). In
between the two, there are pretty, comfortable
rooms that offer good value for the money
(*$63-$80*). What's more, the restaurant serves
tasty food.

Pointe-du-Lac

The **Auberge du Lac Saint-Pierre** (*$180; ℜ,
≈, ≡, ⊛, ◬, ☉; 1911 Route 138, P.O. Box 10,
G0X 1Z0, ☎377-5961, 371-5579 or
1-888-377-5971)* is located in Pointe-de-Lac, a
small village at the north end of Lac Saint-
Pierre, which is actually just a widening in the
Saint-Lawrence. The flora and fauna that make
their home in and around the "lake" are
characteristic of marshy areas. Perched atop a
promontory that slopes down to the shore, this
large inn boasts an outstanding location. It has
comfortable modern rooms, some of which
have a mezzanine for the beds, leaving more
space in the main room. The dining room
serves excellent food (see p 317). There are
bicycles on hand if you feel like exploring the
area; take advantage of them!

Saint-Paulin

Located alongside a river, **Le Baluchon**
(*$97; ☉, ◬, ≈, ℜ, ⊛; 350 Chemin des Trembles,
J0K 2J0, ☎268-2555, 268-5234 or
1-800-789-5968)* is *the* place in the area for
active types. The vast grounds highlight the
beautiful natural surroundings. There are plenty
of ways to occupy your time here: hiking or
skiing along the river or through the woods,
kayaking, canoeing, etc. Guests sleep in one of
two buildings, each containing nearly 40
pleasant and comfortable modern rooms. style.
You can also relax at the well-equipped fitness
centre or tempt your palate in the dining room
(see p 317).

Tour B: Les Bois-Francs

Bécancour

The **Auberge Godefroy** *($150; ⊛, ℜ, ≈, ≡, △, ☉, K; 17575 Boulevard Bécancour, G0X 2T0, ☎233-2200, 233-2288 or 1-800-361-1620)* is an imposing building with lots of windows. During winter, a crackling fire awaits guests in the stately lobby. The 70 rooms are spacious and offer all the comforts one would expect from an establishment in this category. The hotel also has a fitness centre and offers a variety of packages. Go ahead and indulge yourself in the dining room as well (see p 318)!

Drummondville

The **Motel Blanchette** *($55; 225 Boulevard St-Joseph Ouest, J2E 1A9, ☎477-1222 or 1-800-567-3823)* has a good location and pretty, reasonably priced rooms.

The **Hôtellerie Le Dauphin** *($74; ≈, ℜ; 600 Boulevard St-Joseph, J2C 2C1, ☎478-4141, ⇛478-7549)* is located on a very busy street, near a number of shopping centres. It has large, well-kept rooms decorated with modern furnishings.

Victoriaville

The modern **Le Suzor** hotel *($76; 1000 Boulevard Jutras, G6S 1E4, ☎357-1000, ⇛357-5000)* is in a quiet part of town. The pleasant, spacious rooms are equipped with new furniture.

 RESTAURANTS

Tour A: La Mauricie

Trois-Rivières

The **Bolvert** *($; 1556 Rue Royale, ☎373-6161)* is an unpretentious little restaurant serving delicious health-food dishes. The decor is a little bleak but the cuisine is simple and good.

The **Auberge Castel des Près** *(5800 Boulevard Royal, ☎375-4921)* has two different restaurants: **L'Étiquette** *($-$$)* serves bistro-style cuisine and **Chez Claude (Castel des Prés)** *($$-$$$)* offers traditional French cuisine making it an excellent choice in this area. The chef has won a number of culinary awards. The menu includes pasta, meat and fish dishes with rich, flavourful sauces. During the warm weather, guests can enjoy a sheltered outdoor terrace cooled by summer breezes.

Grand-Mère

The **Crêperie de Flore** *($$-$$$; 3580 50e Avenue, ☎533-2020)* has a simple, informal ambiance and specializes in Breton crêpes and veal.

Grandes-Piles

In addition to being charming and comfortable, the **Auberge Le Bôme** *($$$$; 720 2e Avenue, ☎538-2805)* serves French cuisine combined with regional specialties like venison and Arctic trout, with sensational results. An absolute must!

Pointe-du-Lac

If you go to the **Auberge du Lac Saint-Pierre** *($$$-$$$$; 1911 Route 138, ☎377-5971 or 1-888-377-5971)* (see p 316) for dinner, star your evening with a short walk on the shore to work up an appetite, or perhaps have an apéritif on the terrace, with its view of the river. The modern decor of the dining room is a bit cold, but there's nothing bland about the presentation of the dishes, much less their flavour. The menu, made up of French and Québec cuisine, includes trout, salmon, lamb and pheasant, all artfully prepared.

Saint-Paulin

Located on a magnificent estate, **Le Baluchon** *($$$-$$$$; 350 Chemin des Trembles, ☎268-2555 or 1-800-789-5968)* (see p 316) offers choice French and Québec cuisine, as well as a "health-conscious" menu that will leave you feeling anything but deprived. The dining room has a soothing decor and a view of the river.

Tour B: Les Bois-Francs

Bécancour

🦐 The spacious dining room of the **Auberge Godefroy** *($$$-$$$$; 17575 Boulevard Bécancour, ☎233-2200 or 1-800-361-1620)* (see p 317) looks out onto the river. The delicious French cuisine varies from classic to original creations made with regional produce. Succulent desserts!

Victoriaville

Le Perroquet *($; 304 Rue Notre-Dame Est, ☎751-0314)* offers good bistro-style food. The walls in this pleasant restaurant are covered with pictures of parrots. There is also a bar.

The restaurant **Plus Bar** *($; 192 Boulevard Des Bois-Francs Sud, ☎758-9927)* serves a splendid *poutine* (French fries, gravy and curd cheese) deemed one of these best in these parts. You can savour this magnificent "culinary" creation taking in the latest sporting events on a giant screen. Watch out: the "plus" size might be a little more "plus" than you're expecting!

The **Village Mykonos** *($-$$; 6 Rue Tourigny, ☎752-5863)* is a very popular Greek restaurant. The decor is simple yet refined and the prices are affordable. Bring your own wine.

Drummondville

The restaurant of the **Le Dauphin** hotel *($$; 600 Boulevard Saint-Joseph, ☎478-4141 or 1-800-567-0995)* has a good seafood buffet. The helpings are large and there is also an "all you can eat" option. The decor is a little bleak but the atmosphere nice and relaxed.

ENTERTAINMENT

Bars and Nightclubs

Victoriaville

Le Café *(32 Rue Notre-Dame Est)* really lives up to its name; it's an unpretentious place to have a coffee or a beer in the afternoon or evening.

Festivals and Cultural Events

Trois Rivières

The **Grand Prix Player's de Trois-Rivières** *(☎373-9912)*, an Indy Light car race, is held in the city streets in early August. Now-famous drivers like as Jacques Villeneuve, have taken part in this event in the past.

Plessiville

The **Festival de l'Érable** is held every April or beginning of May in Plessisvile. The maple festival is a chance to indulge a sweet tooth and to see the workings of the maple syrup industry.

Drummondville

In mid-July, Drummondville hosts a 10-day **Festival Mondial du Folklore à Drummondville** *(☎472-1184 or 1-800-265-5412)*. The goal of this festival is to encourage exchanges between the different traditions and cultures of the world.

Victoriaville

The **Festival de Musique Actuelle de Victoriaville** *(☎758-9451)* takes place each year in May. This festival is an exploration of new musical forms. Of course, this event won't appeal to everyone, but it is an adventure, for musicians and spectators alike.

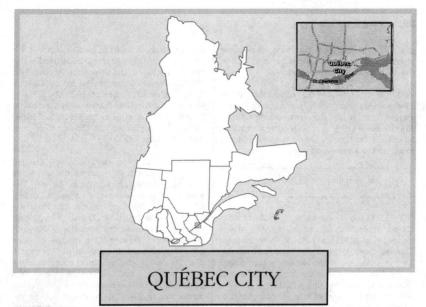

QUÉBEC CITY

Q uébec City ★★★ is a magical place whatever the season. Meandering through the winding streets on a winter evening is an enchanting experience: the snow sparkles under the light of the streetlamps and the whole city looks like a scene from *A Christmas Carol*. Merry makers appear through the window panes of a restaurant, illuminated by the light dancing from the hearth, savouring hearty fare. They've come to join the carnival, or maybe they're setting off on an excursion to the ski slopes of Mont Sainte-Anne.

In the spring and summer, the terraces of Grande-Allée shelter their thirsty patrons under a sea of multicoloured parasols, while out on the Plains of Abraham an elderly woman performs her *Tai Chi* exercises. Fall keeps in reserve its own treasure of special moments to be shared with the inhabitants of the jewel of French America: the spectacular display of the leaves rustling in the fresh breeze; the sight of students dawdling to arrive just in time for the start of a geometry course at the university while the politicians and civil servants pursue their debates over one last coffee before returning to the Parliament buildings.

Québec City stands out as much for the stunning richness of its architectural heritage as for the beauty of its location. The Haute-Ville quarter covers a promontory more than 98 metres high, known as Cap Diamant, and juts out over the St. Lawrence River, which

narrows here to a mere one kilometre. In fact, it is this narrowing of the river which gave the city its name: in Algonquian, *kebec* means "place where the river narrows". Affording an impregnable vantage point, the heights of Cap Diamant dominate the river and the surrounding countryside. From the inception of New France, this rocky peak played an important strategic role and was the site of major fortifications early on. Dubbed the "Gibraltar of North America", today Québec is the only walled city north of Mexico.

The cradle of New France, Québec is a city whose atmosphere and architecture are more reminiscent of Europe than of America. The stone houses that flank its narrow streets and the many spires of its churches and religious institutions evoke the France of the Old Regime. In addition, the old fortifications of Haute-Ville, the Parliament and the grandiose administration buildings attest eloquently to the importance of Québec in the history of the country. Indeed, its historical and architectural richness are such that the city and its historic surroundings were recognized by UNESCO in 1985 as a World Heritage Site, the first in North America.

With over 95% of the population of French ancestry, the capital of Québec is home to an impressive number of excellent restaurants and cafés. It is a lively city all year round, distinguished in the fall by the turning of the leaves, in the winter by its famous carnival, in the spring by the musicians who take to the streets and the newly opened terraces, and in the summer by its summer festival.

Within reach of the city the region offers lovely mountainous landscapes. This chapter contains suggestions for four different walking tours in the city and another tour with other attractions in and around the city, while the next chapter explores the surrounding area.

A Short History of Québec City

During his second expedition, in 1535, Jacques Cartier stopped at Stadacona, a native village located on land that would later become Québec City. Hoping to find precious stones, he christened the sheer and stony escarpment that overlooks the river Cap Diamant, "Cape of Diamonds". At the time, Cartier was on a mission for the King of France, François I, to discover gold as well as a passage to the Orient. After Cartier's three expeditions found neither of these, the King declined to finance further voyages to North America.

A few decades later, the significant profits to be made in the fur trade rekindled France's interest in this far-off land. After the failure of many trading posts both on the coast and in the interior, the area where Québec City now stands was chosen for the establishment of a permanent trading post. In 1608, Samuel de Champlain and his men erected and fortified a series of buildings at the foot of the cape. This first settlement was known as *Abitation*. Despite the extreme harshness of the first winter and the deaths of 20 of the 28 men from scurvy and malnutrition, 1608 marked the beginning of a permanent French presence in North America. Québec City was founded for the fur trade, therefore it initially attracted the interest of French merchants. Little by little, a few peasant families began to establish themselves. Basse-Ville became the centre of commercial activity and the residential area of the colonists. In fact, Québec's lower-town remained its urban and commercial centre until the middle of the 19th century, because the religious institutions of Haute-Ville opposed commercial development. Early on, New France's capital became a prize in the rivalry that pitted France against England. Québec City was captured by the Kirke brothers in 1629, before being returned to France in 1632. Although the city held out against the English siege led by Admiral Phipps in 1690, pressure

from England continued to build throughout the 18th century. The outcome was decided in the famous battle of the Plains of Abraham in 1759, in which British troops led by General Wolfe defeated those of the Marquis de Montcalm. When New France was ceded to the British under the terms of the Treaty of Paris in 1763, the population of Québec City had reached almost 9,000.

Because of its geographic location, Québec City served as the entryway to the colony as well as its principal economic centre. The goods of the commercial triangle linking Canada, the West Indies and London were transhipped in the port of Québec City, which naturally developed an important shipyard. Nevertheless, Québec City began to lose ground rapidly with the growth of Montréal in the 19th century. Following the dredging of the St. Lawrence up to Montréal and the construction of a rail system with Montréal as its centre, Québec City was usurped as the focus of trade and as the foremost economic centre of Canada. Though Montréal became the Canadian metropolis, Québec City nonetheless retained an important role as the provincial capital and as a strategic military base. In the twenties, it even enjoyed a certain prosperity based largely on the shoemaking industry.

The growth of Québec City in the sixties paralleled that of the scope and power of Québec's provincial government. Today, the economy of the sole francophone capital of North America revolves around the civil service.

 FINDING YOUR WAY AROUND

Four walking tours are suggested for getting to know Québec City: **Tour A: Vieux-Québec (Haute-Ville)** ★★★, **Tour B: Vieux-Québec (Basse-Ville)** ★★★, **Tour C: Grande-Allée** ★★ and **Tour D: Saint-Jean-Baptiste** ★.

By Car

Québec City can be reached from Montréal along either shore of the St. Lawrence River. Highway 40 East runs along the north shore, becoming the 440 on the outskirts of Québec City and then Boulevard Charest once you get downtown. On the south shore, Highway 20 runs east until the Pierre-Laporte bridge. Across the bridge, Boulevard Laurier continues in the

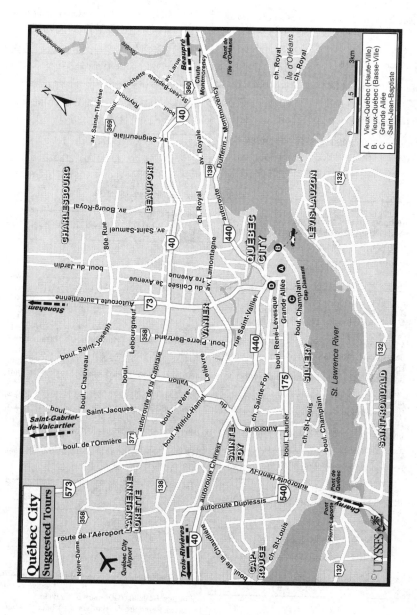

QUÉBEC CITY

Québec City
Suggested Tours

A. Vieux-Québec (Haute-Ville)
B. Vieux-Québec (Basse-Ville)
C. Grande Allée
D. Saint-Jean-Baptiste

© ULYSSES

direction of Québec City, becoming Grande-Allée Est as you enter the downtown area.

Hertz
Airport: ☎871-1571
Québec City: 580 Grande-Allée, ☎647-4949
Vieux-Québec: 44 Côte du Palais ☎694-1224,
☎692-3713

Tilden
Airport: ☎871-1224
Québec City: 295 Rue Saint-Paul, ☎694-1727,
☎694-2174

By Plane

Aéroport Jean-Lesage (see p 48), though smaller than Montréal's airports, does receive international flights.

By Bus

A network of bus routes covers the entire city. A $50 monthly pass allows for unlimited travel. A single trip costs $2 (exact change only) or $1.60 with the purchase of tickets (sold at newspaper stands). Transfers, if needed, should be requested from the driver upon boarding. Take note that most bus routes are in operation between 6am and 12:30am. Fridays and Saturdays, there is additional "late-night" bus service for #800, #801, #7, #11 and #25; all leave from Place d'Youville at 3am. For more information : ☎627-2511.

Bus Station

320 Rue Abraham-Martin (Gare du Palais), ☎525-3000.

Train Station

450 Rue de la Gare-du-Palais, ☎524-4161

By Ferry

The ferry *(adults $1.75; cars $3; 10 Rue des Traversiers, ☎644-3704),* from Lévis to Québec City takes 20 min. As the schedule varies

widely depending on the season, it is best to check the times of crossings when planning a trip.

Ridesharing

Rides are organized to Québec City with Allo-Stop *(☎522-3430)* (see p 56)

Taxis

Taxi Coop: ☎525-5191
Taxi Québec: ☎525-8123

 PRACTICAL INFORMATION

Area code: 418

Tourist Information Office

The information centre of the **Office du Tourisme et des Congrès de la Communauté Urbaine de Québec**, which used to be on Rue d'Auteuil, is now located near the Manège Militaire and the Plains of Abraham. Unfortunately, its opening hours are not very convenient, so stop by during normal business hours: 835 Avenue Wilfrid-Laurier, G1R 2L3, ☎649-2608, ☎692-1481, www.quebec-region.cuq.qc.ca

12 Rue Sainte-Anne, (in front of the Château Frontenac)

Post Office

300 Rue Saint-Paul, ☎694-6176

Banks

Banque Royale: 700 Place d'Youville.
Caisse Populaire Desjardins du Vieux-Québec: 19 Rue des Jardins.

Guided Tours

Located in the tourist information office on Rue Sainte-Anne, **CD Tour** *($15, $24 for two people; 12 Rue Sainte-Anne, ☎990-8687)* rents out portable audio-tours for various parts of the city, including Vieux-Québec, the Colline Parlementaire, Parc-de-l'Artillerie and the Plaines d'Abraham. These tours are recorded on laser disc, enabling visitors to stop where and when they please. In the lively recordings, historic figures are brought back to life to tell visitors about the major events that shaped Québec City.

The **Société Historique de Québec** *($12; 72 Côte de la Montagne, ☎692-0556 or 692-0614)*, on Côte de la Montagne, offers guided tours of Vieux-Québec. There are a number of themes from which to choose, such as "The American Invasion of 1775-1776". These walking tours usually last two to three hours and cover various aspects of the history of Québec City.

Another option is to take a "Québec, Fortified City" walking tour, offered by the **Centre d'Initiation aux Fortifications de Québec** *($7.50; 90 min; mid-May to end of Oct every day 10am to 5pm, mid-Apr to mid-May Wed to Sun 10am to 5pm; ☎648-7016)* (see p 324). These start at the kiosk on Terrasse Dufferin.

 EXPLORING

Coming into Québec City by car, the most common route is via Grande-Allée. After passing through a typical North American style suburb, you come to a rather British-looking part of town with tree-lined streets. Next come the government buildings of the provincial capital, and finally, the imposing medieval-looking gates and behind them the historic streets of the old city, Vieux-Québec.

The numbers beside each attraction refer to the map of the particular tour.

Tour A: Vieux-Québec (Haute-Ville) ★★★ (two days)

Haute-Ville, or upper town, covers the plateau atop Cap Diamant. As the administrative and institutional centre, it is adorned with convents, chapels and public buildings whose construction dates back, in some cases, to the 17th century. The walls of Haute-Ville, dominated by the citadel, surround this section of Vieux-Québec and give it the characteristic look of a stronghold. These same walls long contained the development of the town, yielding a densely built-up bourgeois and aristocratic milieu. With time, the picturesque urban planning of the 19th century contributed to the present-day image of Québec City through the construction of such fantastical buildings as the Château Frontenac and the creation of such public spaces as Terrasse Dufferin, in the *belle époque* spirit.

The Haute-Ville walking tour begins at Porte Saint-Louis, near the parliament buildings.

Porte Saint-Louis (1) *(at the beginning of the street of the same name)*. This gateway is the result of Québec City merchants' pressuring the government between 1870 and 1875 to tear down the wall surrounding the city. The Governor General of Canada at the time, Lord Dufferin, was opposed to the idea and instead put forward a plan drafted by the Irishman William H. Lynn to showcase the walls while improving traffic circulation. The design he submitted exhibits a Victorian romanticism in its use of grand gateways which bring to mind images of medieval castles and horsemen. The pepper-box tower of Porte Saint-Louis, built in 1878, makes for a striking first impression upon arriving in downtown Québec City.

On the right, once inside Porte Saint-Louis, is the **Club de la Garnison** *(97 Rue Saint-Louis)*, reserved for officers of the army, as well as the road leading to the citadel. As a visit to the citadel may require two or three hours, it is best to set aside a separate time to take a tour of the premises (see description at the end of the Haute-Ville walking tour, on p 335).

Lieu Historique National des Fortifications-de-Québec ★. Québec City's first wall was built of earth and wooden posts. It was erected on the west side of the city in 1693, according to the plans of engineer Dubois Berthelot de Beaucours, to protect Québec City from the Iroquois. Work on much stronger stone fortifications began in 1745, according to the plans of engineer Chaussegros de Léry, when England and France entered a new era of conflict. However, the wall was unfinished

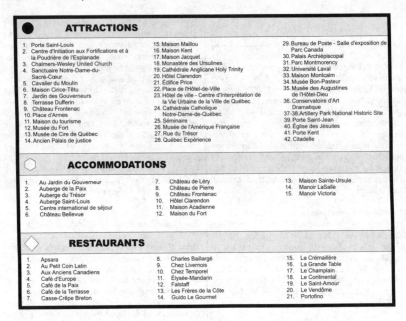

ATTRACTIONS

1. Porte Saint-Louis
2. Centre d'Initiation aux Fortifications et à la Poudrière de l'Esplanade
3. Chalmers-Wesley United Church
4. Sanctuaire Notre-Dame-du-Sacré-Cœur
5. Cavalier du Moulin
6. Maison Cirice-Têtu
7. Jardin des Gouverneurs
8. Terrasse Dufferin
9. Château Frontenac
10. Place d'Armes
11. Maison du tourisme
12. Musée du Fort
13. Musée de Cire de Québec
14. Ancien Palais de justice
15. Maison Maillou
16. Maison Kent
17. Maison Jacquet
18. Monastère des Ursulines
19. Cathédrale Anglicane Holy Trinity
20. Hôtel Clarendon
21. Édifice Price
22. Place de l'Hôtel-de-Ville
23. Hôtel de ville - Centre d'Interprétation de la Vie Urbaine de la Ville de Québec
24. Cathédrale Catholique Notre-Dame-de-Québec
25. Séminaire
26. Musée de l'Amérique Française
27. Rue du Trésor
28. Québec Expérience
29. Bureau de Poste - Salle d'exposition de Parc Canada
30. Palais Archiépiscopal
31. Parc Montmorency
32. Université Laval
33. Maison Montcalm
34. Musée Bon-Pasteur
35. Musée des Augustines de l'Hôtel-Dieu
36. Conservatoire d'Art Dramatique
37-38. Artillery Park National Historic Site
39. Porte Saint-Jean
40. Église des Jésuites
41. Porte Kent
42. Citadelle

ACCOMMODATIONS

1. Au Jardin du Gouverneur
2. Auberge de la Paix
3. Auberge du Trésor
4. Auberge Saint-Louis
5. Centre international de séjour
6. Château Bellevue
7. Château de Léry
8. Château de Pierre
9. Château Frontenac
10. Hôtel Clarendon
11. Maison Acadienne
12. Maison du Fort
13. Maison Sainte-Ursule
14. Manoir LaSalle
15. Manoir Victoria

RESTAURANTS

1. Apsara
2. Au Petit Coin Latin
3. Aux Anciens Canadiens
4. Café d'Europe
5. Café de la Paix
6. Café de la Terrasse
7. Casse-Crêpe Breton
8. Charles Baillargé
9. Chez Livernois
10. Chez Temporel
11. Élysée-Mandarin
12. Falstaff
13. Les Frères de la Côte
14. Guido Le Gourmet
15. La Crémaillère
16. La Grande Table
17. Le Champlain
18. Le Continental
19. Le Saint-Amour
20. Le Vendôme
21. Portofino

when the city was seized by the British in 1759. The British saw to the completion of the project at the end of the 18th century. Work on the citadel began in 1693 to a minor extent. However, the structure as we know it today was essentially built between 1820 and 1832. Nevertheless, the citadel is largely designed along the principles advanced by Vauban in the 17th century, principles that suit the location admirably.

To learn more about these fortifications, visit the **Centre d'iniciation aux fortifications et à la Poudrière de l'Esplanade (2)** *($2.50; mid-May to end of Apr, every day 10am to 5pm; mi-Apr to mid-May, Wed to Sun 10am to 5pm; 100 Rue St-Louis, ☎648-7016)* which displays models and maps outlining the development of Québec City's defense system. Booklets are available with a complete tour of the city's fortifications, and there are also guided tours. Information plaques have been placed along the wall, providing another means of discovering the city's history. The walkway on top of the wall can be reached by using the stairs next to the city gates.

Continue along Rue Saint-Louis and turn right on Rue Sainte-Ursule.

Chalmers-Wesley United Church (3) *(78 Rue Sainte-Ursule)*. Until the end of the 19th century, Québec City had a small but influential community of Scottish Presbyterians, most of whom were involved in shipping and in the lumber trade. This attractive Gothic Revival church is presently used by a variety of groups, testimony to the decline in the Scottish Presbyterian community. The church was built in 1852, according to plans drawn up by John Wells, an architect known for a number of famous buildings, including the Bank of Montreal headquarters. The elegant Gothic Revival spire of the church contributes to the picturesque aspect of the city. The church's organ was restored in 1985. Concerts are presented at the church every Sunday afternoon from the beginning of July until the middle of August. Donations are appreciated.

The **Sanctuaire Notre-Dame-du-Sacré-Cœur (4)** *(free admission; open every day 7am to 8pm; 71 Rue Sainte-Ursule, ☎692-3787)* faces Chalmers-Wesley United Church. The sanctuary was originally built for the Sacré Cœur missionaries. This place of worship, erected in 1910 based on the drafts of François-Xavier Berlinguet, is now open to everyone. The

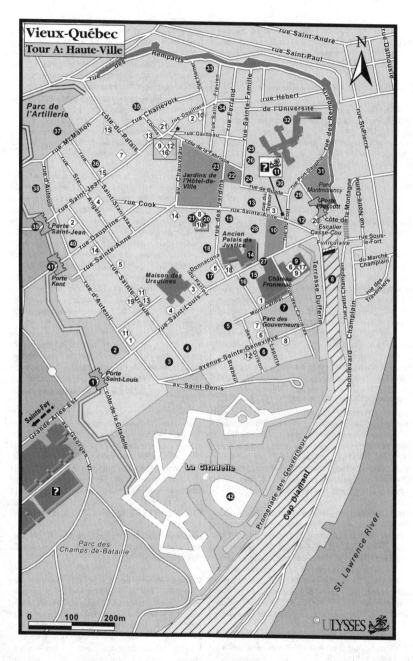

sanctuary has a Gothic Revival façade. Its two rather narrow steeples seem dwarfed by the size of the building. The interior of the structure, with its stained glass windows and murals, is more attractive.

Turn left on Avenue Sainte-Geneviève.

A short detour down Rue Mont-Carmel (to the left) brings you to one of the remnants of Québec City's earliest fortifications, located in an out of the way spot behind a row of houses. The **Cavalier du Moulin (5)**, was built in 1693 according to plans of engineer Dubois Bertholot de Beaucours. It is a redoubt set within the city walls from which it would be possible to destroy them in the event of a successful enemy invasion. The fortification is named for the windmill, or *moulin*, that used to sit on top of it.

Maison Cirice-Têtu ★ (6) *(25 Avenue Sainte-Geneviève).* Besides the city's major historical landmarks, Québec's appeal lies with its smaller, less imposing buildings, each of which has its own separate history. It is enjoyable to simply wander the narrow streets of the old city, taking in the subtleties of architecture so atypical of North America. The Cirice-Têtu house was built in 1852. It was designed by Charles Baillargé, a member of a celebrated family of architects who, beginning in the 18th century, left an important mark on the architecture of Québec City and its surroundings. The Greek Revival façade of the house, a masterpiece of the genre, is tastefully decorated, with palmettes and the discreet use of laurel. The wreathing *piano nobile* has huge bay windows that open onto a single expansive living room in the London style. From the time of its construction, the house incorporated all the modern amenities: central heating, hot running water, and multiple bathrooms.

The charming square known as **Jardin des Gouverneurs ★ (7)** was originally the private garden of the governor of New France. The square was laid out in 1647 for Charles Huault de Montmagny to the west of Château Saint-Louis, the residence of the governor. A monument to opposing military leaders Wolfe and Montcalm, both of whom died on the battlefields of the Plains of Abraham, was erected during the restoration of the garden in 1827.

Walking along **Terrasse Dufferin ★★★ (8)**, overlooking the St. Lawrence, provides an interesting sensation compared to the pavement we are used to. It was built in 1879 at the request of the Governor General of the time, Lord Dufferin. The boardwalk's open-air pavilions and ornate streetlamps were designed by Charles Baillargé and were inspired by the style of French urban architecture common under Napoleon III. Terrasse Dufferin is one of Québec City's most popular sights and is the preferred meeting place for young people. The view of the river, the south shore and Île d'Orléans is magnificent. During the winter months, a huge ice slide is set up at the western end of the boardwalk.

Terrasse Dufferin is located where the Château Saint-Louis, the long-destroyed elaborate residence of the governor of New France, used to stand. Built at the very edge of the escarpment, this three-story building had a long, private stone terrace on the river side while the main entrance, consisting of a fortified façade, opened onto Place d'Armes and featured pavilions with imperial-type roofs. The château was built in the 17th century by architect François de la Joue and was enlarged in 1719 by engineer Chausegros de Léry. Its rooms, linked one to the other, were the scene of elegant receptions given for French nobility. Plans for the future of the entire continent were drawn up in this building. Château Saint-Louis was badly damaged in the British bombardment of the city at the time of the conquest and was later remodelled according to British tastes before being destroyed by fire in 1834.

There are two monuments at the far end of Terrasse Dufferin. One is dedicated to the memory of Samuel de Champlain, the founder of Québec City and father of New France. It was designed by Parisian sculptor Paul Chevré and erected in 1898. The second monument informs visitors that Vieux-Québec was recognized as a World Heritage Site by UNESCO in 1985. Québec City is the first city in North America to be included on this list. A staircase just to the left of the Champlain monument leads to the Place Royale quarter in Basse-Ville.

Château Frontenac ★★★ (9) *(1 Rue des Carrières).* The first half of the 19th century saw the emergence of Québec City's tourism industry when the romantic European nature of the city began to attract growing numbers of American visitors. In 1890, the Canadian Pacific Railway company, under Cornelius Van Horne, decided to create a chain of distinguished hotels across Canada. The first of

QUÉBEC CITY

Château Frontenac

these hotels was the Château Frontenac, named in honour of one of the best-known governors of New France, Louis de Buade, Comte de Frontenac (1622-1698).

To visitors, the magnificent Château Frontenac, symbol of the province's capital city, is probably the most famous sight in Québec. Ironically, the hotel was designed by an American architect, Bruce Price (1845-1903), known for his New York skyscrapers. The look of the hotel, which combines certain elements seen in Scottish manors and others seen in the chateau of the Loire Valley in France, has come to be considered a national archetype style called Château style. Bruce Price, who also designed Montréal's Windsor train station and the famous Tuxedo Park development near New York, was inspired by the picturesque location chosen for the hotel and by the mix of French and English cultures in Canada.

The Château Frontenac was built in stages. The first section was completed in 1893 and three sections were later added, the most important of these being the central tower (1923), the work of architects Edward and William Sutherland Maxwell. To fully appreciate the Château, one must go inside to explore the main hall, decorated in a style popular in 18th-century Parisian *hôtels particuliers*, and visit the Bar Maritime in the large main tower overlooking the river. The Château Frontenac has been the location of a number of important events in history. In 1944, the Québec Conference was held at the Château Frontenac. At this historic meeting, American President Franklin D. Roosevelt, British Prime Minister Winston Churchill and Canadian Prime Minister Mackenzie King met to discuss the future of post-war Europe. On the way out of the courtyard is a stone with the inscription of the Order of Malta, dated 1647, the only remaining piece of Château Saint-Louis.

Until the construction of the citadel, **Place d'Armes ★ (10)** was a military parade ground. It became a public square in 1832. In 1916, the *Monument de la Foi* (Monument of Faith) was erected in Place d'Armes to mark the tricentennial of the arrival in Québec of the Récollet religious order. Abbot Adolphe Garneau's statue rests on a base designed by David Ouellet.

At the other end of the square are the Maison du Tourisme (a tourist information centre) and two museums. The back of the Anglican Cathedral of the Holy Trinity (see p 329) is also visible from here.

The **Maison du Tourisme (11)** *(12 Rue Sainte-Anne)* is located in the former Union Hotel, a white building with a copper roof. A group of wealthy Québécois saw the need for a luxury hotel in Québec City and commissioned British architect Edward Cannon to head the project which was completed in 1803.

On either side of the Maison du Tourisme are two popular tourist attractions. Using an elaborate model of the city, along with a sound and light show, the **Musée du Fort (12)** *(adults $5.50; summer every day 11am to 6pm; early Sep to end of Nov, Mon to Fri 10am to 5pm, Sat and Sun 11am to 5pm; winter Mon to Fri 10am to 5pm, Sat and Sun 11am to 5pm, closed Mon to Fri between noon and 2pm; 10 Rue Sainte-Anne; ☎692-2175 or 692-1759)* recreates the six sieges of Québec City, starting with the capture of the town by the Kirke brothers in 1629 and ending with the American invasion of 1775.

Musée de Cire de Québec (13) *(adults $4; summer every day 9am to 10pm, rest of the year every day 10am to 5pm; 22 Rue Sainte-Anne ☎692-2289)* displays wax likenesses of 80 individuals who played important roles in the history of Québec and North America. These are the creations of artists from the Grévin museum in Paris.

Return to Rue St-Louis

Ancien Palais de Justice ★ (14) *(12 Rue Saint-Louis)*. This is the city's original courthouse, built in 1883 according to the plans of Eugène-Étienne Taché, architect of the parliament buildings. The courthouse resembles the parliament in a number of ways. Its French Renaissance Revival design preceded the Château style as the "official" style of the city's major building projects. The interior of the building was renovated between 1922 and 1930; it has several large rooms with attractive woodwork. Since 1987, the Ancien Palais de Justice building has been used by Québec's Ministry of Finance.

Maison Maillou (15) *(17 Rue Saint-Louis)* is the location of the seat of Québec's chamber of commerce. This attractive French Regime house was built in 1736 under the direction of architect Jean Maillou. It was saved from destruction after the stock market crash of 1929 lead to the abandoning of plans to enlarge the Château Frontenac.

The history of **Maison Kent (16)** *(24 Rue Saint-Louis)*, once a residence of Queen Victoria's father, the Duke of Kent, is somewhat clouded. There is some disagreement as to whether the house was built in the 17th or 18th century. It is clear, however, from its English sash windows and low-pitched roof, that the house underwent major renovations during the 19th century. The house was the site of the signing of the agreement which gave Québec over to the British in 1759. Ironically, the house is now occupied by France's Consulate General.

Maison Jacquet ★ (17) *(34 Rue Saint-Louis)*, a small, red-roofed building covered in white roughcast dating from 1690, is the oldest house in Haute-Ville; it is the only house in Vieux-Québec that still looks just as it did in the 17th century. The house is distinguished from those built during the following century by its high steep roof covering a living area with a very low ceiling. The house is named for François Jacquet who once owned the land on which it stands. It was constructed by architect François de la Joue in 1690, for his own use. In 1815, the house was acquired by Philippe Aubert de Gaspé, author of the famous novel *Les Anciens Canadiens* (The Canadians of Old). The restaurant that now occupies the house takes its name from this book.

Turn right on Rue du Parloir and right again at Rue Donnacona.

Monastère des Ursulines ★★★ (18) *(18 Rue Donnacona; ☎694-0413)*. In 1535, Sainte Angèle Merici founded the first Ursuline community in Brescia, Italy. After the community had established itself in France, it became a cloistered order dedicated to teaching (1620). With the help of a benefactor, Madame de la Peltrie, the Ursulines arrived in Québec in 1639 and, in 1641, founded a monastery and convent where generations of young girls have received a good education. The Ursuline convent is the longest running girls' school in North America. Only the museum and chapel, a small part of the huge Ursuline complex, where several dozen nuns still live, are open to the public.

The Sainte-Ursuline chapel was rebuilt in 1901 on the site of the original 1722 chapel. Part of the magnificent interior decoration of the first chapel, created by Pierre-Nöel Levasseur between 1726 and 1736, survived and is present in the newer structure. The work includes a pulpit surmounted by a trumpeting angel and a beautiful altarpiece in the Louis XIV style. The tabernacle of the high altar, embellished with fine gilding applied by the Ursuline nuns. The Sacred Heart tabernacle, is a masterpiece of the genre, is attributed to Jaques Leblond, also known as Latour, and dates from around 1770. Some of the paintings that decorate the church come from the collection of Father Jean-Louis Desjardins, a former chaplin of the Ursulines. In 1820, Desjardins bought several dozen paintings from an art dealer in Paris. The paintings had previously hung in Paris churches but were removed during the French Revolution. Works from this collection can still be seen in churches all over Québec. At the entrance hangs *Jésus chez Simon le Pharisien* (Jesus with Simon the Pharisee) by Philippe de Champaigne, and on the right of the nave hangs *La Parabole des Dix Vierges* (The Parable of the Ten Virgins), by Pierre de Cortone.

The chapel is the burial place of the Marquis de Montcalm, leader of the French troops at the critical Battle of the Plains of Abraham. Like his rival, General Wolfe, Montcalm was fatally injured in the fighting. In an adjoining chapel is the tomb of Mère Marie de l'Incarnation, the founder of the Ursuline monastery in Québec. An opening provides a view of the nuns chancel, rebuilt in 1902 by David Ouellet who outfitted it with cupolas. An interesting painting by an unknown artist, *La France Apportant la Foi aux Indiens de la Nouvelle-France* (France Bringing Faith to the Natives of New France), also hangs in this section of the chapel.

The entrance to **Musée des Ursulines** *(adults $3; May to Aug, Tue to Sat 1pm to 5pm, Sun 12:30pm to 5pm; Sep to Apr, Tue to Sun 1pm to 4:30pm; 12 Rue Donnacona, ☎694-0694)* is across from the chapel. The museum outlines nearly four centuries of Ursuline history. On view are various works of art, Louis XIII furniture, impressive embroideries made of gold thread, and 18th-century altar cloths and church robes. Even the skull of Marquis de Montcalm is on display!

The **Anglican Cathedral of the Holy Trinity ★★ (19)** *(31 Rue des Jardins)* was built following the British acquisition of Québec, when a small group of British administrators and military officers established themselves in Québec City. These men wanted to distinguish their presence through the construction of prestigious buildings with typically British designs. However, their small numbers resulted in the slow progress of this vision until the beginning of the 19th century when work began on an Anglican cathedral designed by Majors Robe and Hall, two military engineers. The Palladian-style church was completed in 1804. This significant example of non-French architecture changed the look of the city. The church was the first Anglican cathedral built outside Britain and, in its elegant simplicity, is a good example of British colonial architecture. The roof was made steeper in 1815 so that it would not be weighted down by snow.

The cathedral's interior, more sober than that of most Catholic churches, is adorned with various generous gifts from King George III, including several pieces of silverware and pews made of English oak from the forests of Windsor. The bishop's chair is said to have been carved from an elm tree under which Samuel de Champlain liked to sit. Stained-glass windows and commemorative plaques have been added to the decor of the church over the years.

Continue along Rue des Jardins. To the right is a cobblestone section of Rue Sainte-Anne and on the left is the Hôtel Clarendon and the Price building.

The **Hôtel Clarendon (20)** *(57 Rue Sainte-Anne)* began receiving guests in 1870 in the former Desbarats print shop (1858). It is the oldest hotel still operating in Québec. The Charles Baillargé-designed restaurant on the main floor is also the oldest restaurant in Canada. The Victorian charm of the somber woodwork evokes the *belle époque*. The Hôtel Clarendon was enlarged in 1929 by the addition of a brick tower featuring an Art Deco entrance hall designed by Raoul Chênevert.

The design of **Édifice Price ★ (21)** *(65 Rue Sainte-Anne)* manages to adhere to traditional North American skyscraper architecture and yet does not look out of place among the historic buildings of Haute-Ville. Architects Ross and MacDonald of Montréal gave the building a tall yet discreet silhouette when they designed it in 1929. It features a copper roof typical of Château architecture. The main hall of the building, a fine example of Art Deco design, is covered in polished travertine and bronze bas-reliefs depicting the various activities of the

Price company, which specialized in the production of paper.

Walk back up to Rue des Jardins.

The next stop is quaint **Maison Antoine-Vanfelson** at 17 Rue des Jardins., built in 1780. A talented silversmith by the name of Laurent Amiot had a workshop here in the 19th century. The rooms on the second floor of this building feature wonderful Louis XV woodwork.

Place de l'Hôtel-de-Ville ★ (22), a small square, was the location of the Notre-Dame market in the 18th century. A monument in honour of Cardinal Taschereau, created by André Vermare, was erected here in 1923.

The American Romanesque Revival influence seen in the **Hôtel de Ville (23)** *(2 Rue des Jardins)* stands out in a city where French and British traditions have always predominated in the construction of public buildings. The building was completed in 1895 following disagreements among the mayor and the city councillors as to a building plan. Sadly, a Jesuit college dating from 1666 was demolished to make room for the city hall. Under the pleasant gardens outside the building, where popular events are held in the summer, is an underground parking lot, a much needed addition in this city of narrow streets.

Centre d'Interprétation de la Vie Urbaine de la Ville de Québec *(free admission; end of June to Labour Day, every day 10am to 5pm; rest of the year Tue to Sun 10am to 5pm; 43 Côte de la Fabrique, ☎691-4606).* This information centre on urban life in Québec is located in the basement of City Hall. It addresses questions of urban development and planning. An interesting model of the city provides an understanding of the layout of the area.

Cathédrale Catholique Notre-Dame-de-Québec ★★★ (24) *(at the other end of Place de l'Hôtel-de-Ville).* The history of Québec City's cathedral underscores the problems faced by builders in New France and the determination of the Québécois in the face of the worst circumstances. The cathedral as it exists today is the result of numerous phases of construction and a number of tragedies which left the church in ruins on two occasions. The first church on this site was built in 1632 under the orders of Samuel de Champlain, who was buried nearby four years later. This wooden church was replaced in 1647 by Église Notre-Dame-de-la-Paix, a stone church in the shape of a roman cross that would later serve as the model for many rural parish churches. In 1674, New France was assigned its first bishop in residence. Monseigneur François-Xavier de Montmorency-Laval (1623-1708) decided that this small church, after renovations befitting its status as the heart of such an enormous ministry, would become the seat of the Catholic Church in Québec. A grandiose plan was commissioned from architect Claude Baillif, which, despite personal financial contributions from Louis XIV, was eventually scaled-down. Only the base of the west tower survives from this period. In 1742, the bishop had the church remodelled according to the plans of engineer Gaspard Chaussegros de Léry, who is responsible for its present layout, featuring an extended nave illuminated from above. The cathedral resembles many urban churches built in France during the same period.

Baillargé or Baillairgé

Recent historical studies have prompted us to use the name Baillairgé to designate this famous family of Québec architects. However, when referring to primary sources, namely, documents they signed with their own hands, one sees that they used both Baillargé and Baillairgé. Don't be surprised, therefore, if you see both; the reference is always to the same family.

During the siege of Québec, in 1759, the cathedral was bombarded and reduced to ruins. It was not rebuilt until the status of Catholics in Québec was settled by the British crown. The oldest Catholic parish north of Mexico was finally allowed to begin the reconstruction of its church in 1770, using the 1742 plans. The work was directed by Jean Baillargé (1726-1805), a member of the well-known family of architects and craftsmen. This marked the beginning of the Baillargé family's extended, fervent involvement with the reconstruction and renovation of the church. In 1789, the decoration of the church interior was entrusted to Jean Baillargé's son François (1759-1830), who had recently returned from three years of studying architecture in Paris at the Académie Royale. He designed the chancel's beautiful gilt baldaquin with winged caryatids four years later. The high altar, the first in Québec to be designed to look like the façade of a Basilica, was put into place in 1797. The addition of baroque pews and a plaster vault created an interesting contrast. Thus completed, the spectacular interior emphasized the use of gilding, wood and white plasterwork according to typically Québécois traditions.

In 1843, Thomas Baillargé (1791-1859), the son of François, created the present neoclassical façade and attempted to put up a steeple on the east side of the church. Work on the steeple was halted at the halfway point when it was discovered that the 17th-century foundations were not strong enough. Charles Baillargé (1826-1906), Thomas Baillargé's cousin, designed the wrought iron gate around the front square in 1858. Between 1920 and 1922, the church was carefully restored, but just a few weeks after the work was completed a fire seriously damaged the building. Raoul Chênevert and Maxime Roisin, who had already come to Québec from Paris to take on the reconstruction of the Basilica in Sainte-Anne-de-Beaupré, were put in charge of yet another restoration of the cathedral. In 1959, a mausoleum was put into place in the basement of the church. It holds the remains of Québec bishops and various governors (Frontenac, Vaudreuil, de Callière). In recent years, several masters' paintings hanging in the church have been stolen, leaving bare walls and an increased emphasis on ensuring the security of the remaining paintings, including the beautiful *Saint-Jérôme,* by Jacques-Louis David (1780), now at the Musée de l'Amérique Française.

Feux Sacrés *($7; beginning of May to mid-Oct, every day at 3:30pm, 5pm, 6:30pm and 8pm; Oct to May, Thu to Sat, at 6:30pm and 8pm; 20 Rue Buade,* ☎*694-0665),* a sound and light show, is set up inside the cathedral. It illustrates a page of Québec's history with the aid of three-dimensional effects on three screens. Shows are in French and English simultanously.

Séminaire de Québec ★★★ (25) *(end of Jun to end of Aug, contact the museum for the schedule of guided tours; 2 Côte de la Fabrique,* ☎*692-2843).* During the 17th century, this religious complex was an oasis of European civilization in a rugged and hostile territory. To get an idea of how it must have appeared to students of the day, go through the old gate (decorated with the seminary's coat of arms) and into the courtyard before proceeding through the opposite entryway to the reception desk. The seminary was founded in 1663 by Monseigneur Francois de Laval, on orders from the Séminaire des Missions Étrangères de Paris (Seminary of Foreign Missions), with which it

remained affiliated until 1763. As headquarters of the clergy throughout the colony, it was at the seminary that future priests studied, that parochial funds were administered, and that ministerial appointments were made. Louis XIV's Minister, Colbert, further required the seminary to establish a smaller school devoted to the conversion and education of native people. Following the British Conquest and the subsequent banishing of the Jesuits, the seminary became a college devoted to classical education. It also served as housing for the bishop of Québec after his palace was destroyed by the bombardment. In 1852, the seminary founded the Université Laval, the first French-language university in North America. Today most of Laval's campus is located in Sainte-Foy. The vast collection of buildings of the seminary is home to a priests' residence facing the river, a private school and the Faculty of Architecture of Université Laval, which returned to its former location in 1987.

Today's seminary is the result of rebuilding efforts following numerous fires and bombardments. Across from the old gate can be seen the wing devoted to the offices of the Procurator, complete with sundial. During the 1690 attack of Admiral Phipps, it was in the vaulted cellars of this wing that the citizens of Québec City took refuge. It also contains the private chapel of Monseigneur Briand (1785), decorated with sculpted olive branches by Pierre Emond. Forming a right angle with the chapel is the beautiful parlor wing, constructed in 1696. The use of segmented arch windows in this attractive building betrays the direct influence of French models prior to the adaptation to the climate of Québec.

The guided tours leaving from the reception centre at 2 Côte de la Fabrique include visits to the apartments of the seminary, the cellars, the chapel of Monseigneur Briand, and the exterior chapel built in 1890 to replace the original one from 1752 that burned down in 1888. In order to avoid any such recurrence, the interior, which is similar to that of Église de la Trinité in Paris, was covered over in tin and zinc and painted in *trompe-l'oeil,* following the design of Paul Alexandre de Cardonnel and Joseph-Ferdinand Peachy. The chapel contains the most significant collection of relics in North America, including relics of Saint-Augustine and Saint-Anselm, of the martyrs of Tonkin, of Saint Charles Borromé and of Ignatius of Loyola. Some relics are both large and authentic while others are rather small and dubious. On the left is a funeral chapel housing a tomb containing the remains of Monseigneur de Laval, the first Bishop of North America.

To get to Musée de l'Amérique Française, follow Rue Sainte-Famille which follows the seminary and turn right on Rue de l'Université.

Musée de l'Amérique Française ★ (26) *($3; end of Jun to early Sep, every day, 10am to 5pm; early Sep to end of Jun, Tue to Sun, 10am to 5pm; 2 Côte- de-la-Fabrique, ☎692-2843)* is a museum devoted to the history of French America. It contains a wealth of over 450,000 artifacts including silverware, paintings, oriental art and numismatics, as well as scientific instruments, collected for educational purposes over the course of the last three centuries by the priests of the seminary. The museum occupies five floors of what used to be the residences of the Université Laval. The first Egyptian mummy brought to America is on view, as are several items that belonged to Monseigneur de Laval.

On returning to Place de l'Hôtel-de-Ville, turn left on Rue Buade

The old **Holt-Renfrew** store *(43 Rue Buade)*, which opened in 1837, faces the cathedral. Originally concerned with the sale of furs, which they supply by appointment to Her Majesty the Queen, Holt's held the exclusive rights for the Canadian distribution of Dior and Saint-Laurent creations for a long time. Holt's is now closed, having given way to the boutiques of the **Promenades du Vieux-Québec**.

A little further on is the entrance to **Rue du Trésor (27)** that also leads to Place d'Armes and Rue Sainte-Anne. Artists come here to sell paintings, drawings and silkscreens, many of which depict views of Québec City.

Québec Expérience (28) *($6.75; mid-May to mid-Oct, every day 10am to 10pm; mid-Oct to mid-May, Sun to Thu 10am to 5pm, Fri to Sat 10am to 10pm; 8 Rue du Trésor, 3rd floor, G1R 4L9, ☎694-4000)* is an elaborate show about the history of Québec City. This lively three-dimensional multimedia presentation takes viewers back in time to relive the great moments in the city's history through its important historical figures. A wonderful way to learn about Québec City's past, these half-hour shows are a big hit with the kids. Presented in both French and English.

The **Bureau de Poste ★ (29)** *(3 Rue Buade)*, Canada's first post office opened in Québec City in 1837. It was for a long time housed in the old Hôtel du Chien d'Or, a solid dwelling built around 1753 for a wealthy Bordeaux merchant who ordered a bas-relief depicting a dog gnawing a bone executed above the doorway. The following inscription appeared underneath the bas-relief, which was relocated to the pediment of the present post office in 1872: *Je suis un chien qui ronge l'os, en le rongeant je prends mon repos. Un temps viendra qui n'est pas venu où je mordrai qui m'aura mordu*, roughly, "I am a dog gnawing a bone, as I gnaw, I rest at home. Though it's not yet here there'll come a time when those who bit me will be paid in kind". It is said that the message was destined for Intendant Bigot, a swindler if ever there was one, who was so outraged he had the Bordeaux merchant killed.

The dome of the post office and the façade overlooking the river were added at the beginning of the 20th century. The building was renamed **Édifice Louis-Saint-Laurent**, in honour of the former Prime Minister of Canada. Besides the traditional post and philatelic services *(free admission; Mon to Fri 8am to 4:30pm, Sat and Sun 10am to 5pm; 3 Rue Buade, ☎648-4177)* was added to illustrate Canada's natural and historical heritage.

Facing the post office stands a monument to Monseigneur François de Montmorency Laval (1623-1708), the first Bishop of Québec, whose diocese covered two thirds of the North American continent. Designed by Philippe Hébert and erected in 1908, the monument boasts an attractive staircase leading to Côte de la Montagne and from there to Basse-Ville.

The Laval Bishop's monument is located directly in front of **Palais Archiépiscopal (30)** *(2 Rue Port-Dauphin)* or archbishopric, which was rebuilt by Thomas Baillargé in 1844. The first archbishopric stood in what is now Parc Montmorency. Designed by Claude Baillif and built between 1692 and 1700, the original palace was, by all accounts, one of the most gorgeous of its kind in the kingdom. Drawings show an impressive building, complete with a recessed chapel whose interior was reminiscent of Paris's Val de Grace. Though the chapel was bombarded and lost in 1759, the rest of the building was restored and then occupied by the Legislative Assembly of Lower Canada from 1792 to 1840. It was demolished in 1848 to make room for the new parliamentary buildings, which went up in flames only four years later.

Parc Montmorency ★ (31) was laid out in 1875 after the city walls were lowered along Rue des Remparts and the Governor General of Canada, Lord Dufferin, discovered the magnificent view from the promontory. George-Etienne Cartier, Prime Minister of the Dominion of Canada and one of the Fathers of Confederation is honoured with a statue here, as are Louis Hébert, Guillaume Couillard and Marie Rollet, some of the original farmers of New France. These last three disembarked in 1617 and were granted the fiefdom of Sault-au-Matelot, on the future site of the seminary, in 1623. These attractive bronzes are the work of Montréal sculptor Alfred Laliberté.

Continue along the ramparts.

The halls of the old **Université Laval ★ (32)** can be seen through a gap in the wall of the ramparts. Built in 1856 in the gardens of the seminary, they were completed in 1875 with the addition of an impressive mansard roof surmounted by three silver lanterns. When the spotlights shine on them at night, it creates the atmosphere of a royal gala.

Following Rue des Remparts, Basse-Ville, or lower town, comes into view. The patrician manors of the street along the ramparts provide a picturesque backdrop for the old Latin quarter which extends behind them. The narrow streets and 18th century houses of the quarter are well worth a detour.

Montcalm's Maison (33) *(45 to 51 Rue des Remparts)* was originally a very large residence constructed in 1727; it is now divided into three houses. The home of the Marquis de Montcalm at the time of the Battle of the Plains of Abraham, the building subsequently served to house the officers of the British Army before being subdivided and returned to private use. In the first half of the 19th century, many houses in Québec were covered in the sort of imitation stone boards that still protect the masonry of the Montcalm house. Because of this example, it was believed that the covering lent a more refined look to the houses.

Near the corner of Rue Saint-Flavien and Rue Couillard is the small Musée des Soeurs du Bon-Pasteur.

Musée Bon-Pasteur ★ (34) *(free admission; Jul and Aug, Tue and Sun, 1pm to 5pm; Sep to Jun Sun to Thu, 1pm to 5pm; 14 Rue Couillard, ☎694-0243),* founded in 1993, tells the story of the Bon Pasteur (meaning "Good

Shepherd") community of nuns, which has been serving the poor of Québec City since 1850. The museum is located in the Béthanie house, an eclectic brick structure built around 1887 to shelter unwed mothers and their children. The museum occupies three floors of an 1878 addition and houses furniture as well as sacred objects manufactured or collected by the nuns.

Turn right on Rue Hamel and then left on Rue Charlevoix.

The Augustinian nurses founded their first convent in Québec in Sillery. Uneasy about the Iroquois, they relocated to Québec City in 1642 and began construction of the present complex, the **Chapelle et Musée de l'Hôtel-Dieu ★★ (35)** *(32 Rue Charlevoix),* which includes a convent, a hospital and a chapel. Rebuilt several times, today's buildings mostly date from the 20th century. The oldest remaining part is the 1756 convent, built on the vaulted foundations from 1695, hidden behind the 1800 chapel. This chapel was erected using material from various French buildings destroyed during the Seven Years' War. The stone was taken from the palace of the intendant, while its first ornaments came from the 17th-century Jesuit church. Today, only the iron balustrade of the bell tower bears witness to the original chapel. The present neoclassical façade was designed by Thomas Baillargé in 1839 after he completed the new interior in 1835. The nun's chancel can be seen to the right. Abbot Louis-Joseph Desjardins used the chapel as an auction house in 1817 and again in 1821, after he purchased the collection of a bankrupt Parisian banker who had amassed works confiscated from Paris churches during the French Revolution. *La Vision de Sainte-Thérèse d'Avila* (Saint Theresa of Avila's Vision), a work by François-Guillaume Ménageot which originally hung in the Carmel de Saint-Denis near Paris, can be seen in one of the side altars.

Musée des Augustines de l'Hôtel-Dieu *(free admission; Tue to Sat, 9:30am to 12am and 1:30pm to 5pm; Sun 1:30pm to 5pm; 32 Rue Charlevoix, ☎692-2492).* This museum traces the history of the Augustinian community in New France through pieces of furniture, paintings, and medical instruments. On display are the chest that contained the meagre belongings of the founders (pre-1639), as well as pieces from the Château Saint-Louis, the residence of the first governors under the French Regime, including portraits of Louis XIV and of Cardinal Richelieu. Upon request, visitors can see the chapel and the vaulted cellars. The remains of Blessed Marie-Catherine de Saint-Augustin, the founder of the community in New France, are kept in an adjoining chapel, as is a beautiful gilded reliquary in the Louis XIV style, sculpted in 1717 by Noël Levasseur.

Follow the small street opposite the chapel (Rue Collins). At the corner of Rue Saint-Jean is a pleasant view of Côte de la Fabrique, with the Hôtel de Ville on the right and Cathédrale Notre-Dame in the background on the left. Turn right on Rue Saint-Jean, a pleasant commercial street in the heart of Vieux-Québec.

A short detour to the left down Rue Saint-Stanislas gives a view of the old Methodist Church *(42 Rue Saint-Stanislas)*, a beautiful Gothic Revival building of 1850. Today it houses the **Institut Canadien**, a centre for literature and the arts. Before the Quiet Revolution of the 1960s, this centre was the focus of many a contentious dispute with the clergy over its "audacious" choice of books. The institute is home to a theatre and a branch of the municipal library.

The neighbouring building, number 44, is the **Ancienne Prison de Québec**, the old jail, built in 1808 according to plans drawn up by François Baillargé. In 1868, it was renovated to accommodate Morrin College, affiliated to Montréal's McGill University. This venerable institution of English-speaking Québec also houses the library of the **Québec Literary and Historical Society**, a learned society founded in 1824. The building on the corner of Rue Cook and Rue Dauphine surmounted by a palladian steeple is **St. Andrew's Presbyterian Church**, completed in 1811.

Returning to Rue Saint-Jean, cross in the direction of the Conservatoire d'Art Dramatique.

The **Conservatoire d'Art Dramatique (36)** *(9 Rue Saint-Stanislas)* occupies what used to be Holy Trinity Chapel, built in 1824 according to the plans of Georges Blaiklock. Its elegant, sparse, neoclassical architecture has housed the theatre school since 1970.

Turn left on Rue McMahon, and continue on to the reception and information centre of the Artillery Park.

Artillery Park National Historic Site ★★ (37-38)
($3; hours vary according to the season; 2 Rue d'Auteuil, ☎648-4205), also called Lieu Historique National du Parc-de-l'Artillerie, takes up part of an enormous military emplacement running alongside the walls of the city. The reception and information centre is located in the old foundry, where munitions were manufactured until 1964. On display is a fascinating model of Québec City built between 1795 and 1810 by military engineer Jean-Baptiste Duberger for strategic planning. The model has only recently been returned to Québec City, after having been sent to England in 1813. It is an unparalleled source of information on the layout of the city in the years following the British Conquest.

The walk continues with a visit to the Dauphine redoubt, a beautiful white roughcast building near Rue McMahon. In 1712, military engineer Dubois Berthelot de Beaucours drafted plans for the redoubt which was completed by Chaussegros de Léry in 1747. A redoubt is an independent fortified structure that serves as a retreat in case the troops are obliged to fall back. The redoubt was never really used for this purpose but rather as military barracks. Behind it can be seen several barracks and an old cartridge factory constructed by the British in the 19th century. The officer's barracks (1820) which has been converted into a children's centre for heritage interpretation makes a nice end to the visit.

Walk back up Rue d'Auteuil.

The newest of Québec City's gates, **Porte Saint-Jean (39)** actually has rather ancient origins. As of 1693 it was one of only three entrances to the city. It was reinforced by Chaussegros de Léry in 1757, and then rebuilt by the British. To satisfy merchants who were clamouring for the total destruction of the walls, a "modern" gate equipped with tandem carriage tunnels and corresponding pedestrian passageways was erected in 1867. However, this structure did not fit in with Lord Dufferin's romantic vision of the city and was thus eliminated in 1898. The present gate did not replace it until 1936.

Number 29, on the left, is an old Anglican orphanage built for the Society for Promoting Christian Knowledge in 1824, and was the first Gothic Revival style building in Québec City. Its architecture was portentous, as it inaugurated the romantic current that would eventually permeate the city.

The last of Québec's Jesuits died in 1800, his community having been banished by the British and then, in 1774, by the Pope himself. The community was resuscitated in 1814, however, and returned to Québec in 1840. Since its college and church on Place de l'Hôtel-de-Ville were no longer available, they were welcomed by the Congregationists, a brotherhood founded by the Jesuit Ponert in 1657 with a view to propagating the cult of the Virgin. These latter parishioners were able to erect the **Église des Jésuites ★ (40)** *(Rue d'Auteuil, at the corner of Rue Dauphine).*

François Baillargé designed the plans for the church which was completed in 1818. The façade was redone in 1930. The decoration of the interior began with the construction of the counterfeit vaulting. Its centrepiece is Pierre-Noël Levasseur's altar of 1770. Since 1925, the Jesuit church has been Québec's sanctuary for the worship of Canada's martyred saints.

Porte Kent (41), like Porte Saint-Louis, is the result of Lord Dufferin's romantic vision of the city. The plans for this gate, Vieux-Québec's prettiest, were drawn up in 1878 by Charles Baillargé, following the ideas of Irishman William H. Lynn.

Climb the stairway to the top of Porte Kent and walk along the wall towards Porte Saint-Louis.

On the other side of the walls can be seen the **Hôtel du Parlement** (see p 342) as well as several patrician homes along the Rue d'Auteuil. Number 69, the **Maison McGreevy** stands out by its sheer size. The house is the work of Thomas Fuller, the architect of the Parliament Buildings in Ottawa, as well as of New York's State Capitol. It was built in 1868 by McGreevy, a construction entrepreneur who also built Canada's first Parliament Buildings. Behind the rather commercial-looking façade of yellow Nepean sandstone is a perfectly preserved Victorian interior.

Climb down from the wall at Porte Saint-Louis. Côte de la Citadelle is on the other side of Rue Saint-Louis.

Citadelle ★★★ (42) *(at the far end of the Côte de la Citadelle; ☎694-2815).* Québec City's citadel represents three centuries of North American military history and is still in use. Since 1920, it has housed the Royal 22nd Regiment of the Canadian Army, a regiment distinguished for its bravery during World War II. Within the circumference of the

enclosure are some 25 buildings including the officer's mess, the hospital, the prison, and the official residence of the Governor General of Canada, as well as the first observatory in Canada. The citadel's history began in 1693, when Engineer Dubois Berthelot de Beaucours had the Cap Diamant redoubt built at the highest point of Québec City's defensive system, some 100 metres above the level of the river. This solid construction is today included inside the King's bastion.

Throughout the 18th century, French and then British engineers developed projects for a citadel that remained unfulfilled. Chaussegros de Léry's powderhouse of 1750, which now houses the Museum of the Royal 22nd Regiment, and the temporary excavation works to the west (1783) are the only works of any scope accomplished during this period. The citadel that appears today was built between 1820 and 1832 according to the plans of Colonel Elias Walker Durnford. Dubbed the "Gibraltar of America", and built according to North principles expounded by Vauban in the 17th century, the citadel has never borne the brunt of a single cannonball, though it has acted as an important element of dissuasion.

Musée du Royal 22ᵉ Régiment *($5; mid-Mar and Apr, every day 10am to 4pm; mid-May to mid-Jun, every day 9am to 5pm, mid-Jun to Labour Day, every day 9am to 6pm; Sep 9am to 6pm, Oct 10am to 3pm).* This museum offers an interesting collection of arms, uniforms, insignia and military documents spanning almost 400 years. It is possible to go on a guided tour of the whole installation, to witness the changing of the guard, the retreat, and the firing of the cannon. The changing of the guard lasts 35 minutes and takes place every day from mid-June to the beginning of September, barring rain. The retreat lasts 30 minutes and can be seen through July and August, on Tuesday, Thursday, Saturday, and Sunday at 7pm, barring rain. The firing of the cannon takes place every day at noon and at 9:30pm at the Bastion du Prince de Galles.

Tour B : Vieux-Québec (Basse-Ville) ★★★ (two days)

Vieux-Québec's port and commercial area, Basse-Ville, or lower town, is a narrow U-shaped piece of land wedged between the waters of the St. Lawrence and the Cap Diamant escarpment. The cradle of New France, Basse-Ville's Place Royale is where, in

1608, Samuel de Champlain (1567-1635) founded the settlement he called *Abitation* that would become Québec City. In the summer of 1759, three quarters of Basse-Ville was badly damaged by British bombardment. It took twenty years to repair and rebuild the houses. In the 19th century, the construction of multiple embankments allowed the expansion of the town and the linking by road of the area around Place Royale with the area around the intendant's palace. The decline of the port at the beginning of the 20th century led to the gradual abandonment of Place Royale; restoration work began in 1959.

The Basse-Ville walking tour begins at Porte Prescott, which straddles Côte de la Montagne. Those who aren't much for walking would be well advised to take the funicular from Terrasse Dufferin, if it is in operation, and to begin the tour at the start of Rue Petit-Champlain.

Funiculaire (1) *(☎692-1132)*. The funicular began operating in November of 1879. It was put into place by entrepreneur W. A. Griffith in order to bring the lower and upper towns closer together. It is an outdoor elevator that obviates the need to take the *Escalier Casse-Cou*, "break-neck stairway", or to go around Côte de la Montagne. Due to an unfortunate accident that occurred in the summer of 1996, the funicular is being completely overhauled and should be back in operation in April 1998. In the meantime, the business owners of Petit-Champlain have set up a shuttle service between their neighbourhood and Haute-Ville.

Porte Prescott (2) *(Côte de la Montagne)* can be reached from Côte de la Montagne or from Terrasse Dufferin by means of a stairway and a charming footbridge on the left of the funicular's entryway. This discreetly post-modern structure was built in 1983 according to the draughts of the architectural firm of Gauthier, Guité, Roy, who sought to evoke the 1797 gate by Gother Mann. It allows pedestrians to cross directly from Terrasse Dufferin to Parc Montmorency.

Go down Côte de la Montagne and take the Escalier Casse-Cou on the right.

The **Escalier Casse-Cou (3)** *(Côte de la Montagne)* (literally, "the break-neck strairway") has been here since 1682. Until the beginning of the 20th century, it had been made of planks that were in constant need of repair or replacement. At the foot of the stairway is **Rue du Petit-Champlain**, a narrow

pedestrian street flanked by charming craft shops and pleasant cafés located in 17th and 18th century houses. Some of the houses at the foot of the cape were destroyed by rockslides prior to the reinforcement of the cliff in the 19th century.

At the foot of the Escalier Casse-Cou, a small *economusée* unveils the secrets of glass-blowing. At **Atelier Verrerie La Mailloche (4)** *(free admission; summer, Wed to Sun 10am to 4:30pm; Oct to May, Mon to Fri 10am to 4:30pm; 58 Rue Sous-le-Fort, G1K 3G8, ☎694-0445 or 694-1571)*, visitors can observe the fascinating spectacle of artisans shaping molten glass according to traditional techniques. The finished products are sold in a shop on the second floor (see p 363).

Maison Louis-Jolliet ★ (5) *(16 Rue du Petit-Champlain)* is one of the earliest houses of Vieux-Québec (1683) and one of the few works of Claude Baillif still standing. The house was built after the great fire of 1682, which destroyed Basse-Ville. It was this tragedy that prompted the authorities to require that stone be used in building. The fire also paved the way for some improvements in urban planning: roads were straightened and Place Royale was created. Louis Jolliet (1645-1700) was the man who, along with Father Marquette, discovered the Mississippi and explored Hudson Bay. During the last years of his life, he taught hydrography at the Séminaire de Québec. The interior of the house was completely gutted and now contains the lower platform of the funicular (see above).

Follow Rue du Petit-Champlain as far as the stairway on the left leading to Boulevard Champlain. Looking back up from the base of the stairs provides an interesting perspective of the Château Frontenac.

Maison Demers ★ (6) *(28 Boulevard Champlain)* was built in 1689 by mason Jean Lerouge. This impressive residence is an example of the bourgeois style of Québec's Basse-Ville. A two-story residential façade gives on to Rue du Petit-Champlain while the rear, which was used as a warehouse, extends down another two stories to open directly onto l'Anse du Cul-de-Sac (all but the first floor are original).

The cove called l'Anse du Cul-de-Sal, also known as the Anse aux Barques, was Québec City's first port. In 1745, Intendant Gilles Hocquart ordered the construction of a major

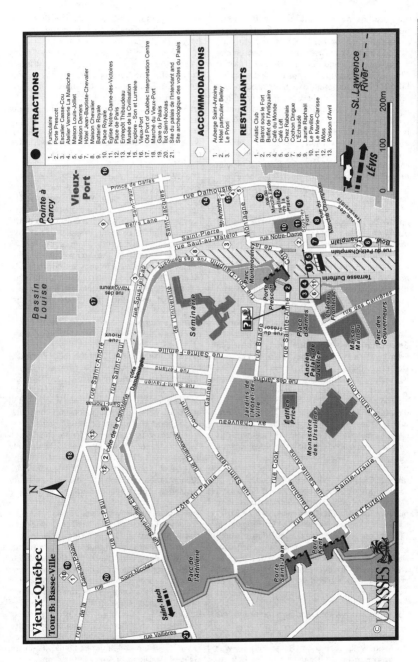

Vieux-Québec

Tour B: Basse-Ville

● **ATTRACTIONS**

1. Funiculaire
2. Porte Prescott
3. Escalier Casse-Cou
4. Atelier Verrerie La Mailloche
5. Maison Louis-Jolliet
6. Maison Demers
7. Hôtel Jean-Baptiste-Chevalier
8. Maison Chevalier
9. Batterie Royale
10. Place Royale
11. Église Notre-Dame-des-Victoires
12. Place de Paris
13. Entrepôt Thibaudeau
14. Musée de la Civilisation
15. Explore – Son et Lumière
16. Vieux-Port
17. Old Port of Québec Interpretation Centre
18. Marché du Vieux-Port
19. Gare du Palais
20. Îlot Saint-Nicolas
21. Site du palais de l'Intendant and Site archéologique des voûtes du Palais

⬡ **ACCOMMODATIONS**

1. Auberge Saint-Antoine
2. Hôtel particulier Belley
3. Le Priori

◇ **RESTAURANTS**

1. Aviatic Club
2. Bistrot sous le Fort
3. Buffet de l'Antiquaire
4. Café du Monde
5. Café Loft
6. Chez Rabelais
7. Cochon Dingue
8. L'Échaudé
9. Laurie Raphaël
10. Le Pavillon
11. Le Marie-Clarisse
12. Möss
13. Poisson d'Avril

0   100   200m

St. Lawrence River

LÉVIS

N

Bassin Louise

Pointe à Carcy

Vieux-Port

© ULYSSES

shipyard in the western part of the cove. Several French battleships were built there using Canadian lumber. In 1854, the terminus of the Grand Trunk railway was built on the embankments, and in 1858 the Marché Champlain went up, only to be destroyed by fire in 1899. Although it is now filled in and built-up, one can still distinguish traces of this natural harbour by examining the older urban arrangement. The location is presently occupied by administrative buildings and by the terminus of the Québec-Lévis ferry. A short return trip on the ferry provides a spectacular view of the ensemble of Vieux-Québec. Taking the ferry in the winter affords a rare chance to come face to face with the ice floes of the St. Lawrence (see p 322).

Follow Boulevard Champlain east as far as Rue du Marché-Champlain. The ferry boards from the south end of this road.

Hôtel Jean-Baptiste-Chevalier ★★ (7) *(60 Rue du Marché-Champlain)* is not a hotel but rather the townhouse of a wealthy family. The first building of the Place Royale area to be restored, the *hôtel* is in reality three separate houses from three different periods: **Maison de l'Armateur Chevalier** (home of Chevalier the Shipowner), built in a square in 1752; **Maison Frérot**, with a mansard roof (1683); and **Maison Dolbec**, dating from 1713. These houses were all repaired or partially rebuilt after the British Conquest. As a group, they were rescued from deterioration in 1955 by Gérard Morisset, the director of the *Inventaire des Oeuvres d'Art*, who suggested that they be purchased and restored by the government of Québec. This decision had a domino effect and prevented the demolition of Place Royale.

Maison Chevalier (8) *(free admission; end of Jun to early Oct, every day 10am to 6pm; early Oct to end of Jun, Sat and Sun 10am to 5pm; 60 Rue du Marché-Champlain, ☎643-2158)* harbours an annex of the Musée de la Civilisation, where an interesting exhibit portrays the daily lives of the merchants of New France. The exhibit features furniture as well as items of everyday use. The original, stately Louis XV woodwork (circa 1764) can also be seen.

Take Rue Notre-Dame, and turn right onto Rue Sous-le-Fort.

With no walls to protect Basse-Ville, it was necessary to find other means of defending it from the cannon-fire of ships in the river.

Following the attack by Admiral Phipps in 1690, it was decided to set up the **Batterie Royale ★ (9)** *(at the far end of Rue Sous-le-Fort)*, according to a plan drawn up by Claude Baillif. The strategic position of the battery allowed for the bombardment of any enemy ships foolhardy enough to venture into the narrowing of the river in front of the city. The ruins of the battery, long hidden under storehouses, were discovered in 1974. The crenellations, removed in the 19th century, were reconstructed, as was the wooden portal, discernible in a sketch from 1699.

The two rough stone houses on Rue Saint-Pierre, next to the battery, were built for Charles Guillemin in the early 18th century. The narrowness of the house on the left shows just how precious land was in the Basse-Ville of the French Regime. Each lot, irregular or not, had to be used. A little further along, at number 25 Rue Saint-Pierre, is the Louis-Fornel house, where a number of artefacts are on display in vaults. This vaulted basement was built in the 17th century from the ruins of Champlain's stronghold, and extends right under the square.

Continue along Rue Saint-Pierre, and turn left on Rue de la Place to go up to Place Royale.

Place Royale ★★★ (10) is the most European quarter of any city in North America. It resembles a village in northwestern France. Place Royale is laden with symbolism, as it was on this very spot that New France was founded in 1608. After many unsuccessful attempts, this became the official departure point of the French exploits in America. Under the French Regime, Place Royale was the only densely populated area in a vast and untamed colony. Today, it contains the most significant concentration of 17th and 18th century buildings in the Americas north of Mexico.

The square itself was laid out in 1673 by Governor Frontenac as a market. It took the place of the garden of the Champlain's *Abitation*, a stronghold that went up in flames in 1682, along with the rest of Basse-Ville. In 1686, Intendant Jean Bochart de Champigny erected a bronze bust of Louis XIV in the middle of the square, hence the name of the square, Place Royale. In 1928, François Bokanowski, then the French Minister of Commerce and Communications, presented Québécois Athanase David with a bronze replica of the marble bust of Louis XIV in the Gallerie de Diane at Versailles to replace the missing statue. The bronze, by Alexis Rudier, was not set up until 1931, for fear of offending England.

Under the French Regime, the square attracted many merchants and shippers who commissioned the building of attractive residences. The tall house on the southwest corner of the square and on Rue de la Place was built in 1754 for the formidable businesswoman Anne-Marie Barbel, widow of Louis Fornel. At the time, she owned a pottery factory on Rivière Saint-Charles and held the lease of the lucrative trading post at Tadoussac. **Maison Dumont** *(1 Place Royale)* was designed in 1689 by the tireless Claude Baillif for the vintner Eustache Lambert Dumont. The house incorporated elements of the old store of the *Compagnie des Habitants* (1647). Visitors can see its huge vaulted basement now used, as it was in the past, to store casks and bottles of wine. Turned into an inn in the 19th century, the house was the favourite stopping place of American President Howard Taft (1857-1930) on his way to his annual summer vacation in La Malbaie.

Maison Bruneau-Rageot-Drapeau, at number 3A, is a house built in 1763 using the walls of the old Nicolas Jérémie house. Jérémie was a Montagnais interpreter and a clerk at the fur-trading posts of Hudson Bay. He also specialized in the sale of various goods imported from La Rochelle.

Maison Paradis, on Rue Notre-Dame, houses the **Atelier du Patrimoine Vivant** *(free admission; end of Jun to mid-Oct, every day 10am to 5pm; 42 Rue Notre-Dame, ☎647-1598)*. In these studios, various artisans hone their skills using traditional methods.

Small, unpretentious **Église Notre-Dame-des-Victoires ★★ (11)** *(mid-May to mid-Oct, every day 9am to 4:30pm, closed Sat in case of weddings; Place Royale)* is the oldest church in Canada. Designed by Claude Baillif, it dates from 1688. It was built on the foundations of Champlain's *Abitation*, and incorporates some of its walls. Initially dedicated to the Baby Jesus, it was rechristened Notre-Dame-de-la-Victoire after Admiral Phipps' attack of 1690 failed. It was later renamed Notre-Dame-des-Victoires (the plural) in memory of the misfortune of British Admiral Walker, whose fleet ran aground on Île-aux-Oeufs during a storm in 1711. The bombardments of the conquest left nothing standing but the walls of the church, spoiling the Levasseurs' lovely interior. The church was restored in 1766, but

was not fully rebuilt until the current steeple was added in 1861.

Raphaël Giroux is responsible for most of the present interior, which was undertaken between 1854 and 1857, but the strange "fortress" tabernacle of the main altar is a later work by David Ouellet (1878). Lastly, in 1888, Jean Tardivel painted the historical scenes on the vault and on the wall of the chancel. What are most striking, though, are the various pieces in the church: the *ex-voto* (an offering) which hangs from the centre of the vault depicting the *Brézé*, a ship that came to Canada in 1664 carrying soldiers of the Carignan Regiment; and the beautiful tabernacle in the Sainte-Geneviève chapel, attributed to Pierre-Noël Levasseur (circa 1730). Among the paintings are works by Boyermans and Van Loo, originally from the collection of the Abbot Desjardins.

Proceed down Rue de la Place until it opens onto Place de Paris.

Place de Paris ★ (12) *(along Rue du Marché-Finlay)* is an elegant and sophisticated mix of contemporary art and traditional surroundings conceived by Québécois architect Jean Jobin in 1987. A large sculpture by French artist Jean-Pierre Raynault dominates the centre of the square. The work was presented by Jacques Chirac, the Mayor of Paris, on behalf of his city, when he came to Québec City. Entitled *Dialogue avec l'Histoire* (Dialogue with History), the black granite and white marble work is said to evoke the first human presence in the area and forms a pair with the bust of Louis XIV, visible in the background. Québécois have dubbed it the Colossus of Québec because of its imposing dimensions. From the square, which was once a market, there is a splendid view of the Batterie Royale, the Château Frontenac, and the St. Lawrence River.

Entrepôt Thibaudeau (13) *(215 Rue du Marché-Finlay)* is a huge building whose stone façade fronts onto Rue Dalhousie. It represents the last prosperous days of the area before its decline at the end of the 19th century. The Second Empire building is distinguished by its mansard roof and by its segmental arch openings. It was built in 1880, following the plans of Joseph-Ferdinand Peachy, for Isidore Thibaudeau, the president and founder of the Banque Nationale and an importer of European novelties. The building was renovated to house the **Centre d'Information de Place-Royale** *(free admission; early Jun to end of Sep, every day*

10am to 6pm, ☎643-6631), where the various artefacts that were found on the site during archeological digs are displayed, and which presents **Place-Royale, 400 Ans d'Histoire**, an exhibition that retraces the events that shapted the urban development of Basse-Ville and Place Royale. Visitors are also provided with information about the various activities in and around the square. Tours of the quarter with either a guide or an audio-guide also leave from the centre.

Head back up the street towards Rue Saint-Pierre and turn right.

Further along at number 92, is yet another imposing merchant's house, **Maison Estèbe** (1752). It is now part of the Musée de la Civilisation, whose smooth stone walls can be seen along the Rue Saint-Pierre. Guillaume Estèbe was a businessman and the director of the Saint-Maurice ironworks at Trois-Rivières. Having participated in a number of unsavoury schemes with Intendant Bigot during the Seven Years' War, he was locked-up in the Bastille for a few months on charges of embezzlement. The house, where he lived for five years with his wife and 14 children, is built on an embankment that used to front onto a large private wharf corresponding today to the courtyard of the museum. The courtyard is accessible through the gateway on the left. The 21-room interior escaped the bombardments of 1759. Some of the rooms feature handsome Louis XV woodwork. On the corner of Rue Saint-Jacques is the old **Banque de Québec** building (Edward Staveley, architect, 1861). Across the street, the old **Banque Molson** occupies an 18th-century house.

Turn right onto Rue Saint-Jacques. The entrance to the Musée de la Civilisation is on Rue Dalhousie, on the right.

The **Musée de la Civilisation** ★★ **(14)** *($6; Tue free admission, except in summer; end of Jun to early Sep, every day 10am to 7pm; early Sep to end of Jun, every day 10am to 5pm; 85 Rue Dalhousie, ☎643-2158)* is housed in a building, completed in 1988, that interprets the traditional architecture of Québec City with its stylized roof, dormer windows and a belltower which evokes those of the surroundings. The architect Moshe Safdie, who also designed the revolutionary Habitat '67 in Montreal, Ottawa's National Gallery and Vancouver's Public Library, has created a sculptural building with a monumental exterior staircase at its centre. The lobby provides a charming view of Maison

Estèbe and its wharf while preserving a contemporary look that is underlined by Astri Reuch's sculpture, *La Débâcle*.

The ten rooms of this "sociological" museum present a collection of everyday objects relating to the Québec culture of today and of yesteryear. The random grouping of this extensive collection tends to overwhelm, so it is a good idea to select a few rooms that seem particularly interesting. Some of the more remarkable items are the aboriginal artefacts, the large French Regime fishing craft unearthed during excavations for the Museum itself, some highly ornate 19th-century horse-drawn hearses, and some Chinese objets d'art and pieces of furniture, including an imperial bed, from the collection of the Jesuits.

Explore - Son et Lumière (15) *($5.50; end of Jun to early Sep, every day 1pm to 4:30pm; spring and fall, every day 10am to 5pm; 63 Rue Dalhousie, ☎692-2175)* uses multimedia technology to recount the voyages of such great European explorers of the Americas as Cartier and Champlain.

Take Rue Dalhousie northeast towards the old port. On the left is a lavish beaux-arts fire station dating from 1912, with a tower styled after that of the Parliament, that now houses **Ex Machina**, a multi-disciplinary artistic production centre founded by Robert Lepage. Continue on to Rue Saint-André to reach the old port.

Vieux-Port ★ (16) *(160 Rue Dalhousie)*. The old port is often criticized for being overly American in a city of European sensibility. It was refurbished by the Canadian government on the occasion of the maritime celebration, "Québec 1534-1984". There are various metallic structures designed to enliven the promenade, at the end of which is the handsome **Édifice de la Douane** (1856), the old customs building, designed by William Thomas of Toronto. All of the port area between Place Royale and the entrance of **Bassin Louise** is known as **Pointe-à-Carcy**.

Continue along **Rue Saint-Paul**, between the fashionable cafés and the antique shops. On the corner of Saint-Pierre is the imposing **Canadian Imperial Bank of Commerce** (CIBC) building, which houses an art gallery. A little further along on the left is the entrance to Rue du Sault-au-Matelot, which leads to Rue Sous-le-Cap, a narrow passageway that was once wedged between the St. Lawrence and the Cap

Diamant escarpment. For a long time, this was the only way to get to the intendant's palace from Place Royale. Not having enough space, the residents of the road built overhead walkways to get from one building to another.

To get to the Centre d'Interprétation du Vieux-Port-de-Québec, turn right on Rue Rioux and continue to Rue Saint-André.

Centre d'Interpretation du Vieux-Port-de-Québec (17) *($2.75; early May to early Sep, every day 10am to 5pm; Sep to end of Oct, every day noon to 4pm; 100 Rue Saint-André, ☎648-3300).* In the days of sail, Québec City was one of the most important gateways to America, since many vessels could not make their way any further against the current. Its bustling port was surrounded by shipyards that made great use of plentiful and high-quality Canadian lumber. The first royal shipyards appeared under the French Regime in the cove known as l'Anse du Cul-de-Sac. The Napoleonic blockade of 1806 forced the British to turn to their Canadian colony for wood and for the construction of battleships. This gave the impetus to a number of shipyards and made fortunes for a number of their owners. The interprative Centre at this National Historic Site concentrates on these flourishing days of navigation in Québec.

Marché du Vieux-Port ★ (18) *(corner of Rue Saint-Thomas and Rue Saint-André).* Most of Québec City's public markets were shut down in the sixties, because they had become obsolete in an age of air-conditioned supermarkets and frozen food. However, people continued to want fruit and vegetables fresh from the farm as well as the contact with the farmers. Moreover, the market was one of the only non-aseptic places people could congregate. Thus, the markets gradually began to reappear at the beginning of the eighties. Marché du Vieux-Port was built in 1987 by the architectural partners Belzile, Brassard, Galienne and Lavoie. It is the successor to two other Basse-Ville markets, Finlay and Champlain, that no longer exist. In the summer, the market is a pleasant place to stroll and take in the view of the Marina Bassin Louise at the edge of the market.

Walk back towards Rue Saint-Paul, and continue on to the corner of Rue Saint-Nicolas in the heart of the Palais quarter on either side of Palais de l'Intendant.

For over 50 years, the citizens of Québec City clamoured for a train station worthy of their city. Canadian Pacific finally fulfilled their wish in 1915. Designed by New York architect Harry Edward Prindle in the same style as the Château Frontenac, the **Gare du Palais ★ (19)** *(Rue de la Gare)* gives visitors a taste of the romance and charm that await in Québec City. The 18-metre-high arrival hall that extends behind the giant window of the façade is bathed by sunlight passing through the leaded glass skylight of the roof. The faïence tiles and multicoloured bricks of the walls lend a striking aspect to the whole. The station was closed for almost ten years (from 1976 to 1985) at the time when railway companies were imitating airlines and moving their stations to the suburbs. Fortunately, it was reopened, with great pomp, and now houses the bus and train stations. The building on the right is Raoul Chênevert's 1938 post office. It illustrates the persistence of the Château style of architecture that is so emblematic of the city.

L'Îlot Saint-Nicolas (20) *(Rue Saint-Paul at the corner of Rue Saint-Nicolas).* The block bordered by Ruelle de l'Ancien-Chantier, Rue Saint-Vallier Est, Rue Saint-Paul and Rue Saint-Nicolas is known as l'Îlot Saint Nicolas. It was restored with verve by architects De Blois, Côté, Leahy. The handsome stone building on the corner and the two others behind it on Rue Saint-Nicolas housed the famous **Cabaret Chez Gérard** from 1938 to 1978. It was here that Charles Trenet, Rina Ketty and many other famous French singers performed, and Charles Aznavour got his start here. In the bohemian days of the 1950s, he sang here every night for many months for a mere pittance.

The big Scottish brick building with the pinnacle inscribed "**Les Maisons Lecourt**" was put up across from l'Îlot Saint-Nicolas using the remnants of the "royal store" of Intendant Bigot. Nicknamed *La Fripone* (The rogue's) because of the extortionary prices exacted from the miserable populace by Bigot and his accomplices, the location was one of only two in the city during the French Regime where one could moor a boat (the other being l'Anse du Cul-de-Sac). In the 17th century, warehouses and wharfs were built along the estuary of the Saint-Charles, as was a shipyard with a drydock that bequeathed the street its name, Rue de l'Ancien-Chantier, meaning old shipyard.

Walk back up Rue Saint-Nicolas, turn right on Rue Saint-Vallier Est, and take the pedestrian path on the right.

The **Site du Palais de l'Intendant ★ (21)** *(free admission; end of May to end of Oct, Tue to Sun 10am to 5pm; end of Jun to Labour Day, and every day 10am to 5pm; 8 Rue Vallière, ☎691-6092)* the **Centre d'Interpretation Archéologique** are part of **l'Îlot des Palais** and the **Site Archéologique des Voûtes du Palais (19)**, (the palace vaults archeological site). The intendant oversaw the day to day affairs of the colony. Near his residence were grouped the royal stores, the few state enterprises and the prison. With so many opportunities to enrich himself, it was only natural that his should be the most splendid mansion in New France. The remains of one wing of the palace can still be seen in the shape of the segment of brown brick foundation wall that is now aboveground. The location was originally that of the brewery set up by the first intendant, Jean Talon (1625-1694). Talon exerted himself greatly in the effort to populate and develop the colony. For his pains, he was made secretary ot thr king's cabinet upon his return to France. His brewery was replaced by a palace designed by engineer La Guer Morville in 1716. This elegant building had a classical entrance in cut stone that gave onto a horseshoe-shaped staircase. Twenty or so ceremonial rooms, arranged linearly one after the other, served for receptions and for the meetings of the Conseil Supérieur.

The palace was spared British cannon-fire only to be burned to the ground during the American invasion of 1775-76. The arches of its cellars were used as the foundation of the Boswell brewery in 1872, bringing the site full circle. Visitors are free to inspect the cellars, where the **Centre d'Interpretation Archéologique**, the archeological information centre, is located. The centre displays artefacts and ruins of the site itself.

To return to Haute-Ville, climb Côte du Palais at the end of Rue Saint-Nicolas.

Tour C: Grande Allée ★★
(one day)

Grande Allée appears on 17th-century maps, but it was not built up until the first half of the 19th century, when the city grew beyond its walls. Grande Allée was originally a country road linking the town to Chemin du Roi and thereby to Montréal. At that time, it was bordered by the large agricultural properties of the nobility and clergy of the French Regime. After the British Conquest, many of the domains were turned into country estates of English merchants who set their manors well back from the road. Then the neoclassical town spilled over into the area before the Victorian city had a chance to stamp the landscape with its distinctive style. Today's Grande Allée is the most pleasant route into the downtown area and the focus of extramural Haute-Ville. Despite the fact that it links the capital's various ministries, it is a cheery street as many of the bourgeois houses which front onto it have been converted into restaurants and bars.

This walking tour starts at Porte Saint-Louis and gradually works its way away from the walled city.

On the right is Paul Chevré's monument to the historian François-Xavier Garneau. In the background, against the ramparts and opposite the Parliament, is where the Carnaval's ice castle is sculpted each year and the site of the annual Summer festival. On the right is the war memorial in front of which Remembrance Day ceremonies are held (November 11th).

The **Hôtel du Parlement ★★★ (1)** *(free admission; guided tours every day end of Jun to early Sep, 9am and 4:30pm; early Sep to Jun, Mon to Fri, 9am to 4:30pm; at the corner of Dufferin and Grande Allée, ☎643-7239)* is known to Québécois as l'Assemblée Nationale, the National Assembly. The seat of the government of Québec, this imposing building was erected between 1877 and 1886. It has a lavish French Renaissance Revival exterior intended to reflect the unique cultural status of Québec in the North American context. Eugène-Étienne Taché (1836-1912) looked to the Louvre for his inspiration in both the plan of the quadrangular building and its decor. Originally destined to incorporate the two houses of parliament characteristic of the British system of government, as well as all of the ministries, it is today part of a group of buildings on either side of Grande Allée.

The numerous statues of the parliament's main façade constitute a sort of pantheon of Québec. The 22 bronzes of important figures in the history of the nation were cast by such well-known artists as Louis-Philippe Hébert and Alfred Laliberté. A raised inscription on the wall near the central passage identifies the statues. In front of the main entrance a bronze by Hébert entitled *La Halte dans la Forêt*

Hôtel du Parlement

(The Pause in the Forest) depicts an aboriginal family. The work, which is meant to honour the original inhabitants of Québec, was displayed at Paris's World's Fair in 1889. *Le Pêcheur à la Nigog* (Fisherman at the Nigog), by the same artist, hangs in the niche by the fountain.

The building's interior is a veritable compendium of the icons of Québec's history. The handsome woodwork is in the tradition of religious architecture. The members of parliament called *députés*, sit in the National Assembly, or Salon Bleu (Blue Chamber), where Charles Huot's painting, *La Première Séance de l'Assemblée Législative du Bas-Canada en 1792* (The First Session of the Legislative Assembly of Lower Canada in 1792), hangs over the chair of the president of the Assembly. A large work by the same artist covers the ceiling and evokes the motto of Québec, *Je me souviens* (I remember). The Salon Rouge (Red Chamber), intended for the Conseil Législatif, an unelected body eliminated in 1968, is now used for parliamentary commissions. A painting entitled *Le Conseil Souverain* (The Sovereign Council), a souvenir of the mode of government in the days of New France, graces this chamber. Several of the windows of the parliament building boast gorgeous Art-Nouveau stained glass by master glazier Henri Perdriau, a native of Saint-Pierre de Montélimar in Vendée, France. Undeniably, the most spectacular is the arch that adorns the entrance to the elegant Le restaurant Parlementaire (see p 359). This feature was

designed by architect Omer Marchand in 1917. The debates of the National Assembly are open to the public, but a pass must first be obtained.

Thanks to the new **Centre des Congrès de Québec (2)** *(900 Boulevard René-Lévesque Est, 2e étage, P.O. Box 37060, G1R 2B5, ☎644-4000 or 644-6455)*, inaugurated just north of the Hôtel du Parlement in 1996, an entire dreary-looking section of Boulevard René-Lévesque (formerly Boulevard Saint-Cyrille) was refurbished. The street, which runs between Parliament Hill and the impressive convention centre and between the Hilton Québec and Radisson Gouverneurs hotels (see p 354) and Place Québec shopping centre, is no longer divided by a wall and has been adorned with trees. On the Parliament side, **Promenade des Premiers Ministres** is lined with information panels providing all sorts of detail about the premiers who have shaped Québec since 1867. On the other side of the street lies **Promenade Desjardins**, dedicated to a single man, Alphonse Desjardins. At the entrance of the convention centre, there is a kinetic sculpture entitled *Le Quatuor d'Airain* (Bronze Quartet).

Follow Grande Allée as far as Rue de la Chevrotière.

There are two other statues on the grounds of the Parliament: one of Honoré Mercier, Premier of Québec from 1887 to 1891, and one of Maurice Duplessis, Premier during the *grande noirceur* or "great darkness" (1936-1939 and

1944-1959). The latter was long kept in storage for political reasons.

The dizzying growth of the civil service during the Quiet Revolution of the 1960s compelled the government to construct several modern buildings to house its various ministries. A row of beautiful Second Empire houses was demolished to make way for **Complexes H and J (3)** *(on Grande Allée opposite the Hôtel du Parlement)*. Dubbed "the bunker" by Québécois, Pierre Saint-Gelais' 1970 building houses the office of the premier of the provincial government.

Place George V and the **Manège Militaire ★ (4-6)** *(opposite Parc Le Pigeonnier)*. This expanse of lawn is used as the training area and parade ground of the military's equestrians. There are cannons and a statue in memory of the two soldiers who perished attempting to douse the flames of the 1889 fire in the suburb of Saint-Sauveur. Otherwise, the grounds serve mainly to highlight the amusing Château-style façade of the Manège Militaire, the Military Riding Academy, built in 1888 and designed by Eugène-Étienne Taché, the architect of the Hôtel du Parlement.

Parc Le Pigeonnier (5) *(between Rue Saint-Augustin and Rue d'Artigny)* and **Complexe G,** which appears in the background, together occupy the site of the old Saint-Louis quarter, today almost entirely vanished. Parc Le Pigeonnier was laid out for open-air shows. It takes its name, which means dovecote, from the interesting concrete structure placed in the middle, after an idea of landscape architects Schreiber and Williams, in 1973.

A little further to the west, the fabric of the old city is again in evidence. **Terrasse Stadacona** *(numbers 640 to 664)*, on the right, is a neoclassical row of townhouses on the English model: the multiple houses share a common façade. These houses date from 1847, and have now been turned into bars and restaurants with terraces sheltered by multitudes of parasols. Opposite *(numbers 661 to 695)* is a group of Second Empire houses that dates from 1882, a period when Grande Allée was the fashionable street in Québec City. These houses show the influence of the parliamentary buildings on the residential architecture of the quarter. Three other houses on Grande Allée are worth mentioning for the eclecticism of their façades: **Maison du Manufacturier de Chaussures W. A. Marsh** *(number 625)*, house of a prominent shoe manufacturer, designed in 1899 by Toronto architect Charles John Gibson; **Maison Garneau-Meredith** *(numbers 600 to 614)* of the same year; and **Maison William Price,** a real little Romeo and Juliet style place which is, unfortunately, dwarfed by the hotel **Le Concorde.** The revolving restaurant (see p 359) of this hotel affords a magnificent view of Haute-Ville and the Plains of Abraham (see p 355).

In little **Parc Montcalm (7)**, next to the hotel, there is a statue commemorating the general's death on September 13, 1759, at the Battle of the Plains of Abraham. The **statue of French General Charles de Gaulle** (1890-1970), which faces away from Montcalm, created quite a controversy when it was erected in the spring of 1997. Farther along, at the entrance to the Plains of Abraham, **Jardin Jeanne-d'Arc** boasts magnificent flowerbeds and a statue of Joan of Arc astride a spirited charger.

Turn right on Rue de la Chevrotière.

Behind the austere façade of the mother house of the Soeurs du Bon-Pasteur, a community devoted to the education of abandoned and delinquent girls, is the charming, Baroque Revival style **Chapelle Historique Bon-Pasteur ★★ (8)** *(free admission; Jul and Aug, Tue to Sat, 1:30pm to 4:30pm; 1080 Rue de la Chevrotière)*. Designed by Charles Baillargé in 1866, this tall, narrow chapel houses an authentic baroque tabernacle dating from 1730. Pierre-Noël Levasseur's masterpiece of New France carving is surrounded by devotional miniatures hung on pilasters by the nuns.

Atop the 31 stories of **Édifice Marie-Guyart** of Complexe G (dubbed the "stovepipe" by Québécois), the **Observatoire de la Galerie d'Art Anima G** *(free admission; Mon to Fri 10am to 4pm; Sat, Sun and holidays, 1pm to 5pm; 1033 Rue De La Chevrotière, ☎644-9841)*, provides a splendid view of Québec City and the surrounding area.

Go back and take a right on Rue Saint-Amable. Walk along as far as Parc de l'Amérique Française.

The **Parc de l'Amérique Française (9)** is a recent creation dedicated to French America. It faces the head office of the Laurentien Insurance Company and is centered around a collection of flags of the various francophone communities of America. The **Grand Théâtre (10)**

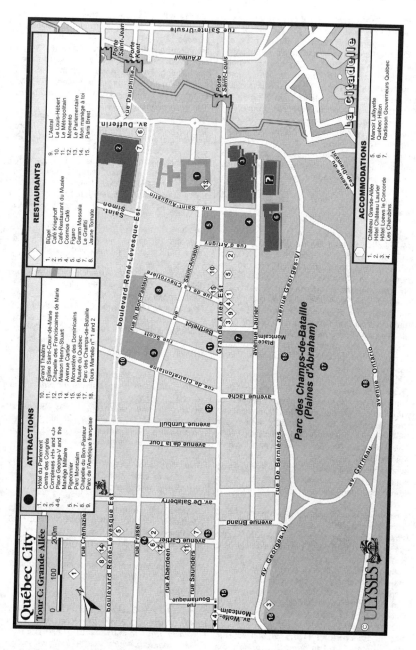

Québec City

Tour C: Grande Allée

0   100   200m

ATTRACTIONS

1. Hôtel du Parlement
2. Centre des Congrès
3. Complexes «H» and «J»
4.-6. Place George-V and the Manège Militaire
5. Pigeonnier
7. Parc Montcalm
8. Chapelle du Bon-Pasteur
9. Parc de l'Amérique française
10. Grand Théâtre
11. Église Saint-Cœur-de-Marie
12. Chapelle des Franciscaines de Marie
13. Maison Henry-Stuart
14. Avenue Cartier
15. Monastère des Dominicains
16. Musée du Québec
17. Parc des Champs-de-Bataille
18. Tours Martello n° 1 and 2

RESTAURANTS

1. Bügel
2. Café Krieghoff
3. Café-Restaurant du Musée
4. Cosmos Café
5. Figaro
6. Garam Massala
7. Le Graffiti
8. Jaune Tomate
9. L'Astral
10. Le Louis-Hébert
11. Le Métropolitain
12. Momento
13. Le Parlementaire
14. Mon manège à toi
15. Paris Brest

ACCOMMODATIONS

1. Château Grande-Allée
2. Hôtel Château Laurier
3. Hôtel Loews le Concorde
4. Les Chérubins
5. Manoir Lafayette
6. Québec-Hilton
7. Radisson Gouverneurs Québec

Parc des Champs-de-Bataille
(Plaines d'Abraham)

© ULYSSES

(269 Boulevard René-Lévesque Est,
☎*643-8131)* is located at the far end of the
park. Inaugurated in 1971, the theatre of Polish
architect Victor Prus was to be a meeting place
for the cream of Québec City society. There
was quite a scandal, therefore, when Jordi
Bonet's mural was unveiled and the assembled
crowd could read the lines from a poem by
Claude Péloquin: *Vous êtes pas tannés de
mourir, bande de caves*, which roughly
translates, "You bunch of straights ain't sick of
dying". The theatre has two halls (Louis-
Fréchette and Octave-Crémazie) and stages the
concerts of the symphony orchestra as well as
theatre, dance and variety shows.

*Turn left on Rue Scott to get back to the
Grande Allée.*

Église Saint-Cœur de Marie (11) *(530 Grande
Allée Est)* was built for the Eudists in 1919
after the design of Ludger Robitaille. It looks
more martial than devotional due to its
bartizans, machicolations and towers, rather
like a Mediterranean fortress with big archways
knocked out of it. Across the way is the most
outlandish row of Second Empire houses still
standing in Québec City *(455-555 Grande Allée
Est)*, **Terrasse Frontenac**. Its slender, fantastical
peaks look like something from a fairy tale.
They are the product of Joseph-Ferdinand
Peachy's imagination (1895).

Chapelle des Franciscaines de Marie ★ (12) is
the chapel of a community of nuns devoted to
the adoration of the Lord. They commissioned
the Sanctuaire de l'Adoration Perpétuelle
(Sanctuary of Perpetual Adoration) in 1901.
This exuberant Baroque Revival chapel invites
the faithful to prayer and celebrates the
everlasting presence of God. It features a small
columned cupola supported by angels and a
sumptuous marble baldaquin.

Several handsome, bourgeois houses dating
from the early 20th century face the chapel.
Among them, at numbers 433-435, is the
residence of John Holt, proprietor of the Holt
Renfrew stores. Both this and the neighbouring
house, number 425, are styled after Scottish
manors. Undeniably the most elegant in its mild
Flemish and Oriental eclecticism is the house of
Judge P. A. Choquette, designed by architect
Georges-Émile Tanguay.

Maison Henry-Stuart (13) *($5; Jun to Aug,
Wed to Mon 11am to 5pm; Sep to May, Sun
1pm to 5pm; 82 Grande Allée Ouest,*
☎*647-4347)*, on the corner of Cartier and

Grande Allée, is one of the few remaining
Regency style Anglo-Norman cottages in
Québec City. This type of colonial British
architecture is distinguished by a large pavilion
roof overhanging a low verandah surrounding
the building. The house was built in 1849 and
used to mark the border between city and
country; its original garden still surrounds it.
The interior boasts several pieces of furniture
from the Saint-Jean-Port-Joli manor and has
been practically untouched since 1911. More
or less closed to the public for a number of
years, Maison Henry-Stuart and its garden,
which belongs to the organisation "Jardins du
Québec", now welcome visitors. The house is
home to the Conseil des Monuments et Sites
de Québec, which offers guided tours. Tea is
even served here on summer afternoons now.

Avenue Cartier (14), visible on the right,
regroups a large number of bars and
restaurants that are popular with locals.

In the area of the American-style **Maison
Pollack** *(1 Grande Allée Ouest)* is the
Renaissance Revival **Maison des Dames
Protestantes** *(111 Grande Allée Ouest)*, built in
1862 by architect Michel Lecourt. Also nearby
is **Maison Krieghoff** *(115 Grande-Allée Ouest)*,
which was occupied in 1859 by the Dutch
painter Cornelius Krieghoff.

Monastère des Dominicains ★ (15) *(175
Grande Allée Ouest, not open to the public)* and
its church are relatively recent realizations that
testify to the persistence and historical
exactitude of 20th-century Gothic Revival
architecture. This sober building of British
character incites reverence and meditation.

*Turn left on Avenue Wolfe-Montcalm the
entrance to both Parc Champs-de-Bataille and
the Musée du Québec.*

Located at the roundabout is the **Monument to
General Wolfe**, victor of the decisive Battle of
the Plains of Abraham. It is said to stand on the
exact spot where he fell. The 1832 monument
has been the object of countless
demonstrations and acts of vandalism. Toppled
again in 1963, it was rebuilt, this time with an
inscription in French.

The **Musée de Québec ★★★ (16)** *($5.75; late
May to early Sep, every day 10am to 5:45pm,
Wed to 9:45pm; early Sep to late May, Tue to
Sun 11am to 5:45pm, Wed to 8:45pm; 1 Ave-
nue Wolfe-Montcalm,* ☎*643-2150)* was
renovated and enlarged in 1992. The older,

Musée du Québec

west-facing building is on the right. Parallel to Avenue Wolfe-Montcalm, the entrance is dominated by a glass tower similar to that of the Musée de la Civilisation. The 1933 Classical Revival edifice is subterraneously linked with the old prison on the left. The latter has been cleverly restored to house exhibits, and has been rebaptized Édifice Ballairgé in honour of its architect. Some of the cells have been preserved.

A visit to this important museum allows one to become acquainted with the painting, sculpture and silverwork of Québec from the time of New France to today. The collections of religious art gathered from rural parishes of Québec are particularly interesting. Also on display are official documents, including the original surrender of Québec (1759). The museum frequently hosts temporary exhibits from the United States and Europe.

On the first floor of the museum's Édifice Baillargé is the **Centre d'Interprétation du Parc des Champs-de-Bataille Nationaux** (National Battlefield Park Interpretive Centre) *($2; mid-May to early Sep, every day 10am to 5:30pm,* *early Sep to mid-May, Tue to Sun 11am to 5:30pm; Édifice Baillargé, level 1, ☎648-5641)*, which exhibits a reconstruction of the Battle of the Plains of Abraham and a model of the subsequent development of the area. They also offer guided tours of the plains.

Turn left on Avenue Georges VI and right on Avenue Garneau.

Parc des Champs-de-Bataille ★★ (17) takes visitors back to July 1759: the British fleet, commanded by General Wolfe arrives in front of Québec City. The attack is launched almost immediately. In total, almost 40,000 cannonballs crash down on the besieged city. As the season grows short, the British must come to a decision before they are surprised by French reinforcements or trapped in the December freeze-up. On the 13th of September, under cover of the night, British troops scale the Cap Diamant escarpment west of the fortifications. The ravines which here and there cut into the otherwise uniform mass of the escarpment allow them to climb and to remain concealed. By morning, the troops have taken position in the fields of **Abraham Martin**, hence the name of the battlefield and the park. The French are astonished, as they had anticipated a direct attack on the citadel. Their troops, with the aid of a few hundred Indian warriors, throw themselves against the British. The generals of both sides are slain, and the battle draws to a close in bloody chaos. New France is lost!

Parc des Champs-de-Bataille, where the battle took place, was created in 1908 to commemorate the event. At 101 hectares, the park affords Québécois a superb recreational space. Previously occupied by a military training ground, the Ursulines and a few farms, the area of the park was laid out between 1929 and 1939 according to the plans of landscape architect Frederick Todd. This project provided work for thousands of Québécois during the Depression. The statue of Jeanne-d'Arc, surrounded by an attractive garden, honours the memory of the soldiers who fell in New France during the Seven Years' War.

The **Tours Martello** ★ **(18)**, two towers designed by the eponymous engineer, are characteristic of British defenses at the beginning of the 19th century. Tower number 1 (1808) is visible on the edge of Avenue Ontario; number 2 (1815) blends into the surrounding buildings on the corner of Avenue Laurier and Avenue Taché.

Tour Martello

This is the end of the Grande Allée walking tour. To return to the walled city, follow Avenue Ontario east to Avenue Georges VI or take Avenue du Cap-Diamant (in the hilly part of the park) to **Promenade des Gouverneurs**. *The promenade follows the citadel and overlooks the Cap Diamant escarpment, winding up at Terrasse Dufferin. This route affords stunning views over the city, the St. Lawrence River and the south shore.*

Tour D: Saint-Jean-Baptiste ★ (two hours)

A student hangout complete with bars, theatres and boutiques, the Saint-Jean-Baptiste quarter is perched on a hillside between Haute-Ville and Basse-Ville. The abundance of pitched and mansard roofs is reminiscent of parts of the old city, but the orthogonal layout of the streets is quintessentially North American. Despite a terrible fire in 1845, this old Québec City suburb retains several examples of wooden constructions, forbidden inside the walls of the city.

The Saint-Jean-Baptiste tour begins at Porte Saint-Jean, near Place d'Youville. It threads along Rue Saint-Jean, the main artery of the neighbourhood.

At the beginning of the 20th century, Québec City was in dire need of a new auditorium, its Académie de Musique having burnt to the ground in March of 1900. With the help of private enterprise, the mayor undertook to find a new location. The Canadian Government, owner of the fortifications, offered to furnish a strip of land along the walls of the city. While narrow, the lot grew wider as it grew deeper, making possible the construction of a fitting hall, the **Capitole** ★ **(1)** *(972 Rue Saint-Jean)*. W. S. Painter, the ingenious Detroit architect already at work on the expansion of the Château Frontenac, devised a plan for a curved façade, giving the building a monumental air despite the restriction of the lot. Inaugurated in 1903 as the Auditorium de Québec, the building is one of the most astonishing beaux-arts realizations in the country.

In 1927, the famous American cinema architect Thomas W. Lamb converted the auditorium into a sumptuous 1,700 seat cinema. Renamed the Théâtre Capitole, the auditorium nevertheless served as a venue for shows until the construction of the Grand Théâtre in 1971. Abandoned for a few years, the Capitole was

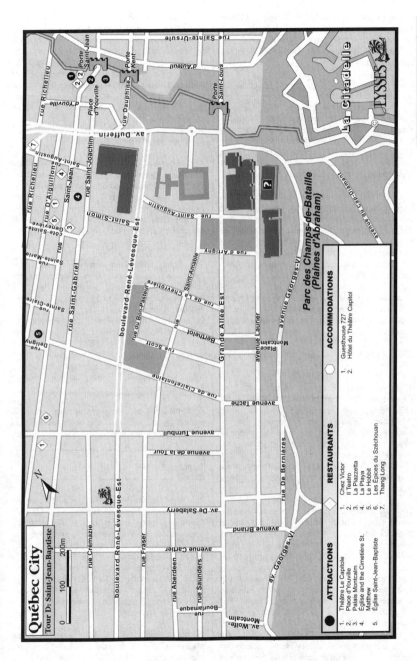

Québec City

Tour D: Saint-Jean-Baptiste

0   100   200m

N

rue Richelieu

rue Crémazie

boulevard René-Lévesque Est

rue Fraser

avenue Cartier

rue Aberdeen

rue Saunders

rue Bourlamaque

av. Wolfe-Montcalm

rue de la Tour

avenue Turnbull

av. De Salaberry

avenue Briand

av. Georges-VI

rue De Bernières

avenue Taché

rue de Claire-Fontaine

rue Scott

rue Berthelot

rue de La Chevrotière

rue du Bon-Pasteur

rue Saint-Amable

rue d'Artigny

Grande Allée Est

avenue Laurier

Place Montcalm

avenue Georges-VI

boulevard René-Lévesque Est

rue Saint-Gabriel

rue Sainte-Claire

rue Sainte-Marie

rue Deligny

Côte Sainte-Geneviève

rue Saint-Augustin

rue Saint-Simon

rue Saint-Joachim

rue Saint-Jean

rue D'Aiguillon

rue Saint-Augustin

av. Dufferin

d'Youville

Place d'Youville

rue du Dauphine

Porte Saint-Jean

Porte Kent

Porte Saint-Louis

d'Auteuil

rue Sainte-Ursule

La Citadelle

ULYSSES

Parc des Champs-de-Bataille (Plaines d'Abraham)

avenue du Cap-Diamant

ATTRACTIONS
1. Théâtre Le Capitole
2. Place d'Youville
3. Palais Montcalm
4. Église and the Cimetière St. Matthew
5. Église Saint-Jean-Baptiste

RESTAURANTS
1. Chez Victor
2. Il Teatro
3. La Piazzetta
4. La Playa
5. Le Hobbit
6. Les Épices du Széchouan
7. Thang Long

ACCOMMODATIONS
1. Guesthouse 727
2. Hôtel du Théâtre Capitol

entirely refurbished in 1992 by architect Denis Saint-Louis. The building now houses a dinner-theatre in the hall, and a luxury hotel (see p 355) and a restaurant (see p 360) in the curved façade.

Place d'Youville (2) is the public space at the entrance of the old section of town. Formerly an important market square, it is today a bustling crossroads and cultural forum. A recent redevelopment has given the square a large promenade area with trees and benches. The counterscarp wall, part of the fortifications removed in the 20th century, has been highlighted by the use of black granite blocks.

The Montcalm Market was levelled in 1932 in order to build the multifunctional space called the **Palais Montcalm (3)** *(995 Place d'Youville)*. Also known as the Monument National, this is the venue of choice for political rallies and demonstrations of all kinds. The auditorium has a sparse architecture which draws on both neoclassical and Art-Deco schools.

Chapelle du Couvent des Soeurs de la Charité (1856) is visible on leaving Place d'Youville. Its delicate Gothic Revival façade is dwarfed by two huge towers.

Cross Avenue Dufferin and continue along Rue St-Jean.

There has been a cemetery on the site of the **Church and Cemetery of Saint Matthew ★ (4)** *(755 Rue Saint-Jean)* since 1771, when Protestants, whether French Hugenot, English Anglican or Scottish Presbyterian, banded together to found a protestant graveyard. Several 19th-century tombstones are still standing. Recently, the gravestones were carefully restored, and the cemetery is now a public garden.

Located on the congruous portion of the site, along Rue Saint-Jean, is a lovely Anglican church. Its Gothic Revival architecture was influenced by the Ecclesiologists, an influential school of Anglican thought that sought to re-establish ties with the traditions of the Middle Ages. In its design, and even in its materials, it looks more like an ancient village church than a Victorian church with a gothic decor. The nave was first put up in 1848; then, in 1870, William Tutin Thomas, the Montreal architect who designed the Canadian Centre for Architecture's Shaughnessy House, drafted an enlargement, giving the church its present bell tower and interior. Québec's Anglican

community dwindled in the 20th century, leading to the abandonment of the church. In 1980, it was cleverly converted into a branch of the municipal library. Several of the adornments crafted by British artists have been retained: Percy Bacon's handsome oak choir enclosure, Felix Morgan's alabaster pulpit, and Clutterbuck's beautiful stained glass. The sober vault with its exposed beams is also noteworthy.

Continue along Rue Saint-Jean.

At number 699, **Épicerie J.-A.-Moisan** *(699 Rue St-Jean)* was founded in 1871 and claims to be the "oldest grocery store in North America". It does in fact look like a general store from yesteryear with its wooden floor and shelves, old advertisements and many tin cans. Relish the past by stocking up on the fresh, appetizing products it offers.

The **Église Saint-Jean-Baptiste ★ (5)** *(Rue Saint-Jean on the corner of Rue de Ligny)* stands out as Joseph Ferdinand Peachy's masterpiece. A disciple of French eclecticism, Peachy was an unconditional admirer of the Église de la Trinité in Paris. The resemblance here is striking, as much in the portico as in the interior. Completed in 1885, the building caused the bankruptcy of its architect, who was, unfortunately, held responsible for cracks that appeared in the façade during construction.

A stroll through the surrounding hillside's streets gives a sense of the day-to-day life of Québec City's residents.

 PARKS

Parc des Champs-de-Bataille (see p 347), better known as the **Plains of Abraham**, is Québec City's undisputed park of parks. This immense green space covers about 100 hectares and stretches all the way to the Cap Diamant, which slopes down to the river. It is a magnificent place for local residents to enjoy all sorts of outdoor activities. Strollers and picnickers abound here during summer, but there is enough space for everyone to enjoy a little peace and quiet.

With its big trees and lawns, **Domaine Maizerets** *(free admission; 2000 Boulevard Montmorency, ☎691-2385)* is the perfect place for a leisurely stroll. Gardening buffs will love the arboretum and the landscaping; the Domaine also belongs to the "Jardins du Québec" organization. A number of historic buildings can also be found here, including the château that houses a small exhibition on the history of the estate. All sorts of outdoor activities can be enjoyed here in both summer and winter. Outdoor concerts, plays and conferences on ornithology and other subjects are held at the Domaine Maizerets year-round.

 OUTDOOR ACTIVITIES

 Cycling

Québec City does not have many bike paths. Still, certain paths are worth mentioning, such as the one leading from the Vieux-Port to Beauport and the one that follows part of the Rivière Saint-Charles. In addition, motorists have to make room for cyclists on some streets. Take note, however, that efforts are being made to develop a bike-path network in the city. Finally, parks like the Plains of Abraham are pleasant places for cycling and even have trails suitable for mountain bikes.

Cyclo Services Voyages *($25 per day; Hangar du Vieux-Port, 84 Rue Prince-de-Galles, ☎692-4052 or 692-4146)*, **Vélo Passe-Sport Plein Air** *($25 per day; 77A Rue Ste-Anne, 100 Rue Saint-André, ☎692-3643, ⇔621-0371)* and the **Auberge de la Paix** *($20 per day; 31 Rue Couillard, ☎694-0735)* all rent out bicycles. The first two also organize bike trips in and around Québec City.

 Cruises

For those interested in seeing Québec City and its surroundings from different angles, the *Louis-Jolliet (cruises at 11:30am, 2pm, 3pm and 7:30pm; ☎692-1159)*, berthed at the port of Québec City, offers cruises throughout the summer. The daytime cruises last an hour and a half and take passengers to the foot of Montmorency Falls, while the evening cruises go to the tip of Ile d'Orléans and include dinner in one of the boat's two dining rooms. These starlight cruises, which last several hours, always include live music, and you can dance the night away on the ship's deck!

Croisières de la Famille Dufour *($85 to $140; ☎827-8836, 827-8206 or 800-463-5250)* take passengers to the lovely region of Charlevoix, to Pointe-au-Pic, to Ile-aux-Coudres and even to the heart of the breathtaking Saguenay fjord aboard a big, modern catamaran.

 In-Line Skating

On the **Plains of Abraham**, in front of the Musée du Québec, there is a big, paved rink for in-line skating. Scores of children and adults wearing protective helmets can be seen blading around the track on fine summer days. Equipment rentals are available at a small stand by the rink.

Vélo Passe-Sport Plein air *($25 per day; 77A Rue Sainte-Anne, 100 Rue Saint-André, ☎801-1920)* and **Cyclo Services Voyages** *($25 per day; Hangar du Vieux-Port, 84 Rue Prince-de-Galles, ☎692-4052)* also rent out in-line skates.

 Jogging

Again, the place to go is the **Plains of Abraham**. The big, flat track in front of the Musée du Québec is a good place for a run, though people also go jogging on the paved streets and trails.

 Ice Skating

From early fall to late spring, a small skating rink occupies the centre of **Place d'Youville**, complete with music-blaring loudspeakers. Skaters also have access to an indoor area equipped with restrooms *(every day noon to 10pm, ☎691-4685)*. In the heart of winter, snow-covered Place d'Youville takes on a magical air, as skaters glide around frost-covered Porte-Saint-Jean, around the illuminated Capitole and around lampposts draped with Christmas decorations in the background.

Once it has iced over, **Rivière Saint-Charles** is maintained for skating. When the weather permits, a lovely skating rink winds several kilometres between the neighbourhoods of Limoilou and Saint-Roch, in Basse-Ville. The Marina Saint-Roch *(Mon to Fri noon to 9pm,*

Sat and Sun 10am to 9pm; 691-7188) offers skaters a heated place to rest.

Each winter, an ice rink is laid out on **Terrasse Dufferin**, enabling skaters to swirl about at the foot of the Château Frontenac, with a view of the icy river. You can put on your gear at the kiosk *(mid-Dec to mid-Mar, every day 11am to 11pm, ☎692-2955)*, which also rents out skates *($2; mid-Dec to mid-Mar, Mon to Fri 1pm to 4pm, Sat and Sun 10am to 4pm, some nights 6pm to 9pm)*.

A lovely skating rink winds beneath the trees of **Domaine Maizerets** *(free admission; 2000 Boulevard Montmorency, ☎691-2385)* (see p 350). There's a small chalet nearby where you can take off your skates and warm up next to a wood stove. Skate rentals *($2; mid-Dec to mid-Mar, Mon to Fri 1pm to 4pm, Sat and Sun 10am to 4pm)*.

 Cross-country Skiing

The snow-covered **Plains of Abraham** provide an enchanting setting for cross-country skiing. Trails crisscross the park from one end to the other, threading their way through the trees or leading across a headland with views of the icy river. All right in the heart of the city!

Some extremely pleasant cross-country trails can also be found at **Domaine Maizerets** *(free admission; 2000 Boulevard Montmorency, ☎691-2385)* (see p 350). At the starting point, there is a little chalet heated with a wood-burning stove. Equipment rentals *($2; mid-Dec to mid-Mar, Mon to Fri 1pm to 4pm, Sat and Sun 10am to 4pm)* are available.

 Tobogganing

The hills of the **Plains of Abraham** are wonderful for sledding. Bundle up well and follow the kids pulling toboggans to find the best spots!

During winter, a hill is created on **Terrasse Dufferin**. You can glide down it comfortably seated on a toboggan. First purchase your tickets at the little stand in the middle of the terrace *($1 per ride; mid-Dec to mid-Mar, every day 11am to 11pm; 692-2955)*, then grab a toboggan and climb to the top of the slide.

Once you get there, make sure to take a look around: the view is magnificent!

 ACCOMMODATIONS

Québec City has an abundance of hotels and accommodations of all kinds. In Vieux-Québec, many old historic houses have been converted into small hotels. They are often charming but can run a bit short on comfort. Many of the rooms in these establishments, for example, do not have private bathrooms. During the winter, many hotels offer special room rates on weekends. However, in the summer, it is best to reserve a room well in advance. During the winter carnival, which takes place in February, a large influx of visitors can also make finding a room difficult.

Hospitalité Canada Tours is a free telephone service operated by the Maison du Tourisme de Québec *(12 Rue Ste-Anne, ☎694-1602 or 1-800-665-1528)*. Depending on what kind of accommodations you're looking for, the staff will suggest various places belonging to the network and even make reservations for you.

Tour A: Vieux-Québec (Haute-Ville)

The **Centre Internationale de Séjour** youth hostel *($17 Canadians, $20 non-Canadians; 19 Rue Sainte-Ursule, G1R 4E1, ☎1-800-461-8585, ☎694-0755)* has 250 beds for young people during the summer months. The rooms can accommodate from three to eight people, the dormitories from 10 to 12, and there are also private double rooms.

Behind its lovely white facade in Vieux-Québec, **Auberge de la Paix** *($18 bkfst incl., plus $2 for bedding if you don't have your own; sb, K; 31 Rue Couillard, G1R 3T4, ☎694-0735)* has a youth-hostel atmosphere. It has a total of 59 beds in rooms able to accommodate from two to eight people, as well as a kitchenette and a living room. The pretty back yard is all abloom. Children welcome!

Manoir LaSalle *($45; 18 Rue Sainte-Ursule, G1R 4C9, ☎692-9953)* is a small hotel with 11 rooms, one of which has a private bathroom. This red brick building is exemplary of an architectural style typical of some of the first homes built in the city.

Ulysses' Favourites

For the friendly atmosphere:
Auberge Saint-Antoine (p 354), Hôtel Particulier Belley (p 354) and Auberge de la Paix (p 352)

For history buffs:
Château Frontenac (p 354) and Hôtel Clarendon (p 354)

For the views:
Château Frontenac (p 354), Hôtel Loews Le Concorde (p 355) and Château Bellevue (p 353)

For the decor:
Hôtel du Théâtre (p 355), Auberge Saint-Antoine (p 354) and Le Priori (p 354)

For businesspeople:
Québec Hilton (p 355), Hôtel Loews Le Concorde (p 355) and Radisson Québec (p 354)

Maison Sainte-Ursule (*$47; 40 Rue Sainte-Ursule, G1R 4E2, ☎694-9794*) is a pretty little house with green shutters. Unfortunately, the rooms are a bit lopsided and drab. In the off-season, rooms can be had here at very good prices.

Located on busy Rue Saint-Louis, **Auberge Saint-Louis** (*$49 sb, $79 pb, bkfst incl; ℜ, ≡; 48 Rue Saint-Louis, G1R 3Z3, ☎692-2424, ⁓692-3797*) is a pleasant, small hotel. Room prices vary according to amenities offered. Less expensive rooms do not have private bathrooms. The hotel is well maintained.

Maison du Fort (*$69 bkfst incl.; ≡; 21 Rue Sainte-Geneviève, G1R 4B1, ☎692-4375*) is located in a quiet area and overlooks Parc des Gouverneurs. This attractive, small hotel has pleasant rooms. Service is very friendly, making for an enjoyable stay.

A number of old houses on Rue Sainte-Ursule have been made into hotels. Among these, **Maison Acadienne** (*$77; ⊚, ≡, K; 43 Rue Sainte-Ursule, G1R 4E4, ☎694-0280*) is easily spotted by its large, white facade. The rooms are rather lacklustre, although some of them have been renovated.

Also next to Parc des Gouverneurs, overlooking the river, the **Château de Léry** (*$78 bkfst incl.; ≡; 8 Rue Laporte, G1R 4M9, ☎692-2692 or 1-800-363-0036, ⁓692-5231*) has comfortable rooms. Rooms facing the street have a good view. This hotel is in a quiet neighbourhood in

the old part of the city but is just a few minutes walk from the bustle of downtown.

Au Jardin du Gouverneur (*$90 bkfst incl.; ≡; 16 Rue Mont-Carmel, G1R 4A3, ☎692-1704, ⁓692-1713*) is a charming little hotel in small blue and white house opposite Parc des Gouverneurs. Rooms are a good size but the decor is nothing special. No smoking.

Auberge du Trésor (*$90, $169 ½b; ℜ; 20 Rue Sainte-Anne, G1R 3X2, ☎694-1876*) was built in 1676. Renovated many times since then, it maintains an impressive appearance. Rooms are modern and comfortable. All rooms have private bathrooms and colour televisions.

Château de Pierre (*$89, ≡; 17 Avenue Sainte-Geneviève, G1R 4A8, ☎694-0429*). The ostentatious entrance of this hotel is quite striking though somewhat flashy. The rooms are comfortable.

The **Château Bellevue** hotel (*$99; 16 Rue Laporte, G1R 4M9, ☎692-2473 or 1-800-463-2617, ⁓692-4876*) has an impressive view of the river. The rooms are reasonable but equipped with uninteresting modern furniture.

Manoir Victoria (*$115, $185 ½b; ≡, ≈, ⊘, ◌, ℜ, K; 44 Côte du Palais, G1R 4H8, ☎692-1030, 692-3822 or 1-800-463-6283*) is a 145-room hotel nestled on Côte du Palais. Decorated in true Victorian style, it succeeds in being both chic and very comfortable. The lobby, at the top of a long flight of stairs, is inviting and contains both a bar and a dining room. Manoir Victoria offers well-equipped suites and a number of cultural and sports packages.

Built in 1870, the **Clarendon** *($140 bkfst incl., $190 ½b; ≡, ℜ, ௯; 57 Rue Sainte-Anne, G1R 3X4, ☎1-800-463-5250, ☎692-4652, ≈692-4652)* is one of the oldest hotels in the city. The hotel has an unpretentious exterior while the elegant interior is decorated in Art Deco style. The entrance hall is very attractive. Over the years, the rooms in this hotel have been renovated many times and are spacious and comfortable. This a very good place to stay in Vieux-Québec (see also p 329).

The **Château Frontenac** *($189 bkfst incl., $249 ½b; ℜ, ≡, ௯, ®, ≈, ◔; 1 Rue des Carrières, G1R 4P5, ☎1-800-268-9420, ☎692-3861, ≈692-1751)* is by far the most prestigious hotel in Québec City (see p 326). Its elegant entrance hall is decorated with wood panelling and warm colours. The reception, unfortunately, is often somewhat cooler. The rooms are decorated with classic refinement and are very comfortable. A new wing has recently been completed and, besides guest rooms, houses an indoor pool.

Tour B: Vieux-Québec (Basse-Ville)

The pleasant **Hôtel Particulier Belley** *($45-$65; K; 249 Rue Saint-Paul, G1K 3W5, ☎692-1694, ≈692-1696)* stands opposite the market at the Vieux-Port. A hotel since 1877, this handsome building will leave you with fond memories for years to come. It has eight simply decorated, cozy rooms, some with exposed brick walls, others with wooden beams and skylights. The ground floor is home to a bar called Taverne Belley (see p 361), whose breakfasts and lunches, served in two lovely rooms, are very popular with locals. A number of extremely comfortable and attractively decorated lodgings, some with terraces, are also available in another house across the street. These may be rented by the night, by the week or by the month.

The **Priori** *($125 bkfst incl.; ®, ℜ; 15 Rue du Saul-au-Matelot, G1K 3Y7, ☎522-8108, ≈692-0883)* is located on a quiet street in Basse-Ville. The building is very old but has been renovated in a very modern style. The

decor successfully contrasts the old stone walls of the building with up-to-date furnishings. The appearance is striking and even the elevator is distinctive. The Priori is highly recommended.

Auberge Sainte-Antoine *($189 bkfst incl.; ®, ≡; 10 Rue Saint-Antoine, G1K 4C9, ☎692-2211, ≈ 692-1177)* is located near the Musée de la Civilisation. This lovely hotel is divided into two buildings. Guests enter through a tastefully renovated old stone building. The entrance hall is distinguished by exposed wooden beams, stone walls and a beautiful fireplace. The hotel serves breakfast. Each room is decorated according to a different theme and has its own unique charm.

Tour C: Grande Allée

A warm welcome awaits at **Les Chérubins** *($55-$60 bkfst incl.; sb; 1185 Avenue Murray, G1S 3B7, ☎684-8833)*, a B&B with three clean, bright and cozy guest rooms, just steps away from the Plains of Abraham. Guests also enjoy the use of two full bathrooms, a small living room containing documentation on the city's cultural and athletic activities, and a small yard strewn with flowers.

Manoir Lafayette *($89; ≡, ℜ; 661 Grande Allée Est, G1R 2K4, ☎522-2652, ≈ 522-4400)* is attractive and elegant. The hotel was renovated recently and some rooms are equipped with comfortable antique furniture. The Lafayette has an excellent location.

The **Chateau Grande Allée** *($99; 601 Grande Allée Est, G1R 2K4, ☎647-4433, ≈ 646-7553)* is a recent addition to the busy Grande Allée. The well-kept rooms are so large that they look under-furnished. Making up for this slight shortcoming are various features, including large bathrooms.

The **Hotel Château Laurier** *($99; ≡, ℜ; 695 Grande Allée Est, G1R 2K4, ☎522-8108, ≈524-8768)* is an old house with a handsome stone exterior. Unfortunately, the rooms are equipped with particularly uninteresting furniture and lack charm.

The **Radisson Gouverneurs Québec** *($109; ≈, ≡, ◔, ௯, ◬, ℜ; 690 Boulevard Rene-Lévesque Est, G1R 5A8, ☎647-1717 or 1-800-910-1111, ≈647-2146)* is located close to Vieux-Québec. This hotel has over 350 rooms, all nicely decorated. Regular rooms are furnished with slightly rustic but elegant pine furniture. The hotel's heated outdoor pool is open all year.

 Also just outside Vieux-Québec is the **Hôtel Loews Le Concorde** *($165; ᕻ, ≡, ≈, ⊙, △, ℛ; 1225 Place Montcalm, G1R 4W6, ☎647-2222, ⊶647-4710)*. It is part of the Loews hotel chain and has spacious, comfortable rooms with spectacular views of Québec City and the surrounding area. There is a revolving restaurant on top of the hotel.

Located just outside Vieux-Québec, the **Québec Hilton** *($170; ≈, ⊙, △, ℛ, ᕻ; 3 Place Québec, G1K 7M9, ☎647-2411, ⊶647-6488)* offers rooms with the kind of comfort associated with an international hotel chain. The lobby is connected to the Place Québec shopping mall.

Tour D: Saint-Jean-Baptiste

In the heart of Québec City's gay neighbourhood, the friendly **Guesthouse 727** *($59 sb, $79 pb, bkfst incl.; 727 Rue d'Aiguillon, ☎648-6766)* has a welcoming and relaxed atmosphere. Some of the rooms are furnished with antiques, and a few have VCRs.

 Adjoining the newly renovated theatre is the **Hôtel du Théâtre Capitole** *($135; ℛ, ≡, ⊚; 972 Rue Saint-Jean, G1R, ☎694-9930 ⊶647-2146)*. The hotel is located in the part of the building surrounding the theatre. While not luxurious, the room's are amusing, the decor resembling a stage set. At the entrance is the restaurant Il Teatro (see p 360).

Near the Airport (L'Ancienne-Lorette)

The area near the airport has no particularly interesting hotels, and most visitors only stay a single night in this region.

The **Château Repotel** *($70 bkfst incl.; ⊚, ≡, ᕻ; 6555 Boulevard Wilfred Hamel, G2E 5W3, ☎872-1111, ⊶872-5989)* is a pleasant enough place. Rooms here are not luxurious but they are comfortable and have large bathrooms.

The **Comfortel Québec** *($82 bkfst incl.; ⊚, ≡, ᕻ; 6500 Boulevard Wilfred Hamel, G2E 2J1, ☎877-4777, 877-0013)*, as the name suggests, is indeed comfortable. Rooms are

spacious and furnished with decent, modern furniture.

The **Comfort Inn L'Ancienne-Lorette** *($83; ≡, ᕻ; 1255 Autoroute Duplessis, G2G 2B4, ☎872-5900)* is a recent addition to the choice of airport hotels. The rooms are reasonably attractive.

✕ RESTAURANTS

Tour A: Vieux-Québec (Haute-Ville)

Little **Casse-Crêpe Breton** *($; 1136 Rue Saint-Jean)* draws big crowds. Though it has been expanded, patrons still have to line up for a taste of its delicious meal-in-one crêpes. Prepared right before your eyes, these are filled with your favourite ingredients by waitresses who manage to keep smiling in the midst of all the hubbub. High-backed, upholstered seats help lend the place a warm atmosphere.

 At **Chez Temporel** *($; 25 Rue Couillard)* all the food is prepared on the premises. Whether you opt for a butter croissant, a *croque-monsieur*, a salad or the special of the day, you can be sure that it will be fresh and tasty. To top it all off, the place serves some of the best espresso in town! The waiters and waitresses sometimes have more work than they can handle, but a touch of understanding on your part will be rewarded a hundred times over. Tucked away in a bend in little Rue Couillard, the two-story Temporel has been welcoming people of all ages and all stripes for over 20 years now. Open early in the morning to late at night.

The **Petit Coin Latin** *($; 8½ Rue Sainte-Ursule, ☎692-2022)* serves home-style cooking in an ambiance reminiscent of a Parisian café. The decor is dominated by parlour chairs and mirrors, creating a relaxed, convivial atmosphere. The menu includes *croûtons au fromage*, quiche and pâté. You can also snack on *raclette* (a kind of fondue), served at tables on small burners with potatoes and deli meats.

Delicious! During summer, a pretty outdoor seating area enclosed by stone walls is open out back; to get there from the street, use the carriage entrance.

Ulysses' Favourites

Québec City's finest tables:
Laurie Raphaël (p 358), Le Saint-Amour (p 357), La Grande Table (p 357), La Closerie (p 360) and Le Champlain (p 357)

For the romantic atmosphere:
Le Saint-Amour (p 357), Graffiti (p 360) and La Crémaillère (p 357).

For the terrace:
Il Teatro (p 360) and Le Saint-Amour (p 357)

For Québec cuisine:
Aux Anciens Canadiens (p 357) and Le Parlementaire (p 359)

For the views:
L'Astral (p 359), Café de la Terrasse (p 356) and Café-Resto du Musée (p 359)

For the decor:
Marie Clarisse (p 358), Le Falstaff (p 356) and La Playa (p 360)

The best cafés:
Chez Temporel (p 355), Café Krieghoff (p 359) and Le Hobbit (p 360)

The **Falstaff** *($-$$; closed Mon and Tue; 1200 Rue St-Jean, ☎694-0618)* serves authentic German cuisine in a relaxed, Bavarian atmosphere beneath the vaults of Maison Serge-Bruyère. The food does justice to the restaurant's reputation (see La Grande Table, p 357). Fireplace and valet parking.

Just a short walk from Porte Saint-Louis, the **Apsara** *($$; 71 Rue d'Auteuil, ☎694-0232)* offers south east Asian cuisine. Reasonably priced, full meals can be had both at midday and in the evening.

The **Frères de la Côte** *($$; 1190 Rue Saint-Jean, ☎692-5445)* serves delectable bistro fare, including pasta, grill, and thin-crust pizzas baked in a wood-burning oven and topped with delicious fresh ingredients. All-you-can-eat mussels and fries on certain evenings. The atmosphere is lively and laid-back, and the place is often packed, which is only fitting here on bustling Rue Saint-Jean. Guests can take in the action outside through the restaurant's big windows.

The **Portofino** *($$-$$$; 54 Rue Couillard, ☎692-8888)* was designed in the image of a typical Italian trattoria. A long bar, blue water glasses, mirrors on the wall and soccer banners on the ceiling help create a warm, lively atmosphere. Don't be surprised if the owner greets you with a kiss! To top it all off, there are the mouthwatering aromas of the food, also authentically Italian. During the tourist season, the place is always full. Valet parking.

Chez Livernois *($$-$$$; 1200 Rue Saint-Jean, ☎694-0618)* is a bistro located inside Maison Serge-Bruyère. It is named for photographer Jules Livernois, who set up his studio in this imposing 19th-century house in 1889. The excellent cuisine consists mainly of pasta and grill dishes, and the atmosphere is a bit more relaxed than at La Grande Table (see p 357).

Café de la Paix *($$$; 44 Rue Desjardins, ☎692-1430)* occupies a narrow space a few steps down from the sidewalk on little Rue Desjardins. It has been around for years and enjoys a solid reputation among Québec City residents. The menu features traditional French cuisine, such as frog's legs, beef Wellington, rabbit with mustard and grilled salmon.

Café de la Terrasse *($$$; 1 Rue des Carrières, ☎692-3861)*, in the Château Frontenac, has picture windows looking out onto Terrasse Dufferin. Attractive decor and delicious French cuisine.

The **Charles Baillargé** restaurant *($$$, 57 Rue Sainte-Anne, ☎692-2480)* is located on the main floor of the beautiful Hôtel Clarendon (see p 354). Discriminating diners come here for excellent, classic French cuisine served in comfortable surroundings.

Le Continental *($$$; closed Sun; 26 Rue Saint-Louis, ☎694-9995)*, just steps away from the Château Frontenac, is one of the oldest restaurants in Québec City. The continental cuisine includes seafood, lamb, duck, etc. Service *au guéridon* (cart service) in a large, comfortable dining room.

The **Élysée-Mandarin** *($$$; 65 Rue d'Auteuil, ☎692-0909)*, which also boasts prime locations in Montréal and Paris, serves excellent Szechuan, Cantonese and Mandarin cuisine in a decor featuring a small indoor garden and Chinese sculptures and vases. The food is always succulent and the service, extremely courteous. If you are in a group, try the tasting menu: it would be a shame not to sample as many of the dishes as possible!

Located halfway up Côte de la Montagne, **Le Vendôme** *($$$; 36 Côte de la Montagne, ☎692-0557)* is one of the oldest restaurants in Québec City. It serves classic French dishes like Chateaubriand, *coq au vin* and duck *à l'orange* in an intimate decor.

Located in one of the oldest houses in Québec City, the restaurant **Aux Anciens Canadiens** *($$$-$$$$, 34 Rue Saint-Louis, ☎692-1627)* serves up-scale versions of traditional Québec specialities. Dishes include ham with maple syrup, pork and beans and blueberry pie (see also Maison Jacquet, p 328).

Café d'Europe *($$$-$$$$; 27 Rue Sainte-Angèle, ☎692-3835)* has a sober, slightly outdated decor. There is limited space, and when the place is busy, the noise level gets pretty high. The service is courteous, with a personal touch. Sophisticated French and Italian cuisine presented in a traditional manner and served in generous portions. The flambée dishes are masterfully served, and the smooth, flavourful sauces make for an unforgettable culinary experience.

The **Crémaillère** *($$$-$$$$, 21 Rue Saint-Stanislas, corner of Rue St-Jean, ☎692-2216)* is a friendly place serving various types of European cuisines. A certain attention to detail makes dining here very enjoyable. The

restaurant's comfortable decor adds to its charm.

Guido Le Gourmet *($$$-$$$$; 73 Rue Sainte-Anne, ☎692-3856)* will transport you to the world of fine dining. The menu, made up of French and Italian cuisine, includes quail, veal, salmon and other delicacies from both land and sea. Chic decor. The large, lovely plates on the table are a good indication of the pleasure that awaits. Brunch on weekends.

Le Saint-Amour *($$$-$$$$; 48 Rue Sainte-Ursule, ☎694-0667)* has been one of the best restaurants in Québec for several years now. Chef and co-owner Jean-Luc Boulay creates succulent, innovative cuisine that is a feast for both the eyes and the palate. The desserts concocted in the *chocolaterie*, on the second floor, are positively divine. A truly gastronomic experience! To top it all off, the place is beautiful, comfortable and has a warm atmosphere. The solarium, open year-round and decorated with all sorts of flowers and other plants, brightens up the decor. On fine summer days, its roof is removed, transforming it into a sun-drenched patio. Valet parking.

Le Champlain *($$$$; 1 Rue des Carrières, ☎692-3861)* is the Château Frontenac's restaurant. Needless to say, its decor is extremely luxurious, in keeping with the opulence of the rest of the hotel. The outstanding French cuisine also does justice to the Château's reputation. Chef Jean Soular, whose recipes have been published, endeavours to add an original touch to these classic dishes. Impeccable service provided by waiters in uniform.

La Grande Table *($$$$; 1200 Rue Saint-Jean, ☎694-0618)*, in Maison Serge-Bruyère, has a solid reputation that extends far beyond the walls of the old city. Located on the top floor of a historic house between Couillard and Garneau Streets, it serves gourmet French cuisine that delights both the eye and the palate. The attractive decor includes paintings by Québec artists. Valet parking.

Tour B: Vieux-Québec (Basse-Ville)

Buffet de l'Antiquaire *($; 95 Rue Saint-Paul, ☎692-2661)* is a pleasant snack bar that serves home-style cooking. As indicated by its name, it is located in the heart of the antique-dealers' quarter and is a good place to take a little break while treasure-hunting. It is also one of the first restaurants to open in the morning (6am).

Café Loft *($; 49 Rue Dalhousie, ☎692-4864)* looks quite like a small loft, with its garage doors that are left open in the summertime. Located a stone's throw away from the Musée de la Civilisation, it is a good place for a post-museum stop. You can give your feet a rest and enjoy a cup of coffee and a snack while watching the action at the Vieux-Port.

The **Cochon Dingue** *($-$$; 46 Boulevard Champlain, ☎692-2013)* is a charming café-bistro located between Boulevard Champlain and Rue du Petit-Champlain. Mirrors and a checkerboard floor make for a fun, attractive decor. The menu features bistro fare, such as *steak-frites* and *moules-frites* combos (steak and fries or mussels and fries). The desserts will send you into raptures. The Cochon Dingue has two other locations, one on the Grande Allée Tour *(46 Boulevard René-Lévesque Ouest, ☎523-2013)* and another in Sillery, outside Québec City *(1326 Avenue Maguire, ☎684-2013)*.

Bistrot Sous le Fort *($$; 48 Rue Sous le Fort, ☎694-0852)* has a somewhat stark decor and is frequented largely by tourists. The restaurant serves delicious, reasonably priced Québécois cuisine.

Café du Monde *($$-$$$; 57 Rue Dalhousie, ☎692-4455)* is a large Parisian-style brasserie serving dishes one would expect from such a place, including steak tartar and *magret de canard* (duck filet). There is a singles bar at the entrance. The waiters, dressed in long aprons, are attentive.

Môss *($$-$$$; 255 Rue Saint-Paul, ☎692-0265)* is a Belgian bistro. Its decor is somewhat cold, with black tables, brick walls, a stainless-steel counter and halogen lights, but its *moules-frites* combo, grill dishes and desserts made with Belgian chocolate are delicious.

Poisson d'Avril *($$-$$$; 115 Rue Saint-André, ☎692-1010)* has moved to the Vieux-Port. Its new home is an old house whose stone walls and wooden beams lend it a great deal of charm. The decor is enhanced by clever lighting and also by the shell-patterned fabric on the

chairs. The menu includes well-prepared pasta, grill and seafood dishes. Try the mussels.

There are two restaurants in the magnificent Gare du Palais. The **Aviatic Club** *($$-$$$; 450 de la Gare-du-Palais, ☎522-3555)* takes you back in time thanks to its mid-19th-century English decor featuring rattan armchairs, burgundy curtains, palm trees and a cosmopolitan menu. **Le Pavillon** *($$-$$$; 450 de la Gare-du-Palais, ☎522-0133)*, for its part, has a modern decor with sky-high ceilings and serves good Italian cuisine presented with an innovative flair. The service and clientele at both places are a bit on the pretentious side, but the lively atmosphere is pleasant nonetheless.

Two good restaurants are perched on picturesque Escalier Casse-Cou, which leads to Rue du Petit-Champlain. On the top floor, two-story **Chez Rabelais** *($$$; closed for lunch; 2 Rue du Petit-Champlain, ☎694-9460)* serves French cuisine, with an emphasis on seafood. A little lower down is **Marie Clarisse** *($$$; 12 Rue du Petit-Champlain, ☎692-0857)*, where everything, save the stone walls, is as blue as the sea – and with good reason: seafood and fish are the house specialties. These divinely prepared dishes are served to guests in a lovely dining room that has been very ornately decorated. When the cold weather sets in, a crackling fire warms the air.

L'Échaudé *($$$-$$$$; 73 Rue Sault-au-Matelot, ☎692-1299)* is an appealing restaurant with an Art Deco decor featuring a checkerboard floor and a mirrored wall. Relaxed atmosphere. Sophisticated cuisine prepared daily with fresh ingredients from the market.

The chef and co-owner of **Laurie Raphäel** *($$$-$$$$; 17 Rue Dalhousie, ☎692-4555)*, Daniel Vézina, was named the best chef in Québec in 1997. The same year, a book of his tempting recipes was published. When creating his mouthwatering dishes, Vézina draws inspiration from culinary traditions from all over the world, preparing sweetbreads, scallops, ostrich, etc., in innovative ways. It goes without saying, therefore, that the food at Laurie Raphaël is delicious! In May 1996 the restaurant moved into newer, more spacious quarters with a semi-circular exterior glass wall. The chic decor includes creamy white curtains, sand- and earth-tones and a few decorative, wrought-iron objects.

Tour C: Grande Allée

Craving a bagel? You'll find all different kinds at **Bügel** *($; 164 Rue Crémazie Ouest, ☎523-7666)*, a bagel bakery on pretty little Rue Crémazie. In a warm atmosphere enhanced by the aroma of a wood fire, you can snack on bagels with salami, cream cheese or veggie pâté and stock up on goodies to take back home.

Named after the Dutch-born artist whose former home stands at the end of Avenue Cartier (see p 346), **Café Krieghoff** *($; 1809 Avenue Cartier, ☎521-3711)* occupies an old house on the same street. It serves tasty light fare (quiche, salads, etc.) and also has a good daily menu. The casual, convivial atmosphere is reminiscent of a Northern European café. During summer, its two outdoor seating areas are often packed.

The electric, futuristic decor of the **Cosmos Café** *($-$$; 575 Grande-Allée Est, ☎692-1316)* promises a good time in a hip atmosphere. Burgers, sandwiches and salads with a cosmopolitan flavour.

Visitors who want to rub shoulders with members of Québec's National Assembly eat breakfast at Le **Parlementaire** *($-$$; closed Sat and Sun; at the corner of Dufferin and Grande Allée, ☎643-6640)*. The menu features European and Québécois dishes. The restaurant is often packed, particularly at lunch, but the food is good. Open only for breakfast and lunch.

A pretty yellow and red restaurant called the **Jaune Tomate** *($$; 120 Boulevard René-Lévesque Ouest, ☎523-8777)* just opened on Boulevard René-Lévesque, right near Avenue Cartier. It serves good Italian cuisine in a country-style decor. The eggplant Parmesan, to name but one item on the menu, is excellent.

Inside the Musée du Québec, you'll find the pleasant **Café-Restaurant du Musée** *($$-$$$; 1 Avenue Wolfe-Montcalm, ☎644-6780)*. Run by a nearby hotel-management school, the restaurant makes it a top priority to offer well-prepared food and outstanding service. Guests can gaze out at the Plains of Abraham and at the river through big picture windows; during summer, the same view can be enjoyed on the patio.

Le Momento *($$-$$$; 1144 Av. Cartier, ☎647-1313)* is decorated in modern fashion with warm colours and adorned with a fresco taken from a Boticelli painting. As you may have guessed, they serve refined, original Italian cuisine that is sure to offer some pleasant surprises. Basil, oregano, dried tomatoes, capers, olives and the rest: the sauces are rich, but not excessively, and savoury. The marinated salmon is prepared just perfectly to melt in your mouth.

Mon Manège à Toi *($$-$$$; 102 Boulevard Réne Lévesque Ouest, corner Cartier, ☎649-0478)* is a Belgian restaurant with exquisite food inspired by Belgian and French cuisine. Service is efficient and friendly and the atmosphere is comfortable. The decor is an elegant mix of bistro and bourgeois elements. This spot is well-worth a visit.

At **Paris Brest** *($$-$$$;, 590 Grande Allée Est, corner De La Cherotière, ☎529-2243)*, French cuisine is the specialty of the house. Prepared with care, the food here will satisfy the most demanding gourmets. In summer, the restaurant opens its small terrace which looks onto Grande Allée.

At the **Garam Massala** *($$$; 1114 Avenue Cartier, ☎522-4979)*, you can savour curry, tandoori and other spicy dishes from the Indian repertoire. Though the restaurant has the disadvantage of being located in a basement, its decor is nonetheless attractive. Pleasant Indian music adds to the ambiance.

Le Louis-Hébert *($$$; 668 Grande Allée Est, ☎525-7812)*, a chic restaurant with a plush decor, serves French cuisine and delectable seafood. There is a solarium be decked with greenery at the back. Courteous, attentive service.

Le Métropolitain *($$$; closed for lunch Sat and Sun; 1188 Avenue Cartier, ☎649-1096)* is the place to go for sushi in Québec City. These delicious Japanese morsels make for a real feast. Other oriental specialties, including fish and seafood dishes, are available here as well. The restaurant used to be located in the basement of another building and had a big sign at the entrance similar to those adorning certain metro stops in Paris. Its new, two-story quarters are brighter.

Located at the top of one of the city's largest hotels, the revolving **L'Astral** restaurant *($$$-*

$$$; Hotel Loews Le Concorde, 1225 Place Montcalm, ☎647-2222) serves excellent French food and provides a stunning view of the river, the Plains of Abraham, the Laurentian mountains and the city. It takes about one hour for the restaurant to revolve completely. This is a particularly good place to go for Sunday brunch.

La Closerie *($$$-$$$$; 966 Boulevard René-Lévesque Ouest, ☎687-9975)* serves fine French cuisine. The chef, who has a well-established reputation, creates meals from fresh, prime quality ingredients. The exterior of the townhouse, located at a distance from tourist attractions, is no indication of what's inside – a gorgeous, intimate decor that makes for some pleasurable moments.

The old-fashioned decor of **Graffiti** *($$$-$$$$; 1191 Rue Cartier, ☎529-4949)*, which is distinguished by exposed beams and brick walls, creates a warm ambience. Graffiti serves excellent French cuisine.

Tour D: Saint-Jean-Baptiste

Located in a basement with a retro decor, **Chez Victor** *($; 145 Rue Saint-Jean, ☎529-7702)* serves up salads and burgers – and not just any old burgers! The menu offers several different kinds (including a delicious veggie burger), all big, juicy and served with fresh toppings. The homemade fries are sublime! Cordial service.

Thang Long *($; 869 Côte d'Abraham, ☎524-0572)*, perched on Côte d'Abraham, is tiny, but its menu will transport you to Vietnam, Thailand, China and even Japan! The decor of this neighbourhood restaurant is simple and unpretentious; the cuisine, truly up to the mark, and the service, very attentive. Try one of the meal-size soups – comfort food at bargain prices!

🦞 **Le Hobbit** *($-$$; 700 Rue Saint-Jean, ☎647-2677)* has occupied an old house in the Saint-Jean-Baptiste neighbourhood for years, and its stone walls, checkerboard floor and big windows that look out onto bustling Rue Saint-Jean have lost none of their appeal. There are two sections: the first is a café-style room where you can linger over an espresso and have a light meal; the second, a dining room whose delicious menu changes daily and is

never disappointing. Works by local artists are displayed here regularly.

For exotic cuisine whose succulent flavours live up to its enticing aromas, try **Les Épices du Széchouan** *($$; 215 Rue Saint-Jean, ☎648-6440)*, which occupies an old house in the Saint-Jean-Baptiste quarter. Its pretty decor is enhanced by a thousand and one Chinese bibelots. One table, with a banquette, is nestled beneath a corbelled wall. The house is set back a bit from the street, so be careful not to miss it!

The layout of modern-looking **Piazzetta** *($$; 707 Rue Saint-Jean, ☎529-7489; 1191 Rue Cartier, ☎649-8896)* does not allow for intimate dining. The restaurant is generally crowded but lively. An infinite variety of European-style pizzas is served. There are many franchises of this restaurant all over Québec, this one is the original and is in a house on Rue Saint-Jean.

La Playa *($$-$$$; 780 Rue Saint-Jean, ☎522-3989)*, a small restaurant with a beautiful, cozy decor, offers Californian cuisine and dishes from other sunny climes. Top billing on the menu goes to pasta served with flavourful sauces including one made with tandoori chicken. The restaurant also has a table d'hôte featuring delicious meat and fish dishes. During summer, guests can dine on a charming little patio out back.

Il Teatro *($$$; 972 Rue Saint-Jean, ☎694-9996)*, inside the magnificent Théâtre Capitole, serves excellent Italian cuisine in a lovely dining room with a long bar at its far end and big, sparkling windows all around. The courteous service is on a par with the delicious food. During summer, guests can dine in a small outdoor seating area sheltered from the hustle and bustle of Place d'Youville.

  ENTERTAINMENT

Bars and Nightclubs

There is no cover charge at most bars and nightclubs in Québec City, except when they are hosting a special event or a show. During winter, most places require customers to check their coats, which costs a dollar or two.

Tour A: Vieux-Québec (Haute-Ville)

All different kinds of musicians perform at **Le d'Auteuil** *(25 Rue d'Auteuil)*, which occupies an old chapel most of whose architecture remains intact.

Le Chanteuteuil *(1001 Rue Saint-Jean)*, at the foot of the hill on Rue d'Auteuil, is a pleasant bistro. People spend hours here chatting away, seated at bench-tables around bottles of wine or beers.

The oldest hotel in the city houses the **Emprise** *(Hôtel Clarendon, 57 Rue Sainte-Anne; see p 354)*. This elegant bar is recommended to jazz fans. There is no cover charge.

Hidden away beneath Le d'Auteuil, **La Fourmi Atomik** *(33 Rue d'Auteuil)* is *the* underground bar in Québec City. There is a different musical theme every night, from black beat, punk rock, alternative and 80s techno to the latest releases. During summer, the patio is always packed.

During summer, the sounds of people having a good time emanate from the open windows of **Petit Paris** *(48 Côte de la Fabrique)*, where *chansonniers* perform for an appreciative crowd.

The **Saint-Alexandre** *(1087 Rue Saint-Jean)* is a typical English pub serves 175 types of beer, 19 of which are on tap. The decor is appealing and the ambiance pleasant.

Tucked away in the basement of a building on Rue Saint-Angèle, the **Sainte-Angèle** *(26 Rue Sainte-Angèle)* looks like an English pub. It's decor is a bit worn, but the place is still comfortable. The space is cramped, but that doesn't stop local residents of all different ages from packing in here. Regulars sit at the bar and chat with the bartender. Good selection of reasonably priced scotches and cocktails.

Tour B: Vieux-Québec (Basse-Ville)

L'Innox *(37 Rue Saint-André)* is a big place at the Vieux-Port that brews good beer and serves other drinks. Its lager, *blanche* (white) and *rousse* (red) beers are all as delicious as can be. There is also a small *économusée* on the premises.

Pape George *(8 Rue Cul-de-Sac)* is a pleasant wine bar. Beneath the vaults of an old house in Petit Champlain, guests can sample a wide variety of wines while nibbling on snacks like cheese and *charcuteries*. The atmosphere is warm, especially when there's a *chansonnier* to heat things up.

Taverne Belley *(249 Rue Saint-Paul)*, in front of the Marché du Vieux-Port, has a few typical tavern features, such as a pool table and small, round, metal tables. The decor of its two rooms is both warm and fun, with colourful paintings hanging across exposed brick walls. A tiny fireplace warms the air nicely during winter.

Le Troubadour *(29 Rue Saint-Paul)*, near Place Royale, is nestled beneath a vaulted ceiling. The place is made entirely of stone, combined with the long white candles stuck in bottles on the wooden tables, makes you feel as if you've stepped back in time to the Middle Ages. During winter, a crackling fire helps banish the cold.

Tour C : Grande Allée

Chez Dagobert *(600 Grande Allée Est)* is an immense and popular disco located in an old stone house. There is always a crowd and there is no cover-charge.

Chez Maurice *(575 Grande Allée Est)*, which occupies an old house on Grande Allée, is a big, chic, trendy discotheque. The place to go to see and be seen and dance to the latest hits. Chez Maurice hosts theme nights as well, including a very popular disco night. Inside, you'll also find a cigar room called **Chez Charlotte**, which truly merits the label *bar digestif* (cocktail lounge)!

Little **Jules et Jim** *(1060 Avenue Cartier)* has graced Avenue Cartier for several years now. It has a smooth atmosphere, with banquettes and low tables reminiscent of Paris in the 1920s.

Le Merlin *(1175 Avenue Cartier)*, on lively Avenue Cartier, is frequented by a thirtysomething crowd who come here to dance. In the basement, **Le Turf**, an English pub, serves imported beer to fashionable regulars. It is also possible to eat at Le Merlin.

Tour D: Saint-Jean-Baptiste

The **Fou Bar** *(519 Rue Saint-Jean)* is an appealing place with a regular clientele who come here to drink, chat with friends or check out the current works of art on display.

Gay and Lesbian Clubs

L'Amour Sorcier *(789 Côte Sainte-Geneviève)* is a small bar in the Saint-Jean-Baptiste quarter. The atmosphere really heats up here sometimes. During summer, it has a pretty patio.

The gay disco **Ballon Rouge** *(811 Rue Saint-Jean)* has an exclusively male clientele. Its several rooms each have their own particular ambience.

Drague *(804 Rue St-Augustin)* is a large, loud, smoky tavern for men only.

Theatres

The Québec City edition of French-language magazine *Voir* is distributed free of charge and provides information on the principal events of the city.

Music

The **Orchestre Symphonique de Québec**, Canada's oldest symphony orchestra, performs regularly at the Grand Théâtre de Québec *(269 Boulevard René-Lévesque Ouest, ☎643-8131)*, where you can also catch the **Opéra de Québec**.

Theatres

Grand Théâtre de Québec: 269 Boulevard René Lévesque Est, ☎643-8131. This theatre has two halls.

Le Palais Montcalm: 995 Place d'Youville, ☎691-2399, ticket service ☎670-9011.

Théâtre de la Bordée: 1143 Rue Saint-Jean, ☎694-9721, ticket service ☎694-9631.

Théâtre Capitole: 972 Rue Saint-Jean, ☎694-4444.

Le Périscope, 2 Rue Crémazie Est, ☎529-2183.

Théâtre de la Bordée, 1143 Rue Saint-Jean, ☎694-9631.

Théâtre du Trident, at the Grand Théâtre de Québec, 269 Boulevard René-Lévesque Ouest, ☎643-8131.

Movie Theatres

Cinéma de Paris: Place d'Youville, ☎694-0891

Les Galeries: 5401 Boulevard des Galeries, ☎628-2455

Place Charest: 500 Rue Dupont, ☎529-9745

Spectator Sports

The now defunct NHL team Les Nordiques used to play on the indoor skating rink surrounded by stepped rows of seats of the **Colisée** *(250 Boulevard Wilfrid-Hamel, Parc de l'Exposition, ☎691-7211)* (unfortunately, the team was sold and moved to Denver, Colorado in 1995). The building, erected in 1950, was designed by Robert Blatter. The Rafales, members of the International Hockey League, play here. Shows are presented occasionally as well.

Right next door is the **Hippodrome du Québec** *(ExpoCité, 250 Boulevard Wilfrid-Hamel, ☎524-5283)* where fans can watch horse races.

Festivals and Cultural Events

Carnaval de Québec *(☎626-3716)*, Québec City's winter carnival, takes place annually during the first two weeks of February. It is an opportunity for visitors and residents of Québec City to celebrate the beauty of winter. It is also a good way to add a little life to a cold winter that often seem interminable. Various activities are organized. Some of the most popular include night-time parades, canoe races over the partially frozen St. Lawrence River and the international ice and snow sculpture contests on the Plains of Abraham and in front of the carved ice castle at Place du Parlement. This can be a bitterly cold period of the year, so dressing very warmly is essential.

The **Festival d'Été de Québec** *(mid-Jul; ☎692-4540)* is generally held for 10 days in early July, when music, songs, dancing and other kinds of entertainment from all over the world liven up Québec City. The festival has everything it takes to be the city's most important cultural event. The outdoor shows are particularly popular.

Place du Parlement houses the **Plein Art** *(late Jul; every day 10am to 11pm;* ☎*694-0260)* exhibit from the end of July to the start of August. All kinds of arts and crafts are displayed and sold.

People from the Québec City region have been enjoying themselves at **Expo-Québec** *(Parc d'ExpoCité,* ☎*691-7110)* every August for 50 years now. This huge fair, complete with an amuseument park, is held in front of the coliseum for about 10 days at the end of the month.

During Carnaval (see above), the city hosts a number of sporting events, including the **Tournoi International de Hockey Pee-wee de Québec** *(*☎*524-3311).*

 SHOPPING

Bookstores

La Maison Anglaise:
Place de la Cité, Sainte-Foy,
☎654-9523.
The best selection of English books around Québec City.

Librairie Ulysse:
4 Boulevard René-Lévesque Est,
☎529-5349; travel bookshop

CDs and Cassettes

Sillons Le Disquaire: 1149 Avenue Cartier, ☎524-8352.

Archambault: 1095 Rue Saint-Jean, Vieux-Québec, ☎694-2088

Craft Shops and Artisans' Studios

Atelier La Pomme: 47 Rue Sous-le-Fort, ☎692-2875. Leather goods.

Boutique Sachem: 17 Rue Desjardins, ☎692-3056. Native crafts.

Galerie-Boutique Métiers d'Art: 29 Rue Notre-Dame, Place Royale, ☎694-0267. Québec-made crafts.

Galerie d'Art Indien Cinq Nations: 25½ Rue du Petit-Champlain, ☎692-3329. Native crafts.

Les Trois Colombes: 46 Rue Saint-Louis, ☎694-1114. Handcrafted items and quality clothing.

L'Oiseau du Paradis: 80 Rue du Petit-Champlain, ☎692-2679. Paper and paper objects.

Pot-en-Ciel: 27 Rue du Petit-Champlain, ☎692-1743. Ceramics.

Verrerie d'Art Réjean Burns: 156 Rue St-Paul, ☎694-0013. Stained glass, lamps.

Verrerie La Mailloche: Escalier Casse-cou, ☎694-0445. Shop-made glass objects.

Ladieswear

La Cache: 1150 Rue Saint-Jean, Vieux-Québec, ☎692-0398.

Les Vêteries: 33½ Rue du Petit-Champlain, ☎694-1215.

Simons: 20 Côte de la Fabrique, ☎692-3630.

Menswear

François Côté Collection: 35 Rue Buade, ☎692-6016.

Louis Laflamme: 1192 Rue Saint-Jean, ☎692-3774.

Jewellery and Decorative Arts

Lazuli: 774 Rue Saint-Jean, ☎525-6528.

Origines: 54 Côte de la Fabrique, Vieux-Québec, ☎694-9257.

Pierres Vives: 23½ Rue du Petit-Champlain, ☎692-5566.

Louis Perrier Joaillier: 48 Rue du Petit-Champlain, ☎692-4633.

Outdoor Clothing and Equipment

L'Aventurier: 710 Rue Bouvier, ☎624-9088. Clothing, accessories, kayaks.

Azimut: 1194 Avenue Cartier, ☎648-9500. Clothing and accessories.

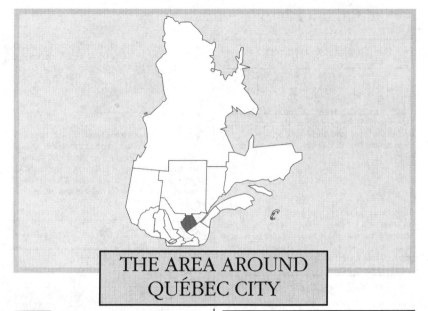

THE AREA AROUND QUÉBEC CITY

nder the French Regime, Québec City was the main urban centre of New France and was the seat of the colonial administration. To supply produce to the city and its institutions, farms were introduced to the area in the middle of the 17th century. The farming region on the periphery of the city was the first populated rural zone in the St-Lawrence Valley. Traces of the first seigneuries granted to settlers in New France are still visible in this historically rich rural area. The farmhouses are the oldest of New France and the descendants of their first residents are now scattered across the American continent.

 FINDING YOUR WAY AROUND

Four tours are suggested for the area surrounding Québec City: **Tour A: The Côte de Beaupré ★★**, **Tour B: Île d'Orléans ★★**, **Tour C: The Chemin du Roy ★★** and **Tour D: The Rivière Jacques-Cartier ★**. With the exception of the Jacques-Cartier tour, which is longer and extends further into the wilderness, these excursions can all be done as day trips from Québec City.

Tour A: The Côte de Beaupré

By Car

From Québec City, take the Autoroute Dufferin-Montmorency (Hwy 440) towards Beauport (Exit 24), then take Rue d'Estimauville. Turn right on Chemin Royal (Route 360), which becomes Avenue Royale, and which will lead you throughout the tour.

By Bus

Sainte-Anne-de-Beaupré *(9687 boul. Ste-Anne, Irving, ☎827-5169)* is accessible by bus *(320 Rue Abrahamm-Martin, ☎525-3000)*.

If you do not have a car at your disposal, the only way to reach the Parc du Mont-Sainte-Anne, the Grand Canyon des Chutes Sainte-Anne and the Cap-Tourmente National Wildlife Area is by bus from Québec City to Sainte-Anne-de-Beaupré, and then taxi for the remaining 6 kilometres in each case.

Public Transportation

Bus number 53 leaves from Place Jacques-Cartier *($ 1.85, Rue du Roi, at the corner of Rue de la Couronne)* and drops visitors near the Chute Montmorency.

Tour B: Île d'Orléans

By Car

From Québec, take Autoroute Dufferin-Montmorency (Hwy 440) to the Pont de l'Île. Cross the river and turn right on Route 368, also called Chemin Royal, which circles the island.

By Bus

There is no public transportation or bus service on or to Île d'Orléans. Some private companies organize tours of the island; in order to explore the island on your own and at your own pace you will need a car or bicycle.

Tour C: The Chemin du Roy

By Car

From Québec City, head west on Grande-Allée, which eventually becomes Chemin Saint-Louis from Bagatelle to Sillery. After following Chemin St-Louis to Cap-Rouge, take Route 138, which you will follow for the rest of the tour. It is also possible to follow this tour in the opposite direction, in other words, starting from Montréal (Exit 236 off Highway 40), or to add a visit to the village of La Pérade included in the Mauricie tour (see p 307) in the Mauricie–Bois-Francs region.

Bus Station

Sainte-Foy: 925 De Rochebelle, ☎650-0087.

By Ferry

Sainte-Foy: 3255 Chemin de la Gare (corner Chemin St-Louis), ☎658-8792.

Tour D: The Rivière Jacques-Cartier

By Car

From Québec City, take Côte d'Abraham, turn right on Rue de la Couronne, then follow Autoroute Laurentienne (Hwy 73) to Exit 150.

Turn right on 80e Rue Ouest, which leads to the heart of the Trait-Carré in Charlesbourg. Highway 175 leads to Parc de la Jacques Cartier.

By Bus

To reach Wendake from Québec City, take bus #801, the métrobus, whose stops are clearly indicated (for example, at Place d'Youville). From the Charlesbourg terminus, take bus #72 to Wendake. The historic village of Onhoüa Chetek8e is north of the reserve and accessible by taxi.

 PRACTICAL INFORMATION

Area code: 418

Tourist Information Offices

Regional Office

Centre d'Information de l'Office du Tourisme et des Congrès de la Communauté Urbaine de Québec 3300 Avenue des Hôtels, Québec, G1W 5A8, ☎651-2882, ⌐651-7135, www.quebec_region.cuq.qc.ca

Tour A: Côté de Beaupré

Sainte-Anne-de-Beaupré: 9310 Boulevard Ste-Anne, ☎827-5281.

Tour B: L'île d'Orléans

Île d'Orléans: 490 Côte du Pont, Saint-Pierre, ☎ 828-9411

Tour C: Chemin du Roy

Deschambault: 12 Rue des Pins, ☎285-4616.

Tour D: Jacques-Cartier

Charlesbourg: 7960 Boulevard Henri-Bourassa, ☎624-7720.

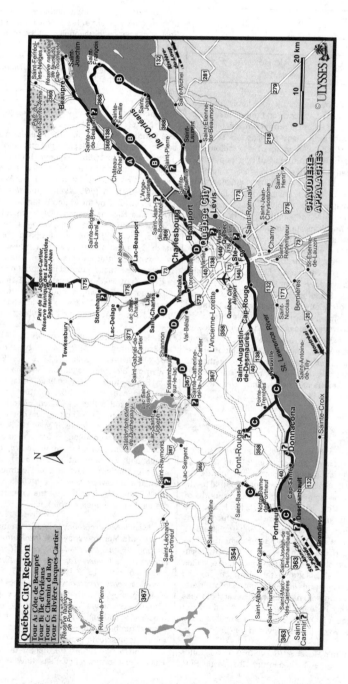

Québec City Region

Tour A: Côte de Beaupré
Tour B: Île d'Orléans
Tour C: Le Chemin du Roy
Tour D: Rivière Jacques-Cartier

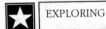

EXPLORING

Tour A: The Côte de Beaupré ★★
(one day)

This long, narrow strip of land, nestled between the St-Lawrence and the undeveloped wilderness of the Laurentian massif, is the ancestral home of many families whose roots go back to the beginning of the colony. It illustrates how the spread of the population was limited to the riverside in many regions of Québec, and recalls the fragility of development in the era of New France. From Beauport to Saint-Joachim, the colony's first road, the Chemin du Roy, or king's road, built under orders from Monseigneur de Laval during the 17th century, follows the Beaupré shore. A typical style characterized by a raised main floor covered in stucco, long balconies with intricately carved wood balusters and lace-curtained windows is repeated in houses along this road. Since about 1960, however, the suburbs of Québec City have gradually taken over the shore, marring the simple beauty of the area. Nevertheless, the Chemin du Roy is still an extremely pleasant route; whether rounding a cape, making one last jaunt in the Laurentians, or exploring the plains of the St. Lawrence, this route offers magnificent views of the mountains, fields, the river and Île d'Orléans.

Beauport ★ (pop. 72,259)

Three types of urban development have shaped Beauport over the course of its history. Originally an agricultural settlement, in the 19th century it became an important industrial town, finally evolving into one of the main suburbs of Québec City in the 1960s. In 1634, the Beauport seigneury, from which the present city grew, was granted to Robert Giffard, a doctor and surgeon from the Perche region of France. In the next few years, he enthusiastically set about building a manor house, a mill, and a small village, establishing one of the largest seigneuries in New France. Unfortunately, wars and fires have claimed several of these buildings, notably the huge fortified manor house built in 1642, containing a chapel and a prison, which burned down in 1879.

The **Chemin Royal ★** *(Route 360)* corresponds to the original 17th century Chemin du Roy, and follows both the upper and lower sections of the Côte de Beaupré. It traverses the former Beauport seigneury diagonally, which explains the angled placement of the buildings along the road. Many of these homes are ancestral houses, such as the **Maison Marcoux** constructed in the 18th century *(588 Avenue Royale).*

Turn right on Rue du Couvent to find parking.

The **Bourg du Fargy ★** district of Beauport was set up as a fortified village in the middle of the 17th century. In 1669, Seigneur Giffard drew up an ambitious plan for the town which even included a market square. The **Maison Bellanger-Girardin** *(600 Avenue Royale)*, constructed in 1727 by the Marcoux family on land granted to Nicolas Bellanger of Normandy, is one of the last remaining vestiges of the original town. The house, designed for the harsh Canadian climate, has just a few small windows and thick doors. Since 1984, the building has housed a tourist information office, and the Centre d'Art et d'Histoire de Beauport. A group of Edwardian houses on Rue du Couvent (circa 1910) offers an interesting contrast to the French Regime era style.

The large white house known as **Manoir Montmorency** *(2490 Avenue Royale, ☎663-3330)* was built in 1780 for British governor, Sir John Haldimand. At the end of the 18th century, the house became famous as the residence of the Duke of Kent, son of George III and father of Queen Victoria. The manor, which once housed a hotel, was severely damages by fire in May 1993. It has been restored according to the original plans and now hosts an information centre, a few shops and a restaurant (see p 387), which offers exceptional view of the Montmorency Falls, the St-Lawrence and Île d'Orléans. The small Sainte-Marie chapel on the property and the gardens are open to the public.

The Manoir Montmorency is nestled in the **Parc de la Chute Montmorency ★★** *(free admission, parking $6, cablecar $4 one-way $6 return; accessible all year; for opening hours and parking ☎663-2877, ↻663-1666, www.chutemontmorency.qc.ca).* The Rivière Montmorency, which has its source in the Laurentians, flows along peacefully until it reaches a sudden 83-metre drop, at which point it tumbles into a void, creating one of the most impressive natural phenomena in Québec. One and a half times the height of Niagara Falls, the Montmorency Falls flow at a rate which can reach 125,000 litres-per-second during the spring thaw. Samuel de Champlain, the founder of Québec City, was impressed by the falls and named them after the viceroy of New France, Charles, Duc de Montmorency. During the 19th century, the falls became a fashionable leisure area for the well-to-do of the region who would arrive in horse-drawn carriages or sleighs.

To take in this magnificent spectacle, a park has been set up, and a tour of the falls is possible. From the manor follow the pretty cliff walk, location of the Baronne lookout. You'll soon reach two bridges, the Pont Au-dessus de la Chute and the Pont Au-dessus de la Faille, which bass the falls and the fault respectively, with spectacular results. Once in the park you'll find picnic tables and a playground. The bottom of the falls are reached by the 487-step panoramic staircase or the trail. The cable-car provides a relaxing and picturesque means of regaining the top. In winter, steam freezes into a cone of ice, called a sugar-loaf, making a good ice-wall that anyone feeling adventurous can climb.

The lower part of the park is also accessible by car, though a complicated detour is required: continue along Avenue Royale, turn right on Côte de l'Église, then right again on Highway 40. The parking lot is on the right. To get back to Avenue Royale, take Boulevard Sainte-Anne west, Côte Saint-Grégoire and finally Boulevard des Chutes to the right.

Take Chemin Royal heading east.

The **Maison Laurent-dit-Lortie** ★ *(3200 Chemin Royal)* was originally constructed at the end of the 17th century. At the beginning of the following century, it was acquired by Jean Laurent-dit-Lortie. His descendants are still living in the house. The imposing size of the building is the result of successive additions, while the steep slope of the roof is indicative of the age of the original structure. The finely carved wood of the balcony, typical of the region, was probably installed around 1880.

Saint-Jean-de-Boischatel (pop. 3,662)

The municipality of Saint-Jean-de-Boischatel is located on former estate lands which were administered by the government and later granted to Jean Le Barbier in 1654. This land was set up as a fief in 1677, by Charles Aubert de la Chesnaye who had recently acquired it.

Dubbed The Fief of Charleville, the district maintained its agricultural vocation until the beginning of the 1970s, when suburban development overtook the area.

The **Manoir de Charleville** ★ *(5580 Avenue Royale)* is one of the oldest standing buildings in Canada. It was constructed in 1670 for the farmer hired by the capital administration. The building's low profile, high gabled roof and small windows are typical of very old buildings in Québec. Unfortunately, the neighbouring property has recently been built up, partially obscuring this venerable site. The ancestor of the Trudel families of Québec moved into the building at the end of the 17th century. After 150 years, the house passed into the hands of the Huot family, who lived there until 1964.

L'Ange-Gardien (pop. 2,952)

Agriculture is still an important industry in Ange-Gardien, one of the oldest parishes on the Côte de Beaupré. The village boasts a number of century-old houses and has beautiful views of Île d'Orléans.

The **Chapelles de Procession** ★ built on either side of the village church *(6357 Avenue Royale)*, are the oldest such chapels still standing in Québec, having been built during the French Regime in about 1750. These charming small buildings served as altars of repose during the Corpus Christi Processions.

On small Rue de la Mairie stands the **Maison Laberge** *(24 Rue de la Mairie)*, the ancestral home of the Laberge family. Built in 1674, it has been added to many times since then. Twelve generations of this family, whose descendants now live all over Québec, inhabited this house until 1970.

Château-Richer ★ (pop. 3,802)

Under the French Regime, Château-Richer was the nerve centre of the immense Beaupré seigneury, which extended from Saint-Jean-de-Boischatel to Baie-Saint-Paul in the Charlevoix region. Conceded in 1636 by the Compagnie des Cents Associés, this seigneury was granted to the Séminaire de Québec thirty years later, and stayed in their hands until the abolition of seigneurial tenure in 1854. In the 17th century, the directors of the seminary constructed Château Richer, a veritable castle endowed with a tower used as a prison. The building, which was bombarded during the British Conquest, was practically in ruins when it was finally totally demolished around 1860.

The village's location is charming and picturesque, highlighted by the striking placement of the church on a promontory. Throughout the village, small wooden signs have been posted in front of historical buildings indicating any distinctive architectural features and when they were built.

The **Centre d'Interprétation de la Côte de Beaupré** ★ *($ 2; Jun to mid-Oct, every day 10am to 5pm; 7007 Avenue Royale, ☎824-3677)*. This information centre is located in the Petit-Pré mill, which is visible from the curve in the road. It has an interesting exhibition on the history and geography of the Côte de Beaupré. A model depicting the development of the region from pre-colonial times to the present day highlights the exhibition. The mill itself was rebuilt right after the British Conquest following a similar design used for the original mill built by the directors of the Séminaire de Québec in 1695.

Take Boulevard Sainte-Anne (Route 138), which runs parallel to the river, to Chemin Royal

For those who are curious about bees and honey, here's an interesting little museum. The **Musée de l'Abeille** *(free admission; "bee safari" $2; May to Oct, every day 9am to 6pm; Nov to Apr, every day 9am to 5pm; 8862 Bd Ste-Anne, ☎824-4411, ⌐824-4422)* offers a brief look into the lives of these tireless workers. Visitors can stroll through at their leisure or receive an introduction to the art of beekeeping by participating in a "bee safari". A beekeeper explains the steps involved in making honey and even mead (honey wine). There's also a pastry shop and a boutique.

Continue on Chemin Royal

Sainte-Anne-de-Beaupré ★ (pop. 3,298)

This long, narrow village is one of the largest pilgrimage sites in North America. In 1658, the first Catholic church on the site was dedicated to Saint Anne after sailors from Brittany, who had prayed to the Virgin Mary's mother, were saved from drowning during a storm on the St-Lawrence. Soon, a great number of pilgrims began to visit the church. The second church, built in 1676, was replaced in 1872 by a huge

temple, which was destroyed by fire in 1922. Finally work began on the present basilica which stands at the centre of a virtual complex of chapels, monasteries and facilities as varied as they are unusual. They include the **Bureau des Bénédictions**, blessings office, and the Cyclorama. Each year, Sainte-Anne-de-Beaupré welcomes more than a million pilgrims, who stay in the hotels and visit the countless souvenir boutiques, of perhaps dubious taste, along Avenue Royale.

To learn more about Québec folklore go to the **Atelier Paré** *(free admission; mid-May to mid-Oct, every day 9am to 5:30pm; mid-Oct to mid-May, Mon to Fri 1pm to 4pm, Sat and Sun 10am to 4pm; 9269 Avenue Royale, ☎827-3992)*. All the works presented at this wood-sculpting museum are inspired by the fascinating world of local legends.

The **Basilique Sainte-Anne-de-Beaupré** ★★★ *(information counter is loctated near the entrance, early May to mid-Sep, every day 8:30am to 5pm; 10018 Avenue Royale, ☎827-3781)*, towering over the small, metal-roofed wooden houses that line the winding road, is surprising not only for its impressive size, but also for the feverish activity it inspires all summer long. The church's granite exterior, which takes on a different colour depending on the ambient light, was designed in the French Romanesque Revival style by Parisian architect Maxime Roisin, who was assisted by Quebecer Louis Napoléon Audet. Its spires rise 91 metres into the sky above the coast, while the nave is 129 m long, and the transepts over 60 metres wide. The wooden statue gilded with copper sitting atop the church's façade was taken from the 1872 church. When the fire destroyed the former basilica, the statue stayed in place while everything collapsed around it.

The basilica's interior is divided into five naves, supported by heavy columns with highly sculpted capitals. The vault of the main nave is adorned with sparkling mosaics designed by French artists Jean Gaudin and Auguste Labouret, recounting the life of Saint Anne. Labouret also created the magnificent stained glass, found all along the perimeter of the basilica. The left transept contains an extraordinary statue of Saint Anne cradling Mary in her right arm. Her tiara reminds the visitor that she is the patron saint the Quebecer. In a beautiful reliquary in the background, visitors can admire the Great Relic, part of Saint Anne's forearm sent over from the San Paolo Fuori le Mura in Rome. Finally, follow the ambulatory around the choir to see the ten radiant chapels built in the 1930s, whose polychromatic architecture is Art-Deco inspired.

Material retrieved after the demolition of the original church in 1676 was used to build the **Chapelle Commémorative** ★ *(free admission; May to Nov, every day 8am to 5pm; alongside Avenue Royale, ☎827-3781)* in 1878. The steeple (1696) was designed by Claude Bailiff, an architect whose numerous other projects in 17th-century New France have all but disappeared, victims of wars and fires. Inside, the high altar comes from the original church built during the French Regime. It is the work of Jacques Leblond-dit-Latour (circa 1700). The chapel is adorned with paintings from the 18th century. The water from the Fontaine de Sainte-Anne, at the foot of the chapel, is said to have healing properties.

La Scala Santa ★ *(free admission; May to mid-Sep, every day 8:30am to 9pm; to the right of the Chapelle du Souvenir)*, a strange yellow and white wooden building (1891), houses a staircase, which pilgrims climb on their knees while reciting prayers. It is a replica of the Scala Santa, the sacred staircase conserved in Rome at San Giovanni in Laterano that Christ climbed to get to the court of Pontius Pilate. An image of the Holy Land is inlaid in each riser.

The **Cyclorama de Jérusalem** ★★ *($6; early May to Oct; every day 8:30am to 8pm, 8 Rue Régina, near the parking lot ☎827-3101)*. This round building with oriental features houses a 360° panorama of Jerusalem on the day of the crucifixion. This immense *trompe l'œuil* painting, measuring 14 metres by 100 metres, was created in Chicago in about 1880 by French artist Paul Philippoteaux and his assistants. A specialist in panoramas, Philippoteaux produced a work of remarkable realism. It was first exhibited in Montréal before being moved to Sainte-Anne-de-Beaupré at the very end of the 19th century. Very few panoramas and cycloramas, so popular at the turn of the century, have survived to the present day.

The **Musée de Sainte Anne** ★ *($6; Apr to Oct, every day 10am to 5pm; Oct to Apr, Sat and Sun 10am to 5pm; 9803 Boulevard Ste-Anne, ☎827-6873, ⊷827-6870)* is dedicated to sacred art honouring the mother of the Virgin Mary. These interestingly diverse pieces were acquired over many years from the basilica but have only recently been put on display for the public. Sculptures, paintings, mosaics, stained-glass windows and goldworks are dedicated to the cult of Saint Anne, as well as written works expressing prayers or thanks for favours obtained. The history of pilgrimages to Sainte-Anne-de-Beaupré are also explained. The exhibition is attractively presented and spread over two floors.

Follow Avenue Royale to Saint-Joachim (Cap Tourmente). Cross Route 138, and go through the municipality of Beaupré. Turn right on Rue de l'Église in Saint-Joachim.

Other recommended destinations in the region include the **Station Mont-Sainte-Anne** (see p 381) and the charming village of **Saint-Ferréol-les-Neiges** on Route 360 E., which branches off Avenue Royale at Beaupré.

Saint-Ferréol-les-Neiges (pop. 2,092)

At the east end of Saint-Ferréol-les-Neiges is **Les Sept Chutes** hydro-electric complex *($6.50; late May to late Jun 10am to 5pm; late Jun to beginning of Sep 9am to 7pm; Sep to mid-Oct, Sat and Sun 10am to 5pm; 4520 Avenue Royale, ☎826-3139, ⊷826-1630)*, which was active from 1916 to 1984 and has since been transformed into an information centre. You can learn about the stages of hydroelectric production and about the lives of people who worked in such powerstations. There are also paths along the Sainte-Anne-du-Nord river to the impressive, 130-metre-high falls.

Grand Canyon des Chutes Sainte-Anne, see p 381.

Saint-Joachim (pop. 1,489)

The village of Saint-Joachim was originally located on the banks of the river, near the farm belonging to the Séminaire du Québec. The town was burned to the ground during the British Conquest (1759). In the years that followed it was rebuilt on its present site, safe from the line of cannon fire. Because of its isolation, at the foot of Mont-Sainte-Anne, it has succeeded in keeping some of its rural charm.

The first church in Saint Joachim, the **Église Saint-Joachim** ★★ *(165 Rue de l'Église)* (17th century) was burned by British troops in 1759. The present church, rebuilt inland along with the rest of the village, was completed in 1779.

Unfortunately, the façade was redone in 1895, and has no aesthetic connection with the rest of the building. In fact from the outside, this church is not exceptional, the interior, however, remains a veritable masterpiece of religious art in Québec.

Once inside the church, the visitor's eye is drawn to the chancel and its triumphal altarpiece composed of a high altar, older than the rest of the decor (1785) and above which hangs a painting by the Abbé Aide-Créquy entitled *Saint-Joachim et la Vierge* (Saint Joachim and the Virgin) (1779).

Beyond the church, turn left on Chemin du Cap.

Cap Tourmente ★★

The pastoral and fertile land of Cap Tourmente is the eastern-most section of the St-Lawrence plain, before the mountains of the Laurentian Massif reach the shores of the St-Lawrence. The colonization of this area at the beginning of the 17th century represented one of the first attempts to populate New France. Samuel de Champlain, the founder of Québec City, established a farm here in 1626, the ruins of which were recently unearthed. The land of Cap Tourmente was acquired by Monseigneur François de Laval in 1662, and was cultivated by the Société des Sieurs de Caen. Soon the land passed into the hands of the Séminaire de Québec which eventually built a retreat for priests, a school, a summer camp and, most importantly, a huge farm which met the institution's nutritional needs and brought in a substantial income. Following the British Conquest, the seminary moved the seat of its Beaupré seigneury to Cap Tourmente, leaving behind the ruins of the Château Richer. The **Château Bellevue ★** was built between 1777 and 1781. This superb building is endowed with a neoclassical cut stone portal. The property's Saint-Louis-de-Gonsague Chapel (1780) is well hidden in the trees.

Cap Tourmente National Wildlife Area ★★
see p 381.

To return to Québec City, continue along the loop formed by the Cap Tourmente road leading to Saint-Joachim, continue towards Beaupré before taking Route 138 W. It is possible to combine the Côte de Beaupré tour with the visit to Charlevoix described on page 466. To do this head to Route 138 E. via the steep,

winding road northeast of the village of Saint-Joachim. Turn right towards Baie-St-Paul.

Tour B : Île d'Orléans ★★
(one day)

Located in the middle of the St-Lawrence River, downstream from Québec City, this 32 kilometre-by-5-kilometre island is famous for its old-world charm. Of all regions of Québec, the island is the most evocative of life in New France. When Jacques Cartier arrived in 1535, the island was covered in wild vines, which inspired its first name: Île Bacchus. However, it was soon renamed in homage to the Duc d'Orléans. With the exception of Sainte-Pétronille, the parishes on the island were established in the 17th century. The colonization of the entire island followed soon after. In 1970, the government of Québec protected Île d'Orléans as a historic district. The move was made in part to slow down the development that threatened to turn the island into yet another suburb of Québec City, and also as part of a widespread movement among Quebecers to protect the roots of their French ancestry by preserving old churches and houses. Since 1936, the island has been linked to the mainland by a suspension bridge, the Pont de l'Île.

To get to the island from Québec City take the Autoroute Dufferin-Montmorency (Hwy 440) to the Pont de l'Île. Cross the river and turn right on Route 368, also called Chemin Royal, which circles the island.

Sainte-Pétronille ★★ (pop. 1,170)

Paradoxically, Sainte-Pétronille was the site of the first French settlement on Île d'Orléans and is also its most recent parish. In 1648, François de Chavigny de Berchereau and his wife Éléonore de Grandmaison established a farm and a Huron mission here. However, constant Iroquois attacks forced the colonists to move further east, to a spot facing Sainte-Anne-de-Beaupré. It was not until the middle of the 19th century that Sainte-Pétronille was consolidated as a village, as its beautiful location began attracting numerous summer visitors. Anglophone merchants from Québec City built beautiful second homes here, many of which are still standing along the road.

Turn right on Rue Horatio-Walker, which leads to the river banks and to a promenade.

The **Maison Horatio-Walker** ★ *(11 and 13 Rue Horatio-Walker)*. The red brick building and the stucco house beside it were, respectively, the workshop and residence of painter Horatio Walker from 1904 to 1938. The British-born artist liked the French culture and the meditative calm of Île d'Orléans. His workshop, designed by Harry Staveley, remains a good example of English Arts and Crafts architecture.

The Porteous family, of English origin, settled in Québec City at the end of the 18th century. In 1900, they had the **Domaine Porteous** ★ *(253 Chemin Royal)* built. This vast country house surrounded by superb gardens, was christened "La Groisardière". Designed by the Toronto architects Darling and Pearson, the house revived certain aspects of traditional Québec architecture. The most notable of these are the Louis XV-inspired woodwork, and the general proportions used in the design of the house, which are similar to the Manoir Mauvide-Genest in Saint-Jean. Inside, there are many remounted paintings by William Brymner and Maurice Cullen depicting countryside scenes on Île d'Orléans. The building also incorporates *art nouveau* features. The property, which belongs today to the Foyer de Charité Notre-Dame-d'Orléans, a seniors' residence, was expanded between 1961 and 1964 when a new wing and a chapel were added.

Saint-Laurent (pop. 1,612)

Until 1950, Saint-Laurent's main industry was the manufacturing of *chaloupes*, boats and sailboats which were known as the in United States and Europe. Though production of these boats has ceased, some traces of the industry, such as abandoned boatyards, can still be seen off the road, near the banks of the river. The village was founded in 1679, and still has some older buildings, such as the beautiful **Maison Gendreau** built in 1720 *(2387 Chemin Royal, west of the village)* and the **Moulin Gosselin**, which now houses a restaurant *(758 Chemin Royal, east of the village)*.

At the little **Forge à Pique-Assaut** *(free admission; Jun to early Sep, every day 9am to 5pm; Oct to May, Mon to Fri 9am to noon and 1:30pm to 5pm; 2200 Chemin Royal, G0A 3Z0, ☎828-9300)*, you can learn about the blacksmith trade by watching artisans at work in front of a large forge or by taking a guided tour. There's a shop on the second floor (see p 389).

Saint-Jean ★★ (pop. 894)

In the mid-19th century, Saint-Jean was the preferred homebase of nautical pilots who made a living guiding ships through the difficult currents and rocks of the St-Lawrence. Some of their neoclassical or Second Empire houses remain along Chemin Royal and provide evidence of the privileged place held by these seamen who were indispensable to the success of commercial navigation.

The most impressive manor from the French Regime still standing is in Saint-Jean. The **Manoir Mauvide-Genest** ★★ *($ 4; late May to late Sep, every day 10am to 5.30pm, early Sep to mid-Oct by appointment only; 1451 Chemin Royal, ☎829-2630)* was built in 1734 for Jean Mauvide, the Royal Doctor, and his wife, Marie-Anne Genest. This beautiful stone building has a rendering coat of white roughcast, in the traditional Norman architectural style. The property officially became a seigneurial manor in the middle of the 18th century, when Mauvide, who had become rich doing business in the Caribbean, bought the southern half of the Île d'Orléans seigneury.

In 1926, Camille Pouliot, descendant of the Genest family, bought the manor house. He then restored it, adding a summer kitchen and a chapel. He later transformed the house into a museum, displaying furniture and objects from traditional daily life. Pouliot was one of the first people to be actively interested in Québec's heritage. The manor still has a museum on the second floor devoted to antique furniture and everyday objects, while the main floor is taken up by a restaurant.

Saint-François ★ (pop. 483)

This, the smallest village on Île d'Orléans, retains many buildings from its past. Some, however, are far from the Chemin Royal and are therefore difficult to see from Route 368. The surrounding countryside is charming, and offers several pleasant panoramic views of the river, Charlevoix and the coast. The famous wild vine that gave the island its first name, Île Bacchus, can also be found in Saint-François.

As you leave the village, on the roadside is an **observation tower** ★★, which offers excellent views to the north and east. Visible are the Îles Madame et au Ruau which mark the meeting point of the fresh water of the St. Lawrence and the salt water of the gulf. Mont Sainte-Anne's ski slopes, Charlevoix on the north shore and the Côte-du-Sud seigneuries on the south shore can also be seen in the distance.

Sainte-Famille ★ (pop. 1,026)

The oldest parish on Île d'Orléans was founded by Monseigneur de Laval in 1666 in order to establish a settlement across the river from Sainte-Anne-de-Beaupré for colonists who had previously settled around Sainte-Pétronille. Sainte-Famille has retained many buildings from the French Regime. Among them is the town's famous church, one of the greatest accomplishments of religious architecture in New France, and the oldest two-towered church in Québec.

The beautiful **Église Sainte-Famille** ★★ *(3915 Chemin Royal)* was built between 1743 and 1747, to replace the original church built in 1669. Inspired by the Église des Jésuites in Québec City, which has since been destroyed, Father Dufrost de la Jemmerais ordered the construction of two towers with imperial roofs which explains the single steeple sitting atop the gable. Other unusual elements such as five alcoves and a sun dial by the entrance (which has since been destroyed) make the building even more original. In the 19th century, new statues were installed in the alcoves, and the imperial roofs gave way to two new steeples, bringing the total number of steeples to three.

Though modified several times, the interior decor retains many interesting elements. Sainte-Famille was a wealthy parish in the 18th century, thus allowing the decoration of the church to begin as soon as the frame of the building was finished. In 1748, Gabriel Gosselin installed the first pulpit, and in 1749 Pierre-Noël Levasseur completed construction of the present tabernacle of the high altar. Louis-Basile David, inspired by the Quévillon school, designed the beautiful coffered vault in 1812. Many paintings adorn the church, among them are *La Sainte Famille* (The Holy Family) painted by Frère Luc during his stay in Canada in 1670, the *Dévotion au Sacré Coeur de Jésus* (Devotion to the Sacred Heart of Jesus, 1766) and *Le Christ en Croix* (Christ on the Cross) by François Baillargé (circa 1802). The church grounds offer a beautiful view of the coast.

Saint-Pierre (pop. 2075)

The most developed parish on Île d'Orléans had already lost some of its charm before the island was declared a historic site. Saint-Pierre is particularly important to the people of Québec, as the home for many years of the renowned poet and singer Félix Leclerc (1914-1988). The singer and songwriter, who penned *P'tit Bonheur*, was the first musician to introduce Quebecois music to Europe. He is buried in the local cemetery.

The loop is now completed. Turn right to return to the mainland.

Tour C : The Chemin du Roy ★★
(one day)

With the exception of Sillery, near Québec City, the towns and villages on this tour are all located along the Chemin du Roy, the first maintained road between Montréal and Québec City and built in 1734. This road, running along the St-Lawrence (some parts parallel to Route 138), and lined with beautiful 18th century French-style houses, churches and windmills, is one of the most picturesque drives in Canada.

Sillery ★★ (pop. 13,082)

This well-to-do suburb of Québec City retains many traces of its varied history, influenced by the town's dramatic topography. There are actually two sections to Sillery, one at the base and the other at the top of a steep cliff which runs from Cap Diamant to Cap-Rouge. In 1637, the Jesuits built a mission in Sillery on the shores of the river, with the idea of converting the Algonquins and Montagnais who came to fish in the coves upriver from Québec City. They named the fortified community for the mission's benefactor, Noël Brûlart de Sillery, an aristocrat who had recently been converted by Vincent de Paul.

By the following century, Sillery was already sought after for its beauty. The Jesuits converted their mission to a country house, and the bishop of Samos built Sillery's first villa (1732). Following the British Conquest, Sillery became the preferred town of administrators, military officers and British merchants, all of whom built themselves luxurious villas on the cliff, in architectural styles then fashionable in England. The splendour of these homes and their vast English gardens were in stark contrast to the simple houses lived in by workers and clustered at the base of the cliff. The occupants of these houses worked in the shipyards, where a fortune was being made building ships out of wood coming down the Outaouais region to supply the British navy during Napoleon's blockade, which began in 1806. The shipyards, set up in Sillery's sheltered coves, had all disappeared before Boulevard Champlain, now running along the river's edge, was built in 1960.

The **Siège Social de L'Industrielle-Alliance** *(1080 Chemin Saint-Louis)* looks like a modern villa, but was actually built as the headquarters for a large insurance company as its headquarters. It is one of the best examples of post-war architecture in Québec. The work of architects Pierre Rinfret and Maurice Bouchard (1950-52) was inspired by houses from the 19th century and is accentuated by a beautiful garden.

The **Bois-de-Coulonge** ★ to the east borders Chemin Saint-Louis. This English park once surrounded the residence of the lieutenant-governor of Québec, the King or Queen's representative in Québec until the title was abolished in 1968. The stately home was destroyed in a fire in 1966, though some of its outbuildings survived, notably the guard's house and the stables. The Saint-Denys stream flows through the eastern end of the grounds at the bottom of a ravine. British troops gained access to the Plains of Abraham, where a historic battle decided the future of New France, by climbing through this ravine. Now Bois de Coulonge, one of the Jardins du Québec, has magnificent gardens and a well-arranged arboretum to walk through.

Bagatelle ★ *($2; Mar to Dec, Tue to Sun 11am to 5pm; 1563, Chemin Saint-Louis* ☎688-8074) was once home to an attaché of the British governor who lived on the neighbouring property of Bois-de-Coulonge. Built in 1848, the villa is a good example of 19th-century Gothic-Revival residential architecture, as interpreted by American Alexander J. Davis. The house and its Victorian garden were impeccably restored in 1984, and are now open to the public. On the grounds, there is an interesting information centre providing background on the villas and large estates of Sillery.

On Avenue Lemoine, which runs along the south side of Bagatelle is the **Spencer Grange Villa**, built in 1849 for Henry Atkinson *(1321 Avenue Lemoine)*. During the Second World War, the building was lived in by Zita de Bourbon-Parme, the dethroned Empress of Austria.

The Gothic-Revival **St. Michael's Church** *(1800 Chemin Saint-Louis)* built in 1852 serves the Anglican congregation of Sillery. Nearby is the **Mount Hermon Protestant Cemetery** and the **Couvent des Soeurs de Sainte-Jeanne-d'Arc** (1917), a huge convent with the look of an imposing castle.

Turn left onto Côte de l'Église.

A short side trip leads the **Cimetière de Sillery**, Sillery's Catholic cemetery, where René Lévesque, founder of the Parti Québécois and Premier of Québec from 1976 to 1984, is buried. To get there, turn right on Avenue Maguire, then left on Boulevard René-Lévesque Ouest.

The **Église Saint-Michel** ★ *(at the corner of Chemin du Foulon and Côte de l'Église)*, Sillery's Catholic church, has many points in common with its Anglican counterpart. To begin with, its patron saint, but also the Gothic-Revival style and the fact that both churches were constructed at the same year (1852). The Catholic church, designed by architect George Browne, is, however, much larger. Inside are five paintings from the famous Desjardins collection. These originally hung in Parisian churches until they were sold in 1792 following the French Revolution and brought to Québec by Abbé Desjardins.

The **Maison des Jésuites de Sillery** ★★ *($2; mid-Mar to late Dec, Tue to Sun 11am to 5pm, Thu to 7pm; 2320 Chemin du Foulon, ☎654-0259, ≈654-0991)* built of stone and covered with white plaster, occupies the former site of a Jesuit mission, a few ruins of which are still visible. In the 17th century, the mission included a fortified stone wall, a chapel, a priest's residence and native housing. As European illnesses, such as smallpox and measles, devastated the indigenous population, the mission was transformed into a hospice in 1702. At the same time work began on the present house, a building with imposing chimney stacks. In 1763, the house was rented to John Brookes and his wife, writer Frances Moore Brookes, who immortalized it as the setting for her novel, *The History of Emily Montague*, published in London in 1769. It was also during this time that the structure was lowered and the windows were made smaller in size, in the New England saltbox tradition. The house now has two stories in front and one in back and is covered with a catslide roof.

By 1824, the main building was being used as a brewery and the chapel had been torn down. The house was later converted to offices for various shipyards. In 1929, the Maison des Jésuites became one of the first three buildings designated as historic by the government of Québec. Since 1948, it has housed a museum detailing the 350-year history of the property.

Continue along Chemin du Foulon, then take Côte à Gignac up the embankment on the right.

On the right at the end of Avenue Kilmarnock stands the villa of the same name. Today it is surrounded by suburban homes. This 1810 villa is one of the oldest in Sillery. On the left on Avenue de la Falaise is one of the first post-war suburbs. It was designed by French urban planner Jacques Gréber in 1948. Turn right on Chemin Saint-Louis.

The **Domaine Cataraqui** ★ *(5$; Tue to Sun 10am to 5pm; 2141 Chemin Saint-Louis, ☎681-3010)* is the best-kept property of its kind still in existence in Sillery. It includes a large neoclassical residence, designed in 1851 by architect Henry Staveley, a winter garden and numerous outbuildings scattered across a beautiful, recently restored garden. The house was built for a wood merchant named Henry Burstall, whose business operated at the bottom of the cliff atop which the house stands. In 1935, Cataraqui became the residence of painter Henry Percival Tudor-Hart and his wife Catherine Rhodes. They sold the property to the Québec government to prevent it being divided up, as many others had been. Today the public can visit the house, one of the Jardins du Québec, and its superb gardens where exhibits and concerts are regularly presented. In the early fall, many concerts are given during the **Festival de Musique Ancienne de Sillery**.

Benmore's *(2071 Chemin Saint-Louis)* very original, Gothic-Revival interior was created in 1834 by architect George Browne, who had just arrived from Ireland. As with many former villas, the house now belongs to a religious community, and was added-on to many times.

Head west on Chemin Saint-Louis.

The **Maison Hamel-Bruneau** *(free admission; Tue to Sun 12:30pm to 5pm, Wed to 9pm; 2608 Chemin Saint-Louis, ☎654-4325)* is a beautiful example of Regency architecture, popular in British colonies at the beginning of the 19th century. This style is characterized by hip roofs with flared eaves covering low wraparound verandas. Graced with French windows, the Maison Hamel-Bruneau, has been carefully restored and transformed into a cultural centre by the town of Sainte-Foy.

Turn left on Avenue du Parc to get to the Aquarium du Québec.

The **Aquarium du Québec** *($8; every day 9am to 5pm; 1675 Avenue des Hôtels, in Sainte-Foy, ☎659-5266)*, home to some 250 species of fish, marine mammals and reptiles, is full of fascinating sights. Of particular interest among the indigenous animals are the four species of seal. The area around the aquarium has walking trails and picnic areas.

Take Chemin Saint-Louis west towards Cap-Rouge, then take Rue Louis-Francœur to the right before turing left down Côte de Cap-Rouge.

Cap-Rouge (pop. 14,738)

Jacques Cartier and the Sieur de Roberval tried to establish a French colony at Cap-Rouge in 1541. They called their encampments Charlesbourg-Royal and France-Roy. The unfortunate souls who came with them, having no idea of how cold Canada could get in January, built frail wood buildings with paper windows! Most died during the winter, victims of the cold or of scurvy, a disease caused by a lack of vitamin C. The others returned to France in the spring.

A plaque has been placed at the **Site Historique de Cap-Rouge** *(at the end of Côte de Cap-Rouge)*, an historic site commemorating the first French colony in America. Cartier and Roberval had intended to make the site a base camp for expeditions heading out in search of a passage to the Orient.

Take Rue Saint-Félix heading west, turn left on Chemin du Lac, then left again on Rang de la Butte, which becomes Route Tessier. Turn left on Route 138 towards Saint-Augustin-de-Desmaures. Continue along Route 138 to Neuville.

Neuville ★ (pop. 1,125)

A vein of limestone, traversing the region from Neuville to Grondines, has been tapped since the French Regime for the construction of prestigious buildings across the province since the French Regime. This explains the large number of rubble-stone houses dotting the villages in the area. Today most of the jobs related to the extraction and cutting of this grey stone are concentrated in the town of Saint-Marc-des-Carrières, west of Deschambault.

The village of Neuville was formerly part of the Pointe-aux-Trembles seigneury, granted to the royal engineer Jean Bourdon, in 1653. The houses of Neuville are built into the hills at varying elevations so that most of them have a view of the St-Lawrence. This terraced layout lends this section of the Chemin du Roy a certain charm.

The **"Château" de Neuville** *(205 Route 138)*, on the left as you enter the village, is a fantastical home built between 1964 and 1972 with materials gathered from the demolition of about a hundred homes along the Grande-Allée in Québec City (see p 342).

The **Maison Darveau** *(50 Route 138)* was built in 1785 for one of the most important stonemasons in Neuville, which explains the presence of the more elaborate stone frames around the windows and doors. In addition to these, the house has a classical portal, which though common in France was quite exceptional.

Turn right on Rue des Érables.

Rue des Érables ★★ has one of the largest concentrations of old stone houses outside Québec's large urban centres. The abundance of the necessary raw material and the homowners' desire to make use of the talents of local builders and stonemasons explains this. Number 500 on Rue des Érables was built for Édouard Larue, who acquired the Neuville seigneury in 1828. The huge house is representative of traditional rural Québec architecture, with its raised stone foundation and gallery covered with flared eaves, running the whole length of the façade.

In 1696 the villagers undertook the construction of the simple **Église Saint-François-de-Sales ★★** *(guided tours; Rue des Érables)*. It was added to and altered during the following

centuries, to the point where the original elements of the building have all but disappeared. A new chancel was built in 1761, the nave was expanded in 1854, and finally, a new façade was added in 1915. The present church is the result of these transformations. The interior of the church houses an impressive piece of baroque art from the period of the French Regime: a wood baldaquin (richly ornamented canopy over the altar) ordered in 1695 for the chapel of the episcopal palace in Québec City.

At the western end of Rue des Érables, take Route 138 to the right. Follow Route 138 W. to Pointe-aux-Trembles, then Donnacona.

Turn right on Rue Notre-Dame, to get to the centre of Donnacona.

Donnacona (pop. 6,304)

A short stop in this paper-industry town dominated by the Domtar Company should include a look at the company's dam on the Rivière Jacques-Cartier, as well as at the nearby Atlantic salmon migration channel.

In the past the Rivière Jacques-Cartier was part of the Atlantic salmon's migratory route. With the construction of dams and the use of the river by the logging industry the number of Atlantic salmon diminished; by 1910 the species had disappeared from the area completely. In 1979, Atlantic salmon were successfully re-introduced. To facilitate the immigration the **Passe Migratoire** was built *($1; late Jun to early Sep every day 9am to 8pm; Rue Notre-Dame, ☎285-2210)*. The channel is an ideal spot from which to watch the salmon swimming upstream. The best time to observe this is during the month of July.

Cross the bridge over the Rivière Jacques-Cartier.

Cap-Santé ★ (pop. 2,857)

This farming village enjoys an enviable setting overlooking the St-Lawrence. Formerly part of the Portneuf seigneury, Cap-Santé came into being at the end of the 17th century and grew slowly. If a typical Quebecois village exists, Cap-Santé is probably it.

The **Site du Fort Jacques-Cartier** *(close to 15 Rue Notre-Dame)*. A plaque by the side of the road indicates the location of the Fort Jacques-Cartier. Erected hastily in 1759, at the peak of the Seven Years' War, the fort was meant to slow down the English on their march towards Montréal. The courageous Chevaliers de Lévis tried desperately to save what remained of New France with these measures. The eventual attack on the fort lasted barely an hour, before the ill-equipped French surrendered. Only archaeological remains of the wood fort have survived. The **Cap-Santé seigneurial manor**, built in about 1740 on the same site, is, however, still standing, well concealed in the woods.

Return to Route 138 on the left.

The construction of the **Église Sainte-Famille** ★★ *(guides tours; Rue du Quai)* went on between 1754 and 1764 under the auspices of curate Joseph Filion, but was seriously disrupted by the British Conquest. In 1759, materials intended for the finishing touches on the building were requisitioned for the construction of Fort Jacques-Cartier. Nevertheless, the completed church, with its two steeples and its high nave lit by two rows of windows, is an ambitious piece of work for its time, and was possibly the largest village church built under the French Regime. The three beautiful wooden statues placed in the alcoves of the façade in 1775 have miraculously survived Québec's harsh climate. The imitation cutstone done in wood covering the stone walls was added in the 19th century. Before stepping inside the church, be sure to visit the wooded cemetery and presbytery built according to plans by Thomas Baillargé in 1850.

Today the **Vieux Chemin** ★, the old road, is nothing more than a simple road passing in front of the church, but it was once part of the Chemin du Roy that linked Montréal and Québec City. Numerous well-preserved 18th-century houses facing the river can still be seen along the road, making it one of the most picturesque drives in Canada.

Drive through **Portneuf** *before stopping in Deschambault.*

Deschambault ★★ (pop. 1,353)

The charming tranquillity of this agricultural village on the banks of the St-Lawrence was a bit disturbed recently by the development of an aluminum smelter. Deschambault was founded

thanks to the efforts of Seigneur Fleury de la Gorgendière who had previously had a church built in nearby Cap Lauzon in 1720. Because the village has grown slowly, it retains its small-town charm.

The **Maison Deschambault** *(128 Route 138)* is visible at the end of a long tree-lined lane. The stone building equipped with fire-break walls was probably built in the late 18th century. It was practically in ruins in 1936 when the Québec government, who owned the building at the time, undertook its restoration, a rarity in an era when many elements of Québec's heritage had already been lost. The building now houses a charming inn (see p 387), and a fine French restaurant (see p 389).

Turn left on Rue de l'Église, which leads to the village square.

The **Église Saint-Joseph** in Deschambault with its large façade adorned with two massive towers set back slightly from the front of the church, is unique in Québec. Instead of the usual gable, the roof of the church has a hipped end adorned with a statue. This solid building, erected between 1835 and 1841, is the work of architect Thomas Baillargé. The original neoclassical steeples were destroyed and replaced during the 20th century with poor imitations of typical New France steeples.

The **Vieux Presbytère** *($1.50; mid-Jun to late Sep every day 10am to 5pm; 117 Rue Saint-Joseph, ☎286-6891)* occupies a prime location behind the church offering a beautiful panoramic view of the river and the south shore. The small presbytery building, set apart in the centre of a large lawn, was built in 1815 to replace the first presbytery dating from 1735. The foundations of the original building are visible near the entrance. In 1955, an antique dealer saved the presbytery from destruction, then, in 1970, a residents' association began using the building as an exhibition centre, demonstrating a dynamic community commitment to preserving its heritage. guide.

Get back on Route 138 W. This section of the Chemin du Roy is lined with many well-preserved traditional Québec residences. Turn right onto Rue de Chavigny.

The magnificent **Moulin de la Chevrotière** ★ *(2$; mid-Jun to early Sep, every day 10am to 5pm; 109 Rue de Chavigny, ☎286-6862)*, a former mill, now houses a facility where tradi

Vieux Presbytère

tional building skills are taught. Every summer, young artisans from around Québec come to learn pre-industrial techniques of working with wood, iron and stone. The imposing building is located on a former section of the Chemin du Roy, renamed Rue de Chavigny in honour of Joseph de Chavigny de la Chevrotière, owner of the fief of the same name and who had this mill built in 1802. The roughcast structure just beside the mill, which houses the forge, is in fact the original mill, built in 1766.

Get back on Route 138 heading towards Grondines.

Grondines ★ (pop. 669)

In the 18th century, the village of Grondines was situated on the banks of the St-Lawrence. In 1831 it was relocated inland to facilitate access and to avoid flooding. Traces of the original village, found between the river and Route 138, show French architectural influences, whereas the core of the present village, centred around Rue Principale, displays decidedly more Victorian influences. The citizens of Grondines showed great concern for their environment during the 1980s, when they fought plans to run hydro-electric lines across the river. The people of Grondines finally won their case. The lines run under the river, keeping the picturesque countryside intact.

The hydro-electric lines *(free admission; guided tours Jun to late Aug, Mon to Fri 10am to 4pm, Sat and Sun 10am to 5pm; access via Exit 254 from Highway 40, then Route 138 towards Grondines, ☎268-8083).* Underwater cables carry electricity from Grondines on the north shore of the St-Lawrence to Lotbinière on the south shore. The laying down of these cables required some very advanced technology, since this was the first time 450 kilovolt continuous current cable was used. The **Centre D'Interpretation d'Hydro Québec** welcomes visitors, and through a series of models and video presentations familiarizes the public with the advantages of this means of transporting electricity.

The remains of the first stone church in Grondines, the **Église Saint-Charles-Borromée ★** *(490 Route 138)* (1716), are visible near the mill. When the village was moved, a new church had to be built. Admired for the churches he designed in the neighbouring parishes, Thomas Baillargé was asked to draw up the plans for a magnificent church. However, funds became very scarce, so much so that the neoclassical structure begun in 1832 remained incomplete. The church steeples were not added until 1894, by which time neoclassicism was no longer in vogue, having given way to Victorian architecture. As a result, the towers, windows and doors were designed in the Gothic-Revival style.

Inside, several interesting paintings are displayed, notably *La Madone du Rosaire* (The Rosary Madonna) by Théophile Hamel above the right lateral altar, and *Saint-Charles-Borromée* by Jean-Baptiste Roy-Audy. The tabernacle of the high altar was sculpted in 1742 by Levasseur. Also of interest is the neoclassical presbytery from 1842, with its beautiful dormer-window-pediment.

Though it lost its imposing presence when it was converted into a lighthouse (a fate shared by many similar buildings) the **Moulin de Grondines** *(770 Rue du Moulin)* is still important as the oldest building of its type still standing. The mill was built in 1672 for the Religieuses Hospitalières de l'Hôtel-Dieu, nuns working as nurses in the main hospital of Québec City, to whom the Grondines seigneury was granted in 1637.

The Chemin du Roy tour ends in Grondines, but could be combined with a visit to the Mauricie–Bois-Francs region, in Sainte-Anne-de-la-Pérade, see p 307

Tour D : Jacques-Cartier ★ (three days)

After a quick tour through some of the first settlements of New France, this itinerary enters the resort regions of the Laurentides, before plunging into the wilderness of the Rivière Jacques-Cartier valley and the Réserve Faunique des Laurentides. Ideal for camping, river rafting and other outdoor activities, the virgin forest of the Rivière Jacques-Cartier is surprisingly close to the city.

Charlesbourg ★ (pop. 73,962)

The Notre-Dame-des-Anges seigneury was granted to the Jesuits in 1626, making it one of the first permanent settlements inhabited by Europeans in Canada. Despite this early settlement and original seigneurial design, few buildings built before the 19th century remain in Charlesbourg. The fragility of early buildings and the push to modernize are possible explanations for this void. Since 1950, Charlesbourg has become one of the main suburbs of Québec City, and has lost much of its original character.

It is best to park near the church and to explore the Trait-Carré on foot.

The **Église Saint-Charles-Borromée** ★★ *(135 80ᵉ Rue Ouest)* revolutionized the art of building in rural Québec. Architect Thomas Baillargé, influenced by the Palladian movement, showed particular innovation in the way he arranged the windows and doors of the façade, to which he added a large pediment. Construction of the church began in 1828 and was uninterrupted. The original design has remained intact since. The magnificent interior decor by Baillargé was done in 1833.

At the corner of Boulevard Henri-Bourassa, is the old Moulin des Jésuites.

The **Moulin des Jésuites** ★ *(free admission; late Jun to mid-Aug, every day 10pm to 9pm; mid-Aug to mid-Jun, Sat and Sun 10am to 5pm; 7960 Boulevard Henri-Bourassa, ☎624-7720 and 624-7740)*. This pretty mill, in roughcast rubble stone, is the oldest building in Charlesbourg. It was built in 1740 by the Jesuits, who were the landowners at the time. After several decades of neglect, the two-story building was restored in 1990, and now houses the **Centre d'Interpretation du Trait-Carré** and a tourist bureau. Concerts and exhibits are also presented here.

A visit to the zoo is always guaranteed to fill both adults and children with wonder. The **Jardin Zoologique du Québec** ★ *($5.50; year-round, every day 9am to 5pm; 9300 Rue de la Faune, Charlesbourg, ☎622-0312, ≈644-9004, www.spsnq.qc.ca)* is on an attractive site overrun by greenery and flowers. In winter the area can be covered on cross-country skis. The buildings that house the animals are made of stone, reminiscent of Quebec's old constructions and include the **Maison des Insectes** *(☎626-0445)*, the insect house, aviaries with over 150 species of birds and a pavilion for big cats and primates. You can also attend seal performances and see many other mammals. All of this can be explored along three trails: the Hibou (owl), Ours (bear) and Orignal (moose). Many educational activities are organized throughout the year.

Take Boulevard Saint-Joseph (the continuation of 80ᵉ Rue Ouest) which eventually becomes Boulevard Bastien.

Wendake ★ (pop. 1,035)

Forced off their land by the Iroquois in the 17th century, 300 Huron families moved to various places around Québec before settling in 1700 in Jeune-Lorette, today known as Wendake. Visitors will be charmed by the winding roads of the village in this native reserve located on the banks of the Rivière Saint-Charles. The museum and gift shop provide a lot of information on the culture of this peaceable and sedentary people.

The **Église Notre-Dame-de-Lorette** ★ *(140 Boulevard Bastien)*, the Huron church, completed in 1730, is reminiscent of the first churches of New France. This humble building with a white plaster façade conceals unexpected treasures in its chancel and in the sacristy. Some of the objects on display were given to the Huron community by the Jesuits, and come from the first chapel in Ancienne-Lorette (late 17th century). Among the works to be seen are several statues by Noël Levasseur, created between 1730 and 1740, an altar-facing depicting a native village, by the Huron sculptor François Vincent (1790) and a beautiful *Vierge à l'Enfant* (Madonna and Child) sculpture, by a Parisian goldsmith (1717). In addition, the church has a reliquary made in 1676, chasubles from the 18th century and various liturgical objects by Paul Manis (circa 1715). However, the most interesting element remains the small, Louis XIII-style gilded tabernacle on the high altar, sculpted by Levasseur in 1722.

The Huron village of **Onhoüa Chetek8e** *($5; late May to early Oct, every day 9am to 5pm; 575 Rue Stanislas-Koska,* ☎*842-4308)* is a replica of a Huron village from the time of early colonization. The traditional design includes wooden longhouses and fences. Visitors are given an introduction to the lifestyle and social organization of the ancient Huron nation. Various native dishes are also served and worth a taste.

Parc de la Falaise et de la Chute Kabir Kouba, see p 382.

Continue on Route 73, which becomes Route 175 and leads to Lac-Beauport.

Lac-Beauport (pop. 4,800)

The Lac-Beauport region is a popular year-round resort area. There are downhill ski centres in the region, including **Le Relais** (see p 385). Vacationners can also enjoy the lake's beautiful beaches.

The Jacques-Cartier tour ends here. To return to Québec City, follow Route 175 S. You could also continue north into the Saguenay - Lac-Saint-Jean tourist region (see p 481).

 PARKS

Tour A: The Côte de Beaupré

Parc de la chute Montmorency, see p 368.

The **Station Mont Sainte-Anne** ★ *(Route 360, C.P. 400, Beaupré, G0A 1E0,* ☎*827-4561,* ☎*827-3121,   www.mont.sainte.anne.com)* cover 77 square kilometres and includes 800-metre-high Mont Sainte-Anne, one of the most beautiful downhill skiing sites in Québec (see p 384). Various other outdoor activities are possible the park has 200 kilometres of mountain bike trails, which become 200 kilometres of cross-country trails in winter. Access to these is $5 per day. Sports equipment is rented on site. There are a few hotels close to the ski hill and to the park.

The **Grand Canyon des Chutes Sainte-Anne** *(40 Côte de la Miche, or 206 Route 138, Beaupré* ☎*827-4057)*. The rushing Rivière Sainte-Anne carves a deep path through the hills near Beaupré and plunges 74 metres into a large pothole 22 metres in width and formed by the resulting water current. Visitors can take in this impressive site from lookouts and a suspension bridges.

The **Cap-Tourmente National Wildlife Area** ★★ *(Saint-Joachim, Apr-Oct* ☎*827-4591, Nov-Apr* ☎*827-3776)* is located on pastoral, fertile land. Each spring and autumn its sand-bars are visited by countless snow geese, who stop to gather strength for their long migration. The reserve also has birdwatching facilities and naturalists on hand to answer your questions about the 250 species of birds and 45 species of mammals you might encounter on the hiking and walking trails that traverse the park.

Tour C: The Chemin du Roy

Northwest of Quebec, the **Réserve Faunique de Portneuf** *(Rivière-à-Pierre,* ☎*323-2028)* offers many kilometres of trails for various outdoor activities including snowmobiling, cross-country skiing and snowshoeing. Lakes and rivers abound in the area. Pleasant little chalets *(reservations ☎1-800-665-6527)*, well equipped for two to eight people, are available to rent.

Tour D: The Rivière Jacques-Cartier

The **Réserve Faunique des Laurentides** *(Route 175 N., Mercier entrance, ☎848-2422)* covers 8,000 square kilometres. This huge wild expanse of forest and rivers is home to a diversified wildlife, including black bears and moose. Hunting and fishing (spotted trout) are permitted at certain times of the year, check with the information desk regarding permits. The reserve has beautiful cross-country ski trails, one-day and overnight hiking trails, and small chalets that can accommodate from two to 17 people and cost around $55 per day. Larger chalets for two people cost around $95. In the summer canoeists can ply the waters of the Rivière Métabetchouane and the Rivière Écorces.

Throughout the year, hordes of visitors come to **Parc de la Jacques-Cartier ★★** *(Route 175 Nord, ☎848-3169)*, located in the Réserve Faunique des Laurentides, 40 kilometres north of Quebec. The area is called Vallée de la Jacques-Cartier, after the river of the same name that runs through it, winding between steep hills. Benefitting from the microclimate caused by the river being hemmed in on both sides, the site is suitable for a number of outdoor activities. The vegetation and wildlife are abundant and diverse. The winding and well-laid-out paths sometimes lead to interesting surprises, like a moose and its offspring foraging for food in a marsh. Before heading out to discover all the riches the site has to offer, you can get information at the nature centre's reception area. Campsites (see p 387), chalets and equipment are all available to rent (see Outdoor Activities).

At the park, specialists organize **Safaris d'Observation de l'Orignal**, moose observation safaris, from mid-September to mid-October as well as **Écoute des Appels Nocturnes des Loups**, nocturnal wolf call-listening sessions *(☎/~848-5099)* at night (7:30pm to midnight) from the beginning of July until mid-October, in order to familiarize people with these animals. Reservations are required for these educational excursions, which usually last three hours; it costs $15 for adults; each of these activities lasts at least three hours and requires that you walk through the forest. Reservations necessary.

Forty-five kilometres from Quebec, on the biggest lake in the region, Lac Saint-Joseph, the **Station Forestière de Duchesnay** *(Ste-Catherine-de-la-Jacques-Cartier, G0A 3M0, ☎875-2122 or 1-800-501-2122)* provides the opportunity to familiarize yourself with the Laurentian Forest. Located on 90 square kilometres of land managed by the Quebec Ministry of Natural Resources, this centre for research on forest flora and fauna is ideal for all sorts of outdoor activities. Long renown for it's cross-country ski trails, it also has hiking trails and a portion of the Jacques-Cartier – Portneuf bicycle path (see p 383). There's also a nature centre that offers activities to promote education and sensitivity.

The **Parc de la Chute et de la Falaise Kabir Kouba** (falls and cliff park) is in the Wendake native village. A few small trails go along the edge of the 40-metre-cliff, at the bottom of which flows the Rivière Saint-Charles.

 OUTDOOR ACTIVITIES

 Cycling

Located in the Vieux-Port de Québec, **Cyclo-Services-Voyages** *(Vieux-Port hangar, beside the Agora, or 1609 Boulevard de l'Entente, G1S 2V3, ☎692-4052)* is a company that offers a series of cycling excusions around the city. They also offer bike rental *($6 per hour)*.

Tour A: Côte de Beaupré

A bicycle path runs from the Vieux-Port of Québec City to Parc de la Chute Montmorency, passing through Beauport on the way. Also, roads such as Chemin du Roy, on the Côte de Beaupré and Île d'Orléans *(bike rental at the Le Vieux-Presbytère guesthouse, see p 386)*, are meant to be shared between motorists and cyclists. Caution is always in order, but these trips are definitely worth the effort.

Tour D: Jacques-Cartier

In 1997, a brand new bicycle path was inaugurated in the Quebec region. Following

---

the route of old railway lines, the **Piste Jacques-Cartier - Portneuf** *(100 Rue St-Jacques, C.P. 238, St-Raymond, G0A 4G0, ☎337-7525, ₌337-8017)* crosses through the Réserve Faunique Portneuf and the Station Forestière Duchesnay (where you can park your car and rent bicycles, see p 386), and borders certain lakes in the area. Including the most recent additions, it is 63 kilometres in length, stretching from Rivière-à-Pierre to Shanon. Its magical setting and safe passage have already attracted many cyclists. In winter, the path is used for snowmobiling.

In **Parc de la Jacques-Cartier** *(free admission; Route 175 Nord, ☎848-3169)* (see p 382), the trails are for both hikers and mountain-biking enthusiasts. Bike rental is available.

Hiking

Tour A: Côte-de-Beaupré

At **Cap Tourmente** *(St-Joachim-de-Montmorency, G0A 3X0, ☎827-4591 or 827-3776)* (see p 381), if your legs allow for it, you can take one of the trails up the cape where you'll get a magnificent view of the river and surrounding countryside. You can also take an equally enjoyable stroll on wooden walkways alone the shore that are adapted for mobility-impaired people.

Tour B: Île d'Orleans

Île d'Orléans is more conducive to cycling than hiking but there are still some trekking opportunities such as on the forest trails of the **Sentiers de l'Isle aux Sorciers** *(1870 Chemin Royal, St-Laurent, ☎828-2163, ₌692-2528)*. You can also go trout fishing.

Tour D: Jacques-Cartier

The trails in **Parc de la Jacques-Cartier** *(free admission; Route 175 N., ☎848-3169)* (see p 382) are favoured by locals. Whether leisurely or steep, the trails lead you to lovely little spots in the forest and reveal magnificent views of the valley and its river.

The **Réserve Faunique de Portneuf** (see p 381), the **Station Forestière Duchesnay** *(Route 360, Beaupré, ☎827-4579 or 827-4561)*, and the **Station Touristique Stoneham**

(1420 Av. du Hibou, Stoneham, G0A 4P0, ☎848-2144) all offer many, very pleasant hiking trails.

Bird-Watching

Tour A: Côte-de-Beaupré

One of the best places for bird-watching in the region is definitely the **Cap Tourmente National Wildlife Area** *(St-Joachim-de-Montmorency, G0A 3X0, ☎827-4591 or 827-3776)* (see p 381). During spring and autumn, the thousands of migrating snow geese that overtake the area are a fascinating sight to behold. Any questions you might have after seeing these creatures up close and in such great numbers can be answered here. The reserve is also home to many other avian species. They are drawn here throughout the year by a number of bird houses and feeders.

Canoeing

Tour D: Jacques-Cartier

You can canoe on the rivers and lakes of the **Réserve Faunique de Portneuf** (see p 381) and down the river at **Parc de la Jacques-Cartier** *(rental $35 per day; Route 175 Nord, ☎848-3169)* (see p 382). Both have canoes for rent and Parc de la Jacques-Cartier also rents river kayaks.

Rafting

Tour D: Jacques-Cartier

In spring and early summer the Rivière Jacques-Cartier has been giving adventurers a good run for their money. Two longstanding companies offer well-supervised rafting expeditions with all the necessary equipment. At **Nouveau Monde Québec** *(three hours $45, per day with breakfast $69; 1440 Chemin du Hibou, C.P. 455, Stoneham, ☎848-4144 or 1-800-267-4144)*, they promise lots of excitement. With **Excursions Jacques-Cartier** *(½ day $45, isothermal suit $16; 978 Av. Jacques-Cartier, Tewkesbury, ☎848-7238, ₌848-5687)*, you can also experience some very exciting runs. Rafting excursions are also offered on the Rivière Batiscan in the **Réserve Faunique de Portneuf** (see p 381).

 Hunting and Fishing

In the Québec City area, you can hunt and fish at **Cap Tourmente** *(☎827-3776)*, the **Réserve Faunique de Portneuf** *(☎323-2021)* and **Parc des Laurentides** *(☎848-2422)* among other places.

 Golf

Tour A: Côte-de-Beaupré

There are two 18-hole courses at the **Mont-Sainte-Anne** *(C.P. 653, Beaupré, GOA 1E0, ☎827-3778, ☎826-0162)* at the foot of the mountain: the Beaupré *($32)* and the Saint-Ferréol *($28)*.

 Tobogganing and Waterslides

Tour D: Jacques-Cartier

You can zip down the hill in winter on an inner-tube at **Club Mont-Tourbillon** *(55 Montée du Golf, Lac-Beauport, ☎849-4418)*. They also offer all sorts of other activities including cross-country skiing. They have a restaurant and a bar.

Winter or summer, the **Village des Sports** *($20; early Jun to late Aug, every day 10am to 7pm; mid-Dec to late Mar, 10am to 10pm; 1860 Bd. Valcartier, St-Gabriel-de-Valcartier, ☎844-3725; take Route 371 N. from Quebec City)* is the undisputed authority when it comes to slides. It's an outdoor-activity centre that offers all the facilities. In the summer, water slides and a wave pool draw huge crowds. In winter, ice slides will help you forget the cold for a little while. There's also snow rafting and skating on a 2.5-kilometre-long ice rink that snakes through the woods. There is a restaurant and a bar.

 Cross-Country Skiing

Tour A: Côte-de-Beaupré

Station Mont-Sainte-Anne *($11.30; Mon to Fri 9am to 4pm, Sat and Sun 8:30am to 4pm; Route 360, C.P. 400, Beaupré, GOA 1E0, ☎827-4561)* has 250 kilometres of well-maintained cross-country ski trails with some heated huts set up along the way. They rent ski equipment *($15 per day)*.

Tour D: Jacques-Cartier

Nestled in the heart of the Réserve Faunique des Laurentides, **Camp Mercier** *($8.50; mid-Nov to late Apr, every day 8:30am to 4pm; Route 175, Réserve Faunique des Laurentides, ☎890-6527 or 1-800-665-6527)* is criss-crossed with 192 kilometres of well-maintained trails in an extremely calm landscape. Given its ideal location, you can ski here from fall to spring. Long routes (up to 68 kilometres) with heated huts offer some interesting opportunities. There are also cottages for rent that can accommodate from two to 14 people *($92 for 2 people)*.

In winter, **Station Forestière Duchesnay** *($4; Ste-Catherine-de-la-Jacques-Cartier, GOA 3M0, ☎875-2147)* is very popular among skiers in the area. There are 125 kilometres of well-maintained trails in this vast forest.

 Downhill Skiing

Tour A: Côte-de-Beaupré

Station Mont-Sainte-Anne *($37.38 per day; Mon 9am to 4pm, Tue to Fri 9am to 10pm, Sat 8:30am to 10pm, Sun 8:30pm to 4pm; Route 360, C.P. 400, Beaupré, GOA 1E0, ☎827-4561, ☎827-3121, www.mont.sainte.anne.com)* is one of the biggest ski resorts in Québec. Among the 51 runs, some reach 625 metres in height and 14 are lit for night skiing. It's also a delight for snowboarders. Instead of buying a regular ticket, you can buy a pass worth a certain number of points, valid for two years, and each time you take the lift, points are deducted. Equipment rentals are also available *(skiing $21 per day, snowboarding $33 per day)*.

Le Relais *($25 per day, 1084 Boulevard du Lac, ☎849-1851)* has 24 downhill skiing trails, all of which are lit for night skiing.

The **Station Touristique Stoneham** *($36; Stoneham, ☎848-2411)* welcomes visitors year-round. In the winter there are 25 runs, 16 of which are lighted. For cross-country skiers there are 30 kilometres of maintained trails, which in the summer are at the disposal of hikers, mountain-bikers and horseback riders.

 Dogsledding

La Banquise des Chukchis *(10 km route $40; 228 Rang St-Georges, St-Basile, G0A 3G0, ☎329-3055)* is a company that offers various day or evening dogsledding packages where you lead the team yourself; one of the packages includes dinner. Friendly atmosphere.

The **Domaine de la Truite du Parc** *(½ day $69; 7600 Boulevard Talbot, Stoneham, ☎848-3732, ⇒848-3732)*, is an outfitter that gives you the chance to drive your own dogsled team. In the summer you can fish for trout.

ACCOMMODATIONS

Tour A: The Côte de Beaupré

Beauport

The **Hôtel Ambassadeur** *($ 75; ℜ; 321 Sainte-Anne, G1E 3L4, ☎666-2828 or 1-800-363-4619, ⇒666-2775)* is on the outskirts of town, away from the sights. The rooms are large and pleasant, and there is a Chinese restaurant on the main floor.

Château-Richer

 For over 50 years, **Auberge Baker** *($59 sb, $85 pb; bkfst incl., ℜ, K; 8790 Avenue Royale, G0A 1N0, ☎666-5509, ⇒824-4412)* has existed in this hundred-year-old Côte-de-Beaupré house. Its stone walls, low ceilings, wood floors and wide-frame windows enchant visitors. The five bedrooms are on the dimly-lit upper floor but there's also a kitchenette, a

bathroom and an adjoining terrace on the same floor. The rooms are meticulously decorated in authentic fashion and furnished with antiques. They serve delicious food (see p 387).

 At the **Auberge du Petit Pré** *($60 bkfst incl.; sb; 7126 Avenue Royale, G0A 1N0, ☎824-3852, ⇒824-3098)*, in an 18th-century house, you will receive be treated well. Their four bedrooms are cosy and tastefully decorated. There's a large picture window which is open when the weather is nice, two lounges, one with a T.V. and the other with a fireplace, as well as two bathrooms with clawfoot tubs. Breakfasts are generous and finely prepared. Also, if requested in advance, the owner will prepare one of his delicious dinners for you. The splendid aroma of the food fills the house and adds to its overall warmth.

Beaupré (Mont Sainte-Anne)

Camping Mont-Sainte-Anne *($18; C.P. 400, Beaupré, G0A 1E0, ☎827-4561 or 826-2323)*, located at Station Mont-Sainte-Anne, has 166 campsites in a wooded area traversed by the Rivière Jean-Larose. Essential services are offered, and, because the campground is close to all the park's outdoor activities, the location is great.

The **Château Mont Sainte-Anne** *($109, $167 ½b; ≈, ☉, △, ℜ, K, ♿; 500 Boulevard Beau-Pré, G0A 1E0, ☎827-5211 or 1-800-463-4467, ⇒827-5072)* is located at the base of the ski-hill; you can not get any closer than this! The rooms are spacious, but the unattractive and out-of-date furniture, makes them seem austere. Each room has a kitchenette, and there is a $ 10 charge to use it. There is also a fitness centre.

Many chalets have recently been built around the base of the Mont Sainte-Anne, in newly developed areas. Among these is the **Hôtel Val des Neiges** *($95, $160 ½b; ≈, ☉, △, ℜ, ♿; 201 Val des Neiges, G0A 1E0, ☎827-5711 or 1-800-463-5250, ⇒827-5997)*. The decor is rustic and the rooms are comfortable. The complex also includes small, well-equipped condos. They also offer cruise packages.

 La Camarine *($98, $240 ½b; ≈, ℜ; 10947 Sainte-Anne, G0A 1E0, ☎827-5703, ⇒827-5430)* faces the Saint-Lawrence River. This charming high-quality inn has thirty rooms. The decor successfully combines the rustic feel

---

Ulysses' Favourites

Accommodations

For a warm reception:
Auberge Chemin du Roy (p 386), Auberge du Petit Pré (p 385)

Restaurants

The Area around Québec City's finest tables:
La Camarine (p 387), La Fenouillère (p 388) and Michelangelo (p 388)

For the views:
Manoir Montmorency (p 387)

For Québec cuisine:
L'Âtre (p 388) and Auberge Baker (p 387)

---

of the house with the more modern wooden furniture. This is a delightful spot.

Tour B: Île d'Orléans

On île d'Orléans, there are about 50 bed and breakfasts! A list can be obtained from the tourist office. There are also a few guesthouses with solid reputations and a campground. There are plenty of options therefore for getting the most out of your stay on this enchanting island.

Camping Orléans *($18; ≈; 357 Chemin Royal, St-François, GOA 3SO, ☎829-2953, ≈829-2563)* has close to 80 campsites, most of which are shaded and offer a view of the river. Many services are offered. There is access to the river bank where you can go for a pleasant walk.

Le Vieux-Presbytère guesthouse *($60 bkfst incl., $118 ½b; pb, sb, ℜ; 1247 Avenue Monseigneur-d'Esgly, St-Pierre, GOA 4EO, ☎828-9723 or 1-888-282-9723, ≈828-2189)* is in fact located in an old presbytery just behind the village church. The structure is predominantly made out of wood and stone. Low ceilings with wide beams, wide-frame windows and antiques such as woven bedcovers and braided rugs take you back to the era of New France. The dining room and the lounge are inviting. It's a tranquil spot with rustic charm.

Le Canard Huppée *($125 bkfst incl., $175 ½b; ℜ; 2198 Chemin Royal, St-Laurent, GOA 3ZO, ☎828-2292 or 1-800-838-2292, ≈828-0966)* has enjoyed a very good reputation over the last few years. Their eight clean, comfortable, country-style rooms are scattered with wooden ducks. The restaurant is also just as renowned and appealing (see p 388). The service is conscientious, and the surrounding, beautiful.

The **Auberge Chaumonot** *($128 bkfst incl., $178 ½B; ≈, ℜ; 425 Chemin Royal, Saint-François, GOA 3SO, ☎829-2735)* is an inn on the south shore of the island, right near the riverbank, with eight rooms. Its receives guests only in the summer. It is located far from the town and the road in a quiet country setting. The rooms, with a rustic decor, are comfortable.

Tour C: The Chemin du Roy

Deschambault

The old Victorian house of the **Auberge Chemin du Roy** *($79 bkfst incl., $119 ½b; ℜ; 106 Rue St-Laurent, GOA 1SO, ☎286-6958)* is on a beautiful piece of land with waterfalls and gardens where good vegetables and lots of flowers grow. There are eight rooms, decorated with lace and antiques, along a narrow winding hallway; the kind of corridor often found in this type of old house. In the warmly decorated dining room, they serve wonderful varied meals. The owners take great care of the property, the house and the guests, right down to the tiniest details.

 The **Maison Deschambault** *($95 bkfst incl., $165 ½b; ℜ; 128 Chemin du Roy, GOA 1SO, ☎286-3386, ⊷286-4064)* offers five luxurious rooms, decorated with flowered patterns and pastel colours. There's also a small bar, a dining room that serves fine cuisine (see p 389), a conference room, and a massage service all in an enchanting old manor house (see p 378). Relaxing in this peaceful setting is no trouble at all.

Tour D: The Rivière Jacques-Cartier

Right in the heart of **Parc de la Jacques-Cartier** *($17.50; Centre d'Accueil et d'Interpretation, Stoneham, GOA 4P0, ☎848-7272)* you can camp in magnificent surroundings. Along the river, there are numerous campsites, some rustic, others with some facilities. And of course there's no lack of things to do!

Wendake

At Wendake, there is a bed and breakfast at the **Maison Aorhenché** *($65-$75 bkfst incl.; pb, sb, K; 90 Rue François-Gros-Louis, GOA 4V0, ☎847-0646, ⊷847-5123)*. A tipi is set up in front of the house where, if you're interested, you can spend the night. The three bedrooms inside, the Tortue (Tortoise), the Ours (Bear) and the Loup (Wolf) are somewhat sparse, and definitely a bit overpriced. Nonetheless, it's a pleasant spot and the hosts are accommodating. Visitors have access to an attractive gallery at the front of the house, a small lounge and all sorts of activities to help you discover native culture.

✗ RESTAURANTS

Tour A: The Côte de Beaupré

Beauport

 The **Manoir Montmorency** *($$$-$$$$; 2490 Avenue Royale, ☎663-3330)* (see p 368) benefits from a superb location above the Montmorency Falls. From the dining room surrounded by bay windows, there's an absolutely magnificent view of the falls, the river and Île d'Orléans. Fine French cuisine, prepared with the best products in the region, is served in pleasant surroundings. A wonderful experience for the view and the food! The entrance fee to the Parc de la Chute Montmorency (where the restaurant is located) and the parking fees are waived upon presentation of your receipt or by mentioning your reservation.

Château-Richer

The **Auberge Baker** *($$-$$$; 8790 Avenue Royale, ☎824-4852 or 824-4478)* (see p 385) has two dining rooms. One has stone walls and a fireplace, whereas the other's decor is somewhat cold. They serve fine traditional Quebec cuisine: game, meat and fowl are well prepared and presented with care.

Sainte-Anne-de-Beaupré

Le **Bistro Ste-Anne** *($$; Promenades Ste-Anne, Route 138, ☎827-5759)*, unfortunately located in a shopping mall, nonetheless serves good Californian food. The pleasant decor and large windows help you forget its location. You can choose among a variety of original snacks, such as *guacamole* with melted brie, salads, pizza and pastas, or you can sample one of their appetizing meal specials.

Beaupré (Mont Sainte-Anne)

 The **La Camarine** Inn *($$$$; 10947 Sainte-Anne, ☎827-5703)* also houses an excellent restaurant which serves Quebecois nouvelle cuisine. The dining room is peaceful, with a simple decor. The innovative dishes are a feast for the senses. In the basement of the inn is another small restaurant, the **Bistro**, which offers the same menu and prices as upstairs; but it is only open in the winter. Equipped with a fireplace, it is a cozy spot for après-ski. It is open in the evening for drinks.

Tour B: Île d'Orléans

In the heat of the summer, the **Petit Baluchon** *($; summer; 1222 Chemin Royal, St-Pierre, ☎828-0122)* offers a decent alternative to restaurants. This self-proclaimed "picnic specialist" offers good food to complement your lunch box.

The dining room at **La Goéliche** *($$$; 22 Chemin du Quai, Ste-Pétronille, ☎828-2248)* is a little small. It's still pleasant though, and you can still get one of the most beautiful views of Quebec City. They serve fine French cuisine: stuffed quail, nuggets of lamb and saddle of hare.

The **Canard Huppé**'s dining room *($$$-$$$$; 2198 Chemin Royal, St-Laurent, ☎828-2292)* serves fine French-inspired cuisine. Prepared with fresh ingredients that abound in the area: island specialties such as duck, trout and maple products, these little dishes will delight the most demanding of palates. Although the room is somewhat dark with forest green being the predominant colour, the country decor is, on the whole, pleasant.

At the **Manoir Mauvide-Genest** *($$$-$$$$; May to Oct; 1451 Chemin Royal, St-Jean, ☎829-2630)*, which also serves as a museum, you'll get a taste of both history and gourmet cuisine. The small dining room, with its stone walls and antique furniture, is altogether charming, making it a pleasure to linger. However, since the restaurant is only open during the summer, it is subject to a regular turnover of chefs which leads to variations in the quality of the food from year to year. At the back there's a lovely café-terrace.

Located in a 17th-century house **L'Âtre** *($$$$; 4403 Chemin Royal, ☎829-2474)* provides a unique atmosphere. The employees, all dressed in period clothing, and the charming old-fashioned decor will make you think you have been transported back in time. The rather pricey menu consists of good traditional Quebecois cuisine.

Tour C: The Chemin du Roy

Sillery

Byrnd *($; 1360 Rue Maguire, ☎527-3844)* is the place to go to for smoked meat and has a variety for all tastes and appetites. There are also items on the menu for those, and too bad for them, who don't want to try the house specialty. The meat is smoked and sliced in front of your eyes, just like at a real delicatessen!

Paparazzi *($$-$$$; 1365 Avenue Maguire, ☎683-8111)* serves Italian dishes. The salad with warm goat-cheese, spinach and caramelized walnuts is a true delight, as are other menu items. The decor is modern and pleasant with pretty tables covered in ceramic tiles set up on various levels.

In Sillery, the restaurant-club **Montego** *($$$-$$$$; 1460 Avenue Maguire, ☎688-7991)* promises a "sunny experience". The warmly decorated interior, the large colourful plates and the food presentation are a pleasure to behold. And the cooking will delight your tastebuds with sweet, hot and spicy flavours inspired by cuisine from California and from other sunny places!

Sainte-Foy

Mille-Feuilles *($$; 1405 Chemin Ste-Foy, ☎681-4520)* is a vegetarian restaurant. They offer good little dishes that are both healthy and delicious, and carefully prepared. Located on a section of Chemin Ste-Foy that has a few shops and restaurants, the decor is a bit cool, but the ambiance is relaxed. They have a little bookstore that sells health books.

At **La Fenouillère** *($$$-$$$$; 3100 Chemin St-Louis, ☎653-3886)* the menu of refined and creative French cuisine promises a succulent dining experience. This restaurant is also proud to possess one of the best wine cellars in Quebec. The decor is simple and comfortable.

The **Michelangelo** *($$$-$$$$; 3111 Chemin Saint-Louis, ☎651-6262)* serves fine Italian cuisine that both smells and tastes wonderful. The classically decorated dining-room, although busy, remains warm and intimate. The courteous and attentive service adds to the pleasure of the food.

Deschambault

Just in front of the village church is the **Bistro Clan Destin** *($-$$; 109 Rue de l'Eglise, ☎286-6617)* with its lovely flowered decor. The menu is varied, and they serve good daily specials.

The restaurant in the **Maison Descham-bault Inn** *($$$-$$$$; 128 Route 138, ☎286-3386, ⊶286-4711)* is well-known for its excellent menu, which consists mainly of fine French cuisine as well as various specialties of the region. The setting is particularly enchanting (see p 378).

Tour D: The Rivière Jacques-Cartier

Wendake

At the Huron village (see p 381), there's a pleasant restaurant whose name means "the meal is ready to serve". **Nek8arre** *($$; Mon to Fri 9am to 5pm; 575 Rue Stanislas-Kosca, ☎842-4308, ⊶842-3473)* introduces you to traditional Huron cooking. Wonderful dishes such as clay trout, caribou or venison *brochettes* with mushrooms accompanied by wild rice and corn, are some of the items on the menu. The wood tables have little texts explaining the eating habits of native cultures embedded in them. Numerous objects scattered here and there will arouse your curiosity, and luckily, the waitresses act as part-time "ethnologists" and can answer your questions. All this in a pleasant atmosphere. The entry fee to the village will be waived if you're only going to restaurant.

ENTERTAINMENT

Theatres

There are many good summer theatres in the area to liven up the beautiful evenings. Here are a few companies to look out for (consult local newspapers for listings). **Théâtre de la Fenière** *(1500 Rue de la Fenière, Ancienne-Lorette, ☎872-1424)*, **Théâtre d'Été de l'île d'Orléans** *(342 Avenue du Galendart, St-Pierre, Île d'Orléans, ☎828-0937)*, **Théâtre d'Été de Stoneham** *(1420 Avenue du Hibou, Stoneham, ☎848-2411)*.

The **Moulin Marcoux** *(1 Boulevard Notre-Dame, Pont-Rouge, ☎873-2027)* presents various shows and exhibitions.

The **Salle Albert-Rousseau** in the Sainte-Foy cegep *(2410 Chemin Ste-Foy, Ste-Foy, ☎659-6710)* presents excellent plays and shows throughout the year.

Festivals and Cultural Events

Beauport

Throughout the summer, on Wednesday and Saturday nights, the Parc de la Chute Montmorency comes to life with the **Grands Feux Loto-Québec** *(☎523-3389 or 1-800-923-3389)*. This magical fireworks display takes place over the falls. Fleets of small boats gather on the river to admire the show.

SHOPPING

Tour B: Île d'Orléans

Île d'Orléans has a handful of craft shops, antique dealers and cabinet-making studios. One of these, the **Corporation des Artisans de l'île** *(☎828-2519)*, is located in the Saint-Pierre church. There are about half a dozen art galleries on the island too, many in the village of Saint-Jean.

The shop of the **Forge à Pique-Assaut** *(2200 Chemin Royal, St-Laurent, ☎828-9300)* (see p 373) sells various forged-metal objects, from candlesticks and knick-knacks to furniture. They also sell other crafts.

The **Chocolaterie de l'Île d'Orléans** *(196 Chemin Royal, Ste-Pétronille, ☎828-2252)* offers a whole range of little delectable treats. Their home-made ice-cream is also delicious.

AROUND QUÉBEC CITY

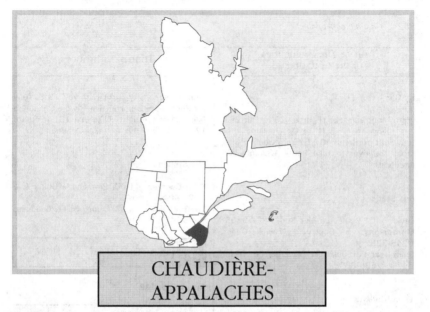

CHAUDIÈRE-APPALACHES

T he Chaudière-Appalaches region is made up of several small areas with very distinct geographical features. Located opposite Québec City, on the south shore of the St-Lawrence, it stretches across a vast fertile plain before slowly climbing into the foothills of the Appalachian Mountains, all the way to the American border. The Rivière Chaudière, which originates in Lac Mégantic, runs through the centre of this region, then flows into the St-Lawrence across from Québec City.

A pretty pastoral landscape unfolds along the river between Leclercville and Saint-Roch-des-Aulnaies, an area occupied very early on by the French. There are attractive villages, including Saint-Jean-Port-Joli, an important provincial crafts centre. Out in the gulf adventure awaits in the Archipel de l'Île-aux-Grues.

Further south, the picturesque Beauce region extends along the banks of the Rivière Chaudière. The river rises dramatically in the spring, flooding some of the villages along its banks almost every year, providing muddied local inhabitants with the nickname "*jarrets noirs*", which translates somewhat inelegantly as "black hamstrings". The discovery of gold nuggets in the river bed attracted prospectors to the area in the middle of the last century. Farms have prospered in the rolling green hills of the Beauce for hundreds of years. Church steeples announce the presence of little villages, scattered evenly across the local countryside. The Beauce region is also home to Québec's largest concentration of maple groves, making it the true realm of the *cabane à sucre*, sugar shack. The spring thaw gets the flowing and signals the sugaring-off season. Local inhabitants, called Beaucerons, are also known for their sense of tradition and hospitality.

The asbestos region, located a little further west of the Rivière Chaudière, around Thetford Mines, has a fairly varied landscape, punctuated with impressive open-cut-mines.

 FINDING YOUR WAY AROUND

Two tours have been laid out for the Chaudière-Appalaches region: **Tour A: The Seigneuries of the Côte-du-Sud ★★**, which runs along the St. Lawrence from Leclercville to Saint-Roch-des-Aulnaies, and **Tour B: The Beauce ★**, which will lead visitors through the valley of the Rivière Chaudière and the asbestos region.

Tour A: The Seigneuries of the Côte-du-Sud

By Car

From Montréal, take Highway 20 to Exit 253, and follow the 265 N. to Deschaillons, then turn right on Route 132 E. From Québec City, cross the river to take Route 132 in either direction.

Bus Stations

Lévis: 5401 Boulevard Rive-Sud, ☎837-5805
Montmagny: 5 Boulevard Taché Ouest, ☎248-3292
Saint-Jean-Port-Joli: 27 Avenue de Gaspé Ouest, ☎598-6808

Train Stations

Lévis: 5995 Rue St-Laurent, ☎833-8056
Montmagny: 4 Rue de la Station, ☎248-7875

By Ferry

The ferry between Québec City and Lévis *($1.75; car $3, ☎644-3704)* takes only 15 minutes. The schedule is subject to change, but there are frequent crossings.

The ferry to Île aux Grues, the **Grue des Îles** *(free; ☎248-3549)*, leaves from the Montmagny dock and takes about 20 minutes. The schedule varies with the tide.

The following companies also ferry people to Île aux Grues or to Grosse Île. The boats of **Taxi des Îles** *($15 round-trip to Île aux Grues; 124 Rue Saint-Louis, Montmagny, G5V 1M8, ☎ 248-2818)* are recognizable by their yellow and black colour scheme and frequently travel to the islands from the Montmagny dock. **Croisières Lachance** *($16 round-trip to Île aux Grues; 110 de la Marina, Berthier-sur-Mer, G0R 1EO, ☎ 259-2140 or 1-888-476-7734)*, has two boats, one of them a pleasure steamer, and offers ferry service and cruises between Montmagny or Berthier-sur-Mer and the islands.

Tour B: La Beauce

From Québec City, take Highway 73 S. (use the Pont Pierre Laporte). The Rivière Chaudière falls are on the right. Take Exit 101 to Route 173 and follow this to Vallée-Jonction.

Bus Stations

Saint-Georges: 11655 Promenade Chaudière, ☎228-4040.
Thetford Mines: 127 Rue Saint-Alphonse, ☎335-5120.

 PRACTICAL INFORMATION

Area Code: 418

Tourist Information Offices

Regional Office

Association Touristique Chaudière-Appalaches 800 Autoroute Jean-Lesage, St-Nicolas, G7A 1C9, ☎831-4411, ≈831-8442, www.chaudapp.qc.ca

Tour A: The Seigneuries of the Côte-du-Sud

Lévis: 7 Mgr Gosselin, ☎838-4126.
Montmagny: 45 Avenue du Quai, C.P. 71 G5V 3S3, ☎248-9196 or 1-800-463-5643, ≈248-1436.
Saint-Jean-Port-Joli: 7 Place de l'Église, G0R 3G0, ☎598-3747, ≈598-3085.

Tour B: La Beauce

Saint-Georges: 11700 Boulevard Lacroix, G5Y 1L3, ☎227-4642, ≈228-2255.
Thetford Mines: 682 Rue Monfette Nord, G6G 7G9, ☎335-7141, ≈338-4984.

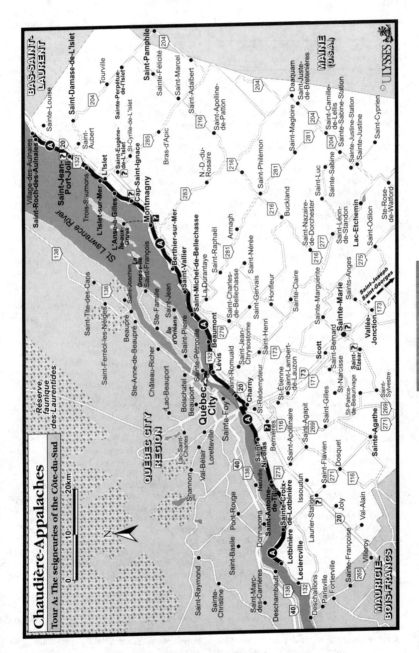

Chaudière-Appalaches
Tour A: The seigneuries of the Côte-du-Sud

© ULYSSES

EXPLORING

Tour A: The Seigneuries of the Côte-du-Sud ★★ (two days)

This tour is dotted with charming villages at regular intervals along the majestic St-Lawrence. It encompasses both the Rive-Sud of Québec City and the Côte-du-Sud (the southern shore and coast), gradually taking on a maritime flavour as the river widens. In many places, visitors will enjoy stunning views of this vast stretch of water as its colour varies with the time of day and temperature, as well as Île d'Orléans and the mountains of Charlevoix. The tour also features a few of the loveliest examples of traditional architecture in Québec, including churches, seigneurial manors, mills, or old houses, whose windows open onto vast open spaces. It is perhaps this region that best represents rural Québec.

Lotbinière ★ (pop. 1,040)

Granted to René-Louis Chartier de Lotbinière in 1672, the seigneury of Lotbinière is one of the few estates to have always remained in the hands of the same family. Because he had a seat on the Conseil Souverain, the sovereign council, the first seigneur did not actually live on the premises; but he did see to it that the land and the village of Lotbinière were developed. At the heart of Lotbinière, which quickly became one of the most important villages in the region, visitors will find a number of old houses made of stone and wood. This area is now protected by the provincial government.

Turn right on Route du Vieux-Moulin in order to see the Moulin du Portage.

Moulin du Portage ★ *(Rang Saint-François).* This flour mill, built in 1815 for Michel-Eustache-Gaspard-Alain Chartier de Lotbinière, lies in a pastoral setting on the banks of the Rivière du Chêne. Visitors can enjoy a pleasant walk or a picnic in the park surrounding the mill.

Along with its presbytery and former convent, the monumental **Église Saint-Louis ★★** *(7510 Rue Marie-Victorin)*, set parallel to the St-Lawrence, provides a lovely setting in which to enjoy a view of the river. The present

building is the fourth Catholic church to be built in the seigneury of Lotbinière. Designed by François Baillargé, it was begun in 1818. The spires, as well as the crown of the façade, are the result of modifications made in 1888. Its polychromatic exterior—white walls, blue steeples and red roof—creates a surprising (and very French) tricolour effect.

The decor of the church is a masterpiece of traditional religious art in Québec. Without question, the key piece is the neoclassical reredos shaped like a triumphal arch, sculpted by Thomas Baillargé in 1824. In the middle of it hang three paintings dating back to 1730, which are attributed to Frère François Brékenmacher, a Récollet monk from the Montréal monastery. The organ in the jube, originally intended for the Anglican cathedral in Québec City, was built in London by the Elliott Company in 1802. Too high for the Anglican church, it was put into storage before being acquired by Père Faucher, the parish priest, in 1846. A century later, it was restored and equipped for electric power by the Casavant Company of Saint-Hyacinthe.

Before reaching the village of Sainte-Croix, turn left on Route de la Pointe-Platon to the Domaine Joly de Lotbinière.

Sainte-Croix (pop. 1,719)

The Chartier de Lotbinière lineage dates back to the 11th century. In the service of French kings for many generations, the family preserved its contacts with the motherland once established in Canada, despite the British Conquest and the distance between the two lands. In 1828, Julie-Christine Chartier de Lotbinière married Pierre-Gustave Joly, a rich Huguenot merchant from Montréal. In 1840, Joly purchased a part of the Sainte-Croix land from the Québec City Ursulines in order to build a seigneurial manor there, which would be known as the Manoir de la Pointe Platon, or the Domaine Joly de Lotbinière.

Domaine Joly de Lotbinière ★★ *($4.50; late Jun to Sep, every day 10am to 6pm; mid-May to late Jun and Sep to mid-Oct on weekends; Route de la Pointe-Platon, ☎926-2462)* is part of the Jardins de Québec association. The main attraction here is the superb setting on the banks of the St-Lawrence. It is especially worthwhile to take the footpaths to the beach in order to gaze out at the river, the slate cliffs and the opposite shore, where the Église de

Domaine Joly de Lotbinière

CHAUDIÈRE-
APPALACHES

Cap Santé is visible. Numerous rare century-old trees, floral arrangements and bird gardens adorn the grounds of the estate. There is also a boutique and café with a patio. The manor, which was built in 1840 to overlook the river, is designed as a villa with wraparound verandas. Though the interior is disappointing, it does include a small exhibition on the family of the Marquis de Lotbinière. Visitors will learn, for example, that the son of Pierre-Gustave Joly, Henri-Gustave, was born in Épernay (France), and later became Premier of Québec (1878-79), federal Revenue Minister and finally Lieutenant-Governor of British Columbia. The Domaine Joly de Lotbinière came under the care of the provincial government in 1967, when the last seigneur, Edmond Joly de Lotbinière, had to vacate the premises.

Upon leaving the parking lot, turn left on the road leading to Route 132 E.

Église Sainte-Croix *(alongside Route 132 E.).* The Université Laval's agronomical centre is the economic mainspring for the village of Sainte-Croix. The village is dominated by its granite Baroque Revival church, built in 1911. The church has a coffered ceiling that is typical of the Belle Époque.

Continue along Route 132 E. Turn left on Chemin de Tilly, which leads to the centre of Saint-Antoine-de-Tilly.

Saint-Antoine-de-Tilly ★ (pop. 1,410)

In 1702, Noël Legardeur de Tilly acquired the seigneury of Auteuil, which now bears his name. The hamlet has evolved into the peaceful village looking over the river that visitors will find today. Saint-Antoine-de-Tilly still has a few small ship-building companies.

The present façade of **Église Saint-Antoine ★** *(3870 Chemin de Tilly),* added in 1902, masks the building erected at the end of the 18th century. The interior, decorated by André Pâquet between 1837 and 1840, highlights several beautiful paintings purchased during sales after the French Revolution, including *La Sainte Famille* (The Holy Family), or *Intérieur de Nazareth* (Inside Nazareth), by Aubin Vouet, which once adorned the abbey church of Saint-Germain-des-Prés in Paris, and *La Visitation* (The Visitation), by A. Oudry. Other particularly noteworthy works include *Jésus au Milieu des Docteurs* (Jesus Surrounded by Doctors) by Samuel Massé and *Saint François d'Assise* (St. Francis of Assisi), by Frère Luc. A stroll through the neighbouring cemetery offers a lovely view of the St-Lawrence and the church in silhouette.

Manoir de Tilly *(3854 Chemin de Tilly)*. Four generations of the Tilly family lived in this manor, built at the end of the 18th century. The building, now an inn, has a low veranda with delicate wood trellises. A little further along lies the Manoir Dionne, with a veranda decorated with wrought iron. This was the residence of Henriette de Tilly, wife of merchant Charles François Dionne whose family owned a number of seigneuries on the Côte du Sud (southern coast).

Continue east on Chemin de Tilly, which leads back to Route 132 E.

Parc de la Chute de la Chaudière ★ *(Highway 73, Exit 130)*, see p 408.

*Continue along Route 132 E., through **Saint-Nicolas**, a former resort area. Follow the signs for Route 132 E. to **Saint-Romuald**, then Lévis. Drivers should pay particular attention near the Pont de Québec, where the interchanges are frequent.*

Turn left on Côte du Passage in order to reach Vieux-Lévis, best explored on foot. Turn left on Rue Desjardins, then left again on Rue William-Tremblay, which leads to the Terrasse de Lévis.

Lévis ★★ (pop. 42,635)

Founded by Henry Caldwell in 1826, Lévis developed rapidly during the second half of the 19th century, due to the introduction of the railroad (1854) and the establishment of several local shipyards, supplied with wood by sawmills owned by the Price and Hamilton families. Because there was no railway line on the north shore of the St-Lawrence at the time, some of Québec City's shipping activities were transfered to Lévis. Originally known as Ville d'Aubigny, Lévis was given its present name in 1861, in memory of Chevalier François de Lévis, who defeated the British in the Battle of Sainte-Foy in 1760. The upper part of the city, consisting mostly of administrative buildings, offers some interesting views of Vieux-Québec, located on the opposite side of the river, while the very narrow lower part welcomes the trains and the ferry linking Lévis to the provincial capital. Lévis merged with its neighbour, **Lauzon**, in 1990.

Built during the stock market crash of 1929, the **Terrasse de Lévis** ★★ *(Rue William-Tremblay)* offers spectacular views not only of downtown Lévis, but also of Québec City. Visitors will note, for example, Vieux-Québec's Place Royale, located alongside the river, and the Château Frontenac and Haute-Ville above. A few modern skyscrapers stand out in the background, the tallest being the Édifice Marie-Guyart, located on Québec City's Parliament Hill.

Turn right on Rue Carrier. The Maison Alphonse-Desjardins, former home of the founder of the Mouvement Desjardins credit union, stands at the corner of Rue Mont-Marie and Rue Guénette.

Maison Alphonse-Desjardins *(free admission; Mon to Fri 10am to noon and 1pm to 4:30pm, Sat and Sun noon to 5pm; 6 Rue du Mont-Marie, ☎835-2090)*. Alphonse Desjardins (1854-1920) was a stubborn man. Eager for the advancement of the French-Canadian people, he struggled for many years to promote the concept of the *caisse populaire* (credit union), a cooperative financial institution controlled by its members, and by all the small investors who hold accounts there. In the family kitchen of his house on Rue Mont-Marie, Desjardins and his wife Dorimène conceived the idea and set up the first *caisse populaire*. The Caisses Desjardins aroused suspicion at first, but eventually became an important economic lever. Today there are more than 1,200 across Québec, with more than 5 million members.

The Gothic Revival house where the Desjardins lived for nearly 40 years was built in 1882. It was beautifully restored on its 100th anniversary and converted into an information centre which focuses on Desjardins's career and achievements. Visitors can watch a video and see several restored rooms. The offices of the Société Historique Alphonse-Desjardins are located on the second floor.

Église Notre-Dame-de-la-Victoire ★ *(18 Rue Notre-Dame)*. In 1851, a parish priest named Joseph Déziel proposed building a large Catholic church to serve the flourishing town. Thomas Baillargé, the architect of so many churches in the Québec City area, drew up the plans. His buildings express a complete mastery of the neoclassical vocabulary of Québec where French and English styles converge. The interior, divided into three naves, has high columned galleries. On the grounds of the church, there is a plaque marking the exact

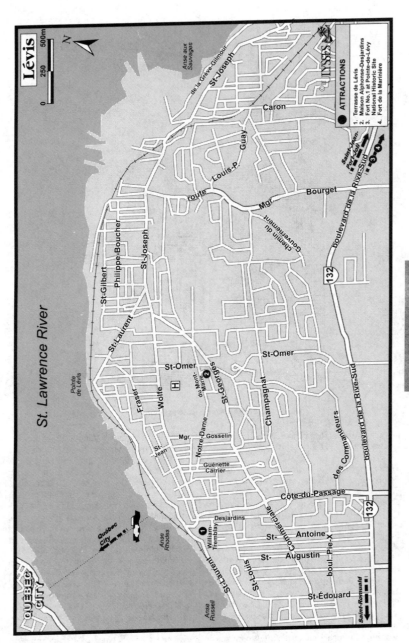

Maison Alphonse Desjardins

location of the English cannons that bombarded Québec City in 1759.

Those interested in visiting the Fort No.1 at Pointe de Lévy N.H.S. should take Route 132 E., then turn left on Chemin du Gouvernement. Otherwise, take Côte du Passage (away from the river) and turn left on Rue Saint-Georges, which becomes Rue Saint-Joseph in Vieux-Lauzon.

The **Fort No.1 at Pointe de Lévy National Historic Site ★** *($2.75; mid-May to mid-June, Sun to Fri 9am to 4pm; mid-Jun to late Aug, every day 10am to 5pm; early Sep to late Oct, Sun noon to 4pm; 41 Chemin du Gouvernement, ☎835-5182)* is also called the Lieu Historique National du Fort-Numéro-Un. Fearing a surprise attack from the Americans at the end of the Civil War, the British (and later

Canadian) government built three separate forts in Lévis, which were incorporated into Québec City's defence system. Only Fort No.1 remains intact. Made of earth and stone, it illustrates the evolution of fortified structures in the 19th century, when military techniques were advancing rapidly. Visitors will be particularly interested by the rifled bore, an imposing piece of ordnance, as well as the vaulted pillboxes and the caponiers, masonry structures intended to ditch the moat. The site also includes an exhibition on the history of the fort. Finally, from the top of the wall, visitors can enjoy a lovely view of Québec City and Île d'Orléans. A little farther along are the remnants of **Fort de la Martinière** *($2; May to Oct, every day 9am to 4pm; Nov to Apr, Mon to Fri 9am to 4pm; 9805 Bd. de la Rive-Sud, ☎833-6620)* which also offers an exhibition of various implements of war. The grounds have picnic areas.

Église Saint-Joseph-de-Lauzon ★ *(Rue Saint-Joseph)*. Lauzon was once the nucleus of the seigneury of the same name, granted to Jean de Lauzon, Governor of New France, in 1636. The parish of Saint-Joseph, founded in 1673, is the oldest on Québec City's entire Rive-Sud. At the time, it encompassed the territory now occupied by Lévis, Saint-Romuald and Saint-Nicolas. The original church, destroyed by a fire in 1830, was replaced soon after by the present one, yet another design by the Baillargé family. Particularly notable are the two procession chapels located on either side of the church, the **Chapelle Sainte-Anne** (1789) and the **Chapelle Saint-François-Xavier** (1822). The **MIL Davie shipyard** lies opposite the latter.

Rue Saint-Joseph leads back to Route 132 E. (also known as Boulevard de la Rive-Sud). Continue on to Beaumont. A road on the left leads to the centre of the village.

Beaumont ★ (pop. 2,030)

The Côte-du-Sud, does in fact correspond to the southern coast (*côte sud*) of the St-Lawrence estuary, and begins technically at Beaumont. With its silver-roofed churches, procession chapels for Corpus Christi and manors set in a landscape that seems larger than life, this is true French-Canadian country. The seigneury of Beaumont (1672) is a fine example of the regional heritage.

The beautiful little **Église Saint-Étienne** ★★ *(Chemin du Domaine)*, built in 1733, is one of the oldest churches still standing in Québec. It faces straight down the axis of the main road, which curves inland just afterwards, forming a small triangular plaza in front of the church square. This formation is typical of classical 18th century French town planning. In 1759, during the British Conquest, the British posted General Wolfe's proclamation decreeing the fall of New France on Beaumont's church. The villagers hastened to tear up the document. To punish them, General Moncton, who was responsible for the deportation of the Acadians in 1755, ordered his soldiers to set fire to the church. They held flaming torches to the door three times, with no success. According to legend, each attempt was thwarted when a mysterious hand "miraculously" extinguished the flames.

Take Chemin du Domaine going east, until it intersects with Route 132 E. The Moulin de Beaumont lies a little further on the left.

Moulin de Beaumont ★ *($5; early May to late Jun, Sat and Sun 10am to 4:30pm; late June to early Sep, Tue to Sun 10am to 4:30pm; early Sep to late Oct, Sat and Sun 10am to 4:30pm; 2 Rue du Fleuve, Route 132, ☎833-1867)*. The mill was built in 1821 on a plateau halfway down the waterfall in Maillou, and only its upper floors are visible from the road. The grounds of the mill, which include a picnic area, slope gradually down toward the St-Lawrence, offering lovely views of Île d'Orléans and the mountains on the opposite shore. There is even a staircase leading down to the tidal flats and the ruins of an older mill, the Moulin Péan. Visitors can purchase muffins and bread made with flour milled on the premises. Both are baked using traditional methods. A video tells the history of the mill as well as an account of the archeological digs that have been carried out on the site.

Continue along Route 132 E. to Berthier-sur-Mer.

Berthier-sur-Mer ★ (pop. 1,132)

This village is aptly named (Berthier by the Sea) because on arriving here from the west, visitors catch their first whiff of sea air. Now that Île d'Orléans has faded into the background, the river, with its blue waves, starts to look like the ocean. On a clear day, typical sights include the mountains of Charlevoix, just opposite, or the fully equipped sailing harbour of this small summer resort founded back in the seigneurial era. Seigneur Dénéchaud's manor, built in the early 19th century, was destroyed by fire in 1992 after nearly 40 years of neglect.

From Berthier-sur-Mer, visitors can set off on a cruise of the St-Lawrence, around the Archipel de l'Isle-aux-Grues, also known as the Archipel de Montmagny. The trip includes a visit to the Grosse-Île National Historic Site, as well as Île aux Grues itself (see descriptions below). Similar cruises also leave from Montmagny, 15 kilometres further east.

Montmagny (pop. 11,830)

The **Centre Éducatif des Migrations** ★ *($6; late Apr to mid-Nov, every day 9:30am to 5:30pm; 53 Rue du Bassin-Nord, ☎248-4565)* is located near the former seigneurial mill, which has been converted into a residence. This information centre on bird migrations deals with the *sauvagine*, or snow goose; it also has a theatre

Moulin de Beaumont

presenting a sound and light show about the colonization of the region and the arrival of immigrants at Grosse-Île. Though the link between these two subjects seems somewhat tenuous, the exhibits and the show are extremely instructive.

Cross Boulevard Taché and pick up Rue du Bassin-Sud, which soon connects with Rue Saint-Ignace. After crossing one bridge, turn right on Rue de la Fabrique. Go over another bridge, then turn left on Rue Saint-Jean-Baptiste.

Visitors will notice that the centre of Montmagny, like that of most towns in Québec (as opposed to Europe), faces neither of the rivers that run alongside it. This is because waterways are a source of cold wind in the winter, and of flooding and ice-jams during the spring thaw. In the past, rivers were viewed from a strictly utilitarian angle and valued only for the purposes of transportation, industry and dumping waste. This means their banks were not equipped with sidewalks.

Maison Historique Sir Étienne-Pascal-Taché *(mid-May to Sep, Mon to Fri 10am to 5pm, Sat and Sun 10am to 4pm; 37 Avenue Sainte-Marie, ☎248-7927)* Rue Saint-Jean-Baptiste and Rue Saint-Thomas meet at a point west of the church and are lined with a number of cafés, terraces and attractive shops in old houses. Avenue Sainte-Marie provides access to the beautiful and historic Taché house, hidden behind commercial buildings. The manor, built in 1759, was the home of Sir Étienne Pascal Taché (1795-1865), Prime Minister of United Canada for a few years. He had the two picturesque towers looking out over the river added to the building.

Head back to Rue de la Fabrique and turn left, then take a right on Boulevard Taché, and another left on Avenue du Quai.

Grosse Île and the Irish Memorial National Historic Site ★★ *(guided tours only; May to Oct; ☎248-8888 or 1-800-463-6769)* is also called the Lieu Historique National de la Grosse-Île-et-le-Mémorial-des-Irlandais. An excursion to Grosse Île is to step back into the sad history of North American immigration. Fleeing epidemics and famine, Irish emigrants to Canada were particularly numerous from the 1830s to the 1850s. In order to limit the spread of cholera and typhus in the New World, authorities required transatlantic passengers to submit to a quarantine before allowing them to disembark at the port of Québec. Grosse Île was the logical location for this isolation camp, far enough from the mainland to effectively sequester its residents, but close enough to be convenient. On this "Quarantine Island" each prospective immigrant was inspected with a fine-tooth comb. Travellers in good health stayed in "hotels", the luxury of which depended on the class of the berths they had occupied on the ships. The sick were immediately hospitalized.

In total, four million European immigrants passed through the port of Québec between 1832 and 1937. It is impossible to ascertain how many of these resided for a period on Grosse Île, but close to 7,000 people perished there. In 1847, the year of the Great Potato Famine, a principle cause of Irish emigration, the typhus epidemic was particularly virulent and especially hard on Irish immigrants. In memory of this sad year, people of Irish descent have made pilgrimages to Grosse Île every year since 1909. A Celtic cross stands on the island, in memory of those who came here and of those unfortunates who did not survive the experience.

The guided tour of Grosse Île, part of which is made on a small motorized train, reveals the natural beauty of the island and its human-made structures. The barracks still stand, as does the imposing disinfection building, recently opened to the public for the first time. Together, these buildings recount a page of the history of this part of the continent.

Île aux Grues ★★ is the only island of the Isle-aux-Grues archipelago that is inhabited year round. It is an excellent spot for watching snow geese in the spring, for hunting in autumn, and for walking in summer. In winter the island is locked in by ice and residents can only access the mainland by airplane. A few rural inns dot this 10-kilometre-long agricultural island. A bicycle trip through its golden wheat fields along the river is one of the most pleasant ways to explore the area. The island is also accessible by car thanks to the Grue des Îles ferry (see p 392). At the centre of the island is the village of **Saint-Antoine-de-l'Isle-aux-Grues**, with its little church and its lovely houses. There is a craft shop, a cheese store that sells a delicious locally produced cheese, and a small museum that reveals past and present traditions of island life. To the east is the **Manoir Seigneurial McPherson-LeMoine**, which was rebuilt for Louis Liénard Villemonde Beaujeu after the island was sacked by the British army in 1759. This attractive house, fronted by a long gallery, was the summer home of historian James McPherson-LeMoine at the end of the 19th century. Today it is the haven of painter Jean-Paul Riopelle.

There is a small tourist information stand at the end of the dock that is staffed during the high season. If you plan to spend a few days on the island bring enough cash since there is only one small bank on the island and it does not have an automatic teller machine.

Continue along Route 132 E. to Cap-Saint-Ignace. Turn right on the village road (Rue du Manoir).

Cap-Saint-Ignace (pop. 2,983)

The **Manoir Gamache ★** *(not open to visitors; 120 Rue du Manoir, on the right at the entrance to the village)* was built in 1744 as a chapel and presbytery. Miraculously spared during the British Conquest, it became the residence of Seigneur Gamache shortly thereafter. The manor, with its thick, low square masonry and its high roof pierced with dormer windows, is typical of rural architecture built under the French Regime. The only rather unconventional element is the main door, that faces inland instead of the river. Recent landscaping showcases this extremely well-restored manor *(now private property)*.

Église Saint-Ignace ★ *(in the centre of the village)* was rebuilt between 1880 and 1894 as a replacement for the original church erected in 1772. Its long nave, lack of transepts, corner pinnacles and magnificent gilded interior with columned side galleries, make it one of the most interesting buildings ever designed by David Ouellet. This Québec City architect did a great deal of work in the Beauce, the Bas-Saint-Laurent and Gaspésie regions.

Continue along the old village road, then turn left to get back on Route 132.

L'Islet-sur-Mer ★ (pop. 1,950)

As its name, which translate as Islet by the Sea, suggests this village's activities centre around the sea. Since the 18th century, local residents have been handing down the occupations of sailor and captain on the St. Lawrence from father to son. Some have even become highly skilled captains and explorers on distant seas. In 1677, Governor Frontenac granted the seigneury of L'Islet to two families, the Bélangers and the Couillards, who quickly developed their lands. They turned both L'Islet-sur-Mer, on the banks of the St. Lawrence, and L'Islet, further inland, into prosperous communities which still play an important role in the region.

The wind coming in off the sea is a gauge of the immensity of the nearby river. A good place to breathe this sea air is from the front step of the **Église Notre-Dame-de-Bonsecours ★★** *(15 Rue des Pionniers Est, Route 132).* The present church, begun in 1768, is a large stone building with no transepts. The interior decor, executed between 1782 and 1787, reflects the teachings of the Académie Royale d'Architecture in Paris, where the designer François Baillargé had recently been a student. Consequently, unlike earlier churches, the reredos mirrors the shape of the semicircular chancel, itself completely covered with gilded Louis-XV and Louis-XVI-style wood panelling. The coffered ceiling was added in the 19th century, as were the spires on the steeples, which were redone in 1882. The tabernacle was designed by Noël Levasseur and came from the original church in 1728. Above it hangs *L'Annonciation* (The Annunciation), painted by Abbé Aide-Créquy in 1776. The glass doors on the left open onto the former congregationist chapel, added to the church in 1853, where occasional summer exhibitions with religious themes are put on.

With objects related to fishing, ship models, an interpretive centre and two real ships, the **Musée Maritime Bernier ★★** *($7.50; mid-May to mid-Oct, every day 9am to 5pm; the rest of the year, Tue to Fri 9am to noon and 1:30pm to 5pm; 55 Rue des Pionniers Est, ☎247-5001)* recounts the maritime history of the St. Lawrence from the 17th century to the present day. The institution, founded by the Association des Marins du Saint-Laurent,

occupies the former Couvent de l'Islet-sur-Mer (1877) and bears the name of one of the village's most illustrious citizens, Captain J. E. Bernier (1852-1934). Bernier was one of the first individuals to explore the Arctic, thus securing Canadian sovereignty in the far north.

Heading towards Saint-Jean-Port-Joli, visitors will see the **Chapelle des Marins** *(Route des Pionniers)* of L'Islet (1835) on the left, along with the Croix de Tempérance, perched atop a hillock. These symbolic structures are used during the Corpus Christi procession, a tradition over three centuries old, revived a few years ago following the restoration of a number of chapels in villages along the Côte-du-Sud. This celebration takes place in early evening on the second Sunday in June. It involves parish guards in costume, the penance of the Vatican and the Sacred Heart, the monstrance and the Blessed Sacrament. The priest in all his finery is sheltered by a gold-embroidered baldaquin and followed by the congregation carrying candles, as he makes stops in front of the procession chapels. This event, dedicated to the Adoration of the Blessed Sacrament, is particularly spectacular in L'Islet-sur-Mer.

Saint-Jean-Port-Joli ★ (pop. 3,414)

Saint-Jean-Port-Joli has become synonymous with handicrafts, specifically wood carving. The origins of this run back to the Bourgault family, who made their living carving wood in the early 20th century. On the way into the town, Route 132 is lined with an impressive number of shops, where visitors can purchase a wooden-pipe-smoking grandfather or knitting woman. Museums exhibit the finest pieces. Though the handicraft business is flourishing now more than ever, the village is also known for its church, and for Philippe Aubert de Gaspé's novel *Les Anciens Canadiens* (Canadians of Old), written at the seigneurial manor.

The **Site of Philippe Aubert de Gaspé's Manor** *(710 de Gaspé Ouest).* The original manor of Saint-Jean-Port-Joli on this site was destroyed in the British Conquest. Another manor was built in 1764 on the same foundations and according to the same design as the first, but unfortunately burned down in 1909. All that remains is the bread oven by the side of the road. Philippe Aubert de Gaspé (1786-1871), Seigneur de Saint-Jean-Port-Joli, withdrew to his manor to write *Les Anciens Canadiens,* published in 1863. Considered the first French

Canadian novel, the book's literary significance is as great as its ethnological interest, as it describes daily life at the end of the seigneurial era.

In a building so unattractive that it seems like more of a caricature of traditional architecture in Québec, the **Musée des Anciens Canadiens** *($4; mid-May to late Jun, every day 9am to 5pm; Jul and Aug, 8:30am to 9pm; Sep and Oct, 9am to 6pm; Nov to mid-May by appointment only; 332 Avenue de Gaspé Ouest, ☎598-3392 or 598-6829)* exhibits a series of wood carvings depicting local traditions.

Maison Médard-Bourgault ★ *($2.50; mid-Jun to early Sep, every day 11am to 5pm; 322 Avenue de Gaspé Ouest, ☎598-3880)*. Médard Bourgault (1877-1967) was the first of a line of famous sculptors from Saint-Jean-Port-Joli. When he bought this house in 1920, the master-mariner gave up navigating in order to devote himself entirely to woodcarving. As the years went by, he carved the walls and the furniture, producing a highly personal work of art.

The **Économusée Les Bateaux Leclerc** *(mid-Jun to early Sep, every day 9am to 9pm; 307 Avenue de Gaspé Ouest, ☎ 598-3273)* exhibits the work of artisans who, for generations, have been creating miniature reproductions of boats that have navigated the St. Lawrence River. During the week it is possible to watch the artists at work. The front of the house is adorned with a tall mural sculpture that seems taken right out of a fairy tale.

The charming **Église Saint-Jean-Baptiste** ★★ *(2 Avenue de Gaspé Ouest)*, built between 1779 and 1781, is recognizable by its bright red roof topped by two steeples, placed in a way altogether uncommon in Québec architecture: one in the front, the other in the back at the beginning of the apse. The church has a remarkable interior made of carved, gilded wood. Pierre Noël Levasseur's rocaille tabernacle, crowned with a wood shell supported by columns, comes from the original chapel and dates back to 1740. The building of side galleries on the nave in order to increase the number of pews is somewhat rare in Québec. Those in Saint-Jean-Port-Joli, dating back to 1845, are the only ones to have survived the waves of renovation and restoration of the past 40 years.

Continue along Route 132 to Saint-Roch-des-Aulnaies.

Saint-Roch-des-Aulnaies ★★ (pop. 1,110)

This pretty village on the banks of the St. Lawrence is actually made up of two neighbourhoods. The one around the church is called Saint-Roch-des-Aulnaies, while the other, not far from the manor, is known as the Village des Aulnaies. The name Aulnaies refers to the abundance of alder trees (*aulnes*) all along the Rivière Ferrée, which powers the seigneurial mill. Nicolas Juchereau, the son of Jean Juchereau, Sieur de Maur from Perche, was granted the seigneury in 1656. Most of the old residences in Saint-Roch-des-Aulnaies are exceptionally large, a sign that local inhabitants enjoyed a certain degree of prosperity in the 19th century.

The manor and its mill are located on the right, after the bridge that spans the Rivière Ferrée.

Seigneurie des Aulnaies ★★ *($5; mid-Jun to early Sep, every day 9am to 6pm; early Sep to mid-Oct; every day, 10am to 4pm; 525 Chemin de la Seigneurie, ☎354-2800)*. The Dionne estate has been transformed into a fascinating information centre, focusing on the seigneurial era. Visitors are greeted in the former miller's house, converted into a shop and café whose menu includes pancakes and muffins made with flour ground in the neighbouring mill, a large stone structure rebuilt in 1842 on the site of an older mill. Guided tours of the mill in operation enable visitors to understand its complex gearing system, set in motion by the Rivière Ferrée. Its main wheel is the largest in Québec.

A long staircase leads to the manor, which stands on a promontory. Like the manor in Lotbinière, this looks more like a charming villa than an austere seigneurial residence. Interactive display units, set up in different rooms in the basement, provide a detailed explanation of the principles behind the seigneurial system and its impact on the rural landscape of Québec. The more sober main floor contains reception rooms furnished according to 19th century tastes.

The Chaudière-Appalaches tourist area ends here, but the Côte-du-Sud continues all the way up to Rivière-du-Loup. We recommend combining this tour with one entitled **The**

CHAUDIÈRE-APPALACHES

Kamouraska Region ★★, which leads through the Bas-Saint-Laurent region (see p 416).

To return to Québec City or Montréal quickly, head west on Highway 20, located just behind the village of Saint-Roch-des-Aulnaies.

Tour B: La Beauce ★ (two days)

After the French Regime's timid attempts at colonization, Beauce, or as it was called frequently in the 18th century, Nouvelle-Beauce, enjoyed a boom, due to the opening of the Kennebec road (between 1810 and 1830), and then the railway (1870-1895). Both linked Québec and its capital to New England, passing through the valley of the Rivière Chaudière on the way. Agricultural hamlets all along this route flourished, becoming prosperous little industrial towns by the end of the 19th century. Known for their enterprising spirit and favoured by fortune, the Beaucerons founded a number of businesses whose names, such as Vachon-Culinar and Canam-Manac, are now well known in Québec.

Continue on Highway 73 and then Route 173, which runs alongside the Rivière Chaudière to the American border. This road was named Route du Président-Kennedy in honour of the man whose memory is dear to the tens of thousands of Americans who take Route 173 each year to Québec City. Near Saint-Joseph, leave Route 173 in order to drive along the river to the centre of town.

Saint-Joseph-de-Beauce ★ (pop. 3,247)

In Saint-Joseph, visitors will find a plaque commemorating Route du Président-Kennedy, renamed in 1970 (*347 Avenue du Palais*). This major artery's modest origins date back to 1737, when Beauce's first seigneurs were asked to open a road between the newly cleared lands and Lévis, located on Québec City's Rive-Sud. In 1758, this original road was replaced by the wider, straighter Route Justinienne. It was not until 1830 that the road was extended over the border to Jackman, Maine.

Saint-Joseph is renowned for its extremely well-preserved group of religious buildings erected at the end of the 19th century on a hillock a good distance from the river; safe from floods. The first houses built alongside the

Chaudière have long since been destroyed or, in some cases, moved to higher ground. This explains why the banks of the river are only slightly developed today.

The Romanesque Revival **Église Saint-Joseph** and its **Presbytery ★** *(Rue Sainte-Christine)*, built out of stone in 1865, are the work of François-Xavier Berlinguet and Joseph-Ferdinand Peachy, two architects from Québec City. The presbytery was designed by George-Émile Tanguay upon his return from a trip to France in the 1880s, an era marking the peak of the French Renaissance Revival style in the Paris region. Tanguay drew his inspiration from this style for the brick and stone presbytery, a veritable little palace for the parish priest and his curates.

The **Musée Marius-Barbeau ★** *($3.75; Mon to Fri 8:30am to 4:30pm; Sat and Sun 10am to 4pm; 139 Rue Sainte-Christine, ☎397-4039)* focuses on the history of the Beauce region and explains the different stages of development in the Vallée de la Chaudière, from the first seigneuries, through the 19th-century gold rush, to the building of major communication routes. The arts and popular traditions studied by Beauceron ethnologist and folklorist Marius Barbeau are also prominently displayed. The building itself is the former convent of the Sisters of Charity (1887), a handsome polychromatic brick edifice built in the Second Empire style. Its neighbour to the south is the former orphanage, now used by social organizations.

Continue to Saint-Georges.

Saint-Georges (pop. 20,043)

Divided into Saint-Georges-Ouest and Saint-Georges-Est, on either side of the Rivière Chaudière, this industrial capital of the Beauce region is reminiscent of a New England manufacturing town. A German-born merchant by the name of Georges Pfotzer is considered the true father of Saint-Georges for having taken advantage of the opening of the Lévis-Jackman route in 1830 in order to launch the forest industry here. In the early 20th century, the Dionne Spinning Mill and various shoe manufacturers established themselves in the region, creating a significant increase in population. Today, Saint-Georges is a sprawling city. Though the outskirts are somewhat grim, there are a few treasures nestled in the centre of town.

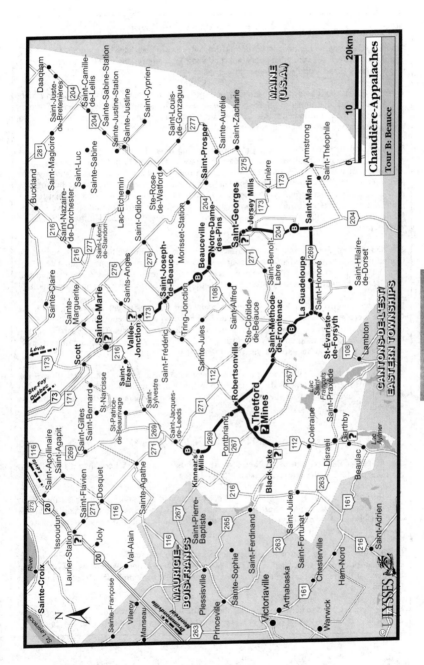

Chaudière-Appalaches
Tour B: Beauce

CHAUDIÈRE-
APPALACHES

Alphonse Desjardins (1854-1920)

Alphonse Desjardins was born in Lévis in 1854, where 40 years later he founded the Caisse Populaire de Lévis, the first in an important movement of credit unions that has grown into the present-day Caisses Populaires Desjardins.

The injustice of the loan system of the day prompted Desjardins create a savings organization that would meet the needs of small-scale investors. Credit unions already existed in Europe; by adapting their methods to the Québec situation, Desjardins concretized his idea of a cooperative system in which community solidarity could benefit all of its members.

Desjardins spent three years refining his project during time off from his position as a House of Commons reporter in Ottawa. During parliamentary breaks he returned to his home in Lévis. At the end of the year 1900 he convinced certain town notables that his project was viable and, on the 6th of December, these men held a meeting during which the establishment of a new savings and loan company was proposed. During the first years of this new institution, members came to deposit their nest eggs right at the Desjardins family home, on Rue du Mont-Marie, where Alphonse, or in his absence his wife Dorimène, would advise them and record their deposits.

The founders of the Caisses Populaires at first insisted that the credit union's activities be limited to the parish, but when they encouraged the creation of new unions, requests came in from all over the province. Since these were cooperatives, they were created by the demand of citizens who were interested in working together to get better savings and fairer credit.

Desjardins toured Québec for several years explaining his idea to volunteers. In 1909, 22 Caisses were active throughout the province; the hundredth was inaugurated in 1912. Each credit union functioned independently under Desjardins's guidance. Three years later the Québec government adopted a law permitting the Caisses Populaires to amalgamate in a larger movement that could help sustain member branches in difficulty.

At the end of his life, Alphonse Desjardins was just as involved as ever in the activities of the Caisses Populaires. He who had so much faith in the human spirit of cooperation left behind a popular movement that today has close to five million members in 1,200 Caisses across Québec.

Joseph-Elzéar Bernier (1852-1934)

Joseph-Elzéar Bernier, one of Québec's most famous sailors, was born into a long line of captains in 1852 in the pretty village of L'Islet-sur-Mer.

In 1869, at the age of 17 years, Joseph-Elzéar was named captain of a ship called the *Saint-Joseph* that was previously piloted by his father, making him the youngest captain in the world. During the following years, he navigated all of the oceans and seas on Earth, setting speed records along the way.

In 1904 he made the first of his exploratory voyages to the Arctic Ocean, financed by the Canadian government. A plaque on the Melville Peninsula commemorates his crowning achievement, the appropriation of this arctic territory in the name of the government of Canada.

Bernier then returned to commercial navigation in the Arctic and on the St. Lawrence. Until the end of his life, at the age of 82 years, he maintained a close relationship with the sea.

The **Église Saint-Georges** ★★ *(1ʳᵉ Avenue, in Saint-Georges-Ouest)* stands on a promontory overlooking the Rivière Chaudière. Begun in 1900, it is unquestionably Québec City architect David Ouellet's masterpiece (built in collaboration with Pierre Lévesque). The art of the Belle Époque is beautifully represented here by the central steeple towering 75 metres and the magnificent three-level interior, which has been lavishly sculpted and gilded. In front of the church stands an imposing statue entitled *Saint Georges Terrassant le Dragon* (St. George Bringing Down the Dragon). This is a fibreglass copy of the fragile original. Louis Jobin's original metal-covered wooden (1909), is now exhibited at the Musée du Québec in Québec City.

Parc des Sept-Chutes see p 408

The **Barrage Sartigan** *(on the way out of town)* was built in 1967 in order to regulate the flow of the Rivière Chaudière, and limit spring flooding as much as possible.

Take Route 173 S. to Jersey Mills, and bear right on Route 204 to drive along the Rivière Chaudière to Saint-Martin. Turn right on Route 269, which leads to La Guadeloupe and Saint-Évariste-de-Forsyth, get back on Route 108, in the heart of Haute-Beauce.

Saint-Évariste-de-Forsyth (pop. 626)

Haute-Beauce is an isolated region, made up of high plateaus, that were cultivated for the first time at the end of the 19th century. Its villages are new and sparsely populated, but residents are friendly and warm-hearted. Saint-Évariste looks out over the surrounding landscape, offering lovely views of neighbouring farms and maple groves.

Musée et Centre Régional d'Interprétation de la Haute-Beauce ★ *($3; mid-Jun to late Oct, every day 9am to 5pm; Sep to late Nov, 9am to 4pm, 325 Rue Principale, ☎459-3195)*. The nucleus of this ethnographic and artistic institution dear to the inhabitants of the Haute-Beauce is the former presbytery of Saint-Éva-riste (1906). Like many presbyteries in Québec, it was considered too large and too expensive to maintain adequately for a dispersed and aging clergy, and so had to be put to a new use. The building houses a collection of about 1,600 everyday objects (Collection Napoléon Bolduc) depicting local customs.

Get back on Route 269 and head north toward Saint-Méthode-de-Frontenac. In Robertsonville, turn left onto Route 112 to visit the asbestos region.

Thetford Mines (pop. 18,669)

Asbestos is a strange ore with a whitish, fibrous appearance that is valued for its insulating properties and heat resistance. It was discovered in the region in 1876, promoting the development of a portion of Québec that had previously been considered extremely remote. Large American and Canadian companies developed the mines in Asbestos, Black Lake and Thetford Mines (before the mines were nationalized in the early 1980s), building industrial empires which made Québec one of the highest-ranking producers of asbestos in the world.

The **Musée Minéralogique et Minier de la Région de l'Amiante** *($4.50; late Jun to early Sep, every day 9.30am to 6pm; the rest of the year, Tue to Fri 10am to noon and 1pm to 5pm, Sat and Sun 1pm to 5pm; 671 Boulevard Smith Sud, ☎335-2123)* houses superb collections of rocks and minerals from all over the world, including samples of asbestos taken from 25 different countries. There are also exhibits explaining the development of the mines and the different characteristics of rocks and minerals found in Québec.

Mine Tours ★★ *($10; late Jun to early Sep, every day at 1:30pm; Jul 1:30pm and 3:30pm; 682 Rue Mofette N., ☎335-7141 and 335-6511)* provide a unique opportunity to see an asbestos mine in operation. In addition to visiting extraction sites and going down into an open-cut mine, participants can attend an information session on asbestos-based products.

Parc de Récréation de Frontenac ★, see p 408.

The neighbouring municipality of **Black Lake** *(8 km southwest, along Route 112)* has one of the most impressive mining landscapes in America.

Return to Route 269 and head north toward Kinnear's Mills and Saint-Jacques-de-Leeds. The isolated hamlet of Kinnear's Mills, located off the main road, is worth a short visit.

CHAUDIÈRE-APPALACHES

Kinnear's Mills (pop. 380)

Between 1810 and 1830, the British colonial government established townships with English-sounding names on territory that hadn't yet been distributed under the seigneurial system. The village of Kinnear's Mills, located on the banks of the Rivière Osgoode, was founded by Scottish settlers in 1821. It is home to a surprising number of churches of different denominations reflecting the region's ethnic diversity—a Presbyterian church (1873), a Methodist church (1876), an Anglican church (1897), and a more recent Catholic church.

Continue on to Saint-Jacques-de-Leeds to visit a few more charming churches before heading back to Québec City.

 PARKS

Tour A: The Seigneuries of the Côte-du-Sud

Parc de la Chute de la Chaudière ★ *(Highway 73, Exit 130)*. Head out of Québec City via the Pont Pierre-Laporte. Once over the river, follow the signs for the Chutes (waterfalls). The Rivière Chaudière originates in Lac Mégantic. One hundred eighty-five kilometres long, it flows into the St. Lawrence just after the falls, the result of an unusual geological formation: a highly resistant layer of sandstone lying within a series of sedimentary rocks formed over 570 million years ago. The area encompassing the falls was set aside as a park by the provincial government. From the footbridge stretching over the Rivière Chaudière, visitors can enjoy an impressive view of the falls. In the spring, the rate of flow reaches nearly 1,700,000 l/sec, 15 times more than usual, making this the most magnificent time to see the falls.

A road just next to Motel-Restaurant de la Plage Berthier-sur-Mer. Although not very large, this beach does offer beautiful sand and a peaceful atmosphere in which to enjoy the river. Facing the beach is a little island, and the view of the opposite bank is magnificent. The western end of the beach is blocked off by rocks from atop which the view is even more breathtaking.

Tour B: La Beauce

The **Parc des Sept-Chutes** *(free admission; early Jun to early Sep, every day 9am to 9pm; 1ère Avenue Ouest, ☎228-6070)*, not to be confused with the one in Saint-Féréol-les-Neiges, has hiking trails, an outdoor swimming pool, a miniature zoo and a number of other facilities for outdoor activities.

Located on the shores of Lac Saint-François, the **Parc de Récréation de Frontenac** *(9 Route Rurale 3, ☎422-2136)* has a number of picnic areas, beaches and nature trails. Visitors can also enjoy canoe-camping and a variety of other water sports here. Boats may be rented on site. Most of this park is located in the Eastern Townships region, see p 217.

Parc de la Chute Sainte-Agathe *($5 per car, $15 for camping; 341 Gosford Ouest, ☎599-2294)* is a wonderful place for swimming and hiking. In certain spots, you have to be pretty resourceful and hop from rock to rock to get to the water, but a little beach has been laid out so that everyone can enjoy the very refreshing cascades and pools of Rivière Palmer. From the shore there is a charming view of a covered bridge across the falls.

 OUTDOOR ACTIVITIES

 Hiking

Tour B: La Beauce

At **Parc de la Chute Sainte-Agathe** *(341 Gosford Ouest, Ste-Agathe, ☎599-2294)* hikers can stroll along the banks of Rivière Palmer and through the surrounding woods.

Lovely forest walks and strolls on the shore of Lac Saint-François await at **Parc de Frontenac** *(9 Route Rurale 3, ☎422-2136)*

 Sea-Kayaking

Tour A: The Seigneuries of the Côte-du-Sud

Sea-kayaking is one of the most wonderful ways to discover nature through sport. Literally sitting on the water, you cannot miss all sorts of marvels that would otherwise be hidden. In the Côte-du-Sud region, sea kayaks are becoming more common sights on the river. If you are already among the faithful and have your own kayak, many launches are accessible. If you would like to rent a kayak, some businesses that provide generally good service have recently popped up in the area. One of these, **Explore** *($35 for 3- to 4-hour introduction; Marina de Saint-Michel-de-Bellechasse, ☎/≈884-2441 or 1-888-839-7567)* has been active for five years in Saint-Michel-de-Bellechasse and offers a variety of attractive packages.

Montmagny's bay is sheltered from the strong winds and currents of the river. It is perfect spot for beginners to test the water and gradually familiarize themselves with their crafts before heading for deeper water, and it is the departure point for excursions along the banks of the river and to the islands of the Isle-aux-Grues archipelago offered by the team at **Kayak-Eau-Fleuve** *($30 per day; 22 Av. des Canotiers, G5V 2B7, ☎248-3173)*. River kayaks and canoes are also available for rental.

 Bird-Watching

Tour A: The Seigneuries of the Côte-du-Sud

The area around the Montmagny dock is a Zone d'Exploitation Contrôlée (ZEC), a protected snow goose reserve. In the spring and fall it is literally overrun with these beautiful migrating birds, turning the sand bars into seas of white.

The Ducks Unlimited organization protects a marshy area called the **Marais de Montmagny**, at the end of Chemin des Prés in Montmagny. Many duck species inhabit this marsh, in such numbers that they are easy to spot.

 Bicycling

Tour A: The Seigneuries of the Côte-du-Sud

Île aux Grues is ideal for bicycle rides. Its small, flat roads follow the river and through vast wheat fields, offering breathtaking views! **Taxi des Îles** *($15 per day; ☎248-2818)* rents bicycles at the docks of Montmagny and of Île aux Grues.

Tour B: La Beauce

A beautiful bicycle path begins in **Saint-Georges** and runs along the west and east sides of the Rivière Chaudière all the way to Notre-Dame-les-Pins and Saint-Jean-de-la-Lande, uncovering hidden treasures of the Beauce that are well worth a pedal push or two! And if you run into a snag along the way, Saint-Georges is home to Procycle, the largest bicycle manufacturer in Canada!

 Golf

Tour A: The Seigneuries of the Côte-du-Sud

Golf de l'Auberivière *($25, $30 weekends; 777 Rue Alexandre, Lévis, G6V 7M5, ☎835-0480)* is located a few minutes from the bridges to Quebec City in a lovely green space crisscrossed by two rivers and dotted with little lakes. This course has the advantage of being easily and quickly accessible.

 ACCOMMODATIONS

Tour A: The Seigneuries of the Côte-du-Sud

Saint-Antoine-de-Tilly

La Maison Normand *($60 bkfst incl.; 3894 Chemin de Tilly, G0S 2C0, ☎886-2218)* is a lovely residence dating back to 1894, that has been tastefully renovated. It has a magnificent living room with a piano, and a pretty terrace in the back. The hosts are extremely friendly, and the breakfasts are both copious and delicious.

Manoir de Tilly *($175 ½b; ⊖, ⊛, ℜ: 3854 Chemin de Tilly, C.P. 28, G0S 2C0, ☎886-2407 or 1-888-862-6647, ≈886-2585)* is a historic home that dates from 1788. The rooms that are available to guests are not, however, in the older part of the building, but in a modern wing that nonetheless offers all of the comfort and peace one could desire. Each room has a fireplace and a beautiful view. The service is attentive and the dining room offers fine cuisine (see p 411). The inn also has a gym and conference rooms.

Beaumont

Perched high on a hill and surrounded by trees, the **Manoir de Beaumont** *($100 bkfst incl.; ≈; 485 Route du Fleuve, G0R 1C0, ☎833-5635, ≈833-7891)* offers bed-and-breakfast accommodations in perfect calm and comfort. Its five rooms are attractively decorated in period style, matching the house itself. A large, sunny living room and a swimming pool are at guests' disposal.

Montmagny

The **Manoir des Érables** *($99, $196 ½b; ⊗, ≈, ⊛, ℜ; 220 Boulevard Taché E., G5V 1G5, ☎248-0100 or 1-800-563-0200, ≈248-9507)* is an old, English-style seigneurial abode. The opulence of its period decor and the warm, courteous welcome it lends make guests feel like royalty. The rooms are beautiful and comfortable, and many of them have fireplaces. On the ground floor there is pleasant cigar lounge decorated with hunting trophies where guests can choose from a great variety of scotches and cigars. There is also a dining room and a bistro (see p 412), both of which serve excellent cuisine. Motel rooms under the maples, set off from the hotel, and a few rooms in a lodge that is just as inviting as the manor itself are also available.

Île aux Grues

On Île aux Grues, two inns, a few campgrounds and some bed and breakfasts can accommodate visitors who want to stay over and witness the archipelago's magnificent sunsets. Lodgers at **Chez Bibiane** *($35 bkfst incl.; sb; G0R 1P0, ☎248-6173)* are subject to a warm welcome from the live-in hosts who are discreet but not averse to conversation with guests who want to learn more about islanders and island life. The house's four small guestrooms are simply decorated. Breakfast, served in a room overlooking the river, includes fresh island cheese. The hosts also run a dairy farm on their land and, come autumn, a snow-goose hunting outfitter.

Saint-Eugène de l'Islet

Auberge des Glacis *($165 ½b; ℜ; 46 Route Tortue, G0R 1X0, ☎247-7486, ≈247-7182)* has a special charm about it, set

as it is in an old seigneurial mill at the end of a tree-lined lane. Each of the comfortable rooms has a name and its own unique decor. Delicious French cuisine is featured in the dining room (see p 412). The stone walls and wood-framed windows of the mill have been preserved as part of the finery of the establishment, which whose property includes a lake, bird-watching trails, a small terrace, and, of course, the river. This is an especially peaceful spot, perfect for relaxation.

L'Islet-sur-Mer

A renovated house that dates back to 1754, the **Auberge La Marguerite** *($138 ½b; ≈, ℜ, tv; 88 Route 132 E., G0R 1B0, ☎247-5454)* has managed to recapture that charm of days gone by. The eight rooms, named after the schooners that were once this region's claim to fame, are comfortable and tastefully decorated. Make sure not to miss breakfast!

Saint-Jean-Port-Joli

La Demi-lieue campground *($17; ≈; 589 Av. de Gaspé E., G0R 3G0, ☎589-6108, ≈589-9558)* occupies a former seigneury that is exactly one half-league-long (a half league, the literal translation of the campground's name, is equivalent to about one and a half miles), providing ample space for all to enjoy this beautiful riverside spot. All necessary services are provided, including a security guard.

In an old, red and white house with four corner towers and a wraparound with a view of the river, the inn at **Maison de L'Ermitage** *($65 bkfst incl.; sb; 56 Rue de l'Hermitage, G0R 1G0, ☎598-7553)* offers five cozy rooms and a tasty breakfast. The house is full of sunny spots furnished for reading and relaxing, and its yard slopes down to the river. The annual Sculpture festival held just next door (see p 413).

Tour B: La Beauce

Saint-Joseph-de-Beauce

Near Saint-Joseph, **Camping Seigneurial** *($10; 221 Route 276, G0S 2V0, ☎397-5953)* numbers 60 campsites beside a river and its

---

Ulysses' Favourites

Accommodations

For a warm reception:
La Maison Normand (p 409) and Manoir des Érables (p 410)

Restaurants

Chaudière–Appalaches' finest tables:
Manoir de Tilly (p 411), Manoir des Érables (p 412) Auberge des Glacis (p 412) and La Table des Père Nature (p 412)

For the terrace:
Bistro Saint-Gabriel (p 412)

For the view:
La Paysanne (p 412)

---

rapids. Swimming and many other activities are possible in this lovely setting.

The **Motel Bellevue** *($40; ℜ; 1150 Avenue du Palais, GOS 2V0, ☎397-6132, ≈397-4779)* is located on the outskirts of town. Very ordinary-looking, it has rooms decorated with plywood furniture. The adjacent restaurant serves good breakfasts.

Saint-Georges

Auberge-Motel Benedict-Arnold *($59; ≈, ≡, ℜ; 18255 Bd. Lacroix, G5Y 5B8, ☎228-5558 or 1-800-463-5057, ≈227-2941)* has been a well-known stopover near the United States border for many generations. The inn has over 50 rooms, each of them decorated with privacy in mind. Motel rooms are also available. Two dining rooms offer quality fare. The staff is very obliging.

 RESTAURANTS

Tour A: The Seigneuries of the Côte-du-Sud

Lotbinière

Set in a Victorian house, **La Romaine** *($$; 7406 Rue Marie-Victorin, ☎796-2723)* offers a good little menu for lunch and dinner, featuring fresh, locally produced foodstuffs. In the summertime, the set menu always includes fish and seafood. Service is friendly and unpretentious.

Saint-Antoine-de-Tilly

The restaurant of **Manoir de Tilly** *($$$$; 3854 Chemin de Tilly, ☎886-2407)* proposes refined French cuisine with a base of local products such as lamb and duck or, for more imaginative dishes, ostrich and deer. The renovated dining room preserves not even a hint of the historic building, but it is pleasant nonetheless. In it, diners savour carefully prepared and finely presented dishes complemented by the view through the large windows on the north wall.

Lévis

Lévis is home to a link in the popular **Piazzeta** *($-$$; 5410 Boulevard de la Rive-Sud, ☎835-5545)* restaurant chain; this one unfortunately located in a rather commercial setting along Route 132 with none of the charm of Vieux-Lévis. Nonetheless, the ambiance is pleasant. Delicious, creatively garnished thin-crust pizza and tasty side dishes such as prosciutto and melon are served.

CHAUDIÈRE-APPALACHES

Beaumont

Jardins des Muses *($; 57 du Domaine,* ☎*833-6916)* is an altogether charming shop and café. Regional products are sold and tasted in a relaxed atmosphere.

Montmagny

🦞 **Bistro Saint-Gabriel** *($$; 220 Boulevard Taché Est,* ☎*248-0100)* occupies the basement of the Manoir des Érables (see p 410). The old walls, made of very large stones, and the low ceiling confer on the spot a very unique atmosphere. During the summer, meals are served in the open air, on a terrace where fish and meat are grilled before your eyes.

🦞 The dining room of **Manoir des Érables** *($$$$; 220 Boulevard Taché E.,* ☎*248-0100)* (see p 410) features fish and game. Goose, sturgeon, burbot, lamb and pheasant are lovingly prepared in traditional French style. Served in the inn's magnificent dining room, these local foods enchant guests, who, in fall and winter, dine in the warm glow of a fireplace. One of the finest restaurants in the region.

Île aux Grues

Visitors to Île aux Grues can replenish themselves either at the good fast-food stand near the dock or in the dining room of one of the island's two inns. On the west side of the island, the hull of a large, beached ship proclaims: *"Oh! que ma quille éclate, Oh! que j'aille à la mer"* ("Oh! my keel is bursting, Oh! I must go to sea"). The **Bateau Ivre**, literally the drunken ship, *($-$$;* ☎*248-0129)* has been nourishing and entertaining islanders and visitors alike for the twenty years that it has been here. Honest family cooking is served, and on some evenings a small band serenades diners. All of this takes place in the ship's interior, which has been left pretty much as it was when it sailed the seas and which has, it should go without saying, a beautiful view of the river!

Saint-Eugène-de-l'Islet

🦞 **Auberge des Glacis** *($$$; 46 Route Tortue,* ☎*247-7486)* serves fine French cuisine

that is likely to become one of the best memories of any trip! The dining room, in a historic mill (see p 410), is bright and pleasantly laid out. Diners savour meat and fish dishes as easy on the eyes as they are on the taste buds. The restaurant also serves a light lunch, which may be enjoyed on a riverside terrace.

L'Islet-sur-Mer

The restaurant **La Paysanne** *($$$; 497 Rue des Pionniers E.,* ☎*247-7276)* is set right on the riverbank and so offers a spectacular view of the St. Lawrence and the north shore. The fine French cuisine plays on regional flavours and is attractively presented.

St-Jean-Port-Joli

The **Coureuse des Grèves** *($$; 300 Route de l'Église,* ☎*598-9111)* is a friendly restaurant-café in a very attractive old house named for a seafarers' legend. Tasty light meals such as spinach squares served with celeriac salad are served. In summer, diners take advantage of a large sheltered patio. This is a popular spot, and the service is business-like but courteous. The upstairs bar is also quite a draw in the evening.

Tour B: La Beauce

Saint-Georges

The new restaurant-bar **Il Mondo** *($$; 11615 1ʳᵉ Avenue,* ☎*228-4133)* presents a lovely decor in the latest style with ceramic, wood and wrought-iron elements. Internationally inspired cuisine, including nachos and pannini, is featured, as is delicious coffee from a popular Montreal roaster. If you order a bowl of coffee be forewarned – it will be garnished with marshmallows!

🦞 **La Table du Père Nature** *($$-$$$; 10735 1ʳᵉ Avenue,* ☎*227-0888)* is definitely one of the best restaurants in town. Guests enjoy innovative French cuisine prepared with skill and sophistication. Just reading the menu is enough to make your mouth water. The restaurant occasionally serves game.

ENTERTAINMENT

 SHOPPING

Bars and Nightclubs

Tour A: The Seigneuries of the Côte-du-Sud

Montmagny

L'Autre Bar *(Wed to Sat; 118 Rue Saint-Jean-Baptiste)* is set in a former post office. This nightclub attracts crowds of young people on weekends with its black and blue decor and its terrace. An attractive fresco on the bar's western wall brightens the terrace.

Saint-Georges

The **Vieux Saint-Georges** *(11655 1ʳᵉ Avenue, ☎228-3651)* is located inside a big, beautiful house. Its magnificent terrace is a great place to have a drink on a lovely summer evening.

Festivals and Cultural Events

Montmagny

In the fall, snow geese leave the northern breeding grounds where they have spent the summer and head south toward more clement climates. On the way, they stop on the banks of the St. Lawrence River, especially in spots that provide abundant food for them, like the sand bars of Montmagny. These avian visitors are the perfect excuse to celebrate the **Festival de l'Oie Blanche** *(☎284-3954)*, which features all sorts of activities related to watching and learning about these beautiful migrating birds.

Saint-Jean-Port-Joli

Every year, at the end of June, Saint-Jean-Port-Joli welcomes sculptors from all over the world to the lively **Fête Internationale de la Sculpture** *(☎598-7288)*. Renowned artists create works before your eyes, some of which are then exhibited throughout the summer.

Lévis

Vieux-Lévis is a great place for a leisurely stroll, especially because it is home to **Chocolats Favoris** *(32 Av. Bégin, ☎833-2287)*, where they make and sell delicious, irresistible chocolate treats and ices that can be enjoyed on their terrace.

Saint-Jean-Port-Joli

Saint-Jean-Port-Joli is renowned for its crafts and many of its shops offer the products of local artisans – if this sort of shopping interests you, this town has much to offer. There are also a few second-hand stores here, to the delight of treasure hunters, many of them along Route 132.

At **Boutique Jacques-Bourgault** *(326 Av. de Gaspé Ouest)*, between Musée des Anciens Canadiens and Maison Médard-Bourgaut, the son of the latter sells contemporary and religious art.

Artisanat Chamard *(mid-Mar to late Dec, 8am to 5pm; 601 Avenue de Gaspé Est, ☎598-3425)*, whose fine reputation dates back nearly half a century, sells woven goods and ceramics, as well as native and Inuit works of art.

CHAUDIÈRE-APPALACHES

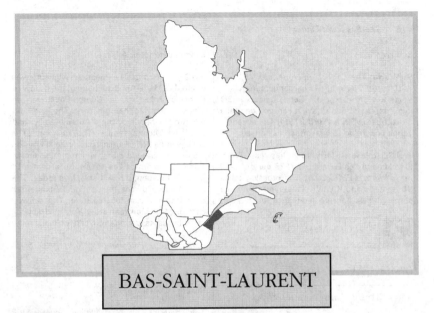

BAS-SAINT-LAURENT

T he picturesque Bas-Saint-Laurent region extends east along the St. Lawrence River from the little town of La Pocatière to the village of Sainte-Luce, and south to the borders of the United States and New Brunswick. Besides the particularly fertile agricultural land next to the river, much of the Bas-Saint-Laurent is composed of farming and forestry development areas stretched over gently rolling hills glittering with lakes and streams.

A permanent European presence in the Bas-Saint-Laurent region began with the founding of New France and continued in stages that corresponded to the development of different economic activities. Before the end of the 17th century, colonists attracted by the fur trade founded trading posts at Rivière-du-Loup, Bic, Cabano and Notre-Dame-du-Lac. Much of the fertile lands along the St. Lawrence River Valley were cleared and cultivated at the beginning of the following century. The lay-out of farms in the region still reflects the seigneurial system originally used to divide land among peasant farmers. Inland areas, used for agriculture and forestry, were first colonized around 1850. There was a final wave of settlers during the depression of the 1930s, when unemployed city dwellers took refuge in the country. The various stages of colonization are reflected in the area's rich architectural heritage.

 FINDING YOUR WAY AROUND

One tour, of **the Kamouraska Region ★★**, follows the St. Lawrence River from La Pocatière to Sainte-Luce and features sweeping views of the river and the mountains of the Charlevoix and Saguenay regions.

By Car

Get off Highway 20 and take Route 132 E. Highways 232, 185 and 289 run through the Bas-St-Laurent, allowing you to penetrate the heart of this region and see its spectacular forests and valleys.

Bus Stations

Rivière-du-Loup: 83 Boulevard Cartier, ☎862-4884.
Rimouski: 90 Rue Leonidas, ☎723-4923

Train Stations

La Pocatière: 95 Rue Principale, ☎856-2424.
Rimouski: 57 de l'Évèché Est, ☎722-4737.
Rivière-du-Loup: 615 Rue Lafontaine, ☎867-1525.
Trois-Pistoles: 231 Rue de la Gare, ☎851-2881.

By Ferry

Isle-Verte: The *La Richardière* (adults $5, cars $20, ☎989-2843) ferries passengers from Isle-Verte to Notre-Dame-des-Sept-Douleurs in 30 ' minutes. If you don't have a car, you can take a taxi-boat ($6.50; ☎898-2199). The schedule varies according to season, so call ahead.

Trois-Pistoles: A ferry runs between Trois-Pistoles and Les Escoumins ($25 per car, $10 per person; ☎233-2202). The crossing takes 90 minutes and if you're lucky you might see some whales. Reserve in advance for summer.

 PRACTICAL INFORMATION

Area code: 418

Tourist Information Offices

Regional Office

Association Touristique du Bas-St-Laurent 189 Rue Hôtel-de-Ville, Rivière-du-Loup, G5R 5C4, ☎867-3015 or 1-800-563-5268, ⁓867-3245, www.tourismebas-st-laurent.com.

The Kamouraska Region

Saint-Fabien: 33, Route 132 Ouest, G0L 2Z0, ☎869-3333.
Rimouski: 50 Rue St-Germain Ouest, G5L 4B5, ☎723-2322 or 1-800-746-6875.

 EXPLORING

The Kamouraska Region ★★

This tour begins near Kamouraska, but leads much further afield. However, as the region is best known as the setting of Anne Hébert's novel *Kamouraska,* this name also graces this tour, which is a logical extension of the Seigneuries of the Côte-du-Sud tour through the Chaudière-Appalaches region (see p 394). Together, the two tours give a good overall picture of the Côte-du-Sud region.

Take Route 132 E. to La Pocatière.

La Pocatière (pop. 4,925)

In 1672, the former La Pocatière seigneury was granted to Marie-Anne Juchereau, the widow of François Pollet de la Combe-Pocatière, an officer in the Carignan regiment. The land later fell into the hands of the d'Auteuil family, and then the Dionne family. The opening of a college in La Pocatière in 1827 followed by the creation of Canada's first agricultural school in 1859, transformed the town into a centre of higher education, a role it still plays today. The main factory of the multinational Bombardier corporation is also located here. The subway cars used in Montréal, New York and several other big cities around the world are made here.

Take Avenue Painchaud to Route 132 E. to Rivière-Ouelle.

Rivière-Ouelle (pop. 1,350)

This charming village, straddling the river after which it is named, was founded in 1672 by Seigneur Francois de la Souteillerie. In 1690, a naval detachment under the command of British admiral William Phipps tried to land at Rivière-Ouelle, and was immediately driven back by about 40 colonists led by the Abbé Pierre de Francheville.

Take Route 132 E. to Saint-Denis.

Saint-Denis (pop. 500)

A typical village in the heart of the Kamouraska Region, Saint-Denis is dominated by its church. Next to the church lies a monument honouring Abbé Édouard Quertier (1796-1872), the founder of the "Croix Noire de la *Tempérance*" (Black Cross of Temperance). It was Monseigneur de Forbin-Janson's tour of Canada in 1840-41 that led him to found the movement. He solemnly awarded a black cross to each person who promised to stop drinking.

Kamouraska ★★ (pop. 760)

On January 31, 1839, the young Seigneur of Kamouraska, Achille Taché, was murdered by a former friend, Doctor Holmes. The Seigneur's wife had plotted with Holmes, her lover, to do away with her husband and flee to distant lands. The incident inspired Anne Hébert's novel *Kamouraska,* which was made into a film

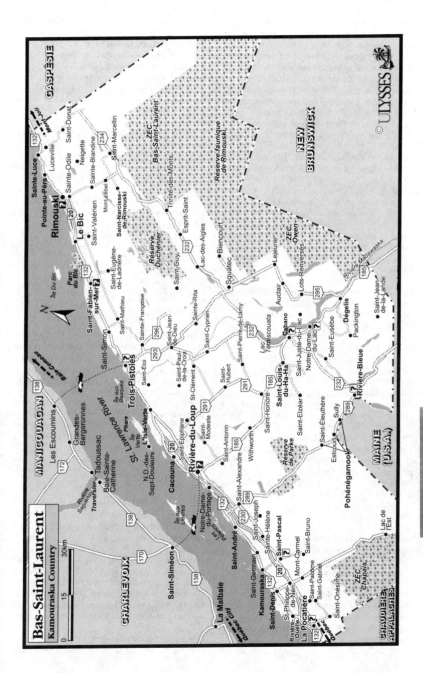

BAS-SAINT-LAURENT

by prominent Québécois director Claude Jutra. The novel, and later the film, brought a level of fame to the village. Kamouraska, an Algonquin word meaning "bulrushes by the water" earned a place in the colourful history of rural Québec. For many years, the village was the easternmost trading post on the Côte-du-Sud. Kamouraska stands on several ranges of rocky hillocks that provide a striking contrast to the adjacent coastal plain. The unusual rocky terrain, a remnant of ancient mountains long worn down by glaciers, is typical of the area.

The **former Palais de Justice** *($3; early Jun to Labour Day, every day 10am to 5pm; 111 Avenue Morel, ☎492-9458)*, designed by architect Élzéar Charest, was built in 1888 on the site of the first courthouse in eastern Québec. Its medieval-style architecture sets it apart from other North American courts that are usually neoclassical in style. The five islands of the Kamouraska archipelago can be seen in the distance from the front steps of the Palais.

To fully appreciate the charm of the village, head down the street facing the Palais de Justice and take narrow Avenue Leblanc to the pier.

The **Musée de Kamouraska** *($4; end of Jun to Labour Day, every day 9am to 5pm; Sep to mid-Dec, Mon to Fri 9am to 5pm, Sat and Sun 1 pm to 4:30pm; 69 Avenue Morel, ☎492-9783)*, which focuses on ethnology, history and local traditions, is housed inside the former Couvent de Kamouraska. Its exhibits are similar to those at the Musée de La Pocatière, though less elaborate. A number of historical artefacts from the region are on display, including a beautiful reredos designed by François-Noël Levasseur (1734); it was taken from the former village church. The present **church**, facing the museum, was built in 1914, following a design by Joseph-Pierre Ouellet.

Maison Amable-Dionne *(no visitors allowed inside; located east of the church)*. Amable Dionne was a merchant who acquired a number of seigneuries in the Côte-du-Sud area during the first half of the 19th century. His manor house in La Pocatière is gone, but his residence in Kamouraska, built in 1802, is still standing. Located east of the church, it is a long building with a neoclassical decor added around 1850.

For a look at the interior of the region, take the road between Kamouraska and Saint-Pascal.

Domaine Seigneurial Taché ★ *($2.50; mid-Jun to early Sep, every day 9:30am to 8pm; 4 Avenue Morel, ☎492-3768)*. The Taché family acquired the Kamouraska seigneury in 1790. Shortly thereafter, they built this manor, the scene of the now famous local drama described above.

If you're interested in learning about eels, stop by the **Site d'Interprétation de l'Anguille** *($4; mid-May to mid-Oct, every day 9am to 6pm; 205 Avenue Morel, ☎492-3935)*, which offers guided tours and fishing trips. The tours last about 30 minutes. Eel fishing plays an important role in the local economy: 78% of the eels fished in the Bas-Saint-Laurent are caught in Kamouraska. These snakelike fish account for 97% of local fishing industry. The fishing season runs from September to the end of October.

Head back to Route 132 and turn right.

Saint-Pascal ★ (pop. 4,130)

Berceau de Kamouraska *(Route 132 Est, 3 km east of Kamouraska)*. A small chapel marks the site of the original village of Kamouraska, founded in 1674 by Sieur Morel de la Durantaye. In 1790, a powerful earthquake destroyed the village, which was rebuilt on the present site. Just off Route 132 is Saint-Germain-de-Kamouraska, and the ruins of the Manoir de la Pointe-Sèche (1835), one of the oldest and once the most elegant Regency cottage in Québec.

Saint-André ★ (pop. 1,467)

The countryside around Saint-André is a dramatic mix of steep hills plunging straight into the river and expansive fields. The tidal flats are typically lined with tall wooden fences strung with eel nets set up on the tidal flats. The nearby rocky slopes of the Îles Pèlerins provide a striking backdrop. The islands are home to thousands of birds (including cormorants and black guillemots) and a penguin colony. If you are lucky, you might even catch a glimpse of a beluga whale or peregrine falcon.

The **Église Saint-André** ★★ *(Jun to Sep, every day 9am to 5pm; 128 Rue Principale,*

Typical house in the region

☎493-2152), built between 1805 and 1811, is one of the oldest churches in the region. Its Récollet design, characterized by an absence of side chapels and a narrowing of the nave around the chancels and a flat caveat, differs from the Latin cross design usually found in Québec churches.

Halte Écologique des Battures du Kamouraska, see p 424.

Falaises d'Escalade de Saint-André, see p 425.

Rivière-du-Loup ★ (pop. 14,354)

Rivière-du-Loup is set on several ranges of rolling hills. It has become one of the most important towns in the Bas-Saint-Laurent region. Its strategic location made it a marine communication centre for the Atlantic, the St. Lawrence, Lac Témiscouata and the St. John River in New Brunswick. Later, it was an important railway centre, when the town was the eastern terminus of the Canadian train network. Rivière-du-Loup is the turn-off point for the road to New Brunswick and is linked by ferry to Saint-Siméon on the north shore of the river.

In order to fully enjoy your visit to Rivière-du-Loup, it is better to park your car on Rue Fraser and explore the town on foot. In addition to the

tour suggested here, the local tourist office has put up a series of signs explaining the history of the town and its buildings.

Manoir Fraser ★ *($3.50; late Jun to mid-Oct, every day 10am to 5pm; 32 Rue Fraser,* ☎867-3906). The Rivière du Loup seigneury was granted to a wealthy Québec merchant named Charles Aubert de la Chesnaye in 1673. It later passed through several owners, all of whom showed little interest in the remote region. The house, originally built in 1830 for Timothy Donahue, became the Fraser family residence in 1835. In 1888, it was modified to suit contemporary tastes by Québec architect Georges-Émile Tanguay. The house was renovated in June 1997 with the help of local residents, and it is now open to the public with guided tours as well as a multi-media presentation of an official dinner of the time.

Turn right on Rue du Domaine, then turn left on Rue Lafontaine.

Église Saint-Patrice ★ *(121 Rue Lafontaine)* was rebuilt in 1883 on the site of an earlier church erected in 1855. It houses several treasures, including a representation of the stations of the cross designed by Charles Huot, stained-glass windows created by the Castle company (1901) and statues by Louis Jobin. Rue de la Cour, in front of the church, leads to

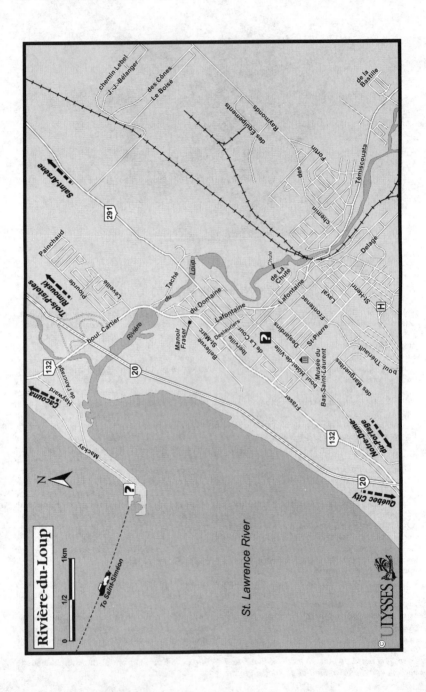

Rivière-du-Loup

St. Lawrence River

To Saint-Siméon

Québec City

Notre-Dame du-Portage

Cacouna

Trois-Pistoles Rimouski

Saint-Arsène

chemin Lebel
J.-J.-Bélanger
des Cônes
Le Boisé

de la Bastille

des Équipements
Raymonds

Fortin

des

chemin

Témiscouata

Delage

Painchaud

Leveille
plourde

Chute
de La
Chute

Lafontaine

Laval

St-Henri

H

Taché

du Loup

Rivière

du Domaine

Lafontaine

Fronenae

boul. Cartier

Manoir
Fraser

Bellevue
St-Marc
Iberville

Deslauriers

Desjardins

St-Pierre

de La Cour.

boul. Hôtel-de-Ville

Musée du
Bas-Saint-Laurent

boul. Thériault

des Marguerites

132

20

Hayward

de l'Ancrage

Mackay

Fraser

132

20

N

0   1/2   1km

© ULYSSES

the **Palais de Justice** *(33 Rue de la Cour)*, the courthouse constructed in 1882 by architect Pierre Gauvreau. A number of judges and lawyers built beautiful houses along the shady streets nearby.

Head back toward Rue Fraser on Rue Deslauriers from the Palais de Justice.

The **Musée du Bas-Saint-Laurent** ★ *($3.50; all year, every day, 1pm to 5pm, Wed to 9pm; 300 Rue Saint-Pierre, ☎862-7547)* displays objects characteristic of the region, and holds contemporary art exhibits (these are often more interesting). The building itself, made of concrete, is a work of modern Brutalist architecture.

Cacouna ★ (pop. 2,028)

Cacouna is an Algonquin word meaning 'land of the porcupine'. The Victorian villas scattered throughout the village are reminders of a golden age of vacationing in Québec, when Cacouna was a favourite summer resort among the Montréal elite. In 1840, people began to spend summers in the village, drawn by the scenery and the saltwater of the St. Lawrence (which were said to have healing properties). While the grand hotels of the 19th century, such as St. Lawrence Hall, have disappeared, Cacouna is still geared towards tourism and recreational activities.

Built for shipowner Sir Hugh Montague Allan and his family, **Villa Montrose** ★ *(no visitors allowed; 700 Rue Principale, ☎862-7889)* is now a prayer house. Its American Colonial Revival architecture demonstrates the influence of New England's seaside resorts on their Canadian counterparts.

Another of Cacouna's noteworthy houses is **Pine Cottage** *(no visitors allowed inside; 520 Rue Principale)*, also known as Château Vert. It was built in 1867 for the Molsons (a family of brewers, bankers and entrepreneurs from Montréal), and is an excellent example of Gothic Revival residential architecture, little of which remains in Québec.

Église Saint-Georges and its Presbytery ★ *(455 Route de l'Église, ☎862-4338)*. The presbytery, built in 1838, displays architecture typical of farmhouses in the Montréal region, characterized by decorative firebreak walls, a roof with a fairly gentle pitch and straight eaves. The Église Saint-Georges, designed by

Louis-Thomas Berlinguet, was built in 1845. The church represents the culmination of a long architectural tradition in Québec that disappeared when new building styles inspired by the past were introduced to rural parishes. Visitors won't want to miss its richly decorated interior containing a number of particularly interesting pieces, including gilded altars executed by François-Xavier Berlinguet in 1852 (when he was only 22 years old), stained-glass windows made by Maison Léonard of Québec City in 1897 and paintings by Roman artists Porta (over the high altar) and Pasqualoni (in the right chapel).

Site Ornithologique du Marais du Gros-Cacouna, see p 426.

Isle-Verte ★ (pop. 1,740)

The village of Isle-Verte was once an important centre of activity in the Bas-Saint-Laurent region; several buildings remain from this period. For its part, life in the surrounding countryside follows a traditional pattern that keeps time with the continuing rhythm of the tides. Just off shore lies Île Verte, the island, named by the explorer Jacques Cartier, who, upon spotting the lush island, exclaimed, *"Quelle île verte!"*, literally "What a green island!". The only island in the Bas-Saint-Laurent inhabited year-round, Île Verte is more easily accessible than the other islands in the area (see below).

Though 12 kilometres long, only 40 people live on **Île Verte**. Its isolation and constant winds have discouraged many colonists over the years. Basque fishermen (Île aux Basques lies nearby), however, made use of the island from very early on. French missionaries were also a presence on the island; they were there to convert the Malecite natives who came to the island every year to trade and fish. Around 1920, the island enjoyed an economic boom when the region became a source of a type of sea moss, which was dried and used to stuff mattresses and carriage seats.

Visitors to the island have the opportunity to watch sturgeon and herring being salted in little smokehouses, test excellent local lamb, watch beluga and blue whales and photograph the waterfowl, black ducks and herons. The **Lighthouse** ★★ *(free admission; Jun to Oct, every day 10am to 5pm; Route du Phare, ☎898-2757)*, or *phare*, located on the eastern tip of the island, is the oldest on the

St. Lawrence (built in 1806). Five generations of the Lindsay family tended the lighthouse from 1827 to 1964. From the top of the tower, the view can seem almost endless.

Baie de L'Isle-Verte National Wildlife Area ★, see p 424.

Continue on Route 132 E. to Trois-Pistoles.

Trois-Pistoles (pop. 3,995)

According to legend, a French sailor passing through the region in the 17th century dropped his silver tumbler, worth three pistols, in the nearby river, giving the river its unusual name. The name was adopted by the small industrial town that sprung up next to the river.

When the colossal **Église Notre-Dame-des-Neiges ★★** *(mid-May to mid-Sep, every day 9am to 6pm; mid-Oct to mid-May, 1pm to 5pm; 30 Rue Notre-Dame Est, ☎851-4949)* was built in 1887, the citizens of Trois-Pistols believed their church would soon be named the cathedral of the diocese. This explains the size and splendor of the building, topped by three silver steeples. The honour eventually fell to the Rimouski church, the masterpiece of architect David Ouellet, to the great dismay of the congregation of Notre-Dame-des-Neiges. An Ottawa canon by the name of Georges Bouillon, designed the elaborate Roman Byzantine interior decor.

Île aux Basques ★★, see p 424.

Continue on Route 132 E. After Saint-Simon, turn left on Route de Saint-Fabien-sur-Mer to approach the water, or right on Route Saint-Fabien.

Saint-Fabien-sur-Mer (pop. 1,910) and **Le Bic ★★** (3,190 inhab)

The landscape in this area becomes rugged, giving visitors a test of the Gaspé region farther east. In Saint-Fabien-sur-Mer, a line of cottages is wedged between the beach and a 200-metre high cliff. An octagonally-shaped barn built around 1888, is located inland in the village of Saint-Fabien. This type of farm building, originated in the United States and, while interesting, proved relatively impractical and enjoyed limited popularity in Cluébec.

*To get to the beautiful **Parc du Bic ★★** (see p 424), continue along Route 132 E., then turn left on Chemin de l'Orignal.*

The road skirts the village of Le Bic before reaching Rimouski, the largest urban centre in the Bas-Saint-Laurent.

Rimouski ★ (pop. 32,397)

At the end of the 17th century, a French merchant named René Lepage, originally from Auxerre, France, undertook the monumental task of clearing the Rimouski seigneury. The land thus became the eastern-most area on the Gulf of St. Lawrence to be colonized under the French Regime. In 1919, the Abitibi-Price company opened a factory, turning the town into an important wood processing centre. Today, Rimouski is considered the administrative capital of eastern Québec, and prides itself on being on the cutting edge of the arts. Rimouski means "Land of the moose" in Micmac.

Musée Régional de Rirnouski ★ *($4; Jun to Sep, Wed to Sun 10am to 9pm; the rest of the year, Wed to Sun 12pm to 5pm, Thu to 9pm; 35 Boulevard Saint-Germain Ouest, ☎724-2272).* This museum of art and ethnology is housed in the former Église Saint-Germain, built between 1823 and 1827. The simple church, with its bell tower set in the centre of the roof, is reminiscent of churches built under the French Regime. The town's **Cathédrale St-Germain**, which houses a Casavant organ, and immense **Palais Épiscopal**, built in 1901, are located nearby. In a neighbouring park is a monument honouring Seigneur Lepage.

Continue on Route 132 E., which is known by different names here Boulevard Saint-Germain Ouest, then Boulevard René-Lepage, and finally Boulevard du Rivage.

The **Maison Lamontagne ★** *($3; mid-May to mid-Oct, every day 9am to 6pm; 707 Boulevard du Rivage, ☎722-8388)* is one of the only buildings east of Kamouraska dating back to the French Regime, and is one of the rare examples of half-timber architecture found in Canada. The left part of the house, an alternating sequence of posts and rough masonry filler made of stones and clay, dates from 1745, while the right part was added at the beginning of the 19th century. There is an

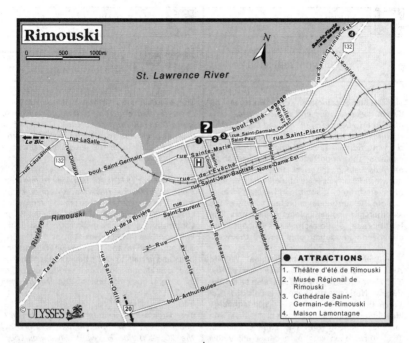

Rimouski

St. Lawrence River

Le Bic

ATTRACTIONS
1. Théâtre d'été de Rimouski
2. Musée Régional de Rimouski
3. Cathédrale Saint-Germain-de-Rimouski
4. Maison Lamontagne

© ULYSSES

exhibition on the architecture and antique furniture of the house inside.

The **Canyon des Portes de l'Enfer** *($5; mid-May to mid-Oct, every day 10am to 5pm; Saint-Narcisse-de-Rimouski, 5.6 km along a dirt road, ☎750-1586)* is a fascinating natural spectacle, especially in winter. Literally, the "gates of hell", this canyon starts at the 18-metre Grand Saut falls, and stretches nearly five kilometres on either side of the Rivière Rimouski, with cliffs reaching as high as 90 metres in places. Guided boat tours are conducted in the canyon.

The next stop on the tour is Pointe-au-Père, Turn left on Rue Père Nouvel, then right on Rue du Phare.

Pointe-au-Père (4,197 inhab.)

Musée de la Mer and the **Pointe-au-Père Lighthouse National Historic Sight ★★** *($5.50; mid-Jun to end of Aug, every day 9am to 6pm; Sep to mid-Oct, every day 10am to 5pm; 1034 Rue du Phare Ouest, ☎724-6214)*, also known as the Lieu Nationale Historique du Phare-Pointe-au-Père. It was off the shores of Pointe-au-Père that the *Empress of Ireland* went down

in 1914, claiming the lives of 1,012 people. The Musée de la Mer houses a fascinating collection of objects recovered from the wreck and provides a detailed account of the tragedy. The nearby lighthouse, which is open to the public, marks the exact spot where the river officially becomes the Gulf of St. Lawrence.

The **monument to the *Empress of Ireland*** *(on the old road, by the shore)*. On the night of May 23, 1914, about a thousand people perished when the *Empress of Ireland*, a Canadian Pacific ocean liner that provided service between Québec City and England, went down in the middle of the St. Lawrence. The liner had collided with a coal ship in the thick fog that occasionally blankets the river. This monument marks the burial place of just a few of the tragedy's many victims.

BAS-SAINT-LAURENT

PARKS

 OUTDOORS

The Kamouraska Region

 Cruises and Whale-watching

The **Halte Écologique des Battures du Kamouraska** *($3.50; end of Jun to mid-Oct, Mon to Fri 10am to 6pm, Sat and Sun 9:30am to 8pm; reservations needed during the rest of the year; Route 132 E., St-André, ☎493-2604)* explains the importance of the wetlands, *battures*, along the river that serves as a habitat for many species of birds and a number of invertebrates. Visitors can have a picnic or explore the surroundings on foot to new of the salt marshes and local plants and animals. The facility has a 65-metre-high lookout that commands an unobstructed view of the river.

The **Baie de L'Isle-Verte National Wildlife Area** ★ *(mid Jun to mid Sep, with reservations; 371 Route 132, ☎898-2629)* is also called the Réserve Nationale de Faune de la Baie de L'Isle-Verte. It protects extensive grasslands that are ideal breeding grounds for the black duck, and marshes teeming with tiny aquatic animals. Trails have been set up to better enjoy this exceptional site.

The Société Provencher offers excursions to **Île aux Basques** ★★ *($12; Marina de Trois-Pistols, ☎851-1202)*, which it safeguards as an ornithological preserve. Bird-watchers will certainly enjoy a trip here. The island is also of historical interest. A few years ago, facilities used by Basque fishermen were discovered. They came here on whaling expeditions in the 15th century, over 100 years before the explorer Jacques Cartier ever set foot on the island. The remains of ovens used to melt whale blubber are also visible et several places on the riverbanks.

Parc du Bic ★★ *(free admission; closed to cars in winter; for a schedule of summer activities, contact reception, ☎869-3502)* is an area of 33 square kilometres and features a jumble of coves, jutting shoreline, promontories, hills, escarpments and marshes, as well as deep bays rich in a tremendously wide variety of plant and animal life. The park is a good place for hiking, cross-country skiing and mountain biking, and also has an information centre.

The **Excursions du Littoral** *($30; Jun to Oct, every day 9am and 1pm; 518 Route du Fleuve, Notre-Dame-du-Portage, ☎862-1366)* offer visitors a chance to observe grey seals and migratory birds near the Îles Pélerins during a three-hour cruise.

The **Duvetnor** *($10-$40; mid-May to mid-Sep, every day; 200 Rue Hayward, Rivière-du-Loup, ☎867-1660)* company offers a variety of cruises. You can visit the Îles du Bas-Saint-Laurent and see black guillemots, eider ducks and razorbills. The cruises start at the Rivière-du-Loup marina and last anywhere from an hour and a half to eight hours, depending on your destination. You can even stay overnight in a lighthouse on one of the islands (see p 427).

The **Croisières Navimex** *($35; Jul to Oct, departures at 9am, 1pm and 5pm, Exit 507 of the 20, 200 Rue Hayward, Rivière-du-Loup, ☎867-3361)* take passengers on whale-watching cruises aboard the *Cavalier des Mers*. You'll get to see belugas, lesser rorquals and maybe even a blue whale. Make sure to bring some warm clothing. The cruises last about three and a half hours.

The **Excursions dans les Îles du Bic** *($25; Jun to Sep; Parc du Bic marina, ☎736-5739)* enable visitors to explore the islets, cliffs and reefs of the Bic. During this two-hour cruise, you'll see lots of birds, as well as grey and common seals.

Écomertours Nord-Sud *(606 des Ardennes, Rimouski, G5L 3M3, ☎724-6227, 724-2527 or 1-888-724-8687)* offer a variety of packages that showcase the river and the islands dotting it as far as the Gulf of St. Lawrence and the Basse-Côte-Nord. The boat used for these cruises, which range in length from two to eight days, is called the *Écho des Mers* (Echo of the Seas). It can carry up to 49 passengers and about 15 crew members and has comfortable cabins. These "ecotours" are led by specialists whose aim is to familiarize passengers with the region's flora and fauna. If you go all the way to the Basse-Côte-Nord, you'll have a chance to meet with the people

Île du Pot-à-l'Eau-de-Vie

who live there as well. The company also offers more adventurous kayaking and scuba-diving packages. The cruises start at the Rimouski Est dock.

 Cycling

The Kamouraska Region

The **Parc du Bic** *(Route 132, 21 km west of downtown Rimouski, in Saint-Fabien and Bic,* ☎869-3502) is without question the most beautiful place in the region to go mountain biking. It has 14 kilometres of maintained trails. Unfortunately, it is no longer possible to scale the Pic Champlain by bike. You can hike up to take in the sunset, though.

The **Parc Beauséjour** *(Boulevard de la Rivière, Route 132, Rimouski,* ☎724-3167) has lots of bike paths. The **Sentier du Littoral** and the **Sentier de la Rivière Rimouski** *(less than 2 km from downtown,* ☎723-0480) offer seven kilometres of superb mountain-bike trails along the Rivière Rimouski and through a swamp.

 Rock-Climbing

There is a magnificent place to go climbing in Saint-André-de-Kamouraska. Besides being composed of an extremely hard stone that makes them safe to climb, the climbing cliffs known as the **Falaises d'Escalade de Saint-André** offer those daring enough to scale them an extraordinary view of the area. Follow the signs to get there.

 Kayaking

The Kamouraska Region

Kayak-O-Tour *($25 per day with no guide, $30 per half-day with guide; Trois-Pistoles,* ☎851-4551) rents out sea kayaks and offers guided tours of the river, along the coast and around the islands near Trois-Pistoles.

Kayak Orca *($35 per day with guide; Jun to Sep every day; Le Bic marina, Route 132,* ☎732-5232) arranges solo and tandem sea kayak excursions, helping visitors explore the Parc du Bic, its beaches, ponds and cliffs. Sunset outings take place from 5:30pm to 8:30pm.

BAS-SAINT-LAURENT

The **Club de Kayak de Mer de Saint-Germain-de-Kamouraska** *($50/four hours with guide; 431 Rue Principale, GOL 3G0, ☎492-2854)* rents out kayaks and arranges guided excursions on the river. The river and the plains are particularly beautiful in this area.

Bird-Watching

The **Site Ornithologique du Marais du Gros-Cacouna** is a lovely place to go birding. Located at the port of Cacouna, it is the fruit of an effort to harmonize local port activities with the natural riches of this marshy environment. If you'd like to take part in a two-hour guided tour of the area, contact the Société de Conservation de la Baie de l'Isle-Verte *(☎898-2629)*.

Île Verte and its marshes are perfect for birdwatching. Thanks to the extraordinarily rich plant and animal life here, all sorts of pleasant surprises await visitors. The **Baie de L'Isle-Verte National Wildlife Area** (see p 424), crisscrossed by hiking trails, is particularly well-suited to wildlife observation.

The **Parc du Bic** (see p 424) is also frequented by several species of water and forest birds. You're sure to see some if you take a hike on the park's trails.

Fishing

The Kamouraska Area

The **Société d'Aménagement de la Rivière Ouelle** *(Route 230, at the bridge over the Rivière Ouelle, ☎852-3097)* has some 40 manmade. For a 40-kilometre stretch, the Rivière Ouelle is paradise for salmon fishing. The river has been stocked with thousands of young salmon (parr) over the past few years, and its banks afford some splendid panoramic views. You can also enlist the services of a guide.

Cross-Country Skiing

The Kamouraska Area

The **Station de Ski Val-Neigette** *($4; via Route 232, Sainte-Blandine, eight min from*

downtown Rimouski, ☎735-2800) has 34 kilometres of cross-country trails.

The **Parc du Mont-Comi** *($4.50; R.R. #2, Saint-Donat-de-Rimouski, 31 km southeast of downtown Rimouski, ☎739-4858)* has 25 kilometres of cross-country trails.

ACCOMMODATIONS

The Kamouraska Region

Rivière-Ouelle

The **Fleur des Bois** *($65-$80; year-round, ≈; 103 Route du Quai, ☎856-1201 or 1-800-463-1201, ≈856-5580)* inn offers unrivalled comfort and serenity in a remote setting. Moved to its present site at the turn of the century, this old house boasts remarkable architecture. Inside, the chandeliers from the former Czechoslovakia and the front door, made of bevelled glass, are sure to catch your attention. The rooms are characterized by the same warmth that emanates from the rest of the house. The sunsets on the river are quite simply magnificent.

Kamouraska

The **Motel Cap Blanc** *($50; K, tv; 300 Avenue Morel, GOL 1MO, ☎492-2919)* has simple, comfortable rooms with lovely views of the river. Pets are allowed.

Saint-André

A large house dating from the late 19th century, **La Solaillerie** *($60 bkfst incl.; sb, ℜ; 112 Rue Principale, GOL 2HO, ☎493-2914)* has a magnificent white façade and a big wraparound porch on the second story. Inside, the sumptuous decor evokes the era in which the house. The five guest rooms are cozy, comfortable and tastefully decorated in pure "old inn" tradition: one even has a canopy bed! Each has a sink and a claw-footed bathtub and offers a lovely view of the river. There are plans to construct an outbuilding with six well-equipped rooms. As far as the cuisine is concerned, gourmets can expect some delightful surprises (see p 429).

Ulysses' Favourites

Accommodations

For the ambiance:
La Solaillerie (p 426).

For tranquillity:
La Fleur des Bois (p 426).

For history buffs:
Le Phare de l'Île du Pot à l'Eau-de-Vie (p 427).

Restaurants

Bas-St-Laurent's finest tables::
La Solaillerie (p 429) and Auberge du Mange Grenouille (p 429).

For the terrace:
Restaurant-Café-Bistrot Chez Denis (p 428).

For Québec cuisine:
La Solaillerie (p 429).

Rivière-du-Loup

The **Auberge de Jeunesse Internationale** in Rivière-du-Loup (*$24; 46 Rue Hôtel-de-Ville, G5R IL5, ☎862-7566 or 1-800-461-8585*) is a youth hostel that offers the most affordable accommodation in town. The rooms are simple but clean.

The **Auberge de la Pointe** (*$70; ≈, △, ⊙, ℜ, tv; 10 Boulevard Cartier, G5R 3Y7, ☎862-3514 or 1-800-463-1222, ≈862-1882*) is particularly well located. In addition to comfortable rooms, guests can indulge in a hydrotherapy, algotherapy or massage therapy sessions, and enjoy spectacular sunsets from the balcony. There is also a summer theatre.

Îles du Pot à L'Eau-de-Vie

The **Phare de l'Île du Pot à L'Eau-de-Vie** (*$135 per person, ½b incl. Cruise; 200 Rue Hayward, RIvière-du-Loup, G5R 3Y9, ☎862-9454, ≈867-3639*), a lighthouse on an island in the middle of the St. Lawrence, exposes its white façade and red roof to the four winds. Owned by Duvetnor, a non-profit organization dedicated to protecting birds, the Pot à L'Eau-de-Vie archipelago is swarming with water birds, Duvetnor offers package rates that include accommodations, meals and a cruise on the river with a naturalist guide. The lighthouse, over a century old, has been carefully restored. It has three cozy guestrooms The food is delicious. If you're looking for a peaceful atmosphere, this is the place to stay.

Saint-Antonin

Camping Chez Jean (*$13, Exit 499 from Highway 20, 434 Rue Principale, ☎418-862-3081*) is a campground with 73 sites, a swimming pool, laundry facilities and a snack bar.

Île Verte

On lovely Île Verte, **La Maison des Phares** (*$55 bkfst incl; sb, K; Chemin du Phare, GOL 1KO, ☎898-2730*) offers you the pleasure of staying in one of the two former lighthouse-keeper houses.

Trois-Pistoles

Motel Trois-Pistoles (*$50; ℜ, tv; 64 Route 132 Ouest, GOL 4KO, ☎851-2563*) has 32 comfortable rooms, some affording a lovely view of the river; the sunsets from this spot are absolutely magnificent.

BAS-SAINT-LAURENT

La Ferme Paysagée *($70 fb; from Trois-Pistoles, turn right onto the Route 293 S. and continue 4 km past the church of St-Jean de-Dieu, ☎963-3315),* a bed and breakfast on a farm, is popular with families and animal lovers. Deer, goats, sheep and even llamas are all kept on the farm.

Saint-Simon

Built in 1830, the charming **Auberge Saint-Simon** *($56; mid-May to mid-Oct; ℜ; Route 132, 18 Rue Principale, GOL 4CO, ☎738-2971)* is a large house with a mansard roof typical of its period. The nine tastefully-decorated rooms are rich in historical atmosphere.

Le Bic

Camping Bic *($16; Parc du Bic, Route 132, ☎736-4711)* has 100 campsites in magnificent Parc du Bic, where all kinds of outdoor activities are possible. Unfortunately, the noise from the highway can be heard in most of these campsites, even though the road is not visible from them.

The nine-room **Auberge du Mange Grenouille** *($50-$80 bkfst incl.; ℜ; 148 Rue Sainte-Cécile, GOL 1SO, ☎736-5656)* has a good reputation in Québec and beyond. Guests are warmly welcomed, served succulent food, and stay in 15 cozy rooms decorated with antiques. The inn also hosts murder-mystery parties.

Rimouski

Camping Le Bocage *($13-$15; 124 Route 132 W. ☎739-3125)* is a campground located near a lake with 23 attractive sites.

The **Hôtel Rimouski** *($85; ≈, ≡, ℜ, tv; 225 Boulevard René-Lepage Est, G5L IP2, ☎725-5000 or 1-800-463-0755, ≈725-5725)* has a somewhat unique design; its big staircase and long pool in the lobby will appeal to many visitors. Children under 18 can stay in their parents' room for free.

Pointe-au-Père

Auberge La Marée Douce *($50 bkfst incl., $85 for rooms in the new modern wing,* $125 ½b; ℜ; 1329 Boulevard Sainte-Anne, G5R 8X7, ☎722-0822, ≈736-5167)* is a riverside inn located in Pointe-au-Père, near the Musée de la Mer. Built in 1860, it has comfortable rooms, each with its own decor.

Sainte-Luce

The **Auberge Sainte-Luce** *($55; 46 Route du Fleuve Ouest, GOK 1PO, ☎739-4955, ≈739-4923)* is a converted hundred-year-old house with simple but comfortable rooms. Guests also have access to a lookout and a beach.

RESTAURANTS

The Kamouraska Region

La Pocatière

Martinet Plaza *($$; Exit 444, ☎856-2610),* on Route 20, is a small restaurant that serves breaded chicken, seafood and grilled meats. It is open 24 hours a day.

The **Restaurant-Café-Bistrot Chez Denis** *($$-$$$; 421 4e Avenue, ☎856-4063),* also known as La Maison Lambert, is housed in a pretty ancestral home with a terrace that can accommodate up to 150 people. Smoked salmon, seafood and roast beef are featured on the menu. The service is attentive and prices reasonable.

Rivière-Ouelle

The **Auberge Fleur des Bois** *($$-$$$; 103 Route du Quai, ☎856-1201 or 1-800-463-1201)* serves veal, poultry and fish dishes in an elegant dining room with an understated decor. The food is both delicious and carefully presented, and the service, very attentive. With all this, a wonderful meal is virtually guaranteed. To top it off, you can admire the scores of Saint-Jean-Port-Joli carvings that line the walls.

Saint-André

🦞 The dining room at **La Solaillerie** *($$$; 112 Rue Principale, ☎493-2914)* has been carefully decorated to highlight the historic character of the old house in which it is located. In this inviting setting, guests savour excellent cuisine lovingly prepared and served by the owners of the inn. Drawing his inspiration from the French culinary repertoire, the chef uses fresh regional foodstuffs like quail, lamb and fresh and smoked salmon to create new dishes according to his fancy.

Rivière-du-Loup

The **Saint-Patrice** *($$$, 169 Rue Fraser, ☎862-9895)* is one of the best restaurants in town. Fish, seafood, rabbit and lamb are specialities. Another restaurant at the same address, **Le Novello** *($$)*, serves pasta and thin-crust pizza in a bistro setting.

The restaurants in the Hôtel Lévesque, **La Terrasse** and **La Distinction** *($$, 171 Rue Fraser, ☎862-2790 or 862-6927)*, serve a variety of delicious Italian dishes, as well as smoked salmon prepared according to a traditional method in the hotel's smokehouse.

Trois-Pistoles

The café/restaurant **L'Ensolleillé** *($; 138 Rue Notre-Dame Ouest, ☎851-2889)* is a vegetarian restaurant with a very simple à la carte menu. The three-course lunch and dinner menus are a good deal.

Michalie *($$, 55 Rue Notre-Dame Est, ☎851-4011)* is a charming little restaurant serving some of the best regional cuisine to be found, as well as gourmet Italian food.

Saint-Fabien

🦞 In the warm, traditional atmosphere of the **Auberge Saint-Simon** *($$$-$$$$; 18 Rue Principale, ☎738-2971)*, guests will enjoy another excellent Bas-Saint-Laurent dining experience. Rabbit, lamb, halibut and seafood are paired with fresh vegetables grown in the restaurant garden.

Le Bic

🦞 The **Auberge du Mange Grenouille** *($$$-$$$$; 148 Sainte-Cécile, ☎736-5656)* is one of the best restaurants in the Bas-Saint-Laurent. It was once a general store and is decorated with old furniture carefully chosen to complement the architecture. Guests are offered a choice of six daily tables d'hôte that include fowl, lamb and fish dishes. Everything served here is delicious, and the service is always attentive.

Rimouski

For a quick bite and a bottle of imported beer, try **Le Mix** *($, 50 Boulevard Saint-Germain Est, ☎722-5025)*, a restaurant, bar and boutique in one.

The **Café-Bistro Le Saint-Louis** *($$; 97 Rue St-Louis, ☎723-7979)* looks just like its Parisian cousins, and is filled with all the same aromas. It offers a large selection of imported beer and microbrews. The menu, which changes daily, is delicious, and the dishes are served in a pleasant atmosphere.

If you're in the mood for Thai, Vietnamese or Cambodian food, head to **Le Lotus** *($$; bring your own wine; 143 Rue Belzile, ☎725-0822)*, which serves delicious, very exotic and well-presented dishes. Every day, in addition to the à la carte menu, guests have the choice between a Mandarin dinner, a gastronomic dinner and a super gastronomic dinner, each of which includes four or five courses.

Serge Pouly *($$; 284 Rue Saint-Germain Est, ☎723-3038)* serves game, seafood, steak and French specialties. The relaxed atmosphere and attentive service make this the perfect place for an intimate dinner for two.

  ENTERTAINMENT

Bars and Nightclubs

Rivière-du-Loup

If you like nightclubs, make sure to go to **Le Jet** *(409 Rue Lafontaine)*, where the atmosphere really heats up on weekends.

Rimouski

The music and outdoor seating at the **Sens Unique** *(160 Avenue de la Cathédrale)* make this one of the most appealing places in Rimouski. The widely varied clientele ranges in age from 18 to 45.

Theatres

Le Bic

The **Théâtre Les Gens d'en Bas** *($20-$22; Route du Golf, 16 km west of downtown Rimouski,* ☎*736-4141)* puts on at least one play each summer. The performances are held from Tuesday to Saturday at 8:30pm at the Grange-Théâtre du Bic, which boasts a magnificent natural setting.

Festivals and Cultural Events

Rimouski

The **Festi-Jazz** *(*☎*724-7844)* is a series of some 20 shows by jazz musicians from Québec and abroad. Some shows are presented in bars and theatres, others on the street. The festival lasts four days and is always held on Labour Day weekend (the first weekend of September).

The **Carrousel International du Film de Rimouski** *(*☎*722-0103)* is a film festival for the younger generation. It takes place the third week of September and lasts for seven days, during which about 40 movies are shown. The screenings are held at the Centre Civique in the afternoon and in the evening.

 SHOPPING

La Samare *(102b Rue St-Germain Ouest, Rimouski,* ☎*723-0242)* has a large array of articles made of fish skin, as well as a wide selection of carvings, vases and knick-knacks, all handcrafted by Inuit artisans.

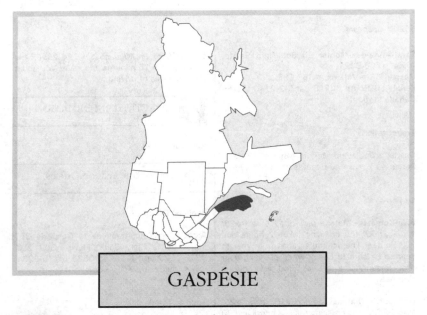

GASPÉSIE

T he shores of the vast Gaspé peninsula are washed by the waters of Baie des Chaleurs, the St. Lawrence River and the Gulf of St. Lawrence. Many Quebecers cherish unforgettable memories of their travels in this mythical land in the easternmost part of Québec. People dream of touring Gaspésie and discovering its magnificent coastal landscape, where the Monts Chic-Chocs plunge abruptly into the cold waters of the St. Lawrence. They dream of going all the way to the famous Rocher Percé, heading out to sea toward Île Bonaventure, visiting the extraordinary Forillon National Park, and then slowly returning along Baie des Chaleurs and through the valley of Rivière Matapédia in the hinterland. This beautiful part of Québec, with its strikingly picturesque scenery, is inhabited by friendly, fascinating people, who still rely mainly on the sea for their living. The majority of Gaspesians live in small villages along the coast, leaving the centre of the peninsula covered with dense Boreal forest. The highest peak in southern Québec lies here, in the part of the Appalachians known as the Chic-Chocs.

The word *Gaspé* means "land's end" in the language of the Micmacs, who have been living in this region for thousands of years. Despite its isolation, the peninsula has attracted fishermen from many different places over the centuries, particularly Acadians driven from their lands by the English in 1755. Its population is now primarily francophone.

Gaspésie's main attractions are its rugged, mountainous landscape and the Gulf of St. Lawrence which is so huge that it might as well be the ocean. The coastline is studded with a string of fishing villages, leaving the interior devoid of towns and roads, much as it was when Jacques Cartier arrived in 1534.

 FINDING YOUR WAY AROUND

The two tours in this chapter follow the coastline. **Tour A: The Peninsula ★★** and **Tour B: Baie des Chaleurs ★**.

Tour A: The Peninsula

By Car

Take Route 132 E. to Grand-Métis. The tour hugs the shore of the St. Lawrence River all the way to Percé, passing through Matane, Sainte-Anne-des-Monts and Gaspé. Once in L'Anse-Pleureuse, you can take a detour through Murdochville.

Bus Stations

Matane: 750 Avenue du Phare O., ☎562-1177 (Irving station).

Saint-Anne-des-Monts: 90 Boulevard Sainte-Anne, ☎763-3321.
Gaspé: 2 Rue Adams, ☎368-1888.
Percé: 50 Route 132 O., ☎782-2140 (Petro-Canada station)

Train Stations

Gaspé: 3 Boulevard Marina, ☎368-4313
Percé: 44 L'Anse au Beaufils, ☎782-2747

By Ferry

Baie-Comeau - Matane *(adults $10, cars $26; ☎562-2500)* the crossing takes 2 hours and 30 minutes. The schedule varies from year to year so be sure to check when planning your trip. Reservations are a good idea during summer.

Godbout - Matane *(adults $10, cars $26; ☎562-2500)* the crossing takes 2 hours and 30 minutes. Reservations are a good idea during summer.

Tour B: Baie des Chaleurs

By Car

This tour picks up where the preceding one left off. It starts in Paspébiac in Route 132 and follows the this highway along the shore of the Baie des Chaleurs. In Matapédia, the tour heads inland to Causapscal.

Bus Stations

Bonaventure: 118 Rue Grand Pré, ☎534-2053 (Motel Grand-Pré).
Carleton: 561 Rue Perron, ☎364-7000.
Amqui: 9 Boulevard Saint-Benoit, ☎629-4898.

Train Stations

Bonaventure: 217 Rue de la Gare, ☎534-3517
Carleton: 116 Rue de la Gare, ☎364-7734
Matapédia: 10 Rue MacDonnell, ☎865-2327

By Ferry

Miguasha - Dalhousie *(cars $13; mid-Jun to mid-Sep, on the hour as of 8am in Dalhousie and 6:30am in Miguasha; ☎794-2596)* the crossing take 15 minutes and saves you about 70 kilometres of driving.

 PRACTICAL INFORMATION

Area code: 418

Tourist Information Offices

Regional Office

Association Touristique de la Gaspésie 357 Route de la Mer, Sainte-Flavie, G0J 2L0, ☎775-2223 or 1-800-463-0323, ⇒775-2234, www.tourisme.gaspesie.qc.ca.

Tour A: The Peninsula

Sainte-Flavie: 357 Route de la Mer, G0J 2L0, ☎775-2223, ⇒775-2234.
Matane: 968 Avenue du Phare O., G4W 3P5, ☎562-1065.
Gaspé: 27 Boulevard York E., ☎368-6335.

Tour B: Baie des Chaleurs

Percé: 142 Route 132 O., G0C 2L0, ☎782-5448.
Carleton: 629 Boulevard Perron, G0C 1J0, ☎364-3544.
Pointe-à-la-Croix: 1830 Rue Principale G0C 1L0, ☎788-5670.

 EXPLORING

Tour A: The Peninsula ★★
(two to three days)

Europeans were fishing in the Gulf of the St. Lawrence before they even set foot the North American continent. Today, not a trace remains of the camps they set up along the coast, but it is possible to imagine their reaction to this unknown continent and their encounters with the native population. While touring the peninsula, visitors will pass alongside steep cliffs before reaching the hospitable areas where Jacques Cartier took possession of the land in the name of the King of France.

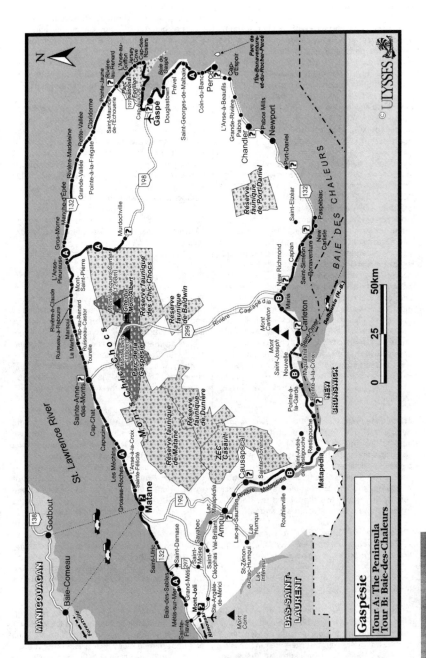

Gaspésie
Tour A: The Peninsula
Tour B: Baie-des-Chaleurs

© ULYSSES

Grand-Métis ★(pop. 327)

Grand-Métis is blessed with a micro-climate which attracted wealthy summer visitors to the area in the past, and also made it possible for horticulturist Elsie Reford to plant a landscape garden here. The garden is now the town's main attraction. It contains a number of species of trees and flowers that cannot be found anywhere else at this latitude in North America. The word "Métis" is derived from the Malecite name for the area, "Mitis" meaning "little poplar".

The **Jardins de Métis ★★** *($6; early Jun to late Aug, every day 8:30am to 6:30pm; Sep and Oct, every day 8:30am to 5pm; 200 Route 132,* ☎*775-2221,* ≈*775-6201).* In 1927, Elsie Stephen Meighen Reford inherited an estate from her uncle, Lord Mount Stephen, who had made his fortune by investing in the Canadian Pacific transcontinental railroad. The following year, she began laying out a landscape garden which she maintained and expanded until her death in 1954. Seven years later, the government of Québec purchased the estate and opened it to the public. The garden is divided into eight distinct ornamental sections-the Floral Massif, the Rock Garden, the Rhododendron Garden, the Royal Walkway, the Primrose Garden, the Crab Apple Garden, *the Muret* (low wall) overlooking Baie de Mitis, and the Underbrush which contains a collection of indigenous plants. The mosquitoes are pretty voracious here, so don't forget your insect repellent.

The **Musée de la Villa Reford ★★** *(Jun to mid-Sep, every day 9:30am to 6:30pm; in the Jardins de Métis,* ☎*775-3165),* a 37-room villa set in the midst of the Jardins de Métis, offers a glimpse of what life was like for turn-of-the-century Métissiens. Visitors can tour a number of rooms, the servants' quarters, the chapel, the general store, the school and the doctor's office. There is also a restaurant and gift shop.

Continue along Route 132 E. towards Matane. A brief detour through Métis-sur-Mer provides an opportunity to get closer to the water.

Métis-sur-Mer ★ (pop. 250)

At the turn of the 20th century, this resort area, also known as Métis Beach, was a favourite among the professor's of Montréal's McGill University, who rented elegant seaside cottages here for the summer vacation. Wealthy Anglo-Saxon families also built large New-England-style homes in the area, attracted by the beauty of the landscape and the presence of a small Scottish community, established here in 1820 by John McNider, the seigneur of Métis. The village's harmonious appearance and high-quality wooden architecture set it apart from the surrounding municipalities.

Most Scots are members of the Presbyterian Church, the official church of Scotland, though a number of communities merged with the Methodists in the early 20th century to form the United Church; Métis-sur-Mer was one of these. Erected in 1874, the **Presbyterian Chapel** *(on the way into the village)* resembles a colonial Catholic church, due to the shape of its doors, windows and bell tower.

The road then leads through Les Boules and the charming village of Baie-des-Sables before reaching Saint-Ulric.

Matane (pop. 12,725)

The main attraction in Matane, whose name means "Beaver Pond" in Micmac, is the salmon and the famous local shrimp, cause for an annual festival. The town is the region's administrative centre and economic mainspring, due to its diversified industry based on fishing, lumber, cement-making, oil refining and shipping. During World War II, German submarines came all the way to the town pier.

The Old Lighthouse *(968 Avenue du Phare),* built in 1911 and no longer in use, greets visitors on their way into town. The lighthouse keeper's house now serves as a tourist office and miniature museum of local history.

The Rivière Matane runs through the centre of town. Here, visitors will find the **Barrage Mathieu-D'Amours ★** *(near Parc des Îles),* a dam, along with a **migratory passage** *($2)* intended to help salmon swim upriver to spawn. From an observation area located below water level, visitors can take in the fascinating spectacle of the salmon struggling furiously against the current. At nearby **Parc des Îles**, there is a beach, a picnic area and an outdoor theatre.

Église Saint-Jérôme ★ *(527 Avenue Saint-Jérôme).* Religious architecture in Québec was greatly influenced by a French monk and architect named Dom Bellot. However, before this man had even made his first trip to Canada

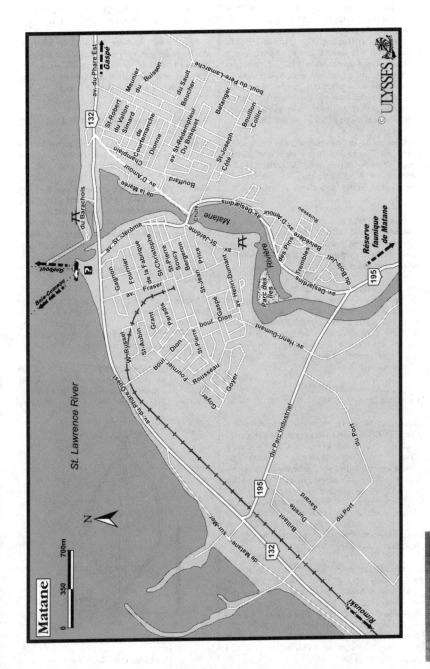

Matane

in 1934, two architects by the name of Paul Rousseau and Philippe Côté had built Église Saint-Jérôme, one of the precursors of modern religions art in Québec. The architect re-used the walls of the town's former church, which was consumed by flames in 1932. As the ruins of the devastated church were too fragile to support the new structure, the full weight of the roof was placed on large, concrete parabolic arches. In the chancel, visitors will is a large mural by painter Lucien Martial.

La Couleur de la Gaspésie ★ *($1; late Jun to early Sep, Tue to Sun 2pm to 4pm and 7pm to 9pm; Matane town hall, 230 Avenue St-Jérôme, ☎562-2333)* displays about 50 paintings of Gaspé landscapes by artist Claude Picher.

Visitors can take an optional trip inland to the Réserve Faunique de Matane, a wildlife preserve located about an hour's drive from town. For information on the Réserve Faunique de Matane see p 444.

Return to Route 132 E. On the way to Cap-Chat and Sainte-Anne-des-Monts, the road runs alongside charming fishing villages with evocative names, like Sainte-Félicité, L'Anse-à-la Croix (Cross Cove), Grosses-Roches (Big Rocks), Les Méchins (a derivative of the French word for mean "méchant") and Capucins (Capuchins).

Cap-Chat (pop. 2,907)

According to some, this little town owes its name to Champlain, who christened the area 'Cap de Chatte' in honour of Commander de Chatte, the King's Lieutenant-General. Still others maintain that the name was inspired by a rock near the lighthouse, which is shaped like a crouching cet *(chat is the French word for a cat)*. Erected in 1916, **Église Saint-Norbert** is the only sizable monument in the centre of town. Romanesque-Revival in style, it is one of only a few churches east of Matane that is not built out of wood.

Electricity can be produced in a variety of ways. One of the most original and least employed methods is without question the wind turbine or *éolienne* in French. The **Éolienne de Cap-Chat** ★ *($6; late Jun to early Sep, every day 8:30am to 5.30pm; Route 132, ☎786-5719)*, which stands 110 metres high, is the largest and most powerful vertical axis wind turbine in the world.

The **lighthouse** and the **Centre d'interprétation du Vent et de la Mer, Le Tryton** *($6; mid-May to mid-Oct, every day 8:30am to 9pm, Route du Phare, near Cap-Chat, ☎786-5507)*. Located alongside a lighthouse built in 1871, the centre traces the history of Cap-Chat and its ties to the wind and the Gulf of St. Lawrence. There are pleasant trails leading to the sea.

Sainte-Anne-des-Monts ★ (pop. 5,616)

There are several interesting buildings in this town, including **Église Sainte-Anne**, executed by Louis-Napoléon Audet in 1939, and the former Palais de Justice (courthouse), now the **Hôtel de Ville** (town hall), which was erected in 1885. Visitors will also find a number of lovely residences, built for various ship captains and industrialists. One of these is the historic Maison Lamontagne. Sainte-Anne-des-Monts is the point of departure for excursions to Rivière Sainte-Anne and the forests of Parc de la Gaspésie and the Réserve Faunique des Chic-Choc.

At **Explorama** *(admission fee; every day 9am to 9pm; 1 1ᵉ Avenue O., ☎763-2500)*, visitors can learn more about the Gaspé peninsula and its close links to the sea and the mountains through interpretive activities.

A large Anglo-Norman cottage nicknamed the "château" by the inhabitants of Sainte-Anne-des-Monts, **Maison Lamontagne** ★ *(170 1ʳᵉ Avenue Est)* stands atop a promontory

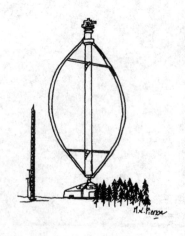

Éolienne de Cap-Chat

overlooking the St. Lawrence. It was built in 1873 for Joseph Théodore Lamontagne, who owned numerous lumber camps in Gaspésie, and exported his products to the United States and Europe. Poet Blanche Lamontagne-Beauregard used to spend her summer vacations in these enchanting surroundings. The house was converted into a restaurant and inn after 1930.

From here, it is possible to set off on a side-trip into the heart of the peninsula. To do so, take Route 299, which leads to the entrance of Parc de la Gaspésie ★★★ (see p 444).

Back on Route 132, visitors will pass through the villages of Tourelle, Ruisseau-Castor and Cap-au-Renard on the way to La Martre.

From La Martre to L'Anse-Pleureuse ★★

With its **wooden church** (1914) and **lighthouse** (1906), La Martre is a typical fishing village, located on the edge of the coastal plain. Beyond this point, the coast becomes much steeper and more jagged. The road zigzags into deep bays and out onto windswept capes. In a number of places, it passes so close to the sea that the waves lap at the asphalt in rough weather. It is worthwhile exploring some of the few roads leading inland from the villages, especially particularly the gravel roads alongside Rivière à Claude and Rivière Mont-Saint-Pierre, in order to fully appreciate the ruggedness of the landscape and the mightiness of the rivers.

Centre d'Interprétation des Phares ★ *($2; early Jun to early Sep, every day 9am to 5pm; 10 Avenue du Phare; ☎288-5698).* In the red octagonal former lighthouse and the equally colourful lighthouse keeper's house, there is an interesting exhibit on the history and operation of lighthouses in Gaspésie.

The road then leads through Marsoui, Ruisseau-à-Rebours, Rivière-à-Claude, Mont-Saint-Pierre, where you will find launching pads for hang gliding, and finally, a village whose name is like something out of a ghost story, L'Anse-Pleureuse (Weeping Cove). From here, it is possible to take a side trip along to Murdochville, the so-called "copper capital" of Québec, and the only sizable inland town in Gaspésie (Route 198).

Murdochville (pop. 1,713)

Murdochville is a "new town", established in the middle of the forest, 40 kilometres from civilization. It dates back only to 1951, when a company named Gaspésie Mines decided to mine the extensive copper deposits in this isolated region. The company built the town according to a relatively precise plan. In 1957, the Murdochville miners went on a difficult strike, demanding recognition of their right to form a union and thus marking one of the most important chapters in the history of trade unionism in Québec. The mine and its information centre are the only attractions in this town, which is otherwise somewhat depressing.

A trip to the **Centre d'interprétation du Cuivre ★** *($6; mid-Jun to early Sep, every day 10am to 4pm; 345 Route 198; ☎784-3335)* is an unusual experience because visitors are required to don a miner's uniform supplied by the centre before heading into a real underground gallery. The objects on display illustrate the history of copper mining and the techniques involved in extracting the metal from the earth.

Head back towards Anse-Pleureuse. Turn right on to Route 132, which leads through a number of other little villages with colourful names, such as Gros-Morne (Big Hill), Manche-d'Épée (Sword Handle), Pointe-à-la-Frégate (Frigate Point) and L'Échouerie (in French "echouer" means to run aground).

L'Anse-au-Griffon ★ (pop. 995)

Starting after the British conquest of New France in 1760, a small group of Anglo-Norman merchants from the island of Jersey took control of commercial fishing in Gaspésie. One of these individuals, John LeBoutillier, built warehouses for salt, flour and dried cod in L'Anse-au-Griffon around 1840, and then began exporting cod to Spain, Italy and Brazil.

Maison LeBoutillier ★ *(free admission, $2 for tour; late Jun to early Sep, every day 8am to 9pm; 578 Boulevard Griffon; ☎892-5150).* This beautiful wooden house, painted bright yellow, was built in 1840 to serve as a residence and office for the managers of LeBoutillier's company, which employed up to 2,500 people in the region in 1860. Its roof has arched eaves, like those found on houses in

GASPÉSIE

Kamouraska (see p 416). Inside, there is a café, a craft shop and an information centre.

After passing through Jersey Cove, you'll reach Cap-des-Rosiers, gateway to the southern portion of Forillon National Park, where the landscape is more uneven, and the sea makes its existence ever more conspicuous.

Cap-des-Rosiers ★ (pop. 525)

Located in a magnificent setting, Cap-des-Rosiers has been the scene of many shipwrecks. Two monuments have been erected in remembrance of one in particular, that of the sailing ship *Carriks,* which claimed the lives of 87 of the 200 or so Irish immigrants aboard. The victims were buried in the local cemetery, while most of the survivors settled in Cap-des-Rosiers, giving the community a surprising new character. Irish names, such as Kavanagh and Whalen, are still common in the area. It was also from atop this cape that the French spotted General Wolfe's fleet heading for Québec City in 1759.

Forillon National Park ★★★, see p 445, 446.

The road skirts round Cap Gaspé, then leads into the bay of the same name, where jagged cliff suddenly give way to gentle valleys streaked with rivers.

Gaspé ★ (pop. 16,670)

It was here that Jacques Cartier claimed Canada for King Francis I of France in early July 1534. But it was not until the beginning of the 18th century that the first fishing post was established in Gaspé, and the town itself didn't develop until the end of that century. Throughout the 19th century, the lives of an entire population of poorly-educated, destitute French-Canadian and Acadian fishermen were regulated by the large fishing companies run by the merchants from the island of Jersey. During World War II, Gaspé prepared to become the Royal Navy's main base in the event of a German invasion of Great Britain, which explains why there are a few military installations around the bay. Today, Gaspé is the most important town on the peninsula, in addition to being the region's administrative centre. The city follows the waterfront in a narrow ribbon of development.

In 1977, upon the initiative of the local historical society, the **Musée de la Gaspésie ★★** *($3.50; late Jun to early Sep, every day 8:30am to 8:30pm; early Sep to mid-Oct, Mon to Fri 9am to 5pm, Sat and Sun noon to 5pm; mid-Oct to late Jun, Tue to Fri 9am to 5pm; 80 Boulevard Gaspé, ☎368-5710)* was erected on Pointe Jacques Cartier, overlooking Baie de Gaspé. A museum of history and popular tradition, it houses a permanent exhibit entitled *Un Peuple de la Mer* (A People of the Sea), tracing life in Gaspésie from the first native inhabitants, members of the Micmac tribe, all the way up to the present day. Temporary exhibit are also featured in the museum.

Next to the museum lies a superb **monument to Jacques Cartier,** executed by the Bourgault family of Saint-Jean-Port-Joli. The six bronze stele are inscribed with descriptions of Cartier arriving in Canada, taking possession of the land, and meeting the Amerindians for the first time.

Take Boulevard Gaspé to Rue Jacques-Cartier.

Cathédrale du Christ-Roi ★ *(20 Rue de la Cathédrale),* the only wooden cathedral in North America, has a contemporary design characteristic of Californian "shed" architecture, that is foreign to the east coast of the continent. Designed by Montréal architect Gérard Notebaert, it was erected in 1968 on the foundations of an earlier basilica, which was begun in 1932 to commemorate the 400th anniversary of Jacques Cartier's arrival in Canada, but was never completed due to a lack of funds. The interior is bathed in soft light from a lovely stained glass window by Claude Théberge, who made it with antique glass. Visitors will also find a fresco showing Jacques Cartier taking possession of Canada, which was received as a gift from France in 1934.

The Ash Inn ★ *(188 Rue de la Reine)* a former residence, built in 1885 for Dr. William Wakeham, the famous arctic explorer, is one of the only 19th-century stone houses in all of Gaspésie.

Nearly one million salmon and speckled trout are born annually at the **Centre de Pisciculture de Gaspé ★** *($3.50; early Jun to mid-Sep, every day 9am to 4pm; 686 Boulevard York O., ☎368-3395).* It was founded in 1875, making it the oldest agriculture centre in Québec. In 1938, it was moved into these buildings,

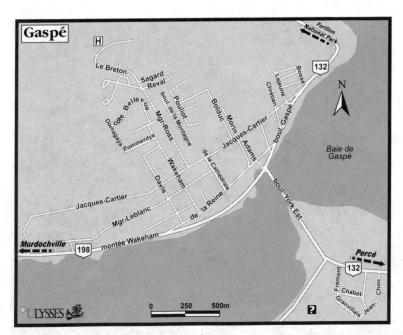

whose design was inspired by the traditional architecture of Québec.

Heading out of Gaspé, visitors will get back on Route 132, which leads to Percé. On the way, the road runs along the southern side of Baie de Gaspé, with its charming Anglo-Saxon Protestant villages, some of which were settled by small communities of American Loyalists, others by British immigrants. The British colonial government intentionally populated these distant regions with settlers who were staunchly loyal to the King of England, in hopes of strengthening its position throughout Québec and promoting the rapid assimilation of the French-Canadian population.

Continue along Route 132 to Percé.

Percé ★★ (pop. 4,120)

A famous tourist destination, Percé lies in a beautiful setting, which has unfortunately been somewhat marred by the booming hotel industry. The majestic scenery features several naturel phenomena, the most important being the famous Rocher Percé, which is to Québec what the Sugar Loaf is to Brazil. Since the

beginning of the 20th century, artists have been flocking to Percé every summer, charmed by the beautiful landscape and the local inhabitants.

Percé was an important gathering place for the natives, until the Denys family established a seasonal fishing camp here in the 17th century, attracting French and Basque fishermen. In 1781, Charles Robin, a powerful merchant from the island of Jersey, founded a fishing business in L'Anse du Sud, at which point a number of Loyalists and Irish and immigrants from Guernsey joined the French- Canadian population. At the time, the area's permanent population was still very small compared to the seasonal population working in Robin's flimsy buildings. Percé was also the main fishing port on Québec coast throughout the 19th century. The tourist industry took over in the 20th century, especially after Route 132 was built in 1929. Life in Percé nevertheless retains a precarious, seasonal quality.

Upon arriving in Percé, visitors are greeted by the arresting sight of the famous **Rocher Percé ★★★**, a wall of rock measuring 400 metres in length and 88 metres in height

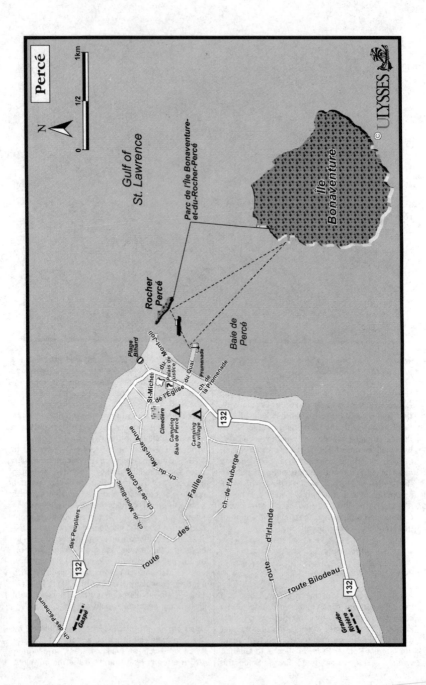

at its tallest point. Its name, which translates as pierced rock, comes from the two entirely natural arched openings at its base. Only one of these openings remains today, since the eastern part of the rock collapsed in the mid-19th century. At low tide, starting from Plage du Mont Joli, it is possible to walk around the rock and admire the majestic surroundings and the thousands of fossils trapped in the limestone *(inquire about the time of day and duration of the tides beforehand)*.

The **Musée Le Chafaud** ★ *($2; Jun to late Sep, every day 10am to 10pm; 145 Rue Principale, ☎782-5100)* occupies the largest building at Charles Robin's old plant in Percé. The *chafaud* is a building where fish was processed and stored. Today, it houses an exhibition on the local heritage, and is also used for various activities linked to the visual arts. The icehouse and salt shed still stand near the quay. On the other side of the street, are the "Bell House", topped by a bell once used to call employees to work; the former company store, with its gabled roof and sawed wood ornaments, and finally an old barn, which serves as the local arts centre.

At the Percé docks, there are a number of boats that take people out to **Parc de l'Île Bonaventure** ★★. During the high season, there are frequent departures from 8am to 5pm. Often, the crossing includes a short ride around the island and Rocher Percé, so that passengers can get a good look at the park's natural attractions. Most of these outfits let you spend as long as you want on the island and come back on any of their boats, which travel back and forth regularly between the island and the mainland.

Parc de l'Île Bonaventure ★★ see p 445.

The **Centre d'interprétation de Percé** *(free admission; early Jun to mid-Oct, every day 9am to 5pm)* shows a short film on the history of Île Bonaventure and the gannets that nest there. Visitors will also find an exhibition area, saltwater aquariums and two short footpaths. Finally, there is a shop run by the local bird-watching, which sells books and souvenirs.

The tour of the peninsula ends et Percé. In order to make a complete circle and return to Québec City or Montréal without having to double back, the most pleasant way is to combine the tour of the peninsula with the following tour of Baie des Chaleurs.

Tour B: Baie des Chaleurs ★
(two days)

In 1604-06, Samuel de Champlain and Sieur de Monts founded the settlements of Île Sainte-Croix and Port-Royal, which were then populated by colonists from Poitou (France), thus marking the origins of Acadie (Acadia), a vast colony corresponding to the territory now occupied by Nova Scotia, Prince Edward Island and New Brunswick. In 1755, during the Seven Years' War, the British captured the Acadians, whom they subsequently deported to faraway regions. A number of those who survived the trip attempted to return to their lands, which had been confiscated and then granted to new British colonists. Some settled in Louisiana, others in Québec, mostly in the Baie des Chaleurs area. Ironically, these Acadians were soon joined by Irish, Scottish and English immigrants, with whom they lived in relative peace, turning the area into a patchwork of French and English villages.

This tour leads through gentler landscapes and more farmlands than the tour of the peninsula. Visitors will also discover sandy beaches washed by calmer, warmer waters than those off Percé. The bay itself penetrates deep into the territory, creating a natural border between New Brunswick, to the south, and Québec, to the north. This route can serve as a springboard for a tour of the Îles de la Madeleine or Canada's Atlantic provinces.

Take Route 132 to Paspébiac

Paspébiac (pop. 3,141)

This little industrial town used to be the headquarters of the Robin company, which specialized in processing and exporting cod. The business was founded in 1766 by Charles Robin, a merchant from the island of Jersey, and then expanded to several spots along the coast of Gaspésie and even along the Côte-Nord. In 1791, Robin added a shipyard to his facilities in Paspébiac, in order to build vessels to transport fish to Europe. Around 1840, the company began to face fierce competition from an enterprise owned by John LeBoutillier, one of Robin's former employees. Then, the failure of the Bank of Jersey in 1886 had a severe impact on fishing enterprises in Gaspésie, which never regained their former power.

The **Site Historique du Banc-de-Paspébiac ★★**
($5; Jun to early Sep, every day 9am to 6pm;
Route du Banc, ☎752-6229). A *banc* is a strip
of sand and gravel used for drying fish.
Paspébiac's *banc*, along with the town's deep,
well-protected natural port, lent itself to the
development of a fishing industry. In 1964,
there were still some 70 buildings from the
Robin and LeBoutillier companies on the *banc*.
That year, however, most of them were
destroyed by a fire. The eight surviving
buildings have been carefully restored in this
historic site and are open to the public.

Most of these buildings were erected in the
19th century. Particularly noteworthy sights
include the forge, the former carpenter's shop,
the kitchens, the Robin company offices, a
powder magazine and the 'B.B.' (1850), a
structure with a high pointed roof used for
storing cod. Some of the buildings house
thematic exhibitions on shipbuilding, the
international fish market and the history of the
Jersey companies. The site also includes a
shop and a restaurant with typical regional
dishes.

New Carlisle ★ (pop. 1,674)

The New Carlisle region was settled by
American Loyalists, who came here after the
1783 signing of the Treaty of Versailles, under
which Great Britain recognized the
independence of the United States. The
charming village, with its four churches of
different denominations, is not unlike those of
New England. A visit to New Carlisle wouldn't
be complete without a tour of its three
Protestant churches, which are a great source
of pride to the villagers. They are located along
Route 132, which becomes Rue Principale, in
the centre of the village.

Gothic Revival in style, **St. Andrew's Anglican
Church** was built around 1890. Larger than
most churches of its denomination in villages of
comparable size, it bears witness to the
importance of the Anglican community in New
Carlisle. **Zion United Church**, which hardly has
any members left, has a curious shape, while
Knox Presbyterian Church, in the Scottish
tradition, has a typical 1850s design.

There are only a few 19th-century bourgeois
residences in Gaspésie, a region of fishermen
and forestry workers, **Maison Hamilton ★**
*($2.50; mid-Jun to late Aug, every day 10am
to noon 1pm to 4:30pm; 115 Rue Principale,*

☎752-6498) is one of these. The stone
foundations makes it even more remarkable. Its
somewhat austere façade adheres to the
neoclassical doctrine of the period. The house
erected in 1852 for lawyer and deputy John
Robinson Hamilton, is still occupied but the
present owners have opened it to the public.
Inside, visitors will discover a lovely assortment
of Victorian furniture, including a piano dating
back to 1840.

Much humbler than Maison Hamilton is the
birthplace of René Lévesque (1922-1987) *(not
open to visitors; 16 Mount Sorel).* Premier of
Québec from 1976 to 1985, Lévesque was the
driving force behind the nationalisation of
electricity in Québec, and the founder of the
Parti Québécois. This house bears witness to
the cultural intermingling between the French
and the English that took place in the region
during the 19th century, when New Carlisle
was the administrative centre of Baie des
Chaleurs.

Continue along Route 132 to Bonaventure.

Bonaventure ★ (pop. 3,000)

This village was founded by Acadians taking
refuge at the mouth of the Rivière Bonaventure
(one of the best salmon rivers in North
America) after Restigouche fell to the British in
1760. Today, Bonaventure is a bastion of
Acadian culture in the Baie des Chaleurs area,
as well as being home to a small seaside resort,
with a sandy beach and a deep water port. It is
also the only place in the world where visitors
will find goods made out of fish leather (wallets
and purses).

An estimated one million Quebecers are of
Acadian descent. The **Musée Acadien du
Québec ★** *($3.50; late Jun to early Sep, every
day 9am to 8pm; rest of the year, Mon to Fri
9am to noon and 1pm to 5pm; Sat and Sun
1pm to 5pm; 95 Avenue Port-Royal,
☎534-4000)* recounts the odyssey of Acadians
living in Québec and elsewhere in North
America. The permanent collection includes
18th-century furniture, period paintings and
photographs, and an audiovisual presentation
of Acadian ethnography, which gives visitors
an excellent idea of the spread of Acadian
culture in North America. The museum
occupies the village's old church hall, a large
wooden building painted blue and white, dating
back to 1914.

The construction of **Église Saint-Bonaventure** ★ *(100* Avenue Port-Royal) was begun in 1860, the same year the Catholic clergy finally started establishing parishes in the Baie des Chaleurs region, considered very remote in those days. The building's façade was modified in 1919 according to a design by architect Pierre Lévesque. Its very colourful interior is decorated with remounted paintings by Georges S. Dorval of Québec City, as well as a number of wooden ornaments made to look like marble.

Grotte de Saint-Elzéar, see p 445.

Return to Route 132 and turn right, towards New Richmond. Take a left off of the main road, onto Boulevard Perron Ouest.

New Richmond ★ (pop. 4,100)

The first English colonists in Gaspésie settled here after the conquest of 1760. They were soon joined by Loyalists, and then Irish and Scottish immigrants. This strong Anglo-Saxon presence is evident in the architecture of New Richmond, with its tidy streets studded with little Protestant churches of various denominations.

Located on Pointe Duthie, on your way into the village, the **Gaspésian British Heritage Centre** ★ *($5; early Jun to early Sep, every day 9am to 6pm; 351 Boulevard Perron O., ☎392-4487)* is made up of buildings from the Baie des Chaleurs area, which were saved from demolition, transported to the grounds of the former Carswell estate and restored in order to house thematic exhibitions on Gaspesians of Anglo-Saxon extraction. Each structure illustrates a different group's arrival in the area: the vestiges of the Carswell residence are devoted to the British settlers; a Loyalist camp to those faithful subjects who came here in August 1784; a house and a grain warehouse to the Scottish immigrants, and another house to the Irish. Finally, in the last clearing, visitors will find the Willet house which evokes the region's industrial development et the end of the 19th century.

St. Andrew's Presbyterian Church ★ *(211 Boulevard Perron Ouest)*, in the centre of New Richmond is one of the oldest churches in the Baie des Chaleurs area, built in 1839 according to a design by Robert Bash. After a number of Protestant communities merged together in the 20th century, St. Andrew's became part of the United Church of Canada.

Carleton ★ (pop. 2,883)

Carleton, like Bonaventure, is a stronghold of Acadian culture in Québec, and a seaside resort with a lovely sandy beach washed by calm waters, which are warmer than elsewhere in Gaspésie and account for the name of the bay *(chaleur* means warmth). The Mountains rising up behind the town give it a distinctive character. Carleton was founded in 1756 by Acadian refugees, who were joined by deportees returning from exile. Originally known as Tracadièche, the little town was renamed in the 19th century by the elite of British extraction, in honour of Sir Guy Carleton, Canada's third governor.

Église Saint-Joseph ★ *(764 Boulevard Perron)* is one of the oldest Catholic churches in Gaspésie. Begun in 1849, it wasn't actually finished until 1917. It houses a tabernacle attributed to François Baillargé (1828), which was given to the parish at an undetermined date. The main vault is adorned with remounted paintings by Charles Huot.

Follow Rue du Quai (perpendicular to the 132) toward the sea; after the Saint-Barnabé (a bar in a beached boat) take the gravel road and stop near the **observation tower**. Climb to the top of the tower, equipped with a telescope for bird-watching. A guide is on hand to provide visitors with information on ornithology.

Miguasha

Palaeontology buffs will surely be interested in **Parc de Miguasha** ★★ *(free admission; early Jun to late Sep, every day 9am to 6pm; 231 Miguasha O., Nouvelle, ☎794-2475)*, the second largest fossil site in the world. The park's **palaeontology museum** displays fossils discovered in the surrounding cliffs, which formed the bottom of a lagoon 370 million years ago. The information centre houses a permanent collection of many interesting specimens. In the laboratory visitors can learn the methods used to remove fossils from the rock and identify them. The park also has an amphitheatre, used for audiovisual presentations.

GASPÉSIE

West of Miguasha, Baie des Chaleurs narrows considerably all the way to the mouth of the Rivière Ristigouche which flows into it.

Pointe-à-la-Croix (pop. 1,840)

On April 10, 1760, a French fleet set off from Bordeaux on its way to Canada, with the goal of liberating New France from the English. Only three ships reached Baie des Chaleurs, the others having fallen victim to English canons as they headed out of the Gironde. The *Machault, Bienfaisant* and *Marquis-de-Malauze,* vessels weighing an average of 350 tons, survived but the English troops caught up with the French at the mouth of the Ristigouche in Baie des Chaleurs. A battle broke out, and the English defeated the French fleet within a few hours.

At the **Battle of Restigouche National Historic Site ★** *($3.50; early Jun to mid-Oct, every day 9am to 5pm; Route 132, ☎788-5676),* also called the Lieu Historique National de la Bataille de la Restigouche, visitors can see a collection of objects recovered from the wreckage of the battle between these ships, as well as a few pieces of the frigate *Machault.* An interesting audiovisual recreation illustrates the different stages of the confrontation.

Between Pointe-à-la-Croix and Restigouche, there is a bridge that stretches across Baie des Chaleurs, linking Québec to New Brunswick.

Causapscal (pop. 2,144)

The Matapédia, one of the best salmon rivers in North America, flows through the centre of Causapscal with its towering sawmills. Every year, fans of sport fishing come to the area. Salmon fishing and exclusive rights to the river have been a source of longstanding conflict between the local population and private clubs. Causapscal, whose name means Rocky Point in Micmac, was founded in 1839 after a post house known as La Fourche (The Fork) was opened at the junction of the Matapédia and the Causapscal.

Site Historique Matamajaw ★ *($3.75; Jun to Sep, every day 9am to 8pm; 48 Rue Saint-Jacques Sud, ☎756-5999).* In 1873, Donald Smith, the future Lord Mount Stephen, acquired the fishing rights to the Matapédia. A few years later, he sold the rights to the Matamajaw Salmon Club. In general, members of clubs like this were American or English

Canadian businessmen, who spent three or four days a year here in the middle of the woods, in a relaxing, holiday atmosphere. These individuals were offered the ultimate luxury of sending their catch home in refrigerated railway cars which waited for them at the Causapscal station. The club stopped operating around 1950, and the buildings on the Matamajaw property were listed as historical monuments and opened to the public after 1975. Here, visitors can see an exhibition on club life and the history of salmon fishing. There are trails leading to **Parc Les Fourches** where the Matapédia and Causapscal rivers meet and you can see fishers at work.

*The road then leads through **Mont-Joli**, which offers a lovely view of the St. Lawrence River, before coming full circle at the departure point of Tour A.*

 PARKS

Tour A: The Peninsula

The **Réserve Faunique de Matane** *(257 Saint-Jérôme, ☎562-3700)* is a series of wooded hills and mountains, stretching over an area of 1,284 square kilometres, and strewn with lakes and rivers excellent for salmon fishing.

Parc de la Gaspésie ★★★ *(free admission; year-round, every day 8am to 8pm; 124 1re Avenue O., ☎763-3301)* covers an area of 800 square kilometres, and encompasses the famous Monts Chic-Chocs. It was established in 1937, in an effort to heighten public awareness regarding nature conservation in Gaspésie. The park is composed of conservation zones, devoted to the protection of the region's natural riches, and an ambient zone, made up of a network of roads, trails and lodgings. The Chic-Chocs form the northernmost section of the Appalachian Mountains. They stretch over 90 kilometres, from Matane to the foot of Mont Albert. The McGerrigle Mountains lie perpendicular to the Chic-Chocs, covering an area of 100 square kilometres. The park's trails run through three levels of terrain, leading all the way to the summits of the four highest mountains in the area, Mont Jacques-Cartier, Mont Richardson, Mont Albert and Mont Xalibu. This is the only place in Québec where white-tailed deer (in the rich vegetation of the first level), moose (in the

Boreal forest) and caribou (in the tundra, at the top of the mountains) co-exist. Hikers are required to register before setting out.

The **Gîte du Mont-Albert** (see p 448) lies in the centre of the park. A *gîte* only in name, it is a very comfortable inn, known for its fine cuisine, delicate wooden architecture inspired by the French Regime, and stunning panoramic view. Erected in 1950, the main building houses the dining room and 17 rooms, while numerous little cottages in the same style are scattered across the hillside (☎1-800-463-0860).

The motto of **Forillon National Park** ★★★ *($2.50 per person, $6 family; early Jun to mid-Oct, every day 9am to 4pm; 122 Boulevard Gaspé; ☎368-5505)* is "harmony between man, land and sea". Many an outdoor enthusiast daydreams about this series of forests, mountains and cliff-lined shores all crisscrossed by hiking trails. Home to a fairly wide range of animals, this national park abounds in foxes, bears, moose, porcupines and other mammals. Over 200 species of birds live here, including herring gulls, cormorants, finches, larks and gannets. Depending on the season, visitors might catch a glimpse of whales or seals from the paths along the coast. A variety of rare plants also lie hidden away in Forillon National Park, contributing to a greater understanding of the soil in which they grow. Visitors will find not only natural surroundings here in the park, but also traces of human activity. This vast area (245 square kilometres) once included four little villages. The 200 families inhabiting them were relocated – not without a fight – when the park was established in 1970. The buildings of the greatest ethnological interest were kept and restored, namely the ten or so **Maisons de Grande-Grave**, the **Phare de Cap-Gaspé** (the lighthouse), the **former Protestant Church of Petit-Gaspé** and the **Fort Péninsule**, part of the fortifications erected during World War II to protect Canada from attacks by German submarines.

Particularly notable buildings in Grande-Grave, originally populated by Anglo-Norman immigrants from the island of Jersey, in the English Channel, include the **Magasin Hyman** (1845). The store's interior has been carefully reconstructed to evoke the early 20th century, while the **Ferme Blanchette** at the seaside could easily grace a postcard. All of these are either fully or partly open to the public.

At **Parc de l'Île Bonaventure** ★★ *(transportation fee, but free admission to the island itself; early Jun to late Aug, every day 8:30am to 5pm; early Sep to mid-Oct, every day 9am to 4pm; 4 Rue du Quai, ☎782-2240, ☎782-2241)*, visitors will find large bird colonies, as well as numerous footpaths lined with rustic houses. The trails range from 2.8 to 4.9 kilometres in length, and cover a total of 15 kilometres. Due to the aridity of the surroundings, there are no stinging insects on the island. There is also no water along the trails, so be sure to bring a canteen. All trails end at an impressive bird sanctuary, where some 200,000 birds, including about 55,000 gannets, form a wildlife exhibition.

Created in 1953, the **Réserve Faunique de Port-Daniel** *(8 km from Route 132 from Port-Daniel, ☎396-2789 or in Québec City ☎418-752-2211)* is teeming with wildlife. Covering an area of 65 square kilometres, it is laced with trails and strewn with lakes and cabins. To top it all off, there are some gorgeous views to drink in from some of its lookouts.

The **Grotte de Saint-Elzéar** *($37, children 8 and older only; early Jun to late Oct, first tour leaves at 8am; 198 Rue de l'Église Saint-Elzéar, ☎534-4335)* introduces visitors to 500,000 years of Gaspesian history. This speleological and geomorphological journey offers participants the opportunity to visit the two largest caves in Québec. Warm clothing and a good pair of shoes are required, as the temperature is a steady 4°C.

 OUTDOORS

 Hiking

Tour A: The Peninsula

Parc de la Gaspésie *(free admission; every day 8am to 8pm; 10 Boulevard Ste-Anne, Ste-Anne-des-Monts, ☎763-3301)* has an outstanding network of hiking trails. On the same outing, you can pass through four different kinds of forests: a boreal forest, a forest coniferous, a subalpine forest made up of miniature trees and finally the tundra on the mountaintops. We especially recommend the Mont Jacques-Cartier (difficult) and Mont Albert (very difficult) trails. The Lac aux

Américains trail is an excellent choice for novice hikers.

Forillon National Park *($2.50 per person, $6 per family; early Jun to mid-Oct, every day 9am to 4pm; 122 Boulevard Gaspé, Gaspé, ☎368-5505)*, with its cliffs sculpted by the sea and its extraordinary landscape, is a wonderful place to go hiking. A number of the trails are suitable for children.

 Kayaking

Tour A: The Peninsula

Carrefour Aventure *($10 per hour, $35 per day; 106 Rue Cloutier, ☎797-5033 or 800-463-2210)*, at Mont-Saint-Pierre, rents out sea kayaks (accessories included).

Tour B: Baie des Chaleurs

In Bonaventure, **Cime Aventure** *(☎534-2333 or 1-800-790-2463)* arranges kayak trips ranging in length from a few hours to six days.

 Bird-watching

Tour A: The Peninsula

The **Jardins de Métis**, in Grand-Métis, are teeming with bird life - in the clearings, on the lawns, in the gardens, in the wooded area and near the river.

The **Baie des Capucins**, a saltwater marsh, is home to a multitude of birds, which can be observed during a stroll along the path that follows its shores.

The **Parc de la Gaspésie** boasts over 150 avian species, who nest in different climates. You can observe them easily from the trails running through the park. Every Monday, Parc Ami Chic Chocs organizes a four-hour bird-watching excursion, which starts at 7am at the shop in the interpretive centre.

Île Bonaventure (see p 445), a protected nesting ground for cormorants and gannets, is a wonderful place to go birding.

Tour B: Baie des Chaleurs

The **Carleton lagoon** is an excellent place to observe wildfowl, terns and great herons. There is a large colony of terns on the south end of the Carleton bank. A small observation tower, complete with information panels, makes it easy to get a good look at the birds.

 Cruises and Whale-watching

Tour A: The Peninsula

Croisières Découverte *($16; mid-Jun to mid-Sep; at the Cap-des-Rosiers harbour, Forillon National Park, ☎892-5629)* takes passengers out on the *Félix-Leclerc* to see a seal colony and the birds that nest in the cliffs. A guide is present on all cruises, which last nearly two hours. If you're lucky, you might get to see some whales. Make sure to dress warmly, as the wind is often very cold. The departure schedule varies greatly depending on the date, so call beforehand.

Observation Littoral Percé *($30; mid-May to mid-Oct; near the Hôtel Normandie; Route 132, Percé, ☎782-5359)* hosts whale-watching excursions. With a little luck, you might also meet up with a school of white dolphins. Don't expect to see whale tails like those in photographs; usually, only the whale's back is visible, and often the animal is far away. The companies that organize these excursions must adhere to strict laws and have to pay large fines if they don't keep their distance. The outings start early in the morning and last two to three hours. Make sure to bundle up and wear a good windbreaker.

 Fishing

Tour A: The Peninsula

The **Réserve Faunique de Port-Daniel** *(8 km from Route 132 from Port-Daniel, ☎396-2789 or in Québec City ☎890-6527)* is strewn with about 20 lakes where you can go trout fishing. You have the choice between day-tripping it to the preserve or staying in one of the lakeshore cabins, which must be reserved 48 hours in advance. In the latter case, you'll have a rowboat at your disposal.

In **Causapscal**, the welcome centre
(☎756-6174) in front of the Site Historique
Matamajaw issues fishing permits for the
Matapédia and Causapscal rivers.

Dogsledding

Tour A: The Peninsula

Dogsledding Expeditions *($550 and up; 38
Rang de la Coulée, Saint-Luc, Matane,
G0J2XO, ☎566-2176, ≈566-2176)*. These
three- to five-day packages include transportation from the airport or the Mont-Joli train
station, an excursion on horseback, a guide and
team for each person, as well as all meals and
sleeping arrangements. Groups are limited to
six people. One-day and half-day excursions are
also available for $100 and $60 respectively.
These prices include one meal and a guide with
a team of 10 to 12 dogs.

Cross-country Skiing

Tour A: The Peninsula

The **Station de Ski Val-d'Irène** *($3.50 per
person; 115 Route Val d'Irène, G0J 2P0,
☎629-3450)* boasts the best snow conditions
in Québec. There are only 7 kilometres of
maintained trails here, however. You can also
take trail no. 3, which is not maintained.

ACCOMMODATIONS

Tour A: The Peninsula

Sainte-Flavie

The **Motel Gaspésiana** *($75; ℜ, ≡, ◎;
460 Route de la Mer, G0J 2L0, ☎775-7233,
≈775-9227)* has well-equipped, soundproofed
rooms which are actually quite pleasant, thanks
to their big windows.

Grand-Métis

The **Motel Métis** *($50; ≈; 220 Route 132,
☎775-6473)* offers new, simple, modern
rooms. Closed during winter.

Métis-sur-Mer

The **Camping Annie** *($14; ≈; 1352 Route 132,
G0J 1W0, ☎936-3825)* has 150 sites, 58 of
which are equipped with hook-ups for RVs.
There are hiking trails and bike paths right
nearby. Located eight kilometres from the
Jardins de Métis, this is a very friendly,
welcoming place.

Though it is known mainly for its restaurant
(see p 450), the motel **Au Coin de la Baie** *($65-
$80; tv, K, ℜ; ☎936-3855, ≈836-3112)* also
has 14 lovely, renovated rooms.

Matane

Located in the CÉGEP de Matane, the **Logis-
Vacances** *($37; ≈, ◎, K; 616 Saint-
Rédempteur; ☎562-1240)* welcome tourists
during the summer season. Guests have access
to a gymnasium, a small kitchen, a laundry
room, tennis courts and a TV room.
Apartments composed of six separate rooms
are also available for the modest sum of $55.

Located near the snowmobile route, the **Motel
La Vigie** *($60; ≡, ℜ; 1600 Avenue du Phare O.,
G4W 3M6, ☎562-3664, ≈562-2930)* offers
simple rooms in a modern setting.

Visitors will find the perfect place to relax at
the confluence of the St. Lawrence and Matane
rivers, namely, **L'Auberge de La Seigneurie**
*($70 bkfst incl.; 621 Rue Saint-Jérôme,
G4W 3M9, ☎562-0021, ≈562-4455)*, an inn
with comfortable rooms, located on the former
site of the Fraser seigneury.

The **Hôtel des Gouverneurs** *($150; ℜ, ≈,
△, ◎; 250 Avenue du Phare E., G4W 3N4;
☎566-2651 or 1-888-910-1111, ≈562-7365)*
makes a charming first impression. Upon
arrival, visitors will notice the care that has
been taken to make the place both attractive
and comfortable. The wooden spiral staircase
and leather armchairs are just a hint of what
lies further on. On their way through the
restaurant and bar, guests will enjoy an
exquisite view of the St. Lawrence. The rooms
on the 3rd floor are among the newest in the
hotel, which also has a tennis court and a golf
course.

Ulysses' Favourites

Accommodations

For nature-lovers:
Gîte du Mont-Albert (p 448).

For history buffs:
Maison du Juge Thompson (p 449).

For tranquillity:
Auberge du Parc (p 449).

For the views:
Auberge du Gargantua (p 449).

Restaurants

Gaspésie's finest tables:
Au Coin de la Baie (p 450), La Normandie (p 451), Auberge à Percé (p 451), La Belle Hélène (p 450) and Gîte du Mont-Albert (p 450).

For Québec cuisine:
Ateliers Plein Soleil (p 450).

Parc de la Gaspésie

There are a number of different **campgrounds** (*$16; mid-Jun to late Sep)* in Parc de la Gaspésie, as well as 19 **cabins** *($59-$169)* able to accommodate four, six or eight people *(☎763-2288 or 1-888-270-4483, ⇌763-7803)*.

For panorama views, head to the **Gîte du Mont-Albert** *($85; ≈, ◌; ☎763-2288 or 888-270-4483, ⇌ 763-7803)*, located in Parc de la Gaspésie. The building is U-shaped, so each comfortable room offers a sweeping view of Mont Albert and Mont McGerrigle.

Mont-Saint-Pierre

The **Auberge de Jeunesse Les Vagues** *($15 per person; ℜ; 84 Rue Place Cloutier, GOE 1VO, ☎797-2851)* offers very simple and inexpensive hostel accommodations. This is a convenient base for excursions to Mont Jacques-Cartier and Parc de la Gaspésie.

Forillon National Park

There are four campgrounds in the park, with a total of 368 sites. To reserve one, dial ☎368-6050 *(May to late Jul, Mon to Fri 9:30am to noon and 1pm to 3:30pm, or from April on write to Forillon National Park, P.O. Box 1220, Gaspé, GOC 1RO)*. Only half the sites may be reserved; for the rest, the park follows a first come, first served policy. The **Camping Des-Rosiers** *($15; Jun 11 to 10 Oct; Secteur Nord)*, a partially wooded area by the sea, has 155 tent and RV sites *(42 with electricity: $18)*. The **Camping Bon-Ami** *($15;*

Jun 11 to Sep 5; Secteur Sud) has 135 tent and RV sites on a wooded stretch of land covered with fine gravel.

Cap-aux-Os

Located at the entrance to Forillon National Park, the **Auberge de Jeunesse de Cap-aux-Os** *($24-$28 per person; ℜ; 2095 Boulevard Grande-Grève, GOE 1JO; ☎892-5153)* is the perfect hostel for visitors on a tight budget. The atmosphere is truly convivial in both the cafeteria and the large living room. Activities organized.

Gaspé

The **residence hall of the CÉGEP de la Gaspésie et des Îles** *($36 a night or $180 a week; 94 Rue Jacques-Cartier, C.P. 2004, GOC 1RO; ☎368-2749)* rents out its rooms between June 15 and August 15. Guests are provided with a kitchenette, bedding, towels and dishes.

Situated between Forillon National Park and downtown Gaspé, the **Motel Fort Ramsay** *($60; K, ℜ, ℝ; 254 Boulevard Gaspé, GOC 1RO, ☎368-5094)* offers simple rooms that are somewhat noisy, due to the proximity of the road.

The **Auberge des Commandants** *($80; ℜ; 178 Rue de la Reine, GOC 1RO, ☎368-3355, ⇌368-1702)* is downtown, next to a shopping centre. The rooms are pleasant and comfortable.

Fort Prével

🦞 Like the Gîte du Mont-Albert, the **Auberge Fort-Prével** *($78; ≈,ℜ; halfway between Gaspé and Percé, 30 min from Forillon;* ☎*364-2281,* ⚏*368-1364)* is run by the Société des Établissements de Plein Air du Québec. The Fort Prével battery was used during the Second World War and an interpretive trail tells its story. There are 54 rooms and 13 equipped cottages ($135). Great views of the sea.

Percé

The **Camping du Gargantua** *($16; 222 Route des Failles,* ☎*782-2852)* is definitely the most beautiful campground in the Percé area. It offers a view not only of Rocher Percé and the sea, but also of the verdant surrounding mountains.

🦞 The **Auberge du Gargantua** *($45; ℜ; Jun to mid-Oct; 222 Route des Failles, G0L 2L0,* ☎*782-2852,* ⚏*782-5229)* has been looking out over Percé from atop its promontory for 30 years now and is well-known to anyone familiar with the Gaspé peninsula. Its restaurant (see p 451) is one of the best in the region, and its location and view are unforgettable. The small, motel-style rooms are simply decorated but comfortable.

🦞 The hotel-motel **La Normandie** *($58-$125; ℜ, ≈; 221 Route 132 O., G0C 2L0,* ☎*782-2112 or 1-888-463-0820,* ⚏*782-2337)* has a well established reputation in Percé. During the high season, this luxury establishment is full most of the time. Both the restaurant and the rooms offer a view of the famous Rocher Percé.

The **Chalets au Pie de l'Aurore** *($62-$98; Route 132,* ☎*782-2166 or 1-800-463-4212)* are located above the coast north of Percé, overlooking the entire town. Each cottage has an attractive terrace, a kitchenette, a bedroom and a living room with a fireplace.

Tour B: Baie des Chaleurs

Paspébiac

🦞 The **Auberge du Parc** *($150; ⌂, ℜ, ≈; 68 Boulevard Notre-Dame, G0C 2K0;* ☎*752-*3555 or 1-800-463-0890, ⚏752-6406) occupies a 19th-century manor erected by the Robin company. It stands in the midst of a wooded area, providing a perfect place to relax. Whirlpools, body wraps, therapeutic massages, acupressure and a saltwater pool enhance the stay.

New Carlisle

🦞 There's a pretty room waiting for you at the **Maison du Juge Thompson** *($60 bkfst incl.; Jul and Aug; 105 Rue Principale,* ☎*752-6308 or 752-5744),* a lovely old villa dating from 1844, complete with walking paths and a beautiful period garden. You can relax and admire the sea on the veranda. The tasty English-style breakfasts are an added bonus.

Carleton

Located near the sea and the beach, the **Camping Carleton** *($14; banc de Larocque,* ☎*364-3992)* is open from mid-June to early September. Despite the lack of shady sites, this is a very calm pleasant place.

The **Hotel-Motel Baie Bleue** *($90-$105; ℜ; 682 Boulevard Perron,* ☎*364-3355 or 1-800-463-9099,* ⚏*364-6165)* has one hundred modern and well-maintained rooms.

The **Centre de Thalassothérapie Aqua-Mer** *($1095 for seven days, including treatments, meals and return transportation from Charlo airport in New Brunswick; ≈;* ☎*364-7055 or 1-800-463-0867,* ⚏*364-7351)* located in an enchanting setting, offers a number of seven-day packages.

Pointe-à-la-Garde

The **Auberge de Jeunesse** and **Château Bahia** *($24 per person; ℜ; 152 Boulevard Perron, G0C 2M0,* ☎*788-2048)* are set back from the road, halfway between Carleton and Matapédia. This youth hoste is a great place to relax. During the high season, the clientele consists mainly of Europeans. Guests are offered high-quality regional dishes such as fresh salmon and maple-flavoured ham, all at modest prices, and may sleep either in the hostel or in the château behind it.

GASPÉSIE

Causapscal

Open between June and September, the **Camping Municipal Saint-Jacques** *($18; ≈; 601 Rue Saint-Jacques Nord, ☎756-5621 or 756-3996)* contains 48 sites for tents and trailers.

La Coulée Douce *($50 sb, $66 pb; ℜ; 21 Rue Soudreau, GOJ 1JO, ☎756-5270, ≈756-3001)* is open from June to September, as well as during the winter, depending on the demand. The former residence of a parish priest, this pleasant little family inn lies in the heart of the Matapédia valley. The rooms are cozily decorated with old furniture.

 RESTAURANTS

Tour A: The Peninsula

Grand-Métis

The restaurant **Les Ateliers Plein Soleil** *($-$$; Jardins de Métis)* takes pride in making sure everything is perfect: the waiters and waitresses, dressed in period clothing, are attentive; the decor is picturesque and the Métis and Québécois cuisine is served in generous portions.

Métis-sur-Mer

The restaurant **Au Coin de la Baie** *($$$; 1140 Route 132, ☎936-3855)* opens its doors between May and September. Here, visitors can treat themselves to smoked salmon royale and "cedar" sorbet. The wine list is excellent.

Matane

The **Pizzeria Italia** *($-$$; toward downtown, at the corner of Rue Saint-Pierre and Rue Saint-Jérôme; ☎562-3646)* serves pizza made with fresh top-quality ingrédients and an interesting choice of toppings.

The restaurant **Le Vieux Rafiot** *($$-$$$; 1415 Avenue du Phare, alongside Route 132, ☎562-8080)* attracts lots of visitors to its incredible dining room, which is divided into three sections by partitions with portholes and decorated with paintings by local artists. In addition to the novel decor, guests can enjoy a variety of delicious dishes.

At **La Maison Sous le Vent** *($$$$; 1014 du Phare O., ☎562-7611)*, opened in 1992, you will dine on exquisite refined cuisine; beef, lamb and fish are prepared with wine, herbs and citrus fruits.

Cap-Chat

The **Fleur de Lys** *($$-$$$; 184 Route 132 Est, ☎786-5518)* invites visitors to savour dishes prepared fresh every day. Warm welcome.

Parc de la Gaspésie

The **Gîte du Mont-Albert** *($$$$; ☎762-2288)* offers innovative seafood dishes that are definitely worth a try. During the Game Festival, in September, you can sample more unusual meats like guinea hen, bison and partridge.

Gaspé

The bistro/bar **Brise-Brise** *($-$$; 2 Côte Cartier, Place Jacques-Cartier, ☎368-1456)* is probably the nicest café in Gaspé. The menu includes sausages, seafood, salads and sandwiches. The place also features an assortment of beer and coffee, an enjoyable happy hour, live shows all summer long, and dancing late into the evening.

Varnished wooden tables and chairs give the **Bourlingueur** *($-$$; 207 Rue de la Reine, ☎368-4323)* the look of an old English pub. This is a large, friendly place, where visitors can enjoy a relaxing meal of Canadian or Chinese food. Try the Cantonese-style lobster.

The café-restaurant **La Belle Hélène** *($$$-$$$$; 135A Rue de la Reine, ☎368-1455)* serves what is undoubtedly the best food in the entire Gaspé area. The menu includes not only fish and seafood, but also Breton crepes and originally-prepared game. For dessert, try the maple syrup and hazelnut pie. The service is pleasant, and the music, exquisite. The tables are decorated with bouquets of regional flowers.

Fort Prével

At **Fort Prével** *($$$-$$$$; 2053 Boulevard Douglas, ☎368-2281 or 1-888-377-3835)* (see p 449) guests are not only plunged into an historic atmosphere, but also get to savour delicious French and Québec cuisine. These skillfully prepared and elegantly presented dishes are served to guests in a huge dining room. The menu includes fish and seafood, of course, as well as all sorts of specialties that could turn any gourmet green with envy.

Percé

La Maison du Pêcheur *($$-$$$; ☎782-5331)* lies right in the heart of the village. It is two restaurants in one; on the second floor, there is a *crêperie* which looks out on the sea and also serves breakfast, while the third floor is reserved for dinner guests. The prices are a little high, but everything is first-rate.

Though there are lots of restaurants in Percé, few fall into the gourmet category. One that does, however, is the **Auberge à Percé** *($$$; 1 Promenade du Bord de Mer, ☎782-5055 or 1-888-782-5055)*, which serves divinely prepared scallops, lobster, fish and red meat. The restaurant's charming address seems tailor-made for the beautiful setting.

Regarded by many as one of the best restaurants in Percé, **La Normandie** *($$$$; 221 Route 132 O.; ☎782-2112)* serves delicious food in an altogether charming spot. Diners rave about the *feuilleté de homard au champagne* lobster in puff pastry with champagne) and the *pétoncles à l'ail* (scallops with garlic). The restaurant also features an extensive wine list.

The decor of the **Auberge Gargantua** *($$$$; 222 Rue des Failles; ☎782-2852)* is reminiscent of the French countryside where the owners were born. The dining room offers a splendid view of the surrounding mountains, so be sure to arrive early enough enjoy it. The dishes are all gargantuan and delicious, and usually include an appetizer of periwinkle, a plate of raw vegetables, and soup. Guests choose their main dish from a long list, ranging from salmon to snow crab, to a selection of game.

Tour B: Baie des Chaleurs

Bonaventure

The **Café Acadien** *($$-$$$; early Jun to mid-Sep; 168 Rue Beaubassin, ☎534-4276)* serves good food in a charming setting. Open throughout the summer season, this place is very popular with locals and tourists alike, which might explain why the prices are a little high.

Carleton

La Seigneurie *($$-$$$; 482 Boulevard Perron; ☎364-3355)*, the restaurant in the Hôtel-Motel Baie Bleue, serves a wide variety of delicious dishes based on game, fish and seafood. The view from the dining room is superb.

La Maison Monti *($$$-$$$$; 840 Boulevard Perron, ☎364-6181)* is the former residence of Honoré Bernard, known as Monti, a rich prospector who returned to Carleton after living out west for a while. The glassed-in dining room is comfortable, and the atmosphere, pleasant. The menu is made up of game, fish and seafood. The service is friendly and attentive.

Causapscal

La Cantine Linda *($; 391 Rue Saint-Jacques N., ☎756-5022)* serves simple, quick dishes.

  ENTERTAINMENT

Bars and Nightclubs

Gaspé

La Voûte *(114 Rue de la Reine)* caters mainly to students. The bar is busiest from 6pm to midnight. *Chansonniers* perform here regularly. On the second floor, there is a bar for people 25 and up.

GASPÉSIE

Theatres

Petite-Vallée

The **Théâtre du Café de la Vieille Forge** *($12; Jun to late Aug, next to the Maison LeBreux; 4 Longue-Pointe,* ☎*393-2222)* puts on plays with a Gaspésian or Québécois flavour and featuring local actors. Touring professional comedians and singers also give shows here throughout the summer.

Carleton

The **Théâtre La Moluque** *($20; mid-Jul to late Aug, Tue to Sat 8:30am; Route 132, downtown; 586 Boulevard Perron,* ☎*364-7151)* puts on professional stage productions. New and stock plays are both performed here.

Festivals and Cultural Events

Matane

Matane's famous shrimp is prized by seafood-lovers far beyond Gaspésie. The **Festival de la Crevette** *(*☎*562-0404)* is held in its honour each year at the end of June.

Mont-Saint-Pierre

Mont-Saint-Pierre's **Fête du Vol Libre** *(*☎*797-2222)* celebrates the town's vocation as a sky-diving centre. Sky-divers from all over come here to swoop about over the bay throughout the summer, but at the end of July, when this activity-filled festival takes place, they really turn out in force.

 SHOPPING

Tour A: The Peninsula

Grand-Métis

Les Ateliers Plein Soleil *(every day 9am to 6:30pm; Jardins de Métis,* ☎*775-3165)*, a group of artisans from Grand-Métis, runs the Maison Reford. They make all sorts of hand-woven tablecloths, doilies and napkins, which may be purchased in their shop, along with herbs, locally produced honey and home-made tomato ketchup.

Percé

Thanks to its central location, you can't miss the Place du Quai, a cluster of over 30 shops and restaurants, as well as a laundromat and an S.A.Q. (liquor store).

Causapscal

Le Kiosque d'Artisanat de la Matapédia *(early Jun to mid-Oct, every day 9am to 9pm; 51 Rue Saint-Jacques Sud,* ☎*756-3062)* has a wide choice of fabrics and knitwear, toys, jewellery, home-made preserves made with wild fruit and all sorts of other souvenirs to take back home. Local artisans have joined forces to offer customers items that truly reflect the traditions of the region.

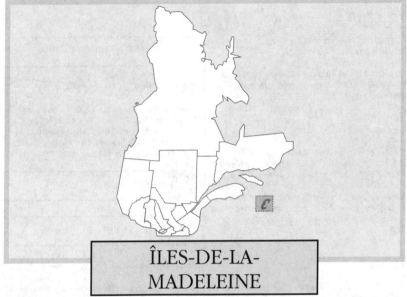

ÎLES-DE-LA-MADELEINE

The Îles-de-la-Madeleine (sometimes referred to in English as the Magdalen Islands) emerge from the middle of the Gulf of St. Lawrence more than 200 kilometres from the Gaspé Peninsula. They constitute a 65-kilometre-long archipelago of about a dozen islands, many connected to one another by long sand dunes. Swept by winds from the open sea, these small islands offer superb colourful scenery. The golden dunes and the long wild beaches blend with the red sandstone cliffs and the blue sea. Villages with brightly painted houses, lighthouses and harbours add the finishing touches to the islands' beautiful scenery.

The 15,000 *Madelinots* (as residents are called) have always earned their livelihood from the sea, and continue to do so today by fishing for crab, bottom-feeding fish, mackerel and lobster. The population, mostly of French origin, live on seven islands of the archipelago: Île de la Grande Entrée, Grosse Île, Île aux Loups, Île du Havre aux Maisons, Île du Cap aux Meules, Île du Havre Aubert and Île d'Entrée. Among them, only Île d'Entrée, where a few families with Scottish roots live, is not attached by land to the rest of the archipelago.

The Îles-de-la-Madeleine archipelago was first inhabited sporadically by Micmac tribes, also called the 'Indians of the Sea'. As of the 15th century, the islands were visited regularly by walrus and seal hunters, fishers and whalers, most of Breton or Basque descent. In 1534,

Jacques Cartier came upon the islands during his first North American expedition. Permanent occupancy did not begin until after 1755 when Acadian families took refuge here after having escaped deportation. Following the British Conquest, the Îles-de-la-Madeleine were annexed to the province of Newfoundland before being integrated into Québec territory in 1774. A few years later, in 1798, King Georges III granted Admiral Isaac Coffin the title of seigneur of the Îles-de-la-Madeleine, initiating a dismal period for the inhabitants of the archipelago. He and his family ruled the land despotically until 1895, when a Québec law allowed the Madelinots to buy back their land.

 FINDING YOUR WAY AROUND

By Car

Of the seven inhabited islands of the Îles-de-la-Madeleine, six are linked together by Route 199. The tour we have proposed brings visitors to each island to unveil some of the hidden treasures.

The seventh island, Île d'Éntrée, is only accessible by boat, and is a trip in itself. The *S. P. Bonaventure* (☎986-5705) boat leaves the Cap-aux-Meules pier from Monday to Saturday, and the trip takes approximately one hour.

Car rentals are available for visitors who want to drive around the islands.

Cap-aux-Meules Honda: 199 Rue La Vernière, ☎418-986-4085. They also rent motorcycles.

Tilden: Airport, ☎418-969-2590

By Plane

Air Alliance *(☎418-969-2888 or 800-361-8620)* and **Inter-Canadian** *(☎800-665-1177)* both offer daily flights to the Îles-de-la-Madeleine. Most flights make stopovers in Cluébec, Mont-Joli or Gaspé, so count on a four-hour trip. Considerable price reductions can be found by booking well in advance.

By Ferry

The *M.V. Lucy Maud Montgomery* ferry *($33.75, car $65, motorcycle $22.50, bicycle $7.75; ☎418-986-6600 or 888-986-3278, ≈986-5101)* leaves from Souris (Prince Edward Island) and reaches Cap-aux-Meules in about five hours. Try to reserve in advance if possible; if not, arrive at the pier a few hours before departure, or to be extra sure, go to Souris the day before your departure and reserve seats. Ask for the ferry crossing schedule, as it changes from one season to the next.

The cargo and passenger vessel *CTMA Voyageur ($480 one-way in high season, includes meals; ☎418-986-6600)* leaves the port of Montréal every Sunday and sails down the St-Laurent to the Îles-de-la-Madeleine; the boat can take about 15 people, and the trip takes 48 hours.

By Bicycle

Bikes are, without a doubt, the best way to visit the islands. Here is bike rental outfit:

Le Pédalier: 365 Chemin Principal, Cap-aux-Meules, ☎418-986-2965.

 PRACTICAL INFORMATION

Area code: 418

Tourist Information Office

Regional Office

Association Touristique des Îles de la Madeleine: 128 Chemin du Débarcadère, Cap-aux-Meules, ☎986-2245, ≈986-2327, www.ilesdelamadeleine.com; mailing address: C.P. 1028, Cap-aux-Meules, GOB 1BO.

 EXPLORING

Tour of the Islands ★★

Île du Cap aux Meules (pop. 1,648)

Our tour begins on **Île du Cap aux Meules ★**, since it is the archipelago's most populated island as well as the docking point for all the ferries (Cap-aux-Meules). Home to the region's major infrastructures, (hospital, high school, CÉGEP), this island is the centre of local economic activity. This activity does not take away from the island's charm, however, with the brightly painted houses that some say allow sailors to see their homes from the sea.

Cap-aux-Meules, the only urban centre of the archipelago (also the only town to have a traffic light) has experienced major development over the past few years. Many buildings have been constructed quickly, leaving little room for aestheticism. A few of the traditional houses still stand, notably the Sumarah warehouse and smokehouse complex *(along the sea, facing the Banque Nationale)*.

A climb to the top of the **Butte du Vent ★★** reveals a superb panorama of the island and the gulf.

The beautiful **Chemin de Gros-Cap ★★**, south of Cap-aux-Meules, runs alongside the Baie de Plaisance and offers breathtaking scenery. If possible, stop at the **Pêcherie Gros-Cap**, where the employees can be seen at work in this fish processing plant.

Head back and take Chemin de L'Étang-du-Nord to Étang-du-Nord.

For a long time, **Étang-du-Nord** was home to almost half the Îles-de-la-Madeleine population

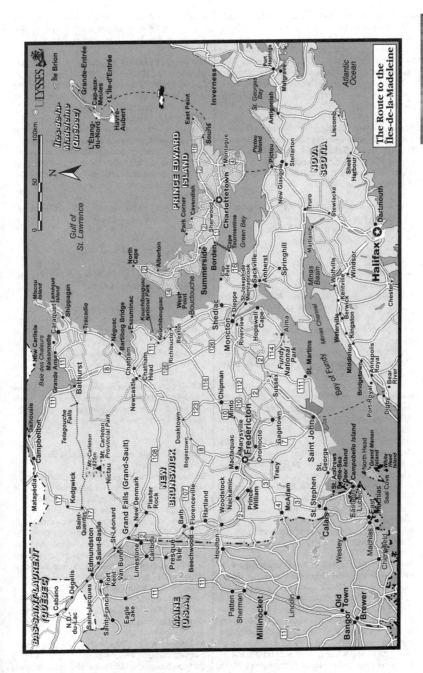

The Route to the
Îles-de-la-Madeleine

and it constituted the largest fishing village. With the foundation of Cap-aux-Meules (1959) and Fatima (1954), however, it lost a significant part of its population, and now only has a bit more than 3,000 inhabitants. The municipality, with its beautiful port, welcomes many visitors every year who come to take advantage of the region's tranquillity and natural beauty.

North of Étang-du-Nord, visitors can take in a splendid view by walking along the magnificent **Falaises de la Belle Anse** ★★. There is an impressive sight of the violent waves crashing relentlessly along the coast, from the top of this rocky escarpment.

Return to Étang-du-Nord and take Chemin de L'Étang-du-Nord to the Highway 199 junction, take this road toward Havre-Aubert, it crosses the Dune du Havre aux Basques.

Île du Havre Aubert

The beautiful **Île du Havre Aubert** ★★★, dotted with beaches, hills and forests, has managed to keep its picturesque charm. From early on it was home to various colonies. Even today, buildings testify to these early colonial years. Prior to this, it was populated by Micmac communities, and relics have been discovered.

Havre-Aubert, the first stop on the island, stretches along the sea, and benefits from a large bay, ideal for fishing. Apart from the magnificent scenery, the most interesting attraction is without a doubt the **La Grave** ★★★ area, which has developed along a pebbly beach and gets its charm from the traditional cedar-shingled houses. It is the heart of a lively area, and home to several cultural events. Boutiques and cafés line the streets, which are always enjoyable, even in bad weather. The few buildings along the sea were originally stores and warehouses that received the fish caught by locals.

For anyone interested in the fascinating world of marine life, the **Aquarium des Îles-de-la-Madeleine** ★ *($3.50; mid-Jun to late Aug, every day 10am to 9pm; 982, Route 199, La Grave, ☎937-2277)* is a real treat. Here visitors can observe (and even touch) many different marine species, such as lobsters, crabs, sea urchins, eels, a ray, as well as a multitude of other fish and shells. The second floor has more of an educational atmosphere with

exhibits explaining the various fishing techniques used throughout the years by the islands' fishermen.

The **Musée de la Mer** ★ *(adults $3.50; late Jun to late Aug, Mon to Fri 9am to 6pm, Sat to Sun 10am to 6pm; late Aug to late Jun, Mon to Fri 9am to noon and 1pm to 5pm, Sat to Sun 1pm to 5pm; 1023 Pointe Shea, Hwy 199, ☎937-5711)* recounts the history of the populating of the islands as well as the relationship that links the Madelinots' destiny to the sea. Visitors also have the opportunity to explore the world of fishing and navigation, as well as discover some of the myths and legends that surround the sea.

When leaving Havre-Aubert, follow Chemin du Sable to Sandy Hook Dune.

Sandy Hook Dune ★★★ (see p 459)

Return along Chemin du Sable and take Chemin du Bassin to Étang-des-Caps.

The road that runs along the sea between the Pointe à Marichite and the Étang-des-Caps offers a magnificent view ★★ of the Gulf of St. Lawrence. From the small village of **L'Étang-des-Caps**, the small Île Corps Mort is visible in the distance on clear days.

Return via Chemin de la Montagne, and follow Chemin du Bassin, then return towards Île du Cap aux Meules by taking Highway 199, which leads to Île du Havre aux Maisons.

Île du Havre aux Maisons (pop. 2,259)

Île du Havre aux Maisons ★★ is characterized by its bare landscape and its small attractive villages with pretty little houses scattered along the winding roads. The steep cliffs at the southern end of the island overlook the gulf and offer a fascinating view of this immense stretch of water. The Dune du Nord and the Dune du Sud are two long strips of land found at both extremities of the island, and are home to beautiful beaches. In the centre of the town also named **Havre-aux-Maisons** stands the Vieux Couvent (old convent) and the presbytery; the town is also the island's main centre of activity.

La Méduse ★ *(37 Chemin de la Carrière, Havre-aux-Maisons, ☎969-4245)* glass-blowing factory opens its doors to visitors, allowing

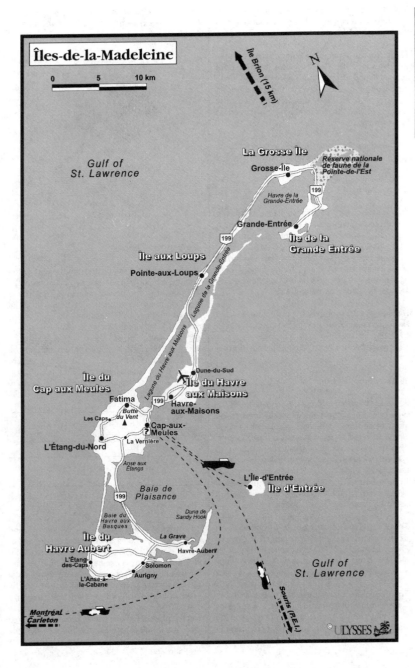

Îles-de-la-Madeleine

0   5   10 km

Île Brion (15 km)

N

Gulf of
St. Lawrence

La Grosse Île

Grosse-Île

Réserve nationale
de faune de la
Pointe-de-l'Est

Havre de la
Grande-Entrée

199

Grande-Entrée

199

Île aux Loups

Pointe-aux-Loups

Île de la
Grande Entrée

Lagune de la Grande-Entrée

Laguna du Havre aux Maisons

Dune-du-Sud

Île du
Cap aux Meules

Île du Havre
aux Maisons

Fatima

199

Havre-
aux-Maisons

Butte
du Vent

Les Caps

Cap-aux-
Meules

L'Étang-du-Nord

La Vernière

Anse aux
Étangs

Baie de
Plaisance

L'Île-d'Entrée

Île d'Entrée

Baie du
Havre aux
Basques

Dune de
Sandy Hook

199

Île du
Havre Aubert

La Grave

Havre-Aubert

L'Étang-
des-Caps

Solomon

L'Anse-à-
la-Cabane

Aurigny

Gulf of
St. Lawrence

Montréal
Carleton

Souris (P.E.I.)

© ULYSSES

them to see the glass-blowers et work. Next to the workshop is a small boutique that displays the items made there.

The scenic Chemin de la Pointe-Basse crosses the south of the island along the Baie de Plaisance and offers beautiful lookouts. A small path along the road, between the Cap à Adrien and the Cap à Alfred, descends towards the sea, revealing the charming natural haven of Pointe-Basse.

Continue along Highway 199, which leads to Grosse Île by crossing Île aux Loups.

Grosse Île (pop. 575)

The rcoky coasts of **Grosse Île** have caused numerous shipwrecks, the survivors of which have settled here. A good number of these accidental colonists were Scottish, and approximately 500 of them still live here today. Most earn their living from fishing and agriculture; some also work in the Seleine saltworks, which opened in 1983.

Highway 199 continues until the **Pointe-de-l'Est National Wildlife Area ★** (see below).

Follow Highway 199 to Île de la Grande Entrée.

Île de la Grande Entrée (pop. 733)

Île de la Grande Entrée ★, colonized in 1870, was the last of the Îles-de-la-Madeleine to be inhabited. Upon arriving, cross Pointe Old-Harry, to check out a striking view of the gulf. This tip of the island was named in honor of Harry Clark, who was the area's only inhabitant for many years. The island's main town, **Grande-Entrée**, has an active port that serves as a departure point for many brightly painted fishing boats, usually for lobster fishing.

The **Old Harry School** *(Jun to Aug, Mon to Fri 8am to noon and 1pm to 4pm; 787 Chemin Principal, ☎985-2116)* is a reproduction of an old-fashioned schoolhouse. A quick tour includes old photos and paraphernalia.

To know more about the lives of seals, visit the **Centre d'interprétation du phoque ★** *(Jun to Aug, every day 11am to 6pm; 377 Route 199; ☎985-2833)* where various exhibits explain the lifestyle of these mammals.

To get to Île d'Entrée, which can be seen in a full day visit take the ferry from the Cap-aux-Meules dock.

Lobster Trap

Île d'Entrée

Île d'Entrée ★★ stands out from the rest of the islands not only because of its geographic location (it is the only inhabited island that is not linked to the others), but because of its population (some 200 residents, all of Scottish descent). This small community lives almost entirely from the sea, and has managed to settle on this land despite the waves and the wind. The island has its own infrastructure to meets the needs of its residents (electricity, roads, and telephone). An incredible serenity prevails on this undulating islet.

 PARKS AND BEACHES

Parks

Grosse Île

The eastern tip, made up of dunes and beaches, is home to the rich bird life typical of these islands. It is one of the best sites for spotting various species, such as the rare piping plover (which only nests on the islands) the northern pintail, the betted kingfisher, the atlantic puffin and the horned lark, but take care not to damage the nesting sites (generally clearly marked). This entire zone is protected by the **Pointe-de-l'Est National Wildlife Area ★**, also known as the Réserve Nationale de Faune de la Pointe-de-l'Est.

Beaches

Île du Cap aux Meules

The **Plage de l'Hôpital**, located along the Dune du Nord, is a good place to go for a dip and watch the seals. You'll also find the wreckage of a ship here. It should be noted that the currents become dangerous toward Pointe-aux-Loups. The Anse the l'Hôpital, Cap de l'Hôpital, Plage de l'Hôpital and Étang-de-l'Hôpital are all named after a boat that came into the cove (*anse*) carrying passengers suffering from a contagious illness (typhus). The boat was put into quarantine, and only doctors and nurses were allowed on board.

Île du Havre Aubert

Like a long strip of sand stretching into the gulf, **Sandy Hook Dune ★★★** is several kilometres long and its beach is among the nicest on the islands. This spot is a favourite with nudists, who come to swim in complete tranquillity.

The **Plage de l'Ouest ★** stretches from the northwest part of Île du Havre Aubert to the southwest part of Île du Cap aux Meules. Perfect for swimming and shell collecting, it is renowned for its magnificent sunsets.

Île du Havre aux Maisons

The **plage de la Dune du Sud ★** offers several kilometres of beach, great for swimming.

Grosse Île

One of the most beautiful beaches of the islands, the **Plage de la Grande Échouerie ★★**, stretches for about 10 kilometres in the Pointe-de-l'Est wildlife area.

 OUTDOORS

 Scuba-Diving

Aventure Plongée des Iles-de-la-Madeleine *(near the tourist office, Cap-aux-Meules, ☎986-6475*

or 986-3899) rents outs snorkeling and scuba diving equipment and can refill your oxygen tank. It also offers lessons and organizes excursions.

 Fishing

Visitors can take part in fishing trips organized by the **Excursions de Pêche des Îles** *(early Jun to mid-Sep; Quai de Cap-aux-Meules, ☎986-4745)*, who also offer boat trips to Île d'Entrée and Île du Havre Aubert. All fishing equipment and instructions are provided on the boat.

The **Pourvoirie Mako** *(Grande-Entrée, ☎985-2895)* organizes shark-fishing excursions around the islands.

  Sailing and Windsurfing

L'Istorlet *(weekly rentals possible, Île du Havre Albert, ☎937-5266)* offers sailing and windsurfing courses and rents out small boats. Its safe and calm location, near the Bassin, makes it the ideal spot for beginners or first-timers to try this sport. Expect to spend $30 per hour for sailling and $20 per hour for windsurfing.

 Cruises

A boat ride on the *Le Ponton III* of the **Excursions de la Lagune** *($20; daily departures in the summer at 11am, 2pm, and 6pm; Île du Havre aux Maisons, ☎969-4550 or 969-2088)*, is an exciting two-hour trip on the waves, during which visitors can observe the sea floot and occasionally some shellfish through the boat's glass bottom.

La Gaspésienne 26 ($40; Mon-Sat during the tourist season; La Grave marina, Ile du Havre Aubert, ☎937-2213), a schooner, is one of a handful of the 50 *Gaspésiennes* to have been restored. A veritable floating work of art, this schooner will carry you off to contemplate the sea in absolute silence. There are two cruises per day, each four hours long.

The *Blanchons*

The symbol of the eco-tourist industry on the Iles-de-la-Madeleine, the *blanchon* is a young seal or "*loup-marin*" (sea-wolf), as the islanders call these mammals. During the first weeks of March, after a long journey along the shores of Labrador and through the Gulf of St. Lawrence, the seals give birth on the ice floes around the Îles-de-la-Madeleine. Nearly three million seals make this trip each year. Once the young have been weaned, the animals head back up to the Arctic, where they spend the greater part of their lives.

The seals actually reach the islands in January, after following the shores of Labrador for about four months. They stay in the gulf for two or three months, building up their fatty tissue. The month of March is marked by the birth of thousands of these little fur-balls that touched the hearts of people around in the 1970s, when environmental groups demonstrated against the seal-hunt. The *blanchons* have to be a month and a half old before they can take their first dive, which makes it easy to observe them. During this period, the *blanchons* grow at an astonishing pace; in the 12 days they are suckled by their mothers, they triple their weight. Seal's milk is actually five times as rich as cow's milk.

The *blanchons* are no longer threatened by hunting, but adult seals are still hunted. When it comes to fish, these animals are formidable predators. Some fishermen even hold them responsible for the depleted fish stocks. Madelinots and Newfoundlanders thus kill nearly 50,000 seals a year. In spite of that, seals are from being an endangered species. In response to pressure from the fishermen, the federal government has revived seal hunting by setting the quotas at 200,000 a year.

 Birdwatching

During the "échouerie" nature walks *(Thu to Sun, in the morning)* organized by the **Club Vacances "Les Iles"** *(Grande-Entrée, ☎985-2833)*, you'll have a chance to see the nests of some whistling plovers, an endangered species. It is important that observers spend no more than 10 or 15 minutes near the nests; otherwise, they might disrupt the birds. At the beach, you'll see guillemots soaring through the air.

 Hiking

The **Club Vacances 'Les Îles'** *(Grande-Entrée, ☎985-2833)* organizes nature walks to help visitors discover the various ecosystems found on the Îles-de-la-Madeleine.

 Horseback Riding

La Chevauchée des Iles *($15 per hour in the forest, $25 for two hours in the forest and on the beach; Jun to Sep; Étang-des-Caps, Ile du*
Havre Aubert, ☎937-2368) organizes riding excursions in the forest and on the beach. Pony rides for the kids cost $15 for a quarter of an hour. Reservations required. Visitors will also find a small zoo containing exotic species like nandus and pygmy goats.

 Sea Kayaking

Aventure Plein Air *(1252 Route 199, L'Étang-du-Nord, Ile de Cap aux Meules, ☎986-5781 or 986-6161)* rents out kayaks *($40 per day)*, organizes guided kayak trips and offers a number of packages. Two-hour guided tours of the caves and cliffs *($25 per person)* at 9am, noon, 3pm and 6pm.

Cime Aventure *($1000; Ile de Cap aux Meules, ☎1-800-790-2463)* hosts six-day kayak trips around the islands. Fixed departure dates.

 ACCOMMODATIONS

Île du Cap aux Meules

The **Le Barachois** campground *($16; ℜ; Fatima, ☎986- 6065, or 986-5678)* can accommodate tents or campers in its 80 sites that are also sheltered from the wind. Located in the middle of a small wooded area along the sea, it has a peaceful atmosphere.

The very warm welcome at the **Auberge Chez Sam** *($35; sb; 1767 Chemin de L'Etang-du-Nord, L'Étang-du-Nord, GOS 1EO, ☎986-5780)* will quickly make guests feel et home. There are five attractive and well-kept rooms here.

Auberge Maison du Cap-Vert *($49 bkfst incl.; year round; 202 Chemin L'Aucoin, P.O. Box 521, Fatima, GOB 1KO, ☎986-5331)* is a family inn with five absolutely charming rooms with comfy beds and a unique decor. This place has managed to carve out an enviable place for itself on the island inn scene in just a short period of time. With its delicious, all-you-can-eat breakfasts, this place is definitely a good deal.

Visitors might first be surprised to find that the **Château Madelinot** *($109; ℜ, ≈, ℝ, ⊗, △; 323 Highway 199, C.P.44, GOB 180, ☎986-3695, or 1-800-661-4537, ⇒986-6437)* is really a large house. But the comfortable rooms and superb view of the sea make it easy to forget this first impression. The château offers many services including a saltwater spa and a large swimming pool, and is without a doubt the most well-known accommodation on the islands.

Île du Havre Aubert

The **Plage du Golfe** campground *($15; 535 Chemin du Bassin, GOS 1AO, ☎937-5115, ⇒937-5572)* has more than 70 sites, some of which accommodate trailers.

Located close to La Grave, **La Marée Haute** *($60; sb, ℜ; 25 Chemin des Fumoirs, GOB 1J0, ☎937-2492)*, is a lovely little inn where guests receive an extremely warm welcome. The rooms are cosy and attractively decorated. One of the owners also cooks; you won't regret trying one of these lovingly and meticulously prepared dishes. The view from the inn is absolutely ravishing!

The **Havre Sur Mer** inn *($95; ℜ; 1197 Chemin du Bassin, L'Anse à la Cabane, GOS 1AO, ☎937-5675, ⇒937-2540)*, near the cliff's edge, enjoys a magnificent location. The rooms have a communal terrace from which everybody can enjoy the beautiful view. The inn is decorated with antique furniture, and attracts many visitors. If you are interested in staying here, it is best to make reservations in advance.

Île du Havre aux Maisons

The **Au Vieux Couvent** hotel *($40; ℜ; 292 Highway 199, Havre-aux-Maisons, GOS 1KO, ☎969-2233, ⇒969-4693)* was built during the First World War and served first as a convent, then as a school. Today it has been converted into a quaint hotel with approximately ten rooms, some of which (the corner rooms) have a nice view of the sea.

Set up in a charming hundred-year-old house, the **La P'tite Baie** inn *($70 bkfst incl.; 187 Highway 199, Havre-aux-Maisons, GOS 1EO, ☎969-4073, ⇒969-4900)* is made of wood and enjoys a warm and comfortable atmosphere. The impeccable rooms offer a superb view of the surrounding area.

Île de la Grande Entrée

The **Grande-Entrée** campground of the **Club Vacances "Les Îles"** *($12; Grande-Entrée, GOS 1HO, ☎985-2833)* is equipped with 40 sites, eight set up for trailers. A dormitory is available for visitors on rainy days.

The **Club Vacances "Les Îles"** *($236 per person, ½b for 3 days including all activities; Grande-Entrée, ☎985-2833 or 1-888-537-4537, ⇒985-2226)*, in addition to offering comfortable rooms, organizes several activities and excursions so that visitors can discover the area's natural riches. Guests can also take advantage of the cafeteria for their meals, where they are served generous portions of food.

Île d'Entrée

There are very few accommodation options on this island. There is, however, the possibility of staying with the local inhabitants et **Chez McLean** *($45; GOB 1CO, ☎986-4541)*. It is a house built over 60 years ago that has managed to keep its character of yesteryear.

Ulysses' Favourites

Accommodations

For history buffs:
  Hôtel au Vieux Couvent (see p 461)

For the reception:
  Auberge Chez Sam (p 461)

For the views:
  Hôtel Au Vieux Couvent (p 461), Château Madelinot (p 461), La Marée Haute (p 461) and Auberge Havre sur Mer (p 461).

Restaurants

The islands' finest tables:
  La Table des Roy (p 462) and La Marée Haute (p 462).

For the warm ambiance:
  Café de la Grave (p 462)

For Québec cuisine:
  La Saline (p 462) and La P'tite Baie (p 463)

RESTAURANTS

Île du Cap aux Meules

Le Bistrot *($-$$; 169 Chemin Principal, Cap-aux-Meules, ☎986-2435)* is a small but lively café that serves good hearty meals. Crepes stuffed with lobster, and seafood submarines are just some of the house specialties.

The **P'tit Café** *($$; ☎986-2130)*, in the Château Madelinot (see p 461), serves Sunday brunch from 10am to 1:30pm. Those with a taste for novelty can order seafood, red meat or chicken cooked on a hot stone. The menu includes a large selection of appetizers, soups and charbroiled offerings. In addition to a view of the sea, the decor is enhanced by temporary exhibitions by artists from the islands and elsewhere in Québec.

 Since 1978, the **La Table des Roy** *($$$$; mid-May to mid-Sep from 6pm, closed Mon; La Vernière, ☎986-3004)*, restaurant has offered refined cuisine to delight every visitor's tastebuds. The seafood, prepared in a multitude of ways, such as grilled scallops and lobster with *coralline sauce,* naturally highlights this tempting menu. The dining room is

charming and adds a particular style to this excellent restaurant that also offers dishes adorned with edible flowers and plants of the islands. It is advised to reserve in advance.

Île du Havre Aubert

Decorated like an old general store, the **Café de la Grave** *($$; early May to end of Oct 8:30am to 3pm; Havre-Aubert, ☎937-5765)* has one of the most pleasant atmospheres, and on days when the weather is bad, you can spend hours here chatting. In addition to muffins, croissants and a wide variety of coffees, the menu offers healthy and sometimes unusual dishes, such as *pâté de loup marin,* which are always good. This café is delightfully welcoming and will leave you with lasting memories.

A former salting shed in La Grave, **La Saline** *($$-$$$; 1009 Route 199, ☎937-2230)* serves excellent regional cuisine. *Loup-marin,* cod, mussels, shrimp and other saltwater treats appear on the menu. Guests also get to enjoy a splendid view of the sea.

The chef and co-owner of **La Marée Haute** *($$$; 25 Chemin des Fumoirs, ☎937-2492)*, knows how bring out the best in fish and seafood. In this pretty inn, you can sample sea perch, shark or mackerel while drinking in the magnificent view. You can taste the ocean in these dishes, whose expertly enhanced flavour will send you into raptures. The menu also includes a few equally well-prepared meat dishes and some succulent desserts.

Île du Havre aux Maisons

La P'tite Baie *($$$; year round; 187 Route 199, ☎969-4073)* serves well-prepared grill, seafood and fish, as well as a number of beef, pork and chicken dishes. *Loup-marin* is served up here in season. In addition to the à la carte menu, there is a table-d'hôte with a choice of two main dishes. The service is courteous and a great deal of care has gone into the decor.

There are two restaurants in the Hôtel Au Vieux Couvent (see p 461). **La Moulière** *($$$; 8am to 10pm; 292 Highway 199, ☎969-2233)*, located on the main floor, occupies a large room that formerly served as a chapel. They serve excellent dishes in a lively atmosphere. **Rest-O-Bar** *($$)* is found on the same floor, in a room (former parlour) that extends onto a terrace overlooking the sea. Hamburgers and mussels are among the dishes served in this restaurant, which is just as popular as La Moulière.

Grosse Île

Chez B&J *($; year round; 243 Route 199, ☎985-2926)* serves fresh scallops, halibut, lobster salad and fresh fish.

Île de la Grande Entrée

The **Délice de la Mer** *($; early Jun to Sep 11am to 9pm; 907 Route 199, Quai de Grande-Entrée, ☎985-2364)* specializes in simply prepared seafood dishes; the lobster is delicious. Affordable prices and home-made desserts.

ENTERTAINMENT

Bars and Nightclubs

Île du Havre aux Maisons

The **Chez Gaspard** bar et the Hôtel Au Vieux Couvent is set up in a former convent dining hall. Musicians play on some evenings, making the bar lively and noisy.

Festivals and Cultural Events

Île du Cap aux Meules

The **Théâtre de la Parlure** *($17; Jul to Sep, Tue to Sat at 8:30pm; at the Château Madelinot; Cap-aux-Meules, ☎986-4040)* puts on plays with a "Madelinot" flavour all summer long. New plays, variety shows, comedians and pioneers of Québec song can all be seen here.

Ile du Havre Aubert

Located in **La Grave** the **Vieux Treuil** *(Jul and Aug, ☎937-5138)* is a venue for theatre, jazz and classical music. Temporary exhibitions are also presented here.

The **Concours des Châteaux de Sable** (Sand Castle Contest) takes place annually during the month of August on the Havre-Aubert beach. Participants work for hours to build the nicest sand castle. Visitors wanting to put their talent to the test can register by calling Artisans du Sable at ☎937-2917.

SHOPPING

Les Artisans du Sable *(La Grave, Havre-Aubert, ☎937-2917)* offer several sand items, made using a special technique unique to Madelinot artisans. These items, which vary from decorations to lampshades, are wonderful souvenirs of the islands. You can also learn more about sand here.

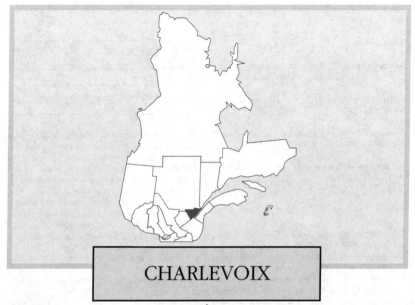

CHARLEVOIX

For years, artists have been captivated by the beauty of the Charlevoix region. From the town of Saint-Joachim to the mouth of the Rivière Saguenay, dramatic mountainous countryside contrasts sharply with the expansive open water of the St. Lawrence. A scattering of charming villages and towns dots the coastline, dwarfed by mountains that fall away into the salt water of the river and steep-sided valleys. Away from the river, Charlevoix is a wild, rugged region where Boreal forest sometimes gives way to taiga. The old houses and churches found throughout the region are vestiges of Charlevoix's history as a French colony. In addition, the division of farmland in the area continues to reflect the seigneurial system of land grants used under the French Regime.

The rich architectural heritage and exceptional geography are complemented by a dazzling variety of flora and fauna. The Charlevoix region was named a "World Biosphere Reserve" in 1988 by UNESCO, and is home to many fascinating animal and plant species. A number of whale species feed at the mouth of the Rivière Saguenay during the summer. In the spring and fall, hundreds of thousands of snow geese make migratory stops, creating a remarkable sight near Cap-Tourmente, farther west. Deep in the hinterland the territory has all the properties of taiga, a remarkable occurrence at this latitude. This area is home to a variety of animal species such as the caribou and the

large Arctic wolf. Charlevoix's plant life is rich in species not found in other parts of eastern Canada.

 FINDING YOUR WAY AROUND

The **Charlevoix** ★★★ tour, set out below, follows the St-Laurent shoreline and includes additional inland excursions. Before leaving, make sure your car is in good condition and remember to have the brakes checked: Charlevoix roads are often steep and winding.

By Car

To get to Charlevoix from Québec City, take Route 138, which is the main road in the region. For a more complete look at the region, consider combining this tour with the Côte de Beaupré tour (see p 368). After crossing a low-lying area close to the St. Lawrence, Route 138 veers into the rolling Charlevoix countryside. This is the southwest extremity of the Laurentides mountains. The north side of the river valley is bordered by the Laurentides for hundreds of miles to the east. Île d'Orléans can be seen from here on clear days.

Bus Stations

Baie-Saint-Paul: 2 Route de l'Équerre (Centre Commercial Le Village), ☎418-435-6569.

Saint-Hilarion: 354 Route 138, ☎418-457-3855.

Clermont: 83 Boulevard Notre-Dame, ☎418-439-3404.

La Malbaie—Pointe-au-Pic: 46 Ste-Catherine, ☎418-665-2264

By Ferry

The ferry to **Île aux Coudres** *(free; ☎418-438-2743)* leaves from Saint-Joseph-de-la-Rive. There is usually a half-hour wait before boarding during the summer months. The crossing takes approximately fifteen minutes; cars can be transported. The 26-kilometre island tour takes about half a day. The roads that runs along the river are ideal for bike rides (bikes can be rented on the island).

Saint-Siméon: The ferry *($10, cars $25; ☎418-638-5530)* from Rivière-du-Loup travels to Saint-Siméon in one hour and five minutes.

Baie-Sainte-Catherine: The ferry *(adults and cars free,* ☎418-235-4395*)* travels between Tadoussac and Baie-Sainte-Catherine in approximately 10 minutes.

 PRACTICAL INFORMATION

Area code: 418

Tourist Information Offices

Regional Office

Association Touristique de Charlevoix: 630 Boulevard de Cornporté, C.P. 275, La Malbaie, G5A 1T8, ☎665-4454 or 1-800-667-2276, ⊷665-3811.

Charlevoix

Baie-Saint-Paul: 444 Boulevard Mgr-de-Laval (Belvédère Baie-Saint-Paul), ☎435-4160.

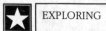 EXPLORING

Charlevoix ★★★ (two days)

The Charlevoix countryside could have been created for giants – the villages tucked into bays or perched atop summits look like dollhouses left behind by a child. Rustic farmhouses and luxurious summer houses are scattered about, and some have been converted into inns. Although Charlevoix was one of the first regions in North America where tourism flourished, further inland it is still a wilderness area of valleys and quiet lakes.

Le Massif ★★★ (see p 476).

Continue along Route 138 to Baie-Saint-Paul.

Baie-Saint-Paul ★★ (pop. 7,335)

Charlevoix's undulating geography has proved a challenge to agricultural development. Under the French Regime, only a few attempts at colonisation were made in this vast region which, along with parts of the Beaupré coast, was overseen by the Séminaire de Québec. Baie-Saint-Paul, at the mouth of the Rivière du Gouffre valley, was home to a few settlers.

Although Charlevoix has some of the planet's oldest rock formations, several major earthquakes have rocked the pastoral region since it was first colonized. The following description by Baptiste Plamondon, then vicar of Baie-Saint-Paul, appeared in the October 22, 1870 edition of the *Journal de Québec:* "It was about half an hour before noon... a tremendous explosion stunned the population. Rather than simply tremble, the earth seemed to boil, such that it caused vertigo... The houses could have been on a volcano, the way they were tossed about. Water gushed fifteen feet into the air through cracks in the ground...'

A bend in the road reveals Baie-Saint-Paul in all its charm, and a slope leads to the heart of the village, which has maintained a quaint small-town atmosphere. Set out on foot along the pleasant Rue Saint-Jean-Baptiste, Rue Saint-Joseph, and Rue Sainte-Anne, where small wooden houses with mansard roofs now house boutiques and cafés. For over 100 years, Baie-Saint-Paul has attracted North American

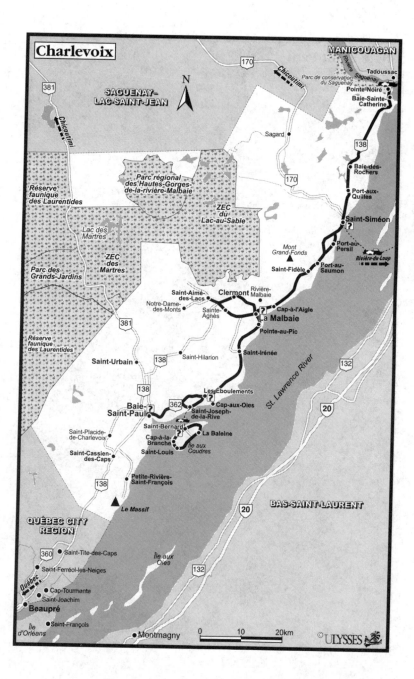

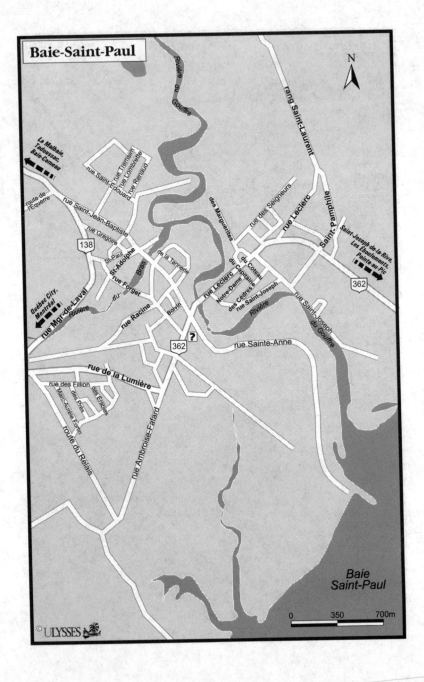

landscape artists, inspired by the mountains and a quality of light particular to Charlevoix. There are many art galleries and art centres in the area that display and sell beautiful Canadian paintings and sculptures. See the **Art-gallery tour**, p 480.

A selection of paintings from Charlevoix artists is displayed in the modern building, the **Centre d'Art de Baie-Saint-Paul ★** *(free admission; late of Jun to late Aug, every day 9am to 7pm; early Sep to late Jun, every day 9am to 5pm; 4 Rue Ambroise-Fafard, ☎435-3681)*, designed in 1967 by architect Jacques DeBlois. A painting and sculpture symposium, where works by young artists are displayed, is held by the Centre every August.

The **Centre d'Exposition de Baie-Saint-Paul ★★** *($3; late Jun to late Aug, every day 9am to 7pm, early Sep to late Jun 9am to 5pm; 23 Rue Ambroise-Fafard, ☎435-3681)* is a museum and gallery, completed in 1992 according to blueprints by architect Pierre Thibault, which houses travelling exhibits from around the world. The Centre also houses the René Richard gallery, where several paintings by this Swiss-born artist are on display (see below).

The **Maison René-Richard ★** *($2.50; every day 10am to 6pm; 58 Rue Saint-Jean-Baptiste, ☎435-5571)*. In the early 20th century, François-Xavier Cimon inherited this house and grounds that extended to the Rivière du Gouffre. The portrait painter Frederick Porter Vinton struck up a friendship with the Cimon family who let him set up a painting workshop on their property. The facility was later used by important artists including Clarence Gagnon, A. Y. Jackson, Frank Johnston, Marc-Aurèle Fortin, and Arthur Lismer. These artists' works can be found in a number of Canadian museums. In 1942, painter René Richard took ownership of the house through his marriage to a Cimon daughter. Since his death in 1983, the property and house have been open to the public. A tour of the grounds provides a fascinating glimpse into the Charlevoix of the 1940s, when artists and collectors from New York and Chicago congregated here during the summer.

The **Centre d'Histoire Naturelle de Charlevoix ★** or **Randonnées Nature-Charlevoix** *($3; late Jun to early Sep, every day 9am to 7pm; early Sep to late Jun, every day 10am to 4pm; 444 Boulevard Mgr-de-Laval (Route 138), ☎435-6275)* explores geological history, flora, fauna, climate, and human history, through the medium of a slide show. The centre is located at the Belvedere Baie St-Paul.

The Laiterie Charlevoix has been accommodating Charlevoix's fourth economuseum, the **Économusée du Fromage ★★** *(free admission; late Jun to Labour Day, every day 8am to 7pm; Sep to Jun, Mon to Fri 8am to 5:30pm, Sat and Sun noon to 4pm; 1151 Boulevard Mgr-de-Laval, ☎435-2184)*, a cheese museum, since 1997. Founded in 1948, this dairy still makes its cheddar cheese the old-fashioned way — by hand. Every day, before 11am, visitors can see cheesemakers in action and get a rudimentary grasp of how cheese is made and ripened. Since 1994, the Laiterie Charlevoix has been producing the delicious "Migneron de Charlevoix" cheese.

From Baie-Saint-Paul, you can take an optional excursion along Routes 138 and 381, in the direction of Saint-Urbain and the Charlevoix hinterland.

Parc des Grands-Jardins ★★ (see p 476).

Return toward Baie-Saint-Paul and take Route 362 heading east. A steep hill leads to the village of Saint-Joseph-de-la-Rive on the right, below Les Éboulements.

Saint-Joseph-de-la-Rive ★ (pop. 225)

The rhythm of life in this village on the St. Lawrence paralleled the rhythm of the river for many generations, as the boats beached along the shore testify eloquently. In recent decades, however, tourism and the craft business have replaced fishing and ship-building as the staples of the economy. East of the dock where the ferry to Île aux Coudres lands, a fine sandy beach tempts swimmers into the chilly salt water. A little wood building in front of the church is a reminder of the fragility of human endeavours within the immense marine landscape of Charlevoix.

The dimensions and white-painted wooden exterior of the **Église Catholique Saint-Joseph ★** *(Chemin de l'Église)* are features reminiscent of the Anglican churches found in Québec's Eastern Townships region. Its interior is decorated with various marine-related objects. For example, the altar is supported by anchors, and the baptistry is actually an immense seashell, retrieved off the coast of

Florida. A recorded presentation dealing with the church's liturgical ornaments is activated by a button on the right-hand side of the entrance.

The **Papeterie Saint-Gilles** ★ *(free admission; May to Dec, every day 8am to 5pm; Jan to May, every day 1am to 5pm; 304 Rue Félix-Antoine-Savard, ☎635-2430)*. This traditional papermaking workshop was founded in 1966 by priest and poet Félix-Antoine Savard (1896-1982, author of *Menaud Maître-Draveur*) with the help of Mark Donohue, a member of a famous Canadian pulp and paper dynasty. Museum guides explain the different stages involved in making paper using 17th century techniques. Saint-Gilles paper has a distinctive thick grain and flower or leaf patterns integrated into each piece, producing a high quality writing paper which is sold on site in various packages.

The **Exposition Maritime** ★★ *($2; mid-May to mid-Oct, every day 9am to5pm; 305 Place de l'Eglise)*, located in a shipyard, recaptures the golden era of the schooner. Visitors are welcome to climb aboard the boats on the premises.

The **Santons de Charlevoix** *(late Jun to early Sep, every day 10am to 5:30pm; mid-May to late Jun and early Sep to mid-Oct, Sat and Sun 10am to 5pm; off season by reservation; ☎635-2521 or 635-2759)*. For a few years now, craftspeople in Saint-Joseph-de-la-Rive have been making *santons,* terracotta figurines representing the Christian nativity scene, including the villagers who gathered around the manger. Setting them apart from other figurines of this kind, the characters are dressed in traditional Québécois garb and the buildings are miniature representations of traditional houses typical of Charlevoix and Île aux Coudres.

Île aux Coudres ★★ (pop. 1,114)

Visitors are sometimes surprised to learn that a number of whale species live in the St. Lawrence. For several generations the economic livelihood of Île aux Coudres centred around whale hunting, mainly belugas, and whale blubber was melted lo produce lamp oil. Ship building, mainly small craft, was also an important regional industry.

Île-aux-Coudres is the municipality that was formed when the villages of Saint-Bernard and Saint-Louis merged *(arrival and departure point on Ile-aux-Coudres)*. The ferry docks at the Quai de Saint-Bernard, where the following tour of the island begins. The dock is the best place to contemplate the Charlevoix mountains. One of the last shipyards still in operation in the region can also be seen from here.

Follow Chemin Royal to Saint-Louis, where it becomes Chemin des Coudriers. Many old schooners are beached along the shore in the area, vestiges of a bygone era. Baie-Saint-Paul can be seen from Cap à Labranche on clear days.

The **Musée Les Voitures d'Eau** ★ *($4; mid-May to mid-Jun and mid-Sep to mid-Oct, Sat and Sun 9:30am to 5pm; mid-Jun to mid-Sep, every day 9:30am to 6pm; Chemin des Coudriers, Saint-Louis, ☎438-2208)* presents exhibits dealing with the history, construction and navigation of the small craft once built in the region. The museum was founded in 1973 by Captain Éloi Perron, who recovered the wreck of the schooner *Mont-Saint-Louis,* now on display.

Turn left onto Chemin du Moulin.

The **Moulins Desgagné** ★★, or **Moulins de l'Isle-aux-Coudres** *($2.50; mid-May to mid-Jun and early Sep to mid-Oct, every day 10am to 5pm; mid-Jun to early Sep, every day 9am to 6:30pm; 247 Chemin du Moulin, Saint-Louis, ☎438-2184)*. It is extremely rare to find a water mill and a windmill operating together. Indeed, the Saint-Louis mills are a unique pair in Québec. The mills, erected in 1825 and 1836 respectively, complement one another by alternately generating power according to prevailing climatic conditions. Along with a forge and milling house, the mills were restored by the Québec government, which has also established on-site information centres. The machinery necessary for operation is still in perfect condition, and is now back at work grinding wheat and buckwheat into flour. Bread is made in an antique wood oven.

Near the end of the tour, visitors will notice posts sticking out of the water close to shore – these are strung with nets used to catch eels.

Take the ferry to Saint-Joseph-de-la-Rive and head to Les Éboulements.

Goélette

Les Éboulements ★ (pop. 1,013)

In 1663, a violent earthquake in the region caused a gigantic landslide; it is said that half a small mountain sank in the river. The village of les Éboulements is named after the event (*éboulements* means landslide in English).

At the entrance to the grounds of the **Manoir de Sales-Laterrière** (*free admission; every day 9am to 11am and 2pm to 4pm; 159 Rue Principale, ☎635-2666*) and the **Moulin Banal ★★** (*$2; late Jun early Sep, 10am to 5pm; 157 Rue Principale, ☎635-2239*) is a wooden processional chapel (circa 1840). It was once located in the village of Saint-Nicolas on the south shore of the St. Lawrence, stands next to the entrance of the grounds. The chapel was reconstructed in 1968, under the auspices of a heritage organization, which also owns the nearby late 18th century seigneurial mill. Visitors cannot enter the red shuttered manor house, as it is currently used as a school by the Brothers of the SacréCoeur.

Head to the village, 1 km to the east.

The name "Tremblay" has become to Québec what the name Dupont is to France, or Smith is to the United States. What is unique about the Tremblays in Québec is that they all have a common colonial ancestor: Pierre Tremblay from Perche, France, who arrived in Québec in approximately 1650 and became seigneur of Les Éboulements. In the 19th century, various Tremblays moved from Charlevoix to settle in the Saguenay and Lac-Saint-Jean regions, which continue to be associated with the

family name. However, Les Éboulements still has the highest concentration of people with the last name "Tremblay" in Québec, and probably the world.

The **Centre d'Interprétation de la Forge Tremblay** (*Jun to Sep, every day 10am to 5pm; 194 Rue Principale, ☎635-1401*). The Tremblay forge (1891), located in the heart of the village, has maintained the same appearance and function as it had in the time of horses and carriages. It is still used by a blacksmith; a tour guide explains how the different tools work. Adjacent to the forge are a selection of boutiques as well as an inn.

Return to Route 132. After a spectacular descent the road then leads to Saint-Irénée. Once at river lever, the entrance to the Forget estate is ahead on the left.

Saint-Irénée ★ (pop. 745)

Saint-Irénée, or Saint-Irénée-les-Bains, as it was known during the Belle Époque, is the gateway to the part of Charlevoix, usually considered the oldest vacation spot in North America. In the late 18th century, British sportsmen were the first Europeans to enjoy the pleasures of the simple life the wild region had to offer. They were followed by wealthy Americans escaping the heat of summer in the United States. Wealthy English- and French-Canadian families also had summer houses with lovely gardens built for them in Charlevoix. Saint-Irénée is renowned for its picture-perfect landscapes and classical music festival (see below).

The **Domaine Forget** ★ *(price and schedule vary according to activity; 398 Chemin Les Bains,* ☎ *452-8111,* ≈ *452-3503, www.cite.net/~dforget/)* was home to Sir Rodolphe Forget (1861-1919), a prominent French-Canadian businessman in the early 20th century. The vast property had its own power plant in addition to a dozen interesting secondary buildings. Unfortunately, the main house, known as 'le château' by the locals, was destroyed by fire in 1961. Inaugurated in the summer of 1996, the **Salle Françoys-Bernier** *(398 Chemin Les Bains, G0T 1V0,* ☎ *452-3535, ext. 820, or 888-DFORGET, ext. 820),* at the Domaine Forget, can accommodate 600 music lovers, who are sure to be delighted by its wonderful acoustics.

Since 1977, the property has been home to the **Académie de Musique et de Danse de Saint-Irénée**, which holds summer sessions. Every summer a classical music festival is held here; it is a major social event in the lives of Charlevoix summer résidents.

Before arriving in Pointe-au-Pic, the road runs next to the **Club de Golf du Manoir Richelieu**, one of the highestrated golf resorts in the world. The club features an 18-hole course, a clubhouse and restaurants. Turn right onto Rue Principale at the bottom of Côte Bellevue.

La Malbaie—Pointe-au-Pic ★ (pop. 5,009)

On his way to Québec City in 1608, Samuel de Champlain anchored in a Charlevoix bay for the night. To his surprise, he awoke the next morning to find his fleet resting on land and not in water. Champlain learned that day what many navigators would come to learn as well: et low tide in this region the water recedes a great distance and will trap any boat not moored in deep enough water. In exasperation, he exclaimed *"Ah! La malle baye!"* (Old French which translates roughly to "Oh what a bad bay!"), inadvertently providing the name for many sites in the region. The towns of Pointe-au-Pic, La Malbaie, and Cap-à-l'Aigle now form a continuous web of streets and houses lining the bay.

The Malbaie seigneurs passed through three sets of hands before being seriously developed. Jean Bourdon received the land for services rendered to the French crown, in 1653. Too busy with his job as prosecutor for the King, he did nothing with it. The seigneury was then granted to Philippe Gaultier de Comporté, in 1672. Following his death, it was sold by his family to merchants Hazeur and Soumande, who harvested wood on the property for the construction of ships in France. The seigneury became crown property in 1724. Exceptionally, it was then granted, under English occupation, to Captain John Nairne and Officer Malcolm Fraser in 1762, who began colonizing it.

Seigneurs Nairne and Fraser initiated a longstanding tradition of hospitality in Charlevoix. They hosted, in their respective manors, friends and even strangers from Scotland and England. Following the example of these seigneurs, French Canadians began welcoming visitors from Montréal and Québec during the summer months. Eventually, larger inns had to be built to accommodate the increasing number of urban vacationers now arriving on steamships that moored et the dock in Pointe-au-Pic. Among the wealthy visitors was American President Howard Taft and his family, who were very fond of Charlevoix.

In the early 20th century, a wave of wealthy Americans and English Canadians built summer houses along **Chemin des Falaises**, a street well worth exploring. The houses reflect popular architectural styles of the period, including the charming Shingle Style characteristic of seaside resorts on the American east coast, which is distinguished by a cedar shingle exterior. Another popular trend at the time was to build houses that resembled 17th-century French manor houses, complete with turrets and shuttered casement windows. Beginning in 1920, the architecture of summer residences started to incorporate traditional local building styles. La Malbaie architect Jean Charles Warren (1869-1929), became known for designing a style of rustic furniture, inspired by local traditions and the English Arts and Crafts movement. Owning one of his creations became a must among summer residents. The most important and impressive building from the turn-of-the-century construction boom is the Manoir Richelieu, et the west end of Chemin des Falaises.

La Malbaie is now the regional administrative centre and, since its amalgamation with the neighbouring municipality of Pointe-au-Pic in 1995, has confirmed its position of strength within the region's tourist industry. It is henceforth officially known as "La Malbaie—Pointe-au-Pic".

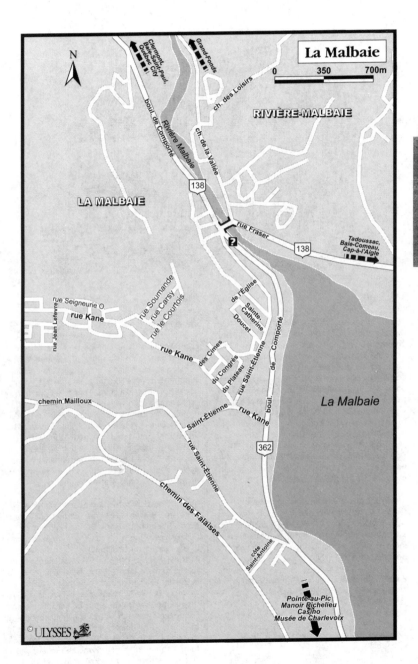

La Malbaie

N

0   350   700m

Clermont, Saint-Paul,
Baie-Saint-
Québec City

Grand-Fonds

ch. des Loisirs

RIVIÈRE-MALBAIE

boul. de Comporté

Rivière Malbaie

ch. de la Vallée

LA MALBAIE

138

rue Fraser

?

138

Tadoussac,
Baie-Comeau,
Cap-à-l'Aigle

de l'Église

rue Seigneurie O.

rue Jean Lefevre

rue Kane

rue Soumande

rue Carsy

rue le Courtois

Sainte-
Catherine

Doucet

de Comporté

rue Kane

des Cimes

du Congrès

du Plateau

rue Saint-Étienne

boul.

La Malbaie

chemin Mailloux

Saint-Étienne

rue Kane

362

rue Saint-Étienne

chemin des Falaises

côte
Saint-Antoine

Pointe-au-Pic
Manoir Richelieu
Casino
Musée de Charlevoix

© ULYSSES

Manoir Richelieu

The original wood building of the **Manoir Richelieu** ★★ *(181 Avenue Richelieu)*, the only grand hotel in Charlevoix to survive, was built in 1899. Destroyed in a fire, however, it was replaced by the current cement building in 1929. The hotel plans were drawn by architect John Smith Archibald in the Château Style. Many famous people have stayed at the hotel, from Charlie Chaplin to the King of Siam, to the Vanderbilt of New York City. The casino is a reconstruction of the Château Ramezay in Montréal. Visitors not staying at the Manoir can nevertheless discreetly walk through its hallways, elegant salons and gardens overlooking the St. Lawrence.

The region's number-one attraction is the **Casino de Charlevoix** *(183 Avenue Richelieu, ☎665-5300 or 1-800-665-2274)*, an attractively designed European-style casino located next to the Manoir Richelieu. Proper dress required.

Parc Régional des Hautes-Gorges-de-la-Rivière-Malbaie ★★ (see p 475).

Mont Grand-Fonds ★ (see p 476).

Return to the main tour at Cap-à-l'Aigle.

Cap-à-l'Aigle (pop. 761)

From Boulevard de Comporté in La Malbaie, visitors can catch a glimpse of a stately stone house sitting high on the Cap-à-l'Aigle escarpment. The building is the old manor house of the Malcolm Fraser seigneurs, a property also known as Mount Murray. It is matched to the east of Rivière Malbaie by the John Nairne seigneury, established west of the waterway and simply named Murray Bay in honour of James Murray, British Governor at the time. Cap-à-l'Aigle, whose tourism industry dates back to the 18th century, forms the heart of the Mount Murray seigneury.

Manoir Fraser ★ *(private property; Route 138).* Malcolm Fraser, like his compatriot John Nairne, belonged to the Fraser Highlanders, a Scottish regiment sent to Canada to participate in the capture of Louisbourg. After the signing of the Treaty of Paris in 1763, putting an end to the Seven Years' War, Nairne and Fraser settled in their seigneuries. Both spoke French; Nairne's family lived in exile in France due to their sympathy for the Stuarts. For its part, the Fraser family was of French origin, descendants of Jules de Berry, who served exquisite strawberries to Charles III, and so created their family name (in French, strawberries are called *fraises*, which later turned into Fraser). The

Manoir Fraser was built for the son of Malcolm Fraser in 1827, according to plans by architect Jean-Baptiste Duléger. Damaged during a fire in 1975, the manor was restored by the Cabot family, owners of the titles to the Cap-à-l'Aigle seigneury since 1902.

Jardins aux Quatre Vents ★★ *(by appointment only, on the left hand side of Route 138)*, on the grounds of the Cabot family estate, is one of the most beautiful private gardens in Québec. The garden is meticulously tended and is expanded annually. Unfortunately it is open to the public for only a few days every year. Strictly speaking, the gardens comprise 22 separate gardens, each one having its own theme. For example, there is the Potager en Terrasses (terraced vegetable garden), the Jardin du Ravin (ravine garden), Les Cascades (waterfalls), and the Lac des Libellules (dragonfly lake). The Quatre Vents (or four winds) garden began in 1928 with the planting of the Jardin Blanc (white garden), where all the flowers are, naturally, white as snow.

Turn right onto Chemin Saint-Raphaël and continue to the junction with Route 138 Est, which travels through Saint-Fidèle and Port-au-Saumon.

Port-au-Persil ★

This small but charming harbour town is set apart by its waterfall, Anglican chapel and winding road that leads through the beautiful mountain landscapes.

Saint-Siméon (pop. 1,040)

From Saint-Siméon, roads lead to the Saguenay region, Côte-Nord, and Québec City. A ferry links the town of Rivière-du-Loup on the south shore of the St. Lawrence.

Baie-Sainte-Catherine ★ (pop. 312)

A tiny village on the north shore of the St. Lawrence, Baie-Saint-Catherine borders a bay on the Saguenay estuary and has a picturesque sandy beach.

PARKS

The newly established **Domaine Charlevoix** *(adults $6; Route362, C.P. 1796, Baie-Saint-Paul, ☎435-2626)*, just outside Baie-Saint-Paul, is a sports centre devoted to various outdoor activities, such as cross-country skiing, hiking and mountain biking. Unfortunately, the trails are not very long. The magnificent lookout onto the St. Lawrence and Île aux Coudres, is the centre's main attraction. There is a small snack bar on the property.

Located at the eastern edge of the Réserve Faunique des Laurentides, the **Parc des Grands-Jardins ★★** *(166 Boulevard de Comporté, Baie-St-Paul, ☎846-2057 and 457-3945)* is rich with flora and fauna characteristic of taiga and tundra, a very unusual occurance at such a southern latitude. Hikes led by naturalises are organized throughout the summer. Caribou have been spotted from some of the trails. The park's Mont du Lac des Cygnes (Swan Lake Mountain) trail is among the most beautiful in Québec. Visitors can also go on canoe-camping trips.

Parc Régional des Hautes-Gorges-de-la-Rivière-Malbaie ★★ *(from Baie-Saint-Paul, take Route 138 to Saint-Aimé-des-Lacs, ☎439-4402)*, which covers over 233 square kilometres of land, was created in order to protect the area from commercial exploitation. Over 800 million years ago, a crack in the earth's crust formed the magnificent gorges after which the park is named; later the terrain was shaped by glaciers. The park features an incredible diversity of vegetation, ranging from maple stands to alpine tundra. The rock faces, some of which are 800 metres high, tower over the river and are used for rock-climbing. The best known climb, 'Pomme d'Or', is a 350-metre high expert-level trail. Other park activities include snowmobiling, hiking (the Acropole trail is particularly scenic), and canoe-camping. The park's rental centre has mountain bikes and canoes. **River boat cruises** are also offered for $20 *(duration: 1 hr 30 min, ☎665-7527)*. A trip down the river is the best way to truly appreciate the park.

On the entrance road to the park, look for a sign on the right-hand side of the road that says *"ZEC des Martres, secteur 7, Lac des Américains'. Nearby* a pedestrian suspension bridge spans Rivière Malbaie. This area is peaceful and deserted, allowing visitors to

CHARLEVOIX

imagine what it might have been like to be one of the first explorers in this region.

OUTDOORS

Downhiill Skiing

The **Massif** ★★★ *($32.25; 1350 Rue Principale; C.P. 47, Petite-Rivière-Saint-François, GOA 2LO, ☎632-5876)* is a ski hill boasting a vertical drop of approximately 700 metres, one of the highest in Québec, making it a popular destination among downhill skiers. Until recently, skiers were brought to the top of the hill by bus. Two mechanical lifts, including a quadruple lift, were installed in order to service more skiers. The mountain can now accommodate up to 2,500 people per day and has 14 intermediate- and advanced-level runs. It is a good idea to reserve lift tickets in advance. The view from atop is mind-blowing.

Parc Régional du Mont Grand-Fonds ★ *($25; 1000 Chemin des Loisirs, La Malbaie, ☎665-0095)* has thirteen 355-metre runs. The longest run is 2,500 metres.

Cross-country Skiing

Mont Grand-Fonds ★ *($8; 1000 Chemin des Loisirs, La Malbaie, ☎665-4405)* has some 160 kilometres of cross-country skiing trails.

The **Génévrier** activity centre *($4.25; 1175 Mgr de Laval, Baie-Sainte-Paul, ☎435-6520)* is located a few kilometres north of Baie-Saint-Paul. It has skating facilites as well as approximately forty cross-country skiing and snowshoeing trails. There are six runs: 4 beginners, one intermediate and one advanced. A skating rink and tobogganing hills have also been set up.

Parc des Grands-Jardins *(3$; 166 Boulevard de Comporté, Baei-St-Paul, ☎435-3101)*. During the winter, 60-kilometre long hiking trails become cross-country skiing and snowshoeing trails. Chalets and shelters are available; they must be reserved with the Parc Régional du Mont Grand-Fonds at ☎1-800-665-6527.

Dogsledding

Le Chenil du Sportif *($120 per day per person, $70 ½ day per person; 65 Rang Ste-Marie, Les Éboulements, ☎635-2592, ⇒635-2256)* organizes excursions that last from half a day to three days and can include ice-fishing and snowshoeing expeditions. Le Chenil du Sportif allows dog-sledding amateurs to lead their team themselves through spectacular natural surroundings, between Les Éboulements and Saint-Hilarion. Guides are experienced and friendly. Day packages include breakfast in a log cabin. There are cabins and trailers for longer stays.

Biking

In La Baleine, on the east coast of the island, **Vel-0-Coudre** *(☎438-2146)* rents out bikes of all kinds; **Roland Harvey Bicyclettes** and **Motel** *(☎438-2343)* offers a smaller selection, but lower rates.

ACCOMMODATIONS

Baie-Saint-Paul

The least expensive place to stay in town is the **Auberge de Jeunesse Le Balcon Vert** *($15; Route 362, GOA 1SO, ☎435-5587)*. This youth hostel offers small chalets that sleep four people, as well as camp sites. It is only open during the summer.

The **Parc des Grands-Jardins** *($14-$20; 166 Boulevard de Comporté, Baie-St-Paul, ☎1-800-665-6527)* rents out small cottages and shelters This park is a popular place for fishing, so if you want to stay here during summer, you'll have to reserve early.

The **Le Genévrier** campground *($20; Route 138, at the Baie-Saint-Paul exit, GOA 1BO, ☎435-6520)* is a vast recreational-tourist complex in perfect harmony with its natural environment. Campers of all stripes are sure to find what they are looking for here. The campground boasts 450 sites, mostly on forested land, for all types of lodging and shelter, from the biggest motorhomes to tents for those who prefer camping in the wild. Several fully equipped, modern and comfortable

---

Ulysses' Favourites

Accommodations

For history buffs:
La Maison (p 477).

For tranquillity:
Auberge des Sablons (p 477).

For the views:
Auberge La Pignoronde (p 477),
Auberge Les Trois Canards (p 477)
and Auberge Des Peupliers (p 478).

Restaurants

Charlevoix's finest tables:
La Pinsonnière (p 479), La Maison
Otis (p 478), Auberge des Peupliers
(p 479), Auberge des Trois Canards
(p 479) and Le Saint-Laurent
(p 479).

For wine connoisseurs:
La Pinsonnière (p 479).

For terraces:
Le Mouton Noir (p 478) and Auberge
des Sablons (p 478).

CHARLEVOIX

---

cottages are situated by the river or lake. In summer, two more rustic but fully equipped log cabins with bedding and showers are also for rent. Every day, an extensive programme of sports and leisure activities is offered. Hiking and mountain-biking trails along the river.

The strange circular building housing the **Auberge la Pignoronde** *($124; $184 ½b; ≈, ℜ; 750 Boulevard Mgr de Laval, GOA 180, ☎435-5505 or 1-800-463-5250)* may be less than appealing from the outside, but the interior decor is quite charming, and the lobby features a welcoming fireplace. There is also an excellent view of the bay.

The **Muse B&B** *($55 bkfst incl., $125 ½b; ℜ; 39 Rue St-Jean-Baptiste, GOA 180, ☎435-6839)*, located in the heart of Baie-Saint-Paul, is set in an old house with a lovely balcony.

The **Auberge La Maison Otis** *($180 ½b; ≈, △, ℜ; 23 Rue St-Jean-Baptiste, GOA 1BO, ☎435-2255)* has a suave ambiance, is tastefully decorated and serves divine food. The old section has small, snug rooms with bunk-beds, whereas in the new section, the rooms are large and cosy. This former bank is an example of classic Québec architecture and is located in the heart of the city.

Île aux Coudres

A long building, with several skylights, the **Cap-aux-Pierres** hotel *($190 ½b; ≈, ℜ; 246 Route*

Principale, La Baleine, GOA 2AO, ☎438-2711 or 1-800-463-5250) offers pleasant rustic rooms.

The **Auberge la Coudrière et Motels** *($158 ½b; ℜ; 280 Route Principale, La Baleine, GOA 2AO, ☎438-2838)* has very comfortable rooms. It is located near the river in a beautiful area perfect for quiet walks.

Saint-Irénée

The charming **Auberge des Sablons** *($168 ½b; sb or pb, ℜ; 223 Chemin Les Bains, GOT 1VO, ☎452-3240)* is a pretty white house with blue shutters, located in a peaceful spot nextto Domaine Forget. The rooms are pleasant, but not all have private bathrooms.

La Malbaie – Pointe-au-Pic

A veritable institution in Quebec, the **Manoir Richelieu** *($69; ≈, K, ℜ; 181 Avenue Richelieu, GOT 1MO, ☎665-4431 or 1-888-270-0111, ≈665-3093)* remains one of the choicest and most highly-rated resorts in Québec. This architectural gem in the Norman style boasts 350 rooms and numerous suites in the rear section. Several boutiques are on the ground floor as is an underground link to the Casino. A good many of the rooms have been renovated since the opening of the Casino.

The **Auberge Les Trois Canards et Motels** *($75.; ℜ, ≈, △; 49 Côte Bellevue, GOT 1MO,*

☎665-3761 or 1-800-461-3761, ₪675-4727) has a magnificent view of the entire region. The inn offers nine rooms, each warmly decorated with a fireplace, thick carpets, and a whirlpool. The motel rooms are not as nice but still offer a great view of the water.

Small charming chalets are available et **Chalets La Remontée** *($75; ≈, K; 15 Côte Bellevue, on the right hand side when descending the coast towards Pointe-Au-Pic village,* ☎665-3757, ₪665-3103). Each chalet is equipped with a kitchenette and can accommodate up to four people.

The rooms in the old wood-framed **Auberge aux Douceurs Belges** *($145 ½b; ℜ; 121 Chemin des Falaises, GOT 1MO,* ☎665-7480) are not particularly soundproof. Nevertheless, those with balconies overlooking the river are great places to pass quiet evenings sipping Belgian beer (specially imported by the inn) and watching the river.

Cap-à-l'Aigle

 The **Auberge des Peupliers** *($172 ½b; △, ℜ; 381 Saint-Raphaël, GOT 180,* ☎665-4423, ₪665-3179) sits on a hillside overlooking the St. Lawrence. The rooms are decorated with wooden furniture that creates a warm, charming atmosphere. The inn also has pleasant, quiet living rooms.

The luxurious **La Pinsonnière** hotel *($130, $230 ½b; △, ≈, ⊙, ℜ; 124 Saint-Raphaël, GOT 180,* ☎665-4431) boasts a wonderful location on a headland overhanging the river. The rooms are tastefully decorated, each different from the next. This is a very pleasant place. Their restaurant is very popular.

✕ RESTAURANTS

Baie-Saint-Paul

The **Pâtisserie Les 2 Sœurs** *($; 48 Rue St-Jean-Baptiste,* ☎435-6591) is a quiet, pleasant place with a healthy menu.

The country decor of the **Le Mouton Noir** restaurant *($; 43 Rue Sainte-Anne,* ☎435-3075) was recently renovated, causing it to lose a bit of its charm. While the restaurant has a good reputation, the food can

be a little unimaginative. Nevertheless, it is a pleasant place with a view of the river.

Graced with an exceptional decor, the dining room of the **Auberge La Pignoronde** *($$$-$$$$; 750 Boulevard Mgr-de-Laval,* ☎435-5505 or 1-800-463-5250) looks out on the vallée du Gouffre and Île aux Coudres. The restaurant serves absolutely delicious fare, where meat, fish and seafood share the stage with panache. Service is particularly attentive.

The finest and most sophisticated of cuisines is featured at **La Maison Otis** *($$$-$$$$; 23 Rue Saint-Jean-Baptiste,* ☎435-2255), which has developed an avant-garde gourmet menu where regional flavours adopt new accents and compositions. In the inviting decor of the oldest part of the inn, where a bank once stood, guests are treated to a delightful culinary experience and a relaxing evening. The service is impeccable, and several ingredients on the menu are home-made. Fine selection of wines.

Saint-Joseph-de-la-Rive

Le Loup-Phoque *($-$$; summer only; 188 Rue Félix-Antoine Savard,* ☎635-2848), is located in an old house, and its varied clientele comes to grab a bite to eat while enjoying the magnificent scenery from the terrace.

The warm and intimate dining rooms of the **La Maison sous les Pins** inn *($$$; 352 Rue F.-A.-Savard,* ☎635-2583) can accommodate about twenty guests that come here to discover the refined aromas emanating from a medley of regional and French dishes, with an emphasis on local products. Friendly reception and romantic ambiance. Non-smoking.

Île aux Coudres

La Mer Veille *($; Pointe de lislet, west side of the island,* ☎438-2149) is a very popular restaurant that serves light meals and an appealing table d'hôte.

Saint-Irénée

Charm, romanticism and good taste are in perfect harmony with culinary quality at the **Auberge des Sablons** *($$$-$$$$; 223 Chemin Les Bains,* ☎452-3594), ensuring a delightful dining experience. Guests here can savour excellent French cuisine while admiring the ocean from the terrace or dining room.

La Malbaie – Pointe-au-Pic

With a most pleasant atmosphere, the **Le Passe Temps** creperie *($$-$$$; 34 Boulevard Bellevue, Route 362, ☎665-7660)* constitutes an excellent choice for both lunch and dinner. The menu features a great variety of buckwheat or whole-wheat flour crêpes as main courses and desserts. The fresh pasta is exquisite, particularly the spaghetti with fresh tomatoes and Migneron cheese. The terrace is also welcome treat.

A spacious house with a nice garden, the **Auberge des Falaises** *($$$-$$$$; 18 Chemin des Falaises, ☎665-3731)* specialises in refined cuisine. The restaurant is among the most popular in the region, and won the *Prix Québécois de la Gastronomie.*

The chefs at the **Auberge des Trois Canards** *($$$$; 49 Côte Bellevue, ☎665-3761 or 1-800-461-3761)* have always been daring and inventive in integrating local ingredients or game with their refined cuisine. Invariably succeeding with panache, they have endowed the restaurant with an enviable nationwide reputation. The service, for its part, is outstanding, and the staff is genuinely cordial and knowledgeable about the dishes served. Good wine list.

For the last few years, the Manoir Richelieu's dining room, **Le Saint-Laurent** *($$$$; 181 Avenue Richelieu, ☎665-3703 or 1-888-294-0111)*, has raised its standards of quality considerably, to the point of making a name for itself as one of the four or five best gourmet restaurants in the area. In addition to its unobstructed view of the river, the glass-walled dining hall boasts a superb menu, generally composed of five-course meals with three choices of meat dishes and three of fish. The Sunday morning brunch is quite an experience in Charlevoix, even for those not staying at the hotel.

Cap-à-l'Aigle

The **Auberge des Peupliers** *($$$-$$$$; 381 Rue Saint-Raphaël, ☎665-4423 or 1-888-282-3743)* has many wonderful

surprises in store for its guests, fruits of its chef's fertile imagination and audacity. Patrons have only to abandon themselves to these intoxicating French and regional flavours, sure to delight any palate.

The food at **La Pinsonnière** *($$$$; 124 Rue Saint-Raphaël, ☎665-4431 or 1-800-387-4431)* has long been considered the height of gastronomic refinement in Charlevoix and, despite increasingly fierce competition, is still worthy of the title in many respects. La Pinsonnière offers a very upscale, classic gourmet menu, worthy of a veritable gustatory experience that requires dedicating an entire evening to. The wine cellar remains the best-stocked in the region and one of the finest in Québec.

  ENTERTAINMENT

Festivals and Cultural Events

Baie-Saint-Paul

The **Symposium de la nouvelle peinture au Canada** *(☎435-3681)* is held annually in Baie-Saint-Paul. Throughout the month of August, visitors can thus admire large-scale works based on a suggested theme and created here by approximately 15 artists from Québec, Canada and abroad.

Enjoying greater success every year, **Rêves d'automne Baie-Saint-Paul** *(☎1-800-761-5150)* takes place during the last week of September and the first week of October. This multidisciplinary festival does everything possible to allow the public to fully appreciate the beauty of Indian summer in Charlevoix, offering a whole series of musical and theatrical performances as well as irresistible gastronomic treats.

Saint-Irénée

Every summer, from mid-June to the end of August, the **Festival international du Domaine Forget** *(☎452-3535 or 1-888-DFORGET)* brings together many classical musicians and vocalists, famous both at home and abroad, who perform on the stage at the Salle Françoys-Bernier (hall), or during musical brunches that take place outside every Sunday. You can request the programme by calling the number above. Season tickets available.

Casino

Pointe-au-Pic

The **Casino de Charlevoix** *(183 Avenue Richelieu, ☎665-5300 or 1-800-665-2274)*, in Pointe-au-Pic, next to the Manoir Richelieu, is a European-style casino. Formal dress required.

 SHOPPING

Baie-Saint-Paul

Baie-Saint-Paul is particularly noteworthy for its **art galleries**. There is a little of everything here, as each shop has its own specialty. Oils, pastels, watercolours, etchings… paintings by big names and the latest artists, originals and reproductions, sculpture and poetry… whatever your heart desires! Take an enjoyable stroll along Rue St-Jean-Baptiste and the neighbouring streets where you'll find countless beautiful galleries staffed by friendly and chatty art dealers.

Saint-Joseph-de-la-Rive

The wonderful paper made at the **Papeterie Saint-Gilles** *(304 Rue Félix-Antoine-Savard, ☎635-2430)* is sold on the premises. The quality of the cotton paper is remarkable. Some of the paper is decorated with maple or fern leaves. You can also purchase a collection of narratives, stories and Québec songs printed on this fine paper.

QUÉBEC ARCHITECTURE

Québec architecture is at once the result of a population
adapting to a difficult climate and a synthesis of French,
British and American influences.
The photos of this section illustrate the various steps
of the history of Québec architecture, including both
simple buildings erected by peasants and elaborate works
designed by world-renowned architects.

The Moulin de La Chevrotière in Deschambault, built in 1802, shows how
French Regime styles persisted in Québec even after the British Conquest of 1760.
Its small-paned casement windows, thick rubble-stone walls and sloped roof
with dormers are all typical of the architecture of New France
from the 17th to the 18th centuries.

For many years, Québec invested all of its creative energies in the interior decors of its churches, which resulted in veritable woodworking masterpieces. The choir of Église de la Visitation du Sault-au-Récollet (Montréal), designed by Philippe Liébert and David-Fleury David between 1764 and 1818, skilfully combines Louis-XV and Louis-XVI styles. The traditional combination of white and gold is embellished with bright colours.

Marché Bonsecours, erected between 1845 and 1850, reflects mid-19th-century British colonial ambitions in Montréal. Its metallic dome, formidable portico, Tuscan pillars and sash windows are typically neoclassical – a very popular style throughout the British Empire during the first half of the 19th century.

Throughout the 19th century, Quebecers endeavoured to adapt to the climactic extremes of the St. Lawrence valley by developing what was to become a traditional Québec architecture. For example, they raised the masonry foundation and adorned their houses with long verandas to prevent snow from piling on window sills. The decreased pitch of the roof kept the snow from falling off, so it could serve as insulation.

Victorian architecture reflects the great prosperity of the second half of the 19th century. Despite many innovations during this period, it nonetheless signalled a return to past forms represented in close to thirty historical styles. This close-up of Christ Church Anglican Cathedral in Montréal, erected in 1859, reveals the clergy's enthusiasm for Medieval styles and its religious fervour.

This lovely house in Saint-Roch-de-l'Achigan (Lanaudière) illustrates the growing influence of American architecture on Québec at the end of the 19th century. The wraparound gallery decorated with machine-turned wood, and the tower covered with fish-scale metal sheet, are typical of the American Queen Anne style.

The former headquarters of the Sun Life Assurance Company in Montréal was built in phases between 1913 and 1933. Its Corinthian columns and crowning balustrades are Beaux-Arts, a style introduced to the Americans at the start of the 20th century by foreign students from the École des Beaux-Arts in Paris. For many years, this building was the largest in the British Empire.

The vernacular urban architecture is the result of massive emigration from the country to the city between 1880 and 1930. In an effort to recreate the verandas of their childhoods, these new arrivals added balconies to their Montréal homes. Direct access to the street was made possible by fancy and winding exterior staircases. These triplexes of Rue Saint-Hubert in Montréal each contain three dwellings with six to eight rooms each.

Lost in the greenery of Mont Royal, the tower of the main pavilion of Université de Montréal, designed in 1926 by architect Ernest Cormier, is a fine example of the Art-Deco style, popular in Québec between 1925 and 1940. Among this style's notable trademarks are its many vertical lines, its tiered elevations and its geometric motifs.

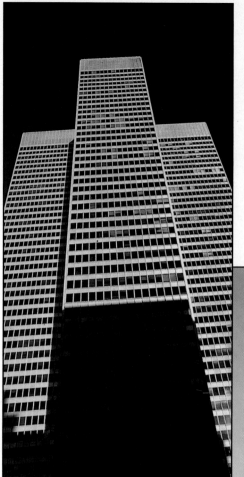

The cruciform tower of Place Ville-Marie is the ultimate symbol of the Quiet Revolution, which made Montréal one of the major centres of modern architecture in the 1960s. The 47-story building, with its aluminum curtain walls, was designed in 1959 by Chinese-American architect Ieoh Ming Pei, who also designed the Pyramide du Louvre in Paris.

The growing interest in integrating the old and the new is one of the main characteristics of contemporary Québec architecture. The design for the Musée d'Archéologie et d'Histoire Pointe-à-la-Callière in Montreal, by architect Dan Hanganu, reflects this with its grey limestone facing, which resembles the neoclassical exteriors of wharehouses in Vieux-Montréal.

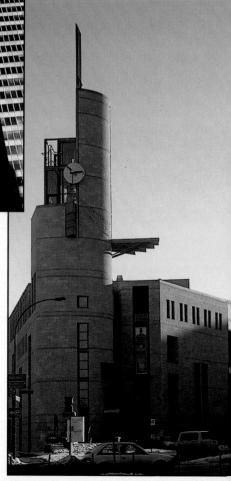

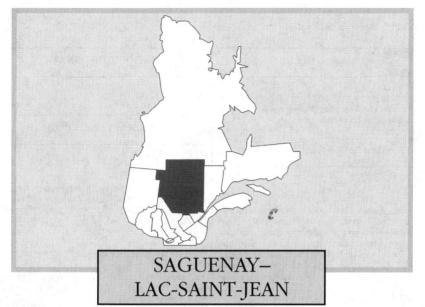

SAGUENAY–
LAC-SAINT-JEAN

Lac Saint-Jean is a veritable inland sea with a diameter of over 35 kilometres; from it flows the Rivière Saguenay, the location of the southernmost fjord in the world. In a way, these two impressive bodies of water form the backbone of this magnificent region. Moving swiftly toward the St. Lawrence River, the Rivière Saguenay flows through a rugged landscape studded with cliffs and mountains. Aboard a cruise ship or from the banks of the river, visitors can enjoy a series of gorgeous panoramic views of this untouched natural setting. The Saguenay is navigable, as far as Chicoutimi, and governed by the eternal rhythm of the tides. Its rich marine animal life includes various species of whale, in the summer. In the heart of the region, visitors will find the bustling city of Chicoutimi, the main urban centre in this part of Québec. The region's first settlers came here in the 19th century, attracted by the beautiful fertile plains and excellent farmland around the lake. The hard life of these pioneers, who were farmers in the summer and lumberjacks in the winter, was immortalized in Louis Hémon's novel *Maria Chapdelaine*. Sweet and delicious blueberries abound in the area and have made the region of Lac Saint-Jean famous. The fruit is so closely identified with the region that Quebecers all over the province have adopted the term *bleuets*, blueberries, as an affectionate nickname for the local inhabitants. Residents of both the Saguenay and Lac Saint-Jean regions are renowned for their friendliness and spirit.

A considerable portion of the local work force is still involved in the same economic activities that brought the original settlers here towards the middle of the last century: forestry development in the Saguenay region and agriculture in the area around Lac Saint-Jean. Other industries have, however, developed since the beginning of the 20th century, in particular aluminum smelters, lured by the abundant supply of hydroelectric power.

Most settlers came from Charlevoix and the Côte-du-Sud regions in the middle of the 19th century, populating the twin regions of Saguenay and Lac-Saint-Jean, which were until then sporadically frequented by nomadic Montagnais tribes, Jesuit missionaries and trappers. The latter were connected with small trading posts established back in the 17th century, which lay sprinkled across densely wooded territory. Everything is large scale in the Saguenay - Lac-Saint-Jean – not only the rivers and the lakes, but also the industrial complexes, which are often open to the public.

A few French Canadian families that originated in the Saguenay–Lac-Saint-Jean region actually became famous for their remarkable fertility The Tremblays, for example, were so prolific that their surname is now closely linked with both areas.

FINDING YOUR WAY AROUND

Two tours have been laid-out for this region.
Tour A: The Saguenay Region ★★ and **Tour B: Circling Lac Saint-Jean ★★**.

Tour A: The Saguenay Region

By Car

From Québec City, take Route 138 E. to Saint-Siméon. Turn left on to Route 170, which passes through the village of Sagard on its way to the Parc du Saguenay. This road continues onto Chicoutimi. It is possible and even recommended to lead up to this tour with a tour of the Charlevoix region, further south (see p 465).

Bus Stations

Chicoutimi: 55 Rue Racine E., ☎543-1403.
Jonquière: 2249 Rue Saint-Hubert, ☎547-2167.

Train Stations

Hébertville: 15 Rue Saint-Louis, ☎343-3383.
Jonquière: 2439 Rue Saint-Dominique, ☎542-9676.

Tour B: Circling Lac Saint-Jean

This tour can easily be done after the Saguenay tour. From Jonquière, take Route 170 W. to Saint-Bruno and then Route 169 around the lake.

Bus Stations

Roberval: 336 Boulevard Marcot (Valentine restaurant), ☎275-1555.
Alma: 439 Rue du Sacré-Cœur (Coq-Rôti restaurant), ☎662-5441.

Train Stations

Chambord: 78 Rue de la Gare, ☎342-6873.

PRACTICAL INFORMATION

Area code: 418

Tourist Information Offices

Regional Office

Association Touristique du Saguenay - Lac-Saint-Jean 198 Rue Racine E., Bureau 210, Chicoutimi, G7H 1R9, ☎543-9778 or 1-800-463-9651, ⚏543-1805.

Tour A: The Saguenay Region

La Baie: 1171 7e Avenue, G7B 1S8, ☎697-5050, ⚏697-5180.
Chicoutimi: see above.
Jonquière: 2665 Boulevard du Royaume, G7S 5B8, ☎548-4004, ⚏548-7348.

Tour B: Circling Lac Saint-Jean

Alma: 715 Rue Harvey O., G8B 7H2, ☎669-5030, ⚏669-5043.
Saint-Félicien: 1209 Boulevard du Sacré-Cœur, C.P. 7, G8K 2R3, ☎679-9888.

EXPLORING

Tour A: The Saguenay Region ★★
(two days)

The "realm of the Saguenay", as its inhabitants often refer to it proudly and without an ounce of modesty, extends on both sides of the Rivière Saguenay and its gargantuan fjord. This region is characterized above all by its grandiose scenery and extraordinary flora and fauna. It was originally exploited for fur, and then wood, before eventually being permanently settled by such companies. Since the beginning of the 20th century, the aluminum industry has flourished on the outskirts of local towns, taking advantage of the abundant supply of hydroelectric power provided by area rivers, and the water ports deep enough to accommodate the ships carrying bauxite, the basic ingredient of the lightweight metal aluminum.

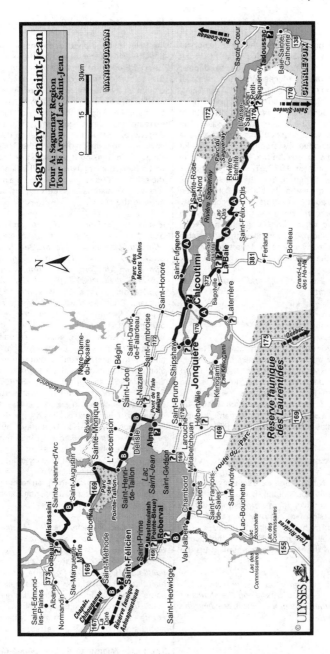

L'Anse-Saint-Jean ★ (pop. 1,340)

In the spring of 1838, the first schooner chartered by the Société des Vingt-et-Un set off from the Charlevoix region to deposit settlers at various places along the banks of the Saguenay. The first stop was L'Anse-Saint-Jean, making this charming village with its many handcrafted bread ovens the oldest municipality in the Saguenay - Lac-Saint-Jean region. Noteworthy attractions include a stone **church,** designed by architect David Ouellet (1890) and a **covered bridge,** known as **Pont du Faubourg,** built in 1929. The village and its bridge are depicted on the back of the Canadian thousand-dollar bill. The **Belvédère de l'Anse de Tabatière** with its a spectacular view of the sheer cliffs along the fjord is also worth a visit. The village boasts a salmon river, a yacht club and hiking and riding trails. It is also one of the many points of departure for river cruises of the Saguenay.

Return to Route 170, and head towards Rivière-Éternité.

Rivière-Éternité ★ (pop. 602)

With a poetic name that translates as Eternity River, how could anyone resist being carried away by the stunning beauty of the Saguenay, especially because Rivière-Éternité is the gateway to **Parc du Saguenay ★★★** (see p 491) and the marvelous **Parc Marin du Saguenay ★★★** (see Manicouagan, p 506), where whales can be observed in their natural habitat.

On the first of the three cliffs that form Cap Trinité, is a statue of the Virgin Mary, christened **Notre-Dame-du-Saguenay.** Carved out of pine by Louis Jobin, it was placed here in 1881 in thanks for a favour granted to a travelling salesman, who was saved from certain death when he fell near the cape. The statue is tall enough (8.5 m) to be clearly visible from the deck of ships coming up the river.

Head back to Route 170. The road leads through Saint-Félix-d'Otis, along the shores of the lake of the same name, before reaching the town of La Baie.

La Baie ★ (pop. 21,647)

La Baie is an industrial town occupying a beautiful site at the far end of the Baie des Ha! Ha! Old French for *impasse* (means dead-end), the colourful term "Ha!Ha!" was supposedly employed by the region's first explorers, who headed into the bay thinking it was a river. The town of La Baie is the result of the 1976 merging of three adjacent municipalities, Bagotville, Port-Alfred and Grande-Baie. The latter was founded in 1838 by the Société des Vingt-et-Un, making it the oldest of the three. At La Baie, the Saguenay is still influenced by the salt-water tides, giving the town a maritime feel. La Baie also has a large **sea port,** which is open to the public.

Musée du Fjord ★ *($3.50; late Jun to early Sep, Mon to Fri 9am to 6pm, Sat and Sun 10am to 6pm; early Sep to late Jun, Mon to Fri 8:30am to noon and 1:30pm to 5pm; Sat and Sun 10am to 5pm; 3346 Boulevard de la Grande-Baie S., ☎697-5077, ☎697-5079).* The Société des Vingt-et-Un was founded in La Malbaie (Charlevoix) in 1837 with the secret aim of finding new farmlands to ease overcrowding on the banks of the St. Lawrence. Under the pretext of cutting wood for the Hudson's Bay Company, the Société cleared the land around a number of coves along the Saguenay, and settled men, women and children there. On June 11, 1838, Thomas Simard's schooner, with the first settlers on board, set anchor in the Baie des Ha! Ha! The colonists disembarked and, under the supervision of Alexis Tremblay, built the region's very first wood cabin (4m x 6m), thus marking the birth of the present town of La Baie. The Musée du Fjord houses an interesting permanent exhibition, describing the settling of the Saguenay region from an ethnographic angle. Temporary art and science exhibits are also presented here each year.

At the **Palais Municipal ★** *($27; late Jun to early Aug, Thu to Sat and some Sun at 8:30pm; 591 5e Rue, ☎544-0404 and 1-800-667-4582),* visitors can see **La Fabuleuse Histoire d'un Royaume**, an elaborate historical pageant similar to those presented in some provincial French towns. Bringing this colourful extravaganza to life involves over 200 actors and 1,400 costumes, along with animals, carriages, lighting effects and sets.

The **Passe Migratoire de la Rivière-à-Mars ★**, built on a part of the river located right in the heart of town, was designed to facilitate the

Pulperie de Chicoutimi

salmons' upriver migration during their spawning period. From the pleasant park that has been laid out in the surrounding area, visitors can watch the salmon and occasionally fish for them ($30 per person).

Take Route 372, west of La Baie, which leads into downtown Chicoutimi. As it is more pleasant to visit this part of the city on foot, we recommend parking in the area around the cathedral, located on Rue Racine.

Chicoutimi ★ (pop. 64,616)

In the language of the Montagnais, "Chicoutimi" means "there where it is deep", a reference to the waters of the Saguenay, which are navigable as far as this city, the most important urban area in the entire Saguenay-Lac-Saint-Jean region. For over 1,000 years, nomadic native tribes used this spot for meetings, festivities and the trading of goods. Starting in 1676, Chicoutimi became one of the most important fur-trading posts in New France. The post remained active up until the mid-19th century, when two industrialists, Peter McLeod and William Price, opened a sawmill nearby (1842). This finally enabled the development of a real town on the site, graced with the presence of three powerful rivers, the Moulin, the Chicoutimi and the Saguenay.

Religious and institutional buildings are predominant in downtown Chicoutimi, who's main commercial thoroughfare is Rue Racine. Very little remained of the 19th century Victorian town after most of Chicoutimi was destroyed by a raging fire in 1912, the rest has been "modernized" or stripped of its character over the past 30 years. Along the streets, visitors will notice shop signs bearing typical Saguenay names, like Tremblay and Claveau, as well as English-sounding names, such as Harvey and Blackburn; this is indicative of a phenomenon found only in this part of the country, the assimilation of English-speaking families into French-speaking society.

The **Cathédrale Saint-François-Xavier** ★ *(514 Rue Racine E.)* has had to be rebuilt on two different occasions, both times due to fire. The present building, erected between 1919 and 1922, was designed by architect Alfred Lamontagne. It is remarkable above all for its high façade, whose two towers, topped with silvered steeples, rise above the old port. In front of the cathedral, visitors will find the former post office, built of pink granite in the Second-Empire style (1905).

Return to your car in order to visit other attractions located further away from downtown. Drive up Rue Bégin, west of the cathedral, then turn right on Rue Price Est. Turn left on Boulevard Saint-Paul, then right on

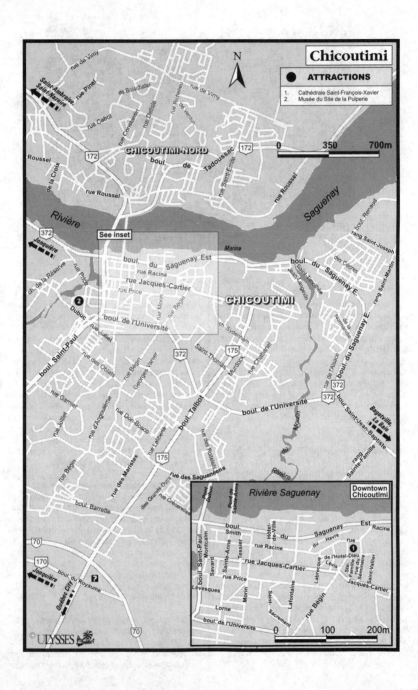

Rue Dubuc. The former home of naive painter Arthur Villeneuve lies on a small street by the name of Rue Taché, located on the left.

At the turn of the 20th century, several large-scale French-Canadian enterprises were established in the Saguenay - Lac-Saint-Jean region, the largest being the pulp mills in Val-Jalbert and Chicoutimi. The **Musée de Site de la Pulperie de Chicoutimi** ★★ *($8.50; mid-May to mid-Oct, every day 9am to 6pm; Jul until 8pm; mid-Oct to late nove, Mon to Fri noon to 4pm; 300 Rue Dubuc, ☎698-3100, ⁓698-3158)* was founded in 1896 by Dominique Guay and then expanded several times by the powerful North American Pulp and Paper Company, directed by Alfred Dubuc. For 20 years, the company was the largest mechanical manufacturer of pulp and paper in Canada, supplying the French, American and British markets. This vast industrial complex, built alongside the turbulent Rivière Chicoutimi, included four pulp mills equipped with turbines and digesters, two hydroelectric stations, a smelter, a repair shop and a railway platform. The decline of pulp prices in 1921 and the crash of 1929 led to the closing of the pulp mill. It remained abandoned until 1980. In the meantime, most of the buildings were ravaged by fire, which, if nothing else, showed the strength of their thick stone walls.

Since 1996, the whole complex has become a gigantic museum covering an area of over 1 hectare. In addition to stopping in at the Maison-Musée du Peintre Arthur-Villeneuve, visitors can go on a 12-stop self-guided tour of the site and take in a thematic exhibition.

Jonquière (pop. 58,734)

In 1847, the Société des Défricheurs (meaning land-clearers) du Saguenay received authorization to set up business alongside Rivière aux Sables. The name Jonquière was chosen in memory of one of the governors of New France, the Marquis de Jonquière. The town's early history is marked by the story of Marguerite Belley of La Malbaie, who escorted three of her sons to Jonquière on horseback to prevent them from being tempted to emigrate to the United States. In 1870, the territory between Jonquière and Saint-Félicien, in the Lac-Saint-Jean region, was destroyed by a major forest fire. It took over 40 years for the region to recover. Today, Jonquière is regarded as an essentially modern town, whose economic mainspring is the Alcan aluminum smelter. This multinational company owns several factories in the Saguenay–Lac-Saint-Jean region, replacing the Price sons and their wood empire as the largest local employer. The towns of Arvida and Kénogami merged with Jonquière in 1975, forming a city large enough to rival nearby Chicoutimi. Jonquière is known for its industrial tours.

The **Centrale Hydroélectrique de Shipshaw** ★★ *(free tour; Jun to Aug, Mon to Fri 1:30pm and 3pm; 1471 Route du Pont, ☎699-1547)*, which began operating in 1931, is a striking example of Art-Deco architecture. It supplies electricity to the local aluminum smelters.

Cross the Aluminum Bridge and turn left on Rue Price.

The **Aluminium Bridge,** opened in 1948, weighs 164 tons, a third of the weight of an identical steel bridge. It was built as a means of promoting aluminum, which at the time was rarely used in construction.

The contemporary-style **Église Notre-Dame-de-Fatima** ★ *(3635 Rue Notre-Dame)*, is renowned as one of the most famous white churches in the Saguenay region. Designed by Paul-Marie Côté and Léonce Gagné, it was erected in 1963. The stained-glass windows by artist Guy Barbeau produce a lovely play of light on the bare concrete interior.

The **Parc et Promenade de la Rivière-aux-Sables** *(2230 Rue de la Rivière-aux-Sables, ☎546-2177)* is the fruit of a major environmental restoration project carried out on the Rivière aux Sables, alongside the largest historic district in town. It links the Place des Nations de la Francité and Place Nikitoutagan to the immediate surroundings of the bridge on Boulevard Harvey. Here, visitors will find Les Halles, where many local market gardeners have stalls. There are a few places to eat in there as well, including an excellent crêpe restaurant. Both pedestrians and cyclists are permitted on the riverside promenade.

Visitors who would like to begin Tour B, Circling Lac Saint-Jean immediately should turn left on Boulevard du Royaume (Route 170 West) from Rue Saint-Dominique, then head towards Larouche and Alma.

SAGUENAY - LAC-SAINT-JEAN

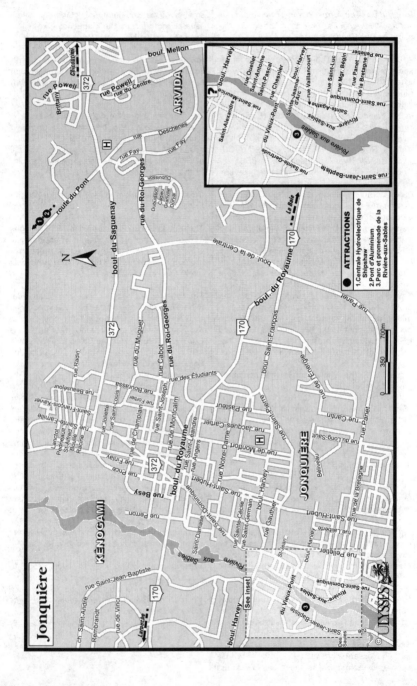

Jonquière

ATTRACTIONS

1. Centrale Hydroélectrique de Shipshaw
2. Pont d'Aluminium
3. Parc et promenade de la Rivière-aux-Sables

Tour B: Circling Lac Saint-Jean ★★
(two days)

Various Montagnais tribes, including the Nation du Porc-Épic (Porcupine Nation), were once attracted to the vast expanse of water known today as Lac Saint-Jean (1,350 square kilometres). Whites were unaware of the lake's existence for many years; it wasn't until 1647 that a Jesuit missionary named Jean de Ouen discovered it on his way to nurse some ailing local inhabitants. Long regarded as an inexhaustible source of fur, this region, with its rich farmlands, sandy beaches and relatively mild climate, was not actually settled until much later, in the second half of the 19th century. In 1926, Lac Saint-Jean's water level increased significantly when dams were built on the Saguenay, leading to the loss of several square kilometres of farmland. The following tour leads visitors around the lake in the same direction as the area was settled, coming almost full circle and ending near the starting point.

Desbiens (pop. 1,380)

Located on either side of the Rivière Métabetchouane, this town is steeped in history. It was settled in 1652 by a Jesuit mission, a fur-trading Post was added in 1676. The trading post, consisted of a store, a chapel and several farm buildings. It prospered until 1880, when the buildings were dismantled and moved to Pointe-Bleue.

Centre d'interprétation de la Métabetchouane ★ *($3.50; late Jun to early Sep, every day 9am to 5pm; early Sep to late Jun, Mon to Fri 9am to 5pm; 243 Rue Hébert, ☎346-5341).* Many excavations have been conducted around the mouth of Rivière Métabetchouane, uncovering various archeological traces of the aboriginals' thousand-year-long habitation of the area, as well as remnants of the Jesuit mission and the fur-trading post. A number of the objects uncovered during these digs are on display at this centre, opened in 1983.

Guides lead visitors through the granite cave known as the **Trou de la Fée** *($6.50, mid-Jun to mid-Aug, every day 9am to 5:30pm; mid to late Aug 10am to 4pm; 1058 Rue Marcellin, ☎346-5632 or 346-5436),* the name means "the fairy's hideaway".

The harsh Québec winter lead Joseph-Armand Bombardier to design a vehicle capable of travelling over vast stretches of snow: the snowmobile. Several models of this vehicle are on display at the **Musée de la Motoneige** *($4; mid-Jun to early Sep, every day 9am to 6pm; 1640 Chemin du Trou-de-la-Fée, ☎346-5368).*

Continue along Route 169 toward Chambord, then Val-Jalbert.

Val-Jalbert

The **Village Historique de Val-Jalbert ★★** *($8.50; mid-May to mid-Jun and early Sep to late Oct, every day 9am to 5pm; mid-Jun to early Sep 9am to 7pm; Route 169, ☎275-3132, ⚏275-5875)* began in 1901, when an industrialist by the name of Damase Jalbert built a pulp mill at the foot of the Rivière Ouiatchouane fails. The enterprise prospered quickly, becoming the most important industrial company run entirely by French Canadians. The drop in pulp prices in 1921, followed by the shift to artificial pulp in the manufacture of paper, forced the mill to close down in 1927, at which point the village was completely deserted by its inhabitants.

Val-Jalbert is a rich slice of North America's industrial heritage. Part of the village still looks like a ghost town, while the rest has been carefully restored to provide visitors with accommodations and an extremely informative interpretation centre. Various viewing areas, linked by a gondola *(adults $3.25),* have been built to enable visitors to fully appreciate the surroundings. There is a campground beside the village, and accommodations are available in some of the restored houses.

Continue along Route 169 to Roberval.

Roberval (pop. 11,929)

This industrial town used to be the crossroads of the railway and the Lac Saint-Jean shipping routes. Today, it is the finishing point of the famous Traversée Internationale du Lac Saint-Jean, a swimming event held each year in July.

The **Centre Historique et Aquatique de Roberval ★** *($5; Jun and Sep, every day noon to 5pm; late Jun to late Aug, 10am to 8pm; 700 Boulevard de la Traversée, ☎275-5550)* enables visitors to familiarize themselves with the history, wildlife and plant life of the Lac-

Saint-Jean region. Particularly noteworthy is the aquarium, where various regional species of fish, including the famous *ouananiche*, a type of fresh-water salmon, have been collected. In a new building with remarkable architecture, visitors can learn about the settlement of the lake's perimeter, as well as great moments in the history of the Traversée du Lac Saint-Jean.

Turn right on the little road that runs alongside the lake towards Mashteuiatsh (Pointe-Bleue).

Mashteuiatsh or Pointe-Bleue ★ (pop. 1,505)

The Montagnais lived in nomadic tribes all around Lac Saint-Jean for over 1,000 years. Advancing colonisation and the forest industry eventually put an end to this way of life.

The **Musée Amérindien ★** *($3; early Jun to late Sep, Mon to Sat 9am to 6pm, Tue and Thu until 9pm, Sun noon to 5pm; 407 Rue Amishk, ☎275-4842, ≈275-7494)* focuses on the customs of the first inhabitants of the Saguenay – Lac-Saint-Jean region. Its temporary exhibitions help acquaint visitors with Canada's other native peoples as well. Significant objects on permanent display include a set of chairs and a table used by the band council, different types of snowshoes and examples of traditional clothing. Artisans skilled in the techniques of their ancestors occasionally gather on the grounds of the museum to pass on their know-how.

Saint-Félicien (pop. 10,656)

At the **Jardin Zoologique de Saint-Félicien ★★** *($17; late May to late Sep, every day 9am to 5pm; Jul until 7pm; Jan and Feb, Sun 9am to 5pm; Mar, Sat and Sun 9am to 5pm; last tour departs at 3:30pm; 2230 Boulevard du Jardin, ☎679-0543 or 1-800-667-5687, ≈679-3647)*, visitors can observe various species of Québec's indigenous wildlife in their natural habitat. What makes this zoo unusual is that the animals are not in cages, but roam about freely, while visitors tour the zoo in small, screened buses. A lumber camp, a fur-trading post, a Montagnais encampment, and a settler's farm have all been reconstructed, and along with the authentic buildings onsite, add a historical feel to this untraditional zoo.

Mistassini (pop. 7,100)

Mistassini is the self-declared blueberry capital of the world. Every year in late July and early August, the town hosts a blueberry festival *(☎276-1241)*, which is as much a reunion of the *Bleuets*, residents of the region, who have scattered across America, as it is a culinary event, featuring delicious chocolate-covered blueberries among other goodies (in season)!

Continue along Route 169 toward Sainte-Jeanne-d'Arc and Péribonka.

Péribonka ★ (pop. 653)

Louis Hémon was born in Brest (France) in 1880. After attending the Lycée Louis-LeGrand in Paris, he obtained his law degree from the Sorbonne. In 1903, he settled in London, where he started his career as a writer. His adventurous spirit eventually led him to Canada. He lived in Québec City, then in Montréal, where he met some investors who wanted to build a railroad in the northern part of the Lac-Saint-Jean region. He headed off to scout out a location, but became fascinated instead by the local inhabitants' daily life. In June 1912, he met Samuel Bédard, who invited him to his home in Péribonka. Hémon helped out on the farm, secretly recording his impressions of the trip in a notebook, these impressions later formed the basis of his masterpiece, the novel *Maria Chapdelaine*.

Hémon did not, however, have time to enjoy his novel's tremendous success; on July 8, 1913, he was hit by a train while walking on the railroad tracks near Chapleau, Ontario, and died a few minutes later in the arms of his travelling companions. *Maria Chapdelaine* was serialized in *Le Temps* in Paris, then published as a novel by Grasset in 1916, and finally translated into several languages. No other work of literature has done so much to make Québec known abroad. The novel was even adapted three times for the screen, by Jean Duvivier in 1934 (with Madeleine Renaud and Jean Gabin), Marc Allégret in 1949 (with Michèle Morgan in the title role) and Gilles Carle in 1983 (with Carole Laure in the title role). Péribonka is a charming village, which serves as the starting point for the swimming race, the Traversée Internationale du Lac Saint-Jean.

Musée Louis-Hémon ★★ *($4.50; Jun to Sep, every day 9am to 5:30pm; Sep to Jun, Mon to*

*Sat 9am to 4pm, Sun 1pm and 5pm;
700 Route 169, ☎374-2177, ⌐374-2516)* is
located in the house where Louis Hémon spent
the summer of 1912 with Samuel Bédard and
his wife Eva (née Bouchard). It is still visible
alongside Route 169 and is one of a few rare
examples of colonial homes in the Lac-Saint-
Jean region to have survived the improvements
in the local standard of living. The extremely
modest house that inspired Hémon was built in
1903. As it was converted into a museum in
1938, its furnishings have remained intact, and
are still laid out in their original positions in the
humble rooms. A large postmodern building
was erected nearby in order to house Hémon's
personal belongings, as well as various
souvenirs of the villagers who inspired his
work, and memorabilia relating to the success
of *Maria Chapdelaine.*

*The road then leads through the villages of
Sainte-Monique, Saint-Henri-de-Taillon (access
to Parc de la Pointe-Taillon) and Delisle. On the
way to Alma, visitors will cross the Saguenay
by the Pont de l'Isle Maligne, which overlooks
the Alcan hydro-electric dam.*

Alma (pop. 26,467)

This industrial town lies along the edge of the
Lac-Saint-Jean region. It is home to a large
aluminum smelter and a paper mill, all
surrounded by working- and middle-class
neighbourhoods. Parc Falaise serves as a
reminder that Alma has been the twin town of
the town of Falaise in Normandy since 1969.

Tour guides at the **Aluminerie Alcan** ★ *(Mon to
Fri before noon, with reservation; 1025 Rue
des Pins Ouest, ☎668-9472)* lead visitors
through the factory and explain the different
steps involved in the making of aluminum.
Visitors sometimes have the opportunity to
watch the aluminum being casted. The tour
lasts about an hour, and participants should
wear long pants, a long-sleeved shirt or
sweater and flat shoes that cover the entire
foot.

Tours of the facilities of the **Papeterie Alma** ★
*(with reservation; 1100 Rue Melançon,
☎668-9400, ext. 9348)* are also offered. The
tour includes a visit to the pulp department and
the machine room and an explanation of the
manufacturing process.

 PARKS

Tour A: The Saguenay Region

The Parc du Saguenay ★★★ *(accessible from
Route 170, ☎272-2267)* extends across a
portion of the shores of the Rivière Saguenay.
It stretches from the banks of the estuary
(located in the Manicouagan tourist region) to
Sainte-Rose-du-Nord. In this area, steep cliffs
plunge into the river, creating a magnificent
landscape. The park has about one-hundred
kilometres of hiking trails, providing visitors
with an excellent opportunity to explore this
fascinating region up close. A few of the more
noteworthy trails include a short, relatively
easy one along the banks of the Saguenay
(1.7 kilometres); the Sentier de la Statue,
which stretches 3.5 kilometres and includes a
difficult uphill climb, and the superb, 25-
kilometre Sentier des Caps, which takes three
days (registration required). During winter, the
trails are used for cross-country skiing.
Accommodation in the form of campsites and
shelters is available.

The **Parc des Monts-Valin** *(accessible by Route
172, 27 km from Chicoutimi, 17 km from
Saint-Fulgence, ☎695-7883 or 695-7897;
Accueil Petit-Séjour ☎674-1200)*, with its lofty
summits, offers a whole slew of activities all
year round. Hiking, mountain biking, canoeing,
cabin stays and sports fishing are the
summertime favourites.

During winter, snowfall reaches record levels of
up to five metres. All this snow turns the trees
into ghostlike figures, hence the legends of the
"Vallée des Fantômes" (Phantom Valley) and
the "Champs de Momies" (Mummy Fields). This
wild and spectacular area, which looks out over
the surrounding region, becomes a mecca for
off-trail and cross-country skiing, snowshoeing
and ice climbing.

Tour B: Circling Lac Saint-Jean

Parc de la Pointe-Taillon ★ *($6.50; 825 3e
Rang Sud, ☎347-5371)* lies on the strip of land,
formed by the Rivière Péribonka, that extends
into Lac Saint-Jean. It is an excellent place to
enjoy water sports, such as canoeing and
sailing, and also has magnificent sandy

beaches. Bicycle paths and hiking trails provide access to the natural beauty of the park.

OUTDOORS

Hiking

Tour A: The Saguenay Region

The **Sentier des Caps** *(after the Pont du Faubourg, turn right on Chemin Thomas Nord and continue for 3 km, L'Anse-St-Jean, ☎272-2267 for reservations)* leads to the foot of one of the concrete pylons supporting Hydro-Québec's first 735 kV line. There are two look-outs, from which hikers can enjoy an extraordinary view of the fjord.

Cruises

Tour A: The Saguenay Region

The cruise-company **La Marjolaine** *($30; Boulevard Saguenay, C.P. 203, Port de Chicoutimi, G7H 5B7, ☎543-7630 or 1-800-363-7248, ⇒693-1701)* organizes cruises on the Saguenay, providing one of the most enjoyable ways to take in the spectacular view of the fjord. The ship sets out from Chicoutimi, en route to Sainte-Rose-du-Nord. Passengers return by bus, except during June and September, when the return trip is by boat. Each cruise lasts an entire day. It is also possible to take the trip in the opposite direction, from Sainte-Rose-du-Nord to Chicoutimi.

See the Manicouagan chapter for more cruises on the Saguenay, p 506.

Ice-Fishing

Tour A: The Saguenay Region

Parc du Saguenay *(accessible from Route 170, ☎272-2267)* and the Rivière Saguenay attract hordes of ice-fishing enthusiasts. From December to mid-March, when the river is frozen, it is covered with fishermen's colourful, little wooden shacks. The river is home to many species of fish, including cod, halibut and

smelt. You can rent the necessary equipment in Rivière-Éternité *(24 Rue Notre-Dame, ☎272-3008)*, La Baie *(1352 Anse-à-Benjamin, ☎544-4176)* and Saint-Fulgence *(953 Boulevard Tadoussac, Chicoutimi, ☎543-2062)*.

Downhill Skiing

Tour A: The Saguenay Region

The **Station Touristique du Mont-Édouard** ★ *($26; L'Anse-St-Jean, ☎272-2927)* has the highest vertical drop in the region (450 m). There are twenty runs for skiers of all different levels of ability.

Cross-Country Skiing

Tour A: The Saguenay Region

Located alongside the Rivière à Mars, seven kilometres from La Baie, the **Centre de Plein Air Bec-Scie** *($5.50; 7400 Chemin des Chutes, C.P. 305, G7B 3R4, ☎697-5132)* has a network of ten trails, four of which are easy, four difficult and two very difficult.

The **Club de Ski le Norvégien** *($5; 4885 Chemin St-Benoît, C.P. 661, Jonquière, ☎542-5822)* has 60 kilometres of trails for skiers of all levels.

ACCOMMODATIONS

Tour A: The Saguenay Region

L'Anse-Saint-Jean

The **Camping de l'Anse** *($25; ☎272-2554 or 272-2633)* not only faces the fjord, but also offers extremely well-equipped sites.

The B&B **L'Anjeannoise** *($45 bkfst incl.; 289 Rue St-Jean-Baptiste, G0V 1J0, ☎272-3437)* a former general store, is as quaint as can be.

Perched atop a cliff along the fjord, the **Gîtes du Fjord** *($88; K, ≈, tv; 344 Rue Saint-Jean Baptiste, G0V 1J0, ☎272-3430 and*

Ulysses' Favourites

Accommodations

For tranquillity:
Maison de la Rivière (p 493)

For businesspeople:
Hôtel des Gouverneurs (p 493)

For a warm atmosphere:
Auberge Presbytère Mont-Lac-Vert (p 494)

For the views:
Maison de la Rivière (p 493) and Auberge des 21 (p 493)

Restaurants

Saguenay - Lac-Saint-Jean's finest tables:
L'Amandier (p 495), Le Bergerac (p 495), Le Doyen (p 494) and Maison de la Rivière (p 494).

For Québec cuisine:
L'Amandier (p 495), Maison de la Rivière (p 494), Le Doyen (p 494) and Le Privilège (p 495).

1-800-561-8060, ☞272-3480) rents out cottages and condominiums, which are ideal for family vacations.

La Baie

🏠 **La Maison de la Rivière** *($50; ℜ, ⊛; 9122 Chemin de la Batture, G7B 3P6, ☎544-2912 or 1-800-363-2078, ☞544-2912)* lies in an enchanting setting, surrounded by beautiful greenery. Its peaceful atmosphere makes it a daydreamers' paradise. Guests are warmly received. Unique, specialized packages focusing on regional and native gastronomy, wild plants, the outdoors, cultural activities, romanticism and alternative medicine. Guide service. Comfortable, tastefully decorated rooms designated by names taken from nature rather than by numbers. Ten of them have private balconies with stunning views of the fjord. Modern architecture with an environmentalist slant.

🏠 The charming **Auberge des 21** *($100; ⊛, ≈, ℜ, tv; 335 Rue Mars, G78 4N1, ☎544-9316, ☞544-3360)* offers a magnificent recently renovated rooms at reasonable view of the Baie des Ha! Ha!. In addition to comfortable

rooms and a health club, to help travellers relax as much as possible.

Chicoutimi

Located in the heart of town, the **Hôtel des Gouverneurs** *($65; ≈, ℜ, ≡, tv; 1303 Boulevard Talbot, G7H 4CI, ☎549-6244 or 1-800-463-2820, ☞549-55227)* is a meeting place frequented by businesspeople looking for rooms with all the modern conveniences.

Jonquière

Though outside the centre of town, the **Hôtel Holiday Inn Saguenay** *($80; ≈, ≡, ℜ, ⊙, tv; 2675 Boulevard du Royaume, G7S 5B8, ☎548-3124, ☞548-1638)* nevertheless very well located on the road between Jonquière and Chicoutimi, and has nice rooms.

Tour B: Circling Lac Saint-Jean

RESTAURANTS

Hébertville

🛶 The **Auberge Presbytère Mont-Lac-Vert**
*($55 bkfst incl.; ℜ; 335 Rang 3, GOW 1S0,
☎344-1548, ⇒344-1013)* lies in a beautiful
setting and has a warm, relaxing atmosphere.
The food, furthermore, has received rave
reviews from many guests.

Val-Jalbert

This ghost town has an outstanding
campground *($20, ☎275-3132)*. A vast stretch
of land, dotted with beautiful natural sites that
will delight fans of rustic camping.

Lodgings and hotel rooms are available in the
historical village *($55, ☎275-3132)*.

Saint-Félicien

As may be gathered from its name, the
Camping du Zoo *($25; ≈; ☎679-1719)* is
located beside the zoo; so you might be
awakened by animal noises at night. It
occupies a large piece of land, and is equipped
with all the necessary facilities.

The **Hôtel du Jardin** *($71; ≈, ≡, ℜ, ⌂, tv;
1400 Boulevard du Jardin, G8K 2N8,
☎679-8422, ⇒679-4459)* offers standard
rooms near the zoo.

Péribonka

Alone on an island, the **Auberge de l'Île-du-
Repos** *($17 per person in dormitory, $83 ½b;
ℜ; Route 169, ☎347-5649)* offers beautiful
surroundings, an environment that stimulates
conversation and a fascinating cultural
programme.

Alma

The **Complexe Touristique de la Dam en Terre**
*($96 for 4 people; 1385 Chemin de la Marina,
G8B 5WI, ☎668-3016)* rents out well-designed
cottages with a beautiful view of Lac Saint-
Jean. Campers can opt for the more
economical campsites.

Tour A: The Saguenay Region

L'Anse-Saint-Jean

At **La Maison des Cévennes** *($$-$$$; 294 Rue
Saint-Jean Baptiste, ☎272-3180)*, guests enjoy
classic French cuisine with a few modern
touches. There are several seafood dishes on
the menu.

The restaurant **Mringouinfre** *($$$; 212 Rue St-
Jean-Baptiste, ☎272-2385)* has a menu of grill
and seafood. Fresh ingredients and an intimate
atmosphere are the highlights here.

La Baie

🛶 With its succulent game dishes, the
restaurant **Le Doyen** *($$-$$$; Auberge des 21,
335 Rue Mars, ☎544-9316)* boasts one of the
region's best menus. The dining room
commands a remarkable, sweeping view of the
Baie des Ha! Ha! The Sunday brunch is
excellent. Run by renowned chef Marcel
Bouchard, who has won numerous regional,
national and international awards, Le Doyen is
making a tangible contribution to the evolution
and refinement of regional cuisine.

🛶 The head chef at **La Maison de la Rivière**
*($$-$$$; 22630 Chemin de la Batture,
☎544-2912)* has developed a menu centred
around aboriginal traditions, regional dishes and
international cuisine. This superb inn lies in an
extremely pleasant setting, featuring a lovely
view of the fjord.

Chicoutimi

La Bougresse *($$; 260 Rue Riverin,
☎543-3178)* distinguishes itself by the variety
and quality of its cuisine, which is always
good. The confidence and loyalty of La
Bougresse's Chicoutimi patrons are the best
possible indication of the quality of the cuisine
served here. The restaurant has regular all-the-
mussels-you-can-eat nights.

The scent of freshly ground coffee permeates
the air at **La Cuisine** *($$; 387 Rue Racine Est,*

☎698-2822). We especially recommend the steak tartare, mussels, rabbit, sweetbreads and "*steak-frites*".

Le Privilège (*$$ wine; 1623 Boulevard St-Jean-Baptiste, ☎698-6262*) ranks among the finest restaurants in the region. A feast for the senses in this picturesque hundred-year-old house. Intuitive cuisine with market fresh ingredients for a lucky few at a time. Friendly and relaxed ambiance and service. Reservations required.

The newly opened **Chez Pachon** (*$$$; 230 Rue Lafontaine, ☎693-0227*), whose chef has already made a name for himself throughout the region, serves gourmet food seasoned with the culinary traditions of France and influenced by regional flavours. House specialties include *cassoulet de Carcassonne, confit de magret de canard*, filet and loin of lamb, sweetbreads, fish and seafood.

Jonquière

Les Pâtes Amato (*$; Faubourg Sagamie shopping centre, Route 170, ☎548-2666*) has acquired a solid reputation; some people apparently go as far as having the company's products delivered to Montréal by airplane! It is now possible to enjoy their excellent pasta in this little restaurant, which has only a few tables.

L'Amandier (*$$; 5219 Chemin Saint-André, ☎542-5395*) has an astonishing dining room decorated with carved plaster and an overabundance of woodwork. The restaurant serves regional cuisine made with fresh ingredients. Somewhat removed from town, it is not easy to find. Reservations required. Good food is joined here by a unique ambiance well-suited to dining among friends: the inviting decor and the hosts' hospitality create a festive mood.

One of the finest restaurants in Jonquière, **Le Bergerac** (*$$$; 3919 Rue Saint-Jean, ☎542-6263*) has developed an excellent repertoire of dishes. Lunchtime menu du jour and evening table d'hôte.

Tour B: Circling Lac Saint-Jean

Saint-Félicien

The fine regional cuisine served at the **Hôtel du Jardin** (*$$-$$$; 1400 Boulevard du Jardin, G8K 2N8, ☎679-8422*) is never disappointing.

Roberval

The **Château Roberval** (*$$-$$$; 1225 Boulevard St-Dominique, ☎272-7511*) is another renowned restaurant. The menu, made up of regional specialties, is full of pleasant surprises.

Alma

People don't come to the **Bar Restaurant Chez Mario Tremblay** (*$$-$$$; 534 Collard Ouest, ☎668-6431*) to enjoy the meal of their life; they are attracted by the owner's reputation as a hockey player and coach, which earned him the nickname '*le bleuet bionique*' (the Bionic Blueberry). This brasserie-style restaurant is a popular gathering place for hockey devotees.

  ENTERTAINMENT

Festivals and Cultural Events

Chicoutimi

The **Carnaval-Souvenir de Chicoutimi** (*mid-Feb; ☎543-4438*) celebrates the customs of winter in days gone by with period costumes and traditional activities.

Roberval

Since 1955, the last week in July has been devoted to the **Traversée Internationale du Lac Saint-Jean** (*☎275-2851*). Swimmers cover the 40 kilometres between Péribonka and Roberval in eight hours, and some even make the return trip in 18 hours.

SAGUENAY - LAC-SAINT-JEAN

SHOPPING

Tour A: The Saguenay Region

Chicoutimi

If you're craving healthy, natural food, **Le Garde-Manger** *(at the corner of Ste-Famille and Hôtel-Dieu, behind the church)* is the perfect place to stock up for a picnic.

Blueberry Patches

Of course, here in the land where three blueberries can just about fill a pie, you might want to check out one of the following blueberry patches:

Bleuetière Au Gros Bleuet 226 Rang 2, 3 kilometres from Falardeau, ☎673-4558.

Bleuetière de Saint-François-de-Sales Chemin du Moulin, 15 kilometres west of the village of Saint-François-de-Sales, ☎348-6642.

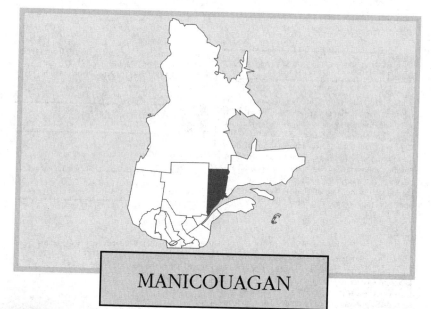

MANICOUAGAN

he Manicouagan region borders the St. Lawrence for some 300 kilometres, extends north into the Laurentian plateau to include the Monts Groulx and the Réservoir Manicouagan, and is joined to the Duplessis region, forming what is called the Côte Nord or north shore. Covered by thick Boreal forest, Manicouagan also has an extensive river system that powers the eight generating stations of the Manic-Outardes hydroelectric complex.

The history of Manicouagan has always been closely linked to the naturel resources of the area. Even before the founding of Québec City, Europeans had set up outposts in the region to trade with Native groups. During the 19th century, forestry became the region's main industry. In 1959, the strong currents of the Rivière aux Outardes and the Rivière Manicouagan were put to use with the construction of eight large generating stations. Completed in 1989, the Manic Outardes complex now produces more than 6,500 megawatts of power and has helped to make Québec a world leader in hydroelectric technology. The complex which houses the largest arch and buttress dams in the world, is now open to visitors.

Route 138 stretches along the coast from the mouth of the Saguenay up to Baie-Trinité, and has beautiful views of steep cliffs and wild beaches. Bird watchers and nature lovers will enjoy the Parc Régional de Pointe-aux-Outardes, home to a multitude of bird species, while more adventurous visitors may want to plan an expedition through the rugged and remote Monts Groulx area. One of the region's main attractions is the Parc Marin du Saguenay (marine park), where a variety of whale species can be spotted during the summer months.

The Côte-Nord was historically an area common to Inuit and various other native groups, mainly because of its huge river system and sea-mammal hunting potential. Before the "discovery" of Canada by Jacques Cartier in 1534, the region was visited by Basque and Breton fishermen hunting for highly valued whale blubber that was melted down on the shore in large ovens. The blubber was later used to make candles and ointments. Although the native presence in the area dates back thousands of years, there are few remaining traces of human habitation from before the 20th century. Today, the region is dotted with small fishing villages as well as pulp and paper and mining towns. Tourism, based mainly on whale watching, has a growing place in the region's economy, and the whales are now protected. Route 138, the backbone of the Côte-Nord tour, provides the opportunity to see long stretches of the immense St. Lawrence; a number of marked trails and minor roads branch off Route 132 along the way, providing access to several roaring rivers. In short, the Côte Nord is an exceptional wilderness area with an interesting history.

FINDING YOUR WAY AROUND

From Tadoussac, the Côte-Nord tour can be linked to the **Charlevoix ★★★** tour (see p 465) or to the **Saguenay ★★** tour (see p 482). To get to Tadoussac, the first stop on the Côte-Nord tour, take the ferry across the mouth of the Saguenay that links Tadoussac to Baie-Sainte-Catherine. Since Tadoussac is small and easy to get a around, explore it on foot. Cars can be left in the Parc du Saguenay parking lot, near the dock where the ferry pulls in.

By Car

From Beauport (near Québec), take Route 138 that runs along the north shore of the Saint Lawrence River to Natashquan, in Duplessis. At Baie-Sainte-Catherine, a ferry crosses the Rivière Saguenay to Tadoussac. To follow the Manicouagan tour, continue on Route 138: You can't go wrong – there's only one highway!

Bus Stations

Tadoussac: 443 Rue Bateau-Passeur, ☎235-4653.
Bergeronnes: 138 Route 138 (Station Irving): ☎232-6330.
Baie-Comeau: 212 Boulevard LaSalle, ☎296-6921.

By Ferry

Except for the Baie-Ste-Catherine—Tadoussac ferry, it is better to reserve a spot a few days in advance in the summer.

Tadoussac: The ferry ride from Baie Sainte-Catherine to Tadoussac *(free, ☎235-4395)* takes only 10 min. The schedule varies greatly from one season to the next, so make sure to double-check the times before planning a trip.

Baie-Comeau: The ferry ride from Baie-Comeau to Matane *(adults $10, cars $27, motorcycles $10, ☎296-2593)* takes 2 hours 30 min.

Godbout: The ferry ride from Godbout to Matane, in Gaspésie *(adults $10, cars, $27, motorcycles $10; ☎568-7575)* takes 2 hours 30 min.

Les Escoumins: There is a ferry from Trois-Pistoles to Les Escoumins *($10, car $25; ☎233-2202)* that lasts one hour and 30 minutes.

 PRACTICAL INFORMATION

Area code: 418

Tourist Information Offices

Regional Office

Association Touritique Régionale de Manicouagan: C.P. 2366, Baie-Comeau, G5C 2T1, ☎589-5319 or 1-888-463-5319, ⇆589-9546.

Tadoussac

Tadoussac: 197 Rue des Pionniers, GOT 2AO; ☎235-4744.
Baie-Comeau: 847 Rue de Puyjalon, G5C 1N3; ☎589-5319 or 888-463-5319.

 EXPLORING

La Côte-Nord ★★

Tadoussac ★★ (pop. 832)

In 1600, eight years before Québec City was founded, Tadoussac was established as a trading post; it was chosen for its strategic location at the mouth of the Saguenay river. Tadoussac was the first permanent white settlement north of Mexico. In 1615, the Récollet religions order established a mission that operated until the mid-19th century. The town's tourism trade received a boost in 1864 when the original Tadoussac Hotel was built to better accommodate the growing number of visitors coming to the area to enjoy the sea air and breathtaking landscape. Although the town is old (by North American standards), it has a look of impermanence, as if a strong wind could sweep the entire town away.

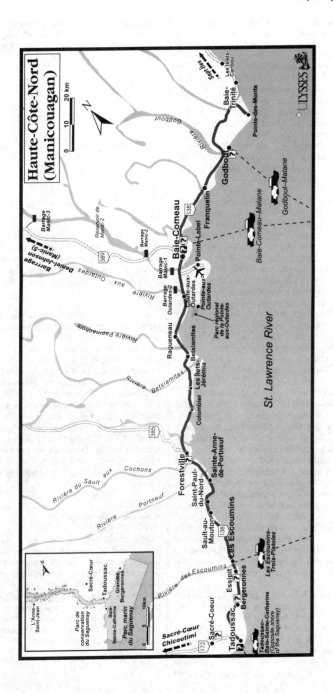

Haute-Côte-Nord (Manicouagan)

MANICOUAGAN

Dominating the town, the **Hôtel Tadoussac ★** *(165 Rue du Bord-de-l'Eau, ☎418-235-4421)* is to this community what the Château Frontenac is to Québec City: its symbol and landmark. The current hotel was built between 1942 and 1949 by the Canada Steamship Lines, following the destruction of the first hotel. Reminiscent of the resort hotels built in New England during the second half of the 19th century, Hôtel Tadoussac is long and low and its weathered wood siding exterior contrasts sharply with the bright red roof. The polished wood panelling and antique furniture that characterize the interior decor reflect traditional rural French-Canadian tastes.

In 1640 the Jesuits took over the Tadoussac mission from the Récollets. Several chapels were built successively on the same site. The one that remains, the **Vieille Chapelle des Indiens** *($1; late Jun to early Sep, every day 9am to 9pm; Rue du Bord-de-l'Eau; ☎235-4324)*, was built in 1747 under Father Claude-Godefroy Coquart of Melun, France. His was a vast ministry that included the parishes of Tadoussac, Saguenay, Lac-Saint-Jean and the rest of the Côte-Nord. The Tadoussac chapel is the oldest wooden chapel in Canada. Its plain interior contains an 18th-century tabernacle designed by Pierre Émond. In the summer of 1997, various events marked the 250th anniversary of the chapel.

American William Hugh Coverdale, president of Canada Steamship Lines during the forties, had a passionate interest in history. In addition to the reconstruction of Hôtel Tadoussac (with 19th-century stylings) in 1942, he ordered the reconstruction of the town's first trading post (also North America's first), originally built in 1600. The **Maison Chauvin ★** *($2.75; mid-Jun to late Sep, every day 9am to 8:30pm; late May to mid-Jun and late Sep to mid-Oct, every day 9am to noon and 3pm to 6pm;157 Rue du Bord-de-l'Eau, ☎235-4657)* is open to visitors; take a look around and try to imagine a time when this was the only building on the continent lived in by Europeans. The building houses an interesting exhibit dealing with the fur trade between France and the Montagnais.

The **Centre d'Interprétation des Mammifères Marins ★** *($4.75; mid-May to late Oct, every day noon to 5pm, late Jun to late Sep, every day 9am to 8pm; 108 Rue de la Cale-Sèche, ☎235-4701)* is an information centre that was created to provide an understanding of the whales that migrate to the region every summer. The centre features skeletons of various sea mammals, video presentations, and an aquarium with specimens of fish species that live in the St. Lawrence; naturalists are on hand to answer questions.

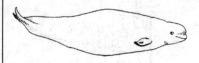

Beluga

Life in Tadoussac has always centred around the sea. The **Musée Molson-Beattie** *(Jul and Aug; Rue de Bateau-Passeur, ☎235-4657)* looks back on the high points in the evolution of the local shipping and shipbuilding industries.

The **Dunes de Sable** (sand dunes) and the **Maison des Dunes ★** are located approximately five kilometres north of Tadoussac. The dunes were formed thousands of years ago as glaciers receded. Although the government now protects the dunes, it is still possible to ski on them at certain times. For information and equipment rental contact the youth hostel or the **Centre d'interprétation des Dunes de Sable** *(free admission; early Jun to mid-Oct, every day 10am to 5pm; Chemin du Moulin-à-Baude, ☎235-4227)*. Turn right onto Rue des Pionniers from Route 138. The dunes are three and a half kilometres farther on. The Maison des Dunes parking lot is located 5.8 kilometres past the turnoff from Route 138.

Bergeronnes ★ (pop. 212)

The municipality of Bergeronnes is made up of the hamlets of Petites-Bergeronnes and Grandes-Bergeronnes, and is the site of an archeological dig. Knives dating back to between 200 and 1100 AD — used by aboriginals to cut seal and whale skins — have been uncovered here. Bergeronnes is also the best spot to observe some of the region's whale species from land; it is here that the blue whales come closest to shore.

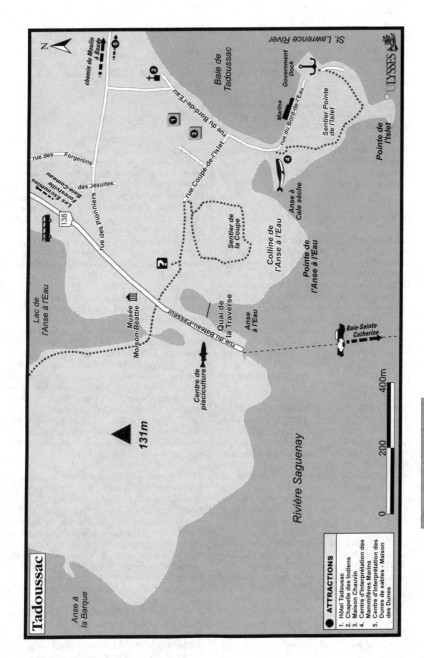

The **Centre D`interpretation Archeo-topo** *($4.75; May to Oct, every day 9am to 6pm; 498 Rue de la Mer, ☎232-6286)* displays objects found during archeological digs carried out on the banks of the St. Lawrence since 1983. Most of these objects are of a certain ethnological interest, but may not fascinate all visitors.

The **Centre d'interprétation et d'observation de Cap-de-Bon-Désir** ★ *($4; mid-Jun to mid-Sep, every day 8am to 8pm; 166 Route 138, ☎232-6751)* is an information and observation centre located around the Cap Bon-Désir lighthouse (still in operation). It has an interesting exhibit on whales as well as a whale observation point.

Les Escoumins ★ (pop. 2,212)

There are several nature trails in Les Escoumins perfect for fishing and observing birds. The area is also known for its scuba diving. The town's metallic cross, planted on a headland jutting into the river, replaces the wooden cross erected by the Montagnais in 1664 commemorating the arrival of missionary father Henri Nouvel. During the American Civil War, Southern officers, separated from their regiment, took refuge in Les Escoumins, while in the Second World War, a group of German soldiers left their submarine under the cover of darkness and went to shore to visit the local fair.

The **Centre des Loisirs Marins** *(admission charge; Mar to Dec; 41 Rue des Pilotes, ☎233-2860 or 233-2727)* caters mainly to a large clientele of divers, but you can also go there simply to watch the divers getting ready or the pilots setting out for the merchant ships. Footbridges provide access to dive sites and picnic areas. The Centre also presents an exhibition on the sea bed. A lookout has been erected so that visitors can observe the sea mammals.

The **Escoumins (Essipit)** native reserve was founded in 1903. The Côte-Nord has long been inhabited by the indigenous Montagnais nation, a nomadic people that lived mainly by hunting and fishing. In the mid-19th century however, many white families from the Îles-de-la-Madeleine and Gaspésie settled in the region, disrupting this way of life and leading to the founding of the reserve. The reserve has nature trails, craft shops and a whale-watching tower.

Pointe-aux-Outardes (pop. 1,070)

Magnificent **Parc Régional de Pointe-aux-Outardes** (see p 506) is at the end of the headland.

Return to Route 138 Est and continue to Baie-Comeau.

Baie-Comeau (pop. 26,905)

In 1936, when Colonel Robert McCormick, publisher and senior editor of *The Chicago Tribune,* no longer wanted to be dependant upon foreign paper-making companies, he chose to build his own paper factory in Baie-Comeau, sparking the transformation of a quiet village into a bustling mill. Over the years, other large companies were attracted to Baie-Comeau by the abundance and low cost of local hydro-electric power. The young town is named after Napoléon Comeau (1845-1923), famed trapper, geologist and naturalist of the Côte-Nord.

Baie-Comeau is divided into two distinct sections, separated by a four-kilometre long rocky strip. The Mingan area, to the west, is the commercial and working-class part of town and is dominated by the Cathédrale Saint-Jean-Eudes *(987 Boulevard Joliet).* The Marquette area, to the east, is the sight of much of the town's heavy industry as well as a number of pleasant residential streets where many mill and factory executives have lived. A ferry regularly crosses the St. Lawrence between Baie-Comeau and Matane. The 2-hour-and-30-minute crossing is a good way to appreciate the huge width of the river in this particular spot (it is over 30 km wide here).

The first hydro-electric dams in Québec were built by private utilities for industrial use and to provide electricity to nearby residents. Some of these companies held monopolies on the energy produced in large regions. Eventually, the Québec government nationalized most of the electric companies in 1964. From then on, Hydro-Québec took over and significantly expanded energy production to attract industries with large energy requirements and export electricity to the United States.

The **Centre d'information d'Hydro-Québec** ★ *(135 Boulevard Comeau, ☎294-3923)* is an information centre on hydro-electricity production in Québec and is a worthwhile stop to make before visiting the Manicouagan

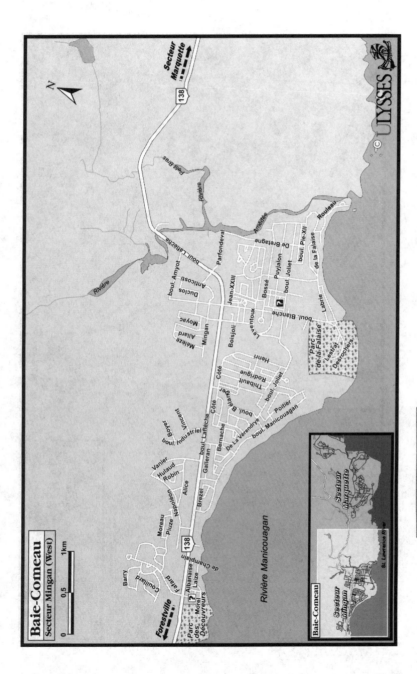

Baie-Comeau
Secteur Mingan (West)

0   0.5   1km

MANICOUAGAN

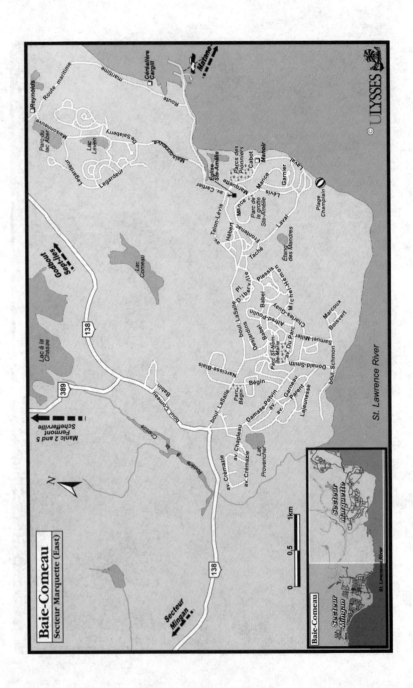

Baie-Comeau
Secteur Marquette (East)

Route maritime

Reynolds

Cédrailière
Cargill

La Matonne

Maisonneuve

Parc du
lac Abel

De Salaberry

Lac
Lévin

Église
Ste-Amélie

Parcs des
Pionniers

Cabot

Manoir

Legardeur

Legardeur

Maisonneuve

av. Cartier

Marquette

Mance

Laval

Garnier

Lévis

Parc de
la grotte
Ste-Amélie

Plage
Champlain

Tolon-Lévis

Hébert

Frontenac

Tache

Laval

Étang
des Mandres

Goubout Iles
Sept-Îles

Lac
Comeau

Pl.
LaSalle

D'Iberville

Plessis

Hamon

boul. LaSalle

Desjardins

Babel

Babel

Alfred-Douin

Charles-Guay

Charles-Michel

Marcoux

Boisvert

138

Parc St-Nom-
de-Marie

av. Du Parc

Samuel-Miller

Narcisse-Blais

Lac à la
Chasse

Parc
Bégin

Bégin

Donald-Smith

boul. Schmon

389

Manic 2 and 5
Fermont
Schefferville

boul. Comeau

Babin

boul. LaSalle

Damase-Potvin

av. Garneau

av. Parent

Lajeunesse

St. Lawrence River

R. de la Chasse

av. Crémazie

av. Chapleau

av. Crémazie

Lac
Provencher

N

0   0.5   1km

138

Secteur
Mingan

Baie-Comeau

Secteur
Marquette

Secteur
Mingan

St. Lawrence River

© ULYSSES

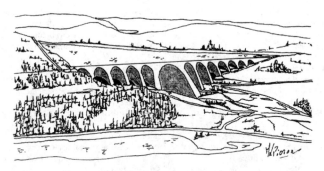

Barrage Daniel Johnson

generating stations. The information presented gives an idea of how best to get around the sometimes overwhelmingly large facilities.

The **Centrales Manic 2 et Manic 5 (Barrage Daniel Johnson)** ★★★ *(free admission; mid-Jun to Labour Day, every day: Manic 2, 9am, 11am, 1pm and 3pm; Manic 5, 9am, 11am, 1:30pm and 3:30pm; 135 Boulevard Comeau, ☎294-3923)*, the generating stations and dam, are located on the Rivière Manicouagan. A 30-minute drive through the beautiful Canadian Shield landscape leads to the first dam of the complex Manic 2, the largest hollow-joint gravity dam in the world. A guided tour of the dam brings visitors inside the imposing structure. A three-hour drive farther north leads to the more impressive Manic 5 and the Daniel-Johnson dam. Built in 1968, the dam is named after a Québec Premier who died on the morning the dam was declared officially completed. With a 214-metre central arch and measuring 1,314 metre in length, it is the largest multiple-arch structure in the world. The dam regulates the water supply to the generating stations of the Manic-Outardes complex. Visitors can walk to the foot of the dam as well as to the top, where there is a magnificent view of the Vallée de la Manicouagan and the reservoir, which measures 2000 square kilometres.

Godbout ★ (pop. 430)

The town of Godbout sits in a picturesque location on a bay. It is a marvellous spot for sport fishing, with both the salt water of the St. Lawrence and the rapids of Riviere Godbout offering good fishing opportunities. It is not surprising that local figure Napoléon Comeau chose to settle here to pursue his activities as

fisherman, guide, and naturalist. Comeau was familiar with traditional native medicines and identified many species of fish unknown to Canadian and American scientists. A plaque in his memory, designed by sculptor Jean Bailleul, is on display near the church.

Most items displayed in the small, private **Musée Amérindien et Inuit** ★ *($2.50; early Jun to end of Oct, every day 9am to 10pm; 134 Rue Pascal-Comeau, ☎568-7724)* do not come from the Côte-Nord, but rather from the Canadian Yukon and Northwest Territories. Nevertheless, these collections of Inuit art, gathered by the founder of the museum, Claude Grenier, are very interesting. Of particular note are the Inuit soapstone carvings.

Turn right onto the small road that leads to Pointe-des-Monts.

Pointe-des-Monts ★

At Pointe-des-Monts, the river widens to look like an ocean (it is almost 100 km wide et Sept Îles). Winds continuously buffet the coastal towns that become farther and farther apart as you travel eastward. Although the area was visited regularly by Europeans during the 16th century, its daunting weather conditions discouraged colonisation. Apart from a few fur-trading posts and one or two missions, established under the French Regime, the first permanent residence in the area, a lighthouse, was built in the 19th century.

After many ships were damaged or lost along the coast near Pointe-des-Monts, Québec port authorities decided, in 1805, to set up lighthouses along the river to reduce the risk of accidents. The Pointe-des-Monts lighthouse,

MANICOUAGAN

built in 1829 and known as the **Phare de Pointe-des-Monts** ★ *($1.50; end of Jun to mid-Sep, every day 9am to 7pm; ☎939-2332 and 589-8408)* was one of these. It has seven floors, circular rooms, a fireplace and recessed cupboards. Today, the building houses a bed and breakfast and an information centre dealing with the lives of lighthouse keepers.

Return to Route 138 and head east.

At this point the Manicouagan region gives way to the more rugged Duplessis region, parts of which resemble northern taiga.

 PARKS

The **Parc du Saguenay** ★★★ *(Tadoussac area)* is located along the St. Lawrence between Tadoussac and Baie des Ha!-Ha! (see also Saguenay section, p 491), near the gulf of the Rivière Saguenay. The park has three hiking trails that wind through the hilly countryside: the Fjord trail, the Colline de l'Anse à l'Eau trail and the Pointe de l'Islet trail. The last of these offers a magnificent view of the St. Lawrence.

The **Parc Marin du Saguenay** ★★★ *(182 Rue de l'Eglise, Tadoussac, ☎235-4703 or 1-800-463-6769)* features the Fjord du Saguenay, the southern-most fjord in the world, and was created to protect the area's exceptional aquatic wildlife. The fjord was carved out by glaciers; it is 276 metres deep near Cap Éternité, and just 10 metres deep at the mouth. The distinctive geography in the fjord, created by glacial deposits, includes a basin where fauna and flora, indigenous to the Arctic, can be found. The top 20 metres of water in the Saguenay is fresh and its temperature varies between 15°C and 18°C, whereas the deeper water is saline and maintains a temperature of approximately 1.5°C. This environment, a remainder of the ancient Goldthwait sea, supports wildlife such as the arctic shark and the beluga, creatures otherwise seen farther north. A number of whale species frequent the region to feed on the marine organisms that proliferate here due to the constant oxygenation in the water. One of these, the blue, reaches lengths of 30 metres and is the largest mammal in the world. Seals and occasionally dolphins can be seen in the park as well. From early on, European fishermen took advantage of the abundance of marine life, with the result that some species were overhunted. Today, visitors can venture

out on the river to observe the whales at close range. However, strict rules have been set to protect the animals from being mistreated, and boats must maintain a certain distance.

The **Parc Régional de Pointe-aux-Outardes** ★ *($4; mid-Jun to late Sep, every day 9am to 6pm; 471 Route Principale, Pointe-aux-Outardes, ☎567-4227)* follows the river and has beautiful beaches. It is mostly known as one of the largest bird migration and nesting sites in Québec. More than 175 species of birds have been identified here. The park also has walking trails, a salt marsh, sand dunes, and stands of red pine.

 OUTDOORS

  Cruises and Whale-watching

Many agencies near the dock organize boat trips onto the river:

Croisières AML *($30; Tadoussac, ☎237-4274)*, offers whale-watching trips in large, comfortable boats that accommodate up to 300 people. The expedition lasts approximately four hours.

For the more adventurous, **Compagnie de la Baie de Tadoussac** *($30; up to four departures every day, Tadoussac, ☎235-4548)* organizes trips in inflatable boats. The boats are smaller than those used by Croisière Navimex, bringing passengers closer to the whales. As a precaution, dry suits, provided by the company, must be worn. The boats may seem a bit crude, but they are quite safe. The air out on the water is significantly colder, so dress warmly. The expedition takes approximately three hours.

The **Croisières Neptune** *(adults $30, children $15; Jun to mid-Oct; 9am, 11:30am, 2pm and 4:30pm; 498 Rue de la Mer, C.P. 194, Bergeronnes, GOT 1G0, ☎232-6716 or 232-6692 during the low season)* whisks thrill-seekers into the heart of the fjord aboard eight-metre long, well-equipped rubber dingies to watch the magnificent sea mammals frolicking about.

Captain Gérard Morneau *(adults $25, ages five to eight $10; Jun 1 to Oct 15, every day 11am; other times may be arranged; three* hours; *539 Route 138, C.P. 435, Les Escoumins, G0T 1K0, ☎233-2771 or 1-800-921-2771)*, who has over 20 years of experience under his belt, favours a friendly, relaxed approach aboard his 10-metre boat, the *Aiglefin*. He seeks out common rorquals and blue whales in their feeding grounds east of Les Escoumins.

The Ross clan of Les Escoumins truly deserve the title **Les Pionniers des Baleines** *(adults $28, children $18; May 15 to Oct 10; Jul 1 to Sep 10: 9am, 11:30am, 2pm, 4:30pm; during the rest of the season: 9:30am and 1:30pm; two and a half hours; 28 Rue de la Réserve, Les Escoumins, ☎233-3274)*, or the "Whale Pioneers", the name of their whale-watching outfit, which now has two inflatable dinghies, each able to accommodate 12 passengers.

Les Croisières Baie-Comeau *(adults $25, children $15; 9am, 1:30pm, 6pm; 194 Rue Laval, Baie-Comeau, ☎294-2300 or 296-2708)* based at the Baie-Comeau marina, near the ferry to Matane, will take you out to explore some magnificent spots along the coast near town. The 7.5-metre outboard stops at the breathtaking Baie de Pancrasse, where passengers can go swimming and tuck into a feast. Seafood dinner in the evening and on weekends (reserve a day ahead).

The **Gîte du Phare de Pointe-des-Monts** *(Route du Vieux Phare, C.P. 101, Baie-Trinité, G0H 1A0, ☎939-2332 or 598-8408 during the low season)* organizes several fascinating excursions, which are a wonderful way to wind up a stay in this extraordinary place. Aboard a rubber dinghy or a small fishing boat, passengers can contemplate the seascape at the beginning of the Gulf of St. Lawrence and observe the sea mammals that live there.

 Sea Kayaking

Sea kayaks are completely different from river kayaks. They are stable enough to be taken out onto the ocean, giving kayakers, alone or in pairs, the freedom to observe whales and seals at very close range. Of course, you'll also need a little luck!

From May to October, the following outfits provide kayak rentals and introductory courses for this kind of adventure, as well as offering one- to five-day guided trips. The rates vary depending on the package: **Azimut Aventure**

(Rue du Bord-de-l'Eau, Tadoussac, ☎235-4128 or 1-800-823-4128), **Mer et Monde** *(53 Rue Principale, Bergeronnes, ☎232-6779)*, and **Explo-Mer** *(Centre des Loisirs Marins, 41 Rue des Pilotes, Les Escoumins, ☎674-1044)*.

 Scuba Diving

Located within the Parc Marin du Saguenay et du Saint-Laurent, the Escoumins area attracts scuba divers year round. Four sites are accessible by land, about 20 others by boat. Divers who venture farther offshore should bear in mind that the strong currents, combined with the movement of the tides, can sweep them away in no time at all. The underwater scenery at the Quai des Pilotes in Les Escoumins is amazing. Huge numbers of anemones, starfish and sea urchins can be seen all along the steep wall.

A network of footbridges provides access to the sites and facilities, while the **Centre des Loisirs Marins des Escoumins** *(mid-Mar to late Dec; 41 Rue des Pilotes, Les Escoumins, ☎233-2860 or 233-2727)* provides information and has changing rooms, showers where you can rinse off your gear, carts and a shop.

The underwater Pointe-des-Monts area is known for its "ship cemetery", as many a boat has gone down in this strategic spot at the base of the gulf ever since Europeans first arrived in the New World. A large portion of Admiral Walker's fleet ran onto the reefs off Île aux Œufs in 1711, and numerous vestiges of those ships can still be found. Some of these wrecks lie only a few metres underwater, making them accessible to novice and intermediate divers.

The **Palm-O-Nord** *(May to Oct, Mon to Fri 8am to 8pm; 144 Rue Crémazie, Baie-Commeau, ☎939-2102 or 292-8279 during the high season, ☎292-2552 during the low season)* dive centre offers the services of an experienced guide, who can take divers to sites in an inflatable dinghy. Viewing of the sea bed through an inverted periscope.

 Hiking

The numerous short and medium-length trails that lace the Tadoussac area are fantastic,

MANICOUAGAN

since they lead through radically different ecosystems.

Tadoussac is also the starting point of one of the most remarkable long trails in Québec: the strikingly beautiful **Sentier du Fjord**. This 12-kilometre, intermediate trail starts near the welcome centre in Parc du Saguenay *(☎235-4238)*, next to the **fish-breeding pond**. For almost its entire length, it offers a view of the mouth of the Saguenay, the cliffs, the capes, the river and the village. There is a rudimentary campground about nine kilometres from the start. When you reach the end of the trail, you can continue hiking to Passe-Pierre, where you'll find another campground, superbly laid out in an idyllic spot.

Aventure Plein Air *(June 1 to Oct 5; 88 Rue Principale, Sacré-Cœur, ☎236-9655)* has a **boat-taxi** for hikers who have to cross the Saguenay on their way to or from Petit-Saguenay. From Anse-de-Roche to Saint-Étienne *($8)* or any other destination *($15)*. The company also organizes guided hikes.

 Bird-watching

The Tadoussac area is one of the best places in Québec to observe birds of prey. It is a potential migratory corridor. Specialists have counted phenomenal numbers of these creatures here. Keep your eyes peeled!

By entering the village on the left-hand access road, before the viaduct, you'll pass the back of the church. Take Rue de la Mer to the little park at **Pointe-à John**, an excellent vantage point from which to view whales and scores of sea and shore bird on the strand. Winter is the most active time of year here.

Most people come to the **Cap-de-Bon-Désir** park *(Bergeronnes)* to watch the whales from the shore, but bird-watchers will find a trail leading to a lookout that offers a magnificent view of the Baie de Bon-Désir, west of the cape.

If you plan on going to the edge of the **marsh in Saint-Paul-du-Nord** to observe the abundant bird life there, the first thing you should do is stop by the **Centre d'Interprétation des Marais Salés** *(435 Route 138, ☎231-1077)*, which is of invaluable assistance in planning any bird-watching activity in the area. The Centre has a self-guided nature trail that makes it easier to tour the salt marsh and helps familiarize visitors with this captivating ecosystem.

Sainte-Anne-de-Portneuf boasts one of the best bird-watching areas in Québec: the **Barre de Portneuf**, also known as the Banc de Portneuf. This four-kilometre-long sandy point, visible from the mainland, is very easy to get to. As many as 15,000 birds have been counted here in one day during the migratory season. The best time to go bird-watching here is from the end of July to the end of September, preferably when the tide is in and the birds are gathered on the inner shore. Access to the sandbank is gained by the parking lot at the north end.

Wide, sandy, wooded Manicouagan peninsula features several attractions: the Baie Henri-Grenier, Pointe-Lebel, Pointe-aux-Outardes and Pointe-Paradis beach, all of which are teeming with shore birds. There is some interesting bird-watching to be done here from mid-April to the end of September.

The area around the **Pointe-des-Monts lighthouse** is known as an excellent place to observe numerous species of sea birds. Because they are so isolated and located so far out into the river, Pointe-des-Monts and its old lighthouse attract scores of red-tailed loons and other divers.

  Hunting and Fishing

Two outfitters organize hunting and fishing trips in the Manicouagan region: **Pourvoirie La Rocheuse** *(214 9e Rue, Forestville, ☎587-4520)* and **Le Chenail du Nord** *(178 Rue Bell, Forestville, ☎766-8757)*.

 Dogsledding

The **Maison Majorique** youth hostel organizes guided dogsled rides *($15 per hour; ☎235-4372 or 235-4863)* (see p 509). Clients are accompanied by a guide and get to "drive".

 Snowmobiling

Les Escapades Nord-Côtières *(Développement Touristique Manicouagan, C.P. 377, Baie-Comeau, ☎296-9369 or 296-8000)* have three exciting snowmobiling adventure packages:

"Caribous du Grand-Nord" (Cariboos of the Great-North) "Côte Blanche" and "Grand Raid Blanc".

ACCOMMODATIONS

Tadoussac

No place offers a more stunning panoramic view than **Camping Tadoussac** (*$17; 428 Rue du Bateau-Passeur, GOT 1AO, ☎235-4501*), which looks out over the bay and the village.

The **Maison Majorique** is Tadoussac's youth hostel (*$16; 158 Rue du Bateau-Passeur, GOT 2AO, ☎235-4372, ≈235-4608*) is located less than one kilometre from the bus station. It has dormitories, private rooms, even campsites in summer, and they offer a whole variety of outdoor activities as well as reasonably priced cafeteria meals.

A small, tastefully decorated hotel, **La Mer Veilleuse** (*$55 bkfst incl.; sb, ℜ; 113 Coupe-de-l'Islet, GOT 2AO, ☎235-4396*) has a nice view of the river. The hotel offers excellent breakfasts, and the service is efficient and courteous.

The **Maison Clauphi** (*$60 bkfst incl.; 188 Rue des Pionniers, GOT 2AO, ☎235-4303*) has an inn, a motel with small rooms, and a few little cabins. It is well-located in the village and offers all sorts of outdoor activities. Bike rentals.

Set up in an old, beautiful home facing the river, the **Maison Hovington** (*$65 bkfst incl.; 285 des Pionniers, ☎235-4466*) offers a superb view. The rooms are well-maintained.

Located by the river, the **Hôtel Tadoussac** (*$129, $260 ½b and cruise; ℜ; 165 Rue du Bord-del'Eau, GOT 2AO, ☎235-4421*) resembles a late 19th-century manor house and is distinguished by its bright red roof. The hotel, made famous as the backdrop for the movie *Hotel New Hampshire*, is not as comfortable as one might expect.

Bergeronnes

Located by the river, the **Camping Bon Désir** (*$17; Route 138, ☎232-6297*) offers an outstanding panoramic view and direct access to the sea for kayakers. You can also enjoy some whale-watching while you're here.

The **Auberge La Rosepierre** (*$70 bkfst incl.; ℜ, ⊛; 66 Rue Principale, GOT 1GO, ☎232-6543 or 232-6215*) is a superb inn with comfortable, elegantly decorated rooms. Various kinds of Québec granite have been incorporated into the structure, a subject the owners wax passionate about. The granite does not create a chilly atmosphere; on the contrary, you'll feel right at home as soon as you arrive. Bike rentals.

Pointe-Lebel

There is a place on the Manicougan peninsula that will seem like heaven on earth to anyone who likes powdery beaches. The **Camping de la Mer** (*$20; ≈, ℜ; 72 Rue Chouinard, GOH 1NO, ☎589-6576 during summer, ☎589-2060 during winter*) is for people who want to enjoy everything the sea and the shore have to offer. Hiking trails, horseback riding, bird-watching and, to top it all off, one of the longest beaches in Québec.

Les Tourne-Pierres (*$60 bkfst incl., $90 1/2 board; 18 Rue Choinard, GOH 1NO, ☎589-5432 or 589-1430*), a pleasant house with a family atmosphere, is an outstanding *gîte*. The hosts are as hospitable as can be and have a passion for their part of the province. Furthermore, the place is located near a unique natural area where you can enjoy a whole slew of outdoor activities.

Baie-Comeau

Anyone who visits Baie-Comeau regularly knows about **La Caravelle** (*$55; ≈, ℜ; 202 Boulevard LaSalle, G4Z 2L6, ☎296-4986, 296-4622 or 1-800-463-4968*), a hotel-motel that looks out over the town from atop a hill. It has 70 renovated rooms, a number of which are available at low rates. Some rooms are equipped with a water bed and some with a fireplace.

What, you might ask, is that splendid house in its own little Garden of Eden right in the middle of town? **Le Petit Château** (*$78 bkfst incl.; ℜ; 2370 Boulevard Laflèche, G5C 1E4, ☎295-3100 or 295-3225*), a *gîte*, has a simple, country atmosphere but is nonetheless inviting.

MANICOUAGAN

Ulysses' Favourites

Accommodations

For history buffs:
>   Hôtel Tadoussac (p 509) and Gîte du Phare de Pointe-des-Monts (p 510).

For a friendly reception:
>   Les Tourne-Pierres (p 509) and Aux Berges (p 510).

For a warm ambiance:
>   Auberge La Rosepierre (p 509).

For outdoor enthusiasts:
>   Maison Majorique (p 509) and Maison Clauphi (p 509).

Restaurants

Manicouagan's finest table:
>   Le Manoir (p 511).

For a romantic atmosphere:
>   La Cache d'Amélie (p 511).

For the terrasse:
>   Les Douceurs de la Côte (p 511) and Petit Château (p 511).

For Québec cuisine:
>   Auberge La Rosepierre (p 510).

The beautiful stone building next to the water is the **Le Manoir** hotel *($85; ℜ; 8 Avenue Cabot, G4Z IL8, ☎296-3391 or 1-800-463-8567, ≈296-1435)*. The hotel offers spacious and bright rooms. Ask for a room overlooking the river.

Godbout

🏨 Any way you look at it, **Aux Berges** *($45 bkfst incl.; sb, ℜ; 180 Rue Pascal-Comeau, G0H 1G0,, ☎568-7748 May to Sep, ☎568-7816 Sep to May)* is one of the best *gîtes* on the Côte-Nord. The rooms are simple and the place is far from luxurious, but the graciousness of the hosts, the tourist services available to guests and the sophisticated regional cuisine make all the difference. This is a place to kick back and relax in the heart of a fascinating village. Aux Berges also rents out log cabins, located near the main building.

Pointe-des-Monts

🏨 The **Gîtes du Phare de Pointe-des-Monts** *($48 bkfst incl.; sb; Route du Vieux Fort, G0H 1A0, ☎939-2332)* offer five comfortable rooms in a setting that has been declared a historic monument. The location, on the banks of the St. Lawrence, makes for an unforgettable stay.

 RESTAURANTS

Tadoussac

Try the **Crêperie La Bolée** *($; 164 Morin, ☎235-4750)* for simple but tasty meals like stuffed crepes. It is also a good place to come later on in the evening for a drink. There is a bakery below the restaurant.

The **Café du Fjord** *($$; 154 Rue du Bateau-Passeur, ☎235-4626)* is located in an uninteresting-looking house, but it is very popular. They offer a seafood buffet for lunch, and nights are livened up with shows or with disco music.

Bergeronnes

🏨 An inn with a unique charm about it, the **Auberge La Rosepierre** *($$-$$$; 66 Rue Principale, ☎232-6543)* (see p 509) has a tastefully decorated dining room with a table d'hôte featuring regional flavours and cooking methods. Naturally, fish and seafood dishes occupy a large part of the menu and are always prepared with flair.

Les Escoumins

In addition to its spectacular view, the **Complexe Hôtelier Pelchat** *($-$$; 445 Route 138, ☎233-2401)* offers the whole range of local seafood dishes, all well prepared.

Forestville

 Les Douceurs de la Côte *($$-$$$; 2370 Boulevard Laflèche, ☎589-4600)* offers a refined cuisine that honours regional flavours. You will surely have a pleasant evening and gourmet dinner in an intimate decor, and weather provided, access to the outdoor terrasse garnished with flowers. They also serve healthy breakfasts.

Baie-Comeau

Les 3 Barils *($; 200 Boulevard LaSalle, ☎296-3681)* is an unpretentious place serving simple fare.

The newly opened Les Deux Fours restaurant *($$; 1257-A Boulevard Laflèche, ☎295-3003)* offers a large variety of dishes. Perfect for family dinners.

 Le Petit Château *($$-$$$; 2370 Boulevard Laflèche, ☎295-3100)* has a sophisticated menu based largely on regional flavours. You'll spend a pleasant and palate-pleasing evening in the intimate dining room, unless the weather is warm enough for you to sit outside amidst the flowers on the terrace. Healthy breakfasts.

 La Cache d'Amélie *($$$-$$$$; 37 Avenue Marquette, G4Z 1K4, ☎296-3722 or 1-800-544-3722)* is *the* place for gastronomic cuisine in Baie-Comeau. In the picturesque former presbytery of the loveliest parish in town, guests enjoy a delightfully intimate atmosphere that enhances their dining experience.

 The hotel restaurant at Le Manoir *($$$-$$$$; 8 Rue Cabot, G4Z 1L8, ☎296-3391 or 1-800-463-8567)* (see p 510) has a well-established reputation. In an extremely inviting and luxurious decor, guests dine on expertly prepared cuisine worthy of the most elaborate praise. A meeting place for businesspeople and industrialists, it will also appeal to tourists, who will enjoy the unique view of the bay and the holiday atmosphere that pervades the outdoor seating area. Outstanding wine list.

Pointe-des-Monts

The Restaurant du Fort de Pointe-des-Monts *($$; Route du Vieux Fort, ☎939-2332)*, located in a quiet little bay, has a menu consisting mainly of fresh seafood dishes. The cuisine is excellent and the service, impeccable.

 ENTERTAINMENT

Bars and Nightclubs

Tadoussac

Find out what acts are booked at the Café du Fjord *(154 Rue du Bateau-Passeur, ☎235-4626)*, where big names in rock, jazz and blues perform from June to the end of August.

Festivals and Cultural Events

Tadoussac

At the beginning of June, the Festival de la Chanson de Tadoussac *(☎235-4392)* is held in various local bars. This string of shows spotlights well-known singers and up-and-coming artists.

Baie-Comeau

In July, Baie-Comeau thrills to the sounds of the Festival International de Jazz et Blues *(☎589-7309)*.

 SHOPPING

Tadoussac

In a village where you can find every kind of souvenir imaginable, the Boutique Nima *(231 Rue des Pionniers, ☎235-4858)* stands for quality, selling magnificent native art.

MANICOUAGAN

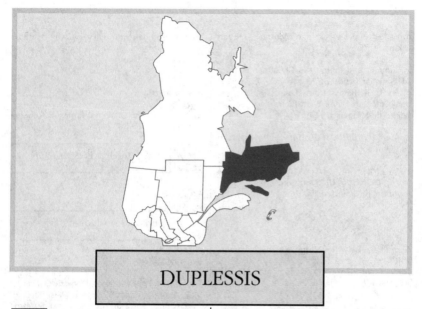

DUPLESSIS

Duplessis is a vast and remote region bound to the south for almost a thousand kilometres by the Gulf of St. Lawrence and to the north by the Labrador border. Its small population of francophones, anglophones and Montagnais is concentrated along the St. Lawrence coast and in a few inland mining towns. The region is far from any large urban centres, and its economy has always been based on natural resources. Aboriginals have lived in the region for thousands of years. In the 16th century Basque and Breton fishermen and whalers set up seasonal posts in the region. Today, the important economic activities are fishing, forestry and iron and titanium mining. Additional jobs are provided by a large aluminum smelter, which was built in Sept-Îles to take advantage of the availability of hydro-electricity.

Duplessis is home to the popular Québec singer Gilles Vigneault, many of whose songs describe life in this corner of the province. From Natashquan eastward the small towns that dot the coast are not linked to the rest of Québec by road. Duplessis is an area of expansive wilderness rich in a variety of flora and fauna. With the added attraction of its remoteness, the region offers excellent hunting and fishing opportunities. Of particular interest to some visitors are the magnificent Île d'Anticosti and the beautiful Mingan archipelago.

The Duplessis region encompasses the middle and lower half of Côte-Nord. To explore this isolated part of Québec we have suggested two tours: **Tour A: Minganie ★** and **Tour B: Gilles Vigneault Country ★★**.

 FINDING YOUR WAY AROUND

Tour A: Minganie

This tour can be linked to the **Côte-Nord ★★** (see p 498) tour of the Manicouagan region. The first town on the tour is Pointe-aux-Anglais, which has been part of the municipality of Rivière-Pentecôte for several years now. The town of Rivière-Pentecôte itself is located 12 kilometres north. This tour ends at Havre-St-Pierre.

By Car

Route 138 provides access to much of this region, before ending at Havre-Saint-Pierre.

By plane

Inter-Canadien (☎ 1-800-665-1177) serves Port-Menier on Île d'Anticosti. There are usually three flights per week from Montréal, through Québec City.

In summer and during the Christmas season, **Air Satellite** *(☎589-8923 or 1-800-463-8512)* offers daily flights from Rimouski, Sept-Îles, Baie-Comeau, Havre-Saint-Pierre and Longue-Pointe-de-Mingan.

Confortair *(☎968-4660)* offers charter flights to Île d'Anticosti.

In summer, **Air Schefferville** *(☎1-800-361-8620)* offers direct flights from Montreal to Schefferville.

Bus Stations

Sept-Îles: 126 Rue Monseigneur Blanche, ☎962-2126.
Havre-Saint-Pierre: 1130 Rue de l'Escale, ☎538-1666.

By Train

QNS&L: ☎962-9411. The train links Sept-Îles to Schefferville and runs once a week. The trip lasts from 10 to 12 hours and crosses the Canadian Shield to the outlying tundra.

By Boat

The *Nordik Express* cargo boat *(adults $40, cars according to their weight between $200 and $400; ☎723-8787 or 1-800-463-0680 from outside area code 418)* leaves from Sept-Îles and travels to Port-Menier, Havre-Saint-Pierre, Natashquan, Kegaska, La Romaine, Harrington Harbour, Tête-à-la-Baleine, La Tabatière, Saint-Augustin, Vieux-Fort and Blanc-Sablon. There is only one departure a week, so check the schedule before planning a trip.

Tour B: Gilles Vigneault Country

In 1996, Route 138 was expanded to reach Natashquan. However, during the summer, only hydroplanes and weekly supply boats from Havre-Saint-Pierre link the inhabitants of the scattered villages farther east to the rest of Québec. In the winter, snow and ice provide a natural route for snowmobiles between villages. The following tour will be of particular interest to those who really love the outdoors and want to get away from the stress and hustle of the city.

Bus Terminal

Natashquan: 183 Chemin d'En Haut (Auberge La Cache), ☎726-3347.

 PRACTICAL INFORMATION

Area code: 418

Tourist Information Offices

Regional Office

Association Touristique Régionale de Duplessis: 312 Avenue Brochu, Sept-Îles, G4R 2W6, ☎962-0808, ☞962-6518, www.bbsi.net/atrd

Tour A: La Minganie

Sept-Îles: 1401, Boulevard Laure Ouest, G4R 4K1, ☎962-1238, ☞968-0022.
Havre-Saint-Pierre: 1081 Rue de la Digue, G0G 1P0, ☎538-2717, ☞538-3439.

Tour B: Gilles Vigneault Country

Natashquan: 33 Allée des Galets, ☎726-3756 (seasonal office)

 EXPLORING

Tour A: Minganie ★
(four days)

Beyond Pointe-des-Monts (in Manicouagan) the region quickly becomes deserted as forests and cliffs give way to windswept coastal plains. Just north of the main road, an uninhabited region begins that stretches to the North Pole and beyond. Minganie takes its name from the islands of the Mingan archipelago and is known for its rushing salmon-filled rivers. Whale hunting attracted the first settlers to the Côte-Nord, but has now been replaced by whale-watching, an activity that can be enjoyed all

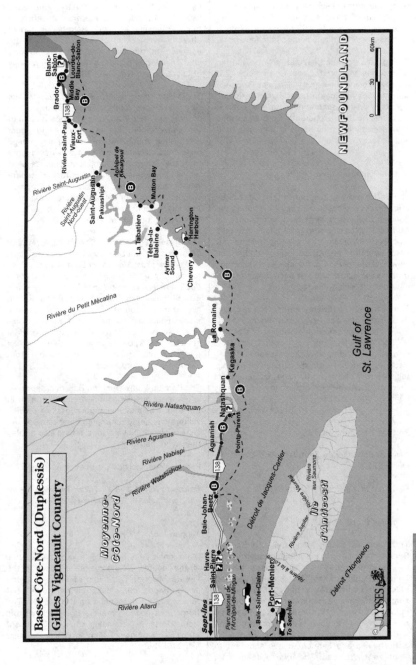

along the coast. Few vestiges of Minganie's colonial past have survived. The long-ago presence of Basque fishermen and French settlers can be confirmed only by archeologists.

During the Second World War, German submarines ventured close to the coast of Minganie, using the same passage as European supply ships and cargo boats. Local residents reported seeing submarines surface not far from their houses. Apparently German soldiers even secretly left their boats to purchase food and liquor.

Rivière-Pentecôte (pop. 790)

The British army attempted to take Canada by force on several occasions. In 1711, during the Spanish Civil War, a large fleet commanded by Admiral Walker was sent from England to take Québec. However, due to fog on the St. Lawrence, the British ships ran aground on the Île-aux-Œufs reefs. Pointe-aux-Anglais, across from Île-aux-Œufs, had just been renamed, it is now part of Rivière-Pentecôte.

The **Écomusée de Rivière-Pentecôte** ★ *($2; end of Jun to early Sep, every day 9am to 5pm; 2088 Rue Mgr Labrie in Pointe-aux-Anglais, ☎799-2262)* features an exhibit on the shipwreck of Admiral Walker's fleet in 1711. Vestiges retrieved from the sunken ships help tell the story of this maritime catastrophe that, thankfully, was followed by many decades of peace.

Port-Cartier (pop. 7,633)

Réserve Faunique de Sept-Îles - Port-Cartier ★ see p 522.

Continue along Route 138 to Sept-Îles.

Sept-Îles (pop. 25,683)

This town extending along the vast Baie de Sept-Îles (45 km^2) is the administrative centre of the Côte Nord. A fur-trading post under the French Regime, Sept-Îles experienced an industrial boom in the early 20th century sparked by the development of the forestry industry. By about 1950, Sept-Îles had become an important relay point in the transport of iron and coal, resources extracted from the Schefferville and Fermont mines and sent to Sept-Îles by railroad. The town's deep-water port is ice-free during the winter and ranks second in Canada after Montréal in terms of tonnage handled annually. Sept-Îles is named after the archipelago of seven islands at the entrance to the bay. The town is a good starting point for exploring the northern regions of Labrador and Nouveau-Québec.

The **Vieux-Poste** ★ *($3.25; late Jun to late Aug, every day 9am to 5pm; Boulevard des Montagnais, ☎968-2070)* is a reconstruction of the important Sept-Îles fur-trading post established during the French Regime. Based on archeological excavations and documents from the period, the compound appears as it would have in the mid-18th century, complete with chapel, stores, houses and protective wooden fence. Montagnais culture is explored through exhibits and according to season, various outdoor activities.

The **Musée Régional de la Côte-Nord** ★ *($3.25; late Jun to Labour Day, every day 9am to 5pm; rest of the year, Mon to Fri 9am to noon, 1pm to 5pm, Sat and Sun 1pm to 5pm; 500 Boulevard Laure, ☎968-2070)*, displays some 40,000 objects of anthropological and artistic importance found during the many archeological digs carried out along the Côte-Nord, as well as stuffed wildlife, aboriginal objects and contemporary artistic works (paintings, sculptures and photographs) from various regions of Québec.

The **Parc du Vieux-Quai**, on Baie des Sept-Îles, is the most popular summer recreation spot in the area. The park has many spots from which visitors can enjoy the magnificent view of the distant islands. Several local artists also display their work here.

Parc de l'Archipel des Sept-Îles ★★ see p 522.

Return to Route 138 E.. After De Grasse, turn right and head to Maliotenam and Moisie.

Mingan (pop. 400)

Montagnais and whites live together in this village located on the mainland opposite the Îles de Mingan. The name Mingan, of Celtic origin *(Maen Cam)*, means "curved stone", and refers to rock formations on the islands. The formations made an impression on early visitors from Brittany, reminding them of ancient stones and dolmens. Mingan is also a major salmon-fishing location.

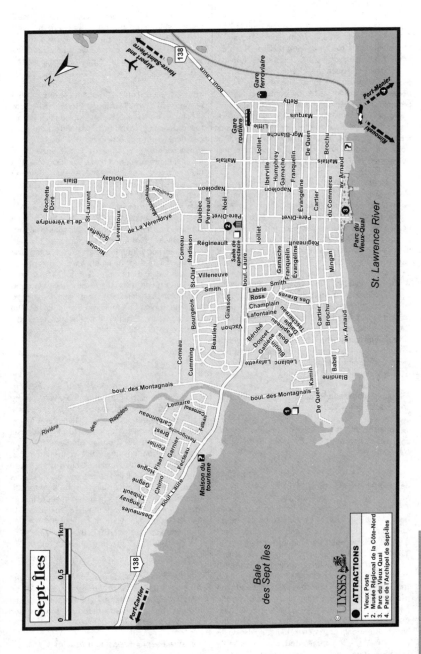

Sept-Îles

0   0.5   1km

ATTRACTIONS

1. Vieux Poste
2. Musée Régional de la Côte-Nord
3. Parc du Vieux Quai
4. Parc de l'Archipel de Sept-Îles

St. Lawrence River

Baie des Sept Îles

Havre-Saint-Pierre ★ (pop. 3,520)

This small picturesque town was founded in 1857 by fishermen from the Îles-de-la Madeleine. In 1948, following the discovery of large titanium deposits 43 kilometres inland, the town's economy was transformed overnight by the QIT-Feret-Titarle company. It became an active industrial centre and port. Since the opening of the Mingan Archipelago National Park Reserve in 1983, Havre-Saint-Pierre has also developed a significant tourism industry. The town is an excellent starting point for visitors who want to explore the Îles de Mingan and the large Île d'Anticosti.

The **Centre Culturel et d'interprétation de Havre-St-Pierre** ★ *(free admission; mid-Jun to early Sep, every day 10am to 10pm; 957 Rue de la Berge, ☎538-2512)* is an information centre in the Clark family's former general store, which has been skilfully restored. Local history is recounted with an exhibit and slide show.

Centre d'Accueil et d'interprétation, Réserve du Parc National de l'Archipel-de-Mingan *(mid-Jun to early Sep, every day 1pm to 5pm and 6pm to 9pm; 975 Rue de l'Escale , ☎538-3285)* is the information centre for the Mingan Archipelago park. Here visitors will find a photo exhibit as well as all the information they will need concerning the flora, fauna and geology of the Mingan islands.

Mingan Archipelago National Park Reserve ★★
see p 522.

Île d'Anticosti is accessible by the Nordik Express cargo boat, or by plane with Inter-Canadian.

Île d'Anticosti ★★ (pop. 340)

The presence of natives on Île d'Anticosti goes back many years. The Montagnais made sporadic visits to the island, but the harsh climate discouraged permanent settlement. In 1542, Basque fishermen named the island "Anti Costa", which roughly means "anti-coast", or "after travelling all this way across the Atlantic, we still haven't reached the mainland!" In 1679, Louis Jolliet was given the island by the King of France for leading important expeditions into the middle of the North American continent. Jolliet's efforts to settle Anticosti were limited by the island's isolation, poor soil and high winds. To make

matters much worse, British troops returning from a failed bid to take Québec City in 1690 were shipwrecked on the island and slaughtered most of the settlers living there. Anticosti is feared by sailors, because more than 400 ships have run aground here since the 17th century.

In 1895, Île d'Anticosti became the exclusive property of Henri Menier, a French chocolate tycoon. The "Cocoa Baron" introduced white-tailed deer and foxes to the island to create a personal hunting preserve. In addition, he established the villages of Baie-Sainte-Claire (later abandoned) and Port-Menier, now the only settlement on the island. Menier governed the island like an absolute monarch reigning over his subjects. He established forestry operations on the island and commissioned a cod-fishing fleet. In 1926, his heirs sold Anticosti to a consortium of Canadian forestry companies named Wayagamack, which continued operations until 1974, when the island was sold to the Québec government and became a wildlife reserve. Not until 1983 were residents given the right to purchase land and houses on the island. Anticosti, still unexplored in parts, holds many surprises, such as the **Grotte à la Patate** (cave) (see p 523), discovered in 1982.

Port-Menier

Port-Menier, where the ferry from Havre-Saint-Pierre docks, is the only inhabited village on the island, with a populations of 340. Most village houses were built during the Menier era, giving the village a certain architectural sameness. Foundations of the **Château Menier** (1899), an elaborate wooden villa, built in the American shingle-style tradition can be seen from Route de Baie-Sainte-Claire. Because the villagers could not adequately maintain the spectacular estate, they set fire to it in 1954, reducing an irreplaceable historical building to ashes. In **Baie-Sainte-Claire**, visitors can see the remains of a lime kiln built in 1897, the only vestige of the short-lived village that once stood on this site.

The **Écomusée d'Anticosti** ★ *(mid-Jun to late Aug, every day 10am to 8pm; Port-Menier, ☎535-0250)* displays photographs taken around the turn of the century, when Henri Menier owned Île d'Anticosti.

Réserve Faunique de l'Île d'Anticosti ★★ see p 523.

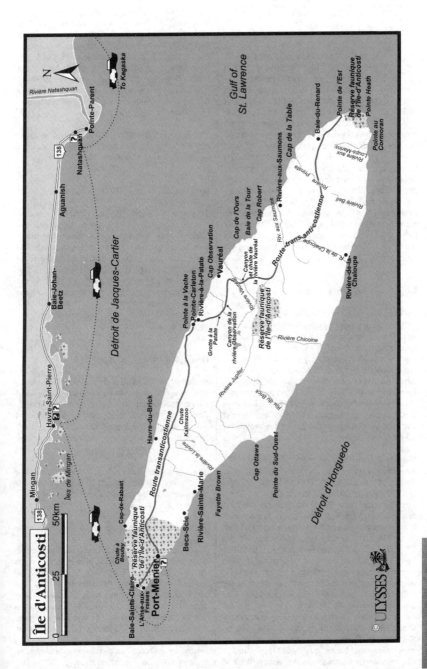

Tour B: Gilles Vigneault Country ★★
(from three to five days)

•

"Mon pays, ce n'est pas un pays, c'est l'hiver", which translates as "My country is not a country, it is winter", is how Gilles Vigneault describes this subarctic part of the world, where icebergs can be seen in the distance in mid-July. Animals such as bears, moose, walrus, seals, and whales can be spotted throughout the region. The area was colonized in the mid-19th century; previously it was visited for some time by fur traders and cod fishing vessels. Francophone, Montagnais and anglophone villages dot the coast. Some of the anglophone villages, originally inhabited by fishermen from the Isle of Jersey (in the English Channel), have very little geographical or sentimental attachment to Québec. The lower Côte-Nord, with its wooden fishing cabins and old docks has retained much of its original character.

Baie-Johan-Beetz (pop. 100)

Originally known as "Piastrebaie", due to its location at the mouth of the Rivière Piashti, this village was renamed after the learned Belgian naturalist Johan Beetz in 1918. Piastrebaie was founded around 1860 by Joseph Tanguay, who, along with his wife, Marguerite Murdock, earned a living here fishing salmon. Over the following years, a number of immigrants from the Îles-de-la-Madeleine arrived. These included the Bourque, Loyseau, Desjardins and Devost families, whose descendants still live mainly on hunting and fishing.

Maison Johan-Beetz ★ (early May to mid-Oct every day, reservations required; ☎539-0137). Johan Beetz was born in 1874 at the Oudenhouven castle in Brabant, Belgium. Grief-stricken over the death of his fiancée, he wanted to take off for the Congo, but a friend convinced him to emigrate to Canada instead. A hunting and fishing fanatic, he visited the Côte-Nord, and soon set up residence. In 1898, he married a Canadian and built this charming Second-Empire-style house, which can be visited by appointment. Beetz painted lovely still-lifes on the doors inside. In 1903, he became something of a pioneer in the fur industry when he started breeding animals for their pelts, which he sold to the Maison Revillon in Paris. Johan Beetz contributed greatly his neighbours' quality of life. Thanks to his university studies, during which he had learned the rudiments of medicine, he became the man of science in whom the villagers placed their trust. Equipped with books and makeshift instruments, he treated as best he could, the ills of the inhabitants of the Côte-Nord. He even managed to save the village from Spanish influenza with a skilfully monitored quarantine. If you ask the elderly people here to tell you about Monsieur Beetz, you'll hear nothing but praise.

The **Refuge d'Oiseaux de Watshishou** ★ (east of the village), the bird sanctuary, houses several colonies of aquatic birds.

Natashquan ★ (pop. 392)

This small fishing village, with its wooden houses buffeted by the wind, is where the famous poet and songwriter Gilles Vigneault was born in 1928. Many of his songs describe the people and scenery of the Côte-Nord. He periodically returns to Natashquan for inspiration, where he still owns a house. In the Montagnais language, Natashquan means "place where bears are hunted". The neighbouring village of Pointe-Parent is inhabited by Montagnais.

Harrington Harbour ★ (pop. 315)

Set apart by its makeshift wooden sidewalks, the modest anglophone fishing village of Harrington Harbour is located on a small island. The rocky terrain ruled out a conventional village lay-out, leading inhabitants to link their houses by slightly elevated wooden footbridges.

Heading east, supply boats wind through a multitude of striking bare and rocky islands that look like something from another planet.

Tête-à-la-Baleine ★ (pop. 350)

Tête-à-la-Baleine, the sixth stop on the supply-boat route, is a picturesque village where seals are still hunted. Fishermen from Tête-à-la-Baleine move to Île Providence during the summer in order to get closer to good fishing sites. However this tradition is quickly falling out of favour, and many of the island homes have been abandoned in the past few years. Some of the cedar-shingled houses can now be rented by visitors. There is also a pretty chapel, built in 1895, on Île Providence.

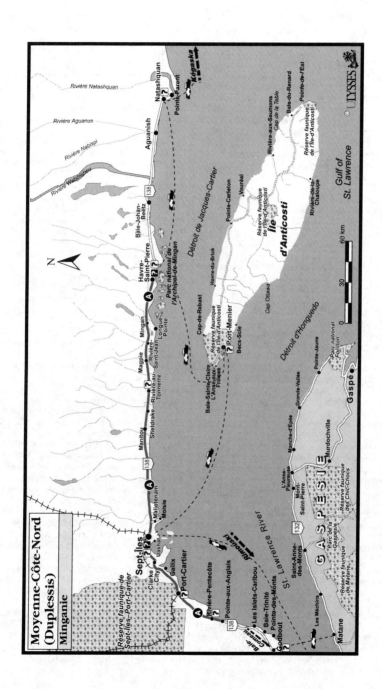

Moyenne-Côte-Nord (Duplessis)
Minganie

*The boat makes stops at Baie-des-Moutons and
La Tabatière before reaching Saint-Augustin.*

Saint-Augustin (pop. 1,010)

Located about twelve kilometres upstream on
the Rivière Saint-Augustin, the town of Saint-
Augustin is the most populous in the lower
north shore. To reach Saint-Augustin, boats
pass through a beautiful estuary, protected to
the west by the Kécarpoui archipelago and to
the east by the Saint-Augustin archipelago. The
Pakuashipi Montagnais community is situated
near the village.

*The boat stops at Vieux-Fort before ending its
voyage in Blanc-Sablon.*

Lourdes-de-Blanc-Sablon (pop. 1,252)

This small fishing village has administrative
offices and a health-care centre that serve this
part of the lower north shore.

The lower north shore is still served by
missionary priests, just as it was during the
colonial era. In 1946, Monseigneur Scheffer
was named first vicar of the Schefferville-
Labrador region. The **Musée Scheffer** *(free
admission; every day 8am to 9pm; in the Église
de Lourdes-de-Blanc-Sablon)* outlines the
history of the Blanc-Sablon region.

Blanc-Sablon (pop. 330)

This isolated region was visited as early as the
16th century by Basque and Portuguese
fishermen. They established camps where they
melted seal blubber and salted cod before
shipping it to Europe. It has been suggested
that Vikings, who are known to have
established a settlement on the nearby island of
Newfoundland, might have set up a village near
Blanc-Sablon around the year 1000. However,
archeological digs have only just begun. Brador,
a fishing camp used by Frenchmen from
Courtemanche, has recently been
reconstructed.

Blanc-Sablon is only 1.5 kilometres from
Labrador, a large, mostly arctic territory. Much
of Labrador was once part of the province of
Québec; it is now the mainland half of the
province of Newfoundland. It is accessible by
road from Blanc-Sablon. The former British
colony of Newfoundland did not become a part
of Canada until 1949. A ferry links Blanc-
Sablon and the island of Newfoundland.

PARKS

Tour A: Minganie

The **Réserve Faunique de Sept-Îles Port-
Cartier** ★ *(24 Boulevard des Îles, Port-Cartier;
☎766-2524)* stretches over 2,422 km² , and is
visited mostly by hunters and anglers. In
addition, the Rivière aux Rochers rapids are
popular with experienced canoeists.

The **Parc Régional de l'Archipel des Sept-
Îles** ★★ is made up of several islands: Petite
Boule, Grande Boule, Dequen, Manowin,
Corossol, Grande Basque and Petite Basque.
There is also an abundance of cod in the area,
making fishing a popular activity. Trails and
camp sites have been set up on Île Grande
Basque. For cruises around the archipelago, see
p 524.

A series of islands and islets stretching over a
95-kilometre long area, the **Mingan Archipelago
National Park Reserve** ★★ *(Havre-St-Pierre,
☎538-3331)* is also called the Réserve de Parc
National de l'Archipel-de-Mingan. It boasts
incredible natural riches. The islands are
characterized by distinctive rock formations,
made up of very soft stratified limestone that
has been sculpted by the waves. The
formations are composed of marine sediment
that was swept into the area some 250 million
years ago from equatorial regions before being
washed up on land and covered by a mantle of
ice, several kilometres thick. As the ice melted
some 7000 years ago, the islands re-emerged
with their impressive stone monoliths. In
addition to this fascinating element, the marine
environment encouraged the development of
varied and unusual plant life. Approximately
200 species of birds nest here, including the
Atlantic puffin, the gannet, and the Arctic tern.
The river is also home to several whale species,
including the blue whale. There are two visitor
information centres, one in Longue-Pointe-de-
Mingan *(124 Rue du Bord-de-la-mer, GOG 1VO,
☎949-2126)* and the other in Havre-Saint-Pierre
(975 Rue de l'Escale, GOG 1PO, ☎538-3285).
Both are open only the summer. There are
camp sites on the island (see p 525). Some of
the islands have hiking trails.

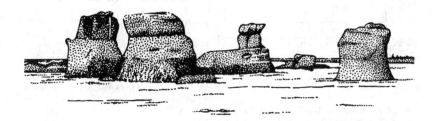

Monoliths of the Mingan Archipelago

In addition to natural attractions, the park also contains the vestiges of a very old native settlement, dating back over 4,000 years. Montagnais from the village of Mingan were the first to visit this spot regularly, to hunt for whales and gather berries.

Apart from the Viking explorers, who are known to have visited the island of Newfoundland, the first Europeans to set foot on Canadian soil are believed to have been Basque and Breton whale hunters, who left evidence of their presence on Mingan islands. Archeologists have found remnants of the circular ovens made of stone and red tile (16th century) they used to melt the whale blubber before exporting it to Europe where it was used to make candles. In 1679, Frenchmen Louis Jolliet and Jacques de Lalande purchased the archipelago for use as a fur-trading post and cod-salting site. The related installations were destroyed by the British during the Conquest (1760).

Measuring 222 kilometres in length and 56 kilometres in width, the **Réserve Faunique de l'île d'Anticosti** ★★ is big enough to accommodate a number of activities including hunting, walking, swimming and fishing. The island has belonged to the Québec government since 1974, but was not open to hikers until 1986. The reserve is very popular among hunters, and is known for its white-tailed deer. Contributing to the magnificent scenery are breathtaking panoramas, long beaches, waterfalls, caves, cliffs, and rivers.

It is possible to visit the reserve and its many natural attractions by car, provided that your vehicle is in good shape, but you'll need a few days. Sixty-five kilometres from Port-Menier,

you'll find a waterfall called **Chute Kalimazoo** *(Ile d'Anticosti)*. A little farther lies **Baie-MacDonald**, named after Peter MacDonald, a fisherman from Nova Scotia, who lived here as a hermit for a number of years. It is said that after falling ill and being treated in Baie-Sainte-Catherine, he walked nearly 120 kilometres in showshoes to get back home. The bay is a magnificent spot, trimmed with a long strip of fine sand. If you continue on the road that runs alongside these magnificent beaches, you'll come to **Pointe Carleton**, whose lighthouse dates from 1918. Nearby, you can see the wreckage of the *M.V. Wilcox*, a minesweeper that ran aground in 1954.

About 12 kilometres from Pointe Carleton, you'll find the road leading to the **Caverne de la Rivière à la Patate**. If your car has four-wheel drive, you can follow the road for two kilometres, then you'll have to walk two more. This cave, which stretches nearly 625 metres, was discovered in 1981 and examined by a team of geographers in 1982.

The **Chute and Canyon de la Vauréal** ★★ are two of the major natural sites on Île Anticosti. The waterfall (*chute*) flows into the canyon from a height of 70 metres, offering a truly breathtaking spectacle. You can take a short *(1 hour)* hike along the river, inside the canyon, to the base of the falls. This will give you a chance to see some magnificent grey limestone cliffs streaked with red and green shale. If you continue 10 kilometres on the main road, you'll come to the turn-off for **Baie de la Tour** ★★, which lies another 14 kilometres away. There, you'll find a long beach with majestic limestone cliffs rising up behind it.

OUTDOORS

  Cruises and Whale-watching

Tour A: Minganie

The **Virée des Iles** *($20; 140 Boulevard Laure Ouest, Sept-Iles,* ☎*968-1818 or 962-1238)*, a three-hour cruise through the Archipel des Sept-Iles, offers a glimpse of the rich marine life of the St. Lawrence, home to many kinds of aquatic mammals, particularly whales. The boat goes to Île Corossol, a large bird sanctuary.

Visitors wishing to tour the Archipel-de-Mingan have a choice of cruises. A little boat by the name of *Le Moyac* *(*☎*949-2069)* stops at several islands; a full cruise costs $30, a half-cruise, $25. **La Tournée des Iles** *($25;* ☎*538-3397)*, another guided cruise, starts at Havre-Saint-Pierre.

For whale-lovers, the most wonderful experience the Côte-Nord has to offer is to set out with the biologists of the **Station de Recherche des Iles de Mingan** for a close encounter with some **humpback whales**. Seated aboard seven-metre, **dinghies** passengers take part in a day of research, which involves identifying the animals by the markings under their tails. Biopsies are occasionally carried out as well, and useful data is compiled. These outings are not recommended for anyone prone to seasickness, however, as they start at the research station at 7am and last a minimum of six hours (sometimes much longer) in turbulent waters.

 Bird-watching

Tour A: Minganie

Amateur ornithologists can observe all sorts of shorebirds, swamp birds and ducks throughout the **Baie de Sept-Iles**. Along the shore, Pointe du Poste, at the end of Rue De Quen; the Vieux-Quai and two stopping places along the 138, west of town, are particularly good spots for bird-watching. Île Corossol is home to various colonies of seabirds, which can be seen during a cruise around the islands in the bay.

The **Mingan Archipelago Natural Park Reserve** boasts many natural wonders found nowhere else in Québec or elsewhere on the eastern part of the continent. This is true of its avian inhabitants. For example, the sanctuary is home to one of the few colonies of puffins in the gulf, on Île aux Perroquets, at the west tip of the archipelago. These birds can be observed during a cruise from Havre-Saint-Pierre, Mingan or Longue-Pointe.

Tour B: Gilles Vigneault Country

At the Refuge d'Oiseaux de Watshishou in Baie-Johan-Beetz, feathered fauna can be observed from walking along wooden walkways.

 Scuba Diving

Tour A: Minganie

Protected by the surrounding islands, the Baie de Sept-Iles is well-suited to scuba diving. Over 75 dive sites of all different levels of difficulty have been inventoried here. Two artificial shipwrecks were even added in 1995. The underwater scenery of the bay is distinguished by its rock walls covered with colourful anemones, as flamboyant as can be in the clear water. **Les Plongeurs du Saint-Laurent** *(209 Avenue Brochu, Sept-Iles,* ☎*968-2028 or 962-4171)* arrange diving excursions in the Baie des Sept-Iles and offer several packages including accommodations, meals, equipment, the services of a guide, transportation and two dives per day. Air station and classes.

 Kayaking

Tour A: Minganie

The **Centre Aventure N R J** *(367 Boulevard Laure, Sept-Iles,* ☎*968-9675)* offers a whole slew of activities for canoeists, kayakers and hikers. Their long list of packages ranges from a tour of the Sept-Iles archipelago to two- to eight-day camping trips.

Excursions Vie à Nature *(Jun to Oct; 116 Rue de la Rive, P.O. Box A7, Magpie, ☎949-2388)* invites visitors to explore the Mingan archipelago *($70 full day with lunch, $35 half-day)* in the company of ecologist guides with extensive knowledge of the natural environment of the islands and the coast. They can also take you kayaking on lakes and rivers in little-known and otherwise inaccessible parts of the region.

Excursions Vie à Nature also runs the **Centre d'Information sur le Kayak de Mer en Mingania** *(Jun to Oct; 116 Rue de la Rive, P.O. Box A7, GOG 1X0, ☎949-2388)*, which can offer advice to kayakers travelling with their own boat and provide them with a special kayaker's map of the Archipel-de-Mingan, as well as various equipment and other items related to sea kayaking.

 Downhill Skiing

Tour A: Minganie

The **Station de Ski Gallix** *(adults $25.50, students $21; mid-Dec to mid-Apr, Wed and Fri 10am to 3:30pm and 6:30pm to 9:45pm, Sat 9am to 3:30pm and 6:30pm to 9:45pm, Sun 9am to 3:30pm; P.O. Box 53, Sept-Iles, G4R 4K3, ☎766-5900)* offers downhill skiers a vertical drop of 185 metres and 22 runs, seven of which are lit for night-skiing.

 Snowmobiling

Tour A: Minganie

La Maison du Portageur *(1947 Rue Boréale, P.O. 1077, Havre-Saint-Oierre, ☎538-3885 or 538-1285)* offers four wonderful excursions in Minganie and on the lower north shore. These one- or two-day snowmobile trips include ice-fishing north of Havre-Saint-Pierre, cultural activities and overnight lodgings.

Tour B: Gilles Vigneault Country

Les Excursions-randonnées Côte-Nord *(1121 Route 138, ☎567-8761)* arrange snowmobile trips from Rivière-Saint-Jean to Blanc-Sablon, on the lower Côte-Nord. Groups of six to eight people.

 ACCOMMODATIONS

Tour A: Minganie

Sept-Îles

Many city-dwellers dream of camping on an unspoiled island in the peaceful wilderness. The **Camping Sauvage de l'Île Grande-Basque** *($20; Jul and Aug; accessible by ferry; Corporation Touristique de Sept-Iles, 1401 Boulevard Laure Ouest, G4R 4K1, ☎962-1238 or 968-1818 in summer, ☎968-0022)* can make such dreams a reality in the magnificent setting of the Baie de Sept-Iles. This island is the closest to the shore, making it a good stopping place for kayakers and canoeists. Firepits; firewood available. No drinking water.

The **Auberge Internationale Le Tangon** *($17 per person, bkfst incl.; K; 555 Avenue Jacques Cartier, G4R 2T8, ☎962-8180)*, the Sept-Iles youth hostel, offers young people an inexpensive place to spend the night, a cozy atmosphere and the opportunity to make some chance acquaintants.

The **Hôtel Sept-iles** *($65; tv, ℜ; 451 Avenue Arnaud, G4R 383, ☎418-962-2581 or 1-800-463-1753)* stands alongside the river and has a pretty view. The rooms are simply decorated but quite comfortable.

Magpie

Set on a mountainside next to the local church, **La Maison du Viking** *($50 bkfst incl.; ℜ; 132 de la Rive, GOG 1X0, ☎949-2822 or 949-2135)* affords a sweeping view of the gulf. For anyone who enjoys peaceful contemplation, this is a wonderful place for an extended stay. If you're looking for more action, the inn organizes numerous outdoor activities, including wildlife observation. To get there, follow the signs on the way into town.

Havre-Saint-Pierre

The **Mingan Archipelago National Park Reserve** *(admission $6 per day; camping $6 to $9 per person per day; 975 Rue de l'Escale, GOG 1P0, ☎538-3285 during the high season,*

Ulysses' Favourites

Accommodations

For history buffs:
Maison Johan-Beetz (p 526).

For a friendly reception:
Auberge Brion (p 527).

For the views:
Maison du Viking (p 525).

For outdoor-enthusiasts:
Auberge de la Minganie (p 526).

Restaurants

Duplessis's finest table:
Le Bon Bistro (p 527).

For terrace:
The Pointe-Carleton dining room (p 527).

For Québec cuisine:
Place Jonathan (p 527), Le Petit Rorqual (p 527) and Chez Julie (p 527).

☎538-3331 *during the low season)* has 34 rudimentary campsites scattered across six islands in the archipelago. Each island has its own distinctive characteristics. Campers looking for solitude and complete tranquillity in a dazzling seascape will find all their wishes fulfilled here. Independence and excellent organizational skills are a must, however. The only amenities on the islands are a platform for tents, restrooms with no running water, tables, cooking grills, firewood and woodsheds. During the tourist season, it is possible to make individual reservations up to seven days in advance and group reservations up to six months in advance. Campers can also try their luck at the auction, held at the visitor information centre in Havre-Saint-Pierre every day at 2:45pm, at which time reserved sites that have not been claimed are re-assigned on a first-come, first-served basis. The maximum stay permitted on one island is six days. There is a water-taxi service for those without their own boat (extra charge). As the temperature is extremely variable, campers are advised to pack plenty of warm, dry clothing. It is also necessary to bring along enough potable water and food for two days more than your scheduled stay, even if you plan to be here for only one day, since boat transportation can be suspended due to bad weather and fog. A wonderful place for sea kayaking.

The friendly **Auberge de la Minganie** youth hostel *($15; K; May to Oct; Route 138, GOG 1PO,* ☎538-2944) is located on the outskirts, beside the Mingan Archipelago National Park Reserve. Visitors arriving by bus can ask the bus driver to let them off here. There are many cultural and outdoor activities here.

You can't miss the **Hôtel-Motel du Havre** *($62; ℜ, K; 970 Boulevard de l'Escale, GOG 1PO,* ☎538-2800 or 538-3438), located at the intersection of the main road and Rue de l'Escale, which runs through town to the docks. This place is definitely *the* big hotel in town. Though some rooms have benefited from recent attempts at renovation, others remain drab and a bit depressing. Friendly service.

Île d'Anticosti

The **Auberge Au Vieux Menier** *($17.50 per person in the dormitory, $45 bkfst incl. in the gîte; sb, ℜ; P.O. Box 112, Port-Menier, GOG 2YO, 535-0111)* falls somewhere between a B&B and a youth hostel. Located on the site of the former Saint-Georges farm. Exhibitions. Low rates.

The **Auberge Port-Menier** *($66; ℜ, ctv; P.O. Box 160, Port-Menier, GOG 2YO,* ☎535-0122 or 535-0204), a venerable institution on the island, offers clean rooms and excellent food in a modest setting. The lobby is decorated with magnificent wooden reliefs from the Château Meunier. The inn serves as the starting point for a number of guided tours. Bicycle rentals.

Tour B: Gilles Vigneault Country

Baie-Johan-Beetz

You can stay at the historic **Maison Johan-Beetz** *($50 bkfst incl.; 15 Johan-Beetz,* ☎539-0137). This truly exceptional hotel is a veritable monument decorated with Beetz's own artwork. The rooms are comfortable but basic.

Natashquan

The **Auberge La Cache** *($85; 183 Chemin d'En Haut, GOG 2EO,* ☎*726-3347,* ⌐*726-3508)* has about ten pleasant rooms.

Kégaska

 A warm welcome in either French or English and a good meal await you at the **Auberge Brion** *($50; Kégaska, GOG 1SO,* ☎*726-3738)*, a truly delightful little family inn. Relaxed atmosphere and attentive service. Open year-round.

As many villages don't have any hotels, a home-stay network has been set up. Local families will welcome you into their houses, enabling you to share in the day-to-day life of the residents of the Côte-Nord:

Aylmer Sound	☎242-2115
Bonne Espérance	☎379-2911
Baie-Johan-Beetz	☎539-0125
Chevery	☎787-2389
Harrington-Harbour	☎795-3376 or
	☎795-3354
Kagaska	☎726-3291
La Tabatière	☎773-2263 or
	☎773-2596
Rivière-St-Paul	☎379-2911
Saint-Augustin	☎947-2501 or
	☎947-2404
Tête-à-la-Baleine	☎242-2115,
	☎242-2045 or
	☎242-2002
Vieux-Fort	☎379-2260

RESTAURANTS

Tour A: Minganie

Sept-îles

The charming **Café du Port** *($-$$; 495 Avenue Brochu,* ☎*962-9311)* prepares simple and delicious dishes. It is one of the area's most popular restaurants.

 The newly opened **Le Bon Bistro** *($$$-$$$; closed Mon; 588 Avenue Brochu,* ☎*968-3777)* is in an old house that is rich in style and character. Seafood dishes and regional cuisine.

Rivière-au-Tonnerre

 Place Jonathan *($-$$; 454 Rue Jacques-Cartier,* ☎*465-2207)* has built itself an enviable reputation all along the Côte-Nord, and the highest honours have been bestowed upon it. This well-deserved praise is due to the quality and freshness of the seafood and fish served here. This is hardly surprising, given that the town is the unofficial capital of crab fishing and lies in the heart of a fishing region unlike any other in the country. Don't expect super-sophisticated gastronomic cuisine here but rather excellent regional fare.

Longue-Pointe

 Le Petit Rorqual *($$; 64 Chemin du Roi,* ☎*949-2240)* is one of the best restaurants on the Côte-Nord. It serves fine regional cuisine, with a natural emphasis on fresh fish and seafood.

Havre-Saint-Pierre

 Chez Julie *($$; 1023 Rue Dulcinée,* ☎*538-3070)* has an excellent reputation for seafood. The coffee shop decor, including vinyl seat covers, does not seem to discourage the customers who flock to the restaurant for seafood and smoked salmon pizzas.

Île d'Anticosti

The **Auberge Au Vieux Menier** *($-$$; Port-Menier,* ☎*535-0111)* and its café/bar serve Anticosti specialties, seafood, home-made baked goods and grilled fare. Outdoor seating available.

 The dining room of the **Pointe-Carleton** *($-$$; SÉPAQ)* is the best and most pleasant place to eat on the island. Whether you're sitting in the bright dining room or outside on the terrace, the view is spectacular and the cuisine, succulent. A different specialty is featured every evening. If you happen to be around on a "Bacchante" night (fisherman's platter), don't miss it.

Tour B: Gilles Vigneault Country

Natashquan

A good meal can be had et the **Auberge La Cache** *($$-$$$; 183 Chemin d'En Haut, ☎726-3347)*; meat and seafood dishes are featured.

Lourdes-de-Blanc-Sablon

The **Restaurant du Lac** *($; ☎461-2112)*, in the Anse-aux-Cailloux motel, serves just about everything, from Italian to Chinese - including seafood, of course.

ENTERTAINMENT

Bars and Nightclubs

Port-Cartier

With its shows, exhibitions, bar and restaurant, the **Graffitti** *(☎766-3513)* dinner theatre is one of the liveliest and most popular places in town.

Sept-Îles

In the heart of town, right alongside the Parc du Vieux-Quai's magnificent promenade, **Le Matamek** *(451 Avenue Arnaud, Hôtel Sept-Iles, back entrance)* is where locals and visitors go for happy hour and lively nights out. The atmosphere is conducive to talking, camaraderie and making new friends. Thirty-something crowd.

If a nice, quiet, honest little place is more up your alley, head to **Le Bon Bistro** *(588 Avenue Brochu)*, which has a good selection of imported beers and microbrews.

SHOPPING

Sept-Îles

Local artists and craftsmen sell their creations at the **Boutique de Souvenirs de la Terrasse du Vieux-Quai** *(during the tourist season; ☎962-4174)* and **Les Abris de la Promenade du Vieux-Quai**, located at the west end of the promenade. **Les Artisans du Platin** *(451 Avenue Arnaud, ☎968-6115)* is another place to check out.

The **Musée Régional de la Côte-Nord** *(500 Boulevard Laure, ☎968-2070)* has a shop with an interesting selection of typical Montagnais crafts.

Île d'Anticosti

Les Artisans d'Anticosti *(June to Sep every day 9am to 7pm, Sep to Dec every day 9am to 2pm; P.O. Box 89, Port-Menier, ☎535-0270)* boast a superb assortment of crafts and deerskin clothing, as well as jewellery made from antlers. T-shirts and maps are also sold here.

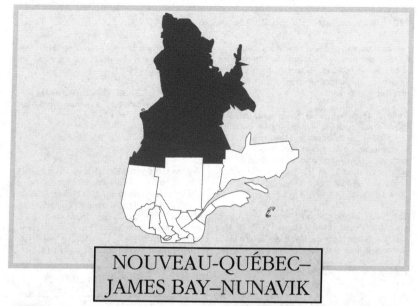

NOUVEAU-QUÉBEC–
JAMES BAY–NUNAVIK

T he geographic area encompassing the tourist regions of Nouveau-Québec and James Bay is a gigantic northern territory stretching from the 49th parallel north to the 62nd parallel, and is known as Québec's far north. It covers more than half of the whole area of Québec. The rough beauty of this barren landscape, its harsh winter climate and its unique tundra vegetation giving way to taiga and then Boreal forest, creates a region completely different from the rest of Québec, leading many Quebecers of the south to imagine it an inhospitable environment. After all, all roads and railways stop about halfway into the region and almost 2,000 kilometres separate Montréal and the village of Ivujivik, the northernmost village in Québec. Some travellers do venture northward, but for the most part this vast territory remains the land of the northern native peoples. The Inuit numbers around 6,850 people in Québec, spread through 14 communities along the shores of Hudson Bay, Hudson Strait and Ungava Bay. This territory is largely administered by the Inuit. In Inuktitut, the language of the Inuit, it is known as Nunavik. The Cree, who number around 10,550, live in nine villages in the taiga, along the shores of James Bay.

From the first days of North American colonization, English and French forces fought for the control of the fur trade across this vast region. Today, and for the last 20 years, it is the government of Québec that has taken a keen interest in the resources of these lands,

namely the massive potential for hydro-electric power contained in certain rivers. Huge hydro-electric dams were constructed in the region of James Bay, now capable of putting out 10,282 megawatts of power.

Northern Québec is not lacking in attractions. The vast wilderness and rich plant and wildlife are attracting nature lovers in growing numbers from all corners of the world.

 FINDING YOUR WAY AROUND

This immense region is divided into four tours: **Tour A: Hydroelectric Projects and Cree Land, Tour B: Hudson Bay Inuit Villages, Tour C: Hudson Strait Inuit Villages, Tour D: Ungava Bay Villages.**

Tour A: Hydroelectric Projects and Cree Land

By Car

The region of Nouveau-Québec – James Bay constitutes 51% of the territory of Québec and counts only about 36,000 inhabitants (Inuit, Cree and non-native). Route 109 penetrates part of this immense territory, travelling from Amos in Abitibi-Témiscamingue to Radisson. It is entirely paved, and practically deserted, along its 600-kilometre route. There is only one rest stop on this highway where you can fill up on food and gas, at Kilometre 381. Preparation is crucial on this leg. In fact, although it is a long one, we recommend that you complete this trip in one day.

Another road heads east-west and accesses the hydroelectric installations of La Grande – LG-2, LG-3, LG-4, Brisay and Caniapiscau – but it is impossible to travel past Kilometre 323 without authorization from Hydro-Québec. The section of road from LG-2 to LG-4 is gravel. There is also a road linking Radisson to Chisasibi and LG-1.

The 437-kilometre-long Route du Nord stretches east from Route 109, linking Chibougamau, Nemiscau, and, at the latitude of Rivière Rupert, Route de la Baie-James. Gasoline is available at the Nemiscau Cree Construction station *(Mon to Sat 7am to 9am and 3pm to 6pm)* and at a gas station at the entrance to the village of Nemiscau *(Mon to Fri 9am to 7pm, Sat and Sun 9am to 3pm)*.

The Route du Nord is an earth and stone road that is especially difficult in summer and on which it is preferable to travel in an all-terrain vehicle. There is constant traffic of heavy-weight trucks on this road and they are not inclined to cede passage – drive defensively and keep to the right. When a truck comes barrelling down the middle of the road, pull over to the right and let it pass. Conditions on the Route du Nord are better in winter when the road surface, although icy, is harder and smoother.

Car Rental

Location Aubé-Tilden: La Grande airport, ☎638-8353, ⌐635-8570.

By Plane

Canadian: in Montreal, ☎(514) 847-2211; in Quebec City, ☎(418) 692-0912. Canadian offers flights to the La Grande/Radisson hydroelectric facilities from Montreal and Quebec City. Fares are reduced for 14-day advance reservation, although the least expensive round-trip fare to the north is usually a minimum of $500.

Air Creebec: ☎825-8355. Air Creebec is the only airline that serves all of the Cree villages of Northern Québec, from Montreal and Val-

d'Or. Fourteen-day advance reservation earns a 50% discount. Regular round-trip fares are a minimum of $450.

Air Inuit: ☎1-800-361-2965. This airline offers service to the Radisson/La Grande hydroelectric facility.

By Bus

Guided tours of the Radisson region are another travel option. **Tour Chantecler** *(2014 Bd. Charest Ouest, Bureau 119, Québec, G1N 4N6, ☎1-800-361-8415)* organizes bus tours from Quebec City to James Bay and the LG-2 hydroelectric dam. The trip usually takes a week and covers a distance of over 1,600 kilometres between Québec and Radisson.

Tours B, C and D

No roads or railroads link the Inuit communities of Nunavik. Car and train travel are out of the question. By air is the only means of transportation between villages in this area.

A small, unpaved road does link the Naskapi village of Kawawachikamach to Schefferville, which is accessible by train or by plane.

By Plane

Air Inuit: ☎1-800-361-2965. This airline serves all the Inuit villages of Northern Québec and Canada. There is a significant discount for travellers who make reservations 14 days in advance. A flight to the far north costs a minimum of $500.

Canadian: ☎1-800-665-1177; links Dorval (just outside Montreal) and Kuujjuarapik and also offers flights to Schefferville.

First Air: ☎1-800-267-1247; serves Kuujjuaq only.

Air Schefferville: ☎1-800-361-8620; direct flights from Montreal to Schefferville during summer.

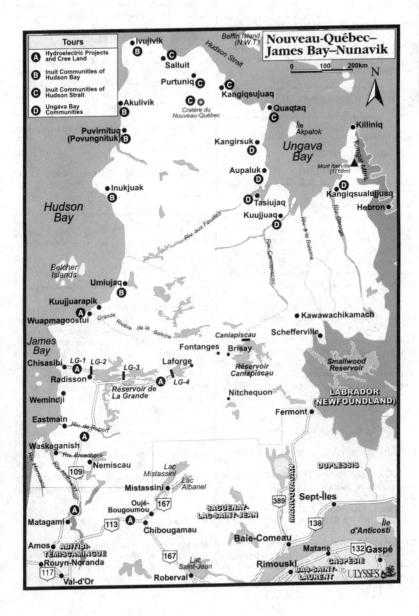

By Train

QNS&L: ☎(418) 962-9411. Once a week, there is train service between Sept-Îles and Schefferville. The trip takes 10 to 12 hours as it crosses the Canadian Shield all the way to the edge of the tundra.

 PRACTICAL INFORMATION

Area code: 819

Tourist Information

The infrastructure for tourism in this region is relatively undeveloped, and it is difficult to travel around in the area, so it is recommended to make all reservations, for hotels and excursions alike, in advance. For exploring this isolated territory, as well as for hunting and fishing trips, it is strongly recommended to hire the services of an outfitter.

Tour A: Hydroelectric Projects and Cree Land

Tourist Information Office: All visitors must stop and register (☎739-4473) at the small office at Kilometre 6 of the road between Matagami and Radisson where they can also make reservations for tours of hydroelectric dams.

Useful Telephone Numbers

Chisasibi Mandow Agency: ☎1-800-771-2733.

Service de Sécurité Civile et Tourisme de la Municipalité de la Baie-James (Municipality of James Bay Tourism and Civil Security Service): 110 Boul. Matagami, C.P. 500, Matagami, J0Y 2A0, ☎(819) 739-2030.

Ministère de l'Environnement et de la Faune: Radisson, ☎(819) 638-8305; Mistissini, ☎(418) 923-3279; Nemiscau, ☎(819) 673-2512; Oujé-Bougoumou, ☎(418) 745-3911.

Tours B, C and D

The three organizations listed below are good contacts for information on the Nunavik region:

L'Association Touristique du Nunavik: B.P. 218, Kuujjuaq, J0M 1C0, ☎ (819) 964-2876, ⊷(819) 964-2002, in Montreal, ☎(514) 695-1686.

La Fédération des Coopératives du Nouveau-Québec: 19950 Clark Graham, Baie-d'Urfé, H9X 3R8, ☎(514) 457-9371, 1-800-363-7610 in Canada, or 1-800-465-9474 in the U.S., ⊷(514) 457-4626.

La Société Makivik (Division du Tourisme): 650 32ᵉ Avenue, Lachine, H8T 3K5, ☎(514) 634-8091.

Naskapi Band of Québec: B.P. 5111, Kawawachikamach, G0G 2Z0, ☎(418) 585-2686, ⊷(418) 585-3130.

 EXPLORING

Tour A: Hydroelectric Projects and Cree Land

Whether its called Moyen Nord, Radissonnie, Baie-James or Cree land, this region, as difficult to define as it is to name, represents the most northerly region of Québec accessible by road. These roads, laid down by dam builders and mine operators, truly opened up the heart of Québec to its southern population while simultaneously giving the native peoples of the north an entry, for better and for worse, to the modern world.

A whole universe opens up here to the traveller who is a bit more daring, who seeks authenticity and a radical change of scenery. Everything is different here: time, climate, wildlife, flora, space, people... No aspect of life here resembles anything found anywhere else.

Matagami (pop. 2,467)

Matagami is a small mining town that was established in 1963. Rich zinc and copper mines attracted residents to this area, the overland entrance way to the James Bay region.

The Hudson Bay Meteorite

If you look at a map of Québec, you'll see that the east of Hudson Bay forms a perfect arc. You'll also see the Belcher Islands, in the centre of the bay. Some scientists attribute this geological formation to the impact of a meteorite. When a meteorite lands, it forms an remarkably round crater. In addition, the force of the impact creates a phenomenon of centrifugal and centripetal waves - a little like what happens when you throw a rock in the water. As these three elements are all present, it is possible to hypothesize that a meteorite hit the middle north of Québec. There are actually a number of sizeable meteoritic craters in Québec: the Cratère du Nouveau-Québec, the semi-crater in Charlevoix, which you can visit, and the largest crater in the province, the Réservoir Manicougan.

If this hypothesis is accurate, the Hudson Bay meteorite was the largest ever to hit the face of the earth. The impact would have been powerful enough to alter the planet's axis and thus cause major climatic changes. In fact, given all the potential repercussions, it could have led to the disappearance of the dinosaurs!

It is impossible, however, to say for certain that this gigantic hollow was created by a meteoritic impact. There is not enough concrete evidence. For example, the presence of rocks similar to those collected on lunar expeditions made it possible to identify the meteorite responsible for the Réservoir Manicougan. Various studies contradict each other when it comes to the Hudson Bay meteorite, however. Consequently, Québec cannot yet claim the largest meteoritic crater on Earth, which is officially in the Gulf of Mexico, around the Yucatan Peninsula. Some scientists attribute Hudson Bay's geological formation to the movement of tectonic plates. Again, though, they have found no proof in the sea bed to support their theory. Perhaps it was caused by the glacier that raged its way through Québec 20,000 years ago. The mystery has yet to be solved.

The Road from Matagami to Radisson

It took 450 days in 1972-73 for Québec labourers to meet the challenge of opening up the 740-kilometre Route de la Baie-James to Chisasibi. The size of the rivers that had to be bridged and the incredible number of lakes that had to be skirted made it a considerable accomplishment indeed. As the road winds northward the landscape changes subtly as black spruce gradually shrink and become frail and stunted.

Nemiscau (pop. 500)

The French began trading for furs as early as 1661 in this historic crossroads and commerce continued to play a determining role in the history of Nemiscau, mainly thanks to the Hudson's Bay Company, which maintained a post here until 1970. At that point this centre of economic activity disappeared and the Cree dispersed to found a beautiful brand-new village on the shores of marvellous Lac Champion in 1979. This recent, well-equipped village has become the administrative centre of the Grand Council of the Cree.

Radisson (pop. 814)

This town was built in 1974 to accommodate the workers from the south who were arriving as part of the James Bay hydro-electric project. During the boom years of construction on the hydro project the population of Radisson was more than 3,000.

If this area interests you, **Voyages Jamésiens** *(96 Rue Albanel, C.P. 914, Radisson, J0Y 2X0, ☎638-6673, ≠638-7080)* offers a weekend trip to James Bay for a little under $700 per person including transportation from Quebec City or Montreal, accommodation and activities. In addition to visits to dams, the tour includes motorized canoe trips on the La Grande river in summer or afternoons of cross-country skiing in winter.

Radisson's main drawing card is the impressive hydro-electric complex. Visitors can tour the **Centrale La Grande-2 (LG-2)** ★★★ *(free admission, year-round Wed, Fri, Sun, reservations required; from Radisson ☎638-8486, from Montréal ☎514-289-2215, elsewhere in Québec ☎1-800-567-7755)*. The tour lasts four hours and includes a tour of the exterior facilities and an information session.

During the sixties the Québec government envisioned a plan to harness the hydro-electric potential of the James Bay region by constructing dams along its rivers. It was not until the seventies that a development project for the damming of the Rivière La Grande (Chisasibi, in Cree), which runs 800 kilometres from east to west before flowing into James Bay, was proposed by then Québec Premier Robert Bourassa. The project was divided into two phases, the first being the construction of three powerful damming centres along the river, namely La Grande-2 (LG-2), La Grande-3 (LG-3) and La Grande-4 (LG-4). Construction began in 1973 and stretched out over several years, since the damming of the river was a complex and involved project. To increase the flow of the Rivière La Grande various waterways were diverted, namely the Eastmain and the Opinaca as well as the Caniapiscau in the east. The source of the Rivière Caniapiscau to the creation of the largest artificial lake in Québec, a reservoir covering more than 4,275 square kilometres.

The La Grande Hydro-electric complex required the construction of dams and dykes. The former were used to close off the river beds and to raise the water level thereby creating falls; the latter were used to stop the rising waters from flowing out via secondary valleys. All of the water is contained and swept up into the intakes, the water is then directed along a series of pipes leading to the turbines which it activates.

On October 27th, 1979 the LG-2 generating station started producing electricity. The other two, the LG-3 and LG-4 generating stations, became operational in 1982 and 1984 respectively. In 1990, these three generating stations were responsible for almost half of Hydro-Québec's total production of electricity. The second phase of the project involves the upgrading of LG-2 (thereby creating the LG-2A generating station, construction of which was completed in 1992), and the construction of four other generating stations, including three on the Rivière Laforge. The Laforge-1 and Brisay stations, or *centrales,* started operation in 1993; La Grande-1 should begin operation in spring 1995 and Laforge-2 in 1996.

The La Grande-2 generating station is the third most powerful in the world (with an installed capacity of 7,634 megawatts), after Itaipu in Brazil, on Paraguay border (installed capacity of 12,600 megawatts), and Guri in Venezuela (installed capacity of 10,000 megawatts).

Installed 137 metres below the ground, La Grande-2 is the largest underground generating station in the world. The dam is 2.8 kilometres long and 162 metres high, supplied by a 2,835-square-kilometre reservoir. For years when the annual rainfall is very high a drainage system of floodgates is necessary. The engineering of such a system involves eight 12-metre-by-20-metre containers, and a 1,500-metre-long and 110-metre-deep collection canal. It has been nicknamed the *escalier des géants* (giant's staircase), since it represents 10 "steps", each about 10 metres high and carved in the rock. When water levels are exceptionally high the system can drain 16,280 cubic metres of water par second, the quivalent of the average flow of the St. Lawrence River. So far the system has rarely been put to use; only between 1979 and 1981 because the turbines inside the generating station were not yet completed and on August 30, 1987, for a couple of hours during a visit by French Prime Minister M. Jacques Chirac. With the opening of LG-2A it will probably be used only once every seventy-five years.

The power station is made up of four levels: the first level houses the machine room, the second the alternators, the third provides access to the spiral containers (inside which are the turbines) and the last level houses the drainage gallery. To absorb the high and low pressure, which builds up when the machines are turned on and off, an equilibrium chamber was built.

The construction of this hydro-electric complex has had very serious repercussions not only for the environment, but for the native populations living off the land in this region. To create the reservoirs, some 11,505 square kilometres of land was flooded, representing 6.5% of the hydrographic basin of the Rivière La Grande river and 2.9% of the Cree hunting grounds. During the whole construction of this hydro-electric mega-project, Hydro-Québec and its subsidiary SEBJ (Société d'Énergie de la Baie James), who's role it is to administer all hydro-electric projects in the area, both carried out environmental-impact studies on this project, and they continue to follow up on their findings. Part of the flooded land was native hunting ground, and the Inuit and Cree who used these lands contested the provincial government's use of their ancestral lands. The negotiations between all the parties involved continued right up to November 11th, 1975, the signing day of the Convention de la Baie James et du Nord Québécois, which established the rights and obligations of the natives, as well as the plan of action of the hydroelectric project. According to the agreement signed by all those concerned, namely the Cree, the Inuit, the Québec and Canadian governments, Hydro-Québec, the SEBJ and the SDBJ, the natives were guaranteed exclusive use of certain lands, as well as guarantees of exclusive hunting, fishing and trapping rights on the land, especially for certain species of animals. Those involved also received greater administrative powers over their lands as well as monetary compensation. Since 1975, 11 supplementary agreements and eight specific accords have been signed to better define each party's rights.

The entrance to the complex is like a terrifying descent into the belly of the earth. The cathedral-sized turbines room is surreal. Megalomaniacs will thrill to the sheer size of this place.

Radisson – Brisay

The Route de la Baie-James does not end in Radisson. From Lac Yasinski (Km 544), the long gravel road continues to Réservoir Caniapiscau and the Brisay dam, the actual geographic centre of Québec.

Chisasibi (pop. 2,800)

A Cree word meaning "the big river", Chisasibi is a modern village that was built in 1981, after the Cree left Île de Fort George. This little village was laid out in keeping with the Cree's matriarchal society, so that the houses stand in small groups, with the mother's house surrounded by those of her daughters. The two-story wooden houses are often completed by a tepee, which serves as the kitchen, as the Cree still prefer to cook their food over a fire rather than on an electric stove. You'll notice that the streets have no names, and that many are dead ends. Don't let this discourage you, however; the Cree are very friendly and quick to help out. The cemetery is also interesting, as it contains examples of two different burial traditions. Traditionally, the Cree buried their dead where they passed away, facing the rising sun. As many people died in the forest, the Cree would build a small fence around the tomb to make it easier to locate. Today, due to the influence of European religions, they bury the dead in a communal cemetery, but the fence tradition has endured. Chisasibi is a dry

community, so don't bring any alcohol with you when you visit, and don't be surprised to see a roadblock a few kilometres before the village; it's a checkpoint.

Île de Fort George

With the increased flow of the Rivière La Grande, the shores of the island are eroding faster than normal. The Cree therefore agreed to move their village to present site of Chisasibi. The island is still of great symbolic importance to them, however. In fact, all the Cree in Canada and their white brothers get together here every August for the **Grand Pow Wow**. Visitors to the island can take the opportunity to sample the traditional Cree lifestyle. You'll sleep on a layer of spruce branches in a tepee and eat as the Cree have for thousands of years. For more information, contact the Mandow Agency (see p 532).

Waskaganish (pop. 1,900)

Founded in 1668 by Médard Couart Des Groseillers, this village was called first Rupert, then Rupert's House and Fort Rupert, in honour of the first governor of the Hudson's Bay Company. Changing hands between the French and the English, this important trading post remained one of the most active up until 1942, the same year the village's infrastructure was put in place.

The traditional campsite **Nuutimesaanaan** (Smokey Hill), where fish and fish eggs (*waakuuch*) were smoked, can be visited.

Eastmain (pop. 445)

Eastmain enjoys a striking view of the mouth of the river and exudes the warmth and welcome of an isolated community.

Wemindji (pop. 900)

The Cree did not establish this community, on the shores of James Bay at the mouth of the Maquatua river until 1959 after leaving Vieux-Comptoir, 45 kilometres to the south. While a large proportion of the population still occupies itself with traditional activities, the Cree have also developed new economic sectors with the creation of a large fox and lynx farm: the Wemindji Cree Fur Ranch. The name Wemindji means "ochre mountain" and the hills surrounding the village contain rich deposits of this mineral which is mixed with grease to make paint.

Oujé-Bougoumou (pop. 450)

This most recently established Cree village is also the most remarkable from many standpoints. After a long, meandering journey from Mistissini to Chibougamau, Lac aux Dorés, Chapais and onward, a group of Cree chose Lac Opémiska for their permanent settlement. Through their determination they gained reservation status and were permitted to draw up plans for a unique and fascinating village. Architect Douglas Cardinal, the creative mind behind the Museum of Civilization in Hull, was entrusted with the task of designing the village. Oujé-Bougoumou is imbued with a profoundly traditional character in spite of the prevalence of the symbolic and the emphasis on vanishing lines. Each residence evokes an ancient teepee, particularly especially in the slope of its roof. The main buildings are especially impressive. The village as a whole is laid out in the shape of a goose, at one end of which stands a reconstructed traditional village that is used for important community events and to accommodate tourists.

In 1995, Oujé-Bougoumou earned official recognition from the United Nations (UN) as one of the 50 villages in the world that best represents the goals of social cooperation, respect for the environment and sustainable development that the UN seeks to promote.

At the village entrance, you will notice an altogether unique building from which rises a column of smoke. This is the **cogeneration plant**, which provides heat to every building in the village with a hot water system fuelled by the waste shavings from the Barrette de Chapais sawmill 26 kilometres away.

Mistissini (pop. 2,600)

At the heart of what was known as Le Domaine du Roi (the king's domain) in the days of the fur trade, halfway between the St. Lawrence Valley and Hudson Bay, Mistissini, along with its immense lake, has been a tremendously important cultural crossroads for centuries. Mistissini is on the southwest tip of Lac Mistissini, on Presqu'île Watson (peninsula), between Baie du Poste and Baie Abatagouche.

With an area of 2,336 square kilometres, **Lac Mistassini** was the largest expanse of water in Québec before the creation of the great reservoirs. It is 161 kilometres long, 19 kilometres wide and as deep as 180 metres in places and it is the main source of Rivière Rupert. Champlain was aware of the lake's existence as early as 1603, but French explorers did not reach it until 1663, when Guillaume Couture accomplished that feat. The Jesuit Charles Albanel crossed it in 1672 in the course of an expedition from Lac Saint-Jean to James Bay.

Whapmagoostui (pop. 600) and Kuujjuarapik ★ (pop. 661)

Here is a truly unique community, as much for its history and geographic location as for its social makeup. In fact, the Cree village of Whapmagoostui sits across from the Inuit village of Kuujjuarapik at the mouth of Grande Rivière de la Baleine on Hudson Bay. This coexistence has persisted for about two centuries around the trading post known as Great Whale or Poste-de-la-Baleine. These villages are actually only one agglomeration divided by what some locals call an imaginary border, which visitors cross completely obliviously. A closer look, however, reveals that the two communities share no public services whatsoever regardless of the harmony between them, not even the new medical clinic (CLSC), that was built right on the boundary line. The Inuit are cared for on one side of the corridor, the Cree on the other, each group on a different day. The best example of integration is the bar, on the Inuit side of town, which is frequented by both communities simultaneously, although each has its own section.

Whapmagoostui is the northernmost Cree village, at the very edge of Cree territory and on the fringes of Inuit territory, which historically has extended all the way to the shores of extraordinary Lac Guillaume-Delisle.

The villages are bordered by a large sandy beach that forms dunes from atop which the magnificent **Îles Manitounuk** are visible. These are representatives of the **Hudson cuestas**, which are characterized by sandy beaches and dunes facing the open water of the bay and spectacular towering cliffs facing the continent.

These constitute refuges for innumerable **birds**, **seals**, **whales** and **belugas**.

Tour B: Inuit Communities of Hudson Bay

Six Inuit villages are dispersed along the Hudson Bay coastline, including Ivujivik, the most northerly community in Québec.

Kuujjuarapik

See above.

Umiujaq ★ (pop. 250)

Situated 160 kilometres north of Kuujjuarapik, the village of Umiujaq was inaugurated in December 1986. The Convention de la Baie-James et du Nord Québécois offered the Inuit of Kuujjuarapik the option of moving to the region of Lac Guillaume-Delisle, in the eventuality of the completion of the Great Whale hydroelectric project. A portion of the residents, fearing the harmful effects of the dam project, voted in favour of a plan to create a new community further north, which became the little village of Umiujaq, in a referendum in October of 1982. After numerous archeological, ecological and land-use studies, construction of the village began in the summer of 1985 and was completed a year and a half later.

Sitting at the foot of a hill "resembling an umiak", a large sealskin boat, Umiujaq looks out onto Hudson Bay.

Inukjuak ★ (pop. 1,222)

Nunavik's second largest village, Inukjuak is set 360 kilometres north of Kuujjuarapik, at the mouth of the Innuksuac river, facing the Hopewell Islands.

The lives of the residents of Inukjuak remain strongly tied to traditional activities. Discovery of a steatite deposit has promoted the art of sculpture; many of the most renowned sculptors in Nunavik live and work in a small studio here.

The oldest buildings in the village are the old Anglican mission and the former trading post,

both of them located behind the Northern store and the cooperative that was founded in 1967.

The **Hopewell Islands**, with their steep cliffs, are well worth closer examination, especially in the springtime when the ice floe, driven by tides and currents, presents itself as an immense field of gigantic, interlocking ice blocks.

Traditional Inuit garb

Puvirnituq (pop. 1,196)

This community is located on the east shore of the Puvirnituq river, about four kilometres from the bay of the same name and 180 kilometres north of Inukjuak. The land surrounding the village forms a plateau of an altitude of about 65 metres.

For the last few years, in an effort to be true to the original pronunciation, the name "Povungnituk" has been written "Puvirnituq". This is an Inuktitut word that means "the place with an odour of high meat", a rather original name that refers to a period when the river was higher than usual and many animals drowned trying to cross it. The odour of the animals' decomposing carcasses on the beach inspired this appellation. Another story tells that an epidemic ravaged a camp here, killing every inhabitant and sparing no one to bury the dead so that when family and friends arrived from neighbouring camps in the spring the air was foul with the odour of decaying bodies.

Akulivik (pop. 393)

The village of Akulivik is 100 kilometres north of Puvirnituq, its closest neighbour, and 650 kilometres north of Kuujjuarapik. It is built on a peninsula that juts into Hudson Bay facing Smith Island. The community is bordered to the south by the mouth of the Illukotat river and to the north by a deep bay that forms a natural harbour, sheltering the village from the wind. This geographic configuration encourages early spring thaws and constitutes prime hunting grounds. Fossilized shells, vestiges of the last ice age, have eroded into crumbs so that the ground has an unusually, sandy quality.

Smith Island, which is part of the Northwest Territories, faces the village a few minutes by boat or snowmobile away. This mountainous island, which offers scenery of a fascinating beauty, is a springtime habitat for thousands of **snow** and **Canada geese**.

Ivujivik (pop. 278)

The most northerly village in Québec, Ivujivik is situated 150 kilometres from Akulivik and 2,140 kilometres from Quebec City. It is nestled in a little cove south of Digges Strait and Digges Islands, in a mountainous region near Cap Wolstenholme. Ivujivik is the site of battling ocean currents at every tide since Hudson Bay and Hudson Strait meet here. Even the name Ivujivik refers to this phenomenon; in Inuktitut it means, "place where strong currents make the ice accumulate".

Tour C: Inuit Communities of Hudson Strait

North of the North, between Hudson Bay and Ungava Bay, on the shores of Hudson Strait are the villages of Salluit, Kangiqsujuaq and Quaqtaq. Surrounded by high plateaus and majestic fjords, these communities offer enchanting natural settings in glorious, wide open spaces.

Salluit ★★ (pop. 1007)

Situated 250 kilometres north of Puvirnituq, 115 kilometres east of Ivujivik and 2,125 kilometres from Quebec City, Salluit is nestled in a valley formed by steep mountains, about ten kilometres from the mouth of the fjord of the same name.

The actual site of Salluit ★★, dominated by jagged mountains and steep hills is absolutely spectacular. Between the sea and the mountains on a magnificent **fjord** ★★, it is one of the most picturesque villages in Nunavik. **Deception Bay**, which the Inuit call Pangaligiak, is famous for its hunting, its excellent fishing and the year-round richness of its wildlife and vegetation.

Kangiqsujuaq ★★ (pop. 460)

Surrounded by majestic mountains at the bottom of a superb valley, Kangiqsujuaq, an Inuktitut word that means "the large bay", stands proudly over the fjord of immense Wakeham Bay.

The most impressive natural tourist attraction of the area, and of Nunavik generally, is without question the **Cratère du Nouveau-Québec** ★★, which the Inuit call Pingualuit. Fewer than 100 kilometres from the village, this gigantic crater has imposing dimensions: its diameter measures 3,770 metres and it is 446 metres deep. Discovered by Chubb, an aviator who was intrigued by its perfectly round shape, the crater was formed by the fall of an enormous meteorite. A research team from the Université de Montréal solved the mystery of its water source – it is not fed by any waterway – when they discovered a subterranean spring in the crater's depths.

On the coastal islands, east of the village, there are remains of **ancient campsites** that date from the Thule era.

Quaqtaq (pop. 290)

Quaqtaq is delimited to the north by mountainous relief and the south and east by low rocky hills, Located 157 kilometres from its nearest neighbour, Kangiqsujjuaq, and 350 kilometres north of Kuujjuaq, the village stretches over a peninsula that juts into Hudson Strait and forms the coast of Diana Bay, known as Tuvaaluk, "the large ice floe", among the Inuit. This point of land also marks the convergence of Hudson Strait and Ungava Bay.

Because the Inuit and their ancestors have occupied this region for almost 2,000 years, many **archeological sites** can be found in the area. The surroundings of **Diana Bay**, an area renowned for its hunting, fishing and wildlife observation, is the habitat of about a thousand

Inukshuk

musk oxen ★. The luckiest visitors to the area occasionally spot **snowy owls**.

Tour D: Ungava Bay Villages

Five Inuit communities sit on the coast of Ungava Bay and form the large region that covers the eastern part of the territory: Kangirsuk, Aupaluk, Tasiujaq, Kangiqsualujjuaq and Kuujjuaq, the administrative capital of Nunavik. The last three of these villages abut the timber line, which adds a whole other dimension to the landscape. East of the bay stand elevated massifs that mark the border between Québec and Labrador. Among these are the Torngat Mountains, the high peaks of Nunavik.

Kangirsuk (pop. 413)

This little community is located on the north shore of Rivière Arnauk, 13 kilometres upstream from Ungava Bay. Once known as Payne Bay and Bellin, the village is 118 kilometres south of Quaqtaq, 230 kilometres north of Kuujjuaq and 1,536 kilometres from Quebec City.

A few **archeological sites** are located near the village, including a large one on **Pamiok Island**. These sites, which are of exceptional quality, open a window on the distant past of the region's first inhabitants. The **Vikings**, notably, visited the Lac Payne area as early as the 11th century. **Artifacts** from this era can be found around the outskirts of Kangirsuk.

Kuujjuaq ★ (pop. 1,427)

Situated 1,304 kilometres north of Quebec City, the administrative, economic and political capital of Nunavik stretches over flat sandy ground on the western shore of Rivière Koksoak, 50 kilometres upstream from its mouth on Ungava Bay. With a population of over 1,400 residents, including a good number of non-natives, Kuujjuaq is the largest Inuit community in Québec.

Today, Kuujjuaq is the administrative centre of the territory of Nunavik and serves as the headquarters of the Administration Régionale de Kativik. Various governmental and regional organizations' have offices here as well. The town's two large landing strips are part of the DEW (Distant Early Warning) line and the village is the hub of air transport in Northern Québec and home to the head offices of many charter airlines.

Kuujjuaq possesses hotels, restaurants, stores, a bank and craft shops and offers most of the services that are available in regional capitals of the South. Tulattavik Hospital provides front line health care services and constitutes the principal medical resource of the Ungava region.

Majestic **Rivière Koksoak ★** is one the marvels of the area. It adds a unique and very picturesque dimension to Kuujjuaq's setting and its tides shape landscapes of fascinating beauty.

Kangiqsualujjuaq ★★★ (pop. 605)

Up until 1959 there was not really a village here; summer camps were established on the coast and winter camps were about 50 kilometres into the interior. The hamlet was created on the initiative of local Inuit who founded the first cooperative in Nouveau-Québec here with the goal of creating a commercial char fishery. Construction of the village began at the very beginning of the 1960s, and the first public services here were organized at that time.

The region attracts one of the largest herds of **caribou ★** in the world. In fact the **Rivière George herd** is the most imposing in Nunavik, with approximately 600,000 head. Kangiqsualujjuaq hunters supply Les Aliments Arctiques du Nunavik, Inc. with a large proportion of the 3,000 kilograms of caribou meat that it puts on the market annually in the region and in the South.

The **Torngat Mountains ★★★**, named for an Inuktitut word that means "mountains of bad spirits", are situated about one hundred kilometres east of the village. Between Ungava Bay and the Atlantic Ocean, at the Québec-Labrador border, they are the tallest mountains in Québec. They stretch over 220 kilometres and are about 100 kilometres across, making them as important a chain as the Alps. Many of the summits reach altitudes of 1,700 metres, including majestic **Mont d'Iberville ★**, which dominates the range with its 1,768-metre height.

Kawawachikamach

Situated 15 kilometres from Schefferville, some 1000 kilometres north of Montreal and just next to the Labrador border, Kawawachikamach is the only Naskapi community in Québec. Related to the Cree and the Montagnais, the Naskapi are also part of the Algonkian language family. Kawawachikamach, a Naskapi word that means "the place where the sinuous river becomes a great lake", is located in a region of exceptional natural beauty and innumerable lakes and rivers.

A nomadic people of great hunters, the Naskapi followed the migration route of the caribou, on which they depended for survival. Following the near disappearance of the caribou from their territory and their increased dependence on trading posts, the Naskapi experienced years of hardship marked by famine starting in 1893. Fleeing hunger and sickness, and assisted by the federal government, a number of families settled near Fort Chimo in 1949. Seven years later, the Naskapi decided to move to the Montagnais community of Matimekosh, near Schefferville, in the hope of bettering their living conditions.

In 1978, the Naskapi, encouraged by the treaty signed three years earlier with the Inuit and the Cree, signed the Convention du Nord-Est Québécois with the federal and provincial governments. The Naskapi thereby abandoned title to their ancestral lands and in return obtained financial compensation, inalienable rights over certain territories and new fishing, hunting and trapping rights. In addition, they decided to establish a community on the shores of Lake Matemace, 15 kilometres northeast of Schefferville. Inaugurated in 1984, the village of Kawawachikamach is equipped with modern equipment for collective use, a dispensary and a shopping centre.

The shutdown of the Iron Ore factory, the main employer of Naskapi men, in 1982 dealt a hard blow to the young community. The Naskapi then turned toward adventure tourism and outfitting to meet their needs. In 1989, they acquired the well-reputed Tuktu hunting and fishing club.

OUTDOORS

Tour A: Hydroelectric Projects and Cree Land

Radisson

Some dream of catching giant fish in untamed wilderness. Others want to hunt caribou in the taiga or simply observe these animals on snowmobile photo-safaris. Still others hope to have the family vacation of a lifetime in a comfortable cottage at the end of the world. **La Pourvoirie Mirage** *(1130 Rue Principale, Tourville, G0R 4M0, ☎418-359-2259, ⌐359-3539)* has created various extremely attractive packages that can make any of these dreams come true.

Whapmagoostui

Aventure Grande-Baleine *(Miguel Simard,* ☎*929-3456,* ⇢*929-3258)* is one of the most reliable and professional organizations in the North. It can put together complete, customized packages year-round.

Chisasabi

The **Agence Mandow de Chisasibi** *(C.P. 30, Chisasibi, JOM JEO,* ☎*819-855-3373 or 1-800-771-CREE,* ⇢*855-3374)* is the best tourism organization in the Cree territory, the best organized and the most reliable, and it offers the greatest variety of products. Under the aegis of the band council, Mandow offers photo-safaris, wildlife observation trips, and snowmobiling, cross-country skiing and canoeing excursions.

Tour B: Inuit Communities of Hudson Bay

Inukjuak

The **Fédération des Coopératives du Nouveau-Québec et Aventures Inuit** *(19950 Clark Graham, Baie-d'Urfé, H9X 3R8,* ☎*514-457-9371, 1-800-363-7610 in Canada or 1-800-465-9474 in the U.S.,* ⇢*514-457-4626)* offers adventure tourism packages in the region of Inukjuak. Notable among these are the opportunities to observe caribou and ptarmigans in their natural habitat, to go ice-fishing for trout and to spend an unforgettable night in an igloo.

Puvirnituq

Puvirnituq is situated on the caribou migration route. Tens of thousands of these animals file through the area over the course of several days, crossing rivers and noisily stamping the ground of the tundra.

Tour C: Inuit Communities of Hudson Strait

Kangiqsujuaq

With the **Fédération des Coopératives du Nouveau-Québec et Aventures Inuit** *(19950 Clark Graham, Baie-d'Urfé, H9X 3R8,* ☎*514-457-9371, 1-800-363-7610 in Canada or 1-800-465-9474 in the U.S.,* ⇢*514-457-4626)* it is possible to head off on an exploratory snowmobile journey to the giant Cratère du Nouveau-Québec.

Quaqtaq

Tommy Angnatuk *(*☎*492-9071)* owns two sea kayaks and organizes expeditions in Diana Bay that head toward the islands of Ungava Bay.

Tour D: Ungava Bay Villages

Tasiujaq (pop. 189)

Tommy Cain and Sons, Finger Lake Lodge *(C.P. 163, Duhamel, JOV 1GO,* ☎*514-971-1800 or 1-800-361-3748)* is an outfitter specialized in trout, salmon and char fishing. In summer they also organize trips down Rivière aux Feuilles in inflatable or standard canoes. In winter they lead snowmobile excursions.

Kuujjuaq

Many outfitters organize trips in the Kuujjuaq area that feature caribou hunting, salmon and char fishing, and extraordinary photo-safaris: **Allen Gordon Outfitting, Wolf Lake Camp** *(B.P. 98, Kuujjuaq, JOM 1CO,* ☎*964-2489, 514-694-4267 in Montreal,* ⇢*514-694-4267).*

Aventures Arctiques *(19950 Clark Graham, Baie-d'Urfé, H9X 3R8,* ☎ *514-457-9371, 1-800-363-7610 in Canada or 1-800-465-9474 in the U.S.,* ⇢*514-457-4626)* organizes ptarmigan hunting and ice-fishing excursions, as well as packages, with or without guides, that include caribou hunting or salmon and char fishing with nights in a camp,.

Kangiqsualujjuaq

Ammarok Outfitters Inc. *(Mark Annanack,* ☎*337-5223)* and their seasoned guide, Mark Annanack, organize adventure tourism excursions. They offer hiking and canoeing packages in the surroundings of the Koroc and George rivers. In winter they offer downhill skiing in the Torngat Mountains as well as cross-country ski trips in the village's surroundings.

The **Fédération des Coopératives du Nouveau-Québec et Aventures Inuit** *(19950 Clark Graham, Baie-d'Urfé, H9X 3R8, ☎514-457-9371, 1-800-363-7610 in Canada or 1-800-465-9474 in the U.S., ⌐514-457-4626)* proposes "archeology-geology-photography" packages, as well as others, led by professionals with overnights spent in very comfortable accommodations.

 ACCOMMODATIONS

Tour A: Hydroelectric Projects and Cree Land

Whapmagoostui

Auberge Sinittivik *(managed by Aventure Grande-Baleine, ☎819-929-3456, ⌐929-3258)* offers 33 clean, modern rooms with televisions, many of them with private bathrooms. Restaurant and bar.

Nemiscau

Nemiscau is disposed of modern and comfortable lodgings at **Hôtel Nemaska** *(☎673-2615)*, in the Cree council building.

Radisson

Two campgrounds are open for the summer months in the Radisson region, **Camping Municipal** *(☎418-276-5675)* and **Camping Saint-Louis** *(☎418-276-4670)*, both of them in Mistissini.

Hôtel-Motel Le Carrefour La Grande *($50; 11 Rue Des Groseillers, ☎819-638-6005)* offers acceptable rooms, some of them equipped with kitchenettes, at reasonable rates.

Auberge Radisson *($100; ☎819-638-7201)* rents modern, comfortable rooms all of which have televisions and private bathrooms.

Chisasibi

Motel Chisasibi *($95 single, $122 double; above the shopping centre, ☎819-855-2838)* disposes of 20 comfortable rooms with private washrooms and televisions. No food service.

Oujé-Bougoumou

Twelve comfortable rooms are available to travellers at **Auberge Cassipit** *(☎418-745-3944)*. The furniture in the main room, the work of Native American artisans from the southern United States, is particularly remarkable. Dining room.

Kuujjuarapik

Hôtel Kuujjuaraapik Inn *($99 plus tax per person, $136 plus tax per person with tv; ☎929-3374, ⌐929-3637)* offers 21 double rooms and a restaurant. The inn also rents snowmobiles.

Tour B: Inuit Communities of Hudson Bay

The **Fédération des Coopératives du Nouveau-Québec** operates most of the hotel establishments in Inuit communities.

Inukjuak

The hotel can accommodate 21 people and offers two rates: $180 plus tax for double occupancy of a room with two single beds or $210 for double occupancy of a room with one large bed and a television. The manager is **Myna Weetaluktuk** *(☎254-8306 or 254-8969 at the co-op)*.

Puvirnituq

Matiusi Tulugak *($180; ☎988-2914 or 988-2983 at the co-op)*. The hotel can lodge up to 20 guests.

Akulivik

The manager is **Evie Luuku** *($180; ☎496-2526 or 496-2002 at the co-op)*.

Tour C: Inuit Communities of Hudson Strait

Salluit

Since the **Fédération des Coopératives du Nouveau-Québec** does not operate any hotels here, there is but one private establishment at which to stay, the **Qavvik Hotel** (☎*255-8500, ··255-8504*), which offers 10 rooms equipped with two small beds each.

Kangiqsujuaq

The only hotel in the village is managed by **Lukasi Napaaluk** (☎*338-3212 or 338-3252 at the co-op*) and can accommodate 14 people.

Quaqtaq

The **Fédération des Coopératives du Nouveau-Québec** runs the only place to stay in Quaqtaq. The manager, **Jusipi Keleutak**, can be contacted at ☎492-9206. The house lodges up to seven guests at a flat rate of $90 plus tax per person.

Tour D: Ungava Bay Villages

Kangirsuk

The only hotel in the community is operated by the **Fédération des Coopératives du Nouveau-Québec**. Its manager, **Maggie Simigak**, can be contacted at ☎935-4382. The house accommodates up to seven guests at a flat rate of $90 plus tax per person.

Aupaluk

There is but one hotel in this small village, operated by the **Fédération des Coopératives du Nouveau-Québec**. Its manager, **Tommy Grey**, can be reached at ☎491-7060. Lodgings consist of a house that can only accommodate six guests, at a flat rate of $90 per person, which sometimes means sharing a room with other travellers. Reservations are strongly recommended.

Kuujjuaq

The **Fédération des Coopératives du Nouveau-Québec** manages one of the two hotels in the village. **Patrice Bernard** operates it and can be contacted at ☎964-2272. It can accommodate 20 people.

Auberge Kuujjuaq Inn (☎*964-2903, ··964-2031*) has 22 double rooms with

televisions and private bathrooms. Count on spending $190 for two people.

Kangiqsualujjuaq

The only hotel establishment in the community is operated by the **Fédération des Coopératives du Nouveau-Québec**. **Tommy Etook**, the manager, can be reached at ☎337-5241. The house can accommodate seven people and offers a flat rate of $90 plus tax per person. The rooms are equipped to receive two to four guests and sometimes must be shared with other travellers.

 RESTAURANTS

Tour A: Hydroelectric Projects and Cree Land

Radisson

Le Radis-Nord (*17 Rue Des Groseillers,* ☎*819-638-7255*) is a general store that sells various foodstuffs and provisions. It is good spot to keep in mind for those planning excursions into the surrounding wilderness.

Restaurant Radisson (*$; 51 Rue Des Groseillers,* ☎*819-638-7387*) offers simple but tasty cuisine and has a liquor license.

The restaurant at **Auberge Radisson** (*$$; in the Pierre-Radisson building,* ☎*819-638-7201*) posts an excellent menu and the service is courteous and congenial.

Chisasibi

Herodier and Son (*Mon to Fri 8am to 7pm, Sat 10am to 5pm; on the ground floor of the shopping centre,* ☎*819-855-2585*) serves breakfast as well as light meals to eat in or take out.

Kuujjuarapik

The Parisian head chef at the restaurant of the **Kuujjuaraapik Inn** (*$$;* ☎*929-3374*) prepares elaborate meals.

Tour B: Inuit Communities of Hudson Bay

Inukjuak

The cafeteria at the adult education centre, **Nunavimmi Pigiursavik** *($$; ☎254-8247)*, is open to the public morning, noon and night. The meals, prepared by cooking students under the guidance of professionals, are varied and balanced.

Puvirnituq

Allie's Coffee Shop *($; ☎988-2600)* serves fast-food-style meals.

Tour C: Inuit Communities of Hudson Strait

Salluit

To satisfy that craving for mussels and scallops, when you're too tired to go out on the water to catch them yourself, contact **Adamie Keatainak Scallops** *(☎255-8971)*, who do their best to satisfy.

Tour D: Ungava Bay Villages

Kuujjuaq

Les Aliments de l'Arctique Inuksiutiit *(☎964-2817)* specializes in the preparation of game.

The **Kuujjuaq Inn** *($$; ☎964-29203)* offers restaurant service. The chef has occasion to prepare freshly caught fish or freshly killed game. Count on spending $15 for a meal.

Kangiqsualujjuaq

There is but one restaurant here, **Julia's Take-Out** *($; ☎337-5430)*, which offers fast-food-style meals.

  ENTERTAINMENT

Kuujjuarapik

Kuujjuarapik is the only village in Nunavik that has a bar. It is open from noon to midnight and dancing is a possibility.

 SHOPPING

Radisson

Inouis *(96 Rue Albanel, ☎819-638-6969)*, a shop that specializes in native art, sells magnificent carvings and pretty pendants.

Chisasibi

A small, extremely interesting shop is set up in the **large teepee**. It has an excellent selection of products created by local artisans.

Kuujjuarapik

The quantity and quality of sculptures produced in Puvirnituq are proportionate to the great interest expressed by members in the village's well-established cooperative movement. Credit and debit (ATM) cards are accepted at the Northern store as well as at the co-op store.

Kuujjuaq

In addition to the cooperative, there are two establishments that exhibit the talents of Inuit artists here. **Innivik Arts and Crafts Shop** *(☎964-2780)* and **Tivi Galleries** *(Kuujjuaq airport, ☎964-2465 or 1-800-964-2465)*.

Kangiqsualujjuaq

Artisans create all sorts of crafts with caribou skin. They have preserved the ancestral art of making mittens, and export a portion of their products to other Inuit villages. Other items of clothing are also made here, like *kamiks*, slippers, coats, and *nasaks*, as are pieces of caribou-antler jewellery.

ENGLISH-FRENCH GLOSSARY

GREETINGS

Hi (casual)	*Salut*
How are you?	*Comment ça va?*
I'm fine	*Ça va bien*
Hello (during the day)	*Bonjour*
Good evening/night	*Bonsoir*
Goodbye, See you later	*Bonjour, Au revoir, à la prochaine*
Yes	*Oui*
No	*Non*
Maybe	*Peut-être*
Please	*S'il vous plaît*
Thank you	*Merci*
You're welcome	*De rien, Bienvenue*
Excuse me	*Excusez-moi*
I am a tourist.	*Je suis touriste*
I am American (m/f)	*Je suis Américain(e)*
I am Canadian (m/f)	*Je suis Canadien(ne)*
I am British	*Je suis Britannique*
I am German (m/f)	*Je suis Allemand(e)*
I am Italian (male/female)	*Je suis Italien(ne)*
I am Belgian	*Je suis Belge*
I am Swiss	*Je suis Suisse*
I am sorry, I don't speak French	*Je suis désolé(e), je ne parle pas français*
Do you speak English?	*Parlez-vous anglais ?*
What is your name?	*Quel est votre nom?*
My name is...	*Je m'appelle...*
friend (m/f)	*ami(e)*
single (m/f)	*celibataire*
married (m/f)	*marié(e)*
divorced (m/f)	*divorcé(e)*
widower/widow	*veuf(ve)*

DIRECTIONS

Is there a tourism office near here?	*Est-ce qu'il y a un bureau de tourisme près d'ici?*
Where is...?	*Où est le/la ... ?*
straight ahead	*tout droit*
to the right	*à droite*
to the left	*à gauche*
beside	*à côté de*
near	*près de*
here	*ici*
there, over there	*là, là-bas*
into, inside	*à l'intérieur*
outside	*à l'extérieur*
in front of	*devant*
behind	*derrière*

GETTING AROUND

airport	*aéroport*
on time	*à l'heure*
late	*en retard*
cancelled	*annulé*
plane	*l'avion*
car	*la voiture*

train	le train
boat	le bateau
bicycle	la bicyclette, le vélo
bus	l'autobus
train station	la gare
bus stop	un arrêt d'autobus
corner	coin
neighbourhood	quartier
square	place
tourist office	bureau de tourisme
bridge	pont
building	immeuble
safe	sécuritaire
fast	rapide
baggage	bagages
schedule	horaire
one way ticket	aller simple
return ticket	aller retour
arrival	arrivée
return	retour
departure	départ
north	nord
south	sud
east	est
west	ouest

CARS

for rent	à louer
a stop	un arrêt
highway	autoroute
no passing	défense de doubler
no parking	stationnement interdit
no exit	impasse
parking	stationnement
pedestrians	piétons
gas	essence
traffic light	feu de circulation
service station	station-service
speed limit	limite de vitesse

MONEY

bank	banque
credit union	caisse populaire
exchange	change
money	argent
I don't have any money	je n'ai pas d'argent
credit card	carte de crédit
traveller's cheques	chèques de voyage
The bill please	l'addition, s'il vous plaît
receipt	reçu

ACCOMMODATION

inn	auberge
youth hostel	auberge de jeunesse
bed and breakfast	gîte
hot water	eau chaude
air conditioning	climatisation
accommodation	logement, hébergement
elevator	ascenseur

bathroom	*toilettes, salle de bain*
bed	*lit*
breakfast	*déjeuner*
bedroom	*chambre*
pool	*piscine*
floor (first, second...)	*étage*
high season	*haute saison*
off season	*basse saison*
fan	*ventilateur*

SHOPPING

open	*ouvert(e)*
closed	*fermé(e)*
How much is this?	*C'est combien?*
I need...	*J'ai besoin de...*
a store	*un magasin*
a department store	*un magasin à rayons*
the market	*le marché*
salesperson (m/f)	*vendeur(se)*
the customer (m/f)	*le / la client(e)*
to buy	*acheter*
to sell	*vendre*
t-shirt	*un t-shirt*
skirt	*une jupe*
shirt	*une chemise*
pants	*des pantalons*
jacket	*un blouson*
blouse	*une blouse*
shoes	*des souliers*
sandals	*des sandales*
hat	*un chapeau*
eyeglasses	*des lunettes*
handbag	*un sac*
gifts	*cadeaux*
local crafts	*artisanat local*
sun protection products	*crèmes solaires*
cosmetics and perfumes	*cosmétiques et parfums*
camera	*appareil photo*
film	*pellicule*
records, cassettes	*disques, cassettes*
newspapers	*journaux*
magazines	*revues, magazines*
batteries	*piles*
watches	*montres*
jewellery	*bijouterie*
gold	*or*
silver	*argent*
precious stones	*pierres précieuses*
wool	*laine*
cotton	*coton*
leather	*cuir*

MISCELLANEOUS

big, tall (person)	*grand(e)*
small, short (person)	*petit(e)*
short (length)	*court(e)*
low	*bas(se)*
fat (person)	*gros(se)*
slim, skinny (person)	*mince*

ENGLISH-FRENCH
GLOSSARY

a little	*peu*
a lot	*beaucoup*
something	*quelque chose*
nothing	*rien*
good	*bon*
bad	*mauvais*
more	*plus*
less	*moins*
big	*grand*
small	*petit*
hot	*chaud*
cold	*froid*
I am ill	*je suis malade*
pharmacy, drugstore	*pharmacie*
I am hungry	*j'ai faim*
I am thirsty	*j'ai soif*
What is this?	*Qu'est-ce que c'est?*
Where?	*Où?*

WEATHER

rain	*pluie*
clouds	*nuages*
sun	*soleil*
It is hot out	*Il fait chaud*
It is cold out	*Il fait froid*

TIME

When?	*Quand?*
What time is it?	*Quelle heure est-il?*
minute	*minute*
hour	*heure*
day	*jour*
week	*semaine*
month	*mois*
year	*année*
yesterday	*hier*
today	*aujourd'hui*
tomorrow	*demain*
morning	*le matin*
afternoon	*l'après-midi*
evening	*le soir*
night	*la nuit*
now	*maintenant*
never	*jamais*
Sunday	*dimanche*
Monday	*lundi*
Tuesday	*mardi*
Wednesday	*mercredi*
Thursday	*jeudi*
Friday	*vendredi*
Saturday	*samedi*
January	*janvier*
February	*février*
March	*mars*
April	*avril*
May	*mai*
June	*juin*
July	*juillet*
August	*août*

September	*septembre*
October	*octobre*
November	*novembre*
December	*décembre*

COMMUNICATION

post office	*bureau de poste*
air mail	*par avion*
stamps	*timbres*
envelope	*enveloppe*
telephone book	*bottin téléphonique*
long distance call	*appel outre-mer*
collect call	*appel collecte*
fax	*télécopieur, fax*
telegram	*télégramme*

ACTIVITIES

swimming	*la baignade*
beach	*plage*
scuba diving	*la plongée sous-marine*
snorkelling	*la plongée-tuba*
fishing	*la pêche*
sailing	*navigation de plaisance*
windsurfing	*la planche à voile*
bicycling	*faire du vélo*
mountain bike	*vélo tout-terrain (VTT)*
horseback riding	*équitation*
hiking	*la randonnée pédestre*
museum or gallery	*musée*
cultural centre	*centre culturel*
cinema	*cinéma*

TOURING

river	*fleuve, rivière*
waterfalls	*chutes*
viewpoint	*belvedère*
hill	*colline*
garden	*jardin*
wildlife reserve	*réserve faunique*
peninsula	*péninsule, presqu'île*
south/north shore	*côte sud/nord*
town or city hall	*hôtel de ville*
court house	*palais de justice*
church	*église*
house	*maison*
manor	*manoir*
bridge	*pont*
dam	*barrage*
workshop	*atelier*
historic site	*lieu historique*
train station	*gare*
stables	*écuries*
convent	*couvent*
door, archway, gate	*porte*
customs house	*douane*
locks	*écluses*
market	*marché*
canal	*canal*
seaway	*voie maritime*

museum	*musée*
cemetery	*cimitière*
mill	*moulin*
windmill	*moulin à vent*
hospital	*Hôtel Dieu*
lighthouse	*phare*
barn	*grange*
waterfall(s)	*chute(s)*
sandbank	*batture*
neighbourhood, region	*faubourg*

NUMBERS

1	*un*
2	*deux*
3	*trois*
4	*quatre*
5	*cinq*
6	*six*
7	*sept*
8	*huit*
9	*neuf*
10	*dix*
11	*onze*
12	*douze*
13	*treize*
14	*quatorze*
15	*quinze*
16	*seize*
17	*dix-sept*
18	*dix-huit*
19	*dix-neuf*
20	*vingt*
21	*vingt-et-un*
22	*vingt-deux*
23	*vingt-trois*
24	*vingt-quatre*
25	*vingt-cinq*
26	*vingt-six*
27	*vingt-sept*
28	*vingt-huit*
29	*vingt-neuf*
30	*trente*
40	*quarante*
50	*cinquante*
60	*soixante*
70	*soixante-dix*
80	*quatre-vingt*
90	*quatre-vingt-dix*
100	*cent*
200	*deux cents*
500	*cinq cents*
1,000	*mille*
10,000	*dix mille*
1,000,000	*un million*

INDEX

INDEX

INDEX

INDEX

INDEX

INDEX

INDEX

INDEX